World Spirituality

Already published

Board of Editors and Advisors

Ewert Cousins, *General Editor*

MODERN
ESOTERIC
SPIRITUALITY

Edited by
Antoine Faivre
and
Jacob Needleman

Associate Editor:
Karen Voss

SCM PRESS LTD

Copyright © 1992 by The Crossroad Publishing Company, New York

ISBN 0-334-02532-X

First British paperback edition published 1993 by SCM Press Ltd
26-30 Tottenham Road   London   N1 4BZ

Printed in the United States of America

Contents

Preface to the Series

THE PRESENT VOLUME is part of a series entitled World Spirituality: An Encyclopedic History of the Religious Quest, which seeks to present the spiritual wisdom of the human race in its historical unfolding. Although each of the volumes can be read on its own terms, taken together they provide a comprehensive picture of the spiritual strivings of the human community as a whole—from prehistoric times, through the great religions, to the meeting of traditions at the present.

Drawing upon the highest level of scholarship around the world, the series gathers together and presents in a single collection the richness of the spiritual heritage of the human race. It is designed to reflect the autonomy of each tradition in its historical development, but at the same time to present the entire story of the human spiritual quest. The first five volumes deal with the spiritualities of archaic peoples in Asia, Europe, Africa, Oceania, and North and South America. Most of these have ceased to exist as living traditions, although some perdure among tribal peoples throughout the world. However, the archaic level of spirituality survives within the later traditions as a foundational stratum, preserved in ritual and myth. Individual volumes or combinations of volumes are devoted to the major traditions: Hindu, Buddhist, Taoist, Confucian, Jewish, Christian, and Islamic. Included within the series are the Jain, Sikh, and Zoroastrian traditions. In order to complete the story, the series includes traditions that have not survived but have exercised important influence on living traditions—such as Egyptian, Sumerian, classical Greek and Roman. A volume is devoted to modern esoteric movements and another to modern secular movements.

Having presented the history of the various traditions, the series devotes two volumes to the meeting of spiritualities. The first surveys the meeting of spiritualities from the past to the present, exploring common themes that

A longer version of this preface may be found in Christian Spirituality: Origins to the Twelfth Century, *the first published volume in the series.*

can provide the basis for a positive encounter, for example, symbols, rituals, techniques. Finally, the series closes with a dictionary of world spirituality.

Each volume is edited by a specialist or a team of specialists who have gathered a number of contributors to write articles in their fields of specialization. As in this volume, the articles are not brief entries but substantial studies of an area of spirituality within a given tradition. An effort has been made to choose editors and contributors who have a cultural and religious grounding within the tradition studied and at the same time possess the scholarly objectivity to present the material to a larger forum of readers. For several years some five hundred scholars around the world have been working on the project.

In the planning of the project, no attempt was made to arrive at a common definition of spirituality that would be accepted by all in precisely the same way. The term "spirituality," or an equivalent, is not found in a number of the traditions. Yet from the outset, there was a consensus among the editors about what was in general intended by the term. It was left to each tradition to clarify its own understanding of this meaning and to the editors to express this in the introduction to their volumes. As a working hypothesis, the following description was used to launch the project:

> The series focuses on that inner dimension of the person called by certain traditions "the spirit." This spiritual core is the deepest center of the person. It is here that the person is open to the transcendent dimension; it is here that the person experiences ultimate reality. The series explores the discovery of this core, the dynamics of its development, and its journey to the ultimate goal. It deals with prayer, spiritual direction, the various maps of the spiritual journey, and the methods of advancement in the spiritual ascent.

By presenting the ancient spiritual wisdom in an academic perspective, the series can fulfill a number of needs. It can provide readers with a spiritual inventory of the richness of their own traditions, informing them at the same time of the richness of other traditions. It can give structure and order, meaning and direction to the vast amount of information with which we are often overwhelmed in the computer age. By drawing the material into the focus of world spirituality, it can provide a perspective for understanding one's place in the larger process. For it may well be that the meeting of spiritual paths—the assimilation not only of one's own spiritual heritage but of that of the human community as a whole—is the distinctive spiritual journey of our time.

EWERT COUSINS

Introduction I

ANTOINE FAIVRE

How can one conceive a collective work dedicated to esotericism when there is no agreement on the meaning of the word? In order to avoid any impression of ambiguity in the title of this collective work, Ewert Cousins, Jacob Needleman, Karen Voss, and I have chosen not to use the noun "esotericism," but instead the phrase "esoteric spirituality," taking it to designate a *range* of spiritual forms. Moreover, we have limited ourselves to the modern period, that is, the last five centuries, except for an introductory chapter that we deemed necessary, devoted to "ancient and medieval roots of modern esoteric movements." Finally we have confined ourselves to the West. Naturally, a definite idea of esotericism has informed our choice of the different contributions here. The present introduction is meant essentially to explain and justify this choice.

The lexical content of the word "esotericism" is small (*eso* signifies "within, "inside," "into"; and *ter* suggests an opposition). Devoid of any particular sense, like any word considered out of context, "esotericism" shows itself to be expandable, transparent, and semantically indeterminate. Accordingly, the point is to investigate not its etymology but its function, which is to evoke a cluster of attitudes, present in comparable forms of spirituality. The question is not what esotericism would be "in itself." No doubt esotericism is not even a domain, in the sense in which one speaks of the domains of painting, or philosophy, or chemistry. It is, rather, a form of thought, and the point is to identify its nature, on the basis of those currents or forms of spirituality which appear to illustrate it. Moreover, the adjective appeared long before the noun, which dates only from the beginning of the nineteenth century; in fact, we might find it preferable to use the adjective and the plural form of the noun whenever possible. In the same way, we might find it preferable to use the plural instead of the singular forms of words like "astrology" and "alchemy." And then how could an abstract definition of esotericism avoid being held hostage to an a priori idea of what it "ought" to be, of its "true" nature—ultimately, in other words, to a philosophical or ideological presupposition?

"Esotericism" generally evokes the idea of "secrecy," of a "discipline of the arcane," of knowledge limited to groups or associations that are called "secret." It is certainly true that things grown most familiar easily lose their charm, that mystery makes for dreams and confers a dimension of depth upon the world—and so esotericists willingly cultivate mystery. This is not to say that we consider this use of the word "esotericism" illegitimate; our object is only to draw attention to the fact that the word now has two meanings. The second, more general meaning is the one that will concern us.

For the most part alchemy is not secret insofar as it has been promulgated by means of an abundant literature, particularly since the sixteenth century. The same holds true for theosophy: the writings of Boehme, particularly representative of theosophy, were intended to circulate in a variety of milieus. Many more examples could be provided. And wherever there are secrets, they are generally open secrets. The etymology of "esotericism" clarifies the second meaning of the word by suggesting that one has access to the comprehension of symbol, of myth, of reality, only through a personal struggle for progressive elucidation on many successive levels, that is, through a form of hermeneutics.

Another inadequate approach to the idea of esotericism is to begin by confusing it with the idea of initiation in general. There exist initiations of every sort, whose meanings and purposes vary enormously, according to their context, be it a matter of individual practices (from master to disciple) or collective practices. Besides, is not initiation a constituent of most religious traditions? Finally, we note the confusion, due sometimes to ignorance and sometimes to an inquisitorial spirit, between esotericism and religious marginality. This confusion leads to misconceptions which various sectarianisms can turn to their advantage and renders any serious approach impossible. Esoteric currents cannot be defined without intellectual dishonesty as being by nature marginal vis-à-vis the churches. What can be labeled as doctrinal within spiritualities of an esoteric character is not properly what constitutes them as such. To start from doctrinal elements would only serve to add to the confusion. That having been said, it is certain that the study of esoteric currents depends on their links with the dominant religion, and that in the Latin West esotericism's relationship with the Catholic and Protestant churches has been and still is difficult.

Therefore, we speak here of esotericism in a sense that is simultaneously more general and more precise. More general, for it does not allow whole aspects of materials possessing elements in common—a kind of factual unity—to escape. More precise, for it does not lose sight of the fact that the forms of spirituality evoked by this word—and which extend beyond, as will be seen shortly, the three overly narrow meanings mentioned above— are joined under the same rubric by Westerners. To be sure, beyond the West there are some words that more or less correspond to this word, but they carry different connotations; they stand for meanings that are too diverse—conceptually too narrow or anthropologically too broad—to be applicable to the domain of spiritualities that concerns us here. In the Far East, and in other cultural areas, esotericism does not even enjoy a status of its own, as it does in the West.

By the term "West" we mean the vast Greco-Roman whole within which Judaism and Christianity have always cohabited with one another, joined by Islam for several centuries. The present reflections and the present col- lection essentially concern most of the great esoteric currents in the modern West, that is, in the Latin West since the end of the fifteenth century. It seems that it is only there, since the beginning of the Renaissance, that people begin wishing to assemble a variety of ancient and medieval mate- rials of the kind that interest us here, in the belief that they were capable of constituting a homogeneous whole. A number of these materials were linked from the beginning of our era to forms of Hellenistic religiosity (Stoicism, Gnosticism, Hermeticism, and neo-Pythagoreanism) and later to the three Abrahamic religions. But in the Renaissance there arose the idea in Marsilio Ficino, Pico della Mirandola, and others of considering them complementary to each other and of seeking common denominators. Thus, Jewish Kabbalah penetrated into the Christian milieu, especially after 1492, and celebrated an unexpected wedding with neo-Alexandrian Hermeticism, while the latter continued to consummate its own wedding with alchemy, in the kind of illuminated atmosphere in which analogical thinking prevails and in a climate in which harmony was more or less universal. There is then born the idea of a *prisca theologia*, a *philosophia occulta*, a *philosophia perennis*, terms that are not entirely interchangeable but nevertheless apply to a particular constellation within the mental universe of the time, a con- stellation that is endowed with relative autonomy and is detached from theology proper. Whether historic or mythic, the representatives of this *philosophia perennis* constitute links in a chain; their names are Moses, Zoroaster, Hermes Trismegistus, Plato, Orpheus, the Sibyls, and still others. Leaving certain nuances aside, we now have that which certain people since the beginning of the nineteenth century have called "tradition" or "esoteric traditions." Our purpose is not to learn whether such a "tradition" really existed, in itself, invisible and hidden behind the veil of the history of events, before the Renaissance, but rather to undertake to grasp this idea as it emerged within images and discourse, that is, as it emerged within the forms of spirituality in which it has clad itself.

Nevertheless, modern Western esotericism is not reducible to this idea of tradition. It appears to be a larger whole whose fundamental components are recoverable from a variegated historical corpus. Before discussing these components, we turn to the corpus. First, three rivers may be seen, the three "traditional sciences," whose appearance does not seem absolutely tied to a particular epoch: alchemy, astrology, and magic (in the Renaissance sense of "*magia,*" more or less linked to an arithmosophy, or science of numbers, related to different forms of musical esotericism). Still flourishing to the present time, these sciences are closely related. Second, a number of streams of thought have opened their depths to reveal relatively retrievable moments (often beginning with "foundational" texts). These streams, which are by no means strangers to the great rivers, begin at the end of the fifteenth century and influence one another: (1) Christian Kabbalah (an adaptation of Jewish Kabbalah); (2) neo-Alexandrian Hermeticism, that is, the discourse inspired by the ideas of the *philosophia perennis* and the "Primordial Tradition"; (3) a Paracelsian and romantic type of philosophy of Nature (a part of German *Naturphilosophie*); and (4) starting from the seventeenth century, theosophy and Rosicrucianism (beginning in Germanic countries), as well as later groups (initiatic societies more or less arising in their wake).

One could be forgiven for thinking that these rivers and streams disappeared with the Renaissance. But when the great epistemological rupture of the seventeenth century was completed, they survived, and nineteenth-century scientism did not force them to dry up. Esotericism is present today more than ever. In the modern era, its tenacious permanence appears as a counterpart to our scientific and secularized vision of the world, but it would be simplistic and mistaken to explain its longevity by a need to react against the reigning episteme. More than a reaction, it is perhaps one of the possible forms assumed by one of the two poles of the human spirit in order to actualize itself, namely, mythic thought, the other pole being what is called rational thought, which in the West is modeled on a logic of the Aristotelian type. This is not a matter of defining esotericism on the basis of the different ways in which esotericists define it themselves; nor, as we have seen, on the basis of sectarian presuppositions concerning what it "ought" to be, as certain people do today who claim to be its representatives and wish to place their little parish church above the others. In contrast, approaching esotericism phenomenologically, as an attitude of mind, as an ensemble of forms of spirituality, allows us to avoid doing violence to historical data. It would do too much violence to these data to attempt to identify ideas that at first glance would appear esoteric simply because some esotericists have considered them so: for example, *magia naturalis* (natural magic) or sophiology (the discourses on the Sophia of the Old Testament). But this would certainly not be the best way to address the question. In fact, if the idea of *magia naturalis* can have a tinge of esoteric coloration, it can also fail to evoke any such thing; it all depends on the authors who are speaking about it. Likewise, in the Latin West, the Divine Wisdom pertains to theology almost as much as to theosophy. This is why we have not organized this work by themes, however interesting and important they might be. We shall regard the "esotericism" of the modern West as an identifiable form of spirituality because of the presence of six fundamental characteristics distributed in varying degrees within its vast concrete historical context. Four of these characteristics are "intrinsic" in the sense that their simultaneous presence is a necessary and sufficient condition for a material studied to be included in the field of esotericism. By nature they are more or less inseparable, as we shall see, but it is important to distinguish them well methodologically. There are two others, which we call "relative," or "nonintrinsic"; these frequently appear alongside the four intrinsic characteristics. The four intrinsic elements are (1) correspondences, (2) living nature, (3) imagination and mediation, and (4) the experience of transmutation.

1. Correspondences. These are symbolic and/or real correspondences between all parts of the visible or invisible universe ("that which is above is like that which is below; that which is below is like that which is above . . ."). Here we rediscover the ancient idea of the microcosm and the macrocosm. These correspondences are considered more or less veiled at first glance, and they are therefore meant to be read, to be decoded. The entire universe is a great theater of mirrors, a set of hieroglyphs to decipher; everything is a sign, everything harbors and manifests mystery. The principles of contradiction, of excluded middle, and of linear causality are supplanted by those of resolution, of included middle, and of synchronicity. Two types of correspondences may be distinguished: first, those that exist in visible or invisible nature, for example, between the seven metals and the seven planets; between the planets and the parts of the human body or character (or society), which constitute the foundation for astrology; and between the material world and the invisible spheres of the celestial and supercelestial realms, etc. Next, there are the correspondences between nature (the cosmos) or even history, and revealed texts; thus, in Jewish or Christian Kabbalah, and in different varieties of *physica sacra;* according to this form of inspired concordism, it is a question of "seeing" that scripture, the (Hebrew or Christian) Bible, for example, and Nature are necessarily in harmony, the knowledge of one furthering the knowledge of the other.

2. *Living nature.* From the idea of correspondences we begin to see that the cosmos is complex, plural, hierarchical. Therefore Nature occupies an essential place within it. Multilayered, rich in potential revelations of all kinds, it must be read as one reads a book. Indeed, the word *magia,* so important in Renaissance imagination, evokes this idea of a Nature seen, known, and felt to be essentially alive in all its parts. Thus understood, "magic" is at once the knowledge of a network of sympathies or antipathies which bind the things of Nature and the concrete implementation of this knowledge (we are reminded of the astral qualities with which the magus charges talismans; of Orphism in all its forms, which are always musical; of the use of stones, metals, and plants propitious for the reestablishment of an upset physical or psychological harmony). Set into this framework, Paracelsianism represents an enormous current with multiple ramifications, ranging from animal magnetism to homeopathy and going through all the forms of *magia naturalis* (a complex notion at the intersection of magic and science). More than practices proper, it is knowledge—in the sense of "gnosis"—which appears to contribute to the basis of an esoteric attitude; knowledge, in the sense in which Goethe makes his Faust say that he burns with the desire "to know the world / in its intimate texture, / To contemplate the active forces and first elements." To this is often added an interpretation of Paul's teaching (Romans 8:19–22), laden with implications for alchemy and for a *Naturphilosophie* of an esoteric character, according to which suffering Nature, subject to exile and vanity, also expects to participate in salvation. In this way there came to be grounded a science of Nature, a gnosis infused with soteriological elements, and a theosophy based on the triangle God–Humanity–Nature from which the theosophist brings forth dramaturgic correspondences, always new and complementary to one another. Nevertheless, since the beginning of the twentieth century, in the wake of an ontologically dualistic metaphysics, we must take note of the appearance of a monistic spiritualism in which Nature (the created world) is neglected, or its very reality denied, under the influence of eastern, notably Hindu, doctrines. Such a view is at odds with Nature; at best, it relegates Nature to a very inferior place and rejects modernity along with the sciences that belong to it. For the observer this is an interesting phenomenon, though it is a derivative current. It must be accorded all the

attention it merits by the importance of the position it occupies in Western esoteric spirituality.

3. *Imagination and mediation.* These two ideas are linked and complementary to each other. The idea of correspondence already presupposes a form of imagination that tends to reveal and use mediation of all kinds, like rituals, symbolic images, mandalas, and intermediary spirits. Hence the importance of angelology in this context, but also of the idea of a "transmitter" in the sense of an "initiator" or "guru" (cf. also the sixth element, "Transmission," below) . Perhaps it is this notion of mediation, above all, which makes the difference between that which is mystical and that which is esoteric. A little simplistically, we might consider that mystics—in the most classic sense—aspire to a more or less complete suppression of images and intermediaries because such things soon become hindrances to the experience of union with God. In contrast, esotericists seem more interested in intermediaries revealed to their interior gaze, by virtue of their creative imagination, which is essentially directed toward union with the divine; esotericists prefer to stay on Jacob's ladder, upon which angels (and doubtless other entities as well) climb and descend, rather than to go beyond. The distinction has only practical value; there is sometimes a great deal of esotericism in the mystics (e.g., Saint Hildegard of Bingen), and a mystical tendency can be seen in many esotericists (e.g., Louis Claude de Saint-Martin).

This, then, is an imagination that allows the use of these intermediaries, symbols, and images for gnostic ends, to penetrate Nature's hieroglyphs, to put the theory of correspondences into active practice, and to discover, to see, and to know the mediating entities between the divine world and Nature. This imagination is a kind of "organ of the soul" by means of which a person can establish cognitive and visionary rapport with an intermediary world, with a mesocosm—with the world which Henry Corbin proposed to call the *"mundus imaginalis."* Here the Arabic influence (Avicenna, Sohravardhi, Ibn Arabi) has exercised a definitive influence in the West, but even without that influence, Paracelsus could have rediscovered quite comparable categories. And it is above all under the inspiration of the *Corpus Hermeticum,* rediscovered at the end of the fifteenth century, that memory and imagination come to be associated to such an extent that they become identical, part of the teaching of Hermes Trismegistus consisting in the "interiorization" of the world, within our *mens:* whence came the "memory arts" cultivated within a glow of magic, during and after the Renaissance. Thus understood, imagination (*imaginatio* is related to "magnet," *magia,* *imago*) is a tool for the knowledge of the self, of the world, of myth; it is the eye of fire penetrating the surface of appearances in order to make meanings, "connections," burst forth, to render the invisible visible (this invisible is the *mundus imaginalis* to which the eye of flesh alone does not give access), and to forge a link with a treasure that contributes to the enlargement of our prosaic vision. Emphasis is placed on vision and certitude rather than on belief and faith. This imagination founds a visionary philosophy, a kind of creative play in which words are read by practitioners of a "phonetic Kabbalah." Above all, it enlivens the theosophical discourse within which it is carried on and emerges out of meditations on the verses of the revealed book, as, for instance, with the imaginative use of the *Zohar* within Jewish Kabbalah, or the great theosophical current in the West that was launched in Germany at the beginning of the seventeenth century.

4. The experience of transmutation. If the notion of transmutation were not considered an essential dimension, the present discussion would scarcely extend beyond the limits of a form of speculative spirituality. Now we know the importance of the initiatic in that which is evoked by words like "esotericism," "gnosis," and "alchemy," even on the most familiar level. However, the term "transformation" would not be adequate here, because it does not necessarily indicate that a thing passes from one level to another or that the very nature of the elements constituting it is modified. "Transmutation," a term borrowed in our context from alchemy, seems more appropriate. We also understand it as "metamorphosis." If one wishes lead to become silver or silver gold, one must not separate knowledge (gnosis) from interior experience, or intellectual activity from active imagination. This illuminated knowledge, which promotes a "second birth," a fundamental idea in modern Western esoteric currents, particularly theosophy, is often called "gnosis" in the general and modern sense of the term. It seems that an important part of the alchemical corpus, particularly after the beginning of the seventeenth century, was directed less toward description of laboratory experiments than toward figurative presentation of this transmutation according to a designated path: *nigredo* (death, decapitation, of the first matter or of the old man), *albedo* (work with white), and *rubedo* (work with red, philosopher's stone). A rapprochement between these three stages and the three phases of the traditional mystic way might be proposed: purgation, illumination, and unification. In such contexts the implication is often that the transmutation takes place in a part of Nature just as much as in the experimenters themselves.

These then are the four basic components on which to rest the methodological approach to modern Western esotericism proposed here. Two more are associated with them. They are "relative" in the sense that they are not indispensable to the definition. Presenting them as two additional necessary conditions would overly restrict the domain we are exploring; these two "relative" elements nevertheless merit specific consideration because they frequently appear juxtaposed with the first four. We have here what could be called the practice of concordance, on the one hand, and of transmission, on the other.

5. *The practice of concordance.*   The practice of concordance is not characteristic of Western esotericism as a whole, but becomes especially apparent at the beginning of the modern era (the end of the fifteenth century, the sixteenth; see above in connection with *philosophia perennis*), and from the end of the nineteenth century in a different and arrogant form. It involves a marked tendency to seek to establish commonalities between two different traditions, sometimes even between all the traditions, with a view to gaining illumination, a gnosis of superior quality. There is, to be sure, a practice of concordance which could be called "exterior," founded on mere recognition of or simple respect for all established religions, which are then studied with a view to investigating points of commonality likely to bring together people of good will in a spirit of active or indifferent tolerance. The present type of concordance is something different. It tends to be more creative and is concerned with individual illumination even more than with collective illumination. It manifests the intention not only to eliminate differences or discover harmonies among diverse religious traditions, but above all to acquire an all-encompassing gnosis, embracing and inflaming different traditions within the same crucible in order to "reveal" to desirous men and women the image of a living and hidden trunk of which particular traditions are only the visible branches. This tendency becomes marked from the nineteenth century on. Its character is a natural consequence of increased knowledge of the Orient, enhanced by the influence of a new academic discipline, "comparative religion," to such an extent that the champions of "traditionalism" (known as "Perennialists" in English) go so far as to postulate and teach the doctrine that there existed a "primordial Tradition," surpassing all other religions or esoteric traditions of humanity.

6. *Transmission.*   To emphasize "transmission" implies that an esoteric teaching can or ought to be transmitted from master to disciple following a channel already dug, abiding by a course already charted. Two ideas are related to this: (a) the validity of knowledge transmitted by a filiation whose authenticity or "regularity" leaves no room for doubt; and (b) initiation, which generally is effected within a master–disciple relationship (one is not initiated alone, or haphazardly; initiation takes place through an initiator,

a guru). We know the importance of these conditions in the genesis and development of secret or discrete initiatic societies in the West.

To study the history of Western esoteric currents would therefore be to take note of the simultaneous presence of their six components in the works and discourses in which these currents appear. These components may be very unequally distributed. Moreover, they are found in music, art, and literature, and not only in explicitly esoteric works; the works devoted to this aspect of Shakespeare's plays, for example, are innumerable. Far from reflecting doctrinal content, the six elements articulated here serve as receptacles within which we can organize different kinds of experiences or imaginings. This aspect cannot be overemphasized. For example, the first element, that of correspondences, brings together thinkers as different as Cornelius Agrippa and Swedenborg; we can locate under this rubric hierarchical views of the Neoplatonic type (the higher is situated hierarchically above the lower) and nonhierarchical views of the neo-Hermetic type (God is found as much in a grain of sand as anywhere else; heliocentrism changes nothing essential, etc.). Or, to take another example, "transformation" can acquire very different theological aspects depending on whether or not belief in the existence of "subtle bodies" intervenes. It seems advantageous, therefore, to study similar constituent elements which have the value of functioning as frameworks for the imaginary, instead of seeking something having to do with particular explicit beliefs and expressions of faith. The advantage is twofold.

The first advantage of this approach is that it facilitates the sketch of a possible outline of the border around the field, a border that is, happily, blurred enough to respect and to promote its interdisciplinary character, which overflows widely into art, the churches, politics, literature, and the history of ideas. (As far as this last is concerned, one of the more interesting aspects of contemporary esotericism is the way in which some of its representatives adapt to modernity, even postmodernity, and others not at all.) Delimiting the field also means not extending it unduly to neighboring areas in spite of actual intersections and obvious proximities. Properly speaking, a phenomenon like the New Age, while interesting today for the sociologist, the psychologist, and the historian of religions, belongs to the study of new religious movements rather than to that of esotericism. (The academy is only beginning to recognize the importance of new religious movements.) In the same way, spiritualism, parapsychology, and sorcery—areas whose connections with modern esoteric currents are often obvious—do not constitute integral parts of these currents.

If the first advantage of this approach appears to me to be that it allows a sketch of the border, the second is that it lets us break with esotericists who speak as "officials," particularly because in our century thoughts or schools often tend to present themselves as esotericism in itself, as the way, as the true Tradition, in opposition to some other ways. Certain of these present as axiomatic the idea that all religious traditions of the world, all expressions of the sacred, are reunited, beyond their differences, in a superior unity—so much that we no longer know if we are still dealing with esotericism or the sacred in general under all its forms, or myth or religion *sub specie aeternitatis*. This tendency is often accompanied by a dogmatic attitude, which confers upon the word "esotericism" a partisan and militant, sometimes even fundamentalist, tone.

Nevertheless, certain of these currents (for example, the neo-Guenonian current, and its development in the school of Frithjof Schuon), however derivative they may be, appear eminently respectable on the intellectual level. Such is not the case with many suspect or lunatic discourses which in our day are proffered by people convinced they possess the truth, and who indulge in shameless appropriation of the word "esotericism." These sorts of discourses lead to a diversion, in the manner of caricature or paranoia, a diversion from the most humanly valid values bequeathed by the esoteric traditions. And then is it surprising that people who are serious but not in touch with the complexity of these problems will be hard put to find their bearings, and sometimes be inclined to look upon such problems with suspicion and irony?

Limitations have not permitted us to devote a separate contribution to each of the aspects of modern esotericism which would have their place in a larger work. We have had to restrict ourselves to some of them only. Besides, the present work is not intended as a general history of Western esotericism. Even so, the reader will perhaps find that it presents certain lacunae. Of these, we attempt here an inventory.

As we have seen above, it is convenient to distinguish "traditional sciences," practiced throughout history, from "currents" proper, which appear at a particular moment. From the "traditional sciences" we have retained only the first two: alchemy and astrology. But of course magic can be considered a form of spirituality, when it is understood in the polymorphic sense mentioned above, in which it is not reduced to practices of the material order. If magic is not the topic of a particular contribution, it is present all the same throughout this volume, implicitly or explicitly. So is its near twin numerology, to which musical esotericism is related.

Among the currents, Jewish Kabbalah constitutes an integral part of the spiritual arena of Western esotericism, but it is already the object of substantial expositions in another volume of this series. At the same time, it was entirely appropriate for Christian Kabbalah to be represented here, and it is. The absence of two great rooms in the present edifice is to be regretted. The first is constituted by what can be called the current of neo-Alexandrian Hermeticism, that is, the reception in the modern era of the *Corpus Hermeticum* and of the collection of texts called the *Hermetica*—for this reception in itself represents an important chapter in the history of Western esotericism to the present day. Although we have not included an article devoted to the topic of neo-Alexandrian Hermeticism, we have ensured that this current is acknowledged in different places throughout the collection. The second missing room is the great Illuminist current in the second half of the eighteenth century and the beginning of the nineteenth, a current that brings together theosophists as different and as substantial as Swedenborg and Saint-Martin, and whose intrinsic spiritual importance and influence within philosophical, literary, and artistic domains are obvious. In any event, like neo-Alexandrian Hermeticism, Illuminism is repeatedly acknowledged and alluded to in many different ways. We would like to have provided genuine bridges or avenues to both of these important aspects of Western spirituality, but we repeat that this is not an exhaustive history; it is not even an exhaustive history of that which is essential.

Here we present to the reader aspects of Western esotericism which are sufficiently varied and sufficiently representative to serve as a thread of Ariadne in a forest where trees often hide the view. We allow ourselves the hope that among the various stones which one finds on these paths of gnosis the reader will be able to discover some which reveal themselves to be not merely objects of curiosity but rather spiritual stones.

Translated by Karen Voss

Introduction II

JACOB NEEDLEMAN

THE SUBJECT MATTER of the present volume offers a unique opportunity to examine the contours and feasibility of the spiritual search in the modern world, a world that has significantly diluted humanity's sensitivity to the language and forms of religious tradition. What are spoken of here as "modern esoteric spiritualities" either deemphasize, redefine, or eliminate altogether the element of *belief* that lies at the basis of what the great Western monotheistic religions demand of the individual. The role that these esoteric teachings give to the faculties of knowing, imagination, observation, and speculation places these movements, at least as regards their overall tone and atmosphere, closer to the modern scientific temperament than to the religions of faith, trust, and hope that have on the whole defined Western religious culture.

Closely related to the above, and equally resonant to the modern temper, is the attention these movements tend to give to the world of nature. Here we find no harsh dichotomy between creation and creator, but rather a multilevel universe in which Spirit acts and calls to humanity within the material world. A study of these teachings, for all their differences, can greatly assist modern persons in their struggle to retrieve their authentic place in nature—without sacrificing all that is beneficent in the achievements of modern science.

A third general feature of these teachings that is intensely relevant to the modern crisis is their psychological thrust. Modern science, having lost the spiritual and metaphysical impetus that shaped its beginnings, has abandoned modern humanity to a universe devoid of consciousness and purpose, while the accelerating breakdown of social and political ideologies has rendered seemingly unattainable the ideal of meaningful human community in an ever-globalizing world. More and more, the modern man or woman has been driven to the individual self as the locus of healing and meaning; we live in a psychological era.

The religious traditions of the West have been of little help in supporting or deepening this quest for self-knowledge initiated by the development of scientific psychology. Although the spirituality of the Western religions contains a profound knowledge of the self, these traditions have on the whole been unable to communicate this knowledge in a language and under conditions that can be accepted by the contemporary secularized seeker. What is needed, and what many "modern esoteric spiritualities" provide–to a greater or lesser extent–is an approach to self-knowledge separable from prior acceptance of a system of religious belief and moralism, while at the same time opening the seeker to the potential immensity of love and wisdom that is inherent in the structure of the human self. That is to say that while their psychological and philosophical language resonates with the scientific tenor of modern psychology, their vision of the nature of the self soars far beyond the ideals of "normality" and "ego-strength" of modern psychology.

What we shall find, then, in the study of these movements, is the hope of a *worldview* for modern people, a sense of the wholeness and purposiveness of reality within which individual human beings are called to discover their own natural place, bringing with them everything of their minds, hearts, and instincts. For example, the doctrine of the microcosm–the human as the universe in miniature–is a common theme among the esoteric teachings treated in this volume, and among its other qualities, this idea has the virtue of theoretically joining the inner life in all its possible levels to the world of nature and beyond, even up to the Creator.

Among the many possible ways of characterizing modernity and the spiritual crisis of our time, perhaps none is more telling than to cite the absence of a coherent worldview embracing both the inner and the outer world. Surely this lack is one of the factors responsible for the alienation and loneliness of our era, as well as its excesses of materialism. The upsurge in recent years of new religious movements in America and the West may surely be understood in part as a rebellion against the unresolved compartmentalization and contradictions existing in modern society with regard to religion, science, education, ethics, technology, art, family life and work, resulting in a pervasive ethical and metaphysical relativism and paranoia. Beginning as a movement among the so-called disaffected youth, the new-religions phenomenon has now spread much closer to the established representatives of social responsibility in our culture.

A survey of the contemporary new-religions phenomenon reveals groups and movements of every stripe and coloration, including many that also speak of themselves as "esoteric." But in order to consider the usage of this term in the contemporary milieu, it is necessary to confront the problem of spiritual authenticity in a setting where time-honored spiritual teachings rub shoulders with invented cults, and where new and powerful expressions of perennial truth may exist alongside shallow imitations of ancient traditions, not to mention the pervasive influence of commercialism and journalistic distortion. All of this together, and much else besides, comprise what is called "new age" culture. Here the problem of authenticity takes many forms, from the difficulty facing the individual seeking an authentic teacher to the task of the scholar analyzing the roots and branches of humanity's perennial religious quest.

In certain essential respects, of course, the seeker and the scholar face entirely different challenges. The former needs to discover if the teacher or teaching is spiritually effective for him or her, without regard to whether or not it bears the "outer" credentials of lineage. The scholar, on the other hand—at least to a large extent—is obliged to set aside his or her own spiritual needs in order to fulfill the social function of contributing to the general fund of accessible human knowledge. The scholar's criterion of authenticity is of necessity more outer—though perhaps never entirely, if the scholar is a human being and not a machine. Unlike the spiritual seeker, the scholar is obliged to give greater weight to "the marks of the Buddha" in the more literal sense of this symbol—namely, considerations involving institutional, theological, sociocultural and externally verifiable historical continuity, though the discernment of even these more outer aspects of religious tradition very often depends on what we might acknowledge as the spiritual intuition. But as a rough characterization, we may say that the seeker is concerned with his or her own inner life, while the scholar is primarily concerned with the object of his or her study—in this case the phenomenon of religion in one or another of its many aspects and manifestations.

For example, there are now dozens, even hundreds, of groups in the United States and Europe that characterize themselves as Buddhist. Some are under the guidance of a master with "credentials," some are not. Which are authentically Buddhist and which are not? Where the scholar asks about the official lineage of the teacher, the seeker asks if the teacher really is inwardly free and capable of transmitting the truth to him or her. The scholar may resist passing such judgments, whereas the seeker is passionately concerned with them. We could say that the scholar attends to the "horizontal" dimension of religion, its forms and manifestations in culture and history; the seeker attends to the "vertical" dimension, understood as the movement within oneself toward inner freedom or, to use other language, toward God.

The scholar looks outward; the seeker looks inward (or "upward"). It is at this point, as I see it, that the idea of esotericism can usefully be introduced. The distinction between the movement toward God and the movement toward the outer world is surely a natural and basic distinction, and in that sense there has always been and there always will be a contrast in human life between functioning effectively and coherently with regard to the external world and, on the other hand, submitting oneself to a more conscious and transcendent reality that is contacted within the self. The possibility of the development within the human person of a presence that contains and reconciles both these movements is, it seems to me, a central defining characteristic recognized and even emphasized by teachings that may authentically be termed *esoteric*.

The inclusion of the "profane," the acceptance of the outer world, of all of human life including the movement toward the outer world, and including the mind and its desire for explanation and verification—to include all of this while at the same time leading the individual toward the divinity within the self, to embrace all these aspects of human life and reality; such a comprehensive spirituality may, I think, be at the heart of what is *esoteric*. Clearly, such a vision of human possibility is to be found within all the recognized religious traditions, but it is almost always in some measure hidden or obscure as compared to the form the tradition takes when it becomes a religion of the people. In every great religious tradition, somewhere—sometimes deeply hidden, sometimes closer to the surface—there is a path that embraces the profane, a path that embraces what the more widespread religion rejects as evil. One need only mention terms like *tantra, vajrayana,* or the Hasidism of the *Likutei Amarim,* or the various spiritual forms emanating from, say, the Brethren of the Common Life in fifteenth-century Holland—examples could be multiplied without limit. One needs to understand how such esotericism exists within each tradition. Indeed, it may be that what we generally call the larger tradition actually exists *within* the esoteric as a movement outward of a highly concentrated spirituality toward the larger world which stands in need of moral ideals, ideas, attitudes, and rules of behavior, and not necessarily the intense interior struggle that leads to the transformation of human nature.

In any case, what we might term the esoteric has bodied itself forth in recent decades as a sacralization of the profane. This has genuine appeal, in general, for a society that has desacralized nature, the human body, action in the world, work, labor, and the mind itself. There is genuine appeal in the resacralization of all that a divisive or "puritanical" or dogmatically doctrinal Christianity had in the early modern era separated off from the value realm of God and goodness. Our modern culture, sickened by technologically and economically driven mass violence on a scale hitherto unknown, disappointed in science and in the universe that science seemed to reveal—a universe without intrinsic meaning or value—alienated by a style of life defined by the continuous production of consumer goods, that is, the continuous creation and satisfaction of humanly peripheral desires— this society could be expected to welcome any conceptually acceptable way of bringing back nature, human labor, family relations, and the functions of the human body into the realm of the sacred.

In this sense, when Oriental religions began to attract Westerners in the late nineteenth and early twentieth centuries, it was partly because neither Hinduism nor Buddhism as it was known in the West demanded rejection of science and the standards of intellectual, philosophical rigor, nor did they emphasize the division between the realm of the spirit and the realm of the profane. The idea of "All is Brahman" or the Allness of the Buddhist Void enabled Western people to include aspects of human life that Christianity had separated itself from or condemned in one mode or another. In short, the Oriental religions brought spirituality without *moralism*. They brought not a rejection of science and the mind but alternate metaphysical explana- tions that in principle met science head-on, without retreating from the need to think and ponder and understand for oneself the world one lived in.

All the more has there been an attraction in recent years to Zen Bud- dhism and the metaphysical symbolism of Tibetan Buddhism; to Sufism as presented in the writings of gifted contemporary expositors who demon- strate its independence from fundamentalistically conceived Islamic doctrine; to Kabbalah and Hasidism, where the tendencies toward moral- ism and secularized intellectualism of modern Western Judaism are absorbed and dissolved in a powerful mythic symbolism and cosmic vision; and to the mysticism of a Meister Eckhart or Hildegard of Bingen.

In this sense, we could say that the deeper aspects of the new-religions phenomenon represent the reemergence within our culture of esotericism in general—the esoteric tradition *within* the world religions quite as much as the esoteric teachings that are identified as existing outside or inde- pendent of the known religious traditions. It is the latter, of course, that are the subject matter of the present volume.

But we cannot yet leave the question of authenticity. The "new age" milieu obviously presents much that is superficial and even absurd under the most time-honored, hallowed, and weighty terms. There is an abun- dance of "esoteric" merchandise, quite as much as there is of "mystical" merchandise—and reference here is not only to objects for sale in shops but to their philosophical and emotional equivalent in the tawdry use of words, ideas, and symbols, the conceptual equivalent of "crystals" and fortune- telling cards. But such aspects of the "new age" phenomenon are only the

most garish and easily recognizable aspect of the lawfully inevitable concomitant of the esoteric sacralization of the profane—namely, the danger,
if one may call it that, of profaning the sacred. At the very same moment,
for example, that nature and the body are, in theory or in practice, brought
into the realm of the sacred through the esoteric vision of the harmonization of the two movements within humanity and the universe, at that very
moment there appears within the individual and within the culture the
tendency to bring the sacred into the realm of the profane.

Surely to protect humanity from this reverse tendency is one of the
reasons why religion has often rigidly held to the separation of the sacred
and the profane. Better to maintain a tense separation of good from evil
than a blending of the two that brings down everything good. Better to
have a relative and just "harshness" that allows a definite level of good to
flourish than a false reconciliation that pollutes and mixes all good with its
opposite.

One cause of this reverse tendency is the erroneous supposition that the
inclusion of all levels in the realm of the inner search, and the goal of a
harmonious relationship between all the parts of human and cosmic nature,
implies the identity of all things, even their sameness. But when the great
teachings of the past speak of the unity of "heaven and earth," they are
speaking not of their identity but of their deeply natural and mutually
fecundating relationship. A true union also implies a true separation, and
the aim of unity refers to a circulating exchange of force among parts that
are, up to a very considerable degree, ineluctably independent as well as
being ultimately one in the service of the Absolute or God-principle. "As
above, so below" by no means entails "as below, so above"! It is when the
levels and separateness of principal forms within reality are clearly seen and
diligently maintained that the divine mutual organic exchange of universal
conscious energy (*Da'at* in Kabbalah) can flow. When this flows, then *all
is one.* Misunderstandings of the nature of unity often occur from a partial
acquaintance with familiar "mystical" statements about oneness with God,
or from partial or hasty reports of mystical experiences by individuals who
may not be sensitive to the whole range of what they themselves have
experienced—who are, as it were, captivated by the intensity of one or
another aspect of their experience and express it imprecisely and without
due care for how it will be heard by others.

But the whole issue of the meaning of the esoteric has many more inner
aspects to it. The esoteric is nothing if not hidden, inner, *secret.* As an outer
symbol of an interior reality, the notion of secrecy refers to the need within
the self to maintain a purity or separation of what is holy from what is
profane, and, in the context of the interior life, this may be taken to mean

the need to prevent one's ordinary, egoistic mind from appropriating the higher, more interior energies of the self. "Do not let the left hand know what the right hand is doing."

What is referred to here is what may be called the question of the conditions under which spiritual ideas and methods can be received by an individual and truly introduced into his or her life. A teaching is far more than words on paper or symbols in stone or on canvas. Ideas can be presented under such conditions as to contradict the very essence of their meaning, or as to provoke emotions and attitudes that effectively prevent the essential nuance of the teaching from being heard. This is an extremely subtle issue, and it is perhaps safe to say that—in our era, certainly—the question of the conditions under which sacred ideas can be heard is very poorly understood where it is even recognized at all. An authentic understanding of secrecy involves the rigorous but deeply compassionate control under which spiritual ideas or methods are made available to the outside world; and those who hold the teachings will not be persuaded to compromise on the basis of the modern assumption that all things should be made available to everyone. It is not that truth is being withheld from whoever seeks it; it is only that measures are taken to ensure that it is exposed only to those who will not so readily distort it or be harmed by it.

It is on this issue that the distinction between the seeker and the scholar needs to be recognized, not only in order to prevent confusion and to prevent pollution of scholarly standards of knowledge, on the one hand, or, on the other hand, in order to protect seekers from imagining that they have inwardly assimilated a truth merely because they can repeat to themselves what someone else has said or written about it, but also to realize that the understanding of any level of esotericism, insofar as it embraces both the outer and the inner movement of the mind, requires that the seeker and the scholar each honor the other. Or, to put it even more precisely: in the study of the esoteric scholars need to allow the seekers *within themselves* to exist; and seekers after esoteric knowledge must, for their part, allow within themselves the validity of the outward, analytic, or critical mind.

The question of authenticity leads us, therefore, to the signal issue of authority. The movements discussed in this volume manifest themselves, as was noted, to one degree or another as independent of "established" orthodoxies. They are all, each in its own way and degree, "spiritualities without credentials." In this aspect, perhaps even more than in any other, they speak to the modern mind, which—as many others have noted—has an allergy to authoritarianism of any kind. They speak to the conceit (not necessarily understood as a pejorative term) of autonomy which forbids the modern person to accept knowingly any ideas, especially spiritual ideas, on faith. They speak to the modern disillusionment with hierarchies of all kinds; they speak to the distrust of privilege; to the feeling for democracy and liberty in all matters; they speak to the need for explanations understandable to logic and sense perception (a canon of knowledge that reflects, epistemologically, the modern idea of equality and the modern distrust of authority). In the context in which we have placed them, the modern esoteric movements, to one degree or another, speak to the modern impulse of persons to see things for themselves, to verify for themselves, to be independent and self-reliant.

We are speaking now about the subjective conditions under which great truth enters a culture—in this case our own. These conditions, spiritually speaking, need to be seen not only as symptoms of an era's malaise (such is the claim of traditionalism), but also as its "language," its mode of crying for help, and, eventually, the channel through which the ever-eternal outpouring of the Way can reach us.

Authenticity, authority, and autonomy. Modern people, as scholars—that is to say, as scientists—cannot be asked to retreat before the seekers. Individuals today must retain their skepticism, their healthy distrust of the world of appearances, especially in the human world and the religious world. Yet the skeptic who was born with the birth of modern science, the Cartesian, the Baconian who must see for himself or herself, must not be separated from the seeker. The scientist must rediscover the heart—not the heart of sensual passion and fantastical dreams but the heart of hope in the sacred dimension of life. Underneath the appearances of pseudo-religiosity and pseudo-godliness there may certainly lie a scientifically determinable world obeying rigorous laws (this is the noble vision of the true scientist). But also: underneath the appearance of a world without objective meaning (the world of scientism) there may lie the noumenal reality of absolute conscious Being calling humanity to return to its own deepest self.

1

Ancient and Medieval Sources of Modern Esoteric Movements

Antoine Faivre

ELOW WILL BE found a succinct history of the currents of thought corresponding to what I have called esotericism in its broader meaning—or what stood for it from the end of antiquity to the beginning of modern times. This history, in the section on the Middle Ages, does not go beyond the Latin world except to consider those influences which had a strong effect on it, such as Jewish esotericism and Arabic and Byzantine philosophy. This history is indispensable for understanding esoteric movements since the Renaissance, for it makes their roots known to us. The generally accepted date for the beginning of modern times, that is, the end of the Middle Ages, is the taking of Constantinople by the Turks in 1453. For the sake of continuity, we will push it up to the end of the fifteenth century.

Esoteric Aspects in the Thought of the Lower Empire

Neo-Pythagoreanism and Stoicism; Philo

In spite of the lack of documents that it left, we know that the neo-Pythagoreanism of the first two centuries profoundly marked Neoplatonism; it has continued to resurface up to our time in various forms of arithmosophy. Numbers open the way to metaphysics, claim Nicomac of Gerase and also Moderatus of Gades, who provided a "numerical" translation of the Platonic teachings. However, the originality of this teaching resides in the fact that it tends to inwardly connect these numbers to a belief in an ordered procession of souls after death, and thus to a whole series of mediating processes of which the planets and stars are the stages. In this manner, the idea of mediation, so characteristic of esoteric thought, is expressed. The most frequently used scale at that time was, from top to bottom, the One, then Intelligibilities or Ideas, the soul, and finally, matter.

1

After death, or during this life, it is a matter of climbing the rungs. Such, very briefly stated, was the reigning conception of this current of ideas, which in this regard was close to that of the Essenes or of Plutarch (46?–120?). The latter is not only the author of *Lives;* he also left a doctrine on the "creation of the soul" in his bold interpretation of *Timaeus.* The writings of Plutarch which describe the rising of souls toward the moon after death are among the finest of this type of imagery in the West which have to do with the cosmicization of the beyond. The Egyptian myths, above all those connected to the cult of Osiris, fascinated this author, whose great worth after all was to have taken the very notion of "myth" seriously— contrary to all those who wanted to see in it only the allegorization of forces and natural phenomena.

If the intermediaries and gradations of neo-Pythagoreanism directly prepare the way for Neoplatonism, it is the same with Stoicism, although for slightly different reasons. The latter lasted for almost six centuries and also impregnated a part of the gnostic and hermetic currents. The aspect of Stoicism which most heralds esoteric thought in the West is without doubt the accent it places on the necessity for knowing the concrete universe by harmoniously combining wisdom and technique. Philosophy and wisdom are themselves considered practices, while Plato and Aristotle classed them among non-"liberal" activities. Stoicism thus teaches the necessity of concrete abilities; it refuses pure speculation and endeavors to understand the organic totality which guarantees the harmony between heavenly and earthly things.

It was also open to popular religion, even to various types of divination. From Zeno to Posidonius, the Stoics defended such religion, for they were sensitive to whatever recalled the harmony and affinity joining the different parts of the universe together. As a corollary, the idea of a passage between opposing forces due to the discovery of intermediary forces assured the harmony of the soul with things. It was a monistic thought, which knew only a homogeneous universe all the parts of which were penetrated by breath. As a matter of fact, Western esotericism would remain fundamentally antidualist, that is, opposed to all forms of ontological dualism, while turning toward both the spiritual and the concrete. It would preserve this trait, which already was a part of Stoic thought—that is, the paradox consisting of conserving commonsense things by transmuting them into manifestations of universal reason.

At the first ray of dawning, Christianity—thus even before the writing of the *Corpus Hermeticum*—also prepared the way for Neoplatonism in the work of Philo of Alexandria (20 B.C.–A.D. 54) For this Alexandrian Jew the transcendent God did not in fact affect the world directly, but through intermediaries, and the soul cannot reach God without them. Now, esotericism, in the final analysis, rests on the idea of mediation in whatever form it cloaks itself. According to Philo, it is the Logos or Word that is the mediator by which God sees the plan of the world and according to which he creates it. Wisdom is also a mediator, with which God mysteriously unites to create the universe. Angels and "demons," airy and fiery, are also mediators, followers, and performers of divine injunctions thanks to whom our souls may rise again to God. With Philo, the characteristic tendency of Neoplatonism is clearly expressed. This consists in investigating and proposing means of attaining an "intelligible" transcendent reality. However, contrary to Stoicism and, of course, to Christianity, the idea of a God coming to the aid of a human remains practically absent.

Philo achieved the synthesis of the Judaic tradition with Greek thought thanks to his eclecticism, common to all Greek Alexandrian thinkers. This eclecticism allowed him to interrelate knowledge and traditions, necessitating the examination of the scriptures on different levels with different possible interpretations of the same text. This was reaffirmed by medieval theology and is one of the functions of esotericism. All the same, Philo would remain unknown to Jewish thinkers, his influence for the most part affecting Christian thought.

Alexandrian Hermetism *

Alexandrian Hermetism—that is, the totality of writings called *Hermetica*—was, much more than Stoicism, a fundamental corpus from which esotericism would draw. One can speak of four new and even rival "religions" from the second century to the fourth: Hermetism, gnosticism, Neoplatonism, and Christianity. Each had much of importance in common with the others. It is known that Alexandria, founded in A.D. 332, developed rapidly to become one of the most important cities of antiquity. There Euclid opened his school of mathematics, in which Archimedes, Hipparchus, Eratosthenes, and Apollonius de Perga studied. But other towns of the delta also became famous. The *Chaldean Oracles,* perhaps the work of Julian the Theurgist, a contemporary of Marcus Aurelius, are in

---

*The word "hermetism" should be used to refer (a) to the Alexandrian texts written in Greek called the *Hermetika,* many of which (like the *Corpus Hermeticum*) are attributed to the legendary Hermes Trismegistus; (b) to the literature directly inspired by such texts and produced later, up to the beginnings of modern times (particularly in the fifteenth to twentieth centuries). The word "hermeticism" should be used in a wider sense, which covers many aspects of Western esotericism, such as alchemy, astrological speculations, and the like.

the same vein as Alexandrian Hermetism. These writings are half Eastern and half Greek, and have a negative theology strongly affirming the transcendence of the Father and theurgic magic. By "theurgy" we mean the knowledge of the theory and practice necessary to connect us with gods and spirits, and not only through raising our understanding but also through concrete rites and material objects that set in motion divine influences where and when we want, thus allowing angelic beings to appear before us. Elements of the *Chaldean Oracles* are found in Marius Victorinus (A.D. 280?–363?), Augustine, Porphyry, Synesius, Iamblichus, Arnobius, and, in the eleventh century, in the Byzantine Psellos. The work of Apuleius of Madaura (125?–170?), who lived and studied mainly in Athens, also flourished during the era of Alexandrian Hermetism. He is the author of the famous *Golden Ass* (or *Metamorphoses*), a Latin novel full of magic, spells, and mysteries.

The *Hermetica* consist of several small scattered works, the most famous being the collection *Corpus Hermeticum*, which left a permanent mark on Western thought. It brings together seventeen treatises written in Greek in the second and third centuries. These treatises (*Poimandres, Asclepius, Kore Kosmu*, etc., to which the so-called *Stobaei Hermetica* were added) are known only from manuscripts dating no earlier than the fourteenth century. Fourteen of them were translated into Latin by Marsilio Ficino in 1463. The Middle Ages had forgotten them, with the exception of the *Aesclepius*. During the Renaissance, Valentin Weigel (1533–1588), the father of German theosophy (Jacob Boehme [1575–1624] being the prince) cites Hermes Trismegistus more than any other author before his time—Pseudo-Dionysius, Eckhart, Plato, and Augustine coming next. These writings are attributed to the "thrice-great" Hermes Trismegistus. Contrary to doctrines focusing on certain similar points, like Mandeanism, the teachings marked with the seal of Hermes were received by the modern Western world less as relics of "bygone days" than as an always-present, living, and revivifying source, inviting one to a continual hermeneutic exegesis.

Modern Western esotericism shares with Alexandrian Hermetism an eclectic orientation together with a certain philosophical perspective and a pervasive reference—which is clear in the corpus—to a scenario of fall and reintegration. This eclectic outlook, the possibility of drawing from diverse currents, gives rise to the notion of *philosophia perennis*—and also includes an emphasis put on the will, at both the divine and human levels. The acts of God are his will, and his essence consists in "willing." Likewise, Germanic theosophy, starting with Jacob Boehme, puts the emphasis on this same primacy of the will of God. The adept, for his part, must "will to know." The optimistic and pessimistic aspects of the *Hermetica* are also found in modern Hermetism—optimism in the possibility of our uniting with the divine by inscribing a representation of the universe in our own "*mens*"; pessimism in the strongly emphasized consequences of the fall on the present state of nature.

The philosophical assumption common to both the *Hermetica* and to modern times is the absence of absolute ontological dualism. In the treatise *Nous to Hermes,* the former instructs the latter to reflect the universe in his own mind, to grasp the divine essence of nature and engrave it within his psyche, which is made possible by the fact that humans possess a divine intellect. This theme of the "mirror," on which "speculating" never stops, is connected to a major common denominator of esotericism, namely, the idea of the universe seen as a book to be read or to decipher. God is known by contemplation of the world; and since the universe is a forest of symbols, it is natural to become interested in everything within it. From this comes the accent the *Hermetica* put on the particular, the *mirabilia,* at the expense of the abstract and the general (see especially the *Cyranides*). This science is not "uninvolved," but it comes to the general through the enriching detour of the concrete and particular. It is already the seed of Paracelsus and the romantic German *Naturphilosophie.* The taste for the concrete and the philosophy of the incarnation offer an obvious compatibility with Christianity. "There is nothing invisible, even among incorporeal beings," for the reproduction of bodies is an "eternal act"; embodiment is "an acting force"—this is what the *Corpus* teaches. Already it is close to *Geistleiblichkeit,* the "spiritual corporeity" of Boehme's and Oetinger's theosophy.

The third point of convergence is the reference to the mythical themes of fall and reintegration. Note that the theme of the fall of humanity by the attraction of the sensual, very prevalent in Western theosophy, is already present in *Poimandres* (the first text of the *Corpus*), where it is said that the enclosing of Adam within the sensual was due to *Eros.* This does not mean contempt for nature; rather it is a cosmosophic theme inviting a regenerative work by way of a reascension. This takes place either through our "intellect," which, connected to intermediary spiritual intelligences, employs them like a spiritual ladder, or by theurgical practices—or both at once. The *Hermetica* thus enables us better to understand the theurgy of John Dee and, in the eighteenth century, that of Martines de Pasqually. The divine essence enclosed within human beings is not such that it can be freed or regenerated by any means one wishes, but only according to precise methods, among which are initiations that can be of various types. The teaching that Alexandrian Hermetism provides on this point implies the belief in an "astrological cosmos," while modern astrology, especially since the seventeenth century, tends more and more to part from initiatory processes and become only a form of divination.

Finally, there is the idea in Alexandrian Hermetism that, because of humanity, the earth itself is susceptible to improvement, to a return to a glorious state, to become truly "active." The spread of this fecund idea was helped by the writings of Saint Paul (Romans 8:19–22): the fall of humanity brings nature in its train, and consequently nature can be regenerated with humanity's help if only it returns to the good. A possible basis perhaps for a metaphysically grounded ecology!

Until 1610 it was believed that these writings were anterior to Christianity and contemporaneous with Moses—thus the aura that surrounds them, especially in the eyes of seekers. Nevertheless, except for the *Asclepius*, of which the Latin version had never been lost, the Middle Ages had no direct knowledge of them. Hermetic alchemy issued from a similar influence and arose in the same environment. It seems that it was unknown in pharaonic Egypt. Within Alexandrian Hellenism or parallel to it, Hermetic alchemy appears to have developed as an extension of Hermetic astrology, proceeding from the notion of a sympathetic correspondence between particular planets and metals. Alexandrian alchemical Hermetism took two directions: one that consisted of working out the processes for creating metallic tinctures and transmutations, and another corresponding to a mysticism expressing itself through natural symbols. Let us retrace the broad stages of this development.

Western alchemy undoubtedly began in Alexandria or, more broadly, in the towns of the Delta. Until about the second century B.C., it was mainly a technique connected with the art of fashioning gold. With Bolos of Mendes, called the Democritean, it takes a philosophical or, more precisely, an esoteric bent in the second century. For the first time, it seemed, doctrine grounded and supported experience. A collection of important writings entitled *Physica and Mystica*, often referred to afterwards, set forth Bolos's ideas. Then in the second and third centuries A.D. we find a series of texts of which only some extracts remain, that are called "apocryphal" by historians, and which answer the need to hold up alchemy as a science revealed by a god, a prophet, or a king of the past. We then come to Zozimos of Panopolis (end of third or beginning of fourth century), who seems to have worked mainly in Alexandria. The twenty-eight books composing the vast compendium dedicated to his sister Theosebia were translated by Berthelot and Ruelle at the end of the last century. They contain an astonishing allegorical symbolism, secrets revealed during visions, a great deal of compilation as well as original writing, all pervaded by a feeling for the spirit of Hermetism and gnosis. And finally, from the fourth to the seventh century, we enter the age of "commentaries" during which the divorce between the practitioners and the "mystics," that is, between those who are seeking practical methods and adepts who are concerned above all with esoteric symbolism, grows ever more pronounced. Those who stand out are Synesius (fourth century), Olympiodorus (sixth century), and Stephanos of Alexandria (610–641). The last, a philosopher, mathematician, astronomer, and in favor at the Byzantine court, considered alchemy essentially a spiritual exercise. Also dating from the seventh century are anonymous commentaries said to be written by the Anepigraph and the Christian. No doubt the *Corpus* of the Greek alchemists, which contained the writings of all these authors and which would later influence the Middle Ages, was completed at the end of that century.

Gnosticism

Is it possible to speak of esotericism with reference to "gnosis," so present in the very first centuries, in the same way that one speaks of alchemy and Alexandrian Hermetism? Certainly, and all the more as this word, in the sense of "knowledge," is above all synonymous with esotericism. Yet the general meaning of the term "gnosis" should remain carefully distinct from the "gnosis" of the beginning of our era, for which it would be best to reserve the term "gnosticism" to avoid confusion. The common theme of the various forms of gnosticism is redemption, the deliverance from evil. It implies the destruction of the universe in which we live, or at least the rising of our souls above this world we must all someday leave. Basilides and Valentinus did not teach a dualist doctrine in which Evil is an ontological principle equal to Good. But in the same period, the second century, Marcion proposed such a dualism, which is also found in many similar systems dealing with this theme; that is, the deliverance by Christ of our divinely created soul which is trapped in this world created by an evil demiurge. The God of the Old Testament is this evil demiurge, whose harmful work was to be corrected by the God of the New Testament. Meditations based on the myths of the biblical Genesis are common to both gnosticism and Hermetic writings. But Hermetism is often optimistic, while gnosticism is always pessimistic. The former execrates the latter for committing the error of seeing, in the whole universe, only the evil work of a perverse creator. The disciples of Hermes Trismegistus are the bitter enemies of the Gnostics, even when they are commenting on myths or doctrinal elements more or less common to both.

Gnosticism and Neoplatonism have something in common, in that both believe that our soul, of divine origin and alien to earthly life, becomes blemished in becoming incarnate and is purified by rising to its origin. This is possible by virtue of a divine potentiality that we possess, and which can be actualized when awakened from without. But by a Neoplatonist like Plotinus, gnosticism is not much appreciated. Plotinus turns away from gnosticism, reproaching it for professing an absolute dualism, for not being satisfied with religious practices, with the ascetic way, and for adding arbitrary metaphysical dramas to these practices.

From the point of view of Judeo-Christian esotericism, gnosticism is looked upon favorably for taking myths very seriously. Mani presents a superb myth that is characteristic of the drama of the "saved savior," a mythological theme that modern esotericism would bring up to date. But Western theosophy, whether Jewish (Kabbalah) or Christian, will always reject ontological dualism and remain aloof from the complicated and fantastic lucubrations which, like those of the gnostic Justinian in the third century, make humanity's fate depend on a metaphysical family quarrel. The gnostic tendency to misuse intermediaries ended up in a hodgepodge of clichés which had short-lived results. Christian esotericism, moreover, could not subscribe to the gnostic idea that Christ is not the Savior in the full sense of the term, but only one who revealed a hidden science, the messenger whose mission was to awaken humanity rather than save it. This absolute dualism has lasted a long time. It is at the root of tenth-century Bulgarian Bogomilism, itself one of the sources of the Catharist movement. Finally, the tragic and humiliating image that Mani gives of the human being is found again in the twentieth century, obviously modified, in Freudian anthropology.

Pagan Neoplatonism

In Platonic thought, there is a clear boundary between the higher and lower worlds, and any idea of help coming from above is excluded. The higher does not come down to us; nor is it necessary, because our soul, surrounded by things here below that remind us of the existence of a higher world, finds the possibility of development within itself. Neoplatonism retains from Plato's thought the belief that, on the one hand, the world of the senses is in opposition to the world of Ideas, that it is the prison from which the soul must be delivered; but, on the other hand, this world of the senses nevertheless takes part in the Ideas insofar as it can transmit "reminiscences" to our soul which bring it out of its dream state. With Plato, Eros goes toward the higher as salvation is the ascension of the soul. Plotinus inserted the doctrine of Eros in the formula dear to Alexandrians: there is an ascension *and* a descent, a double movement which marked the Neoplatonist seal and Western esoteric thought forever.

In the first centuries Neoplatonism is characterized by two tendencies that are not doctrinally distinct from each other but rather correspond to different orientations of certain activities. One is purely intellectual—that of Plotinus, for example, for whom no visible religion is justified by its practices. The other corresponds to the profuse use of myths, rites, and incantations. Neoplatonism saw its greatest period from Plotinus to Damascius, from the second to the sixth century, when it followed a four-fold direction that the historian Jean Trouillard summarized in the following manner: (1) a revival of the great Hellenic doctrines in the light of Platonism; (2) an intense curiosity about the wisdom and religions of the East; (3) a seeking for deliverance as well as for truth; (4) a tendency to set forth a complete spiritual hierarchy, an intransigent transcendence allied with a mystical immanence. Western esotericism followed each of these directions, adapting each of them in its own manner.

Neoplatonic philosophers arose from the well-to-do classes of society, purposely hiding themselves from the ignorant and teaching that philosophy demands a long and difficult initiation. This characteristic is enough, in the eyes of some nowadays, to define esotericism as secretive, as the "disciplina arcani," though esotericism cannot be defined by, or limited to, the notion of secrecy. What appeared at the end of the second century, with the birth of these philosophical circles, is mainly the teaching of a method allowing one to reach an "intelligible" reality and to construct or describe this reality with its structure and connections. Contrary to what Western esotericism will become, the function of this intelligible reality is not to explain the material world but rather to have us leave it in order to see this imperfect region for what it is, and allow us to enter a pure world where knowledge and happiness are possible. Of course, the material reflects the intelligible, but the meaning of the material matters little; the essential thing is to go beyond it and arrive at the world of Ideas. There is no real communication between gods and humans; the divine beings in the myths are indifferent to our fate. This philosophy is above all a method of "describing the metaphysical landscapes to which the soul is transported by a kind of spiritual training" (Emile Bréhier). Human beings are no longer a goal of the universe, as they are in Stoicism and later in esotericism, but only beings trying to contemplate the universal order. Consequently, the interdependence of beings matters little, at least as hermetism and, more broadly speaking, esotericism see it. What counts is the hierarchy of the forms of being, from the most to the least perfect in accordance with our knowledge of the steps to follow in climbing the rungs of the ascending ladder.

We know practically nothing about Ammonius Saccas, except that while teaching in Alexandria (232–243) he was the master of Plotinus and perhaps the first Neoplatonist philosopher. Plotinus lived in Rome from 245 until his death in 270, where he gathered some disciples, including Porphyry, who published Plotinus's works in the form of *Enneads* (a series of lectures dealing with astrology, the manner in which the soul descends into the body and is united with it, memory, etc.). When Plotinus speaks of astrological divination, prayer, or the cult of statues, it is to show that the effectiveness of these practices is due not to the action of a god on the world but to the affinities connecting the parts of the world to each other. A well-performed religious act or an incantation produces its own effects. Whereas Philo's intermediary, the Logos which can punish or reward, concerns itself with human welfare, the Platonic hypostasis cares not at all for our good. This is a fine example, as we have mentioned several times, of the difference between Semitic devotion and Hellenic intellectualism. Plotinus's interest in magic does not express a special taste for nature as a bearer of meanings to decipher; it only shows an interest in rites "which in the last analysis transform every religious act into a magic one" (*Enneads* IV, 4, 38ff.)— which is a characteristic common to this period fond of incantations, writing tablets, and divinations of every kind. The material world is a vast network of magic influences from which only philosophy can escape insofar as it sees itself primarily as a school of purification. Let us remember that Plotinus struggled against the dualism of gnosticism: section IX of the second *Ennead* is entitled "Against those who say that the Demiurge of this world is evil and that the Cosmos is bad."

His disciple Porphyry (273–305), from Tyre, insists on the purifying character of theurgy and in *Images* he discusses the symbolic meaning of statues. The thought of Iamblichus of Chalcis (end of the third century to 330?), who taught under Diocletian and Constantine, dominated the end of Neoplatonism. Like Aristotle, this neo-Pythagorean liked to classify, but in a Platonic way, in order to rediscover the many pagan religious forms in the "intelligible" world. His book, *The Mysteries of Egypt,* composed about 300, is an attempt to justify the literal meaning of theurgy and the "mysteries" as a reaction against a purely "intellectual" road to deliverance. For Plotinus, philosophy was the only way to communicate with higher beings, while Iamblichus's book is a defense of theurgy. It was influential for a long time—on the emperor Julian, on Proclus, and on Pseudo-Dionysius—and it was Proclus who handed it down.

Macrobius, as important as Chalcidius for understanding the Platonism of Chartres in the twelfth century, is the author of a commentary on Cicero's famous "Dream of Scipion" (*De re publica* 6). Entitled *In somnium Scipionis* and written about 300, this book by Macrobius developed Neoplatonist, astrological, and arithmetical ideas found in part in his *Saturnalia.*

The Intellect is conceived as a divine faculty common to both humans and the heavenly bodies. The latter direct human reason in the same way as they make bread rise. The germinating power of plants is connected here with human reason.

The next great name after Iamblichus is that of Proclus of Byzantium (412–485), a theurgist who also taught in Athens. Marinus left us his *Life of Proclus*, an informative biography. Proclus was a great classifier, had an incisive mind, and was the author of numerous commentaries on Plato. He was interested in all the myths and rites and was connected to the school of Iamblichus. In the face of a rising Christianity, Proclus made himself the defender of ancient traditions, but he often referred to esoteric Christianity in his work, and, contrary to Porphyry, he attacked Christianity very little. His *Commentary on Timaeus*, his theories on the World Soul, on "Chaos"— which he considered as sacred as Light, seeing in both the first expression of the Good—his sense of mythic drama (the combat of the Titans against Dionysos, the struggle of the Giants against Zeus, etc.), and his dynamic polarities, served to nourish later theosophical thinking. His conception of polar opposites, for example, had a long influence down through the centuries, for it put the accent on the fruitfulness of antithetical principles. His *Elements of Theology* took up the old idea of Thales: "Everything is full of gods"—to the point that even pebbles have a life, or a purifying quality. Under the influence of the *Chaldean Oracles*, Proclus, like Iamblichus, developed a conception of magic corresponding to a rehabilitation of matter. But above all, the affirmation that there exists a nonempirical form of corporeality ("*oklema*," the vehicle, an idea borrowed from *Timaeus*) anticipates the theosophical idea of a spiritual body, for according to Proclus every soul has a garment made of light, a mediator between body and spirit, able to manifest itself and endowed with an unalterable sensibility. It is close to the idea that Henry Corbin developed concerning Shiite esotericism in speaking of the "subtle body." Proclus truly appears as one of the first representatives of Western esotericism in the sense that he was as concerned with transforming the sensible world as he was with purifying the soul. His influence reached Syria, leaving its mark on the *Liber de causis* (825?) through which this type of thought would return to the West. Through Psellos, and thus later through Gemiste Plethon, it would have an effect on Pico della Mirandola at the dawn of the Renaissance—at the threshold of modern esotericism.

Besides these great writers, Neoplatonism saw various other works and practices. The book by Philostratus, *Life of Apollonius of Tyana* (220?), had already known a lively success in its time, for this novel showed the Pythagorean Apollonius being initiated into all the magic practices of the East. A little before that, Alexander of Abonotica had flourished as a charlatan; Lucianus, in *Alexander,* had devoted himself to unmasking his machinations. From the third century to the fifth, the imperial government issued many laws and edicts against divination and certain forms of sacrifices— while still believing in their effectiveness—that is, against practices that Neoplatonism made more and more bound up with its own teaching. Neoplatonists had a religious veneration for the cosmos which, from the second century to the fourth, expressed itself mainly by a sun cult of the people—as much in the mysteries of Mithra as in the official cult of the *Deus Sol*—the common denominator of almost all the religions of the empire. To this we must add, of course, on the one hand, the influence of the *Chaldean Oracles,* the holy book of Hellenism, about which Proclus said that if it was necessary to burn all the books in the world, this one along with *Timaeus* must be kept, and on the other hand, the alchemical practices so widespread in that period, which also rested on the belief in the unity of beings, on universal affinities. With Greek alchemy we rediscover Hermetism, which is quite natural, since there is a close connection between it and Neoplatonism. This is especially so with Proclus, whose treatise *On Hieratic Art,* based on the theory of affinities, explicitly refers to the "mystic chains"—that of Hermes, for example—which connect plants with the heavenly bodies, and even with animals, and which also belong to the medical-astrological aspect of Hermetism. Neoplatonism dies along with Greek culture: Damascius (470?–544?), one of the very last Neoplatonists, was a devotee of the intense spiritual and mystic life, but he speaks as a philosopher, not as a magician or a theurgist. In this sense, he marks the end of an era. The sixth and seventh centuries would bring in a long period of silence.

The Beginnings of Christian Esotericism

Hellenistic Neoplatonism includes points of doctrine incompatible with Christianity: for example, the divinity of the heavenly bodies (even if Christian esotericism willingly admits the idea of intermediary intellects or directing intelligences), the eternity of the world, and the belief that souls are of divine origin. But this last example could be interpreted in a Christian sense, and the last constituent element of Neoplatonism, the belief in magic, is not completely incompatible. Furthermore, the idea of intermediaries or mediators, such as the human *Intellectus,* related to governing or mediating "intellects," and the corresponding idea of an initiatory peregrination of the soul—along with transformable nature —ascending toward God are not contrary to the teaching of Jesus. This is why Christian esotericism will adopt and affirm clearly Neoplatonistic traits down through the centuries, to the point that they will quickly become inseparable from esotericism itself.

Another influence to be added is that of Hermetism. Lactantius, who converted to Christianity in 300 and then became tutor to the son of Emperor Constantine, considered Hermes Trismegistus a sage inspired by God. Certainly Hermetism knew nothing of the savior nor of a revelation coming from above, and furthermore it tended to accept more or less the idea of an inexorable fate based on the stars, but it nevertheless shared with Christianity a high conception of humanity's place in the universe and in cosmic development. Now, this place is dramatized in Judeo-Christianity, and here the accent is on "drama." The fall of Lucifer, of Adam, the involvement of the universe in the fall, and the final reintegration bring the basic all-embracing myths to life by incorporating into their scenarios a certain number of *dramatis personae* and actions through which all the levels of Being and things are shown to be united with each other, whether it has to do with Heaven, the whole of nature, or humanity. The cosmos of the Greeks was eternal, without a history, or at the most cyclic. Christianity brought in radically new changes which accentuated the dramatic aspects of the Old Testament while at the same interpreting the Greek myths on the level of the individual. Celse, in *A True Speech* (second century), thus reproached Christians for accepting a God not absolutely immutable, one sensitive to pity, and a Christ about whom the accounts do not allow for allegories. Finally, Christianity conceives of human beings as individuals relatively autonomous and independent of the material world, that is, as beings endowed with their own lives, whose roles are not only to think of nothing but the universe but also to work in various ways. A human life is also an existence, which implies responsibility and "talents" to be developed.

This is not the place to enumerate all the elements allowing us to see in primitive Christianity—through the New Testament—a form of esotericism. We will restrict ourselves to just a few of these elements. But at the same time, we must insist that to affirm that its exotericism is nothing more than a betrayal of its original esoteric meaning would be as false as claiming the inverse. Moreover, the several characteristics mentioned here mainly concern one esoteric element among others, that of "secrecy," of the *disciplina arcani* or initiatory degrees; the limitations of this study do not allow for further development. Thus, in the New Testament there are passages such as Mark 4:10ff.; 7:17ff.; 10:10ff., which can be interpreted esoterically. In the same way, Paul speaks to us of knowing the four dimensions (Ephesians 3:17–19), as elsewhere he alludes to the "solid food" that not everyone can bear. It is never a question of a secret knowledge transmitted to the apostles by Christ after his resurrection; but, after all, nothing in the Gospels prevents us from assuming this, and most of the apocryphal gospels do not hesitate to mention it. Furthermore, during the beginnings of the church, one distinguished among beginners, those on the way, and the perfect ones, a triadic classification belonging to almost all initiations. Ambrose tells us that even in the fourth century one did not write nor speak of the Symbol of the Apostles in front of catechumens or heretics. Whether it is a speech of Bishop Cyril of Jerusalem catechizing or the writings of Basil, one always has the impression that an initiatory teaching exists and by "stages."

There is nothing strange in this. How, in fact, is one to make the Trinity, the Eucharist, or the "Son of God" understood to the firstcomer who has never heard anything about them? Such elaborate metaphysical conceptions, inserted in a universal myth, or one derived from it, could not be accessible to everyone right away. It is not enough to be a catechumen in order to have the ability to contemplate what Basil called a "tacit and mystic tradition maintained up to our time." As Raymond Abellio has correctly written: "Democratic by its mystery, Christianity is aristocratic by its gnosis." (Of course, it has nothing to do here with gnosticism.) "This science is not for everyone," said Pseudo-Dionysius, recalling that the apostles set forth truths under the veil of symbols and not in their sublime nudity. To these testimonies we must add the obvious: namely, that there has never been and could never be "secret" sacraments more important than baptism or the Eucharist! Esotericism as something "secret" is nothing more than illuminating ways allowing our intelligence to perceive what is more "inner" within the mysteries. It is nothing more than the analogic way—that is, a higher level of understanding of a sacred document beyond a simply allegorical interpretation. On this complex question, one can consult the study of Jean Daniélou (*Eranos Jahrbuch* 31 [1962]) and the references furnished by Frithjof Schuon (*The Transcendental Unity of Religions*). For the moment, let us leave the final word to Origen: "There are various forms of the Word by which it is revealed to His disciples conforming to each person's degree of light—that is according to one's level of progress towards saintliness" (*Against Celsus* 4.16). All the same, to limit esoteric thought to this one dimension would be, as we have seen, to mutilate it. One cannot repeat too often that in the West the great esoteric current passes through Nature and in no way restricts itself to the question of knowing if such and such a thing is less "secret" or should be kept more "hidden" than another. It is for each to discover for himself or herself what he or she is able to understand. Nature—that is, the whole Cosmos—is part of this hermeneutics, of which the famous passage of the apostle (Romans 8:19–22) bears witness.

The existence of apocryphal gospels has helped us better to perceive certain deep meanings in the canonical texts. Among these writings, we mention only the *Pseudo-Clementines,* which have been attributed to Clement of Rome and which deal with astrology, magic, and angelology. To these texts are added others of a curious appearance, like the *Confession* of Cyprian, a magician of the third century who became bishop of Antioch and died a martyr, in which, as regards his education, he speaks much about demons, pagan mysteries, and natural and occult sciences. But for the development of a Christian esotericism in the full sense of the word, the essential is elsewhere—that is, in the debate that an important part of Christianity took on with philosophy.

We know in fact that the history of Christian thought is inseparable from the need to reconcile faith with certain fundamental teachings of Hellenism. This is particularly true of Christian esotericism. Clement of Alexandria and Origen were very attached to Hellenistic civilization, and it is not by chance that these two thinkers have been continually cited by almost all esotericists up to our time. There was no lack of Christians, however, who emphasized the differences between Christianity and Hellenism, the most important being the fact that Hellenism did not limit the divinity at the same point in the hierarchy of beings. In fact, for Plato and the Stoics, the divine Being extended to the stars, to our world, and even to our souls, whereas Christians limit it to the Trinity. Thus, we see Arnobius, converted in 297, attacking the teaching of Plato according to which souls are fallen divine beings (the famous theory of "reminiscences"). And yet to perceive spirit even in inanimate matter or to strive to see, through innumerable "signatures" scattered throughout nature and discoverable in our soul, the rungs of Jacob's ladder uniting heaven and earth—this is what esotericism is concerned with, and the Greeks had already said much on the subject. In the end, it is a question of reconciling transcendence and immanence.

Pantenus, a Stoic converted to Christianity, created a school in Alexandria successively headed by Clement (160–215) and Origen (185–254), and which undoubtedly represents the first large-scale Christian attempt to compete with the pagan schools. Clement, also a Stoic turned Christian, dared to affirm that Christianity had two Old Testaments, the Hebrew and the Hellenistic. He openly declared that if given the choice between knowledge and eternal salvation he would choose knowledge, all the while knowing that the two cannot be separated (*Stromata* 4.136). In this important work and in other writings, he emphasized more strongly than any other Christian thinker before him, except of course representatives of gnosticism, the importance of this knowledge, that is, of gnosis—understood in the sense it will continue to have in Christian esotericism. Gnosis contains the rule of faith and goes beyond it: "Gnosis . . . is a kind of maturing of man *qua* man. It takes place thanks to the knowledge of divine things. . . . Through it, faith is attained and becomes perfect, it being given that the faithful can become perfect only in this way. . . . One must start from faith and, growing in the grace of God, acquire its knowledge as much as possible" (*Stromata* 7.55).

In this same Alexandrian Christian school, Origen first studied under Ammonius Saccas—the same teacher for whom twenty years later Plotinus in his turn would be the student. Origen left abundant works, of which *De principiis (Peri archon)* is the most important book. It can be said that with Origen, Christian thought became impregnated with Neoplatonism. Fallen souls are pure spirits only having strayed from God, but who, thanks to an appropriate pilgrimage, draw close to him again. Our earthly body is both a punishment and a help on this path (an idea taken up again by modern Christian theosophy). Metaphors of a journey describe the stages of this pilgrimage. Origen laid out and consolidated the basis of an anti-idealism which would remain one of the characteristics of Christian esotericism, namely, the idea that created souls that are completely lacking in bodily form do not exist. Only God is incorporeal; bodies only change in terms of rank and perfection according to their merits. Thus there is no clean break between the human and angelic worlds. The idea of apocatastasis which he upheld—that is, of universal salvation (the devil included)—emphasizes, even though it is arguable, the typically Origenian idea of the integration of Christ's work in a cosmic process; and this integration itself, with or without apocatastasis, will be the strength of modern theosophy. Two other aspects of his work deserve to be mentioned for our purposes. Origen recommends first a constant effort to interpret texts—that is, spiritual hermeneutics—to pass from faith to knowledge (to gnosis), to structure in our mind what is by nature impenetrable. The contents of the scriptures are on three levels: carnal (literal), psychic (moral), and spiritual (mystical and prophetical). It is essential that each of us causes meanings to spring up from the third level within ourselves. Then Origen recommends freedom of investigation. Now this by its very nature is the basis and justification of all theosophy. No more than with Clement, the reducing of faith to gnosis has as its goal to humanize faith by denying its specificity; but this liberty of investigation obviously has meaning only within the fact of revelation.

To this idea of gnosis—which, as we have seen, is distinct from gnosticism—we must join the idea of "tradition," which is not unique to esotericism but still remains inseparable from it. It opens the thought of the high Middle Ages, in the *Commonitorium* by Vincent de Lerins in 354, with the formulation of the rules to be used to distinguish the true tradition in matters of faith. The author attaches great importance to the opinion of the "ancients." Taken up again through the centuries, this idea would encourage and justify the marked tendency of esotericists to study the most varied authors of antiquity, and in a way so general as to allow for all varieties of eclectic notions. But with Vincent de Lerins and in esotericism, it is always a question of seeking common denominators, that is, what is common to all. Western esoteric thought, as well as constituted church theologies, accepts the idea of the growth of tradition—thanks to individual revelations with the theosophs and to doctrinal elucidations having a more collective authority with the theologians. But in both cases, this growth is understood as a succession of developments having no claim to be more than further elucidations. It is a question of maintaining wholeness, whether of doctrine or from inspiration. The whole period of the high Middle Ages is characterized by an intense activity bearing on biblical commentaries and following the rules of Philo's allegorical commentary; namely, that no knowledge exists, whether scientific or philosophical, of which a commentary cannot be turned to account. From this arose an eclecticism, a movement across disciplines, that theology would abandon little by little down through the centuries and especially in modern times. But esotericism would conserve it through its continual denial of any gap or hiatus between revelation of the Book and that of Nature—an affirmation that would characterize in particular what would be called philosophies of nature, in the romantic sense of the term.

From the beginning of the third century until the fourth century, three names appear to represent this neoplatonizing and esotericizing eclecticism in Christian thought: Chalcidius, Synesius, and Nemesius. Chalcidius, still more than Macrobius, contributed to the introduction of Platonic themes in the Middle Ages in an esoteric way. In fact, Chalcidius's translation of *Timaeus* and his commentary on it (300?) would remain the basic Platonic source of the thought of the Middle Ages up to the twelfth century. Synesius (370?-430) would mainly influence the Byzantine period. An African bishop of Cyrene and a friend of Hypatia, he wrote in Greek his *Hymns* and *Letters,* which detail the occult affinities between natural objects. Synesius conceives of the universe as active and dynamic, and he recalls that "knowledge" should be hidden from the ignorant and is thus esoteric. Nemesius, bishop of Emese, lays down a whole universe of meanings. His treatise *De natura hominis* (400?) is one of the first basic Christian writings to view the human being as a microcosm, that is, as a miniature universe, a link between the material and spiritual worlds. The world becomes sacred again through the *anthrōpos.* The ordered universe that

Synesius sees in all visible and invisible created things is a landmark in the history of occult "correspondences."

Esoteric Aspects in the Thought of the Early Middle Ages

Augustinian Ideas; Boethius

The thought of Augustine (354–430), the spiritual and intellectual giant dominating all the early Middle Ages, does not belong to the same esoteric current, but his authority was often cited by its representatives. In fact, if medieval thinking on divine things was able to draw substantial nourishment from the Neoplatonic tradition, it is due in part to Augustine, for he taught that once the soul is noble, harmonious, and ordered, it is capable of seeing the source from which all truth flows. At a lower level, an intelligent soul, united to higher "Intellects," perceives their truth through a light with which we are naturally endowed. Esotericism is thus pleased to find in Augustine the idea of archetypes. Did he not say that the laws of numbers are established in God, that God directs the order of things through Ideas? Numbers and Ideas are certainly not created beings, but behind them works the eternal Wisdom by which the creator made the world. "Ideas are the original forms (*formae principales*), the stable and immutable ground of things. . . . They are a part of divine intelligence" (*De diversis quaestionibus*); and since they are the archetypes of created beings, we have only to try to rise from the reflection to the pattern. We can, through the things of this world, raise ourselves to the creator.

This is by no means a summary of Augustine's thought, but only that aspect of it which most concerns our subject. The end of his life corresponds to the end of pagan teachings in Alexandria (the female philosopher Hypatia was assassinated by Christians in 415). The Egyptian philosophers sought refuge in Athens, where Proclus was teaching, and Alexandrian alchemy passed on to Greece. The end of Augustine's life also corresponded to the beginning of the barbarians' destruction of large cities, that is, to the eventual disappearance of a true Roman civilization. Thus one witnessed the development of a spiritual life that is much more than a pursuit of intellectual culture—from which arose the creation of rather exclusive conventicles recalling those of the era of Philo of Alexandria. In the Christian East, the emphasis was put on metaphysical concerns and the need to understand the intelligible structure of things in a Neoplatonic sense. The West, by contrast, was more concerned with questions having to do with the institution of the church and its hierarchy—and thus with heresies as well (Donatism,

Pelagianism, etc.). The popes seized power with Gregory the Great (540?–604), but without giving any creative impulse to theology; for up to the Middle Ages properly so called, they were almost all politicians and jurists. Little remains, moreover, from ancient Greece, apart from some Aristotle (his logic!), a bit of Plato, and also Lucan, Virgil, and Cicero. Strangely enough, one of the rare great personalities of the period, who does not seem to have been particularly influenced by Hermetism, would nonetheless be frequently referred to in modern esoteric thought—especially in masonic literature. We are talking about Boethius (480–525), the "last of the Romans," who was consul in 510 under Theodoric and was executed after having been accused of magic. It was with him that the problem of nominalism and realism seems to have made its first specific appearance. *The Consolation of Philosophy*, written in prison before his execution, is a moving book that served as a model for innumerable souls in search of true wisdom. Of the greatest importance for us are the names Dionysius the Areopagite and Johannes Scotus Erigena.

Pseudo-Dionysius

Dionysius, called Pseudo-Dionysius since it was known that he was not the person mentioned in the Acts of the Apostles, wrote at the beginning of the sixth century (*Mystical Theology, Divine Names, Celestial Hierarchy*, and *Ecclesiastical Hierarchy*, as well as *Letters*). He contributed to the introduction of numerous Neoplatonic ideas into Christian mysticism. He boasted of having drawn all his philosophy—or, as he called it, "theosophy"—from the scriptures themselves. And, as a matter of fact, theosophs would henceforth consider this to be their task. The negative theology that he worked out placed God above all the "divine names." But the latter remained the keystone of his theosophy, which "imagines" a triple triad of angelic entities in a series of celestial hierarchies that correspond to a state, at least theoretically, in the lower world. After Philo, Clement of Alexandria, Gregory the Great, and Origen, Pseudo-Dionysius is, with the Cappadocians and Augustine, an essential link in the great tradition of Western angelology, later to be followed by Bernard of Clairvaux, Hugh and Richard of Saint Victor, Hildegard of Bingen, Hadewijch, and many others. Angelology is inseparable from the esoteric tradition, which is nourished by intermediaries and mediators, and we know that *angelos* means "messenger." Pseudo-Dionysius gives this theosophy to Christianity along with a carefully worked out mysticism founded on ideas of Plotinus mixed with Christian dogma into a new harmonious alloy, while the Neoplatonism of his predecessors generally remained, more or less, a product of culture. His theosophical thought is impregnated mainly with the ideas of Proclus; it could be that Pseudo-Dionysius was his student, even though he seems closer to Damascius with regard to his negative theology.

Maximus the Confessor, Isidore of Seville, and Johannes Scotus Erigena

Maximus the Confessor, an ascetic author and poet, lived about a century after Pseudo-Dionysius, on whose work he commented. He spoke of the remoteness of God, the return of created beings, of their "restitution"—Western esotericism would use, in the same sense, the word "reintegration"—and showed himself to be more Christ-centered than his master. Because of Maximus's interpretations of Pseudo-Dionysius, the latter's mysticism and theosophy penetrated more deeply into the West to become one of the most important and most precious sources of Christian mysticism and theosophy. Maximus's *Ambigua* contains a passage essential for understanding later anthroposophy (or theosophical anthropology) from the Renaissance on. In fact, one finds here—perhaps explicitly stated for the first time—the celebrated formula of Man as *officina omnium,* a universal repository, which brings together in the human self both the world of the senses and of the mind, and so unifies creation. A little after him, Isidore, bishop of Seville (636) unifies it as well, but more superficially by means of an erudite inventory. Isidore was the author of the famous *Etymologies,* a veritable encyclopedia of the period copied by Raban Maur and read by succeeding generations; Isidore's goal was to draw up a summary of beings and things. To discover an infinite number of signs in nature and to apply oneself in presenting them in the form of vast tables of correspondences was the main characteristic of Isidore and of Western esotericism. One could speak of a veritable "Hermetic aesthetics" in regard to this author, who is in fact representative of a type of thought on the rise in the early Middle Ages that is unlike classical thought, for it is attached to symbols and analogical games.

It was the task of Johannes Scotus Erigena to produce a synthesis of Dionysius and Maximus, and he created one of the most important theological and historical edifices of the early Middle Ages. A monk from Ireland—one of the rare places in the West where philosophical inspiration still breathed and real culture found refuge—Johannes Scotus Erigena became the household scholar of Charles the Bald, in whose court he composed, in Latin, his masterpiece, *On the Division of Nature* or *Periphiseon.* He also wrote commentaries on the writings of Dionysius on divine names, accomplished the exegesis of the *Marriage of Mercury and*

Philology by Martianus Capella in the Palatine court. Johannes Scotus died about 870.

True authority and sane reason can never contradict each other, for both spring from the same source–divine wisdom, the origin of all light. As the title of his masterpiece indicates, Johannes Scotus wished to set down a philosophy of nature. It is not possible to give a useful summary of it in a few lines; we simply recall that in spite of the suspicion and even the interdiction it underwent by ecclesiastical authorities, this philosophy fed the theosophical speculations of many authors up to the period of German idealism in the nineteenth century. The different kinds of "nature" it distinguishes and studies, particularly *natura naturata* and *natura naturans,* "nature created and nature which creates," furnished for posterity a commodious framework that encouraged much inspired thought. Its philosophy of expansion and contraction seems much closer to the dynamics of the Kabbalah than to classical Platonism. Then again, much of the anthropology of Johannes Scotus responds to the *Ambigua* of Maximus, who had presented humanity as summarizing and gathering in itself all of nature to bring it back to its First Cause. If, contrary to Dionysius, Johannes does not use the term "archetype," it is because he prefers *exemplum* and wishes to emphasize the idea of archetypes or living prototypes at work in the *natura creata et creans,* composed of the noblest of all God's creatures. This teaching, which so effectively throws into relief the doctrines of Dionysius, helps us to understand the art of the cathedrals. The theme of Adam's androgynous nature before the fall, which continues through the development of ideas already set out in the work of Maximus, was the Western starting point for a long theosophical tradition on this theme–up to Franz von Baader (1765–1841), who referred several times, moreover, expressly to Johannes Scotus, and even to earlier individuals. The *Periphiseon* is a truly theological and often theosophical "compendium," where ideas and citations taken from Augustine, Boethius, the Cappadocians, Gregory of Nyssa, Gregory of Nazian, Maximus the Confessor, and Pseudo-Dionysius are brought together and united by an eloquent style and the effort of a bold synthesis, all integrated into a powerfully original work.

The "Sepher Yetsira"

It is perhaps not by chance that the first important text of the Kabbalah appeared during the period of Pseudo-Dionysius, at least the first that has come down to us from this essentially oral tradition. We are speaking of the *Sepher Yetsira,* whose theosophy contains analogies with that of the *Celestial Hierarchy* and the *Divine Names.* It is known that the Kabbalah constitutes the essence of Jewish esotericism. If one wishes to understand its importance for the Hebraic religion, one must know that in this religion the mystic, in the sense of union with God, remains quite exceptional. Judaism speaks of the "vision" of God more readily than of "union"; it also speaks of contemplation of divine majesty, and of understanding the mysteries of creation. Vision, contemplation, and active understanding: these are what defines theosophy at this level. The Kabbalah is nothing other than Hebraic theosophy. Its direct historical ancestor is the esoteric tradition called Merkavah (the basic text being Ezekiel 1–3), centered on the idea of an ascension up to the divine "Throne." This tradition of the Merkavah continues from the first century B.C. until the tenth century of our era and presents striking similarities to Hermetism and to certain forms of gnosis. The books called Hekhalot, or "Celestial Palaces," which are essentially initiatory treatises, describe the stages of this ascension in great abundance of detail, revealing at the same time the mysteries of Creation and the geography of the angelical realm. It was only around the fifth or sixth century that the *Sepher Yetsira,* or *Book of the Creation,* an obscure text of not more than a few pages, was written. It aimed to reconcile Hebraic monotheism with certain Neoplatonist views and served as the basis for most of later kabbalistic speculation. Inspired by a source equivalent to that of the Merkavah but more speculative and theosophical, it is based on a complex arithmology teaching the thirty-two ways of Wisdom (Hokhma, or Sophia) by which God created the world, the twenty-two letters of the sacred alphabet, and the ten *sephirot* or primordial numbers, the last six representing the six directions. This treatise's widespread influence and diffusion stand in strong contrast to its size and relative obscurity.

The Presence of Hermetism: The Arab Influence

Let us return to Christianity. It would be a mistake to think that the ecclesiastical authorities were suspicious of all forms of esotericism during this period or that they prohibited them. If alchemy does not have an aura of saintliness, it is because of the fakes and spagyrists who wanted only to enrich themselves; but there are few condemnations of the hermetic art in the ecclesiastical literature of the early Middle Ages, especially since this form of spirituality stayed in the background until the twelfth century. As for astrology, it was practiced together with alchemy by Gerbert (950?–1013), bishop of Reims, who became pope in the year 1000 under the name Sylvester II. He had developed a complex and very detailed astrological system, arising from the schema of Ptolemy, which the West would keep for a long time: the earth, at the center of the universe surrounded by nine concentric spheres, namely, the seven planets, the sphere of the fixed stars, and that of the Prime Mover. In other respects, a more or less christianized Hermetism continued—the Alexandrian hermetic tradition, sometimes mixed with alchemy. Thus the *Liber Hermetis* is the translation of a Greek anthology worked out in the fifth century at the latest, but whose elements are taken from much older works. It deals mainly with astrology, and in particular it contains one of the first detailed and complex descriptions of the system of decans. This book was fundamental for the esotericism of the Middle Ages, during which the *Asclepius* was also known. But is was necessary to wait, as we know, until the dawn of the Renaissance for all of the *Corpus* to be rediscovered and immediately translated into Latin. Alexandrian Hermetism thus kept its influence because of various writings, often just fragments or anthologies: besides the *Liber Hermetis* and *Asclepius,* particularly some translations from the Greek *Cyranides.* Similarly, *The Marriage of Philology and Mercury,* written in the fifth century by the North African Martianus Capella from Madaura, recalls Dionysius the Aeropagite in its hierarchies of spirits. But if this book was the object of real interest in the Christian West, it was not a book particularly inspired by the Bible.

The mass of other hermetic writings of this period came mainly from the Arabs; beginning in 635, Islam, which had greatly expanded, arrived in Spain and did not stop its expansion in the West until 732 at Poitiers (and in 751 in Chinese Turkestan). Its religion, "clear and concise like a desert landscape and not having the Hellenistic taste for complicated speculations on the nature of divine reality" (Emile Bréhier)—which did not prevent it from developing a magnificent theosophy, particularly in the Shiite tradition—favored a rational, atomistic theology without neglecting the study of Aristotle and Neoplatonism. An important fact is that from the ninth century on, much was translated into Arabic, either from Syriac or Greek, and we know that Aristotle's influence dominated. The Arabic interpretation was dictated, however, by two treatises falsely attributed to Aristotle: *The Theology of Aristotle* (translated into Arabic in the ninth century), which contains writings by Plotinus and other Neoplatonists, and the *Liber de causis,* in which texts by Proclus are found. These treatises combine two very different types of thought: the rationalist empiricism of Aristotle, who possessed his own logical method, a form of positivism; and a strongly mythic vision of the world in which spiritual forces reign, and which only intuition can claim to apprehend. The Arabic mind showed itself capable of easily passing from one tendency to the other, which allowed for the development of both. Among the Arabic philosophers whose influence helped steer the West toward the second tendency, we can mention, besides Al-Kindi (ninth century) and Al-Farabi (tenth century), Avicenna (980–1037), for whom knowledge is due to the influence of the "mediating intellect" on minds open to its effect. It was certain that so long as the belief in mediating intellects lasted, there would be room for theosophy in the philosophies of nature and in anthropology, but this belief would be later supplanted, at least formally, by the influence of Averroes (1126–1198), even though he recognized only one mediating intellect.

It was thus due to the Arabs that Hermetism returned to the West, or reached it in a new form. Astrology, chiefly from the tenth century to the thirteenth, was in great part nourished by Arab anthologies, some of which supplemented the teachings about decans in the *Liber Hermetis*. Thus Arabic is the source of the *Book of Images* by Pseudo-Ptolemy, of *Picatrix*, and of the material taken up in the *Lapidary* of King Alphonse of Spain. The astrologer Apomasar (ninth century) transmitted hermetic teachings from Syria to the Latin world. The miniature paintings in the Latin versions of Apomasar, of *Picatrix*, and of the *Astrolabe*, being influenced by astrology, are part of the treasure of Western symbolism and are all the more precious as it was necessary to wait until the eleventh and mainly the twelfth century for an astrological iconography to develop. Alchemy and Hermetism also benefited from these influences, for it was from the Arabs that the famous text *Turba philosophorum*, or *Assembly of Pythagoras*, originated (an anthology perhaps written directly in Arabic) and also the even more famous *Emerald Tablet*. The story of the discovery of the *Emerald Tablet* was published with an account of the creation of the world in a work that the Arabs, around 825, entitled *Book of Secrets of the Creation*, itself taken from the *Liber de Causis*. They attributed the *Book of Secrets of the Creation* to Balinous, that is, to Apollonius of Tyana. A beautiful chapter called "On the Creation of Man," presented as a revelation of Hermes, recalls the *Poimandres* (the work that begins the *Corpus Hermeticum*). The *Emerald Tablet* is found at the end, in the version that would prevail from then on. Still further, there were, among other works, the *Book of the Moon*, in which Apollonius appears as the spokesman of Hermes; the *Golden Flower*, a theurgical work; and finally the hermetic treatise by Thabit ben-qurra, born in Harran in 826, on magical and astrological images, which was highly valued in the West during the Middle Ages. The Arabs also contributed to the spread of medical theories and practices in various forms, including magical and hermetic teaching. Moreover, medicine itself constituted a huge chapter in the history of medieval ideas. We mention only the name of Constantinus Africanus (1015–1087), who was born in Tunis and died at Mount Cassius. He translated and spread medical works of many kinds, from which Hermetism and magic were not excluded.

East and West

We know that intellectual activity in the West did not resume on a wide scale before the end of the eleventh century. Previously, "schools" had been founded in connection with cathedrals (Auxerre, Reims, Paris), which assured that teachings would be preserved and texts copied; but after the conquest of the East by the Arabs, parchment became rare, and it was mainly the religious orders, created from the beginning of the eleventh century, which would copy manuscripts. It was only then that religious iconography began to develop. As this naturally tends toward symbolic forms, one inevitably finds here and there drawings associated with esotericism, especially as there began to appear then more and more figures of man as the microcosm. Many are the manuscripts from the ninth, tenth, and eleventh centuries – and of course from later centuries also – which contain abundant schemas associating the world, the year, humanity, the four seasons, the four humors, the four ages of life, the four winds, and the cardinal points.

Byzantium in the Middle Ages was equal to the task of continuing the Greek tradition, but its intellectuals displayed a marked taste for legal studies, the world of commerce, and a rather rational theology. Ancient Greek thought was mainly the subject of commentaries and scholarly work, which for the most part consisted of comparing Plato and Aristotle. The fall of Rome in 470 made Byzantium the sole capital of the empire, and it remained a cultural and spiritual center for ten centuries. The West, prey to barbarians, was culturally reduced to a few mainly monastic localities in Ireland and northern Italy (Bobbie). During the time of the second separation from Rome, Neoplatonism survived and continued to spread through studies of Plato, for if Photius (820–897) was the great Aristotelian in the city of Constantine, the Platonism of Michel Psellos (1018–1098) tended in a Neoplatonist direction. The great influence of Psellos was felt in the Latin world beginning in the middle of the fifteenth century. He drew his inspiration chiefly from Proclus, but also from Plotinus and Iamblichus. He contributed to the spread of alchemy while distrusting theurgy and restricting himself within a certain rationalism. Apart from this more or less formal philosophy, the Byzantine monasteries favored a mystic current that had certain aspects which were inseparable from Latin esotericism. Thus, John Climacus at Mount Sinai taught, with his "ladder of paradise," the journey up the twenty-nine degrees of contemplation and union, the thirtieth being beyond suffering. And Gregory Palamas of Thessalonica (1296–1359), to which the tradition of the *Philokalia* owes so much, insisted on the increate light, distinct from the Trinity but which emanates from it and which puts the aspirant in communication with God. It is "the highest manifestation of neo-Platonist emanationism within Christianity" (Emile Bréhier).

Neoplatonism and Hermeticism in the Twelfth Century

The Temple, the Cosmos, and Man

The twelfth-century mind was characterized by a "discovery" that helps to understand esoteric thought in modern times. It was the discovery of Nature, which became no longer only a repository of allegories but commanded attention in its own right. In Roman times, this realization favored a return, as we have already seen with Johannes Scotus Erigena, to cosmological themes of Greco-Roman antiquity, that is, to a universe conceived of and represented as an organic whole under the influence of laws to be searched for in the light of analogy. The discovery of these laws would lead to a twofold result: on the one hand, the secularization of the world, which took place to the same degree as one lost the sense of the sacred; and on the other, a long-lasting revival of magic in the sense of "cosmic participation," that is to say, the cosmological themes of *Timaeus* and Neoplatonism, of Pseudo-Dionysius, and of the Hermetic writings. The Hermetism of antiquity and of the early Middle Ages would not have been enough, perhaps, to give Western theosophy, such as it has developed since the Renaissance, the forms that it has taken without this extraordinary outpouring of symbolism during the twelfth century. In science, the fields of medicine and mathematics proved to be the most active in this intellectual revival. But in a general way, there was a systematic and poetic formulation of networks and relations between the realms of visible and invisible creation. The universe was taken over by speculative thought, which endeavored to decipher its living and concrete meanings. Using the word of Jean de Mun, Nature became the "chambermaid" or vicar of God. Matter limits, certainly, but it is not bad in itself, an idea that takes up, following Hermetism, this current of twelfth-century thought in which the flesh is rarely denied—contrary to an appreciable tendency in the thirteenth century to use torture as a relatively normal practice.

God became embodied in stone during this period when the first and perhaps the only truly sacred art in the West arose. The architect of the romanesque churches was God himself. These churches, and above all those of the Cistercian Order, are made of squares, thus symbolizing the cosmos with the four corner pillars representing the four elements. The cities are also built in the form of squares, like the Temple of the Grail, and the central nave is like a body whose transepts form the arms. Man as micro-cosm has the number four and indicates the four cardinal points associated with the four elements and the four rivers of paradise. To pass from the square to the circle is to go from time to eternity, or from divine mani-festation to wholeness. Being the image of a universe in hierarchical expan-sion, and of both the microcosm and macrocosm, the romanesque temple carries humanity and all of creation toward God. Mystery resonates from these living stones; they are like an act of grace from created nature and they call forth fantastic creatures which take their place in the human-cosmic drama. Such a knowledge of relations, uniting God, Man, and the universe, can only be transmitted by a tradition, itself made up of initia-tions or successive stages—a tradition created in workshops. The appren-tices, fellows, and masters employ the trowel, a trinitarian symbol, and also other tools whose rich symbolism, after having been defined during the Gothic period, is perpetuated by the modern esoteric movement of specu-lative Freemasonry.

Romanesque decoration was also fed by an epic feeling. Loyal to the fun-damental inspiration of the Judeo-Christian myth, it favors the triptych (cosmology–cosmogony–eschatology), especially its third apocalyptic volet, by developing a visionary theology full of theophanies and meta-morphoses. Because it is epic and thus narrative—like all living myths esoterically understood—this sculpture confers superhuman dimension on Christ and on the human being as the image of God. The romanesque apocalypse conserved something of the terrors of millenarianism. If the flashing intuitions of Johannes Scotus Erigena did not directly inspire this sculpture, they help us to understand its deepest nature. More than in gothic, one is struck by the number of monsters, their exoticism, their strangeness. To the apparent contradiction between the silent order of the church and this exaltation of the wonders of chaos, alchemy quite naturally provides the key. Romanesque sculpture has us penetrate into an unknown world, into a teratological maze, and at the same time into the secret places of the spiritual life.

The sententiaries, the school of Chartres, and finally the mystical move-ment connected to the monastic orders, characterized the essential religious activity of the century. The sententiaries, who correspond to a kind of codification of Christianity in the form of large theological encyclopedias having a philological and critical spirit, are best represented by the names of Peter Abelard and Peter Lombard. There is little to keep us here, except that in *Ethics* Abelard (1079–1142) speaks of the power that demons can exercise over us because of their knowledge of natural forces. Plants, seeds, trees, and stones harbor forces capable of arousing or soothing our souls.

The philosophical theology of the school of Chartres was a revival of Platonism representing a successful effort to widen the intellectual horizon in a spirit of free investigation. It was less a question of fixing knowledge than of spreading it. Bernard of Chartres, a Platonist, wrote: "We are dwarfs standing on the shoulders of giants; we see more than they, and further. It is not so much that our look is piercing, nor that we are so tall: rather their immense stature elevates us, raises us up." Inspired by *Timaeus*, Bernard Silvester of the same school wrote *De mundi universitate sive megacosmus et microcosmus*, in which he recounts the life of stars, the intermediary angels between the sun and moon, and the sublunary spirits, thus foretelling the "elementary spirits" of Paracelsus, while denying neither astrology nor geomancy. The author teaches that the perceptible universe looks toward a divine reality that it strives to imitate. Here again one thinks of the words of the apostle Paul on invisible perfection (Romans 1:20). The title of this work itself could have been signed by a Renaissance Christian kabbalist. This Platonism of Chartres was interested in nature, the oneness of nature, and the laws of nature, which also appeared in the work of William of Conches (1080–1145), a student of Bernard of Chartres, who spoke much about physics (demanding, moreover, that this science be autonomous), and who spread the teaching of Johannes Scotus Erigena on the World Soul. He also fomulated a list of qualities and natural humors for each planet, as well as their positive and negative influences. Like Bernard Silvester, William endeavored to integrate the Platonist philosophy of nature into Christianity. Other aspects of Platonism can be found in another student of the school of Chartres, Gilbert de la Porrée.

Intensely curious about everything, those in the school of Chartres thoroughly studied all the disciplines they knew, relating them all to each other. By reading Virgil, Boethius, the commentary of Macrobius on the "Dream of Scipion," they discovered, or rediscovered, and then set down, a vast metaphysical and cosmological framework from a Platonist or Neoplatonist viewpoint—when all they knew of Plato was *Timaeus*, having read it in the version of Chalcidius. Certainly, the doctrine of Ideas and the thinking about numbers are of a nature to cast out from our perceptible world into the pure kingdom of archetypes all forms of reality judged to be absolute or true; but the school of Chartres did not succumb to this temptation inherent in true Platonism, and from which Augustine did not escape. Those in the school of Chartres owe to the natural sciences this idea of the integration of the world, and of course their debt to the science of the Arabs is obvious, especially in medicine, which had recently been made accessible to the West. The occult philosophy of the Renaissance is in many ways close to the school of Chartres.

In the mystical movement connected to the monastic orders, there was a picture of the inner life which often recalled Philo, Plotinus, and of course Augustine; but this mysticism is hardly oriented toward speculation. It developed rules of life for the soul and not, as in Plotinus, formulations of a philosophic conception of the universe. As there is no esotericism without speculation, there is no need to dwell on the admirable works of Saint Bernard (1091–1153) and Hugh of Saint-Victor (1096–1141), although for the latter, nature is a field of investigation (cf. chiefly *Didascalion* and *Commentarium in hierarchiam*), and the superb symbolism of Saint Bernard contains countless spiritual pearls, for example: "one can draw honey from stones and oil from rocks."

Alain de Lille, Saint Hildegard, Honorius

Alain de Lille (1128?–1203) was very close in his ideas to the school of Chartres, even though he did not belong to it. Nevertheless, his esoterically colored naturalism remains on the fringe of official teaching. Besides, it is less in the Chartrains themselves than in the popular magical tradition that one sees it integrated, in, for example, the *Roman de la Rose*. Generally, it is physicians who read the signatures; only secondarily is it scholastics. In his masterpiece, *De planctu naturae,* the "universal doctor" represents Nature as a young virgin bearing a diadem decorated with twelve precious gems representing the twelve signs of the zodiac, and seven stones symbolizing the sun and planets. She wears a coat embroidered with every kind of being, the animals being divided into three groups. It is a representation connected to the human being as microcosm, formed from the same parts of nature. Reason is within us like the movement of the sphere of fixed stars, and our emotions, so subject to change, are like the complex movements of the planets. Reason in the head is analogous to God and to heaven; emotion and feelings in the heart to the angels; and the lower part situated in the loins, home of the instincts, is analogous to humanity and the earth as well as to different minerals. The relationship between God and nature is more or less borrowed from Proclus, and he draws from the *Monologium* of Anselm the method of returning to the nature of God using his different attributes as stages, that is, his "Names" as Pseudo-Dionysius understood it. Alain de Lille mentions several times, with commentaries, the image of the sphere of the "Intellect," whose center is everywhere and circumference nowhere, and he becomes the exegete of the iconographic symbolism of the period, especially when he describes the unicorn (*calidissima natura*) calmed by the maiden (*frigida et humida*). With Alain de

Lille we can truly speak of esotericism, but it is perhaps even more true for Hildegard and Honorius.

Saint Hildegard of Bingen (1099–1180), author of *Scivias* and of *Liber divinorum operum simplicis hominis,* developed ideas in many ways similar to the above. She insisted, for example, on the analogy existing between the roundness of the head and the firmament. She was certainly not the only one to do so, but her originality was in presenting a vast and coherent work in which inner and mainly cosmic visions played a large part. This visionary integrated revelations she had into an inspired whole, even to the point where it could be called theosophy, or, more precisely, cosmosophy. Thus the second vision of *Scivias* recounts the harmony of the four elements before the fall of Lucifer. Elsewhere she speaks of the disturbing effect on nature of Adam's sin (*elementa humanis iniquitatibus subvertuntur*), a theme that would be one of the leitmotifs of Western theosophy. Hildegard even goes to the point of saying that the blood of Abel blemished the sun, thus causing pernicious humors to flow out from which venomous snakes were born.

The symbolic cosmos of the twelfth century, the direct ancestor of the many esoteric cosmological representations of the Renaissance, is remarkably illustrated, both philosophically and iconographically, in the *Clavis physicae* of Honorius Augustodunensis. Honorius probably studied in Canterbury under Anselm before retiring to the Irish Benedictine community of Saint James at Regensburg. He left a great number of works. The *Clavis physicae* is "probably one of the most perfect expressions of imaginative activity of 12th-century man, while at the same time being a faithful translation of a representation of the world linked to the system of Plato as interpreted by the Greek fathers and their disciple of the 12th century, Johannes Scotus" (M. T. d'Alverny). This little work is called *Key to Nature* because it claims to reveal nature's secrets. It takes up the idea of Maximus and Johannes Scotus of the human being conceived as *creaturarum omnium officina,* or the organ of all created beings who gathered in himself all creation. Several drawings, and especially a beautiful painting, illustrate the text. In it one sees God descending into the primordial Causes (the intermediaries between God and created being), then into their effects, and manifesting himself in his theophanies, even including inert bodies. A magnificent drawing, rich in symbolic connotations, represents the World Soul seen in light of the cosmobiological tradition of the Stoics as interpreted by Johannes Scotus. Another writing of Honorius, the *Elucidarium,* a kind of catechistic, pedagogic summary, emphasizes a number of symbolic correspondences. This treatise was used for three centuries as a foundation for the education of the clergy and the faithful. In it the author develops, in particular, a definition of the human as microcosm, an idea that had been commonplace for a long time; and his long and detailed list of correspondences between the parts of the human body and the constituent elements of the world has perhaps no antecedent in Western literature (for example, the bones, nails, hair, and senses are related to stones, trees, plants, and animals, which seems to echo Judeo-Hellenistic and Alexandrian thinking). These conceptions are found again in other texts of Honorius such as *Sacramentarium* and *De imagine mundi*. *Clavis physicae* was the subject of a remarkable study in French by M. T. d'Alverny, who equally studied a curious little anonymous treatise in the form of a sermon, the *Peregrinations of the Soul in the Other World*, a bearer of Avicennian and gnostic influences.

Hermeticism and Alchemy

It would be easy to produce many other interesting examples given over to analogies between Man and nature, between the microcosm and the macrocosm; but certain names and titles are more important by virtue of their originality of thought or their influence. The *Liber viginti quatuor philosophorum*, written at the end of the century, is a short text, but in it is found for the first time the image of God conceived of as a sphere whose center is everywhere and circumference nowhere. This book is tinged with Hermetism, and it is the dialogue between Hermes Trismegistus and Asclepius that William d'Auvergne, bishop of Paris, mentions several times in order to recall the existence of a divine power at work in plants and even in stones. Alexander Neckham, foster brother of Richard the Lion-hearted, deserves special mention for the idea he developed according to which human sin has had physical consequences in nature. In his *De naturis rerum*, not only the spots on the moon but also the savage state of most animals and the existence of harmful insects, venomous animals, and sickness are attributed to the fall of Adam. The widespread taste for precious stones, their symbolism and occult properties, finds a fine elucidation in *Liber lapidum seu de gemmis*, a poem of 734 hexameters attributed to Marbed (1095–1123), bishop of Rennes, of which there exist many copies.

Above all, one could not fail to mention the fact that the books of Avicenna (980–1037), contemporaneous with the great works of Ismaelian esotericism, were already partially translated into Latin during the twelfth century. The theory of Avicenna on knowledge is a kind of angelology which lays the foundation for both a cosmology and an anthropology. It could have served as a model for the Western tradition, but immediately found itself up against a destructive criticism, especially on the part of

William d'Auvergne. Thus the way was paved for the demythologizing Averroism in the next century, whereas the doctrine of Avicenna on the intermediary Intelligence which illuminated the human soul offered the West a broadening and deepening of his angelology. To reject the heavenly mediating hierarchies of Creation is to reject angelology and interfere with cosmology.

Concerning astrology, many works could obviously be cited for each period, but in the twelfth century the names Roger of Hereford and John of Spain stand out from the rest. Astrology was not essential at the time, for the world in which people lived then was filled with the divine; individuals tried to situate themselves within this divine life in order to participate in a universal redemption excluding them from the inexorable laws of the heavenly bodies. As was said then by William of Saint-Thierry, it is for humans to become "by grace what God is by nature." Alchemy poses different questions, at least in its spiritualized form as a ritual or a magical act aimed at giving back to a particle of matter a little of the original glory from which the entire world benefited before the fall, or before a succession of falls—with the alchemist himself being included in this transmutation. It is easy to understand that to unravel the intentions of this or that "adept" is not always easy, that is to distinguish the true alchemist from a simple spagyrist or "fake." This is all the more true insofar as the West produced even more "recipes" in the twelfth century than mystical-allegorical accounts, contrary to what was being produced by the Arabs. Furthermore, alchemy was scarcely known in Europe before the twelfth century, having been introduced through Islam by way of Spain. And we know that the introduction of Arabic alchemical texts in Latin enriched the European scientific vocabulary with numerous new terms.

A key event took place in the year 1144 with what could have been the translation, from Arabic into Latin, of an important book on medieval alchemy. Translated by Robert of Chester, archdeacon of Pamplona, who said it was "edited" by Morienus Romanus, a hermit of Jerusalem, for "Calid, king of the Egyptians," it is entitled *Liber de compositione alchemiae quem edidit Morienus Romanus.* Morienus, whose story is told in the book, becomes, because of this book, the first prominent mythic figure of European alchemy. As fundamental for the Hermetic science as the *Emerald Tablet,* the *Liber de compositione alchemiae* contains a romantic story in which Hermes discovers and makes known all the occult arts and sciences since the flood, before Morienus himself discovers them. There are astonishing accounts of initiations, and of course it was often republished, especially in the sixteenth century in the large Corpus of Manget in 1702. Robert of Chester also provided a translation of an Arabic commentary on the *Emerald Tablet*. Among the Arabs and Latins, the reputation of Hermes Trismegistus continued to be confirmed and to grow more than ever, even outside of alchemical literature. He was considered more and more as a fountain of knowledge and wisdom. Thus Roger Bacon could speak of "Hermes Mercurius, the father of philosophers."

At that time, the greatest translators from Arabic into Latin were Gerard of Cremone (1114?–1187), who lived and worked mainly in Toledo, and the learned Englishman Adelard of Bath. Gerard of Cremone translated the *Liber de causis* mentioned above, thus contributing to the spread of Proclus's influence. The first Latin transcription of the *Emerald Tablet* was presented by Hugo Sanctelliensis, bishop of Tarazona in Spain, and published with the *Liber de secretis naturae et occultis rerum causis quem transtulit Apollonius de libris Hermes Trismegisti;* it was once considered by the alchemists as a revealed text only accessible to a few initiates.

In the face of expansion of knowledge in the twelfth century, the system of *artes liberales* also broadened, which benefited alchemy. It was considered, in fact, a divine "art" and would never stop being viewed as such. Being both *ars* and *scientia,* natural science and divine science, it produced many figurative and allegorical expressions, such as those in Macrobius. While mentioning the ultimate principles of matter, those that touch the divine, Macrobius had seen the poetic form as the only acceptable possibility of expression and had said that Nature itself spoke as a poet (*Commentarius in somnium Scipionis* 1.2.17). The alchemy of the twelfth century, and often theology as well, took up again the methods of the *involucrum* used by the poets and philosophers of antiquity, which consisted of using fables to both veil and reveal the divine secrets of Nature.

The Myth of Alexander, the Fedeli d'Amore, and Myths of Chivalry

Hermeticism, in the general sense of the term, does not necessarily refer only to Hermes. The *Story of Alexander,* for example, written in verse during the first third of the century, brings forward characters of which some, like the magician Naptanabus, had been legendary figures already for a long time. The guiding thread of the story rests on the old idea that Aristotle had been Alexander's tutor. If in this tale the exterior of Alexander's tent recalls various kinds of magical practices, the interior is a summary of all the world's knowledge. The seasons are represented there, and the months, the days, the hours, the planets, and finally the geography of the earth, which prefigures the "art of memory," later represented by fine examples during the Renaissance. The marvelous "alexandrine" of this work springs from a syncretism that prepared the way for a resurgence of the myth of the Golden Fleece, a myth whose fertile meaning would be increasingly influential, especially in the eighteenth century but which also was instrumental in the passage from the Middle Ages to the Renaissance. Chronologically situated between Charlemagne and Arthur, Alexander was seen in the civilization of the Middle Ages as an imaginary example of one aiming to conquer the world. Portugal lived this myth out to the full in its expeditions, the enthusiasm for which is difficult to explain solely by economic considerations. In regard to the myth of Alexander, we should also note that there existed numerous pseudo-Aristotelian writings in the twelfth century that were attributed—falsely, of course—to Alexander's "master." They were of various kinds: alchemical, astrological, and pneumatological; or they dealt with the occult properties of stones and plants, or with palmistry and physiognomy. The most famous of these writings was *Secreta secretorum*, a veritable catchall of occultism, containing a great deal of astrology, which presented Aristotle as an ever-present counselor to Alexander. It was one of the most popular books of the Middle Ages.

The initiatory side to all this often stands out quite clearly, and came to the fore in various forms and ways during the twelfth century. Courtly love, for example, was initiatory in the elaborate way in which it exalted "for the first time since the gnostics of the 2nd and 3rd centuries, the spiritual dignity and religious worth of Woman. . . . The soteriological function of love and of Woman was clearly expressed by what was apparently a mainly *literary* movement, but which consisted of an occult and probably initiatory gnosis" (M. Eliade): the Fedeli d'Amore. A veritable secret militia widespread in various countries of Europe, it expressed itself through a cryptic language. The "faithful" dedicated themselves to the "one and only Woman" and to initiation into the mystery of love. Furthermore, there appeared in this century an esotericism in the sense of a secret language or teaching, which probably did not previously exist to the same extent. Like members of religious sects, lovers had their signs, symbols, and passwords.

Initiation, secretness, love, knowledge, and mysticism came together in this mythology of chivalry brought about by this period so rich in spiritual discoveries of every kind. This mythology was going to undergo a cultural destiny more important than its social or political history. Its first great literary expression was formulated around the legendary King Arthur; the writings called *Matière de Bretagne*, being both a receptacle and a living source for the inspirations of the soul and of poetry, crystallized around figures like Arthur, Perceval, Lancelot, and the Fisher King. Much more than in the first Arthurian or Breton stories, symbolism and initiatory

1. *Hermes Trismegistus*, c. 1740. Color painting on wood. Anonymous. The figure wears a red robe; his cloak and hat are blue. He holds the sphere, which is his attribute, and a roll on which the first verse of the *Tablet of Emerald* is written ("Quod est superius est sicut inferius").

scenes are quite evident in the theme of the Grail, which made its first appearance around 1180 with the book by Chretien de Troyes and Robert de Boron. The Grail combines the Western Druidic and Celtic traditions (Ireland, Avalon) with the Christian mysteries. They blend together in Parsifal, or Perceval, and in the Grail, a mythical chalice having strong alchemical connotations (Sun and host, moon and chalice). The symbol of the Grail evokes underground esoteric currents connected to the apocryphal evangelists, especially Nicodemus, who extolled Joseph of Arimathea. And it is not by chance that in this period the rite of the Elevation of the Host was introduced into the Roman Mass. The German knight Wolfram von Eschenbach was the first to author a masterpiece on the inexhaustible themes of the Grail and chivalry: *Parzival*, written between 1200 and 1210. Although there are abundant elements from the East in it, it is nevertheless one of the great Western books. Its esoteric meaning was reaffirmed in a recent study by the researches of H. and R. Kahane, who concluded that the word "grail" (bowl, vase) is derived from the Greek *krater*. Thus this symbol's soteriological function is emphasized, for book 4 of the *Corpus Hermeticum* speaks of a large "crater" sent to earth and filled with understanding by God, and in which Men of Aspiration should bathe themselves to take part in this knowledge and rise again to God. Apart from the word *krater*, the expression *lapis exillis*, also having alchemical connotations, has kindled many investigations as well. The image of a "krater" was used by the Hermeticist Lazarelli during the sixteenth century in his "basin of Hermes" or *Crater Hermetis*.

These mythical expressions are evidently connected to the Knights Templar, created in Jerusalem in 1119 after the first crusade and the taking of Jerusalem (1099). The mission of these knights, who received their rule from Saint Bernard, theoretically consisted of protecting pilgrims. There were certain similarities between the Knights Templar and the Islamic order of the Elders of the Mountain; there certainly were between the former and the Grail, attested to in the *Parzival* of Wolfram. Moreover, the holy land was not only geographic but inner, hidden, and esoteric. It is the meeting place of heaven and earth. To be persuaded of this, it would be enough to visit the Templar convent of Tomar in Portugal. This building, a veritable living organism, bears the mark and testimony of teachings inseparable from the quest for the Grail in its initiatory and symbolic meaning. It is perhaps not at all by chance that the myth of the Fifth Empire appeared at the same time in Portugal. It was born with the independence of the country—due to the victory over the Moors in 1139—when Christ promised Alfonso Henrique that Portugal would receive the Kingdom of the Sea to transmit the Christian message to the world.

We mention again two important factors for understanding the esoteric movements of modern times: the influence of Joachim da Fiore and Jewish esotericism.

Joachim da Fiore; Moses Maimonides; The "Bahir"

The Calabrian abbot Joachim da Fiore (1135?–1202) formulated a vast system of philosophy and universal history based on a ternary scheme. The reign of the Father corresponds to the Old Testament, of the Son to the New, and a third era awaits us, in history itself, namely, a kind of Christian perfection corresponding to the reign of the Holy Spirit—thus, the period of the primrose, then of the rose, and finally of the lily! That he was speaking from a temporal point of view and not an eschatological one in the sense of being "outside of time" is evidenced by the fact that Joachim imagines this third age as having a dramatic end. Divine perfection is reserved, in fact, for the last judgment. These theories became very widespread and had an enormous influence, whose consequences have recently been the subject of a masterly study (H. de Lubac). Joachim da Fiore is the originator of modern philosophies of history, those of Lessing, Hegel, Marx, and others, who secularized, each in his own way, the thought of the Calabrian. But the latter was equally the starting point for speculations on the dates of the third age and on diverse prophecies concerning the future spiritual guides of humanity. Written at the beginning of the eighteenth century, the work of Bengel represents a privileged example, but it takes its place among many others. Finally, this work has strongly reaffirmed the always open nature of prophecy. The ecclesiastical authorities, on the other hand, have tended to declare it officially closed, or at least let it be understood as such. But if the Holy Spirit is called to reign during the last part of human history as Joachim has announced, here and now we can allow it to breathe through us, making us its instrument, that is, to prophesy in the biblical sense of the term. The work of Joachim thus introduces the principle of a great spiritual liberty in each individual soul, since the soul was seen as capable of discovering, with the help of the Spirit whose coming was near, meanings hidden since the beginning of the world. Christian theosophy, a particular form of prophecy, benefited from the teaching of Joachim.

It was mainly in Spain and Morocco that Jewish philosophy developed. The *Fons vitae* by Avicebron (1020?–1070), a thinker from Malaga, which was an important source of Neoplatonism for the Latin West beginning in the twelfth century, was a hierarchical classification of beings from top to bottom on the cosmic ladder. Later, the contemporary of Joachim, Moses

Maimonides (1135-1204)–called Moses of Cordoba, although he lived mainly in Cairo–is a first-rate thinker in the Hebraic tradition. Albert the Great and Thomas Aquinas willingly cited him, for he tried to do for Jewish thought what they themselves were trying to accomplish for Christian thought, that is, harmonize Aristotle and the Bible, philosophy and revelation, a task whose possibility William of Conches had envisioned before them. The thought of Moses Maimonides, as expressed above all in the *Guide to the Perplexed,* is difficult and his system often contradictory. It is not precisely the work of a theosopher. Even so, it is not only a question here of recalling certain points that would influence later esoteric currents, especially through the Christian Kabbalah of the Renaissance. He believed, in fact, that the prophets of the Old Testament had received, besides the texts gathered in the Bible, orally transmitted philosophical revelations which were then lost during the persecutions of the Jewish people. His famous book contains remarkable definitions of a prophet and prophecy, and he twice recounts that our lower world is governed by properties and influences of the heavenly spheres that are animated, conscious, and free. He also holds a specifically gnostic trait–that metaphysical knowledge is necessary to ensure life in the hereafter (*Guide,* III, 51, 54). For certain esoteric traditions, only the accumulation of metaphysical knowledge acquired by us here below is immortal.

Yet it is clearly the Kabbalah that once again gives us the essence of Jewish esotericism. The *Sepher Yetsira* laid the foundations in the fifth and sixth centuries; and in Provence during the twelfth, a collection of old and also more recent kabbalistic materials was produced under the title *Bahir,* which constituted the first account of the Kabbalah properly so-called. Starting from this book, *Bahir,* the kabbalists of Provence steered the Kabbalah in two directions: one toward a gnosis originating in the East, and another toward medieval Neoplatonism. It was in this twofold form that it arrived in Spain, specifically in Gerona. Just as in the previous period of the early Middle Ages, it was less a question of mystical union than of theosophy. Contrary to the Talmud, this theosophy interpreted numbers and letters as a speech addressed to us by Wisdom, from which it strove to know the world through the world's relation to God by way of intermediary links. The most specific thing here, no doubt, is the use of letters as a method of interpretation, which allows one to see in each word of the Torah a higher meaning with various ramifications.

* * *

Great Summae, the Great Work, and New Currents in the Thirteenth Century

New Spiritual Movements; Catharism; Brothers of the Free Spirit; Saint Francis

It was not esotericism that worried the ecclesiastical authorities from the end of the twelfth century through the thirteenth. Theosophy, alchemy, astrology, and Hermetism were scarcely cause for concern by a church whose representatives were themselves impregnated with Neoplatonism. It had all it could handle with heresies of every kind: Waldensians (from the name of Pierre Valdes of Lyon, who, in preaching true evangelistic poverty, denied all ecclesiastical authority), the disciples of Amalrich of Bene around 1200 (the reign of the Spirit being already here, God is present everywhere and not only in the host), Joachimism (the abbot of Fiore had left many disciples upon his death). But above all, the church grappled with the problem of Catharism.

Catharism began to penetrate Western Europe at the beginning of the twelfth century, coming from the Byzantine Empire, and Bulgaria in particular, where this sectarian movement was called Bogomilism (from the name of its founder, Bogomil, who lived in the tenth century). Catharism was characterized by an absolute dualism, which for this reason was not a part of the Western esoteric tradition as we have defined it here. It contained a trait belonging to most examples of ancient gnosticism: the world was created by an evil demiurge, that of the Mosaic Law; matter and flesh are absolutely evil, and in descending to earth Christ took on only the appearance of a body. Pope Innocent III, aided by several great lords and the king of France, undertook a crusade against the Albigensians in 1207 – that is, against the Cathars, established mainly in southwest France, whom he succeeded in crushing through sheer unimaginable cruelty. It was not until around 1330 that the Catharist church ceased to exist in France. To this, the only victorious crusade, France owed its unification as a kingdom, the civilization in southern France its destruction, and Europe the creation of the Inquisition, which, having been decided in 1215 at the Council of Lateran, ended by authorizing torture in 1254. This council condemned the Vaudois, the followers of Joachim, and the disciples of Amaury de Bene – as well as the De divisione naturae by Johannes Scotus Erigena (in 1210), which was suspected of being at the origin of Amaurism. It also condemned Aristotle, more well known then because his work had just been rediscovered.

More than in Catharism, it was among the Brothers of the Free Spirit that certain traits belonging to Western esotericism or to any esotericism could be found, for here the emphasis was placed on knowledge. Under the influence of Amalrich of Bene, who died around 1206, the Brothers of the Free Spirit emphasized the knowledge of salvation rather than the hope of salvation; for knowledge in itself was supposed to produce a salvational effect. Contrary to the Cathars, they preached a doctrine affirming life and universal love, where *agapē* combines with *eros.* Each Christian was considered to be totally a part of the body of Christ. Being a radical mysticism of union, it found one of its best expressions in Marguerite Poret, burned in 1310 as a heretic, whose *Mirror of Simple Souls* is also an esoteric text, in the sense that it was meant only for those who "understood."

In order to canalize the ideal of evangelical poverty that threatened to spread without control and undermine the authority of the church, Innocent III gave Francis of Assisi (1182–1226), whose admirable vocation dates from 1209, the authorization to direct a minor order in 1210. This is an important fact in the history of Christianity, for the Franciscan spirit introduced a love of nature that the Roman mind could not succeed in bringing forth by itself. For the latter, in fact, nature represented mainly a means of knowledge, which explains the curiosity felt for it. But if now love became more important, there was, at the same time paradoxically, a growth in a kind of Puritanism with regard to the body, a tendency that has continued to be felt up to our time. Franciscan love, on the contrary, stimulated the philosophers of nature and the alchemists. Another aspect of the movement of popular evangelical piety recalled the religious Vaudois ideal but was nevertheless tolerated by the religious authorities because of its limited pretensions: this was the creation of women's religious communities, the Beguines, which were organized in the regions of the north. Mechthild of Magdeburg (1207–1282) was among the most well known of them for her book *The Flowing Light of the Godhead,* the first written in German by a woman mystic.

Averroism; The Franciscan Spirit: Saint Bonaventure

The philosophers and theologians at the beginning of the thirteenth century finally had access to almost all of Aristotle's works, thanks to the Latin translations from Arabic and Greek. Interest in them was not prevented by their condemnation; on the contrary, not only were the Greek commentaries of Aristotle's work translated, but also works in Arabic by Al-Kindi, Al-Farabi, Avicenna, and Averroes. Plato was relatively less well known. Averroes (1126–1198) was born in Cordoba; his work, written mainly in Seville and Morocco, had a wide, if posthumous, influence.

Known in Paris from 1230 on, his work began to spread mainly after 1270; it was at this time that Thomas Aquinas wrote on the unity of the intellect, attacking Averroes's ideas, and that the followers of Averroes were condemned. Condemnations were declared also in 1277, in which masters of art such as Siger de Brabant and Boece de Dacie were implicated. The followers of Averroes taught, in fact, that the world and the human species were eternal, that there existed a single intellect for all humans, that free will was impossible, and that God knows nothing more than himself (the denial of providence). Peripateticism, particularly as reexamined by Averroes, gives an image of the universe that corresponds very little to Christianity. If it was able to tempt some Christians desirous of formulating "rational" theologies because of its influence, it was still quite incompatible with esoteric thought. Even apart from Averroes's interpretation, it was for the most part incompatible with dogma, for Peripateticism contained the idea of an eternal and uncreated universe, of a God whose role was limited to being the mover of heaven and the fixed stars, and from whom neither knowledge nor action reached the sublunary world, and finally the belief that the soul disappeared with the body. These two opposing tendencies thus divided the thought of the period. First, the Franciscan mind, nourished by Augustine and mainly represented by Bonaventure, believed it possible to attain at least a reflection of divine reality in a Neoplatonist sense. Reason, according to Augustine's idea of it, was already illumination, for Being by its nature aspires toward new forms, just as matter potentially bears within itself the attributes engendered by form. Second, there was the Dominican mind, issuing from Aristotle and represented by Albert the Great and Thomas Aquinas. Here it was a matter of making a separation in principle between revealed theology and a philosophy that declares its independence from theology as its first working principle, that is, which begins from sensory experience according to a "rational" method. Consequently, intellectual knowledge naturally tends toward abstraction; individuals aspire toward realization by themselves—thus cut off from analogical universal correspondences—and matter passively waits to be formed.

A third tendency, the school of Oxford, can be added to the other two. It shares a wish for universal intuition with the spirit of the school of Chartres of the twelfth century and is represented by Alexander Neckham; Michael Scot, the astronomer and alchemist; Robert Grosseteste, the theologian of light; and Roger Bacon.

Bonaventure (1217–1274), the "seraphic doctor" born near Orvieto, studied theology in Paris, where he later taught, and in 1257 was elected General Minister of the Franciscan Order. Among numerous works, his masterpiece was *The Journey of the Mind to God*. Besides the mystical way,

Nature was paramount in his thought, because for him God was revealed in the realities of the cosmos. Faithful to the basic tendencies of Neoplatonism, he conceived reason as the mediator between faith and an intellectual intuition capable of directly grasping the principle. He sought expressions, images, and traces of divine nature. In this way he was quite different from Thomas Aquinas, who was less sensitive to the vast symbolism which caused the seraphic doctor to consider Nature equal to the Bible as a book to be deciphered. The intelligible world is not, as for Plotinus, an intermediary between God and the perceptible world; it is not a first creation, nor even a creation at all, but God himself as Word or Son. In this sense, Bonaventure is not a Neoplatonist, since there is nothing to fill up the chasm separating the created being from its creator; at the same time, there is nothing to block the soul's return to God. Contrary to Aquinas, but as a Franciscan and in agreement with one of the most widespread ideas of later theosophy, particularly in the work of Jacob Boehme, Bonaventure denied the existence of absolutely pure or disincarnated forms in creation, so that, like humans, the angels themselves are made up of both form and matter. The idea that the physical world does not contain its own explanatory principle within itself and is not autonomous but depends on seminal causes for its functioning and the idea of universal hylomorphy were what characterized this Platonist-Augustinian movement, to which John Peckham (1220–1292) was also connected, and what the contrary Aristotelian movement endeavored to combat.

Some Dominicans; The School of Oxford: Robert Grosseteste, Roger Bacon

If the spirit of modern esotericism is connected to this Franciscan tendency by way of Christian Neoplatonism, it should not be thought that theologies influenced by Aristotelianism are completely without any element of this kind. They approach it by way of mysticism. Two German Dominicans propagating the doctrines of Albert the Great in Cologne were Hugh of Strasburg and Ulrich of Strasburg. The latter represented the transition between Arabic Peripateticism and the work of Meister Eckhart. If, in his treatise on minerals, Albert himself often mentions Hermes Trismegistus, it is to refer as well to alchemy and magic and to distinguish between simple physicians and true alchemists. Thomas Aquinas also believed in alchemy, whose effectiveness he attributed to the use of occult forces having celestial properties. He considered the stars as mediators between the "separated intellects" and our material world, and he tried to respond affirmatively to the question of whether angels caused the stars to move. The higher angels drive the heavenly bodies, a movement that is then transmitted to earthly bodies. Every visible thing has its especially appointed angelic substance. Since God governs lower beings by the intermediary of higher ones, and terrestial bodies by way of the stars, Thomas in no way rejected astrology. He granted that the stars can act on human intelligence and that they help to predict great collective events. But for him, reason aided by faith was more important than intelligence in the esoteric Neoplatonist sense, the *intellectus,* to which he only attributed a "natural" character. Above all, his adoption of Aristotelian categories and the emphasis he put on the sensory origin of knowledge contributed to the desacralization of the latter—and of Nature. Alexander Neckham (?–1217), a member of the school of Oxford, inaugurated the series of "compendiums" of the branches of knowledge of the period—and especially the natural sciences—with his *De naturis rerum,* a precedent for others of the same type. From the same school, Michael Scot demonstrated the fact that astrology in the Middle Ages did not lead to persecution. We will speak of him further on.

The spirit of Oxford blossomed in the work of a professor at the University of Oxford, Bishop Robert Grosseteste (1175–1253). Two characteristics of the English masters of the thirteenth century, Neoplatonism and an interest in science, were quite evident in this precursor of the philosophers of nature of modern times. He wrote on the human being as microcosm, the "Intellects," and divine emanations. What made him so interesting for posterity was his predilection for speculating on the subject of light. In his system, it played a role similar to that of fire in Stoic philosophy. As "first corporeal form" (*Lux*), it accounts for—by its expansion, condensation, or rarefaction—the presence of all the bodies of the universe and the constitution of the world. Grosseteste conceived the idea that a point of light created by God diffused so as to form a sphere having a finite radius—namely, the universe (a hypothesis prefiguring the "big bang"). Upon reaching the limit of its power of diffusion, it gave rise to the firmament, which, in its turn, reflected a light (*lumen*), thus engendering the heavenly bodies and the elements. Another theologian of light—and a Parisian author—Adam Pulchrae Mulieris (a contemporary of William of Auvergne), prefigured several of Grosseteste's intuitions with his *Liber de intelligentiis.* In the second half of the eighteenth century, when theosophy took the form of romantic *Naturphilosophie,* similar speculations were found in the work of Oetinger, the greatest German theosopher of his time, and his disciples. Speaking generally, light is the central point of all cosmosophies.

A work entitled *Summa philosophiae* was wrongly attributed to Grosseteste for a long time. It is an encyclopedia of a Franciscan nature spread out in nineteen books and emphasizing the natural sciences, particularly mineralogy. There is an interesting definition of theosophy in it, for the anonymous author distinguished "philosophers" (Plato, Aristotle), "theosophers," that is, authors inspired by the Holy Scriptures, and "theologians," whose task is to explain theosophy (Dionysius, Ambrose, Jerome, Augustine, Origen, etc.). It also contains a fantastic mythological story dealing with Abraham, Atlas, and Mercury.

An admirer of Grosseteste, the famous Franciscan of Paris and Oxford Roger Bacon (1214–1294) left among other works an *Opus majus* that was characteristic of the spirit of Oxford in that in it he deals with almost everything. Incarcerated for a time by the General of the Franciscans—for political reasons involving the Dominicans, whom he violently attacked—Bacon never stopped struggling against the prudent Thomist constrictions and looked for support from Clement V, whom he saw as the pope predicted by the stars for the conversion of all peoples to Catholicism. In modern times, Bacon is often regarded as a precursor of the experimental method, which gives a false idea of a person completely taken with the doctrine of illumination and the method of experience—two attitudes that are inseparable here, for what he calls "experience" (*experimentum*) should not be taken in its present meaning but in the sense of "work of an expert"; in this quality, *experimentum* refers to practices such as alchemy and astrology. Later, Paracelsus would think in the same way when dealing with "experience" in medicine. This word should be understood in the sense of study and knowledge of hidden "natural" forces, comparable to those which Pierre de Mariscourt tried to unravel. For Bacon, experimental science meant secret traditional science, provided that concrete science and the Holy Scriptures were not separated but connected, for each clarified the other. It was to such a science that Oetinger, after Paracelsus, devoted himself. Bacon also believed in spiritual secrets and in this way anticipated the occult philosophy of the Renaissance with which he shared the impatience of wanting to break the narrow frameworks of formal systems, like those of the Dominicans, which enclosed humanity and the universe. Bacon was not averse to practicing alchemy and astrology from time to time, and he believed in those rare individuals, illuminated by a superior wisdom, who could lead a humanity having need of them in the direction of truth. He believed the stars to be incorruptible and governed in their movements by angelic "intellects." The intermediary intellect which illuminates our minds comes from God and does not constitute a part of the human mind. He believed further that a true philosophy is revealed by God and was conferred upon the patriarchs and upon Solomon.

The Summae: Vincent de Beauvais,
Bartholomew of England, William of Auvergne

Esotericism is not completely absent from the writings of the Dominicans. The *Speculum maius* and especially the chapter *Speculum naturale* (1245?), by Vincent de Beauvais, sub-prior of the monastery of that city, is one in the series of large compendiums of natural science begun by Neckham's *De naturis rerum*. Vincent's book is an account of natural history in the form of an immense commentary on the first chapters of Genesis. One is struck by the importance given to the characters of Greek mythology: Apollo and Mercury are beneficent sorcerers; the gods become patrons of peoples and towns; and stones bear the stamp of the gods. We recall that the mythological sources which the Middle Ages had at its disposal were essentially constituted by *The Marriage of Mercury and Philology* (beginning of the fifth century) by Martianus Capella, the *Commentary on the Dream of Scipio* by Macrobius, as well as the writings of Isidore and of Bede. Another Dominican, who was very credulous in accepting the reality of many popular beliefs, was the author of a large *De natura rerum* in nineteen volumes. This was Thomas of Cantimpre, who borrowed from Neckham the title of his compendium. He can be compared to the Franciscan Bartholomew of England, who wrote *De proprietatibus rerum* around 1230, of which there existed numerous manuscripts and which was translated into several languages. Certainly, compendiums of this type did not always arise from magical inspiration; but by recounting numerous stories and observations on the properties of plants, animals, minerals, and heavenly bodies, they prepared the way for the occult philosophy of the Renaissance, especially because some of them spread over a wide area. These works reflected the forces of intellectual democratization; that is, they corresponded as much to the taste for popularization as to the trend toward encyclopedism, two traits of this gothic century in which the Dominicans also figure prominently owing to *The Golden Legend* by Jacques de Voragine.

The bishop of Paris, William of Auvergne (1180–1249), more clearly demonstrated an esoteric tendency and was perhaps the first Christian doctor of the church in the Latin West to display a solid knowledge of the works attributed to Hermes Trismegistus, at least of those known at the time. He left several treatises, including *De universo,* which more than the others deals with nature itself and provides considerable bibliographical information concerning magic. William of Auvergne also belongs to the long tradition of spiritual thinkers attributing all the evil in the world to human sin. But his work was a break in traditional thought in the sense that he opposed the angelology of Avicenna with a thorough indictment against what is perhaps the essential or specific trait of Western esoteric thought. We will deal with this question later in discussing the work of Averroes in the fourteenth century. On the other hand, the follower of Avicenna Ulrich of Strasburg (?–1277) likened Light to Being and Form and set down his own version of a hierarchy, the foundations having already been laid and developed by Neoplatonism and Pseudo-Dionysius.

Theurgy, Astrology, and Medicine

Among the works of magic in the thirteenth century, there existed Spanish and Latin translations of *Picatrix,* a work compiled in the twelfth century by the Arab Norbar; but mainly there were texts giving credence to the belief that Solomon, thanks to revelations from an angel, had been a magician and the author of various occult treatises. In the thirteenth century, these treatises attributed by legend to Solomon were considered to be in the domain of the *ars notoria,* an art that was supposed to procure knowledge of, or communication with, God through theurgic methods such as the invocation of angels, the use of figures and drawings, or appropriate prayers. In this category of writings, one must place *Liber secretis,* or *Liber juratus,* attributed to a certain Honorius, a book full of names of angels, theurgical prayers, and strange words derived from Hebrew and Chaldean.

Two important figures are of great interest to historians of astrology. Michael Scot (1170?–1232) was the principal translator of Averroes and also astrologer to Frederick II (who summoned seers and soothsayers to his court). This astrologer authored texts considered authoritative in their time but which were criticized for their prodigious amassing of doubtful facts. Dante placed this astrologer in hell, although he was never actually in trouble with the authorities during his lifetime. His master work, *Liber introductorius, Liber particularis, Phisonomia* (in three parts), is characterized by descriptions of the seven planetary rules related to the seven metals, and by astrological diagrams in which names of angels appear. It is an amazing guide to the geography of heaven and earth and the intermediary worlds, and to analogies and correspondences of every kind. Dante did not reserve any better treatment for Guido Bonatti, the other great astrologer, who died around 1300. Bonatti was professor at the University of Bologna and author of *Liber astronomicus,* undoubtedly the century's most important astrological work in Latin. To these works, one must add the treatise *Speculum astronomiae,* attributed by some scholars to Albert the Great and by others to Roger Bacon—but none of this is sure—which remains one of the most interesting treatises of medieval astronomy. This *Speculum* teaches the existence of two eternal principles: the body of heaven and its soul, the latter animating the former. God, or Intellect, is capable of transmitting science and knowledge into sleeping man by the intermediary of a heavenly body. Here again, we are dealing with a variation on the idea of an *intellectus agens*. We are far from the determinism of Averroes then professed by Peter of Abano and Siger of Brabant. The universal law of correspondences was of course applied to various divinatory sciences. The most prominent work in the field of geomancy is the great *Summa* by the Italian Bartholomew of Parme, published in Bologna in 1288 and entirely devoted to this question. The doctrine of correspondences, of homologies and analogies, continually nourished medieval thought and reflection, perhaps more in the thirteenth century than in the century before. This doctrine made famous the names of Gilbert of England (*Compendium medicinae*, around 1230), William of England, and above all, Petrus Hispanus. The last became pope under the name of John XXI and authored the *Thesaurus pauperum*, a medical manual very respected for the duration of the Middle Ages. He scarcely dealt, it is true, with the occult properties of things, but rather with the four elementary qualities: heat, cold, dryness, and humidity — categories which have more or less always been an aspect of alchemical thought.

Alchemical Texts; Arnald of Villanova; The Roman de la Rose; The "Sepher Ha Zohar"

Criticized as both illusory science and boring discourse, alchemy reacted by calling itself a divine science. Consequently, it based the idea of transmutation ever increasingly on that of incarnation, and made more and more references to the Bible. Roger Bacon was not the only Franciscan to become interested in it; Brother Elias, one of the companions of Saint Francis, was removed from his functions as General of the Franciscan Order in 1239 because of his interest in alchemy. Yet it seems that more than any other order the Franciscans had quite a few adepts and sympathizers — a fact that is not at all surprising.

The Latin version of a collection of diverse texts and inspired writings entitled *Secreta secretorum* contained, besides directions for the making of the philosopher's stone, a reproduction of the *Emerald Tablet* with the other texts serving as its commentary. Toward the end of the thirteenth century, two publications circulated that were a source of inspiration for later alchemical literature: the *Turba philosophorum*, mentioned above, and some treatises attributed to Geber. The *Turba* contains various dialogues between a certain number of ancient philosophers (Pythagoras, Socrates, Anaxagoras, Democritus, Parmenides, etc.), giving credit to the idea of a *philosophia prisca* or *perennis,* which would become widely accepted in modern esotericism. The *Summa,* the collection of writings attributed to Geber, includes precepts, generalizations, and aphorisms, some of which turn up again and again as citations in later texts, even up to our time.

The little work *Aurora consurgens* (*The Break of Day*), probably dating from the end of the thirteenth century, is a marvelous spiritual pearl that has recently been the subject of various translations and commentaries. In the Middle Ages, it was attributed to Thomas Aquinas, in the same way that many writings of this kind were attributed to famous authors.

The direct Arabic influence continued to be felt, in alchemy as elsewhere, but practically ceased to exist after 1300. In this period, a brilliant century for Spain under the reign of Alphonse the Wise, the most well-known Iberian alchemist was the Catalan physician Arnald of Villanova (1235?–1312). Influenced by the work of Joachim, he was the author of medical treatises as well as an anti-Thomist pamphlet, *Gladius veritatis adversus Thomistas.* A great traveler enjoying an exalted reputation, a social reformer and diplomat, he left many works on alchemy, including *Rosarium philosophorum.* He seems to have been the first to use the symbolism of the passion of Christ as *exemplum* of the process of transmutation.

The science of Hermes is not missing from the finest literary work of the time, *Le roman de la rose,* composition of which was begun by Guillaume de Lorris and continued by Jean de Meun, extending from 1230 to 1285. Embellished by illuminated miniatures, it portrays a richly allegorical and symbolic universe. Nature is represented as serving the divinity, in accordance with the teaching of Alain de Lille. The quest for the Grail as recounted in *Der junge Titurel* by Albrecht von Schwarzenberg, if not always of an alchemical bent, was at least initiatory. Written a little after 1260, it was an epic of 42,000 verses calling forth the *Imago Templi,* the image of the Temple of Solomon and of the New Jerusalem in all its architectural splendor.

Finally, the Kabbalah was augmented in the thirteenth century by what would remain its most important book, the *Sepher Ha Zohar* or *Book of Splendor,* which appeared in Spain a little after 1275 and would be considered for several centuries, at least in certain communities, one of the three fundamental books of the Jewish religion, next to the Bible and the Talmud. This brilliant compilation owes its existence to Moses de Leon, but for centuries it was believed to have been much older. It represents the summit of Jewish theology, that is, of theoretical mysticism applied to the knowledge and the description of the mysterious works of divinity. Never again would the Sefirothic Tree be the subject of such descriptions and theosophical speculations. It is an inspired text of almost a thousand pages, a hermeneutical text that has been the source for innumerable exegetes. The Christian kabbalists of the Renaissance seized upon it to make their own commentaries, and generations of philosophers of nature as well, for the *Zohar* considerably expands the talmudic position relating to work and ritual so as to develop a mythology of nature, a cosmic dimension that benefited Renaissance philosophy. Since mystical ecstasy plays a less important role in Jewish spirituality than theosophical speculation, it is not surprising that the great mystic Abraham Abulafia, born in Saragossa in 1240, was not very popular. Abulafia's work was very personal because of its mysticism, and his meditation practices were interesting in terms of esotericism in their initiatory and symbolic aspect, which called on bodily techniques, as in yoga.

Gothic Sculpture, The Great Work, and Freemasonry

Diverse spiritual tendencies are expressed through sculpture, one of whose characteristics is to take hold of nature in its concreteness by regarding it in a naturalistic and cosmic way. Animals, plants, and often luxuriant leafage covered many cathedral capitals and columns, as if slices of familiar life were always destined to be transmuted into living stone. It was as if this century that despised flesh wanted nevertheless to bring it back, especially during the late gothic period, when new forms blossomed. One can never say enough about all that Christianity owes to the Franciscan spirit. These forms, captured in sculpture, lost nothing of their reality, for this palingenesis respected detail; Pliny and Aristotle himself were surpassed in terms of precision. Among other documents the period left us, there were the designs, sketches, drawings, and notes of Villard de Honnecourt, the inspired architect who preserved excellent evidence of the workshop and work site, that is, of a melting pot where the constituent elements of a living and varied *prima materia* call and answer each other, combine and intermix, resulting in what is perhaps the unsurpassable alchemical work: the gothic cathedral. Within that forest, heaven and earth consummate a marriage that ancient Greece wanted to celebrate in its statuary; but here the biblical scenes, whether strongly emphasized or only suggested, add a dimension to this marriage that allows one to sense the invisible movements of the divine, human, and cosmic depths. For if the Hellenistic mind used light to set off humanity and arranged statues in an order based on reason, medieval sculpture, like Buddhist iconography, always placed persons, events, and the products of nature cyclically around divine statues.

The tracing of designs and sculpture and all that they aim to represent is not comparable to the power of romanesque art to call forth mystery. We are instead drawn to the gospel of creatures, while waiting for the time when the happily accepted decline of this style restores to human restlessness a larger part of its dramatic motivations. Through partially renouncing monsters, the thirteenth century put aside romanesque demonism, but what it lost in intermediary spirits it gained in an encyclopedic vision. The cathedrals were constructed and embellished at the same time as the great *Summae* or encyclopedias were put together, such as the *Speculum majus* of Vincent de Beauvais, a prime example. "Encyclopedic" means the seeking of meaning in the multiplicity of things and in their relation—but doing so by defining a center, a referential axis, an "East," around which they are organized. Mirror of Nature, Mirror of Science, Mirror of History; this is how such written and architectural works present themselves—they speak of the hierarchical kingdoms of the natural world and of the spiritual life, conferring a musical dimension on the occult rhythm of these universal relations which, if more reassuring than romanesque art, nonetheless continue to transmit a system of symbolic and cosmic values. Even if these forms become more familiar, they still follow the law of numbers and signs; they claim to be nothing other than the concrete expression of God's thought, or at least the rising into God of beings and things. No claim is made that they are necessarily hieroglyphic in nature, contrary to what certain romantics believed who were inclined to see more esotericism in the cathedrals than was there. Nevertheless, there is surely much truth in the interpretations of the alchemist Fulcanelli, whose fine work *Le mystère des cathédrales* (1925) interpreted some details as symbolic keys to the Great Work. Astrological elements were not lacking either, as witnessed by Chartres cathedral's twin towers of the sun and moon, the twelve signs of the zodiac linked to corresponding seasonal tasks in the cathedral at Amiens, and other examples of the same kind.

The masons who built these temples not only possessed practiced skills; the operative aspect of their activity presumed a wide knowledge enriched and deepened by their connection with learned clerics behind the scenes. These artisans came together to form associations. In fact, the system of the Roman corporation, the *collegia,* dismantled by the barbarians, was reestablished little by little in a new form: monastic associations. At the end of the twelfth century, each of these grouped together lay and ecclesiastical master workers and tended to call itself a brotherhood. When these brotherhoods became well-established communities of craftsmen, they were accorded great privileges (monetary favors, freedom of movement, etc.), or "franchises," from which arose their name, "free-craft," with Freemasonry obviously being the most well known example. The guild is a legally constituted autonomous organization. One of its rituals is the *convivium*, or banquet, a tradition preserved in modern Freemasonry. Guilds and brotherhoods were composed of lodges (thus, in Germany, the *Steinmetzen-Brüderschaft* was composed of *Hütten*). The word "corporation" is from modern times, and the *Compagnonnage* properly so called as it is understood today did not appear until the sixteenth century.

Each craft possessed its own saints and initiations, and the patrons of Freemasonry were the two Saint Johns. The apprentices of the guilds and brotherhoods were obligated to follow various technical, moral, and spiritual practices. These obligations, or duties, constitute what is called today the "Old Charges"; the texts that have come down to us on this do not go back beyond the end of the fourteenth century, but they were composed from earlier duties. Two of these works are the *Regius* (1390?) and *Cooke* (1410) manuscripts—the first in 794 verses and the second in prose. They teach that Masonry was created in Egypt by Euclid, then propagated in England, where it goes back to King Ahelstan (tenth century). Geometry, or the writing of God, or again Masonry, born at the beginning of the world, finds itself within universal Becoming. Advice and moral and practical directives were added to this; yet the mythical and symbolic considerations enhance the speculative aspect of these texts, to the point where medieval Masonry tended more and more to accept in its ranks those who were in no way "operatives." They were called "the accepted." It was necessary to wait until 1717 for the London lodges, conscious of the fact that the operative aspect of Masonry was henceforth purely symbolic, to decide to create a different Masonry called "speculative" on the ancient traditional foundation. If 1717 represents the birthdate of Freemasonry as we know it today, its spirit took form with the Constitutions of Anderson in 1723. Now, to write this famous text, Anderson used the *Cooke* manuscript, in which the word "speculative" is found for the first time.

How could medieval Masonry be anything but speculative? On the one hand, the Knights Templar supported and considerably developed the free-crafts and, after the disappearance of the order, entered into the corporations of builders. The Knights Templar were influenced in the East by the Karmates, the Ismaelians, the Fatimites, and the Assassins. Certain historians have found in that a reason for supposing that the foremen of our cathedrals sought to engrave various heretical teachings in the stone. But the heresies of the Knights Templar are fables, and one must have a strong imagination to see the Manichean or Catharist propaganda in cathedral sculpture which some biased authors claim to find. The stones frequently bear the stamp of passwords, and there is every reason to believe that certain secrets remained the privilege of the Masons, but nothing justifies speaking of heresy.

On the other hand, medieval Masonry could not do without its speculative aspect, since its function was precisely to express a universal language in architecture and sculpture. It could not help but consider itself as privileged, since according to the thought of the times, the entire universe was seen as an immense worksite of construction—or rather reconstruction. It was the only corporation that was not of a local nature, thus providing a freedom of movement that ignored frontiers and made it much easier to transmit drawings and ideas. The universal language that it conveyed translated an essentially esoteric and symbolic mode of thought, which remained in the West until the seventeenth century, and in this respect was similar to alchemy and Hermetism. At the dawn of the Middle Ages, Gerbert of Aurillac showed himself capable of being pope, alchemist, and master workman all at the same time; at the other end of this period, the legendary figure of Nicolas Flamel would represent the perfect example of the marriage of architecture, sculpture, and the Great Work.

Alchemy, Mysticism, and What Is at Stake in Philosophy in the Fourteenth Century

Averroes and Avicenna: Nominalism and Realism

Two major facts stand out in the history of philosophical and religious ideas of the fourteenth century. They were a long time in the making, and the result of them both was the far-reaching secularization of the modern world and the increasingly marginal role of esotericism in the eyes of ecclesiastical authorities. When this break was almost complete, that is, from the Renaissance on, the church tended to consider esotericism a competing system of thought. Further on, modern philosophy, a secularized form of theology, would classify it permanently as secondary.

The first fact was the acceptance of Averroes's thought in the Latin world, that is, a break with Avicenna's theory of knowledge; the other was the question of nominalism. Around 1300, the penetration of Arabic texts had been completed. From then on, one worked on what was already translated and known. The philosopher who had the most decisive influence on the Latin fourteenth century was Averroes, the interpreter of Aristotle, translated in turn by Michael Scot. Averroes made a clear distinction between esotericism and exotericism, the complementary nature of which can be understood thanks to a spiritual exegesis, the *ta'wil*. But his cosmology ended up destroying a part of Avicenna's angelology, the intermediary worlds represented by the *angeli* or *animae coelestes*, namely, the domain of the *malakut*, of the world of autonomous images perceived in their own right by the active imagination. By proposing a fundamental homology between *anima coelestis* and *anima humana,* Avicenna taught the existence of an intermediary Intellect, a *dator formarum* branching out in many possible intellects. This comes down to saying, as esotericism often teaches, that our intellect is connected to a superindividual source of light and knowledge. William of Auvergne had previously tried to refute this doctrine, and although Thomas Aquinas willingly accepted that each individual has an intermediary intellect, he refused to accord it the value of a spiritual entity truly distinct from our natural reason. With this, he broke the individual's direct connection with the divine world, whether it be the Holy Spirit, the angel of revelation, or angels in general.

The *animae coelestes* possess active imagination in its pure and perfect state. Humans are also capable of exercising this faculty for their own good, if imperfectly, owing to the connection they are able to maintain with these angelic or mental hierarchies. Their disappearance, in Averroes and his followers, is found in the "Imaginal," where it is reduced to the status of simple imagining. The word "Imaginal" was coined by Henry Corbin, created to distinguish the *mundus imaginalis* from the imagination in the purely subjective or psychic sense of the term. We are also indebted to him for the first systematic account of the disastrous consequences that the adoption of the ideas of Averroes, rather than of Avicenna, had in the Latin world. In the East, and in Iran in particular, the ideas of Avicenna continued to exist, thus inspiring and retaining the spiritual role of symbolic stories. The *ta'wil,* for example, unveils spiritual truths; whereas in the West, it is the novel, a profane literary style, that appears and proliferates. Moreover, once the relation between the individual and the intermediary Intellect is broken, the authority of the church quite naturally substitutes itself for this personal relationship that has no such need of intermediaries; the heavenly intermediaries are quite enough, for they guarantee and establish the autonomy of spiritual individuality as the norm. It was almost inevitable that people would rise against the constituted church, since it did not rest any longer on individual initiation, nor thus on a truly creative freedom. Once socialized, exotericism would even go so far as to forsake what was specifically religious.

Nominalism poses similar problems. We know that it consists of denying the existence of illusory "universals" (*"Universalia sunt nomina post rem"*), whereas realism affirms their reality (*"Universalia sunt realia ante rem"*). For a realist, a species such as the human species constitutes a reality. For a nominalist, this species is only a word, with the sole reality existing in individual human beings. What is at stake in this debate is of great importance to our subject matter, for "traditional" knowledge necessarily sees, in the laws and realities of the sensory world, a collection of analogical and homological replicas of higher celestial or divine worlds. Thus, according to Aristotle himself, the movement of the heavens is only possible by the driving force of eternally existing intellects. This had been connected by the Arabs and Western philosophers of the thirteenth century to a theological cosmology that found an indispensable support in them: the angelical hierarchies, of which Pseudo-Dionysius had, so to speak, mapped the terrain.

It was just this dynamic principle that was attacked in the fourteenth century by the Parisian nominalists and certain Scotists. Having won the debate, they left the way open for the development of modern science, beginning with physics. And celestial mechanics, taken in the same way as terrestrial mechanics, would fill the hole left empty by the departure of the driving force of the Intellects. Thus, the continuity that the traditional dynamics guaranteed between a spiritually structured universe and purely physical and self-sufficient laws was broken. In the eleventh century, Roscelin de Compiegne became the chief exponent of nominalism. In the fourteenth century, this current was represented by Jean Buridan, rector of the University of Paris, and by Nicolas Oresme (?–1382), also a Parisian theologian and bishop of Lisieux. Though the Scotists were non-nominalist, it would be best to mention them here—that is, the disciples of Duns Scotus (1265?–1308), who had tried to erase any trace of the Neoplatonist spirit, and thus of continuity and hierarchy between the various forms of the real. It has been said by Emile Bréhier that Augustine proposed continuity in being and knowledge, Thomas proposed continuity in being but discontinuity in knowledge, and finally Scotism taught discontinuity in being and discontinuity in knowledge. (One asks oneself what Bréhier makes here of the univocacy of Being, a Scotist idea.) To these names must be added that of William of Ockham, whose critical dialectic helped unsettle a number of previous theological conceptions. Ockhamism spread throughout Germany, where a professor at Tübingen, Gabriel Biel (?–1495), would popularize it during the next century. It was the students of Biel, such as Staupitz of the Augustinian order, who would initiate Luther into a nominalism in which God resembled more a capricious and arbitrary principle than an entity working in terms of universal order and good.

Rhenish and Eastern Mysticism:
Meister Eckhart, Palamas

One would have expected to see an opposing current arise that would have been a reawakening of sacred science and theosophy. Although the period seems poor in this respect, a viewpoint contrary to nominalism did exist, and this was mysticism—mainly Rhenish mysticism. But this was not theosophy in the true sense of the word, for it tended to go directly to God without passing through Nature and saw the latter only as being engulfed in divinity. Nevertheless, there was still gnosis, in the full and etymological sense of the term, in Meister Eckhart.

Meister Eckhart (1260–1327), a Dominican and the greatest of the Rhenish mystics, was not without affinities to Plotinus, though he was not directly dependent on him. In fact, we find in him the basic Neoplatonist triptych: the original unity of beings, division (or fall), and return to unity—a very traditional notion, and therefore inseparable from the very idea of esotericism in the West. In Meister Eckhart one finds a reflection of the triads of Proclus, of which William of Moerbeke (1215?–1286) had translated, among other texts, the *Elementatio theologica*, the direct source of the *Liber de causis*. Above the Trinity or *natura naturata* Meister Eckhart conceived the deity (*Gottheit*) or *natura non naturata*. For him, the mystic experience was not a return to the *unio mystica* that Saint Bernard had exalted but to the *Gottheit* or nonmanifested unity. It was possible, according to the Rhenish master, to reintegrate one's ontological identity in God while remaining in the world, a return to a source preceding Adam and even creation. From Augustine, Albert the Great, and his contemporary Dietrich of Freiberg, he borrowed the idea of the "ground of the soul" (*Seelengrund, synteresis*), which corresponds to the unique and privileged place where a being can again find his lost fundamental unity. Knowledge, as he defined it, did not consist in describing things outside of us, but rather in transmuting things that are known, and ourselves, in a return to God. Eckhart radically separated himself from Thomas Aquinas by declaring the *Intellectus* superior to the *esse*, for according to John the evangelist, in the beginning was the Word, that is to say, the *Intellectus*—and not Being. From this teaching, Tauler (1300–1361) and Suso (1300–1365) took mainly rules for living, whereas the thought of Ruysbroek (1293–1381) recalled the piety of Philo, in that he advised Men of Aspiration against penetrating the articles of faith—a not very theosophical attitude.

At the beginning and turning point of the century, the Dominican Dietrich of Freiberg (1250?–1310?), in a magnificent work, developed Neoplatonist themes that also owed much to Proclus. He showed himself to be far from Thomas Aquinas and devoted a large part of his writings to the idea of an active intellect, seeking to demonstrate that the soul has a knowledge of the totality of beings. "The intermediary intellect," he wrote, "is by its essence the pattern of every being *qua* being." Dietrich proposed a series of equations between the intermediary intellect of the Peripatetics and the reflection of God in human beings. A little further into the century, another Dominican, Bertoldus of Morsbruch, was also inspired by Neoplatonism and Proclus.

The mysticism of the Eastern Church was represented mainly by Saint Gregory Palamas (1296–1359), whose theories took on a form of gnosis. He distrusted the imagination, but came back to one of the most cherished ideas of Western theosophy when he taught that the contemplative brings all creation to God through himself. Under his influence, the Byzantine church turned away from the spirit of the Renaissance so that neither humanism nor anything comparable to the Reform could penetrate it. In the Hesychasm of this theologian and his school, there was, moreover, a form of meditation that could rightly be called Christian yoga. It is the prayer of the heart, known well before him in Eastern Christianity; but with the work of Palamas, Hesychasm acquired a real religious status, and Eastern spirituality finally found a theological synthesis. Although this work does not directly belong to the Latin West, it nevertheless left a deep influence, especially at the end of the eighteenth century, on a certain number of Western esotericists, for example, the Russian Alexander Labzine.

Rulman Merswin and the Green Island

The fourteenth century saw a great increase in the number of millenarian and apocalyptic "prophets" and also the development of sects of flagellants, which became especially well known around 1348. They were generally connected to the Brothers of the Free Spirit but were characterized by their ignorance of the efforts made since Pseudo-Dionysius and Johannes Scotus Erigena to adapt Neoplatonism to Christianity. Furthermore, while the *unio mystica* of traditional mysticism is a momentary illumination, the Brothers of the Free Spirit considered themselves permanently transformed and possessing magical powers.

More interesting from our point of view is the development of an ethics of spiritual chivalry. In this connection, one of the most important facts of the century regarding Western esotericism was the appearance in Strasbourg of a group of spiritual seekers called the Friends of God. On the banks of the Ill and under the direction of the laic Rulman Merswin (1307–1382), an ancient cloister sheltered these equally laic Men of Aspiration. The cloister was permanently consecrated to this use in 1369. These seekers of truth were connected in many ways to the Knights of Saint John residing in Rhodes. Rulman Merswin, spiritual leader of the Green Island, was said to receive his instructions from a person whose name he would never reveal and who was spoken of only as "The Friend of God, from Oberland." Merswin corresponded with him, and their letters, conserved up to our day along with various other documents of this spiritual chivalry, constitute a veritable treasure of initiatory mysticism. Who was the Friend of God, from Oberland? Perhaps no one will ever know. However, the fact that after the death of Merswin, the Friends of God stopped receiving any message from the secret guide and master from Oberland led historians to see him and Merswin as one and the same person. But this is of little importance; the essential thing is the existence of this spiritual chivalry, of these "knights in search of knighthood," as Merswin himself called them. As for the Oberland, its geographical location is just as uncertain, for it could just as well be the "high country" of Bern as of Alsace. In any case, the best interpretation is spiritual. We recall once again that it was Merswin who converted Tauler to the interior life, after which Tauler became one of the greatest preachers of any epoch. And Tauler had also read the *Liber de causis* in the translation of William of Moerbeke, thus indirectly coming under the influence of Proclus.

Raymond Lull; Peter of Albano

The three high points of the gnosis of the fourteenth century (in our sense of the word) are the thought of Meister Eckhart, the work of Rulman Merswin connected to the existence of the Friends of God, and the *Ars magna* of Raymond Lull (1235–1310). The latter was more a man of the thirteenth century, but the fourteenth began with the definitive version of his *Ars magna* (1305–1308). Born near Majorca and a member of the third Franciscan Order, Lull spent his entire life looking for an "art" having a universal value. He studied the primal causes or *dignitates Dei,* the divine names or attributes, a project in the tradition revived by Johannes Scotus Erigena. Lull broke with the static schemas the Middle Ages used for describing the various domains of knowledge and their interconnections, and in their place he proposed rather abstract but quite dynamic structures and diagrams instead of genetic and dialectical ones, which rested on letters rather than on images. Now the procedure that consists of combining letters in order to arrive at "knowledge" and illumination is typically Jewish, and particularly kabbalistic. The letters refer to elements representing religious concepts in the widest meaning of the term, as well as items symbolizing the elementary universal structure of the world according to the ideas of the period. The figures of the *Ars magna* are therefore, by their nature and as a consequence, able to be used for theological, medical, or astrological ends! We find divine Entities arranged in ternary structures that descend and reflect themselves in creation. The *Ars* applies to all possible and imaginable levels, from God himself down to the lowest levels of nature, passing through the angels, the stars, and the four elements; and, of course, it is an *ars ascendendi* as well as *descendendi*.

At the end of the thirteenth century and the beginning of the fourteenth, during this period so deeply influenced by scholasticism, the *Ars* of Lull arose in opposition to it as the channel by which medieval Neoplatonism was passed on, just as Johannes Scotus Erigena carried the torch in his way—a dynamic Platonism close to the Jewish Kabbalah then flowering in Spain. It was not surprising that Lull took arms against the Averroism of his time. In 1311 at the Council of Vienna, he tried without success to prevent its being taught in Christian universities. Lull's work would spread over a wide area, but only with the coming of the Renaissance. Nicholas of Cusa, Marsilio Ficino, and Pico della Mirandola drew a good part of their knowledge and methods from it. In a general way, the esotericists of the Renaissance integrated Lullism into the various elements of the hermetic-kabbalistic tradition. Esotericists such as Wronski (1776–1853) and Saint-Yves de'Alveydre (1842–1909) are comparable to Lull because of this "search for the absolute" based on ordered activity, the former by his geometric schemas, and the latter by his famous "Archeometry." From the beginning of the fourteenth century, numerous alchemical treatises appeared under the name of Raymond Lull, often published again in later periods. But all are undoubtedly apocryphal.

Parallel to the astrology of Lull, that of his contemporary Peter of Abano (or of Padua, 1250–1317?)—who had connections with Marco Polo and Michael Savonarola, and who had barely escaped the Inquisition—contains a grandiose conception of nature. Astrological Hermeticism constitutes half of this encyclopedic work, and the *Conciliator* (1303) is its most important book, in which Nature is governed by the stars and the gods are everywhere. Peter of Abano is also the author of a physiognomic treatise that is a classic of its kind. Cecco d'Ascoli, called Francesco Stabili (1269–1327), an Italian poet, scholar, and hermetic astrologist, was less fortunate; his life ended at the stake in Florence. In this first half of the century, astrology was mainly medical in nature, with Agostino of Triente and Geoffroy de Meaux. A "zodiacal man," indicating correspondences between the astrological signs and the parts of the human body, is conserved in the Bayerische Staatsbibliothek of Munich. At the end of the century, one astrological work seemed to dominate the others; it was that of Antonius de Monte Ulmi, *De occultis et manifestis* (or *Liber intellegentiarum*), in which angelology, planetary spirits, necromancy, and theurgy are mixed in an interesting way.

The Alchemists: Dastin,
Bonus, Rupescissa, Flamel

The fourteenth century hosts a growing number of individuals like Thomas of Bologna, court physicians who are at the same time alchemists and astrologers. Like a pilgrim, the alchemist undertakes a journey between two worlds, between the learned world and the world of those who are less educated. He becomes the genuine mediator of different cultures, and it would be of great help if we understood more about the alchemists' social status up until the Renaissance.

Alchemical literature truly flowered and remained plentiful through the Enlightenment. The most famous alchemist, at least during the first half of the century, was the Englishman John Dastin, whose writings have often been confused with those of Arnald of Villanova. Dastin defended alchemy in his letters to the pope at Avignon, John XXII, who reigned from 1316 to 1334. John XXII had condemned alchemy in the papal bull *Spondent quas non exhibent,* specifically with respect to the great quantity of alchemical, or fake, gold circulating as counterfeit money. There also exists a correspondence between Cardinal Orsini and Dastin, as well as two treatises from Dastin's hand: *Libellus aureus* and *Desiderabile desiderium.* Another adept, Petrus Bonus, alias Pierre Lombard (not to be confused with the theologian of the twelfth century), is the author of a famous text, *Pretiosa Margarita Novella de Thesauro ac pretiosissimo Philosophorum Lapide.* Written around 1330, this verbose account reflects an age of overlearned scholasticism but, more important, constitutes a testimony to what the Philosopher's Stone had become—namely, a question of faith, a form of mysticism, and a subject of sermons at least as much as a matter of experience. Armed with his pen and his references more than with metals and retorts, Petrus Bonus was chiefly a theoretician, a thinker who tried to harmonize Aristotle's philosophy with the way of the Great Work.

The writings of the Frenchman Martin Hortulanus also have an obvious symbolic interest; he is the author of a commentary on the *Emerald Tablet*—then often called *Thelesinum* or *Telesim,* or again *Secrets of Hermes*—which compares the alchemical process to the creation of the world. Similar preoccupations are found in Nicolaus de Comitibus, whose *Speculum alchimiae,* which appeared under the name of Arnald of Villanova, contains a dialogue between a master and his disciple. In this, a strong religious note is harmoniously suggested by the astrological considerations.

We have seen that the disciples of Saint Francis were often interested in alchemy. The apostles of poverty would have been surprised to hear the Great Art defined simply as a process for fabricating material gold. On the contrary, their characteristically intense fascination with alchemy confirms rather that it is a question of a spiritual science. In the middle of the fourteenth century, the Franciscan Jean de Rupescissa (or Jean de Roque-taillade) became quite well known owing to his repeated imprisonments, his prophecies on the coming of the Antichrist, and his alchemical treatises. We are indebted to him for a classic of its kind, *De consideratione quintae essentiae,* often translated and republished up to our time, sometimes fraudulently, and which also bears the title *Liber de famulatu philosophiae.* It develops at great length the idea of a "quintessence" at work in each thing, as well as theories on the four elements and on principles. All of this prefigures Paracelsus. Although Rupescissa's alchemy was practical and con-crete, it also dealt with the search for elixirs of eternal youth and was distinctly spiritual and symbolic. His book on the quintessence offers a description of the passion of Christ as an *exemplum* of chemical processes. Of course, one must bear in mind that religious teachers of that period were generally inclined to use the natural sciences to explain spiritual ideas, and in the literature of the period we often find *exempla* taken from the domain of the sacred to illustrate concrete realities.

Other Franciscans shared the same interest, such as Esimenis de Gerone, a visionary follower of Joachim. But the most famous of all medieval alchemists lived somewhat later. He was a Frenchman and not a Franciscan at all, but a layman: Nicolas Flamel (1330–1417). A copyist, bookseller, and Parisian miniature painter, in 1357 he came upon a book that he had seen in a dream, which was signed Abramelin the Jew. To decipher it, he made a pilgrimage to Compostella in 1378, visiting synagogues along the way. In Leon he met Master Canches, a Jewish kabbalist, who became intensely interested in Flamel's quest and decided to accompany him to Paris. But Canches died during the trip without having given his companion a key to interpreting the book. Returning home, Flamel devoted three years to his ovens, finally accomplishing the Great Work in 1382. From then on he endowed chapels, churches, and hospitals, demonstrating great generosity. His wife, Dame Pernelle, is connected to this semilegendary story. The couple was sculpted on the doorway of the chapel Saint Jacques de la Boucherie, whose tower, Tour Saint-Jacques, still stands. Flamel himself recounted his grand gesture in considerable detail. It is for each one to inter-pret as one sees fit, and at the level that corresponds! Flamel's work, *The Book of Hieroglyphic Figures,* probably drafted in 1409, is a commentary on the pages of the mysterious Book of Abraham the Jew. In this connection, we may mention the fact that alchemical treatises with illuminated minia-tures first began to appear in the fourteenth century. The *Book of Secrets of My Lady Alchemy* by Constantinus is among the most interesting.

The Divine Comedy; Alchemy and Literature; The Imagination of Chivalry

There are many who wish to see the *Divine Comedy* (begun in 1302) as an alchemical text. It does not take much effort of imagination to pick out an esoteric theme here and there. The subject of this colossal poem is Dante (1265–1321) himself, but its material is the universe taken as a whole. The celestial and angelic hierarchies, the cone with its Luciferian point at the center of the earth, the concentric circles, and the cyclic images, all of which comprise the book, obviously recall many works already mentioned above. The *Convivio*, another text written in 1304, distinguishes (see 2.1) four meanings of scripture; the fourth is anagogic, that is, esoteric, and it is no doubt the best way to read the *Divine Comedy*. René Guénon spoke in a very convincing way of a relation between the Christianity of Dante and the esoteric Sufism of Ibn Arabi. Moreover, Dante seems to have been one of the disciples of the Fede Santa, a third order of the Knights Templar. We should not forget, however, that in certain respects he is connected to Averroism, for not only does Thomas Aquinas (canonized by John XXII in 1323) have a high place in *Paradise*, but also Siger de Brabant. Be that as it may, the *Divine Comedy* represents the last great compendium of the Middle Ages, after which Christian thought tends more or less to break up into isolated parts.

The popularity of alchemy can be witnessed in one of the *Canterbury Tales* by Chaucer ("The Tale of the Valet and the Canon"), but even more so in literature where the supernatural merges with alchemical thought. "Extravagant alchemy," as Daniel Poirion calls it today, where the fairy mother Melusine "represents matter, the source of all metamorphosis, and thus of all life and all riches." This is exemplified in *La noble histoire de Lusignan* (1392), a novel in prose by Jean d'Arras, a version of which in verse was issued by the bookseller Couldrette a few years later. Here the novel combines with an iconography that flourished soon after in the *Très riches heures du Duc de Berry*. The hermetic art willingly adorned such emblematic iconography later on in the sixteenth and seventeenth centuries. It was also in the fourteenth that playing cards began to be drawn, with one of the first known appearing around 1367; they were important both in divination, and, later with the Tarot, as a support for symbolic meditation. In the novel of Jean d'Arras, the fairylike setting is used less as a framework for the supernatural tales than as a symbolic system of explanation of the world using universal correspondences. Melusine is the World Soul, who recalls the knight Perceval to his duty—for he had left his redemptive mission unfinished. And again, there is the *Roman de Fauvel*, dealing with the macrocosm and the microcosm.

The imaginary journey, the initiatory peregrination, is connected to the knightly quest. The trial and execution of Jacques de Molay, the last Grand Master, mark the end of the Knights Templar in 1314. But the myth of the Temple would cross the centuries affirming its power, especially in Germany four and a half centuries later in the Masonic form of the Strict Observance of the Temple. At the same time, in other related rites, there was a great increase in the number of knightly grades that were surrounded with esotericism. The drama *The Son of the Valley* (1804), the masterpiece of Zacharias Werner that crystallized these romantic aspirations, would be an essential landmark in the history of the expression of chivalry's ideal. When the romantic books of the fourteenth and fifteenth centuries happened to evoke Greco-Roman antiquity, it was to provide the role of a "mirror" for chivalry and heroism. But the pregnant meanings of the myth of the Temple and their continual resurrection express above all the quest of a fraternal and initiatory brotherhood. Finally, the founding of the Militia of Christ in 1319 in Portugal to replace the fallen Order corresponds to a call to maritime discoveries transposable, of course, to the spiritual level. The creation of the Knights Templar, on the other hand, had been connected to a reconquest. It would be shortsighted to attribute the great Portuguese adventure beyond the seas only to the attraction of spices and exotic products.

Philosophy, Art, and the Romanesque in the Esotericism of the Fifteenth Century

The Florentine Academy; Marsilio Ficino

The Neoplatonism of Proclus remained alive in fifteenth-century Byzantium with Gemistus Plethon as its most authoritative representative. From the time of Michael Psellus (1018–1096), the Byzantine university circles had been characterized by an increasingly autonomous philosophical movement—up until the fifteenth century. This independence, maintained despite the constant interchange between Greeks and Latins in their colonies and warehouses around the Aegean Sea—at least since the last crusade at the beginning of the thirteenth century—had contributed to the flowering of the scientific spirit and a definite turning away from occult philosophy. But with Gemistus Plethon, the Neoplatonism of Proclus, which had never been completely abandoned, became once again a subject of interest. Plethon went to Florence for a great "international congress" on philosophy that opened in 1439. For the occasion, he transformed his name (George Gemisthus) to Plethon, a pseudonym already adopted by the author of the book of the *Laws,* an esoteric writing destined for the members of a polytheistic and Platonist secret society. Cardinal Bessarion also contributed to this penetration of Neoplatonism into Italy. It was in this spirit that Cosimo de Medici entrusted the creation of the Platonic Academy in Florence to the quite young Marsilio Ficino (1433–1499) around 1450. Ficino translated Plotinus in 1492, about the same time that Jean Pico della Mirandola (1463–1494) gave his famous theosophical reading of *Heptaplus* on *Genesis.* Above all, Ficino translated the texts of the *Corpus Hermeticum,* attributed to Hermes Trismegistus, into Latin, the entirety of which had just been discovered (the Middle Ages had known only the *Asclepius.*) He accomplished this work at the request of Cosimo himself, who deemed this translation more urgent than translating the complete works of Plato. Ficino finished it in 1463; the complete edition appeared in 1471; and in 1497 he translated the *De mysteriis* of Iamblichus. In *De christiana religione* and *Theologia platonica* (1474–1475), this Florentine Plato, Ficino, developed Neoplatonist themes on the hierarchy of being by expanding in his own way the philosophical and religious irenics of Nicholas of Cusa.

Alexander VI, pope from 1492 to 1503, who supported Pico, had Pinturicchio paint the Borgia apartments in the Vatican with a large fresco abounding in hermetic symbols and zodiacal signs. In 1488, the pavement of Giovanni di Stefano Cathedral in Sienna was encrusted with a beautiful work that can still be seen today: a large Hermes as an old bearded man, dressed in a robe and cloak, wearing a padded miter on his head, and surrounded by various figures—with the inscription *Hermes Mercurius Trismegistus Contemporeanus Moysii.*

Pico della Mirandola
and the "Homo Universalis"

If Western esotericism had been aware of a part of the hermetic writings for a long time, Pico della Mirandola added to the *philosophia perennis,* the Koran, Islamic philosophy, and mainly the Jewish Kabbalah, which the West had scarcely appreciated up to then. Thanks to Pico, for whom the Kabbalah and magic singularly demonstrate the truth of the Christian religion, a Christian Kabbalah came into being and lasted for over two centuries. Thanks to him, and to Marsilio Ficino, the Renaissance would come to know cultural horizons that were not limited to classical antiquity, though, of course, the latter also was studied and rediscovered in a new spirit. Esotericism would form itself into a form of thought to the point of being an integral part of Renaissance philosophy, thus representing one of its essential aspects, a reaction against an overpowering Averroism. It would be to go beyond the scope of this study to take our discussion further, up to the triumph of the Renaissance. We recall that the image of humanity that Pico proposes in his *Oratio de hominis dignitate*, an affirmation of the *homo triumphans*, is a justification of an achieved individuality. Far from being specifically pagan, this ideal also corresponds to a theology of grace. It is an affirmation of the necessity for a total philosophy, of a form of knowledge, that is more than a conquering and aggressive material science. The *magia naturalis* at the end of the fifteenth century also expressed this effort at reconciliation and harmonization. It corresponded to the need to bring nature and religion together, just as Hermeticism in all its forms instigated a religious universalism based on the harmony and peace that Nicholas of Cusa also espoused. In a parallel manner, the *opus alchymicum*, this privileged branch of Hermeticism, continued its work of redeeming humanity and nature.

A figure like Pico, however exceptional, was not without precedent. In the 1440s, a time of intense ferment, a child prodigy by the name of Fernandus de Cordova was reputed to know all languages, to have an astonishing memory, and to possess doctorates in several disciplines! This sort of wandering knight of the universities and the intellect prefigures, even beyond Pico himself, the *homo universalis* of the Renaissance, a universality that favors the eclecticism of esotericism. Astrology, alchemy, and "magical" medicine were already a part of the cultural *corpus* of the pre-Renaissance, a period also influenced, more than previous ones, by the belief in demons and their relation to the secret arts, by the doctrine of occult properties of natural things—from which developed the *magia naturalis*—by physiognomy, by palmistry, etc. It was equally characterized, in a different domain, by a form of mysticism, the *devotio moderna*, which since the fourteenth century proposed a spirituality accessible to all, without theorizing, without meditation, careful to stay within the wake of orthodoxy, and of which the *Imitation of Christ*, attributed to Thomas à Kempis (1380–1471), remains the most well known expression. It was a sad mysticism all the same, practically iconoclastic, necessarily reserved for a few souls marked by the stamp of austerity and not at all for one having an inquiring mind, searching to discover in one movement the wonders of heaven and of the whole universe.

Nicholas of Cusa

In philosophy, the apostle of harmony and peace was Nicholas of Cusa (1401–1464), who by the breadth of his views dominated the period and who influenced to some extent the currents leading to modern esotericism. Nourished on the works of Meister Eckhart and Pseudo-Dionysius, he developed a theory of "opposites" in which the infinitely great coincides with the infinitely small and, as in Bonaventure, divine Oneness coincides with the Trinity. He believed in a total, but not totalitarian, science, which also embraced astrology, an important part of his life, and by which the *ars coincidentiarum*, the esoteric art, is clearly distinguished from the *ars conjecturarum*, the art of common science. The first corresponds to the principle of the intellectual knowledge of things; the second to the principle of contradiction, that of simply rational knowledge. The man from Cusa went to war against a mathematics and logic that were closed and static, and forced science to glimpse the possibility of dynamic forms. This done, he went on in the way of Pythagoras. The Intellect (*Intellectus*) sees opposites unified, while simple reason (*ratio*) declares them to be contrary and irreducible. *Learned Ignorance,* the title of his most well known book, *De docta ignorantia* (1440), is a form of higher knowledge, a gnosis, that of the reconciliation of opposites, or a state of unity among all things. The curve coincides with a straight line, day with night. Aristotelian logic is out-of-date—reduced to the status of an operational method—in this both visible and invisible universe whose center is everywhere and circumference nowhere, as Nicholas of Cusa presents it following the hermetic book of the "XXIV Philosophers." If Pico is the last great follower of Proclus, it might well be that Nicholas of Cusa is the next to last. In him we find the idea that each level of the universal hierarchy of beings contains all possible reality, in each case from a different aspect. He also seems indebted to Proclus for his images of unity and continuity which brings things and their intellectual correspondents together. Applying his theories to various human beliefs, in *De pace fidei* (1453) he draws from them the idea of the fundamental unity of religions in which even the polytheists have their place, since among all the gods, it is always the divinity that they worship.

The Presence of Astrology and Alchemy; Illuminated Miniatures and the Plastic Arts

In the years immediately preceding the Renaissance, few people were as drawn to astrology and to occult arts as the monks—some of whom, of course, provided the era with theologians—and inquisitors. Astrology and medicine went rigorously hand in hand in the work of the monk Jean Ganivet, whose *Amicus medicorum* (1431), which had a remarkably clear style, was republished numerous times. It was a work that was expanded by Conrad Heingarter in the second half of the century. Physiognomy was represented mainly by Michael Savonarola (1384–1464), author of *Mirror of Physiognomy* and grandfather of the Florentine reformer. In the fourteenth century, astrology and the Kabbalah had more importance than alchemy. Johann Trithemius (1462–1516) of Würzburg, one of the fathers of Renaissance occult philosophy and the future master of Paracelsus, was also a precursor of Cornelius Agrippa and left only a modest place for alchemy. If alchemy seemed relatively poor in major works, nevertheless many copies of older treatises appeared.

The Englishman George Ripley dedicated his book *The Compound of Alchemy,* or *Book of the Twelve Doors,* to Edward IV in 1470, and in 1476 *Medulla alchimiae* was dedicated to George Neville, archbishop of York, who also popularized the subject. The writings of George Ripley were often republished as classics of their kind. The famous *Theatrum Chemicum Britannicum,* an anthology introduced by Elias Ashmole in 1652, gave them a favored place. Thomas Norton (?–1477) would also become a classic writer, and with Christophe de Paris, an eclectic popularizer of fourteenth- and fifteenth-century alchemy, would prepare the way for the great "compendiums" and anthologies of the seventeenth century. The treatises of Bernard Trevisanus of Bologna (1406–1490) have also remained classics, like the *Liber de secretissimo philosophorum opere chemico,* which mentions Hermes, and *De chimico miraculo,* a novel about the adventures of a seeker of the Philosopher's Stone. Several books appeared under Trevisanus's name that were not his; and generally there was a great increase in the number of writings attributed to all sorts of people. In this way, the marvelous work of the beginning of the fifteenth century *Les douze clefs de la philosophie hermetique,* a book often pondered over by future generations, had been ascribed to a Benedictine of Erfurt, Basil Valentine, who was also supposed to have discovered antimony. Yet we do not possess the least trace of his existence before the first printing of one of his books in 1602! Alchemy is also present in the court. There exists a treatise attributed to Charles VI, who was interested in the science of Hermes, as were his predecessor Charles V and the Duke of Berry as well.

In Bourges, the palace of Jacques Coeur (1395–1456), the banker of Charles VII, was a *demeure philosophale,* which is still often visited and made the goal of alchemical pilgrimages. Likewise, the Hotel Lallemant in the same city abounds in hermetic symbols and allusions. Finally, the tapestries of the Maiden and the Unicorn—the most beautiful reposing in the

Thermes Museum, the Hotel de Cluny, and in the New York Metropolitan Museum of Art—are part of a "courtly esotericism" having clear alchemical meanings, including traditional opposites like the solar symbol of the lion and the feminine symbol of the moon surrounding the unicorn. Even if alchemical thought did not then produce very many original books, it still invaded the field of the supernatural. Though veiled, it offers itself to our sensibilities in the works of the Flemish painter Heironymus Bosch (1450?-1516?), such as *The Temptation of Saint Anthony* and *The Garden of Eden*, executed during the last years of the century.

A few alchemical treatises with illuminated miniatures, such as the work of Constantinus, had made their appearance in the fourteenth century; but illustrated texts did not really begin to spread until the beginning of the fifteenth century, when two masterpieces of this style were produced: *Aurora consurgens* and, between 1410 and 1419, the *Book of the Holy Trinity*, both recently researched by Barbara Obrist. The second, written in the south of Germany, is a mystical treatise in German in which the Trinity and the passion of Christ become allegories of alchemical ideas, some of which are nonetheless quite matter-of-fact. There exist a beautiful illuminated miniature of the *Ordinall* of Norton, and illuminated texts of Nicolas Valois, whose athanor is still kept in the castle of Flers. Symbols of operative Masonry can be recognized in these manuscripts, like the cubic stone and the compass—which hint at the existence of a rather close relationship between alchemists and corporations of builders. We mention, finally, the superb illuminated miniature produced around 1475 in northern Italy and preserved at the National Library of Florence.

The hermetic symbolism of these manuscripts easily became a part of other works that were not specifically alchemical. The Duke Jean du Berry (1340–1416) was the patron who allowed the Limburg brothers to illuminate their *Très riches heures*. This work contains the famous "anatomical man," where correspondences between the parts of the human body and the planets and signs of the zodiac are shown with a deft hand. Although the fall of the angels was rarely treated by the artists of the period, there was nevertheless a fine example of it in the *Très riches heures*, which recalled the invective of Isaiah against Lucifer: "How did you fall from Heaven, Lucifer, you who so shined in the morning?" Such works are testimony to the love of the occult sciences that Charles V shared with his brothers and to which he devoted himself with his astrologer, Christine de Pisan. The establishing of correspondences between astrological signs and the parts of the human body accelerated in the iconography of the time. There was the *Guildbook of the Barber Surgeons of York* and the *Compost et Kalendrier des Bergers*. Albrecht Dürer was perhaps inspired by these to create his woodblock *The*

Syphilitic in 1496. But there was also the *Book of Bedford* (1423), the reliefs of Agostino de Duccio (Malatestiano Temple at Rimini), the numerous engravings of the "wheels of fortune," and the "months and decans" of Francesco di Cossa in the Schifanoia Palace of the Duke Borso d'Este in Ferrara (around 1470), and the extraordinary Italian manuscript in color *De sphaera.* The Florence cathedral shelters the painting of Domenico de Michelino (1465) that pictures Dante in a cosmic setting. And we have already mentioned Pinturicchio's fresco in the Vatican.

The finest example that the beginning Renaissance left in this domain remains, for us, the *Primavera* of Botticelli, painted in 1478. Of course, the multilayered meanings of this enchanting work do not all reveal themselves in a moment and allow for various interpretations. But far from being contradictory, they complement and clarify each other. It is perhaps a horoscope for the person it was commissioned for, the young cousin of Lorenzo the Magnificent. A hermetic gift quite in Ficino's line of thought, it also brings to mind, according to G. Francastel, the illustrated calendars of the period. Above all, Hermes-Mercury is represented in it, in the form of an angel, the *spiritus mundi,* a *spiritus* or the channel taken by stellar influences, so that Frances A. Yates was able to see a veritable magic talisman in this painting, a "picture of the world."

Philosophical astrology thus expressed the spirit of gothic baroque in vogue at the end of the fourteenth century, in the sense that it expressed the same tendency toward transcendent spiritual forms, with a concomitant refusal of a fixed order. Curiously, it was from this moment on that architectural geometry tended to become set, while previously the cathedrals proscribed straight lines and right angles. But festivals and the romantic prevailed in other domains, at the same time as the obsessional presence of death. Festivals and strange costumes were in fashion under Charles VI, and also that novel of the soul, the *devotio moderna.* Was not Suso above all a novelist of himself? Astrology was the novel of destiny, thanks to which humanity found itself connected to a network of faraway forces; astrology stretched the limits of the individual to cosmic dimensions, thus preparing the way for the great Christian theosophy, mainly German in nature: that of Jacob Boehme (1575–1624), who was prefigured by Valentine Weigel (1533–1588). The fifteenth century became passionately enthusiastic for chivalry, the other form of transcendence which so readily cultivates symbolic emphasis, epic hyperbole, and the bizarre—three characteristics by which the aristocratic milieu likes to define and find itself. But chivalry is not only that; one must, above all, see in it an initiatory model of spirituality.

The Golden Fleece, Initiatory Novels, and Prester John

The year 1429 was marked by an event having a major influence on the esoteric thought of modern times; this was the creation of the Order of the Golden Fleece by Philippe the Good, duke of Burgundy, under the official pretext of fighting the Saracens—which his knights, intact, would never have the occasion to do. The Order possessed a beautiful symbolism in dress and ritual, over which generations of alchemists would ponder, at least up to the eighteenth century. It would also serve, as its name indicates, to revive the myth of Jason in the European imagination, a myth that would serve as a paradigmatic and figurative structure for the alchemical *opus* itself, as a romantic theme of the pre-Renaissance, and as an initiatory schema beginning in the sixteenth century. Around 1460, Raoul Lefevre wrote a novel entitled *History of Jason*, in which, of course, the important thing was the alchemical or spiritual gold, with all the wonders set out in the story bringing one back to this same common denominator.

Parallel to the orders of chivalry, here and there other initiatory orders were also created. Still more than at the court of Duke Jean du Berry, esotericism was expressed a little later at the court of René d'Anjou (1409–1480). King of Naples and Sicily, and of Jerusalem, he founded an order whose slogan was "loz en croissant" ("mounting praise"), but he also wrote works in which esotericism and mysticism unite, as in *Le livre du cuer* [=*coeur*] *d'amour epris* (1457). Artists and writers worked for him in the same spirit of cultural syncretism, among whom was Pierre Chastellain, author of *Temps perdu* (1445), then of *Temps recouvré* (1455), and who practiced alchemy himself, citing the best authors. *The Dream of Polyphilus* (*Hypnerotomachia Poliphilii;* Venice, 1499), by Francisco Colonna, illustrated with beautiful wood engravings, is, at the end of the century, like an allegorical synthesis of these great myths. Again we find, according to the plan borrowed from Dante, the idealized woman, who appears as the guide for man on his quest.

Portugal proceeded on this quest by setting out on very real expeditions after the subjects of Jean II dreamed of the famous Prester John, who continually fed the Lusitanian imagination. The famous Henry the Navigator (1394–1460) goes off in search of this famous person, who is believed to reside in Ethiopia, and who is seen as the guardian of the Grail come from Asia, a secret king, the emperor of the last day. If, in the end, it is a question here of an illusion as compared with "objective" history, a truth of yet another order can be perceived: "Prester John" is the ideal priest king of the kingdom of Saint John" (Henry Corbin). He also heralds Sebastianism, and one can equally see in him the paradigm of the "Unknown Superiors" in whom some believed during the modern era and of which the mythical Christian Rosenkreuz, at the dawn of the seventeenth century, was supposed to be one of the avatars.

As Henry Corbin reminds us, it is not only the memory of a history of events that can teach us about the place where "the two seas join," and where in reality spiritual transmission takes place. Always indispensable at the beginning, names, titles, and chronologies are of little importance and should be considered reference points only. To read esoteric teachings with eyes not only of flesh but of fire, to be connected to one of the traditions that passes these teachings on, is to enter into a "subtle history," the only history where meaning is unveiled. A work is truly "active" only insofar as it allows Tradition to speak in us and for us; insofar as it awakens us by bringing us closer to the eternal presences; and asks us to become awakeners ourselves.

Translated by Michael Allswang

2

Alchemical Esotericism
and the Hermeneutics of Culture

FRANÇOISE BONARDEL

HE ATTEMPT TO DETERMINE the specific place and role of alchemy within modern esoteric movements presents a number of difficulties, stemming from the complex nature of the Art of Hermes, which is at once laboratory practice and illuminative gnosis, and from its mode of transmission, by adept to disciple and by treatises whose reading, as René Alleau has rightly said, constitutes "an initiatic test."[1] But they stem as well from the evolution of its status in the history of ideas, especially since the advent of modern times, that is, since the Renaissance, in which two distinct conceptions of "humanism" confronted each other, and the natural and the divine lights whose unity Marsilio Ficino, Pico de la Mirandola, Cornelius Agrippa, and Paracelsus had worked to maintain were separated by Promethean and Faustian will.

From the seventeenth century, and even in the sixteenth, and regardless of the quality of alchemical treatises that continue to come to light, this traditional art was officially questioned and attacked by the partisans of a rationality that was to extend its control still further in the Age of Enlightenment—so much so that for the majority of "positive minds" of the nineteenth and twentieth centuries, there is no longer any doubt whatever that the art of metallic transmutations, that ancient chimera cultivated by people enamored of the absolute, is definitively lifeless, given the progress of the chemical sciences arising from the work of Lavoisier (1743-1794) showing the existence of simple nontransmutable bodies. The name of alchemy, wrote William Gilbert in 1835, "is now applied only to a science regarded as illusory, which one cannot engage in without ridicule."[2]

Fortified by Boerhaave's (1668-1738) successive discoveries, Cavendish's isolation of hydrogen in 1767, Priestly's discovery of oxygen in 1774, and Black's (1738-1799) introduction of the quantitative method into chemistry, science comes to confirm the doubts that Robert Boyle had already expressed in his attack on the alchemical theory of the four elements in *The Skeptical Chemist* (1661). From that time on, could the Art of Hermes possibly be anything but the work of overheated minds condemning themselves to social and cultural marginality? From the time of Chaucer's *Canterbury Tales* (fourteenth century), does not the quest for the Philosopher's Stone border on farce? What remains of the patient fervor of the adepts in Ben Jonson's *The Alchemist* (1610) or that of the moonstruck character in Honoré de Balzac's *La recherche de l'Absolu* (1834)? How is it possible to continue to speak of a movement, even one classed as esoteric, in a context so resolutely demystifying?

Far from being content with a declaration so summarily negative, in which alchemy would lose its entire *raison d'être* and sink into the order of "curiosities" of the spirit whose hopes it had borne, it is possible on the contrary to hold that this official eviction from the field of "positive" thought was and remains the opportunity for rethinking—theoretically and practically—a place for alchemy's possible survival and the conditions of its ever-vital spiritual and creative fecundity. It is also an opportunity to put an end to what was perhaps only a historical compromise, issuing from its very origin from an art of fire, which led it to link its destiny with what was to become chemistry, to the detriment of its operative and gnostic vocation as *Ars Magna*. Far from having sounded the death knell of hermetic-alchemical thought, symbolism, and practice, modern times have perhaps signaled their resurrection, on a level more essential although for the time being more obscure. The present study will attempt to retrace their underground progress, thus doubly worthy to be called "esoteric."

If we indeed allow, as the majority of the great traditions invite us to do, that esotericism signifies the secret character of a teaching received through initiation,[3] we must then observe that the Enlightenment ideology of progress compelled alchemical esotericism to return to an obscurity that is not only an initiatic demand but a historical constraint. This is why "modern" alchemy, thenceforth "occulted" while as always "occult" (because of its relation to the secret "virtues" of Nature), appears to us to represent a current, a multiform lode *to be found once again* by going through its historical avatars, more than an organized movement which is culturally available by the sole path, inevitably exoteric, that this type of historical approach presupposes.

Moreover, insofar as it reveals "traditional," and therefore atemporal, truths, how can an esotericism—here that of alchemy—reveal itself to be more specifically "modern"? Is not the very modernity of a traditional teaching, at least if René Guénon or Julius Evola are to be believed,[4] a contradiction—indeed, nonsense heavily laden with consequences for a culture that maintains it? By linking these different terms, and still more the spiritual and historical realities to which they refer, are we doing something other than *searching out a place for their coexistence?* Now if traditional civilizations were able to free themselves from the need for such a search, it seems that the latter constitutes on the contrary the specific feature of every esoteric quest undertaken within "modernity."

Furthermore, in order to remain a spokesman for a genuine esotericism—and not only for a passing fashion that contradicts its essential vocation—a movement that claims to leave the domain of sociology or even anthropology for that of gnosis cannot maintain its universality with statistical constants, but only with the quality of spiritual engagement of the "gnostic consciousnesses" that animate it. "It is by no means the 'great currents' which arouse them and make them appear; it is they which bring into being such a current, and then bring about its appearance," Henry Corbin judiciously remarks.[5] One might say as well that a genuinely esoteric movement always surpasses, by its scope, every "science" claiming to give an account of it, without for all that vitiating the diverse approaches to it which may be tried out—historical, psychological, sociological, aesthetic.

If the "man of the Work" which the alchemist always was remains today "the man of desire" whose edification was called for by Louis-Claude de Saint-Martin (1743–1803), one cannot avoid an inquiry into the *renewed forms* taken, throughout the history of modern times, by this desire for the unique incarnated in matter, which is called the Philosopher's Stone, the Elixir of Long Life, the Hermetic Androgyne, or, more simply, the gold of transmutation, within a "modern" cultural context which encourages completely different, more pragmatic fulfillments. For alchemy, A. Waldstein states, "is a 'Saturnian' mysticism in love with deliberation, depth, and concentration, all qualities radically alien to the modern world."[6]

First of all we shall need to be careful about the usage of the word "alchemy" itself, whose scope and meaning vary perceptibly depending on the period referred to. Let us say instead that a "metallurgical mysticism"[7] seems to have accompanied, in the majority of ancient and archaic cultures, the practice of arts of fire, especially metalworking technologies, a mysticism that expresses, paradoxically for modern minds, what Mircea Eliade has called "the sense of the concrete" in these cultures.[8] When, for example, we observe the multiple formulas collected in the *Leyden Papyrus* and the *Stockholm Papyrus* (third century A.D.), to speak only of the Greco-Egyptian branch of alchemy—alloys, goldsmithing of metals and precious stones, tinctures, medicines—we find in them as many manifestations of an *ars* which we still hesitate to classify as *magna,* even if we sometimes already see in them the aim of transformation, purification, and unification that will constitute its originality from the time of its implantation in the West in the twelfth century.

Like tantric yoga in India, Taoism in China, and Chaldean astrology, "alchemy" presents itself immediately as a path where work upon matter and desire for immortality converge, inasmuch as alchemy seeks an inspired mastery of the cosmic energies which it draws back to their glorious destiny. "In the majority of 'traditional' civilizations," writes Maurice Aniane, "alchemy is nothing but the sacrificial science of terrestrial substances, the transfiguring liturgy proper to crafts that concern apparently inanimate nature."[9]

Alchemy, therefore, has never claimed to be a substitute for the great religions and spiritual traditions, but rather to prepare for or accompany their revelation by the *operative way* which is its own, by being responsible for and taking charge of the created world it brings about. According to the cultural context in which it operates, it is evident that this "work," at once material and spiritual, can lead to duplicating a wisdom without transcendence – Taoism, for example – or espousing the sacrificial verticality of Christianity, without any contradiction in terms or impersonal plasticity in the Art of Hermes. Nor is there always perfect agreement, it goes without saying, particularly when alchemy is called upon to secure the demiurgic projects of Faustian Man out to conquer the strictly material universe.

It seems, therefore, that if alchemy occupies a singular place in the history of religions and spiritual traditions, it is as mediator between the realms of matter and Spirit. It implicitly compels each religion not to fail in its essential task of rebinding, *re-ligare,* heaven and earth, to reaffirm its relation to mediation and to the supplications that set it to work. Conversely, alchemy expects from the divine lights not only guidance for its art but the guarantee of its purity. We understand as well why alchemy and Christianity, the religion of incarnation *par excellence,* have constantly been in league with each other in Western history. The necessity for alchemy constantly to rethink its place and its role in relation to the maturing exact sciences is therefore equaled only by its obligation to determine no less constantly and acutely its relations with theosophy.

If the Arabic origin of the word *al-kimiya* is scarcely contested, the interpretation of its English equivalent "alchemy" is already more complex, depending on whether its etymology is Greek, Arabic, or Hebrew. Does it designate the black earth of Egypt, the cradle, symbolic more than historical, of the Great Work? Does it refer to the stage in which matter is brought to Blackness (*Nigredo*) by the work of the Art? Is it more simply an allusion to the art of casting and coloring metals or to a mythical founder named Chymes? All these uncertainties justify the pertinent remark of Mary Anne Atwood, for whom an investigation of this order realizes its own limit at the threshold of this mystery: the moment when the practice of the Art of Hermes begins to render us wiser ourselves.[10] In addition, however, the word *al-kimiya* invites us to consider as primordial—at least for the Western tradition—the Greco-Egyptian derivation, confirmed by the intimate interpenetration of the hermetic and alchemical traditions, both placed under the patronage of Hermes in the West.

But is the Hermes Trismegistus (Thrice Great) of the *Corpus Hermeticum* (second and third centuries A.D.), the prophet and mediator of the Noûs-God, the same as the Hermes of whom the alchemists ceaselessly proclaim themselves "sons"? Without going into the details of such a paternity, we shall mean here by "hermetic," in the very broad sense of the term, simply a teaching of a type that is gnostic (gnosis, knowledge) and visionary, revealed by Hermes Trismegistus and inviting each aspirant to work toward regeneration. While we could have spoken of syncretism, because of the superposition of the doctrines comprising it, we must consider as well that some of them, opposed to all metaphysical dualism, will have no difficulty in finding in the thought and practice of alchemy their privileged extension. Are we not invited, in the *Corpus* of Hermes, to cultivate our bond of "sympathy" with the created universe; to reanimate creation with the power of our Word alone, potentially divine? To safeguard the earth, placed under our protection and that of the sun, this link with the Noûs-God?

Moreover, the *Alchemical Fragments* attributed to Hermes are also present in the corpus of the Greek alchemists (probably compiled in the seventh century A.D. by Theodoros), in which the names of Bolos Democritos, the presumed author of the *Physika et Mystika* (about 200 B.C.), Zozimos of Panopolis (third century A.D.), Synesius, Olympiodoros, Stephanos of Alexandria (seventh century A.D.), and the Persian magus Ostanes stand out. All these "mystical" writings allow us to recognize in alchemy a "daughter of Neo-Platonic gnosis" (Wilhelm Ganzenmüller). This "secret affinity between Gnosis, which teaches the true meaning of philosophical and religious theories . . . and chemistry, which seeks knowledge of properties hidden in nature," had already struck Marcellin Berthelot,[11] as well as Louis Ménard, who published a critical translation of *Poimandres* in 1866. This point of view was to be confirmed in the twentieth century in the works of C. G. Jung. Finally, the diverse writings (on botany, astrology, and medicine) collected under the name of *Kyranides* confirm the vocation of Hermes as magus and healer.

A mythical genealogy also has it that Stephanos of Alexandria was the preceptor of the alchemist Morienus, who himself in turn transmitted his secret knowledge to Prince Khalid (died ca. 704 A.D.). The Latin translation of the Arabic treatise relating this teaching was effected in 1144 by Robert of Chester; accordingly, the *De compositione alchemiae* can be considered the cornerstone of what was to become the Western alchemical tradition, which had thus far been limited to a few technical formulas entered, for example, in the *Mappae clavicula,* the *Compositiones ad tingenda* (tenth century), and the *Schedula diversarum artium* by the monk Theophilus (twelfth century). Other translations followed: that of the *De salibus et aluminibus* of Al-Rhazi (ca. A.D. 825–932) or Rhazes by Gerard of Cremona (1114–1187) as well as that of *The Book of Seventy* of Jabir ibn Hayyan (eighth century), to which were added later the works of his Latin counterpart Geber (thirteenth century), among which the *Summa perfectionis magisterii* remains the most widely known. One must not forget, however, what was to become the "Bible" of Western alchemists, the *Tabula smaragdina* ("that which is above is as that which is below"), whose fame is equaled only by that of the *Turba philosophorum.*

This was also the period of compilations such as the *De proprietatibus rerum* (1240) by Bartholomew the English and the *Quaestiones naturales* by Adelard of Bath (ca. 1070–1142). But original works also begin to emerge, such as the *Ars alchemiae* of Michael Scot (ca. 1175–1234) and the *Speculum maius* of Vincent of Beauvais (ca. 1190–1264). If we refer, therefore, to the first Arabic treatises known in Latin translation and then to the rich literature that was to constitute through the centuries the alchemical corpus, we can agree on a definition of the *Ars Magna* that does not neglect either the predominance of the speculative element in some of the works or the operative in others, and moreover leaves intact the possibility of a christianization of the *processus.*

The Art of Hermes presents itself, indeed, as the preparation ("mise en oeuvre"!) of a matter disclosed as "first" (*prima materia*) at the end of a work of polishing and purification frequently associated, because of its harshness and its dangers, with the struggles of Hercules. In the same way, the alchemist achieves an inversion of signs, entropic until then, and is gradually disclosed as capable of exalting and pondering not only the opposed Principles of the work—Sulfur and Mercury, King and Queen—but the fire within matter and the cosmic fire, with the sole aim of delivering metals from their imperfection and humankind from death, completing and redeeming creation. Alchemy in this respect is only an art of fire, but this is the secret Fire, which is to say the desire maintained by the *anima mundi* even for the heart of the smallest particle of matter. This desire is sometimes associated with the active imagination, alone capable of "informing" and animating matter; it is not a simple support or pretext for spiritualization, but the "place" (the crucible) wherein and instrument whereby transmutation takes place (temporally and spatially), permitting the corporealization of the spirit and the spiritualization of the body. This is the key formula which encapsulates the mystery of the Work and renders alchemy irreducible to any profane chemistry or metallurgy whatever. In any case it is repeated indefatigably in the treatises that succeed one another like links in the same chain, the *Aurea Catena Homeri* by which the hermeticists designate the genealogy that makes them "sons of Hermes," as does the aptitude of the magus to bind heaven and earth, to uncover and put into motion the "sympathies" uniting all created things.

And so they follow one after another: Arnald of Villanova (ca. 1235–1312), presumed author of the wonderful *Rosarium philosophorum;* Roger Bacon (ca. 1214–1294), whose *Opus minus* and *Opus tertium* set forth the secrets of alchemy and accurately portray him as their enthusiastic discoverer; Martin Hortulanus, to whom we owe a commentary on *The Emerald Table* and a celebrated treatise on the Philosopher's Stone; John of Rupescissa (fourteenth century), author of the very famous *Liber quintessentiae;* Raymond Lull, whose title as alchemist is contested despite the fact that he left an *Ars magna* no less famous than his *Testamentum*. And also Petrus Bonus and his *Pretiosa margarita novella* (1330), and Nicolas Flamel (1330?–1417), in whom we see, perhaps excessively, the very incarnation of the alchemist confronted with the *Book of Hieroglyphic Figures*. No "history of alchemy" can omit the names of Bernard Trévisan (1406–1490); Salomon Trismosin, whose name is associated with the wonderfully illustrated *Splendor solis* (fourteenth century); Michael Maier (1568–1622) and his *Atalanta fugiens;* and George Ripley (1415–1490), author of a *Medulla alchimiae* and a *Cantilena,* which C. G. Jung was to cite frequently. How can one ignore Basilius Valentin; Eirenaeus Philalethes and his *Introitus apertus ad occlusum regis palatium;* Jean D'Espagnet (*L'Oeuvre secret de la Philosophie d'Hermès*); Marcantonio Crasselame; Le Cosmopolite; Limoon de Saint-Didier; and all those who, often anonymously, maintained the Word of Hermes in the seventeenth century in the face of the burgeoning discourse of Cartesianism?

The truth is that the repetitive character of the treatises poses for the contemporary investigator an almost insoluble dilemma. Should one take into account only the variations historically detectable from treatise to treatise, from author to author, from century to century, leaving aside that which the alchemists consider to be essential—the atemporality of their Word—thus scorning all of its historical avatars? Or should one begin with this Word, examining it exegetically, and from then on renounce any "history" of alchemy? This was a difficulty of which the Abbot Lenglet du Fresnoy had already become aware in 1732: "The Scholars who apply themselves to

History rightly scorn everything that has to do with this Science; and the Philosophers, occupied solely with their operations, neglect their History, and mix together all the different times."[12] Is it certain that the modern historian of ideas has advanced much on this point? Difficult to classify according to our contemporary scientific criteria, alchemical and more generally hermetic treatises belong nevertheless to three distinct genres.

1. *Treatises comprising the alchemical corpus properly speaking.* These attempt in general to unite, according to the particular genius of the hermetic art, the exigencies of *Ora et labora*, the motto of the old masters. They flowered from the fourteenth century to the eighteenth, diminished in the nineteenth (though the names of Cyliani and Cambriel stand out from this century), and decreased still more in the twentieth, despite the presence of Albert Poisson, Fulcanelli, and Eugène Canseliet, in whom the operative tradition of alchemy persists. Frequently collected into libraries, museums, and other *theatra chemica*[13] during the sixteenth and seventeenth centuries, these treatises are so many angles of approach to the Great Work whose polydimensionality, baffling for the uninitiated, they each reflect in their own manner. But in fact the question, for those able to receive initiation, is how to use them to recover once again that unique Book of Nature of which the work on matter allows progressively active interiorization.

Emphasis is quickly placed on the circulation and conversion of elements in the heart of the vessel (*Turba philosophorum*, Flamel), a vessel that is, moreover, as much that of Nature (mercurial water, called the Water of Hermes) as of art (the vessel of glass). Emphasis will also be placed on the progression of colors of the Work (almost all of the treatises allude to this); on the struggle between the two "natures" (Jean D'Espagnet), still often expressed in terms of the "chemical wedding" of sulfur and mercury, put into play in the baroque era by Johann Valentin Andreae's account in his novel *Chymische Hochzeit Christiani Rosenkreutz* (1616);[14] on the extraction and exaltation of natural "virtues"; and on the analogical relation of microcosm and macrocosm found in Paracelsus and the entire school of natural "magic" in the sixteenth century.

2. *Works of natural philosophy.* These are often described as hermetic, or even "occult," philosophy. The appellation "natural magic" suited one and all, once it was freed from the demonic connotations often associated with the term. "Magic is the mother of eternity, of the essence of all essences, because it makes itself, and is understood in desire,"[15] Jacob Boehme was to say. Among these works, it is proper to give an entirely unique place to the *De occulta philosophia* of H. Cornelius Agrippa (1486–1533), the *Royal*

Chemistry of Oswald Crollius, the *Magiae naturalis libri viginti* (1589) of Giovanni Battista Porta, and above all the enormous work of Paracelsus (1493–1541), greater than that of all other hermetic mages. If alchemy, as technique, is only one of the columns of the Paracelsian edifice, it continues nevertheless to play within it the role of *Ars Magna*. Thus Paracelsus could still write: "The alchemist is the baker who bakes, the vintner who presses, and the weaver at his trade. To each natural thing which grows for the use of man, alchemy permits the attainment of the degree which nature has assigned to it."[16] The people of the hermetic Renaissance refer more frequently to the magician of the *Asclepius* than to the prophet of the *Poimandres*. And if operative alchemy no longer occupies the first place for them, it always informs a vision of the world and orients each magical procedure.

3. *Works of Christian Kabbalah and Theosophy.* Under the influence of Ficino (1433–1499) and Pico de la Mirandola (1463–1494), people began to seek out in the hermetic teaching the most widely "comprehensive" vision of the world, one that could unite the Judeo-Christian and Platonic traditions, root the nascent science of modern times in some ancient wisdom (*prisca theologia*), and thus safeguard the "dignity of man" (Pico de la Mirandola), in danger of fragmentation from the very explosion of knowledge. Thus the movement of the Christian kabbalists was born, for whom alchemy, through its unique art of transmutation, can join forces in striving for the assumption of the glorious body of the resurrection. Jacob Boehme (1575–1624), Heinrich Kunrath (d. 1605), Robert Fludd (1574–1637), and later Karl von Eckartshausen (1752–1803), author of the *Chimische Versuche* (Chemical essays, 1801) and *Die Wolke über dem Heiligthum* (Cloud upon the sanctuary, 1802) were still to remain "alchemists."

What unites these three genres in the face of the oppositions discussed above is the acceptance of a certain philosophy of Nature, without which alchemy would not be possible. But it can also be said, conversely, that a certain vision of nature almost necessarily brings with it thought processes and language "alchemical" in nature. For, in contrast to the proofs which the physical and chemical sciences supposedly bequeathed to the nineteenth century and which are themselves today brought into question by modern conceptions of matter,[17] and in contrast to the recent historicist and neo-scientistic writings of Barbara Obrist,[18] Nature and matter, understood alchemically, can only be one and animated. Any demonstrative process that seeks to prove the opposite is mistaken not only in its manner but also in its mode of observation.

Nature in reality is not a thing for the mind to meditate on in order to extract its laws and so increase its mastery over the created world. It is the divine Mirror thanks to which the reflective possibility of catching a glimpse of itself is offered to each mind that sincerely renounces the inevitably violent appropriation of such an "object." The invocation of Nature as sole mistress of the Work, which punctuates all the treatises on alchemy, was therefore not a concession to a naturalism whose collusion with scientism was only to increase in the course of history; nor was it a return to a primitivism always ideologically suspect. It was, rather, a reference to that supplication which is at once the *materia prima* and the evolutionary and regulatory dynamic of all creative *processus*. Although it is the power of self-regulation, of mediation, and of orientation, Nature requires guidance, accompanied by the Art of Hermes, which elevates its latent "virtues" without ever infringing on its aims or abusively exploiting its resources.

This is why Ganzenmüller could justifiably say that "the alchemists are not Faustian types of people"[19]—considering Faust as the epitome of the "black magician," one who, for the price of his damned soul, thinks he obtains an ever-increasing ascendancy over a world that is in fact devastated, made a wasteland by the rupture with "the Spirit of the earth" generated by this type of conquest. But an evolution is very clearly perceptible in a number of alchemical and hermetical texts of the seventeenth and eighteenth centuries. One finds a decline of symbolism in the service of allegory, a pedagogical desire to strip away the veils, a socialization of spiritual preoccupations, and finally, above all, an insidious slide from the prerogatives of Hermes to those of Prometheus: one no longer assists Nature; one takes it by force and competes against it!

In this respect Goethe's *Faust* Part I (1808) and especially Part II (1832) mark a critical moment in the history of thought, that in which "modern" Faustian Man, breaking definitively with the chthonian energies that had until then been divinized by Spirit, displays before an ever-darkening horizon a look thenceforth perpetually troubled. And if Goethe (1749–1832) was an "alchemist,"[20] this is not only because his extremely concrete knowledge of the principles of the Work enabled him to sprinkle his writings with symbols referring to it or to create a tale like *Das Märchen* (The green serpent, 1795) and above all the drama of *Faust*, following the progression of the phases of transmutation. It is also because he reflected the crisis which was beginning to shake the West and which, imperiling the hermeticist vision of the world and Nature, perhaps also suggested that an escape from it must be found that was itself alchemical, by means of a redemptive turning back of a history doomed to decline[21] on the part of Faustian Man.

2. Frontispiece. Johann Joachim Becher, *Psychosophia oder
Seelen-Weisheit* (Lauenburg, 1707).

Conversely, however, far from having succumbed to scientistic attacks or to Faustian undertakings, the alchemical vision of Nature was to survive and undergo a resurgence in a very large number of works inspired in different respects by the Art of Hermes. We would go so far as to say that the preservation or rediscovery of a philosophy of Nature reveals, in most cases, the sign or trace of at least the potential for an alchemy. From the end of the eighteenth century, however, it appears that a dividing line must be traced, inasmuch as the alchemical tradition gradually loses its official standing even while giving birth, in a manner more difficult to retrieve because of its multiformity, to ramifications that we must now undertake to recognize as "alchemical."

Germany played an incomparable conserving role in this regard. The Hermetic Society of Westphalia, for example, was to carry on its activities from 1796 to 1819, and *Naturphilosophie* constitutes a cultural and spiritual tradition within it. The development of the diverse branches of Freemasonry was also to preserve the permanence of an initiatic way (both operative and speculative) in the West. Again, isolated works proliferated in which the alchemical process, its phases, and its end constitute the often-hidden dynamic of a creation that also belonged to the history of culture — literature, philosophy, aesthetics, etc.

Thus a panoramic view of the nineteenth century, in which scientistic positivism triumphs, nevertheless allows us to observe that alchemy, having changed its terrain and in most cases left the laboratory, continues its progress nonetheless, especially in the first and last quarters of the century. Still, the multiplication of "alchemies" doubtless makes it necessary, each time something presents itself as one, to redefine it and determine its worth, and to attempt to evaluate its soteriological significance in a culture that has become antitraditional. Without this effort, the alchemical process and the symbols of the Work will be used only metaphorically, in the most flatly rhetorical sense of the term and not according to what its etymology (*metaphorein*, "transport") would otherwise suggest: a directed itinerary of the soul through transformations of matter, in a vessel of transmutation.

Romanticism and Generalized Chemical Philosophy

Into a vision of the world that continued to be hermeticist, romanticism frequently integrates symbolic materials having redemptive ends that often remain those of alchemy. We cannot here reconstitute the universe proper to each of these creators, but we can try to display some of the constants as well as the most obvious limits of romanticist alchemy.

Shocked and affronted by the rationalist clarities of the eighteenth century, and in this respect closer to the Illuminists than to the Enlightened, romanticism proceeded toward an inversion of the values of day and night and tended to make of the night the domain in which all revelations arose. From this point of view, it must be observed that all romantic thought, even that which consciously seeks to be "synthetic," is marked by what Gilbert Durand calls the "mystical nocturnal" order of the imaginary[22]—by its uterine involution, its propensity to dream, indeed, by its derealization. It remains therefore to ask whether this involution can be assimilated either to the process of complete transmutation, which would give it value for the Great Work, or to the stage called *Nigredo* (the Work of the Black), which is indeed a passage through the night, but only prefigures a return of dawn by way of the terrors of decomposition, a dawn that alone truly transmutes. Such was romantic ambiguity, at least with regard to alchemical thought, whatever additional superb images might have generated such an involution—Friedrich Hölderlin's, for example: "The night illuminated by stars has become my element. When silence made its abode in the night, as even in the depths of the earth where the mysterious growth of gold occurs, the most beautiful time of my love began. Then the heart once again found its poetic rights."[23]

Beyond the philosophical and literary movement that bears this name, we would be inclined to consider "romantic" every "mystical nocturnal" which, making entrance into and residence within the night a substitute for the Great Work, tends to confuse the means and the ends of the alchemical transmutation and therefore puts it in jeopardy. It is this which bursts forth in Novalis's *Hymnen an die Nacht* (Hymns to the night, 1800), but also in Wagner's *Tristan,* in certain pages of Georg Trakl, and even in André Breton. It is no less true that, disappointed by their times, the romantics sometimes considered their passage through the night to be the promise of a civilizing dawn yet to come. If there is alchemy among them, it is in this eschatological vision of history.

Be that as it may, the great romantic obsession remains the refusal of inertia, material as well as spiritual, and most romantics proclaim their fascination with all forms of vital fluidity, side by side with their desire to belong to the great All, the *En to Pan* of the hermeticists. The romantics hope to find confirmation for what their poetic aspirations instinctively suggest to them in certain scientific theories of the time. Is this not the epoch in which Mesmer (1734–1815) makes his magnetic experiments and Ritter (1776–1810) his discoveries concerning electricity, in which Friedrich Schelling (1775–1854) believes he has found the equivalent of the *anima mundi* in oxygen, in which people are enthralled by Galvanism and the phenomena of clairvoyance (such as those reported by Justinus Kerner in

Die Seherin von Prevost [The seeress of Prevorst, 1829]), in which dreams come to be studied (Gotthilf Heinrich von Schubert published *Symbolik des Traums* [Symbolism of the dream] in 1814) as an opening into a "natural" world lost to the waking state? Finally, the work of the mineralogist A. G. Werner (1750–1817) was to familiarize the entire romantic generation with the alchemical and "geo-gnostic" art of the mine, as is attested by Novalis's *Heinrich von Ofterdingen* as well as E. T. A. Hoffmann's *Die Bergwerke zu Falun* (The mines of Falun, 1818).

Thus there emerges in its turn the romantic conception of "science," which Antoine Faivre rightly defines as "an art of life understood as vital force and an aesthetic of knowledge understood as gnosis."[24] A science eminently poetic and "magical," since far from searching for general and statistically verifiable truths, this art conceives of the veridical and atemporal emergence of eternal Nature only through the quintessence of the instant, which it calls "Pollen," fragment, or "*Witz*" (witticism). It is the romantic Philosopher's Stone, a crystallized time in which antagonisms are resolved, contradictions are dissolved.

But it is reasonable to wonder whether the romantics, having emphasized the rapid conduction of an influx which the internal sense, the imagination, taps like a fluid, and which places it in analogical and sympathetic relation with Nature, may have underestimated the importance of the slow maturation of the Work. It would seem that romantic haste did not always allow the accomplishment that was admirably, and alchemically, formulated by Novalis (1772–1801): "We are here on earth with a mission: it is our vocation to educate the earth."[25]

Finally, one cannot underestimate the influence of alchemy on a theosopher such as Franz von Baader (1765–1841), on a *Naturphilosoph* such as Schelling, indeed on Hegel, because the triad of which the Hegelian dialectic was to become the demonstration and the official mouthpiece is in fact inherited from alchemical thought, through the intermediary of Boehme's theosophy. However, while Baader keeps alive the confrontation of alchemy and Christianity and elaborates a remarkable philosophy of the incarnation which owes as much to one as to the other, Schelling, divided between *Naturphilosophie* and theosophy, hesitates between the vision of a self-sufficient Nature, polarized by extremes, and its subordination to a God still to come, with Hermes its harbinger (*Die Weltalter*–The Ages of the world, 1815). For his part, Hegel definitively chooses the side of history; and whatever the "natural" metaphors that punctuate the odyssey of consciousness in the *Phänomenologie des Geistes* (Phenomenology of spirit, 1807), Nature is no longer considered in the *Encyclopedia* as anything but a dead crystal in which Spirit may contemplate a necessary but limited phase of its own advancement toward totality.

Hermetical Renewal and Hyperchemistry

The diverse forms in which this resurgence is manifested, beginning in the years 1850 to 1860, cannot all be put on the same plane.

The name of Marcellin Berthelot (1827–1907) remains associated with the rediscovery of ancient alchemical texts. He published successively *Les origines de l'alchimie* (1885), *Collection des anciens alchimistes grecs* (1888), and *La Chimie au moyen âge* (1893). We must not forget, however, that Karl Christoph Schmieder had already published *Geschichte der Alchemie* in 1832 and that Hermann Kopp, between 1843 and 1847, had published *Geschichte der Chemie*. Berthelot presents his undertaking as a strictly historical investigation, directed at shedding as much light as possible on the alchemical origins of thenceforth scientific chemistry. The motivations of the scientist are inscribed within the vast humanistic current which, elucidating the archaic foundations of positivist thought, only exalts more thoroughly its value and significance, social and intellectual. Nothing human must remain alien to a scientist worthy of the name—not even the aberrations (alchemical, as it happened) of the human mind. This point of view was shared by E. Chevreul (who also put together a very fine collection of ancient treatises), F. Hoefer, M. Deherrypon, and Louis Figuier, to whom we owe a study on *L'alchemie et les alchimistes* (1854). Such presuppositions explain the disdain of all these scholars for passages they judged too "mystical," their errors of translation, as well as their barely disguised perplexity in the face of the Work's symbolism.

In fact, Berthelot's thought proves to be considerably more complex: that he had been in passing fascinated by his readings seems evident more than once; that he himself had had the ambition to reconstruct, solely on the historical plane, a kind of *Ars Magna* of alchemical-chemical knowledge stands out quite clearly in his remarks. What appears certain is that he also foresaw, no doubt thanks to alchemy, the limits of "positivist" knowledge, recognizing the existence of a necessity just as pressing within the human spirit to have reference to an "ideal" science, open not only to what is currently unknown but also to what cannot be known, which not only serves as a driving force generating new discoveries but satisfies a "gnostic" need. If Berthelot does not pronounce the word it is because positivist orthodoxy imposes its limits on him; but the study of alchemy enabled him to see the possibility of another type of "science," with other forms of relation between theory and practice.

By contrast, the works of Ethan Allen Hitchcock (*Remarks upon Alchemy and the Alchemists,* 1857) and those of Mary Anne Atwood, published about the same time, open certain perspectives closer to contemporary anthropology, comparative history of religions, and Jungian depth psychology than to the views of Berthelot. Indeed, they both affirm in effect that the "subject" of the Work is none other than the human being in search of a superior unity acquired during a "new birth." If there is novelty here, it is found first of all in the act of proclaiming this traditional platitude in a context so little prepared to receive it! Atwood, however, goes further still, suggesting that ancient wisdom no longer dwells in philosophy emptied of all spiritual significance by both rationalism and empiricism. From this point of view, her work *A Suggestive Enquiry into the Hermetic Mystery* (1850) is the first protest raised against Western philosophy's loss of its philosophical dimension.

In the path thus reopened, other works were to follow, such as those of Arthur Edward Waite, *Lives of Alchemystical Philosophers* (1888) and *The Secret Tradition in Alchemy* (1926); H. Stanley Redgrove, *Alchemy: Ancient and Modern* (1911); M. Pattison Muir, *The Story of Alchemy and the Beginnings of Chemistry* (1902); without forgetting the important works of Eduard O. von Lippmann, *Entstehung und Ausbreitung der Alchemie* (1919–1931). Alchemy occupies only a secondary place by contrast in the *summa* of Lynn Thorndike, *History of Magic and Experimental Science* (1923–1958). Finally, we must mention the remarkable contribution made by the collaborators of the journal *Ambix* (1938 to the present) to a better understanding of the history of alchemy.

In the majority of the preceding investigations, with few exceptions, there was no longer a question of taking account of the esoteric significance of alchemy, but rather of studying its origins and historically accessible forms by relating them to chemical science, of which it is considered the ancestor. At the end of the nineteenth century, the neohermeticist and occultist movement, to which hyperchemistry must be linked, seems to proceed in an exactly opposite manner, since it asks that science to guarantee gnosis and to justify its unifying procedures. One might well ask, however, to what extent it did not itself also serve to institute another "positivism," this time spiritualist. But what can one expect of a hermeticism thus exhumed, at the end of the nineteenth century, and what place does alchemy occupy within the "primordial wisdom" being sought after—an alchemy called, moreover, depending on the circumstances, "neo-alchemy," "dynamo-chemistry," "hyperchemistry"?

In the commentaries he devoted to *Poimandres* (1866), Louis Ménard writes that "the books of Hermes Trismegistus are a hyphen between the dogmas of the past and those of the future, and it is in this way that they are connected to current and living questions."[26] Indeed, did not Hermes appear as a god of transitions and exchanges, the mediator and redeemer *par excellence,* he "who explains, appeases and reconciles"? If hermeticism knew in the first centuries of our era, themselves so troubled, how to secure a transition between gnostics and Neoplatonists, can it not once again restore the unity of knowledge, lost through the dissociation between science and spirituality?

Hermeticism, occultism, and indeed theosophy are thus only diversified formulations of a single unique aspiration: the elaboration of a "great synthesis" between wisdom and science, East and West. Hermes is seen as the most "synthetic" of all the gods and prophets of an otherwise highly eclectic pantheon. Thus revised and corrected, hermeticism appears, still more than in the Renaissance, as the most broadly "comprehensive" movement, and is therefore the most receptive to new investigations. Beginning with the resolution, many times affirmed, to struggle against all forms of materialism, dualism, mechanism, people continue either to ask the ancient wisdom to ground and legitimize science or to ask the latter to prove rationally the intuition of the first sages and prophets. A circle so obviously vicious does not seem to shock anyone in this period.

All this leads to a summary amalgam of the great traditions. Christianity, Hinduism, Kabbalah, alchemy are all called upon with the sole end of showing that they all admitted the existence of a unique "ubiquitous agent," flowing through everything and from which everything issued. In other words, they *already* knew that matter was one and living. Issuing from this primordial unity, can the diverse realities be anything other than analogies? The principle of analogy, erected into a unique explanatory principle, is then used and abused, just as are references to the "occult," the vast reservoir of mystery and hope in a world otherwise more and more given over to demystification.

What is to be retained, and according to what criteria, from a production as obsessively repetitive as it is uselessly dazzling? Hardly credible scientifically, hardly rigorous philosophically (whether they are judged from a rational or a traditional point of view changes nothing), often mediocre in literary terms, the works conceived then can nevertheless touch by their very enthusiasm and naïveté, by their awkward desire for spiritual proselytism and for humanitarian and social commitment: such are the concerns of *La clé des grands mystères* by Eliphas Levi (1861), *Essais de sciences maudites* by Stanislas de Guaïta (1890), and *Traité élémentaire de sciences occultes* by Papus (1898) . Moreover, is not everything for them "high" and "great"? Witness *La grande loi* of Maurice Maeterlinck, or his other stories *La grande porte, Le grand secret.* In their spirit, does not the very amplitude of the synthesis thus undertaken reconnect with the no less grandiose project of the *Ars Magna*? Still, it is not enough to evoke, however loftily, the mysterious and the occult in order to constitute a real esotericism; nor is it enough to proclaim one's nostalgia for unity in order to put oneself in a condition to realize it alchemically.

It is clearly among the collaborators of the journal *Hyperchimie* (founded in 1896 by F. Jollivet-Castelot) that we find the most determined effort to demonstrate experimentally the unity of matter to spiritualist ends. Besides the founder, the author of numerous works in praise of neo-alchemy (*Le grand oeuvre alchimique*, 1901; *La science alchimique*, 1904), most of the authors have real laboratory experience: Albert Poisson (*L'initiation alchimique*, 1900); August Strindberg, *Brévaire alchimique, Occult journal, Inferno*); and Theodore Tiffereau (*L'art de faire de l'or*, 1896). "At the dawn of the nineteenth century," writes Jollivet-Castelot, "triumphant materialism, led astray by immoderate love of excessive Analysis, denied Alchemy, the same Alchemy to which this very dying century returns, eager in its decline for mysticism and for synthesis."[27]

Their program is clear: "To militate for the Unity of Matter and therefore the possibility of transmutation."[28] Every experiment capable of proving that "metals are not simple bodies, but rather composite bodies," is favorably welcomed. Unfortunately, Tiffereau's experiments only succeeded in producing an allotropic variety of silver. Unluckily, the evolutionist theories of Darwin are marshaled in defense of hylozoism, while the discoveries of Becquerel and Curie are seen as lending their guarantee to a possible "transmutation" of matter. Rare are those who, like R. Schwaeblé, ask themselves, "But where are this always identical life and this always identical matter taking us? Toward more perfection? Will lead one day be totally transmuted into silver? Will virtue triumph?"[29] To say that ether is perhaps the equivalent of alchemical mercury is really only a verbal substitution if what is essential is left out: the process of inner transformation which allows Nature and humankind to work one for the other toward their "aurification."

It is nevertheless significant that the hermeticists and the hyperchemists had hoped, through the great synthesis, to redirect society toward objectives other than those set down by the socialism and Marxism then rampant. Thus, Louis Lucas wrote in his *Roman alchimique* (1857): "Very fine social ideas are contained in the books of the alchemists. A vast fraternal, humanitarian religion is concealed by their works, although at first they give the impression of being directed toward a profane and material goal." To be sure, the hypothesis of a sudden proliferation of gold, reversing economic and moral values, had at one time shocked adepts and worried or tempted princes. But to realize the social Great Work can also be, because of the unity of matter and the analogies everywhere present between matter and spirit, to incite peoples to "rectify" societies corrupted by individualism and mercantilism—unity reconstructed in this way "working" in turn for a higher cosmic unity.

Such was the most surprising avatar of a hermeticism become "popular," of an alchemy called upon to sustain a social and spiritual transmutation to rival Marxism, but close on the other hand to certain ideals of Charles Fourier (1772–1837) and Joseph Maria Höené-Wronski (1776–1853), which were also, in a way, preoccupations of René Allendy, author of a thesis on alchemy and medicine (1912). The "fatal flaw" of this hermeticist medicine, closer to Jung than to Freud if it must so be situated, the generator of incalculable cultural disasters, is first of all the misunderstanding of our "esoteric" destination, which is to make of us "royal" people.

"Modern" Alchemy and Tradition

An essential question arises, at the end of the previously mentioned research: May we hope for a social and cultural change that would allow collective attainment of the reality of the inner accomplishment, in a nontraditional context like that of modern Western society? It is this central problem with which "traditionalists" such as René Guénon and Julius Evola have grappled. If "alchemy" exists for them, it resides first of all in the aptitude of a culture—that of the West in particular—to perform a salutary "transmutation," capable of reversing the entropic cycle of its decline. Is not the West the place and the time where the sunlight, associated by alchemists with becoming, falls upon the dangerously multiform diversity of "manifestation," which the Great Work must properly reunify and orient after having integrated its creative potential?

The operative Art of Hermes nevertheless occupies only a secondary place in the metaphysical vision of which Guénon has become the spokesman. Thus Eugène Canseliet could legitimately reproach him for having been ignorant of its fundamental texts and overestimated alchemy's relevance to royal initiation, which he regards as subordinate to sacerdotal initiation, a point of view opposed to the one Evola developed in *La tradizione hermetica* (1931), which made of alchemy a solely *cosmological* science, an initiation solely into "little mysteries." No doubt Guénon can also be reproached for having taken little account of operative alchemy, work on "matter" being for him no more than the indirect and secondary continuation of spiritual "transmutation." But is this really transmutation, or transformation?

For Guénon, in fact, alchemy, the technique of hermeticism, could not constitute a true metaphysics, if by that is meant an intuitive science (one of *Intellectus*) that would make it possible to trace back "manifestations" to their "principal" source and thus effect a liberating return toward the "formless." In a way Guénon takes alchemy at its word, which speaks of trans-mutation and not of trans-formation. And his disdain for any philosophy of Nature confirms still further the subordination in which he holds alchemy, dedicated to remain operative only in the intermediary world. Only its symbolism could be transposed, "giving it a truly spiritual and initiatic value."[30] This is why Guénon frequently integrates the symbols of the Work—sulfur and mercury, vessel, crucible-heart—among the *Symboles fondamentaux de la science sacrée* (1962).

Moreover, like Evola, Guénon tended to interpret the alchemical antagonism of "natures" in terms of a heroic battle of the male and solar principle against the dispersing, lunar, and female fascination, whereas it was in fact a matter—as Jung clearly saw—of the *intersecting* of reciprocal properties allowing the constitution of a balanced quaternity of which the "quintessence" is the center. In René Daumal as well, a misunderstanding of the "erotic" dynamic of the Work was to transform the famous "chemical wedding" into "holy war" and orient the poet toward Hindu asceticism more than toward hermetic wisdom.

By contrast, Evola accords more importance to the role of the West as the possible crucible of a Work of spiritual and cultural regeneration still to come (*Rivolta contra il mondo moderno*, 1969), thereby implicitly revaluing the function of the intermediary world. This appears still more clearly in certain remarks of Raymond Abellio (born in 1907), even if he often substitutes the notion of transfiguration for that of transmutation: even if he makes of the background of *La structure absolue* (1977) the equivalent of a neognostic Philosopher's Stone that is too strongly opposed to the "mystical" feminine to be the fruit of a true *coincidentia oppositorum*. He can also conclude that alchemy, "the science of open systems, . . . appears as a simple specific case of a general science of energy still to be disclosed in its universality."[31]

Generally speaking, the "traditionalist" approaches that were thus made to alchemy appear to us, with the exception of those emanating from operative alchemists such as Fulcanelli or Canseliet, to have underestimated the originality of alchemical gnosis and especially the privileged role it could be made to play in the West—to be sure, a place of antitradition, a place where all is rent asunder, but also, because of this very fact, a place where the inversion of signs prefiguring transmutation can be most legible, a place where the cross can at every moment be molded into the crucible. This is illustrated in its own way by the eminently esoteric work of an Ernst

TRAITE'
DE L'EAV DE VIE
OV
ANATOMIE THEORIQVE
ET PRATIQVE
DV VIN,
DIVISE' EN TROIS LIVRES.

Composez autrefois par feu Me I. Brouaut MEDECIN.

Dedié à M^r DE LA CHAMBRE, Conseiller & Medecin du
Roy, & Ordinaire de Monseigneur le CHANCELIER.

A PARIS,

Chez IACQVES DE SENLECQVE, en l'Hostel de Bauieres,
proche la porte de saint Marcel:

OU AV PALAIS,

Chez IEAN HENAVLT, dans la salle Dauphine à l'Ange Gardien.

M. DC. XLVI.
AVEC PRIVILEGE DV ROY.

3. Frontispiece. Jean Brouaut, *Traité de l'eau de vie* (Paris, 1646).

Jünger, for example. Perhaps it would have been necessary to meditate still further on the famous turning of venom into theriac, of which the texts constitute the mystery of the work. In this context, the magisterial work of Henry Corbin (1903–1978) takes its place more and more with each day that passes as that of an "alchemist" in whom the oriental detour invites the West to "work" toward its own reorientation.

This is why the proliferation of "alchemists" throughout the last centuries must not in any way make us forget that a gnostic quest such as that undertaken by the Art of Hermes is first of all a reunifying and orienting enterprise. Numerous historical, anthropological, and aesthetic works have indeed come to counterbalance the reductive influence of scientism and give alchemy back its place in culture. But exactly what place, and for what culture? Is it a question of knowing whether there always exist operative alchemists or of proposing a guided tour of the places that were important to alchemy? Whatever may be the interest in such an undertaking, does it suffice to bring to light the identity of the symbolic and archetypal images found within alchemy, dreams, and artistic works, if the whole of these steps, or each one separately, does not itself engender a more central and vital questioning and does not achieve a *change of plane*, without which it is not esotericism? Is an alchemical quest still possible for a modern person? With what "matter"? For the sake of what "gold"? It is fine to speak of the eternal human, but that may not suffice when it comes to taking account of a datum infinitely more complex and murky—"modernity" as such.

Now it seems that in the contemporary cultural context, particularly the West, this quest is undertaken more through these substitutes for the Great Work, the works of culture, than through the work of the furnace or mysticism. Can the quest in this case be isolated in a hermeneutics *of* and *by* culture? The difficulty of such a situation appears to us to have been foreseen remarkably by the French poet Joë Bousquet (1897–1950):

> Today the Great Work is forgotten, he who follows its paths does not even know that he has entered. And more than one questions himself, in the manner of the Kabbalist who, however, is ignorant of his entire doctrine. If he knew the power which leads him, he would no longer be bewitched. He would make of it a truth, that is to say nothing much: his ignorance has been cooperating in maintaining the principle, and keeping it from being formulated and lost in reasons.[32]

It is in fact in this intermediary zone between total unknowing and the formulation of "reasons" that alchemical esotericism is most often situated, acrobatically and paradoxically. We must now specify the links that unite it to the "poetic."

Alchemy and Creation

Arthur Rimbaud's famous *Alchimie du verbe,* which generated so much exegesis, must in fact be placed in a larger current which makes of Art the "Philosopher's Stone of the 19th century"—to borrow the words of Aloysius Bertrand—an imprecise current, continuing into the twentieth century, through surrealism, for example, or even the work of an Elie Faure. Did not Rimbaud also write a "Quest for the Absolute" (*L'esprit des formes,* 1927), from which André Malraux probably drew his conception of art as "Currency of the Absolute"? And in his work *Portrait de l'artiste en saltimbanque* (1970), Jean Starobinski clearly showed how much the artist, at the end of the nineteenth and the beginning of the twentieth century, prowled the confines of a sacred whose aesthetic conceptions (here aided by the ambiance of nihilism, it must be added) forbid him to make it the end of his quest, thus condemning him to remain a being in limbo, a "prowler at doors" (Homer, *Hymn to Hermes*), like Hermes the psychopomp, who passes through the work of so many creators of that time. Was not Nietzsche the precursor of this ambiguity, a constituent of "modern" art aspiring nevertheless to the status of the Great Work—Nietzsche, for whom creation was the supreme consolation and jubilation, because it alone is capable of throwing over the cruelty of life and Nature "the veil of undefined thought"?[33]

However, if one grasps fully how the art of transition practiced by Novalis as well as Wagner, Nietzsche, Baudelaire, and Mallarmé can be hermetic, one also feels that it needs something more in order to become the Great Work. Is it because art snatches us from death through the affirmation of the (entirely relative) eternity we possess? This is an easy certitude and one that expects no particular legitimation from alchemy. If one wants, on the other hand, to go beyond the recollection of the alchemizing metaphors by which literary criticism decides on the alchemical significance of a work, one must attempt to interrogate both art and alchemy together in three essential directions: (1) the desire of art to be an *Ars Magna;* (2) the "poetic" act as spiritual "work" of an alchemical nature; (3) the transmutative vocation of creation in culture.

This ambition seems to us to be particularly visible in the works of Wagner, Mallarmé, and Proust. To speak of a Wagnerian "alchemy" is legitimate for more than one reason, not only by reference to the "magical" powers exercised by the music of the "old enchanter." For one thing, most Wagnerian heroes search for an "impossible" very similar to the Philosopher's Stone, through the redemption of love, knightly tests, or self-sacrifice. It is this constant, moreover, which gives Wagnerian creation its unity and its amplitude. What is more, Wagner's very conception of musical drama invites one to see in it *a Work:* not a collaboration of heterogeneous elements, skillfully arranged, as Adorno holds, but the polyphonic development of a kind of poetic and musical "seed" (the famous E chord of the Prelude of *Das Rheingold*), from which the drama unfolds, driven by its own antagonisms: the pinnacle of a culture that has gained maturity at the same time as the *Work of Nature.* All these "alchemical" ingredients find in the *Ring* their tattered and yet glorious assumption: the ambiguity of the god Wotan, hesitating between power and love and condemned to destroy that which he loves, is for more reasons than one the drama of our times. To be sure, this is an abortive philosophical journey: the smoking ashes of Valhalla are not the alchemical *Rubedo;* they herald a world for accession to which Brunhilde accepted sacrificial purification by fire.

But Richard Wagner was not the only one to restore the ancient alliance between alchemy and the art of music. Did not Hermann Hesse see in this universal combinatory, which is his *Das Glasperlenspiel* (Glass bead game, 1943), the equivalent of a "sublime alchemy," purging the unessential and redeeming? And it is again music, this "trace of gold," which sets *Demian* (1919) and the *Steppenwolf* (1927) on the path of their "individuation."

No doubt the connections linking Satie, Berg, Scriabin, and Messiaen with musical esotericism are more anecdotal or more generally "mystical." If Edgar Varèse's *Arcana* (1926) is dedicated to Paracelsus, are the sonoral splitting and drifting obtained by *Ionisation* (1931) also comparable to a transmutation? By contrast, the dramatic orchestration achieved by Thomas Mann in *Doktor Faustus* (1947) nicely shows the relationship between the extravagant disorientation of twelve-tone musical space and the diabolically perverse alchemy with which the Faustian West is struggling. Finally, we find even in the *Livre pour quatuor à cordes* (1955) by Pierre Boulez the Mallarmian ambition for the book at once totalizing and "cut into sheets."

Such is not the only aspect of Mallarmian alchemy and its failure: a few grains of gold at the bottom of the cupel, from the confession of the poet himself, broken by his Plutonian journey—falsely initiatic, with respect to alchemy at least, since the eternal thus glimpsed excludes incarnation from that point on. For the inadequacies of language, poetic or not, cannot by themselves explain the Mallarmian impotence. Confounded and devitalized, was not the poet instead guilty of having "disobeyed the slow deliberative pace of natural laws," by wishing in haste "to rejoin the purest glaciers of Aesthetic," after, however, being given the task of making an "Orphic explanation of the Earth"? Thus dismissed, did not Nature, through the poet, loudly affirm that the Work does not exist without her? The greatest paradox, therefore, is that Stephane Mallarmé's quality as an alchemist has been judged on the basis of that (the quintessentialized jewel of the book) which was precisely the stumbling block.

This was a danger escaped by the Proustian Great Work, that Ouroboros within which the reader learns to circulate until the glorious revelation of *Temps retrouvé* is granted, when the Omega engenders the Alpha afresh, when the perfect circle of reading and of writing is reconstituted, transmuting bruised life through the unique confidence of art. For Marcel Proust, although worldly and urbane, nevertheless remained attentive to the humble messages of a Nature which he set about to observe and to deliver from its incomplete state. And if the joyous grace of Eternity recovered was accorded him, it is without doubt because he did not cease to grasp and express the ephemeral truth which a row of hawthorns or reflections from a wet roof were sheltering, and raised these humble specks of creation to their secret royalty. At this cost, which justified so many sacrifices, his complete work also becomes as much a cathedral as the "Work of Nature."

The Poetic Act and the Alchemical Work

Of course, for Rimbaud as well as for Baudelaire or Mallarmé, alchemy, despite its aesthetization, often went hand in hand with the Word. But none of them succeeded in going beyond what Yves Bonnefoy calls a group of "endemic conflicts between writing and incarnation."[34] In alchemical terms, it might be said that the charnel-house of life is what is thrown on the grill of art, to see the phoenix of the Work rise up from it. In vain did Charles Baudelaire proclaim himself the "perfect chemist" (one thinks of his famous "you have given me your mud and I have made gold of it") and at times rediscover "native harmony" by means of "correspondences." His poetic alchemy, admirable to be sure, is nevertheless in conflict with his inability to pry his own life away from Satan Trismegistus, he who "turns gold into iron and paradise into hell."[35] No doubt a sacrificial dimension is inscribed within all authentic creation, but it must also be shown that an art of fire such as that of Hermes cannot be reduced to Promethean theft raised into creative purpose. Such perhaps has been the error of numerous modern "alchemies," their unpardonable sin.

This was a confusion constantly present, for example, in André Breton (1896–1966): one hardly knows whether he was the "son of Hermes" or of Prometheus and his fallacious *Mystique du surhomme* (Carrouges). If references to alchemy—alas, filtered through occultism—dot his work, if there

came to him superb images incontestably sympathetic with the great symbols of the Work, one has a right to wonder if the "flashes of the Philosopher's Stone" thus glimpsed were really capable of transmuting life.
Changing it, perhaps, but to what ends other than the renewal of poetic
excitation itself? Can one make an alchemy of the poetic quest by placing
the scintillating fusion of contraries at its heart, given the work's constant
failure to ripen when a poet is fascinated more by the flash of light than
by the slow, dark work with matter?

Such work, by contrast, never ceased to obsess Rainer Maria Rilke (1875–
1926); it constituted the invisible sap of his poetic alchemy. It was a secret
work, inviting each person to plumb his or her own inalienable secret. It
was a work that went against the current, if one judges it by the measure
of contemporary eagerness and fascination, but a work reflecting the vital
concerns of its time to one who discerns in it one of these unalterable lodes
in which a certain idea of Western esotericism is lodged. It was a work of
fervor and praise, of care and patience, comparable to that of the bee who
gathers "the honey of the visible, in order to store it in the great hive of
gold of the Invisible."[36] This is not an Invisible to relieve the earth of having
to discover its own gravity, but one which rather endows it through the
medium of the poet with a mysterious, angelic density. If all his life Rilke
never ceased to seek out greater accuracy and intimate accord with things,
that is because for him "alchemy" existed only in this implacable yet sweet
distillation, purged of the unessential; in this transmutation by which the
opening of the world, redeemed, can be perceived and accepted in the
perfected heart of the rose, and, in this latter, an absolute truly absolved by
the acquiescence of the poet's gaze.

That is as much as to say—and so much the better—that Rilke could
found a school only by inciting each person to be, poetically. Is this the
reason why Bonnefoy (born in 1923), who is on so many planes so close,
almost never makes reference to him? The wonderful poet of *Du mouve-
ment et de l'immobilité de Douve* (1953) has, in an essential text, "L'acte et
le lieu de la poésie" (1958), as well as in various essays, laid down the foundations of this "passionate gnosis," which is for him poetic alchemy. Distrust-
ful on account of the seductions of language in which the presence can be
undone, aware of having to carry on the Work in a time of finitude and
abandonment by the gods, he assigns to poetic transmutation no less a
mission than that of safeguarding hope. But if transmutation is possible, it
is neither in the usurious exploitation of a "realized" real, impoverished in
the very act, nor in some unknowable Ideal, destructive of incarnation
(Mallarmé). It resides in this very tension wherein lures and thresholds
forever alternate, where the fraternal hand of the poet, given new strength

in and by the Night which inhabits it, succeeds in "reanimating the absolute" in some "true place." Thus poetry brings about "the transmutation of that which is excluded into the possible, of memory into expectation, of desert space into pathway, into hope."[37] In and through it, the inevitable secret of being awaits now and then the threshold of mystery, shared.

For Rilke as for Bonnefoy, but also to different degrees for Jouve, Milosz, Saint John Perse, Bousquet, and Char, poetry is "alchemy" by virtue of the ontological vocation which is its own, by virtue of the safeguarding of being to which it is suited, quite apart from the inevitably partial references to the Great Work which it may include. This is the reason why it occupies a central place in the meditations of Martin Heidegger (1889–1976), in whom it appears to us perfectly legitimate to see one of the last Western "esotericists" – and also an "alchemist" in his way, as much by the vision that was his of the Western night, the augury of an auroral return, in which the age of metaphysics will be completed through being exhausted, by the very nature of its hermeneutics. For the Heideggerian landscape, which at times opens to disclose being, is indeed something like a crucible within which, under the gaze of the thinker-poet, the antagonism of the earth and the world make peace. It is a gaze rendered responsible by the being of which it is the messenger, the guardian. Stripped of the worthless vein of moralizing ore which contains it, responsibility, with regard to the earth in particular, is thus restored to its true dimension, the spiritual.

Creation and Cultural Transmutation

Must we go further still and make of alchemical transmutation, possible in all true creation, the instrument for safeguarding a culture as threatened as that of the West? Is this to say that a creation worthy of the name cannot be confined in the far too narrow sphere of aesthetics, and in a certain way symbolically concerns the destiny of culture, just as the alchemists aimed to save Nature while carrying out the Work on a few particles of matter?

From this point of view, no one has testified more and better than Antonin Artaud (1896–1948) to the decisive importance of a possible "alchemy" of culture. He was closer in this respect to René Daumal (1908–1944) and Roger Gilbert-Lecomte (1907–1943) than to the surrealists. For this work in perpetual loss and suffocation, this quest for a center always refused, just as implacably demonstrates two things: that an "alchemical" process sustains and animates being and that the "loss of the soul" is not an empty phrase: without this mediating process, the circulation of energies between body and spirit is rendered impossible at the same time as all incarnation. On the other hand, in seeking to renew the theater,

Artaud was perfectly aware of participating in the Work alchemically by giving back to the West the crucible-scene where its logomachic history could once again resemble a destiny. This is what he attempted in *Heliogabalus*, as well as in the texts comprising *Le théâtre et son double.* There is certainly an Artaud "case," but one tends quickly to forget that it echoes another "case": that of a culture intellectualized, devitalized, cut off from the "magical" and sacred forces of Nature. It is possible that alchemy alone can enable the synchronic resonance of these two absences and the perception in them of the two forms of a single abortion of the self. This is no doubt why one might wish to relate Artaud to C. G. Jung, as the two faces—one aroused, the other at peace—of the same "contemporary drama."

The very magnitude of the work of Carl Gustav Jung (1875–1961) invites us to consider it, and it alone, as a vast scientific and gnostic movement which, breaking with Freudian dogmatism and leading back to some of the intuitions of Mary Anne Atwood and Herbert Silberer (*Probleme der Mystik und ihrer Symbolik,* 1914) by nourishing them with his colossal culture as well as his clinical observations, is one of the few enterprises of recollection ever undertaken in which alchemy almost constantly provided the thread of Ariadne. But this would be to forget that the name of Jung was associated, during more than a quarter of a century, with the spiritual adventure of the Eranos group (founded by Olga Froebe-Kapteyn), whose "spirit"[38] from 1938 until the present was to attract, from the most diverse quarters, all those whom the contemporary world counts as "gnostics." If there exists an esoteric movement in the twentieth century, certainly this one, on the shores of Lake Majeur, has contributed to maintaining with the greatest discretion a certain complete image of human nature.

If there is ambiguity in Jung's work, it has to its credit that it was the bearer of alchemy, technique, and gnosis, but raising it to the level of a paradox wherein many contemporary seekers can recognize themselves. Does not scientific work, when submitted to the demands and limitations of experimentation, demonstrate that by going to the very end of scientific requirements, one inevitably meets those of gnosis, which alone, retroactively, can explain the scientific process and give it meaning? That which was the stumbling stock for a timid and narrow rationalist consciousness then becomes the cornerstone for those who have meditated on the teachings of alchemy.

For such is undeniably for Jung the essence of the process of transmutation which he calls individuation: to keep alive the paradox of opposites: to bring into dialogue the conscious and the unconscious, and introduce people to their "shadows" without incinerating them; and to chemically marry the *animus* and the *anima,* its psychological transposition. It remains no less true that alchemy was certainly more than the projection of unconscious conflicts onto matter, an enigma for which depth psychology was to provide the key. Classifying alchemy as a form of gnosis, as Jung did, denied it such a restrictive function. So did his constant reference to the idea of Nature, of which Jung is incontestably one of the last philosophers. Is this mysterious power of renewal and transformation reducible to scientific data, this power which symbolizes so well on the plane of matter the *Mercurius* of the alchemists? The work of Jung is above all "alchemical" in that it is a powerful stimulus to "Work according to Nature": not only to liberate impulses repressed by censure and seek to balance them with a perpetually restrictive "reality" but also to find them a vessel and an orientation capable of integrating them and so working toward a greater and more significant plenitude.

The rich perspectives opened, on the psychological as well as the anthropological and spiritual plane, by Jungian "alchemy" have been pursued in the works of Marie-Louise von Franz, Etienne Perrot, and James Hillman. On a decidedly parallel path, the exploration of the imagination undertaken by Gilbert Durand leads him as well to the borders of gnosis, since the contradictory dynamics of the "Hermetica ratio"[39] open it too upon the nuptial mystery of creation. Finally, the erudite work of Mircea Eliade reveals its true dimensions only if it is seen as a great step toward cultural regeneration, offered by way of initiatic baptism to the "theoretical" person of the West. All of them evolve along this difficult crest, more or less visibly traced by alchemy, where the exoteric and the esoteric are henceforth called upon less to repel each other than to fecundate each other.

Translated by Katherine O'Brien and Stephen Voss

Notes

1. René Alleau, "Alchimie," in *Encyclopaedia universalis* 1:596.
2. William Gilbert, "De l'alchimie," extract from *Dictionnaire de physique générale, théorique et appliquée* (Paris: Mame, 1835) 4.
3. See in this connection the work of J. Marquès-Rivière, *Histoire des doctrines ésotériques* (Paris: Payot, 1950) 7ff.
4. A point of view developed by René Guénon in *La Crise du Monde moderne* (1946) and *Le Règne de la Quantité et les Signes des Temps* (1945), and by Julius Evola in *Révolte contre le monde moderne* (French ed. 1972).
5. Henry Corbin, "Le temps d'Eranos," in *Cahier de L'Herne H. Corbin* (Paris, 1981) 287.
6. A. Waldstein, *Lumières de l'alchimie* (Paris: Mame, 1973) 207.
7. Mircea Eliade, *Forgerons et alchimistes* (Paris: Flammarion, 1977) 92.
8. Mircea Eliade, "Metallurgy, Magic and Alchemy," in *Zalmoxis* (Paris, 1938) 85ff.

9. Maurice Aniane, "Notes sur l'alchimie, 'yoga' cosmologique de la chrétienté médié-vale," in *Yoga, science de l'homme intégral* (Paris: Cahiers du Sud, 1953) 243.

10. Mary Anne Atwood, *A Suggestive Enquiry into the Hermetic Mystery* (London, 1850; Belfast, 1918; reprint, s.d. (ca. 1985, cf. p. 4).

11. Marcellin Berthelot, *Les origines de l'alchimie* (Paris: G. Steinnheil, 1885) 66.

12. Abbé N. Lenglet du Fresnoy, *Histoire de la Philosophie Hermétique* (Paris: Couste-telier, 1742) 1:III, Préface.

13. One of the most famous being the *Theatrum chemicum*, vols. 1–3 of which were published in Ursel in 1602 and vols. 4–6 which were published in Strasbourg in 1613, 1622. It comprised 209 treatises: reedited and enlarged, 1659–1661 (facsimile edition, Turin, 1981).

14. See Bernard Gorceix, *La Bible des Rose-Croix* (Paris: Presses universitaires de France, 1969) 71. See the recent translation by Joscelyn Godwin: *The Chemical Wedding of Christian Rosenkreutz* (Grand Rapids: Phanes Press, 1992).

15. Jacob Boehme, *Sämtliche Werke* (Leipzig: J. A. Barth, 1846) "Sex Puncta Mystica," V, I, p. 407.

16. Paracelsus, *Sämtliche Werke* (Munich: O. W. Barth, 1923/33) vol. VIII, "Das Buch Paragranum," p. 181.

17. See, e.g., Fritjof Capra, *The Tao of Physics* (Berkeley, 1975).

18. Barbara Obrist, *Les débuts de l'imagerie alchimique* (Paris: Le Sycomore, 1982).

19. W. Ganzenmüller, *Die Alchemie im Mittelalter* (Paderborn, 1938) 235.

20. See in this connection the work of Ronald D. Gray, *Goethe the Alchemist* (Cambridge, 1952).

21. This is Oswald Spengler's thesis in *Der Untergang des Abendlandes* (1918/1922).

22. Gilbert Durand, *Les structures anthropologiques de l'imaginaire* (Paris: Presses universitaires de France, 1963).

23. Friedrich Hölderlin, "Hyperion" in *Sämtliche Werke* (Frankfurter Ausgabe) 2:666.

24. Antoine Faivre, "Physique et métaphysique de feu chez J. W. Ritter," *Les Etudes philosophiques* no. 1 (1983) 25.

25. Novalis, *Schriften* (Darmsadt, 1960) vol. II, "Blüthenstaub," p. 426.

26. Louis Ménard, *Hermès Trismégiste* (Paris: Didier, 1866) XIII.

27. F. Jollivet-Castelot, *La science alchimique* (Paris: Chacornac, 1904) 344.

28. The title of a pamphlet published by Theodore Tiffereau in 1853 in Paris.

29. R. Schwaeblé, *La divine magie* (Paris, 1918) 147.

30. René Guénon, *Symboles fondamentaux de la science sacrée* (Paris: Gallimard, 1962) 35.

31. Raymond Abellio, *La fin de l'ésotérisme* (Paris: Flammarion, 1973) 195.

32. J. Bousquet, quoted in *J. Bosquet* (Paris: Seghers, 1972) 201.

33. Friedrich Nietzsche, *Gesammelte Werke* (Munich: Musarion Verlag, 1923) vol. VIII, *Menschliches, Allzumenschliches,* p. 151.

34. Yves Bonnefoy, *Le nuage rouge* (Paris: Mercure de France, 1977) 80.

35. Charles Baudelaire, *Oeuvres complètes* (Paris: Gallimard, 1954) 149.

36. Rainer Maria Rilke, *Briefe aus Muzot* (1921/1926) (Leipzig: Insel-Verlag) 335.

37. Yves Bonnefoy, *L'improbable* (Paris: Mercure de France, 1980) 130.

38. Corbin, "Le temps d'Eranos," 256ff.

39. Gilbert Durand, *Science de l'homme et tradition* (Paris: Berg, 1981).

3

Natural Science
in the Age of Romanticism

DIETRICH VON ENGELHARDT

THE AGE OF ROMANTICISM and German Idealism around 1800 represents a particular phase in the history of the natural sciences and their relationship to philosophy.[1] At that time various trends stand side by side and influence one another, and there are different reactions to the modern development of science and above all to the Enlightenment. Romantic natural science is a specific trend that spread especially in Germany, but even there this trend was by no means dominant. Other trends existed: a positivistic trend comparable to that in other areas of science, a transcendental trend influenced by Kant, and a more speculative trend shaped by Schelling and Hegel. Romantic natural science and speculative natural philosophy are particularly dependent on Schelling, but influences from theological and philosophical movements from the past similarly made their mark independently of Schelling.

It is not always possible to make a clear distinction between the romantic and the speculative trends, either in the works of a scholar as a whole or in a particular writing. The scientific condemnation of the nineteenth century did not take account of these differences between the romantic and speculative trends in both transcendental natural philosophy and natural science with a transcendental philosophical basis, or if it did, it did not do so sufficiently. No account was taken of Schelling's and above all Hegel's committed criticism of romantic natural science, and natural philosophy became a derogatory slogan. Hegel, Schelling, romantic natural scientists, and even Kant were lumped together, and Kantianism only partially sparked off new impulses in the second half of the nineteenth century in the assessment of the romantic natural scientists. Right up to the present day not a few historians of science have similarly concealed these differences in scientific positions—usually in unconscious dependence on a positivistic conception of science.

Those involved in romantic natural science include Baader, Eschenmayer, Novalis, Ritter, Troxler, Treviranus, Görres, Schubert, Steffens, Oken, Windischmann, Kieser, Oersted, and Carus; many more names could be added.[2] Romantic natural science is not itself a unity; specific features and individual developments have to be noted: the differences in relationship to Schelling, divergent conceptions of nature and science, different responses to the victory of positivistic natural science in the nineteenth century. The division and typification of the romantic positions remain tasks for future research.

While Schelling is rightly regarded as the founder of speculative natural philosophy around 1800, his proximity to romantic natural philosophy is just as evident. Schelling's work is one of the basic presuppositions for both the romantic and the speculative trends in contemplation of nature. Goethe's natural science, which without doubt is connected with speculative natural philosophy and romantic natural science, combines aesthetics, philosophy, and science. Hegel aptly describes it as "practical consideration of nature"; Goethe's primal phenomena led into a "twilight, spiritual and comprehensible by its simplicity, visible or tangible through its sensory nature."[3] Goethe expressed both distance and proximity in his greeting to Hegel: "The Primal Phenomenon [*Urphänomen*] commends itself to the Absolute."[4] Alexander von Humboldt also occupies a specific place between natural science, natural philosophy, and art; his aim is an "empirical view of nature as a whole in the scientific form of a portrait of nature."[5] Schopenhauer, too, has a particular position in the spectrum of that time, indebted as he is to Kant and Goethe and at the same time in sharp opposition to Hegel and to contemporary natural science.

Friedrich Wilhelm Joseph Schelling

Schelling's natural philosophy[6] leads from inanimate nature to the organic sphere, from matter to human life. The beginning and end of his philosophical construction is the identity of matter and consciousness, of the spirit which gains knowledge and nature which is observed. This identity is meant to make possible an adequate understanding of nature, a grasp of nature that corresponds to nature and does not subject nature to human understanding with external perspectives and practical aims. For Schelling nature is a "development from an original involution"; this can be understood only as the ideal act of an absolute synthesis which represents "as it were the turning point from transcendental to natural philosophy."[7] Natural philosophy, as the "Spinozism of physics,"[8] seeks to give explanations in terms of natural forces and to renounce transcendent explanations.

The autonomy and self-sufficiency of nature are to be recognized: "all its laws are immanent, or, *nature is its own lawgiver* (the autonomy of nature)," and "what takes place in nature must be explained from the active and mobile principles which lie within it, or: *nature is self-sufficient* (the autarky of nature)."[9]

An original dualism in the original identity of nature stresses the multiplicity of phenomena and forces; these phenomena and their connection derive from a series of limitations of production and an ever-new transcending and surpassing of these limitations; they derive from a tendency toward development and at the same time its restraint (*natura naturans = natura naturata*). The individual products of nature are in each instance specific products of the restraint of the infinite productivity of nature. Natural philosophy is teleological dialectic; it must be understood as process, as potentiation, metamorphosis, and analogy.

The phenomena and forces of nature are derived on three levels or stages of potency as different images of the infinite in the finite, as a varied differentiation of the originally undifferentiated and at the same time constantly new undifferentiation. The differences in the individual stages can also be understood as a differentiated relationship between subject and object; the relationship of subject and object prevails throughout nature; even where objectivity is most strongly expressed, subjectivity can still be recognized, and even where the point of highest subjectivity is arrived at, objectivity has not yet disappeared.

The first potency of nature is the derivation of matter and the structure of the world from the three principles of repulsion, attraction, and gravity. According to Schelling a construction of matter and of qualities only from the powers of repulsion and attraction cannot succeed; the principle of gravity is also necessary. The alternatives of atomism and dynamism are overcome in a "dynamic atomism."[10] In the second potency the qualitative nature of the inorganic is deduced with the three principles of magnetism, electricity, and chemistry. The third potency of nature embraces the organic world, including plants, animals, and humankind; here the principles of reproduction, irritability, and sensitivity are decisive. The inorganic and the organic are connected yet independent. The difference in the potencies is not transcended, for all their analogy and unity. The inorganic presupposes the organic and vice versa; a prestabilized harmony embraces both spheres, "a mean which maintains the continuity between the two."[11]

Special interest attaches to the organic. Schelling criticizes making any mechanistic, materialistic thought absolute. Finality stands above causality. In the structure of the world and in nature generally, according to Schelling, purpose and unconscious teleology can be recognized, not just mechanics. The universe is a kind of organism; it is "a causality which has itself as its object."[12] However, the connection between natural phenomena may not be understood in real genetic terms. Schelling is not an early Darwinist: "So the assertion that really the various organizations were formed from one another by a gradual development is the misunderstanding of an idea."[13]

The organism in the narrow sense is like nature as a whole: having itself as an object, being subject and object to itself, maintaining itself in and by opposition. That is the meaning of excitability, which differs from Haller's irritability. As an object, the organism can be conditioned by the external world, but not as a subject; as a subject it constantly reproduces itself anew until its death in the medium of the external world. Physics and chemistry cannot demonstrate the nature of life, but they may not ignore it in the analysis of life. According to Schelling, the organism is the relationship between reality and idea or matter and light. This relationship appears in three forms: as the predominance of the real principle ("the implication of light in matter"), as the predominance of the ideal principle (=the dissolution of matter into light), or as absolute identity. Sensitivity, irritability, and reproduction represent these three possibilities in the sphere of organic corporeality. These three functions are further supplemented by the drive to propagate and the artistic drive of the organism, which represents a modification of the general drive toward formation.

Health and sickness, medical theory and practice also fall within the organic sphere. Medicine stands at the head of the natural sciences: "Medical science is the crown and climax of all the natural sciences."[14] Central importance is attached to the controversy with the medical system of John Brown, which is both acknowledged and also declared to be inadequate on the basis of philosophical deduction. According to Schelling, natural philosophy must be able to provide a further derivation of the excitability presupposed by Brown; that happens by means of the capacity of the organism to deal with external stimuli and renew itself with their help. Sickness is a disruption of the organism as an unbalanced relationship between the three basic functions or basic dimensions of the organism (reproduction, irritability, sensitivity) so that it is now no longer the "pure, untroubled reflection of the universe."[15] The multitude of sicknesses can be put in a philosophical order as "families of sickness," and therapeutic procedures and even medical treatment itself can be understood and systematized in philosophical terms.

Schelling's natural philosophy reflects the state of the natural sciences around 1800. The philosopher was intensively preoccupied with the empirical research of his time; he had heard lectures on science and medicine and, in addition to reading scientific books and articles, had taken part in scientific experiments. But natural philosophy is not natural science or scientific theory and research. When Schelling criticizes the natural sciences he does so more in the sphere of metaphysical presuppositions and theoretical conclusions than in the realm of specific observations. His committed criticism of Bacon, Newton, and Boyle also lies on the metaphysical level. According to Schelling, speculation must be connected with empiricism. Natural philosophy cannot compete with natural science, nor does it seek to; specific observations, discoveries, and technical inventions are not its aim. Natural science is recognized for its contribution to human life. Science can rightly "praise itself for such splendid and striking successes."[16] The decision of science to limit itself to experience is also legitimate. But experience has its limits, and the task of philosophy, which remains constantly related to nature, begins beyond them. Natural philosophy "is nothing but physics, but it is only *speculative* physics."[17] The correctness of the construction made by natural philosophy is demonstrated by the "coincidence of the product appearing in experience with that which has been constructed."[18] Reason may not contradict experience, but it does go beyond it. The general principles of which natural science makes use—such as gravity, light, warmth, electricity, reproduction—cannot in essence be understood by empirical research, by observation and experimentation. That can only happen in philosophy; because of the progress of the natural sciences and the empirical gaps that are constantly there, this derivation can be understood only as "an infinite task."[19] Philosophical theories can be refuted by experience, and deductions can find recognition only as hypotheses. Conversely, natural philosophy can draw attention to inadequate metaphysical conclusions, point to empirical gaps and provide specific stimuli to research. Natural philosophy and natural science come into contact in empiricism; they are different in their foundation and their aims. Incursions from the side of science into the sphere of natural philosophy are as possible as are incursions from the side of natural philosophy into the sphere of natural science; that cannot put the legitimacy of either into question.

In contrast to Hegel, Schelling's reflections on natural philosophy did not result in a conclusion or in an interconnected yet differentiated account of all the spheres of nature. The move away from natural philosophy corresponds to the general drift of the time—around 1815 the climax of the romantic and speculative contemplation of nature had already been passed. In its encyclopedic versions of 1817, 1827, and 1830, Hegel's natural philosophy came too late—too late also to be evaluated in its specific nature by natural scientists and doctors. Schelling repeatedly criticized the romantic natural scientists and physicians of his time and their adoption of his natural philosophy. In 1798 there is a condemnation in the introduction to *The World Soul* of "that spiritless attempt to blot out the multiplicity of natural causes by fictitious identities."[20] In 1803 Schelling complains that the speculative method of his natural philosophy has propagated itself in "weaker subjects" and that in them it has degenerated "into emptiness and a hollow, imitative enthusiasm."[21] Then in 1806 he comments quite generally on outlines of the philosophy of medicine "that none of these attempts has made a completely worthy trial of what a basically natural approach can do in the theory of the healing arts."[22] One can explain everything and yet nothing with general concepts like contraction and expansion, receptivity and activity. The drive toward philosophical generalization must always maintain "the necessary counterbalance in a true experience based on the view of nature,"[23] since otherwise the whole thing will sooner or later collapse. If that happens, however, it will not be the fault of true natural philosophy, but only of these comments. Schelling also distanced himself from the natural philosophy of Hegel, its ontological foundation, its dialectical method, and its specific deductions. In 1807 misunderstanding of his own views and the distortion of them made Schelling renounce further publications: "Since I have seen the misuse which is made of the ideas of natural philosophy, I have resolved to keep to verbal communication over the whole matter until a time when that no longer is a concern."[24]

Principles and Aims

Romantic natural science is like Schelling's speculative natural philosophy or Hegel's metaphysics of nature, and it differs from Kant's transcendental natural philosophy or empirical positivistic natural science. The concept of nature matches the understanding of science among romantic natural scientists; the investigation of nature is always connected with human life, with society and history. Education is unthinkable without knowledge of nature. The views of this movement are not a unity; the distance from Schelling is clear despite all the recognition of his towering significance for a new understanding of nature. The actual form of the science of the time is criticized, but a connection between empiricism and theory, between physics and metaphysics, is thought to be possible in principle. The area and period within which romantic natural science was accepted were limited, but that does not affect its systematic importance. The reaction of the empirical positivistic natural sciences was generally negative, but influences can be traced right down to the present day.

The Concept of Nature
and the Understanding of Science

These two ideas are intrinsically connected. For all their rejection of the concept of knowledge among contemporary natural scientists, which they thought to be too narrow, the romantic natural scientists were convinced that human beings cannot grasp the ultimate elements of nature. They thought that human understanding was limited. According to C. J. H. Windischmann, all natural phenomena are the effects of an activity, but this activity itself cannot be derived further: "The basic cause of this activity lies outside our range of vision, as we can only perceive it and nothing outside it."[25] All attempts to discover the primal ground of all perceptions are therefore fruitless. For I. P. V. Troxler, the absolute which underlies nature and the spirit can be grasped neither by "intellectual contemplation" nor by "belief in reason"; any word for the absolute is only a "sign" of it.[26] Similarly, J. W. Ritter wants to see the recognition of an unsurpassable limit for human knowledge: "The *highest a priori* deduction is a misunderstanding, and human beings are not its master."[27] The Absolute escapes human reason. According to H. C. Oersted, despite its original affinity with the infinite, human reason is "imprisoned in the finite, and cannot completely tear itself away from it";[28] only a weak picture of the whole is possible, and not a complete "explanation." The absolutizing of knowledge is said to have a negative effect on human beings and their relationship to reality: A. C. A. von Eschenmayer fears a loss of faith and a sickness of the soul: "The desire to explain everything and understand everything has sullied the purity of our souls and taken heaven from our eyes."[29]

But the romantic natural scientists are not content with the limitation of human understanding. In their view not only understanding, but faith, feeling, and dreams should contribute to grasping nature. Troxler makes true knowledge arise only from intimation: "Only that knowledge is perfect and complete which springs from intimation and by reflection and experience can form itself into reason; and only that knowledge is living which takes up into itself the knowledge of reflection at all times and at the same time."[30] For many adherents of this movement faith is an essential source of knowledge, and significant insights are communicated to human beings even in dreams. Feeling can also appear as enthusiasm or inspiration, but a communication of this psychological capacity and these states is always striven for by understanding. Romantic natural science is not a one-sided glorification of the irrational.

The conception of human knowledge is also matched by the literary form given to it: romantic natural science appears in unsystematic, fragmentary, aphoristic, and also poetical and mystical form. This form is chosen deliberately; it is meant to reflect what can be understood from nature. Novalis's demand that "the complete form of the sciences must be poetic"[31] takes up the antipathy toward systems widespread among the romantics and follows their striving to combine science and art. According to Novalis, the tendency to investigate nature is often lost "with the discovery of a system," which is only sought "in order to be further raised above the labour of reflection."[32] Romantic natural science seeks to avoid both empirical specialization and speculative systematization. In its implementation, however, the danger of formal constructions could not always be avoided.

The romantic conceptions of nature are based on the identity of nature and spirit; the laws of nature are supposed to correspond to spiritual laws. Von Eschenmayer's "Deduction of the Living Organism" of 1799 is governed by the presupposition "that precisely this object comes under the necessary conditions of self-consciousness."[33] For Troxler the correspondence between nature and spirit follows from the fundamental "animation" of nature:

> Only because a life ensouls and gives body to the universe do the norms which we find in the Spirit correspond to the forms which are evident to the senses; therefore the laws in our intelligence are the same as the forces in nature and what is manifested to the senses is the same as what is expressed by objects.[34]

Görres saw the Spirit as being composed of three potencies, each potency in turn manifesting itself under a positive and a negative aspect: reason, imagination, and motive power are the positive series; and understanding, sense, and excitability the negative series. All can be found again in nature. Reason appears in nature as the sun (positive), understanding as gravity (negative), imagination as electricity (positive), sense as magnetism (negative), motive power as atmosphere (positive), and finally the excitability as fuel (negative).[35] The fact that nature and spirit are identical also increases the possibilities of self-knowledge. To the assertion that matter shows its true nature in heating and in the process of fusion, Ritter adds the conclusion: "So also it is with us. The *warmer* we are, the more we can understand and comprehend; we thaw out."[36] For the romantics, self-knowledge and knowledge of nature are inseparable; each sphere heightens the other. So H. Steffens thinks: "Do you want to investigate nature? Then cast a glance inwards and in the stages of spiritual formation it may be granted to you to see the stages of natural development. Do you want to know yourself? Investigate nature and your actions are those of the Spirit there."[37]

Various scientists begin from an intrinsic relationship between mathematics and nature and refute the supposed hostility of romantic natural science to mathematics. L. Oken sees mathematics as the spiritual expression of what is manifested corporeally in nature: "If we know the main sections, the basic actions, the central pillar of mathesis in number and quality, so we know for certain that the same number and quality of basic actions, main sections, must recur in nature."[38] As elements of "mathesis" on the first level Oken mentions line, circle, and ellipse; as elements of the second level, parabola, hyperbola, and oval; as elements of the third stage, cone, sphere, and synthesis. In nature the phenomena of time and space, the basic forces and the elements, and the three spheres of nature are supposed to correspond to these three stages.

The leading idea is the unity of nature. As in a number of other items, here too naïve views of nature and the romantic concept of nature correspond. The natural and artificial systems and encyclopedic overall accounts of nature from the end of the eighteenth century and the beginning of the nineteenth are attempts to give a general account of nature on an empirical basis. Von Humboldt with his "Kosmos" also takes this line. According to the romantic view, the multiplicity of natural phenomena and the difference between inorganic and organic nature cannot conceal the connection and the unity of nature. The deduction of natural phenomena from a metaphysical basis, derivation from vegetable or organic categories, and attribution to mathematical principles are all different approaches to a contemplation of nature as a whole. Novalis calls for the investigation of inner connections as opposed to the isolating knowledge of the natural sciences: "In physics the phenomena have long been torn from their context and their mutual relations are not pursued. Any phenomenon is a link in an incalculable chain—which understands *all phenomena* as links."[39] Oken compares the essential task of science to nature thus: "just as nature, originally torn apart, attempts to gather itself together again by bringing together the individual members."[40] The mathematical foundation provides evidence for a unity of nature that is not seen or striven for by contemporary science but is even destroyed by it. For Ritter, too, the knowledge of the unity of nature is also the highest goal of the study of nature. "Anyone who finds in infinite nature nothing but one whole, one complete poem, in whose every word, every syllable, the harmony of the whole rings out and nothing destroys it, has won the highest prize of all,"[41] and similarly in his researches G. H. Schubert is guided above all by the link between natural phenomena:

> The history of nature has to do not just with individual, finite, imminently perishable being, but with an imperishable basis of all that can be seen, which

unites it all and gives it soul. It teaches a love which loves in all things, a universal soul which sets everything, even that which is most remote and apart, in a living interplay that gives to all that can be seen, from the firmament of heaven to the ephemeral insect, one rhythm of time and law of life.[42]

Polarity is contrasted with unity, difference with identity. In nature a conflict of opposed principles and powers and manifold forms of its communication are recognized in accordance with the dualism of nature and spirit or, in the human consciousness, of sense perception and understanding. Throughout nature the formal principle of thesis–antithesis or dualism and the overcoming of it is observed. In principle the polar character of nature is derived from the dualism of forces of attraction and repulsion; nature with the wealth of its phenomena is said to have come into being from its conflict and the results of its mediation. F. von Baader supplements the three basic elements by a further principle which in his view first brings movement into nature and makes possible the production of phenomena: "The great lever of nature would remain in eternal rest, i.e. in the O of its action and reality, unless something external, permeating it, from within, brought it into play, and supported it in itself through a reciprocally divided predominance of one action of its forces over the others."[43] Baader's specific position over against romantic natural science and speculative natural philosophy is also to be understood on this basis. For Oken, polarity and constant mediation are indisputable: "At first glance it emerges that earth and air are opposed and that water forms their indifference, similarly metal and sulphur, whose indifference is salt, and thus finally coral and plants, whose supreme crown is the animal world."[44] Ritter derives this fundamental polarity of nature from its original activity:

A proof of the absolute polarity in nature. Nature is an action, and only to this degree is it nature. Now action calls for multiplicity, for only in that way does an action come into being, and with multiplicity action also disappears. Thus every action presupposes difference. But this is contrast, polarity, and as nature is only where action is, so polarity, too, must be everywhere.[45]

Steffens stresses the painful yet necessary fundamental polarity of nature: "all things of the world oppose one another in compulsory tension."[46]

Analogy, series, potency, and metamorphosis play a major role alongside identity and difference; they are valid for all spheres of nature and even individual natural phenomena. Oken associates earth and metal, air and sulphur, water and salt; Steffens describes the attractiveness of nitrogen to oxygen in plants as the "hidden beast."[47] Görres draws analogies in two directions when he not only observes the spiritual in nature but also pursues the natural into the Spirit: "Therefore what is *reason* in our personality is the sun in nature outside; what is *idea* there is light here; the sun *thinks in light,* reason shines in the idea, and shines and sparkles around itself."[48] Even philosophical positions can be understood as analogues of natural phenomena and regularities; Görres describes Fichte's idealism as "leaven" and Schelling's absolute idealism as "atmosphere."[49] In addition to many simple analogies, above all in Ritter there are double and triple analogies. So, for example, he says, "The brain of plants is the earth."[50] Or, "The whole race of cats is the human race and human beings are merely the most noble cats, as it were their sun." Or, "The worms seem to be the maggots of land vegetation, and the amphibia those of water vegetation. Here the earth itself is the animal."[51] The nature and function of romantic natural analogies will have to be investigated in even more detail in the future and compared with the function of analogies in the empirical natural sciences. Life has towering significance: often the proofs of the unity of nature are based on a transference of organic categories to the inorganic. Nature is to reach its consummation in the organic, and the world of corporeal manifestations make contact with the world of the spirit; the organism is to reflect the essence of nature and make a decisive contribution to physical, chemical, and geological phenomena.

For the romantic philosophers the phenomena of nature are in a hierarchical order. Series, potency, and metamorphosis are expressions for this thinking in terms of orders. The gradation of the basic principles produces the multiplicity of phenomena and forces. Ideal genesis determines the ideas, and not a real descent; but the boundaries are not always observed clearly enough. Ritter regards the "spherical" as a potency of iron; from this it follows for him that the earth is "such a potentiated iron," and moreover any solar system is "a *higher* chemical system." It is important to recognize the "affinity," the "transitions" of the planets.[52] The earth and metals that Oken uses in analogies, or air and sulphur, or water and salt, each belong in a series: "but only in a series which runs through a number of stages; so the earths are only debased metals, and the latter elevated earths; so is the air at a lower level, and salt is water at a higher level."[53] The other natural substances are derived from the earth as the principle of the corporeal world; they came into being by metamorphosis from it. Oken explicitly rejects the conception of a real change: "To say that the earth and metal have been elevated to coral conveys as little as to say that the earth as such has really changed into coral, when he asserts above that it has become metal, or air has become sulphur . . . all is to be taken in a philosophical sense."[54] For Oken, higher forms of nature too can undergo metamorphosis and are interrelated as potencies: the insect is "the human eye still hovering free," the snail "his separated hand," and the bird "his ear in the making."[55]

Troxler formulates a general natural philosophical presupposition for the principle of potency: "The eternal is a spontaneous potency . . . and the infinite is the *independent substance* of the living from which *accidents* emerge into time only in the dynamism in which the substance limits the potency, and the *attributes* rise up into space only in the organism in which the potency limits the substance."[56] Steffens, who speaks of a "theory of evolution," regards the digestion of animals as a "depotentiated digestion of plants" and from this hierarchical analogy between vegetable and animal processing of food it follows for him that "the animals extract the animal in plants, and therefore we understand why the herbivorous animals, when they are transformed into carnivorous animals, increase in strength and animal energy, and meat-eating animals decrease when they eat grass."[57] Novalis also puts particular stress on the applicability of the concept of potency in mineralogy: stones in potencies—fossils of different species—stones differing by degree.[58] In principle, in his view science should seek "the degree of vegetability, animality, minerality."[59] Series, metamorphosis, and potency are connected with the analogy; like this, however, they also appear in empirical natural science.

Society and History

In the eyes of the romantic natural scientists, science always also has to have a practical purpose, the improvement of the immediate conditions in which men and women live. Specific application is not condemned; it is even given a theoretical grounding and justification, but it is also clearly evaluated. Pure knowledge is always put above immediate practical interest, and a predominantly utilitarian standpoint is rejected. According to Treviranus, "His perspective is narrow who only considers everything in connection with bodily needs." Spiritual education of the individual, the overcoming of the dichotomy between nature and spirit, the connection between natural knowledge and knowledge of God are to be set above all utilitarian thinking. According to Treviranus, pure knowledge of the self always automatically leads to praxis: "Moreover truth can never remain without influence on human well-being. If we succeed in doscovering it, its applications will come about without our doing."[60]

Science has a central significance for both the individual and society: science and education are essentially connected. The attempts of the Enlightenment to combine the natural sciences and education are continued in a specific way in romanticism and introduced into the discussions about school and university reforms. Whereas because of the multiplicity of material and specialization of disciplines, already by the end of the eighteenth century the incorporation of the insights and theories of the natural sciences into general education had become increasingly problematical, the romantic scientists had found a new way of combining science and education at the level of the metaphysical contemplation of nature and the exemplary. The general concept of education at the time[61] comes conceptually close to these attempts; but there are also differences between neo-humanism and romantic natural science which recall discussions between humanists and natural scientists in the Renaissance. Around 1800 poetry and the graphic arts shared in the metaphysical presuppositions of the natural scientists of the time in their observation of nature, while at the same time transcending appearances. The romantic natural scientists did not understand education to be a comprehensivce knowledge of the details of all the technical disciplines. According to Steffens, all were to have a "general sense" and in addition devote themselves to a specific area "with strict renunciation."[62] Only an ideal and metaphysical natural science could fulfill the presuppositions and claims of an education governed by nature.

Romantic natural science seeks to connect faith and knowledge, knowledge as natural science and the arts, individual behavior, the social world and art, and thus bring together the fundamental dimensions of education. One piece of evidence relating to the connection between science and art is the *Letters on Landscape Painting* (1831; 2nd ed. 1835) by Carus. According to Carus, natural philosophy has produced a specific kind of painting, deepened insights into the connection between science and art, and taught a new way of contemplating the landscape and reproducing it in art. Certainly not every individual is aware of these presuppositions of attractive landscape painting, but without doubt even here an inkling, a feeling for their enjoyment of art is decisive. These effects of a metaphysical contemplation of nature are similarly observed by contemporaries. According to Mme. de Staël, as she writes in her affirmative but reserved report in *De l'Allemagne,* a verdict on romantic natural science must depend on the results; however, what can already be recognized are "the relationships that it establishes between the different branches of studies." On the whole the scholar and the poet, the poet and the natural scientist, and even scientists of different disciplines had nothing to say; romantic natural science led to a change here: "The wise men penetrate nature with the aid of the imagination; the poets find the true beauties of the universe in the sciences. The scholars enrich the poets by memories and the sages by analogies."[63]

According to the view of romantic scientists, natural science should stress morality and general ethics; it should be able to further political order. Natural science should also intervene in the spiritual life of the individual; it should be able to fortify the health of the psyche, have emotional consequences, give support and direction to thought, and drive away superstition. According to Treviranus men and women cannot "attain the highest stage of humanity" through one-sided development but only through the equal development of all their spiritual forces—neither geometricians nor even poets could by themselves provide the basis of education. Treviranus thinks biology particularly suitable for educating human beings: there is probably hardly any other "science which keeps the understanding and at the same time the power of imagination so active and therefore is so appropriate for bringing people to humanity."[64] For Carus, insight into the beauty and regularity of nature will stimulate human beings to "shape our own innermost life to similar harmony and clarity."[65] In "*equal respect* for nature and the spirit" lies "the key to every true art of living."[66] Again and again human development and education are compared to natural phenomena, and their changes to natural forces. According to Carus, "modern man with his unrest and anxious urges" clearly stands apart from oriental life with its "quiet contemplation in the great organic context."[67] Modern reflectivity and the formation of personality also make sense and have their justification, and here too natural phenomena are recalled; the way through errors to the truth is compared to the play of clouds and the breaking through of the sun.

Natural science influences society; here too it has a "use." Education in the natural sciences as understood by the natural scientists of the time of romanticism and Idealism remains related to life, to the concrete life of the individual and to political life generally. According to Steffens, natural science can "in no way be a mere abstract"; it must take hold of the whole of being and determine its direction: "We rightly call those people enthusiasts and useless citizens who, escaping the pressure of day-to-day life, look down on its necessities contemptuously, from what they imagine to be a loftier standpoint."[68] Döllinger recognizes in the present an impulse toward the knowledge of nature which "penetrates deeply into education, has an effect on the development of the powers of the spirit to which maxims of government are conformed, and perhaps cannot remain completely unnoticed even in the definition of affairs of state."[69] According to the view of many romantic natural scientists, state and governments are too closed to the most recent contemplation of nature in ideas, and here their resistance will also find an ally in that natural science which is hostile to metaphysics.

At the time romantic natural science and political radicalism were identified with each other in different ways. The romantic natural scientists were accused of confusing students, leading them astray into false action, and spreading spiritual illness, atheism, political terror, and revolution.

Attempts were made to keep Oken's natural philosophy out of the Prussian universities. Oken was regarded as one of the "wild professors" who along with the "misguided students"[70] had incited people to vandalism and intolerance at the Wartburg feast. Under his presidency "some thirty books are said to have been burned because their content pleased neither the natural philosophers nor the young Solon."[71] Writings by Ancillon, von Haller, Kotzebue, von Kamptz, and also the Napoleonic Code were thrown into the fire. In his speech to all the students, Oken, who did not take part in the burning, called for a student group which stood above all ties of party and state and "as the class of the educated" repeated "the whole state in itself,"[72] finding a common ground which was also determinative in nature and which one day would lead to German unity.

Class divisions and political representation were defined in terms of nature and spirit. Oken based the classes on "human nature," on three central activities: "the physical, the spiritual, and that which is a combination of both, that of courage or bravery." The three states of nurture, teaching, and resistance correspond to these activities; they are natural states, they are "appointed by nature, by philosophy, and by all history."[73] In accordance with his natural science and anthropology, which have a strongly religious stamp, Eschenmayer sees the discussions about the Württemberg Landtag aiming at that inner proportion of the powers of state "in which democracy, aristocracy and autocracy are each assured their full effect, without their preponderances working inimically on one another and against the common good."[74]

The state is limited or spiritualized. According to Görres, in its historical development there is a constant oscillation between absolute despotism and anarchical freedom.[75] For Steffens, time has shown that state and inner freedom "may never fight against and limit one another, that the most open pursuit of the real determination of each calls forth the innermost union in the purest separation."[76] State and spirit must understand their sphere and their limitations. The "understanding of the individual" may not be elevated to be the "norm" for "the organization of the states" if the fanaticism and anarchy of the French Revolution of 1789 are to be avoided, and it is equally wrong for the state to control the world of the Spirit if despotism and lack of education are not to spread and ultimately also bring down the state. Science and art are the supreme legitimation of the state, and they may not be sacrificed to the ideal of an "empty political freedom."[77]

Nature has a history; history is also nature.[78] All natural phenomena undergo development and have changed in time. To understand nature as an organism is to grasp its genesis. These changes, which are always thought of in connection with an ideal system of natural forms, are also said to correspond to the history of the natural sciences and the system of the capacity of the psyche and its modes of knowledge. The historicizing of nature is intrinsically connected with the historicizing of the knowledge of nature; the objective and subjective dimensions of historical consciousness are united, and similarly the history of science and empirical research cannot be separated. The development of natural phenomena is understood as an evolution, a metamorphosis of ideas, a genesis of ideals, and not as a Darwinian real descent. In his *Theory of Evolution*,[79] Steffens derives the multiplicity of plants and animals from a dynamism of expanding and contracting forces as a result of which the "total organization" is realized. Similarly, the genre preserves itself in the decay of the individual; life passes over into death and death into life. Decay and renewal are said to be merely the apparent, external side of nature; according to Carus a "true origin and annihilation are as inconceivable as a limit to the universe."[80]

History is also nature. The understanding of humanity and society would remain inadequate without the insights of the natural sciences. Human beings are subject to development—as individuals and as social beings. Extractions and contractions apply in both the individual and the social spheres; standstills and accelerations, focal points and revolutions in human history can be understood. The individual development of the body, of the powers of courage and understanding, of will and behavior, of health and sickness, is brought about by natural and spiritual potency, but constantly remains related to nature and society generally and to their particular historicity. Just as individual and genre exist in nature, so too for Steffens the human being is to be both anchorite and cosmopolitan and to find a balance between these. Society derives from an impulse which is identical "with the impulse towards formation in nature generally."[81] The particular is acknowledged, but it must also serve the totality. Often inorganic and technical metaphors are associated with lack of freedom and images of organic life with freedom; the machine human is opposed to the living human, the relationship of the individual to the state is explained by the example of the organism and its parts, and the hierarchy of the state by the hierarchy of the realms of nature.

The history of human beings, races, and peoples is generally associated with nature by way of the metaphysical identity of nature and spirit and also indirectly at the level of phenomena. All the epochs of history are given a relative value; the idea of the whole development is decisive. With the end there is a return to the beginning and the totality is realized; the original is found in the copy. The "kingdom of God" is to prevail in a "natural world" which is in the process of establishing itself; art, science, and faith are to become one with life. Like the natural development, the historical development substantially has its foundation at the ideal level; concrete factors are recognized, and finality is set above causality; history is the history of ideas. According to Steffens those historians are to be rejected who want to follow the stream of history "into its dirtiest puddles . . . they call that the study of sources."[82]

The history of nature is made dependent on human history, and conversely human history is made dependent on the history of nature. The mediated history of human beings and nature is to make the beginnings of a new history for both men and nature. This new history will again realize the original identity of human beings and nature, of consciousness and being, which was originally at the basis of everything. Different attitudes to faith condition divergent integrations. Eschenmayer, who rejects the view of some natural philosophers and natural scientists influenced by philosophy, that God manifests himself fully in the phenomena of nature, derives the moral human order from the organic order of nature, "in which the spirit of men, now made free, constructs a realm of its own in world history."[83] The development of nature and of world history, as understood by revalation, is not a progression from the logical idea to the absolute spirit, but begins from the divine "perfection of election" and returns to the divine "well-pleasing."[84]

Nature and humankind have a common destiny. Humans are natural beings, and nature has developed in them up to the spirit. Through the history of natural science human beings increasingly understand their original bond with nature and now themselves begin to be concerned about their formation. The first period of an identity of nature and spirit was followed by the history of nature and the history of the world; this twofold development is now to give way to an era of unity and freedom. In the thought of the romantic natural scientists this process can be called a naturalizing of human beings and a humanizing or idealization of nature. The exploitation and destruction of nature are now to become as impossible as the spiritual crippling of human beings by a denial of nature or even by social concepts remote from nature. The theoretical construction of nature and technical reproduction are regarded as the manifest evidence of this change in world history. Human beings have to take special responsibility for nature, but at the same time this serves to advance their realization of themselves. For Novalis the mission of human beings is the "formation of the earth."[85] Nature will be able to become completely spirit. According to Ritter, nature is to achieve "supreme presence and self-awareness,"[86] through human beings, and the harmony which emanates from it will "make men part of a blessedness which is like that of nature itself"; human beings may never forget that "integrating nature is the goal of their existence."[87] The destruction of nature by human beings confirms Carus in his conviction that "not only does man need the earth for his life and activity, but also *the earth needs man*."[88]

The current alternatives of restoration and revolution, of permanence and change, of history and progress, do not match the self-understanding of the romantic natural scientists. History and system are constantly thought of together, both in the sphere of nature and in the social and spiritual spheres. Development is related to ideas that are realized in a temporal succession and can be put in a systematic order. History is not just a development as progress into the future; in this development there is a return to the beginnings of nature and society. History restores the beginnings at a higher level, actualizes potency, is an ongoing regression, an oscillation, a pulsation, a steady movement. Görres speaks of the "cycloidal progress"[89] or of the fundamental reversal, "that after the progress from the sensory to the super-sensory has arrived at its supreme vertex the progress turns on itself and becomes regression."[90] History is birth and "pregnancy in reverse," which also makes the true historian "seek the rule and the law of the future in the present and the past."[91] Historical knowledge is combined with analysis of the present and prognosis of the future and is the condition of further, true progress.

Internal Differences – Dissociation from Schelling

Where romanticism is concerned, systematizations will always come up against limits. Not only is it possible to mistake transitions from romantic natural science to empirical natural science, but there is varying proximity to or remoteness from speculative natural philosophy. Often individual passages in romanticism are shaped by an immanent connection between phenomenon and concept which is a hallmark of speculative natural philosophy, and natural philosophy is in no way free from statements in which the terms are related more externally to the phenomena and a(n onto)logical basis for the relationship between notion and phenomenon does not seem to have been achieved.

For all their agreement in rejecting an empirical natural science which made itself absolute, the romantic natural philosophers could not conceal the differences in their conception. In reflections on their own standpoint a relationship to Schelling's natural philosophy naturally plays an important role. Görres stresses his independence of Schelling, but he took time to achieve it: "Schelling's powerful nature stimulated me as Plato stimulated him; each is his own product and that of his whole past. I spoke his language because at that time it was not yet spoken very much, but my eccentric nature drove me out of a form: I had to create my own language, for the school could not tolerate me in its closed circles."[92] Görres complains that Oken's early attempt at a survey of the outline of the system of natural philosophy in 1804 is too dependent "on the tight fetters of Schelling's construction,"[93] but says that in principle this work has to be recognized as an important contribution to the development of science. In a review, von Eschenmayer accuses Oken of wanting to see God in nature; it is even to be assumed "that with his doctrine of God he is trying to pull our legs somewhat."[94]

Troxler also distances himself from Schelling in seeking to recognize the foundation of all reality and ideality in "life." Life, he argues, to some extent transcends nature and spirit and "reveals" itself only relatively in these two spheres; in principle it can be recognized "only in its image and counterpart."[95] Troxler regards his "biosophy" as the consummation of the history of philosophy, as the overcoming of the one-sidedness of the critical standpoint of Kant and the subjective and objective idealistic positions of Fichte and Schelling. The principle of biosophy means "recognizing the *Absolute in itself* as *something* both beyond the *Absolute of reason* and beyond the *Absolute of Nature*."[96] For Ritter, Schelling is a one-sided, though necessary, element in the history of natural philsophy; Schelling conceived his natural principles too much in terms of electricity: "he is really a philosophical electrician or an electrical philosopher. We still lack the magnetic side, a magnetic philosopher. The one who combines the two will be a chemical philosopher, and the supreme judge."[97] For Ritter, the attempt to understand the metaphysics of nature solely through human reason, neglecting faith and intimation, is responsible for the basically atheistical character of Schelling's natural philosophy. Steffens accuses Oken and other romantic natural scientists "of being concerned almost exclusively with manifest life and discussing general physics in an extremely sparse way."[98] Without the acceptance and philosophical penetration of the inorganic realms of nature also, however, it is impossible to develop a convincing philosophical basis for the natural sciences. Steffens is aware that the romantic contemplation of nature is constantly in danger of turning into "mere formalism"; he is convinced that it was because Schelling partially succumbed to this danger among the romantics that he was moved "to give up further work in this direction."[99] But formalism is not essential for romantic natural science; it is partly dependent on the almost vain effort to offer another perspective on nature alongside the overwhelming positivist natural science, and it must also be judged a first step toward a more successful future association of form and content or method and object. With other natural scientists

Oken wants to avoid succumbing to the danger of formalism and later wants to be free of initial formal confusions. If natural scientists maintained this charge they would not be doing justice to the essence and aims of natural philosophy or the metaphysical contemplation of nature. They would thus be depriving themselves of the possibility of a serious examination: "It is to be regretted that scholars who rightly used to recognize under the title of natural philosophy nothing but formalities and often fraud, still even now associate the old nonsense with this word and are therefore deaf to self-examination."[100] In the middle of the nineteenth century Schubert similarly confronted inadequate and polemic attacks by the natural scientists:

> They are accustomed in their fantasies to set up a man of straw or some ridiculously dressed scarecrow; to this contraption they give the name of natural philosophy and attribute to it both the wretchness of the straw and the gaudy rags and bits of glass which in fact really came out of their own heads.[101]

Romantic natural science is not a uniform movement. It is one of the prejudices of positivism to think that multiplicity and deviations are possible only in the arts and humanities. Idealistic, theosophical, and aesthetic trends can be distinguished, and even trends that incline more toward natural philosophy and theological mysticism.[102] An even more sophisticated division could be derived from a series of dimensions and aspects: (1) the relationship between empiricism and philosophy or the relationship between fact and metaphysics; (2) the application of formal principles like identity, difference, polarity, analogy, potency, and metamorphosis or even mathematical categories; (3) orientation on particular realms of nature; (4) the relationship between natural science and society and history; (5) the relationship between natural science and art; and (6) the relationship between natural science and religion.

In this perspective meaningful lines of demarcation and interconnections could be marked out both theoretically and historically. Summary decisions and classifications are hardly likely to be successful. The realms of nature and the individual scientific disciplines each need specific analysis and an assessment of their relationship to philosophy, religion, and art, to society and history. Whether it is possible to arrive from this at a level from which these differences can be derived, and on the basis of which the spectrum of romantic natural science can be systematized, is still an open question.

Criticism and Effects

Romantic natural science is an important phase or epoch in the history of modern natural science; it offered committed criticism of the natural science that had become established internationally, and it was itself criticized equally vigorously. In general the movement was always restricted to German countries, though at the same time many adherents can be noted in other countries. Analyses of social history and interpretations in terms of the history of philosophy here face the task of clarifying these differences in the academic situation around 1800. Talk of spiritual compensation for the political dissection of the German Reich is not an adequate explanation, but it certainly has some value; in addition there are individual factors like philosophical and cultural traditions. A social history would also go in detail into the production of romantic natural science and the way in which it was received. The proportion of romantic writings in the publications of the time, their contribution to textbooks, the place given to them in university lectures, and the dissertations they prompted need to be examined[103] and compared with the activities of the empirical positivistic natural scientists. The way in which romantic natural science was noted by the general public and in specific circles of readers and the reviews in the journals of the time need to be investigated.[104] We also need to study the effects of their commitment to romanticism on the social and economic situation of the natural scientists, how far they were encouraged by governments and their relationship to princes and kings.

The really dominant period of romantic natural science—as also of the speculative natural philosophy of Schelling and Hegel—was quite short, amounting to only a few years before and after 1800. The zenith had already been passed around 1815, but the basic studies in natural philosophy appeared only after 1797. The manner and circumstances of this collapse and decline need more detailed investigation, both regarding individual natural scientists and in general. Three types can be recognized: (1) the abandonment of romantic natural science and a move toward empirical positivistic natural science; (2) the abandonment of romantic natural science and a move toward other interests and activities; and (3) a continuation of romantic natural science.

The circumstances of the break-off and decline include internal and external factors that were responsible for the development of natural science in the nineteenth century generally: the expansion of knowledge; technical inventions; professionalism and the imperative of research; the loss of the predominance of theology and philosophy and its replacement by the hegemony of the natural sciences; the increase in scientific journals, societies, and specific research institutions; a change of generation; the war of liberation; the union movement; the 1848 revolution; industrial change and the workers' movement. Some of these external and internal factors are in essence already the conditions of the modern development of science generally, which were given a special boost in the nineteenth century. But an immanent dynamism similarly impelled scientific progress in modern times or, more basically, supported and impelled the theoretical-practical relationship of human beings to nature once it had been established.

The contemporary empirical-positivistic form of natural science is criticized by the romantic natural scientists. They regard it as abstract, mechanistic, arbitrary in its analyses, aimless in its progress; it is said to endanger or destroy the necessary connection between nature and human beings. According to Steffens, in the hands of the physicists nature has become "like a ruin."[105] For Ritter modern science has lost itself in "detail which is approaching its maximum."[106] Oersted too sees the scientific spirit sunk "in a mass of details"[107] and helplessly exposed to the future: "Without marking out a goal, we have no guideline for our powers, and without an unattainable goal, the constant development for which the human race is destined cannot go forward."[108] Mere description and causal analysis and countless independent individual investigations cannot do justice to the human need for insight into the inner unity of all natural phenomena and their connection with the phenomena of consciousness and the world of social history. At the same time a purged natural science which was aware of its limitations would have a necessary function and could be incorporated into the romantic approach. If at the beginning of the nineteenth century, the success of the romantic movement was asserted with self-confidence, in the coming years doubts soon grew. The *de facto* failure of the movement was recognized, but its significance in principle was not denied.

Around 1800 criticism from the empirical-positivistic natural scientists is already aggressive and negative. P. Chenevix regards the attempts of the natural scientists in Germany influenced by philosophy "as an insult to sound human understanding and an attack on reason."[109] G. Cuvier declares their theories to be a "jeu trompeur de l'esprit."[110] Nor is rejection limited to foreign countries. J. F. Blumenbach expresses his reservations; he acknowledges that his philosophical foundation lies in Kantianism. C. F. Kielmeyer, who in France was called the "father of natural philosophy," condemns speculative and metaphysical deductions from natural phenomena and forces.[111] C. W. Hufeland rejects philosophical influence on medicine. F. Wöhler thinks Steffens far too wise to be able to believe the "feverish stuff"[112] that he presents in his lectures and writings. J. Liebig claims to have lost two precious years of his life through romantic natural science; for him it is "the plague, the Black Death of the century."[113] The list can be continued indefinitely, down to the present day. The verdicts are generally sweeping, do not take account of the differences between individual positions, and above all do not distinguish between intention and execution.

Romantic natural science did not want in any way to oppose empiricism; rather, physics and metaphysics were to be combined. The empirical standpoint was to be supplemented, not abolished. The romantic natural scientists were responsible for important discoveries and insights in the organic and inorganic sciences (galvanism, electromagnetism, comparative anatomy, theories of sickness), which were adopted and recognized by contemporary natural science and even later. However, the essential significance of the movement does not lie in these achievements. It would similarly be a positivistic misunderstanding to seek to evaluate and rescue Schelling's and Hegel's natural philosophy on the grounds that they were forerunners of the theories of evolution and relativity. According to the romantic scientists, detail and generalizations, empiricism and theory are to be noted equally. According to Carus, even the small and insignificant phenomena of nature filled the natural scientist "with true esteem, indeed with wonder"; that "tender relationship" to nature was to be preserved which former scientists like Swammerdam, Lyonnet, and Linnaeus had possessed and which could "perhaps also only become quite clear to the one who has come very close to nature through his own work of investigating nature."[114] Ritter wanted "to keep the strictest empiricism in constant harmony with the clearest speculation."[115] For Troxler, science and natural philosophy cannot be separated: "Observation and experience are impossible without inner insight and knowledge, and on the other hand without these, philosophy is torn away from the object which gives it a particular direction, and which is the real condition of its being called philosophy of nature."[116] Natural knowledge can be understood as knowledge of God; for Oersted, nature is "revelation of the united creative power and reason of the deity."[117]

Regarding detail, in the writings of the romantic natural scientists one can constantly find empirical mistakes, exaggerated formalization, and questionable analogies. Metaphysical and empirical levels are often confused or directly juxtaposed. In this respect the speculative natural philosophy of Hegel with its systematic separation and relating of empiricism and metaphysics seems to present fewer problems to an association with positive natural science. The romantic detachment from a conceptual speculative derivation of nature and the spirit, a complete mediation between all opposites, matter and power, matter and consciousness, in turn provides a greater proximity to the present with its skepticism about idealistic dialectic. Moreover, empirical mistakes, rash hypotheses, and overhasty analogies occur in contemporary natural science as they do in any natural science. This in itself cannot fundamentally put in question the principles and aims of the romantic natural scientists.

The end of romantic natural science and speculative natural philosophy does not rule out the possibility of influences down to the present day. Nineteenth- and twentieth-century natural scientists who seem to have rejected resolutely that direction prove to have been influenced by its observation of the principle of life and the idea of development, by its interest in problems of scientific theory and worldview, by its demand for a scientific concept of education. Psychoanalysis, philosophical psychiatry, and antipsychiatry also stand in the tradition of Idealism and romanticism. Marxism and philosophical anthropology have repeatedly drawn attention to the abiding significance of romantic natural science and the natural philosophy of Schelling and Hegel. The growing interest at present in the metaphysical understanding of nature in the period around 1800 is similarly impressive evidence of the influence of romantic natural science.

Perspectives

The metaphysical contemplation of nature in the form of romantic natural science and speculative natural philosophy was valid around 1800 and exercised a variety of influences on all the sciences and arts. This period was of particular significance in the modern development of the natural sciences. Neither internationally nor in German countries did this movement succeed in establishing itself, but its influence can be noted down to the present day. The empirical and positivistic natural sciences, the foundations for which were laid in the Renaissance, can be traced through the concepts and intentions, the hopes and fears of this movement, in the years shortly before 1900 and later in the first half of the twentieth century, by means of the attempts to combine natural science, philosophy, and the world in which human beings live. Romantic natural scientists and speculative natural philosophers criticized the science of their time, but they in no way challenged the value and justification of an empirical approach to nature, though they did reject the absolutizing of its positivistic perspectives, its one-sided stress on mathematical and mechanical-physical principles, and the glorification of experimentation and technology. A metaphysical understanding of nature, the unity of natural phenomena, the association of nature and culture, the derivation of human beings from nature, and their responsiblity for nature were the ideas of these scientists and thinkers, which in their view were in accord with, and indeed had to be in accord with, a science built on observation and experiment, if the future of humanity and nature is not to be equally endangered. The era of romantic natural science around 1800 was a time of unique significance: no use was made of the opportunity to bring nature and humanity into a relationship on the basis of modern natural science which took equal account of the needs of human beings and the preservation of nature.

The history of the nineteenth and twentieth centuries did not fulfill the requirements of the romantic natural scientists, but rather brought out even more sharply the circumstances and relationships that those natural scientists had sought to avoid and overcome. The destruction of nature, the finitude of natural resources, inhuman circumstances, technology and anonymity are the stamp of modern life all over the world, regardless of ideological limits and political systems. Therefore a present that is unwilling to accept this development rightly returns to that period. The connections between the technological and scientific pessimism of our day, between the widespread uncertainty over progress and the criticism of human treatment of nature and the human form, and yet between the motives and convictions of romantic natural science and speculative natural philosophy around 1800 are evident.

In fact the period of romanticism, the concern with romantic natural science and speculative natural philosophy can still, or rather can again, provide vital stimuli today. Return and imitation are impossible. One hundred seventy-five years of scientific development and of social and cultural changes and transformations of individual consciousness cannot be bridged. But the basic insights of that period are of abiding significance: the unity of nature and humanity and their mutual interdependence, the connection between all the realms of nature and thus also all the natural sciences, the integration of the natural sciences into the world of politics and culture, the need to define the direction and aim of scientific progress. These basic insights have not lost their significance even today; they can be a significant guide for the present and its search for expedients and new solutions.

Notes

1. See R. Ayrault, *La genèse du Romantisme;* D. von Engelhardt, "Bibliographie," in *Romantik in Deutschland,* ed. R. Brinkman; A. Faivre, "La philosophie de la nature," in *Histoire de la philosophie,* ed. Y. Belaval, vol. 3; B. Gower, "Speculation in Physics: The History and Practice of 'Naturphilosophie,'" *Studies in the History and Philosophy of Science* 3 (1972–73) 301–56; H. A. M. Snelders, "Romanticism and Naturphilosophie and the Inorganic Natural Sciences 1797–1840," *Studies in Romanticism* 9 (1970) 193–215; W. D. Wetzels, "Aspects of Natural Science," *German Romanticism* 10 (1971) 44–59.

2. See M. Heun, *Die medizinische Zeitschriftenliteratur der Romantik;* E. Hirschfeld, "Romantische Medizin: Zu einer künftigen Geschichte der naturphilosophischen Ära," *Kyklos* 3 (1930) 1–89; H. von Seemen, *Zur Kenntnis der Medizinhistorie.*

3. Hegel to Goethe, 24 February 1821: Hegel, *Briefe* 2:250.

4. Goethe to Hegel, 13 April 1821: Hegel, *Briefe* 2:258.

5. A. von Humboldt, *Kosmos* 1:33.

6. See *Natur. Kunst. Mythos. Beiträge zur Philosophie F. W. J. Schellings,* ed. S. Dietzsch; D. von Engelhardt, "Prinzipien und Ziele der Naturphilosophie Schellings: Situation um 1800 und spätere Wirkungsgeschichte," in *Schelling,* ed. L. Hasler; *Die Philosophie des jungen Schelling,* ed. E. Lange; K. E. Rothschuh, "Schellings Konzept einer natur-philosophischen Medizin," in Rothschuh, *Konzepte der Medizin;* X. Tilliette et al., *Schelling, Scritti.*

7. F. W. J. Schelling, *Erster Entwurf eines Systems der Naturphilosophie,* 268.

8. Schelling, "Einleitung zu dem Entwurf eines Systems der Naturphilosophie," 273.

9. Schelling, *Erster Entwurf,* 17.

10. Ibid., 23.

11. Ibid., 144.

12. Ibid., 145.

13. Ibid., 63.

14. Schelling, "Vorrede zu den Jahrbüchern der Medicin als Wissenschaft," 65.

15. Schelling, *Vorläufige Bezeichnung,* 276.

16. Schelling, "Vortrag in der öffentlichen Sitzung der Akademie am 27. März 1841," 440.

17. Schelling, "Einleitung," 274.

18. Schelling, "Ueber den wahren Begriff der Naturphilosophie," 730.

19. Schelling, "Einleitung," 279.

20. Schelling, "Von der Weltseele," 347–48.

21. Schelling, "Benehmen des Obscurantismus gegen die Naturphilosophie," 606–7.

22. Schelling, "Vorrede," 70.

23. Ibid., 71.

24. Schelling, "Kritische Fragmente," *Jahrbücher der Medicin als Wissenschaft* 2 (1807) 303.

25. C. J. H. Windischmann, "Ueber den einzig möglichen und einzig richtigen Gesichtspunkt aller Naturforschung," *Archiv für die Physiologie* 4 (1800) 290.

26. I. P. V. Troxler, *Elemente der Biosophie,* 28–29.

27. J. W. Ritter, *Fragmente aus dem Nachlasse eines jungen Physikers* 2:173.

28. H. C. Oersted, "Ueber das Studium der allgemeinen Naturlehre," *Journal der Chemie und Physik* 36 (1822) 464.

29. A. C. A. von Eschenmayer, *Einleitung in die Natur und Geschichte,* 29.

30. Troxler, *Biosophie,* 3.

31. Novalis, "Logologische Fragmente," 527.

32. Novalis, *Vermischte Bemerkungen und Blüthenstaub,* 430.

33. A. C. A. von Eschenmayer, "Dedukzion des lebenden Organism," *Magazin zur Vervolkommnung der theoretischen und praktischen Heilkunde* 2 (1799) 3, 327–90.

34. Troxler, *Biosophie,* viii–ix.

35. J. von Görres, *Aphorismen über die Organonomie,* 175–77.

36. Ritter, *Fragmente* 1:33.

37. H. Steffens, "Ueber die Vegetation," in Steffens, *Alt und Neu* 2:102.

38. L. Oken, *Abriss des Systems der Biologie,* 2.

39. Novalis, *Fragmente und Studien,* 574.

40. Oken, *Abriss,* 196.

41. Ritter, *Fragmente* 2:205.

42. G. H. Schubert, *Allgemeine Naturgeschichte,* 4.

43. F. von Baader, *Ueber das pythagoräische Quadrat in der Natur,* 266.

44. Oken, *Abriss,* 9.

45. Ritter, *Fragmente* 1:17–18.

46. Steffens, "Vegetation," 65.

47. Ibid., 91.

48. Görres, *Organonomie,* 175.

49. Ibid., 169.

50. Ritter, *Fragmente* 2:46.

51. Ibid. 2:48.

52. Ibid. 1:41.

53. Oken, *Abriss,* 10.

54. Ibid., 53.

55. Ibid., 199–200.

56. Troxler, *Biosophie,* 93.

57. Steffens, "Vegetation," 44.

58. Novalis, *Das allgemeine Brouillon,* 258.

59. Ibid., 262.

60. G. R. Treviranus, *Biologie oder die Philosophie der lebenden Natur für Naturforscher und Ärzte,* 15.

61. O. F. Bollnow, *Die pädagogische Bedeutung der Romantik;* R. Fiedler, *Die klassische deutsche Bildungsidee.*

62. H. Steffens, *Vorlesungen über die Idee der Universität,* 356.

63. G. de Staël, *De l'Allemagne* 4:270.

64. Treviranus, *Biologie,* 6.

65. C. G. Carus, "Von den Naturreichen, ihrem Leben und ihrer Verwandtschaft," *Zeitschrift für Natur- und Heilkunde* 1 (1820) 1–72.

66. C. G. Carus, *Lebenserinnerungen und Denkwürdigkeiten* 1:257.

67. Ibid. 1:238.

68. Steffens, *Vorlesungen,* 324.

69. I. Döllinger, *Von den Fortschritten, welche die Physiologie seit Haller gemacht hat,* 4.

70. K. A. von Kamptz, in D. G. Kieser, *Das Wartburgfest am 18. Oktober 1817,* 135.

71. *Hamburgischer unpartheyischer Korrespondent,* in Kieser, *Wartburgfest,* 49.

72. Oken, in Kieser, *Wartburgfest,* 113.

73. Ibid., 17.

74. A. C. A. von Eschenmayer, "Reflexionen über den würtembergischen Landtag," *Heidelberger Jahrbücher der Literatur* (1817) 107.

75. J. von Görres, *Wachstum der Historie,* 376.

76. H. Steffens, "Ueber das Verhältnis der Naturphilosophie zur Physik unserer Tage," in Steffens, *Alt und Neu* 1:135.

77. H. Steffens, "Ueber die Bedeutung eines freien Vereins für Wissenschaft und Kunst," in Steffens, *Alt und Neu* 1:157.

78. D. von Engelhardt, *Historisches Bewusstsein in der Naturwissenschaft von der Aufklärung bis zum Positivismus,* 79.

79. H. Steffens, *Beyträge zu einer innern Naturgeschichte der Erde,* 256.

80. C. G. Carus, "Naturreichen," 27.

81. Steffens, "Bedeutung," 155.

82. Ibid., 151.

83. A. C. A. von Eschenmayer, *Grundriss der Naturphilosophie,* 295.

84. Ibid., 300–301.

85. Novalis, *Blüthenstaub,* 427.

86. J. W. Ritter, *Die Physik als Kunst,* 14.

87. Ibid., 3.
88. C. G. Carus, "Naturreichen," 72.
89. Görres, *Wachstum der Historie*, 379.
90. Ibid., 372.
91. Ibid., 379.
92. J. von Görres, "Exposition der Physiologie," 12.
93. J. von Görres, review of Oken, Übersicht des Grundrisses des Systems der Natur-philosophie, *Jenaische Allgemeine Literatur-Zeitung* (March 1805) 472.
94. A. C. A. von Eschenmayer, review of Oken, *Ueber Licht und Wärme, Heidelberger Jahrbücher der Literatur* 3.1.1 (1810) 97–126.
95. Troxler, *Biosophie*, xviii.
96. Ibid., 20.
97. Ritter, *Fragmente* 2:176.
98. Steffens, "Verhältnis," 82.
99. Ibid., 69.
100. Oken, *Lehrbuch des Systems der Naturphilosophie* 2:iv.
101. G. H. Schubert, *Der Erwerb aus einem vergangenen und die Erwartungen von einem zukünftigen Leben* 2:36–37.
102. J. V. Carus, *Geschichte der Zoologie bis auf Joh. Müller und Charl. Darwin*, 587–89; K. E. Rothschuh, "Ansteckende Ideen in der Wissenschaftsgeschichte, gezeigt an der Entstehung und Ausbreitung der romantischen Physiologie," in Rothschuh, *Physiologie im Werden*, 54–58.
103. See Heun, *Die medizinische Zeitschriftenliteratur;* Hirschfeld, "Romantische Medizin: Zu einer künftigen Geschichte der naturphilosophischen Ära," *Kyklos* 3 (1930) 1–89; von Seemen, *Zur Kenntnis der Medizinhistorie*.
104. D. von Engelhardt, "Naturphilosophie im Urteil der *Heidelberger Jahrbücher der Literatur 1808–1832*," *Heidelberger Jahrbücher* 19 (1975) 53–82.
105. H. Steffens, *Zur Geschichte der heutigen Physik*, 118.
106. Ritter, *Fragmente* 2:110.
107. H. C. Oersted, "Der Naturwissenschaft Verhältniss zu Zeitaltern und deren Philosophie," in Oersted, *Der Geist in der Natur*, 326.
108. Oersted, "Studium," 460.
109. P. Chevenix, "Kritische Bemerkungen, Gegenstände der Naturlehre betreffend," *Annalen der Physik* 20 (1805) 448.
110. G. Cuvier, *Histoire des progrès des sciences naturelles* 1:7.
111. C. F. Kielmeyer to G. Cuvier, December 1807: Kielmeyer, *Gesammelte Schriften*, 235–54.
112. F. Wöhler to J. J. Berzelius, 31 March 1825: O. Wallach, ed., *J. J. Berzelius und Fr. Wöhler, Briefwechsel* 1:39.
113. J. Liebig, *Über das Studium der Naturwissenschaften und über den Zustand der Chemie in Preussen*, 29.
114. C. G. Carus, *Lebenserinnerungen* 1:242.
115. Ritter to F. Schlichtegroll, June 1809; F. Klemm und A. Hermann, eds., *Briefe eines romantischen Physikers*, 12.
116. I. P. V. Troxler, *Anthropologie*, 10.
117. Oersted, "Studium," 463.

Bibliography

Ayrault, R. "En vue d'une philosophie de la nature." In R. Ayrault, *La genèse du romantisme allemand 1797–1804*, 2:11–167. Paris: Aubier, 1976.

Baader, F. von. *Ueber das pythagoräische Quadrat in der Natur.* 1798. In *Sämmtliche Werke,* vol. 3. Leipzig: Bethmann, 1852.

Bollnow, O. F. *Die pädagogische Bedeutung der Romantik.* Stuttgart: Klett-Cotta, 1952.

Carus, C. G. "Von den Naturreichen, ihrem Leben und ihrer Verwandtschaft." *Zeitschrift für Natur- und Heilkunde* 1 (1820) 1–72.

———. *Lebenserinnerungen und Denkwürdigkeiten.* 1855/56. 2 vols. Weimar: Kiepenheuer, 1966.

Carus, J. V. *Geschichte der Zoologie bis auf Joh. Müller und Charl. Darwin.* Munich: Oldenbourg, 1872.

Chenevix, P. "Kritische Bemerkungen, Gegenstände der Naturlehre betreffend." *Annalen der Physik* 20 (1805) 417–84.

Cuvier, G. *Histoire des progrès des sciences naturelles, depuis 1789 jusqu'à ce jour.* 4 vols. Paris: Nouvelle edit., 1826–28.

Dietzsch, S., ed. *Natur. Kunst. Mythos. Beiträge zur Philosophie F. W. J. Schellings.* East Berlin: Akademie-Verlag, 1978.

Döllinger, I. *Von den Fortschritten, welche die Physiologie seit Haller gemacht hat.* Munich: Lindauer, 1824.

Engelhardt, D. von. "Bibliographie der Sekundärliteratur zur romantischen Naturforschung und Medizin 1950–1975." In *Romantik in Deutschland,* edited by W. Brinkmann, 307–30. Stuttgart: Metzler, 1978.

———. *Historisches Bewusstsein in der Naturwissenschaft von der Aufklärung bis zum Positivismus.* Freiburg im Breisgau: Alber, 1979.

———. "Naturphilosophie im Urteil der *Heidelberger Jahrbücher der Literatur 1808–1832.*" *Heidelberger Jahrbücher* 19 (1975) 53–82.

———. "Prinzipien und Ziele der Naturphilosophie Schellings–Situation um 1800 und spätere Wirkungsgeschichte." In *Schelling: Seine Bedeutung für eine Philosophie der Natur und der Geschichte,* edited by L. Hasler, 77–98. Stuttgart-Bad Cannstatt: Frommann-Holzboog, 1981.

Eschenmayer, A. C. A. von. "Dedukzion des lebenden Organism." *Magazin zur Vervollkommung der theoretischen praktischen Heilkunde* 2 (1799) 3, 327–90.

———. *Einleitung in die Natur und Geschichte.* Erlangen: Walther, 1806.

———. *Grundriss der Naturphilosophie.* Tübingen: Osiander, 1832.

———. "Reflexionen über den würtembergischen Landtag." *Heidelberger Jahrbücher der Literatur* (1817).

———. Review of Oken, *Ueber Licht und Wärme.* 1809. *Heidelberger Jahrbücher der Literatur* 3.1.1. (1810) 97–126.

Faivre, A. "La philosophie de la nature dans le romantisme allemand." In *Histoire de la philosophie,* edited by Y. Belaval, 3:14–45. Paris: Gallimard, 1974.

Fiedler, R. *Die klassische deutsche Bildungsidee.* 2nd ed. Weinheim: Beltz, 1973.

Görres, J. von. *Aphorismen über die Organonomie.* 1803. In *Gesammelte Schriften,* 2.1:165–333. Cologne: Gilde-Verlag, 1932.

———. "Exposition der Physiologie." 1805. In *Gesammelte Schriften,* 2.2:3–131. Cologne: Bachen, 1934.

———. Review of Oken, *Übersicht des Grundrisses des Systems der Naturphilosophie.* 1804. *Jenaische Allgemeine Literatur-Zeitung* (March 1805).

———. *Wachstum der Historie.* 1808. In *Gesammelte Schriften,* 3:363–440. Cologne: Gilde-Verlag, 1926.

Gower, B., "Speculation in Physics: The History and Practice of 'Naturphilosophie.'" *Studies in the History and Philosophy of Science* 3 (1972–73) 301–56.

Hegel, G. W. F. *Briefe von und an Hegel.* 4 vols. Hamburg: Meiner, 1952ff.

Heun, M. *Die medizinische Zeitschriftenliteratur der Romantik.* Leipzig medical dissertation, 1931.

Hirschfeld, E. "Romantische Medizin: Zu einer künftigen Geschichte der naturphilosophischen Ära." *Kyklos* 3 (1930) 1–89.

Humboldt, A. von. *Kosmos.* 4 vols. Stuttgart and Augsburg: Cotta, 1845–58.

Kielmeyer, C. F. *Gesammelte Schriften.* Berlin: Keiper, 1938.

Kieser, D. G. *Das Wartburgfest am 18. Oktober 1817.* Jena: Frommann, 1818.

Klemm, F., and A. Hermann, eds. *Briefe eines romantischen Physikers: Johann Wilhelm Ritter an Gotthilf Heinrich Schubert und an Karl von Hardenberg.* Munich: Moos, 1966.

Lange, E., ed. *Die Philosophie des jungen Schelling: Beiträge zur Schelling-Rezeption in der DDR.* Weimar: Böhlau, 1977.

Liebig, J. *Über das Studium der Naturwissenschaften und über den Zustand der Chemie in Preussen.* Brunswick: Vieweg, 1840.

Novalis. *Das allgemeine Brouillon.* 1798–99. In *Schriften* 3, 242–478. Darmstadt: Wissenschaftliche Buchgesellschaft, 1968.

——. *Fragmente und Studien.* 1799–1800. In *Schriften* 3, 556–693. Darmstadt: Wissenschaftliche Buchgesellschaft, 1968.

——. "Logologische Fragmente." 1798. In *Schriften* 2, 522–32. Darmstadt: Wissenschaftliche Buchgesellschaft, 1965.

——. *Vermischte Bemerkungen und Blüthenstaub.* 1798. In *Schriften* 2, 412–70. Darmstadt: Wissenschaftliche Buchgesellschaft, 1965.

Oersted, H. C. "Der Naturwissenschaft Verhältniss zu Zeitaltern und deren Philosophie." 1830. In Oersted, *Der Geist in der Natur* 1, 314–47. Leipzig: Lorck, 1854.

——. "Ueber das Studium der allgemeinen Naturlehre." *Journal der Chemie und Physik* 36 (1822) 458–88.

Oken, L. *Abriss des Systems der Biologie.* Göttingen: Vandenhoeck, 1805.

——. *Lehrbuch des Systems der Naturphilosophie.* 3 vols. Jena: Frommann, 1809–11.

——. "Ueber das Grundgesetz und die Landständische Verfassung des Grossherzogthums Sachsen-Weimar-Eisenach." *Isis* (1817) 65–84.

Ritter, J. W. *Fragmente aus dem Nachlasse eines jungen Physikers.* 2 vols. Heidelberg, 1810. Reprint, Heidelberg: Mohr, 1969.

——. *Die Physik als Kunst: Ein Versuch, die Tendenz der Physik aus der Geschichte zu deuten.* Munich: Lindauer, 1806.

Rothschuh, K. E. "Ansteckende Ideen in der Wissenschaftsgeschichte, gezeigt an der Entstehung und Ausbreitung der romantischen Physiologie." 1961. In Rothschuh, *Physiologie im Werden,* 45–58. Stuttgart: Fischer, 1969.

——. "Schellings Konzept einer naturphilosophischen Medizin." In Rothschuh, *Konzepte der Medizin,* 5–15. Stuttgart: Hippokrates, 1978.

Schelling, F. W. J. *Benehmen des Obscurantismus gegen die Naturphilosophie.* 1803. In *Werke* 1, *Ergänzungsband,* 600–617. Munich: Beck, 1956.

——. "Einleitung zu dem Entwurf eines Systems der Naturphilosophie." 1799. In *Werke* 2, 269–326. Munich: Beck, 1927.

——. *Erster Entwurf eines Systems der Naturphilosophie.* 1799. In *Werke* 2, 1–268. Munich: Beck, 1927.

——. "Kritische Fragmente." *Jahrbücher der Medicin als Wissenschaft* 2 (1807) 285–304.

——. "Ueber den wahren Begriff der Naturphilosophie." 1803. In *Werke* 2, 713–37. Munich: Beck, 1927.

——. *Von der Weltseele.* 1798. In *Werke* 1, 413–651. Munich: Beck, 1927.

——. "Vorläufige Bezeichnung des Stankpunkts der Medicin nach Grundsätzen der Naturphilosophie," 1805. In *Sämmtliche Werke*. 1. AbTLG., 7, 260–88.

——. "Vorrede zu den Jahrbüchern der Medicin als Wissenschaft." 1806. In *Werke* 4, 65–73. Munich: Beck, 1927.

——. "Vortrag in der öffentlichen Sitzung der Akademie am 27. März 1841." In *Werke* 4, *Ergänzungsband*, 437–44. Munich: Beck, 1959.

Schubert, G. H. *Allgemeine Naturgeschichte*. Erlangen: Palm u. Enke, 1826.

——. *Der Erwerb aus einem vergangenen und die Erwartungen von einem zukünftigen Leben: Eine Selbstbiographie*. 4 vols. Erlangen: Palm u. Enke, 1854–56.

Seemen, H. von. *Zur Kenntnis der Medizinhistorie in der deutschen Romantik*. Zurich: Füssli, 1926.

Snelders, H. A. M. "Romanticism and Naturphilosophie and the Inorganic Natural Sciences 1797–1840." *Studies in Romanticism* 9 (1970) 193–215.

Staël, G. de. *De l'Allemagne*. 1813. 4 vols. Paris: Hachette, 1959.

Steffens, H. *Beyträge zu einer innern Naturgeschichte der Erde*. Freyberg: Craz, 1801.

——. "Ueber das Verhältnis der Naturphilosophie zur Physik unserer Tage." In Steffens, *Schriften, Alt und Neu*, 1:67–84. Breslau: Max, 1821.

——. "Ueber die Bedeutung eines freien Vereins für Wissenschaft und Kunst." 1817. In Steffens, *Schriften, Alt und Neu*, 1:148–66. Breslau: Max, 1821.

——. "Ueber die Vegetation." In Steffens, *Schriften, Alt und Neu*, vol. 2. Breslau: Max, 1821.

——. *Vorlesungen über die Idee der Universität*. 1808–9. In *Die Idee der deutschen Universität: Die fünf Grundschriften aus der Zeit ihrer Neubegründung durch klassischen Idealismus und romantischen Realismus*, edited by E. Anrich, 309–74. Darmstadt: Wissenschaftliche Buchgesellschaft, 1956.

——. *Zur Geschichte der heutigen Physik*. Breslau: Max, 1829.

Tilliette, X., et al. *Schelling: Scritti*. Padua: Cedam-Casa, 1976.

Treviranus, G. R. *Biologie oder die Philosophie der lebenden Natur für Naturforscher und Ärzte*. Göttingen: Röwer, 1802.

Troxler, I. P. V. *Anthropologie: Ein Vortrag aus dem Jahre 1825*. Glarus, 1968.

——. *Elemente der Biosophie*. Leipzig: Krappe, 1808.

Wallach, O., ed. *J. J. Berzelius und Fr Wöhler, Briefwechsel*. 2 vols. Leipzig, 1901. Reprint, Wiesbaden: Sändig, 1966.

Wetzels, W. D. "Aspects of Natural Science." *German Romanticism* 10 (1971) 44–59.

Windischmann, C. J. H. "Ueber den einzig möglichen und einzig richtigen Gesichtspunkt aller Naturforschung." *Archiv für die Physiologie* 4 (1800) 290–305.

4

Renaissance Kabbalah

G. Mallary Masters

MISUNDERSTOOD, OFTEN IGNORED by all but the most persistent students of the period, the Kabbalah was, nevertheless, a very important aspect of humanistic renewal of knowledge from antiquity. We must not assume from our lofty twentieth-century perspective, however, that the Renaissance understood Jewish mysticism with the same "objectivity" to which we pretend today. As we shall see through the reading of one very typical "popularizing" treatise from early sixteenth-century France and a review of its sources, for Renaissance thinkers, the Kabbalah fit in as but one piece in a puzzle comprising all of human thought from Adam on. A study of one such work clarifies the entire period which it exemplifies.

Jehan Thenaud's *Traité de la Cabale* or *Traité de la Cabale chrétienne*, a manuscript on the Kabbalah, written in French for Francis I about 1521,[1] represents extraordinarily well the impact the Jewish Kabbalah had after the mid-fifteenth century on European religious and philosophical thought for some two or three hundred years. One of the first such treatises, if not the first, in French to summarize and vulgarize earlier Latin humanistic studies, Thenaud's work was commissioned by the king to complement a verse treatise entitled *La Cabale métrifée* he had completed some two years before.[2] Meanwhile Thenaud had undertaken with great effort and personal expense a more thorough study of Hebrew in order to master the secrets of the tradition. What is so striking about the work is that it not only demonstrates the enthusiastic adoption of Kabbalah but also betrays the unilateral prejudices of some Christian adepts of Kabbalah. A summary of the manuscript will show how a professional Christian theologian conceived of Jewish mysticism and how he fitted it into his own tradition.

Guided by Curiosité, whom he has followed, at least for some four books of ninety-four folios, and who has presented him to a learned Hebrew,

132

already a literary type (whose literal historical identity we need not pursue), Thenaud in the guise of a pilgrim seeks the way to heaven. The Hebrew teaches him that Kabbalah means "reception," that is, *an orally revealed tradition passed on from generation to generation.* His initiation is progressive and slow, for the student of Kabbalah must build spiritual experience slowly. That same kind of progression is seen in the Mosaic tabernacle, forerunner of the Solomonic Temple, which represents by its structure four worlds: the elemental, the celestial, the angelic or spiritual, and the microcosmic—corresponding respectively to the entry oriented toward the East; the sanctuary with its altar reserved to the priests; the *sanctum sanctorum,* the Holy of Holies, destined uniquely once a year for the high priest; and, of course, the Human-Man (Adam), who is privileged by the creator to mirror the other three, uniting all in human nature. The nine orders of the angels rule over the highest, most spiritual, angelic world, which dominates the celestial world below; and the latter, in turn, controls through its virtues the elemental world (foll. iii^{ro}–ix^{vo}).

Our learned Hebrew reflects clearly the humanistic work of the late fifteenth and early sixteenth centuries dealing with the Kabbalah. But here and especially in the eight chapters of book 2 he places the kabbalistic doctrines in a context of Aristotelian and Platonic cosmology. It becomes clear that, whereas the Kabbalah may have a privileged position in the Judeo-Christian tradition, here its revealed spirituality is interpreted within a very definite context of all philosophy and spiritual wisdom of classical antiquity, such as it was understood by Renaissance thinkers. The philosophers and poets of Greco-Roman letters stand in equality with kabbalistic cosmologists, from whom we learn of the nature of the universe as well as of the immortality and true nature of souls (foll. ix^{vo}–xl^{vo}).

The third book, drawing once again on kabbalistic humanistic texts, reminds us also of the treatises of Dionysius the Areopagite on the celestial hierarchy. The angelic world, reflecting the divine Trinity, is figured by three triangles of Triumph, Victory, and Virtuous Combat. The nine orders of angels, ruling over the nine celestial spheres, are placed in parallel to Apollo, god of light and spirit, and the nine Muses. Contemplation of these wonders must, of course, be prepared by meditation and progressive initiation (foll. xli^{ro}–lvii^{ro}).

In book 4, our pilgrim into Kabbalah listens as his Hebrew guide defines Kabbalah:

> . . . the science and knowledge of God, as well as of the separated substances, of the spiritual world, and of its secrets. Such knowledge cannot be acquired by exterior senses, nor by experience, reason, demonstration, syllogism, study or any other human and logical means, but only by faith, by illumination

and celestial revelation which moves the free will to believe that which is inspired and to know the aforesaid secrets by the holy and written law of God and also by the figures, names, numbers, symbols, and other ways divinely and supercelestially given and revealed to the fathers, patriarchs, prophets, and doctors of the Hebrews on the divine law. (fol. lvii)

Such a definition has little to do with what we today call practical Kabbalah, more concerned with the "magical" manipulation through kabbalistic knowledge of natural forces; but, for Thenaud, to speculate about the spiritual teachings of Kabbalah is not enough. One must put such contemplative truths into moral practice. Such a goal seems, at first sight at least, far removed from the accomplishment of this book, which is truly the most kabbalistic of all.

Having suggested that the tradition of revelation passed from Adam to Noah, Noah to Moses, who *wrote* the law and *taught verbally* to a limited number the secrets divinely revealed, Thenaud then has the Hebrew guide distinguish between talmudic and kabbalistic interpretation, between the letter and the spirit, between the literal and the *"imagistic."*[3] The talmudists await a literal, historical Messiah who will save Israel in a physical sense; the kabbalists seek a spiritual savior (foll. lvii^{vo}–lx^{vo}). Such is the *received tradition*, taught by the kabbalistic masters and renewed in recent times by Pico della Mirandola, Paulus Ricius or Rici, and Reuchlin (fol. lviii^{vo}).

Now the Hebrew comes to the essence of things. All other languages are made by humans, but Hebrew is the divine language of creation, the language that is "fecund, rich, and full of all secrets whether of geometry, arithmetic, physics, or mathematics" (fol. lx^{vo}). Kabbalistic knowledge, in contrast to the science of the Egyptian and Greek wise men, is the only lasting wisdom, inspiring people to rise in spirit to God himself (fol. lxvii^{ro}).

The twenty-two letters of the alphabet and the five doubled terminal forms divide neatly into three groups of nine each whose mathematical, cosmological, and philosophical significances appear in chart form (fig. 1). It goes without saying that Holy Scriptures, written in Hebrew, contain all grammar, all knowledge. Therefore by transposition, following the example of Pico della Mirandola, one can arrive at the most profound truths. For example, the first verse of Genesis:

הארץ׃	ואת	השמים	את	אלהים	ברא	בראשית	←
terram	et	celum		Deus	creavit	*principio In*	←
earth	the and	heavens	the	God	created	beginning the In	←

According to Pico, this gives the following:

Pater in filio, et per filium principium et finem sive quitem creavit Caput Ignem et fundamentium magni hominis, federe bono.

Chart of Thenaud's
Hebrew Alphabet, Orders, Cosmological Attributes

	Way				*Oxford*	*Thenaud*		
Prudence	Country	Teaching	Seraphim	1	Aleph	Aleph	א	1
	Life	House	Cherubim	2	Beth	Beth	ב	
	Peace	Retribution	Thrones	3	Gimel	Gimel	ג	
Retribution	Wisdom	Door, entry	Powers	4	Daleth	Daleth	ד	
	Seeing	Foyer	Principalities	5	He	He	ה	
	Hearing	Hooked needle	Dominations	6	Waw	Vau	ו	
	Smell	Arms	Virtues	7	Zayin	Sdain	ז	
	Speaking	Fright	Archangels	8	Het	Cheth	ח	
	Infusion	Lead astray	Angels	9	Tet	Theth	ט	
	Sleep, Bed	Praise	Primum mobile	10	Yod	Jod	י	2
	Riches	Palm of hand	Firmament	20	Kaph	Caph	כ	
	Negotiation	Doctrine	Saturn	30	Lamed	Lameth	ל	
	Waters	Water	Jupiter	40	Mem	Men	מ	
	Conduits	Filiation	Mars	50	Nun	Num	נ	
	Spirit	Apposition	Sun	60	Samek	Samach	ס	
	Laughter	Eye	Venus	70	Ayin	Ayin	ע	
	Seed	Mouth	Mercury	80	Pe	Phe	פ	
	Suspicion	Ribs	Moon	90	Sade	Zadik	צ	
	Sleep	Circuit	Elements	100	Kop	Kuph	ק	3
	Grace	Poverty	Elements	200	Res	Res	ר	
	Fire	Teeth	Elements	300	Sin	Schin	ש	
	Power	Signs	Elements	400	Taw	Thaph	ת	
			all mixed	500	Kaph	Caph	ך	
			or	600	Mem	Men	ם	
			elementally	700	Nun	Num	ן	
			composed	800	Pe	Phe	ף	
			things	900	Sade	Zadik	ץ	

The Father by the Son and in the Son Who is the Principal, End and Beginning of all things created the Head, the Fire and the Foundation of the Great Man by good alliance.

The head, seat of reason and of animal powers, signifies the angelic world; fire is the celestial world; the foundation represents the elemental world; and the alliance embodies the union of the other three. The devout recitation of the 150 Psalms has a sure effect on events: for example, *Domine in virtute tua laetabitur rex* ("In thy strength the king rejoices, O Lord" [Ps. 20/21:1]) brings about prosperity and victory in peace, and so on. Thenaud teaches us that there are three parts of Kabbalah: number (*consulto*), weight (*sententia*), and measure. Others name two parts, Sephiroth (numbers) and Shemoth (names)—speculative and practical, respectively. Still others give five parts: rectitude, combination, permutation, *equipollence,* and numeration (foll. lxxi^{ro}–lxxiiii^{vo}).

Following *rectitude,* one reads the first letters of, say, a page to find a sentence revelatory of hidden truth. In *combination,* one combines various letters so as to use them to replace one another: for example, A for B, B for A; C for D, D for C; etc. Or one combines syllables. *Permutation* results from the changing around of all the letters of a sentence, without adding or subtracting any, to give another complete sentence: "Françoys par la grace de Dieu roy de France" ("Francis by the Grace of God King of France") contains "l'Eage d'or d'icy a C. roys durera en France." *Equipollence* is a kind of abbreviated notation or shorthand. *Numeration* is based on numerical equivalences of letters, so that words have equality of number and meaning through mathematical operations. All these methods produce the greatest spiritual truths when applied to Holy Scriptures, especially in Hebrew, but similarly to a lesser degree in Latin or Greek (foll. lxxiiii^{vo}–lxxvi^{ro}).

Thenaud's Hebrew guide cautions him that because of his pupil's limited knowledge of Hebrew, he must avoid profaning the mysteries of the Names of God, and he will instruct him only in a general way. Then, after a brief statement about the three ineffable Names of God revealed by the angel Gabriel or Metatron, he teaches the essence of the kabbalistic doctrine of emanation. Of the three names, the first, Himself (*Hu*), reveals the simple unity of the divine nature; the second, Essence (*Ehieh;* Greek *On;* Latin *Ens*), divine transcendence; and the third, Fire (*Esh;* Greek *Pir;* Latin *Ignis*), reminds of the illuminatory aspects of God, who transforms us by his Spirit into divine sons of light. The ten emanations of the celestial angelic world, from the *Ensoph,* Infinity, are ten spheres: *Kether,* infinite power and crown of the reign of everlasting felicity; *Hochman,* wisdom, God the Son; *Binath,* prudence, intelligence, God the Holy Spirit; *Hesed, misericordia; Geburath,* justice, severity; *Tiphereth,* glory, beauty; *Nerad,* triumph, magnanimity; *Hod,* confession, praise; *Malkuth,* king, superillustrious deity; *Pahad,* furious, fear.[4] While revealing to us mortals the splendor of the divine, to the degree we are capable of perceiving it, these names also warn us of the need for purification before we approach so awesome a study (foll. lxxvi^{ro}–lxxxii^{vo}).

Ritual purificatory bathing, changing of garments, and four days of fasting serve as preparation for our pilgrim prior to his being instructed on the fifth day into the meaning of the unspeakable Tetragrammaton. Those four sacred characters manifest themselves universally in tetrads: the four worlds all have tetradic structures. In the angelic, four princes direct the angelic hosts according to the will of the Eternal Monarch. In the celestial, four triple signs are present with four qualities that cause the four seasons. In the elemental world, the four elements reflect the tetradic nature as well as the four aspects of the microcosm, that is, flesh, spirit, shadow, and soul. Finally, after a long enumeration of other universal reflections of the un-utterable Tetragrammaton, our Hebrew explains the name of God יהוה (Yahweh): *Yod*, 10, is the beginning of all things and the end of all numbers, for unity contains the first tetrad. *He*, 5, contains the 2 of creatures and the 3 of the divine nature, otherness and unity, multiplicity and simplicity. *Waw*, 6, perfection, signifies the celestial and elemental worlds joined together and united, perfected and accomplished by God (foll. lxxxii^{vo}–lxxxvi^{ro}). There follows a discussion of the various names of God and those of the seventy-two angels (foll. lxxxvi–lxxxix^{vo}) and of the ancient practice of kabbalists of purifying themselves by fasting and cere-monious rites during thirty-seven days for the reception of the Spirit who ravished their spirits into mystical ecstasy (foll. lxxxx–lxxxxiv^{vo}).

In the fifth treatise, Thenaud demonstrates clearly the prejudices of his Christian unilateral faith, for Dame Simplicité suddenly separates him from his Hebrew guide and the Holy of Holies of the Temple, saving him from such unenlightened superstition, to lead him to the Church of the Holy Sepulcher in Jerusalem. The walls are lined with the books of the early fathers, so numerous as to outnumber the ancient libraries of Alexandria and Rome, written in Hebrew, Greek, Latin, Arabic, and Aramaic; but of all of them the Roman fathers Ambrose, Augustine, Jerome, and Gregory the Great represent the four fountains of all knowledge. Their works put to shame the teachings of the great philosophers and men of letters of antiquity, for their doctrine founds itself on the essential teaching of the cross, illustrated thus:

The simple faith of the Christian Kabbalah does not need transmutation, *equipollence*, or any of the other operations to teach its doctrines, which are recorded in the divine book seen by Saint John on Patmos (foll. lxxxxv^{ro}–lxxxxvii^{vo}). By Grace, the pilgrim is led on to the holiest of mountains, Calvary, where he has visions of the divine Names subsequently explained by Dame Simplicité in the Chapel of Saint Helen. The three worlds of angelic, celestial, and elemental dimensions are explained now in terms of a series of quadratures that recall the *carmina quadrata* of Rabanus Maurus. In a short sixth treatise dealing with cosmology, Thenaud brings to an end his volume, having run the course of his understanding of Hebrew Kabbalah, only to return to the dogma of Roman theology. Jewish mysticism is at best a preparation for the revelation of Christian faith for which one does not need practical kabbalistic manipulations but uniquely divine grace (foll. lxxxviii^{ro}–cxvi^{vo}).

Now it is clear from this analytical summary what use a professional Christian theologian could make of the Kabbalah. He viewed it much as the early fathers had viewed the Old Testament, as a prefiguration in which law precedes grace, penitence precedes salvation, and so on. Thenaud follows the lead of early humanists such as Pico della Mirandola and Reuchlin, on whose works he draws most heavily. But, as the eminent scholar of Kabbalah Gershom Scholem has shown, it is rather the Jews converted to Christianity during and prior to the fifteenth century who have set the stage,[5] for they interpret kabbalistic texts as prefiguring or containing explicitly doctrines of the Trinity, as seen in the example of the three different letters of the Tetragrammaton. *Yod, waw,* and *he* designate respectively "the Father and the existence of a 'principle without beginning' in God, Son as a principle of the beginning, Holy-Spirit as a spiritual breath emitted by the first two principles."[6] Their tradition, on the one hand, made it easier for converted Jews to accept the teaching of Christianity by finding essential doctrines already revealed in Jewish mystical thought, and, on the other, permitted conservative nonkabbalistic Jews to condemn Kabbalah as non-Jewish. Converted Jews served as teachers for such humanists as Pico, whose instructor Dattilo[7] may serve as the literary type of guide we see in Thenaud.

There is another important concept we must bring again to mind in order to understand better such a use of Kabbalah—namely, the tradition of the *prisca theologia.*[8] In an early form the idea is that the philosopher-god Hermes Trismegistus instructs Asclepius, who transmits the knowledge of "Logos" to Orpheus, Pythagoras, Plato, the Platonists of the Academy, the Neoplatonists, the Alexandrian Platonists, the medieval Platonists, on down to the Platonists of the Renaissance (Ficino, Pico, etc.). Let us now complicate things by adding in Moses. Does he instruct or is he instructed by Hermes? Clearly the whole notion fits better into Christian linear time if it is Moses who transmits (at least partially) *the revealed tradition* (received from Enoch, from Noah, from Adam, from Adonai Elohim)[9] to Hermes. The terms "eclectic" and "syncretistic" are frequently used to explain such a notion of *prisca theologia,* but they betray a nineteenth- or twentieth-century perspective. For the Renaissance these various schools of philosophy were not disparate but rather unified expressions of essentially the same divinely revealed and inspired truth. Thenaud reflects such

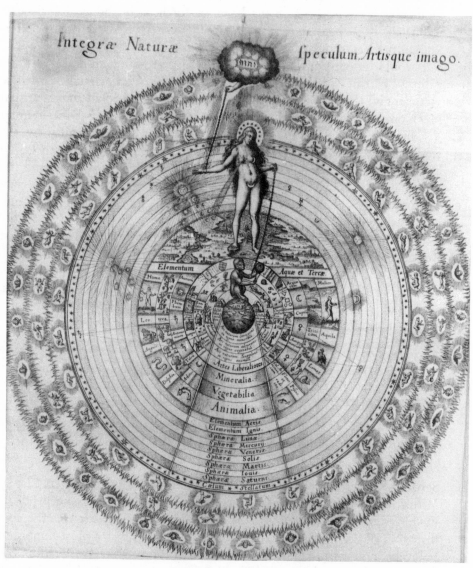

4. "Integra Naturae Speculum Artisque imago" from Robert Fludd, *Uriusque Cosmi Historia*, volume I, a (Oppenheim, 1617), pp. 4-5.

humanist tendencies, but he also demonstrates, as we have seen, those prejudices that led ultimately to overt hostility toward Kabbalah. Consequently, his work, which we have set forth to introduce Renaissance Kabbalah, is perhaps more representative even than those of his better-known predecessors.

It would be presumptuous to pretend to give here a summary of kabbalistic doctrines or of the history of Kabbalah. Earlier studies in these volumes give the origin of the Kabbalah, and Gershom Scholem has written much on this topic.[10] For the Renaissance, the history has been written by Joseph Blau and François Secret and completed more recently by the studies of the *Cahiers de l'Hermetisme* (see n. 5 and n. 9) among others. To acquaint the reader who seeks here an initiation into and to remind the reader already knowledgeable of the Kabbalah, we shall rather now elaborate briefly on Thenaud's sources, while referring the reader to more complete texts and studies.

Giovanni Pico della Mirandola (1463–1494), often cited as the first Renaissance kabbalist, was perhaps, more correctly stated, the first non-Jewish Christian kabbalist.[11] It is undoubtedly he who, in his oration *On the Dignity of Man,* intended as an introduction to his nine hundred theses, establishes from the outset the idea of the *concordance*[12] of Christianity, Jewish Kabbalah, Platonism, Aristotelianism, Pythagoreanism, magic, Zoroastrianism, etc., within a framework of *prisca theologia:*

> For this reason I have not been content to add to the tenets held in common many teachings taken from the ancient theology of Hermes Trismegistus, many from the doctrines of the Chaldeans and of Pythagoras, and many from the occult mysteries of the Hebrews. I have proposed also as subjects for discussion several theses in natural philosophy and in divinity, discovered and studied by me. I have proposed, first of all, a harmony between Plato and Aristotle. . . . (245)

Second, Pico establishes the belief, following perhaps the convert Flavius Mithridate, whom he met in Paris and whose translations he probably used,[13] that "the ancient mysteries of the Hebrews [serve as] . . . the confirmation of the inviolable Catholic faith" (249). This is a most important point, because it sets the stage for subsequent humanistic investigation. But Pico himself states the case admirably:

> When I purchased these [kabbalistic] books at no small cost to myself, when I had read them through with the greatest diligence and with unwearying toil, I saw in them (as God is my witness) not so much the Mosaic as the Christian religion. There is the mystery of the Trinity, there the Incarnation of the Word, there the divinity of the Messiah; there I have read about original sin, its expiation through Christ, the heavenly Jerusalem, the fall of

the devils, the orders of the angels, purgatory, and the punishments of hell, the same things we read daily in Paul and Dionysius, in Jerome and Augustine. But in those parts which concern philosophy you really seem to hear Pythagoras and Plato, whose principles are so closely related to the Christian faith that our Augustine gives immeasurable thanks to God that the books of the Platonists have come into his hands. (252)

Similarly, his definition of Kabbalah as revealed tradition passed on from generation to generation, from God to Moses, and on down the line, serves as the standard for several generations of Renaissance kabbalists.[14] Pico teaches, probably from the *Sepher Yetsirah* or *Book of Creation*, the doctrine of the En-Soph and the Sephiroth, or emanations, as *numerationes*, enumerations. And, more specifically, dealing with the Sephira Shekhinah, representing God living in the world, and with the corporeal world, he places humanity at the center of the world. Through his free will, and because of his divinely given ability to raise himself up or down the hierarchy of being, the Human, Man (Adam), can become like unto Adam Kadmon, celestial Man (Christ).[15] He deals with the kabbalistic mysteries of the Names of God[16] and of the thirty-two paths of wisdom by which God brought about creation. We have already seen this idea in Thenaud, where the thirty-two paths consist of the ten Sephiroth and the twenty-two characters of the alphabet.

Another of Thenaud's sources, Johannes Reuchlin (1455–1522), drew on the work of Pico, which he developed more discursively. In fact, the better known of his two works on the Kabbalah, *De arte cabalistica* (1517), appears in the *Opera omnia* of Pico.[17] His earlier text, *De verbo mirifico* (1494), presents a dialogue among three speakers, Sidonius, an "Epicurean" philosopher; Baruch, a Hebrew thinker; and Capnion (Reuchlin), a Christian, each of whom dominates respectively one of the three days and three books of the work. Now there is obviously a progression from the wisdom of antiquity to that of the Old Testament, in talmudic and kabbalistic perspectives, and to that of Christianity. Similarly the wisdom of antiquity is largely geographical, mathematical, and cosmological (elemental); that of Baruch concerned with the world of emanations from the divine Names, with the paths of creation, with kabbalistic knowledge (celestial); while Capnion concerns himself with ultimate spiritual truths dependent on the pronounceable name of Christ (angelic). It may be indeed true, as Blau points out, that Reuchlin's knowledge of Kabbalah at this stage of his study is limited and contains error; but let us remember that Reuchlin writes from the perspective of *prisca theologia*. He is not interested in pure Kabbalah in historic isolation, but in Kabbalah as only *one* manifestation of spiritual truth whose most absolute expression is revealed in Christ. If, as Blau also suggests, his Kabbalah is more Pythagorean than kabbalistic, does it not result from Reuchlin's seeing Moses and Pythagoras as exponents of the same wisdom? Among the concepts he sets forth here, let us call attention to the following: (1) Reuchlin gives the names of the Sephiroth in part in incorrect order.[18] (2) Hebrew is the oldest of languages, the language used by God for creation, for dialogue with humanity and among human beings and angels; it is the oldest written language, and Moses is the first author (*De verbo* 2.42–43). (3) The mysteries of all creation are expressed in the Tetragrammaton, from which all creation has emanated by divine will (60–72), as is manifest in a long listing of things characterized by the Tetrad. (4) As Capnion explains on the third day, Logos is the wonder-working Word, the name of the Son, Yhsvh, the Pentagrammaton coexisting with God's other name, YHVH, of the time of the law. Yhsvh contains the determinant of the Son, *shin*, the determining element of *Esh*, fire (73–103), one of the main signs of the age of Grace and Spirit.

The *De arte cabalistica*, as Secret points out, elaborates on the *De verbo*, but it is not a mere repetition in form or content.[19] Obviously Reuchlin profited much from his study of Hebrew in the years intervening and established himself as one of Europe's leading Hebraists.[20] Also a three-part work, the *De arte* presents a dialogue among Simeon, who speaks in books 1 and 3 about Kabbalah; Philolaus, a Pythagorean whose "philosophy" determines book 2 in the absence of Simeon, who must observe the Sabbath; and the Muhammadan Marranus, who actively participates on all three days. According to Simeon, "Cabala is an alchemy transforming external perceptions into internal, then into images, opinion, reason, intuition, spirit, and, finally, light. Such a deification is symbolised by the place of the microcosm Tiferet, the great Adam, in the middle of the tree of the Sephiroth. . . . This deification is not obtained without a work of moral and intellectual asceticism."[21] Mathematics and metaphysics do not suffice; maturity in the contemplative way alone, a gift of God, leads us to deification [θεοσις] (*Kabbale* 27–44; *De arte* 115–23). Book 3 clarifies the doctrine of the thirty-two paths of wisdom, that of the number 10 whose radius 5 (the spherical number) when multiplied by 10 (the number of the universe) gives 50, the number of the gates and of the jubilee; and when we add to the gates the number of letters, we arrive at 72, the number of the Names of angels and of God. In this work, Reuchlin distinguishes between practical Kabbalah and spiritual Kabbalah, and he implies, like Pico before him but more pointedly, that the names of angels can be used in kabbalistic magic (*Kabbale* 203–314; *De arte* 210–71).[22]

Another of Thenaud's contemporaries, Heinrich Cornelius Agrippa von Nettesheim (1486–1535), whom he undoubtedly met in the troubled years when the latter served as astrologer to Louise de Savoie, was popularly recognized as Rabelais's necromancer-sorcerer Herr Trippa (*Tiers Livre*, chap. 25). He developed even more fully the supposed magical aspects of Kabbalah.[23] In book 1 (elemental world) Agrippa concerns himself with the nature and virtues of things, of the planets and their sympathies and influences, of the passions of the soul, and of humanity, human nature, and the relationship of human beings as microcosm to macrocosm. In book 2 (intellectual world), Agrippa deals with numbers, so he naturally enumerates at "ten" the ten Names of God and of the Sephiroth (2.13.194–95); at "twelve" the Hebraic Names of God of twelve letters and of the orders of angels and tribes, etc. (14.196–99). He discusses *Notariacon*, values of letters with their mystical meanings (19.209–11) and the related sciences of cosmology and astrology. Book 3 (celestial world) presents religion in its relation to magic and the dependence of the magus on God for his knowledge (chaps. 1–9). In the remaining chapters he talks about the Names of God, angels, and demons, revealing a summary knowledge of kabbalistic teachings, both theoretical or spiritual and practical, which he places together with the teachings of Orpheus, Pythagoras, Zoroaster, and so on, in a context of the occult sciences, demonstrating a clear belief in the possibility of magical practice. His demonic and angelic magic, as Müller-Jahnke notes, is more "Christian" than truly kabbalistic in origin.[24] If Agrippa denounced the study of Kabbalah in his *De vanitate scientiarum* as superstitious allegorizing after the coming of Christ, it is not so much that he really rejected Kabbalah or any of the human sciences per se, but rather that, as the introduction of the *De occulta philosophia* clarifies, all of these sciences must be put in proper perspective. None for and within itself has any validity; collectively they are of value as partial expressions of truth, but Truth as such is only revealed by God in Christian faith. Whatever knowledge we have of it is a gift of God not attained exclusively by our own efforts and not at all by our merit. The fact that Agrippa published the *De occulta* (begun in 1510) in 1533 should be seen less as a vacillation from the *De vanitate* than as a confirmation of the concept given in interpretation of his own statements. In his works Agrippa analyzed extensively two major kabbalistic texts, the *Zohar* and the *Sepher Yetsirah*. Once again we see the study of Kabbalah sublimated to the occult or hermetic sciences as a part of *prisca theologia*.

Yet another of Thenaud's contemporaries of importance for the study of Kabbalah, though probably not for the text of Thenaud himself, Francesco Giorgio or Zorzi (1460–1540) of Venice, composed a much-misunderstood work entitled *De harmonia mundi*, which he dedicated to Clement VII in 1527. The work has an elaborate schema: three books or canticles, each subdivided into eight tones and each tone into an unequal number of chapters. Jacques Fabry, in one of the best evaluations of Giorgio's work to date, calls to our attention the fact that the *De harmonia* presents, perhaps with greater clarity than Pico or Reuchlin, the major ideas of Renaissance kabbalists. It is a work of extreme erudition by a man who spent his time reading and studying not only the philosophers of antiquity and ancient languages but also the fathers of the church and the writings of contemporary *prisci theologi* and *platonici*. Giorgio's book merits close scrutiny and a major study.[25]

The work of the Italian kabbalist Paul Rici, *De coelesti agricultura*, published in 1541, reflects the content of a number of smaller works going back to 1507, among which is his translation of the *Porta Lucis* (1515). For Rici, who is cited by Thenaud, the Kabbalah confirms all major Christian dogmas (Trinity, Virgin Birth, etc.), and he sees it as a most spiritual form of contemplation. Often forgotten by historians of spirituality, Rici's work deserves recognition in the history of the Kabbalah.[26]

Of lesser renown but of more immediate and personal importance for Thenaud was the work and influence of Agostino Giustiniani (1470–1536), called by Francis I to teach in Paris, where he remained until 1522. He published a translation of Maimonides's *Guide for the Perplexed*, a polyglot Psalter (with eight versions for each psalm) with kabbalistically inspired commentaries, and (in 1513) a prayer based on the seventy-two Names of God in Hebrew and Latin. Fabry says of him, "The Kabbalah of A. Giustiniani is not only an affair of grammarians discussing letters and their numeric value, it is also a much richer Cabala quite replete with modulations on the name of God." Clearly another little known spiritualist whose works merit study and editing, Giustiniani remains virtually unknown.[27]

One of the most important figures in the history of Renaissance Kabbalah, Cardinal Egidio (Gilles) da Viterbo (1465–1532), wrote much and translated more; but he published nothing. In 1959 François Secret published two of his most important treatises: the brief *Libellus de litteris hebraici* (1517) and the much longer *Scechina* (1530). Their importance ultimately lies in the clarity and depth of expression about, respectively, the spiritual signification of all the letters of the Hebrew alphabet and of the importance and meaning of the tenth of the Sephiroth, the Shekinah, the indwelling manifestation of God in our midst. The very length of the latter, occupying some 192 manuscript folios or 470 pages in the modern edition, which deals with so narrowly defined a subject, points out the care and study that went into its preparation and the great importance of Hebrew texts for the period. Clearly the treatises dealing with the main kabbalistic themes we have seen elaborate those ideas in greater detail. Viterbo's works were known indirectly in his own day through their influence on Galatino,

Teseo Ambrogio, Widmanstetter, and, less immediately, Postel. Perhaps of even greater importance is Viterbo's own influence on the development and promulgation of Kabbalah through his own circle, for he had in his court or household service both converted and Christian Hebraists, who copied texts and sought out manuscripts, contributing to the building up of one of the finest Hebraic libraries of the Renaissance, unfortunately dispersed after Viterbo's death. If a cardinal, who presented the opening address at the Lateran Council, who served as papal ambassador on many important missions, gave so much attention and time to the study of Kabbalah, in a context of *prisca theologia,* how important an aspect of Renaissance thought it must have been![28]

Among the works and translations of Guillaume Postel (1510–1581), one of the most curious of Renaissance kabbalists, are found the *Zohar,* the *Bahir,* parts of the commentaries of Recanati and the *Beresith Rabba;* commentaries on the Apocalypse and Ruth; the *Absconditorum clavis,* the *De nativitate mediatoris ultima;* his Hebrew/Latin *Candelabrum typicum* (edited in a beautiful modern edition by Secret), among many others. If Postel became one of the best qualified Hebrew and Arabic scholars of his day, his philological accomplishments were offset to a great extent by his "prophetic visions," his hearing of voices, and his very peculiar relationship to Mother Jeanne. He met the latter, a devout charity worker at the Hospital of Saints John and Paul in Venice, where he worked as chaplain; it was she who served as his spiritual mother and guide, illiterate though she was, to understand the *Zohar.* After her death, Postel identified her as the *Venetian Virgin,* the feminine manifestation of the Messiah. Clearly Postel (perhaps possessed by his *anima*), after his visionary crisis, identifies Mother Jeanne with Shekinah as the manifestation of the Son of Man.[29] If one must view his commentaries with caution, his studies of Kabbalah demonstrate to what extent an adept could go in a personal dedication to Kabbalah in the context of *prisca theologia.* His life and much of his work cause him to be regarded with caution, if not suspicion about his sanity. That caution is somewhat typical of the attitude of those not convinced of the value of the so-called esoteric sciences toward their adepts and even their students. If, in our brief survey of early Renaissance Kabbalah, we have dealt with those positively motivated toward the study of the tradition, we must call to our readers' attention the negative viewpoint as well.

Gershom Scholem points out clearly that among the Jews not sympathetic to Kabbalah their hostility made itself manifest against the converts who used Kabbalah to "prove" the tenets of Christianity: such critics argued that Kabbalah was, in effect, non-Jewish. Perhaps their arguments betray the suspicion felt among some conservative orthodox Jews before the more "individualized" direction taken by the Jewish mystics who followed the tradition.[30] It also points up a unilateralism of Jewish belief, comparable to that demonstrated by Thenaud and, among others, Johann Albrecht Widmannstadt (1506–1557). The latter, a colleague of Viterbo and Postel, recounts in his preface to the *Novum testamentum syriacum* (1555) that he had reacted most pointedly to Dattilo's kabbalistic doctrine of universal salvation for all species of creation; such monstrous opinions were for Widmannstadt, who viewed favorably other aspects of Kabbalah, a Trojan horse on the verge of assailing the true church of Christ.[31] Let us recall also the opposition on the part of Pope Innocent VIII and the Roman curia to Pico's *Conclusiones*[32] and the famous quarrel that broke out in Cologne against Reuchlin. The instigator of the latter, a certain Johannes Pfefferkorn, a converted Jew himself, was so outspokenly ardent in his new faith that he acted to persuade Maximilian I to condemn all Hebrew books belonging to Jewish communities to the fire. Subsequently he attacked Reuchlin for his interest in Hebrew and Kabbalah. Agrippa von Nettesheim wrote in defense of Reuchlin's *De verbo* and later, to preclude the attacks of the enemy, wrote an open letter to the Council of Cologne defending the kabbalists before publishing there his *De occulta philosophia*.[33]

In England, interest in the Kabbalah developed slowly and almost cautiously, revealing at the same time an equally negative element. John Colet (1466–1519) was hesitant; John Fisher (1459–1535) defended Kabbalah in his condemnation of Luther; Thomas More translated the life of Pico but did not elaborate at all on Kabbalah; the Frenchman Giles du Guez, librarian to Henry VII and Henry VIII, displayed knowledge (after Reuchlin) of the fifty gates; Everard Digby and John Dee (1527–1608) both demonstrated familiarity with the major Continental kabbalists, the latter going his own kabbalistic way. Reginald Scott (1538–1599), John Rainolds (1549–1607), and Francis Bacon (1561–1626) rejected the papist, superstitious, philosophical, or materialistic aspects of Kabbalah. The most celebrated of the English kabbalists is Robert Fludd (1574–1637), whose *Mosaic philosophy* and *Summum bonum* are a defense of the great Continental kabbalists and of true Kabbalah, which, in the second of these works, he distinguishes as "Bereschith" and "Mercawa" (Notaric and Temurah) from the superstitious Kabbalah of Gematrion, Notaric, and Temurah.[34]

Our study could go on almost endlessly, but we would find, for the most part, a repetition, amplification, or continuation of the work on Kabbalah done by the early humanists, Pico, Reuchlin, Rici, Viterbo, and others. One major exception is the independent development after the exodus from Spain in the Jewish community of Safed (Upper Galilee) of Lurianism. Scholem has dealt amply with the work of Isaac Luria, which would make itself felt on subsequent western European kabbalistic movements, for example, the work of Friedrich Christoph Oetinger (1702–1782). A Lutheran

5. Cover page from Robert Fludd, *Uriusque Cosmi Historia*, volume II (Oppenheim, 1619).

dignitary and theosopher, Oetinger expounded a sacred philosophy heavily inspired by Renaissance Kabbalah, Lurianism, and Jacob Boehme.[35]

* * *

Clearly a major aspect of Renaissance thought, Kabbalah contributed significantly to the renewal of spiritual awareness on the part of Renaissance humanists. They placed the work of the kabbalists either in line with the other sciences they viewed in the tradition of *prisca theologia* or, like Thenaud, they viewed Kabbalah as prefigural, much as the early fathers had treated the Old Testament. Some, such as Pico, Reuchlin, Postel, and others, openly or cautiously, saw in Kabbalah, like Dattilo, an indication of universal salvation. The "magical" or "mystical" aspect of name, letter, number in the creative process was of particular interest to an age concerned with the *imagistic* perspective, where symbolic language as an expression of reality occupied their attention for a few intensive generations before giving way to the rationalism not of Descartes but of the Cartesians. Their enthusiasm brought an end, among at least a small number of Jews and Christians, to the ghettos of the mind, opening the way to sharing a spiritual mysticism vital to both communities.

Notes

1. Paris, Bibliothèque de l'Arsenal, MS fr. 5061, fol. lxxᵛᵒ. There are two other manuscript copies of the work: Geneva, Bibliothèque Municipale, MS fr. 167; Nantes, Bibliothèque Municipale, MS 521 (fr. 355). See G. Mallary Masters, ed., *La Lignée de Saturne de Jehan Thenaud,* 5–38, for a general discussion of the biography and bibliography of Thenaud.

2. Paris, Bibliothèque Nationale, MS fr. 882. For a partial edition of this work, see Joseph Leon Blau, *The Christian Interpretation of the Cabala in the Renaissance.* It is discussed further by François Secret, *Les Kabbalistes chrétiens de la Renaissance,* 153–56.

3. For the difference among *sign, symbol,* and *image,* and the meaning of "imaginal" and "imagistic," see James Hillman, "An Inquiry into Image," *Spring* (1977) 62–88; "Further Notes on Images," *Spring* (1978) 152–82; and "Image Sense," *Spring* (1979) 130–43.

4. Compare Reuchlin's treatment below, n. 18.

5. Gershom Scholem, "Considérations sur l'Histoire des débuts de la Kabbale chrétienne," in *Kabbalistes chrétiens,* ed. Antoine Faivre and Frédérick Tristan, 17–46.

6. Ibid., 26.

7. Ibid.

8. Daniel P. Walker, "Orpheus the Theologian and Renaissance Platonists," *Journal of the Warburg and Courtauld Institutes* 16 (1953) 100–120; idem, "The *Prisca Theologia* in France," *Journal of the Warburg and Courtauld Institutes* 17 (1954) 204–59.

9. Jacques Fabry, "La Kabbale chrétienne en Italie," in *Kabbalistes chrétiens,* ed. Faivre and Tristan, 63; and G. Mallary Masters, *Rabelaisian Dialectic and the Platonic Hermetic Tradition,* 2–3. See also François Secret, "Lectures de Platon et d'Aristote à

la Renaissance: Aristote et les Kabbalistes chrétiens de la Renaissance," in *XVIe colloque international de Tours: Platon et Aristote à la Renaissance,* 277–91.

10. See *Jewish Spirituality from the Bible through the Middle Ages,* ed. Arthur Green (World Spirituality 13; New York: Crossroad, 1986) chaps. 11, 12, 14, 15; *Jewish Spirituality from the Sixteenth-century Revival to the Present,* ed. Arthur Green (World Spirituality 14; New York: Crossroad, 1987) chaps. 1, 2; Gershom Scholem, *Major Trends in Jewish Mysticim;* idem, *On the Kabbalah and its Symbolism.* See also François Secret, *Le Zôhar chez les Kabbalistes chrétiens de la Renaissance.*

11. Scholem, "Considérations sur l'Histoire," 19–26.

12. The term "concordance," used by Hermann Greive ("La Kabbale chrétienne de Jean Pic de la Mirandole," *Kabbalistes chrétiens,* ed. Faivre and Tristan, 159–79) captures marvelously well the spirit of the nonsyncretistic conception of *prisca theologia.* The text of the *Oration on the Dignity of Man* is cited from the translation of Elizabeth Livermore Forbes, in *The Renaissance Philosophy of Man,* ed. Ernst Cassirer, Paul Oskar Kristeller, and John Herman Randall, 223–54.

13. Greive, "Kabbale chrétienne de Pic," 161 and passim; and Chaim Wirszubski, "L'Ancien et le nouveau, dans la confirmation kabbalistique du christianisme par Pic de la Mirandole," *Kabbalistes chrétiens,* ed. Faivre and Tristan, 181–93, who studies in detail Kabbalah as proof of Christian doctrines in the 900 *Theses* or *Conclusiones.*

14. Giovanni Pico della Mirandola, *Apologia, Opera omnia* (1557–1573), ed. Cesare Vasoli, 1:166–81.

15. *Conclusiones, Opera omnia* 1:80–83, 106–13; *De hominis dignitate, Opera omnia* 1:314–24; and Greive, "Kabbale chrétienne de Pic," 168.

16. *Conclusiones, Opera omnia* 1:80–83, 106–13; and Greive, "Kabbale chrétienne de Pic," 171–72.

17. *Opera omnia* 1:733–899. The Friedrich Frommann Verlag published at Stuttgart-Bad Cannstatt in 1964 a facsimile of the *De arte cabalistica, 1517* together with the *De verbo mirifico, 1494.* François Secret published at Aubier Montaigne (Paris, 1973), a translation of the *De arte, La Kabbale,* in the series Pardès, ed. Georges Vajda, with an excellent introduction and critical notes.

18. Blau, *Christian Interpretation,* 47. The chapter "Pythagoras redivivus" (pp. 41–64) deals with Reuchlin; note 28 (pp. 46–47) corrects the listing of the Sephiroth thus:

Correct form

	(1) KETER	
(3) BINAH		(2) CHOCHMAN
(5) GEBURAH (or PACHAD)		(4) CHESED
	(6) TIPHERETH	
(8) HOD		(7) NETZAH
	(9) YESOD	
	(10) MALCHUTH	

Reuchlin's List

	(1) KETER	
(3) BINAH		(2) CHOCHMAN
(5) HOD		(4) NETZAH
	(6) TIPHERETH	
(8) MALCHUTH		(7) GEBURAH
	(9) CHESED	
	(10) PACHAD	

19. Secret, "Introduction," in Reuchlin, *La Kabbale,* trans. Secret, 7–17.

20. Ibid., 6–8; Blau, *Christian Interpretation,* 41–50, esp. p. 50.

21. Secret, *Kabbalistes chrétiens,* 57–58.

22. Ibid., 60–69.

23. Wolf-Dieter Müller-Jahncke, "Agrippa von Nettesheim et la Kabbale," in *Kabbalistes chrétiens,* ed. Faivre and Tristan, 197–209. The best studies on Agrippa are those of Auguste Prost (*Les sciences et les arts occultes au XVIᵉ siècle: Corneille Agrippa, sa vie et ses oeuvres)* and Charles G. Nauert, Jr. (*Agrippa and the Crisis of Renaissance Thought).* His works have been edited in a two-volume facsimile of the 1600(?) Lyons text at Hildesheim and New York by Georg Olms Verlag in 1970: *Opera.* It is possible that Thenaud may have known Agrippa's work, but obviously only in manuscript form or by word of mouth, given the publication date. He does not, however, give much indication of interest in the magical arts per se. And, of course, his own text, though subsequently revised in at least one manuscript, was completed before Agrippa came to the French court. Did, as Secret suggests (*Kabbalistes chrétiens,* 156–57), Thenaud rather influence Agrippa in his *De vanitate?*

24. Müller-Jahncke, "Agrippa," 200–204.

25. Fabry, "La Kabbale chrétienne en Italie"; see also *L'Harmonie du monde, divisée en trois cantiques: Oeuvre singulier, et plein d'admirable érudition,* trans. Guy Le Fèvre de la Boderie. Pico's *Heptaplus* is also given in translation.

26. Secret, *Kabbalistes chrétiens,* 87–99; Fabry, "La Kabbale chrétienne en Italie," 54–57.

27. Fabry, "La Kabbale chrétienne en Italie," 70; Secret, *Kabbalistes chrétiens,* 99–102, 105.

28. Secret, *Kabbalistes chrétiens,* 106–21; and his introduction (pp. 9–20) in the first of the two volumes of his edition of Viterbo's works, Edizione Nazionale die Classici del Pensiero Italiano, ser. 2, 10. On Galatino, see Anna Morisi, "Galatino et la Kabbale chrétienne," in *Kabbalistes chrétiens,* ed. Faivre and Tristan, 211–31.

29. Secret, *Kabbalistes chrétiens,* 171–86; idem, *Le Zôhar,* 6, 51–78, 104–14; W. J. Bouwsma, *Concordia mundi, The Career and Thought of Guillaume Postel.* An extensive bibliography of Postel's works and of the critical studies on them is given by Secret, *Kabbalistes chrétiens;* see also his "Notes sur G. Postel," *Bibliothèque d'Humanisme et Renaissance* 35 (1973) 85–101; 37 (1975) 101–32.

30. Scholem, "Considérations," 19–20; idem, *Major Trends,* 1–39, 287–324; see also Secret, "*L'Ensis Pauli* de Paulus de Heredia," *Sefarad* 26 (1966) 79–102, 253–71.

31. Scholem, "Considérations," 20–21; Secret, *Kabbalistes chrétiens,* 121–26; idem, "Un cheval de Troie dans l'église du Christ: La Kabbale chrétienne," in *Aspects du libertinisme au XVIᵉ siècle,* 153–66.

32. Secret, *Kabbalistes chrétiens,* 32–38.

33. Müller-Jahncke, "Agrippa," 197–205.

34. Secret, *Kabbalistes chrétiens,* 228–38; Serge Hutin, "Note sur la création chez trois kabbalistes chrétiens anglais: Robert Fludd, Henry More et Isaac Newton," in *Kabbalistes chrétiens,* ed Faivre and Tristan, 149–56.

35. Pierre Deghaye, "*La Philosophie sacrée* d'Oetinger," in *Kabbalistes chrétiens,* ed. Faivre and Tristan, 233–78; Scholem, *Major Trends,* 238, 244–86, 405, 407–15; Ernst Benz, "La Kabbale chrétienne en Allemagne, du XVIᵉ au XVIIIᵉ siècle," in *Kabbalistes chrétiens,* ed. Faivre and Tristan, 89–148. For a more complete perspective on both major and minor kabbalists not touched on here, consult the works of Blau and Secret and the very useful volume of Cahiers de l'Hermétisme cited here (*Kabbalistes chrétiens)* as well as others in the series dealing with Kabbalah and other hermetic sciences. The

following studies, among many others, by Secret are especially useful also: "La Kabbale chez Du Bartas et son commentateur Claude Duret," *Studi francesi* no. 7 (1959) 1–11; "Les 'Annotationes decem in sacram Scripturam' de Petrus Antonius Beuter," *Sefarad* 29 (1969) 319–32; "Un Kabbaliste chrétien oublié: Jean Phelippeaux, jésuite du XVIIᵉ siècle," *Annuaire de l'E.P.H.E.*, Section des Sciences Religieuses 82:7–34; "Notes pour l'histoire des juifs en France et les hébraïsants chrétiens," *Revue des études juives* 134.1–2 (1975) 81–100; "Histoire de l'Esotérisme chrétien," in *Problèmes et méthodes d'histoire des religions*, 243–50; "Notes sur les hébraïsants chrétiens et les Juifs en France," *Revue des études juives* 126.4 (1967) 417–33; "Notes sur quelques kabbalistes chrétiens," *Bibliothèque d'Humanisme et Renaissance* 36 (1974) 67–82. The series of reviews, articles, and studies published in *ARIES*, Association pour la Recherche et l'Information sur l'Esotérisme (Neuilly-sur-Seine: La Table d'Émeraude Éditeur), published since 1982 under the direction of Antoine Faivre, Pierre Deghaye, and Roland Edighoffer, are most helpful for the latest work on Renaissance (and later) Kabbalah and other hermetic sciences. See also the study of Frances A. Yates, *Giordano Bruno and the Hermetic Tradition*, and the French translation, *Giordano Bruno et la tradition hermétique*.

Bibliography

Sources

Agrippa von Nettesheim, Heinrich Cornelius. *Opera*. Facsimile of 1600(?) Lyons text. 2 vols. Hildesheim and New York: Georg Olms Verlag, 1970.

Georges, François (Francesco Giorgio). *L'Harmonie du monde, divisée en trois cantiques: Oeuvre singulier, et plein d'admirable érudition*. Translated by Guy Le Fèvre de la Boderie. Paris: Jean Macé, 1579. New edition in facsimile: Neuilly/Seine: Arma Artis, 1978. Georges (Giorgio) is also the author of *Problemata* (1536), another important work of Christian Kabbalah, and of a long poem in Italian, *L'Elegante Poema* (a manuscript that was not published until 1991; see *L'Elegante Poema*, edited by Jean-Francois Maillard [Paris: Archè, 1992]).

Pico della Mirandola, Giovanni. *Heptaplus*. Translated by Guy Le Fèvre de la Boderie. In François Georges, *L'Harmonie du monde*.

———. *Opera omnia* (1557–1573). Edited by Cesare Vasoli. Vol. 1. Hildesheim: Olms, 1969.

———. "Oration on the Dignity of Man." Translated by Elizabeth Livermore Forbes. In *The Renaissance Philosophy of Man*, edited by Ernst Cassirer, Paul Oskar Kristeller, and John Herman Randall, 223–54. Chicago: University of Chicago Press, [1961].

Reuchlin, Johannes. *De arte cabalistica, 1517. De verbo mirifico, 1494*. Facsimile. Stuttgart-Bad Cannstatt: Friedrich Frommann Verlag, 1964.

———. [*De arte cabalistica*]. *La Kabbale*. Translated by François Secret. Pardès. Edited by Georges Vajda. Paris: Aubier Montaigne, 1973.

Thenaud. *La Cabale métrifée*. Paris, Bibliothèque Nationale, ms fr. 882.

———. *Traité de la Cabale* or *Traité de la Cabale chrétienne*.

(1) Paris, Bibliothèque de l'Arsenal, ms fr. 5061.

(2) Geneva, Bibliothèque Municipale, ms fr. 167.

(3) Nantes, Bibliothèque Municipale, ms 521 (fr. 355).

Viterbo, Egidio da. *Scechina e Libellus de litteris hebraicis.* Edited by François Secret. Edizione nazionale dei classici del pensiero italiano, ser. 2, 10–11. 2 vols. Rome: Centro internazionale di studi umanistici, 1959.

Studies

ARIES. Association pour la Recherche et l'Information sur l'Esotérisme. Edited by Antoine Faivre, Pierre Deghaye, and Roland Edighoffer. Neuilly-sur-Seine: La Table d'Émeraude Éditeur, 1985–.

Benz, Ernst. "La Kabbale chrétienne en Allemagne, du XVIe au XVIIIe siècle." In *Kabbalistes chrétiens,* edited by Antoine Faivre and Frédérick Tristan, 89–148. Cahiers de l'Hermétisme. Paris: Albin Michel, 1979.

Blau, Joseph Leon. *The Christian Interpretation of the Cabala in the Renaissance.* Port Washington, NY: Kennikat, [1965].

Bouwsma, W. J. *Concordia mundi, The Career and Thought of Guillaume Postel.* Cambridge: Harvard University Press, 1957.

Deghaye, Pierre. "La Philosophie sacrée d'Oetinger." In *Kabbalistes chrétiens,* 233–78.

Fabry, Jacques. "La Kabbale chrétienne en Italie." In *Kabbalistes chrétiens,* 49–64.

Greive, Hermann. "La Kabbale chrétienne de Jean Pic de la Mirandole." In *Kabbalistes chrétiens,* 159–79.

Hillman, James. "Further Notes on Images." *Spring* (1978) 152–82.

———. "Image Sense." *Spring* (1979) 130–43.

———. "An Inquiry into Image." *Spring* (1977) 62–88.

Hutin, Serge. "Note sur la création chez trois kabbalistes chrétiens anglais: Robert Fludd, Henry More et Isaac Newton." In *Kabbalistes chrétiens,* 149–56.

Kabbalistes chrétiens. Edited by Antoine Faivre and Frédérick Tristan. Cahiers de l'Hermétisme. Paris: Albin Michel, 1979.

Masters, G. Mallary, ed. *La Lignée de Saturne de Jehan Thenaud.* Travaux d'Humanisme et Renaissance 130. Geneva: Droz, 1973.

———. *Rabelaisian Dialectic and the Platonic Hermetic Tradition.* Albany: SUNY Press, 1969.

Morisi, Anna. "Galatino et la Kabbale chrétienne." In *Kabbalistes chrétiens,* 211–31.

Müller-Jahncke, Wolf-Dieter. "Agrippa von Nettesheim et la Kabbale." In *Kabbalistes chrétiens,* 197–209.

Nauert, Charles G., Jr. *Agrippa and the Crisis of Renaissance Thought.* Illinois Studies in the Social Sciences 55. Urbana: University of Illinois Press, 1965.

Prost, Auguste. *Les sciences et les arts occultes au XVIe siècle: Corneille Agrippa, sa vie et ses oeuvres.* 2 vols. Paris: Champion, 1881, 1882.

Scholem, Gershom. "Considérations sur l'Histoire des débuts de la Kabbale chrétienne." In *Kabbalistes chrétiens,* 17–46.

———. *Major Trends in Jewish Mysticism.* New York: Schocken, 1961.

———. *On the Kabbalah and its Symbolism.* New York: Schocken, 1965.

Secret, François. "Les 'Annotationes decem in sacram Scripturam' de Petrus Antonius Beuter." *Sefarad* 29 (1969) 319–32.

———. "Un cheval de Troie dans l'église du Christ: La Kabbale chrétienne." In *Aspects du libertinisme au XVIe siècle,* 153–66. De Pétrarque à Descartes 30. Paris: Vrin, 1974.

———. "L'*Ensis Pauli* de Paulus de Heredia." *Sefarad* 26 (1966) 79–102, 253–71.

———. "Histoire de l'Esotérisme chrétien." In *Problèmes et méthodes d'histoire des religions,* 243–50. Ecole pratique des hautes études, Ve section: Sciences religieuses. Paris: Presses universitaires de France, 1968.

———. "La Kabbale chez Du Bartas et son commentateur Claude Duret." *Studi francesi* no. 7 (1959) 1–11.

———. "Un Kabbaliste chrétien oublié: Jean Phelippeaux, jésuite du XVIIᵉ siècle." *Annuaire de l'E.P.H.E.*, Section des Sciences Religieuses 82:7–34.

———. *Les Kabbalistes chrétiens de la Renaissance.* Paris: Dunod, 1964.

———. "Lectures de Platon et d'Aristote à la Renaissance: Aristote et les Kabbalistes chrétiens de la Renaissance." In *XVIᵉ colloque international de Tours: Platon et Aristote à la Renaissance*, 277–91. De Pétrarque à Descartes 32. Paris: Vrin, 1976.

———. "Notes pour l'histoire des juifs en France et les hébraïsants chrétiens." *Revue des études juives* 134.1–2 (1975) 81–100.

———. "Notes sur G. Postel." *Bibliothèque d'Humanisme et Renaissance* 35 (1973) 85–101; 37 (1975) 101–132.

———. "Notes sur les hébraïsants chrétiens et les Juifs en France." *Revue des études juives* 126.4 (1967) 417–33.

———. "Notes sur quelques kabbalistes chrétiens." *Bibliothèque d'Humanisme et Renaissance* 36 (1974) 67–82.

———. *Le Zôhar chez les Kabbalistes chrétiens de la Renaissance.* Paris: Mouton, 1964.

Vasoli, Cesare. "L'Hermétisme à Venise, de Giorgio à Patrizi." In *Présence d'Hermès Trismégiste*, 120–52. Cahiers de l'Hermétisme. Paris: Albin Michel, 1988.

Walker, Daniel P. "Orpheus the Theologian and Renaissance Platonists." *Journal of the Warburg and Courtauld Institutes* 16 (1953) 100–120.

———. "The *Prisca Theologia* in France." *Journal of the Warburg and Courtauld Institutes* 17 (1954) 204–59.

Wirszubski, Chaim. "L'Ancien et le nouveau, dans la confirmation kabbalistique du christianisme par Pic de la Mirandole." In *Kabbalistes chrétiens*, 181–93.

Yates, Frances A. *Giordano Bruno and the Hermetic Tradition.* Chicago: University of Chicago Press, 1964.

———. *Giordano Bruno et la tradition hermétique.* Foreword by Antoine Faivre. Paris: Dervy, 1988. French translation of 1964 English edition.

Zambelli, Paola. *L'ambigua natura della magia.* Milan: Arnoldo Mondadori, 1991.

5

Paracelsus and His Followers

HEINRICH SCHIPPERGES

IN THE TRANSITION from Middle Ages to modern times we encounter one of the most fascinating figures of cultural history, Theophrastus von Hohenheim (1493–1541), who later called himself Paracelsus. He was a physician, philosopher, and theologian whose view of the world was supported and permeated by a spirituality that is concrete through and through.

Paracelsus's picture of the world and humankind is based on a thoroughly spiritual natural philosophy that comprehends all the phenomena of history and society. This does not in any way—as in the nineteenth century—result in a universally binding single science with its methodological dogmatism, to which subsequently psychosocial aspects could be added only as a compensatory principle. In contrast to such an axiomatically reduced, monocular way of thinking, Paracelsus sketches out a large-scale table of categories of medical thought and action and thus spins a thread which alone can show a way out of the labyrinth in which the Minotaur is in control, the *monoculus* with his one-eyed gaze and his methodological terror.

Nowhere are the increasing methodological scientific constriction of human nature, and also the methodological possibilities of understanding the whole person, healthy or sick, displayed more clearly than in the medicine of Paracelsus. But here too it is already possible to see with terrifying clarity the gap between the increasingly firm nucleus of the sciences and the suppressed sciences: a division, or even more a breach, which in modern times was to lead to the dichotomy between the natural sciences and the humanities.

Since the middle of the sixteenth century the anatomical age has developed with increasing consistency a specialized structural theory (morphology), a highly differentiated functional theory (physiology), and a complex theory of disease (pathology), which from the middle of the nineteenth century was extended into a general pathology that was obligatory for all medical disciplines. By contrast, in Paracelsus the intrinsic correspondence between human beings and nature is seen quite clearly when he recognizes and confesses "that the philosopher finds nothing other in heaven and in earth than what he also finds in human beings, and that the physician does not find anything other in human beings than what heaven and earth also have." In human beings there is the sign of all things; the human being is like a particularly finely polished diamond, in which all the world is reflected.

Paracelsus says that the ministry of the physician is to avert distress in this world of misery; however, such a healing art is necessary for the healthy as well as the sick, for all of us. The physician's ministry to human beings is "to preserve the body in health and to restore the sick person to his former health." The healing art is applied anthropology.

In this survey of the system of Paracelsus and his disciples I shall limit myself to the sixteenth and seventeenth centuries and only refer in passing to their effects on the eighteenth and nineteenth centuries. "Paracelsism" as a whole, however—and thus also the basic question of the "authentic" Paracelsus—is a phenomenon that can in no way be approached adequately by the history of modern science, far less be solved as a problem.

A survey of the "disciples of Paracelsus" in terms of the history of science will not be able to arrive at any convincing documentation unless it briefly but also clearly presupposes the foundations and guidelines of the "authentic" Paracelsus. So first I shall discuss the foundations of the *Corpus Paracelsicum*, and then turn to the distortion of Paracelsus in the sixteenth and seventeenth centuries, finally considering the influence of Paracelsism in the early modern period. Here I shall refer only to investigations of the life and work of Paracelsus.[1]

The Foundations of the *Corpus Paracelsicum*

In Paracelsus's worldview, the role of the physician is of central significance. From the perspective of his office in the world we first become aware of the characteristic dimensions of his system of medicine, a many-layered healing art, which has found specific representation in the nature and effects of the *arcana*. I shall therefore quite deliberately begin this introduction to the foundations of Paracelsus's medicine and natural philosophy with the question of the role of the physician in this world of distress and misery.

The Role of the Physician in Paracelsus

At the center of the cosmos created and well ordered by God, the physician finds the sick person as a suffering human being who, while being the center of the universe, a "point of heaven and earth," a complete "extract from the whole *machina mundi*" ("machine of the world"), is also a being that is extremely frail and fragile, "born to misfortune"; one therefore cannot be one's own shepherd, but needs a helper. In this fundamental need the physician, who is as it were "the God of the microcosm," gives the sick person professional aid. For just as God, the great physician, himself heals the fragility of things in the powerful "sphere of the world," so God has commanded the "physician of the microcosm" equally to avert distress, "by acting as the great physician instructs him."

Just as the physician as it were "draws out" the power and the nature of a healing from the herb, so now human beings seem to be "drawn out" of the great cosmos, as a microcosm which as God's creation contains both good and evil and therefore cannot be separated—as by the later Paracelsists—into different bodies or into an "elemental" and a "spiritual" principle. Here, where it is a question of the role of the physician in the "noblest creation," opinions are clearly divided.

Visible nature is therefore none other than the composer of the body, whether healthy or sick. In the "light of nature" the physician is to get to know the dramaturgically moved natural event, in order to walk the "way of the *arcana*." So the cosmos, and thus nature, is completely directed toward human beings. With this move toward nature, Paracelsus clearly opposes the pathological concept of humors in Greek and Arab medicine to build his house of medicine anew—on four pillars.

In this utterly corporeal worldview, health and sickness are the two leading examples that constantly serve to illuminate each other. Human beings, "born to fall," are by nature involved in this "fragility." The order of the microcosm includes as it were an immanent instability in which nature "itself quivers" (IV, 534). For, as we read in the *Labyrinthus medicorum errantium* (Labyrinth of the perplexed physicists), human beings are "burdened with all kinds of sickness and subject to them all as soon as they emerge from their mother's body and even in their mother's womb." Powers of construction and destruction, factors of risk and restitution, are here always simultaneously at work; the *destructor sanitatis* is naturally always accompanied by the *conservator sanitatis*. "Because man's own enemy is already imprisoned in his body at birth, he must be surrounded by sickness and death." From knowledge of the regularities of the macrocosm the physician may then also heal or assuage the injuries of the microcosm. His ministry is to avert distress.

Paracelsus attempted his reform of medicine on the basis of this quite special role of the physician; with his new medicine he strove for a new universalist ideal of education which makes the physician "whole," experienced in all the faculties of *studium generale,* concerned for that universal, saving political aversion of the distress of his time.

In his "*Septem Defensiones* (Seven defenses)," Paracelsus defends the originality of his new conception with great passion; he does not want it to be confused with the thought and language of the antiquated scholastics: "It has been objected that I give the diseases new names which no one can understand. Why did I not stick to the old names?" To this he gives the succinct reply: "How can I use the old names, especially as they do not derive from the origin of the disease?" (XI, 135). Now for Paracelsus, the origin of the disease is not a simple one but has five divisions; it is a mode of being, a fivefold *ens*. These five *entia* confront us with no less than the closed circle of human life with all its crises, and thus with the anthropological conception of an all-embracing order and way of life in days of health as well as days of sickness.

In contrast to modern thought, with its preexisting axioms and ideas reduced to models, which tends to distort reality, Paracelsus develops a broad table of categories of medical thought and action. Paracelsus sees them as no more and no less than the "five princes" which rule our life (see table 1 below).

Table 1. The Five Entia

ENS ASTRORUM   ENS VENENI
(Historical field)   (Toxic situation)

ENS NATURALE
(Constitution)

ENS SPIRITUALE
(Social sphere)

ENS DEI

The System of Healing Knowledge

The first category of our existential constitution described by the physician Paracelsus is the *ens astrorum*. By this he does not mean the influence of the stars on earthly history but rather the historical and cosmological framework which governs and supports human beings in their environment and with their history. We have to learn not only the "physical course of nature" but also the "course of heaven" within us. We are to note this "entry of heaven into us" and be prepared for this heaven "to take bodily form in us." Only in this way do we experience the regularity of this world, "the insertion of heaven." Human beings and their history are involved in a great cosmic event. The world encounters us not just as environment or heredity; in addition to the world of nature there is a whole world of time, of coming into being and passing away, of history and destiny. Each of us has his or her own space-time and many thousands of ways in it; each of us matures toward his or her consummation. Only as time goes on do we become aware of the full riches of reality "without ceasing until the end of the world" (II, 317).

Experiences of such an extent and depth mean that Paracelsus's theory of disease cannot recognize an unhistorical natural order. It is time that changes everything and makes it rise up again like a cloud (VII, 188). For Paracelsus, what produces disease is not the stellar constellation but the "star within," an incorporeal ideal principle: "And that which is not *corpus*, the same is sickness, and that which is *corpus* is not sickness" (VIII, 161). It is the "inner firmament" that makes the physician the origin and course of all sicknesses. Only to this degree does each disease have its "star." One must know "how heaven rules disease and how it rules medicine" (VIII, 170). But the "inner astra" produce not only diseases but also cures.

Finally, however, the structure of time also shows us the "term" appointed for us and the fundamental decay in things, the possible reversal and change of all natural forces—that obliteration and suppression of the original nature which makes the pathos of human existence more comprehensible and marks the facticity of death. "Time is the cause of corruption"; it shows the pathos of our existence in all its drama, and it points to the final end in death. The physician must therefore in all things "be mindful of time, so that he knows time, how he is to defend himself against it and how he is to govern it. It is not enough to note the present day, but also the morrow and all the future thereafter from the points of the hour to the terminus, and to see in time what is still to be done" (IV, 495).

What is to be done in our time span in the world is shown by the second constitution of being, the *ens veneni*, the essence of poison. God has certainly made all things in the world perfect in relation to themselves, but he has left them imperfect in relation to their mutual uses. Depending on the terms of reference, anything can be "poison." "It is only the dose which makes a poison not a poison." Human beings need a protector to cope with these poisons—in food, in medicine, in every aspect of life.

The *ens veneni* first of all deals with the question whether there is not still a mystery of nature as a whole in poison (XI, 136). Again comes the clear answer: poison too is part of nature and therefore should not be despised. But everything should be used for that for which it is in order and ordained. Anyone who despises a poison does not know the power that is really present in the poison. Now such a mysterious reality must be explained more closely: if one were to explain every poison correctly, what would there be in nature that was *not* poison? All things are poison, and nothing is without poison: only the dose makes something not poison (XI, 138).

In order to cope with this toxic atmosphere, human beings need an environmental protection, the "alchemist," who distinguishes poison from what is good. So not only should medicines with their toxic substances be under constant supervision, but energetic and comprehensive countermeasures are also called for to combat the side effects, for even food as such is broadly impregnated with such unwanted concomitant effects and is a toxic landscape that becomes increasingly pernicious. The world of natural matter is certainly ours, but it has not yet been fully made ready; it is still completely hidden in slag. Therefore it is the task of alchemy, the "art of Vulcan," to separate the useless from the useful in order to bring the world to its *ultima materia* and thus its wholeness. Nature in itself does not produce anything that is already perfect in its place: "Man must perfect it, and this perfection is called alchemy."

The dynamic structure of Paracelsus's table of categories emerges particularly impressively at the third level, the *ens naturale*, our natural constitution anchored in the body. From the three principles of our corporeal substance—salt, sulphur, and mercury—we learn not only the "cause, origin and knowledge of diseases," their etiology, but also their signs and properties, their pathogenetic course, and "what a physician needs to know" from them (IX, 40) in order to avert distress. "For although human beings are made of nothing, they are made into something which has a threefold division. These three make up the whole man and are man himself, and he is them" (IX, 40). The three substances are called sulphur, mercury, and salt, and each in its specific composition forms a concrete totality, a *corpus*.[2]

Now these three substances give us not only the structures of matter but also the processes of illnesses and the phases of cures. "So too with life: first we are shredded by God and divided into three substances, then we are painted with life which gives us our standing, walking and all our movement—and in a flash it is all over again."

The natural course of our life takes place against this theoretical background, which is indeed largely laid down and predetermined by our constitution. Human beings enter life burdened with every kind of sickness.

But from birth they also already have their natural physician. "And as he has the *destructor sanitatis* of nature, so too he has the *conservator sanitatis* of nature" (XI, 197). Both macrocosm and microcosm, as it were, intrinsically cope with this antagonistic principle to some degree: "Just as the external world acts in its nature, so too in human beings we are to note the quarrelsome and the peaceful, the warlike and the restful (falcons and doves). For where the firmament and the elements are, as in the macrocosm, there for certain are also peace and unrest" (XI, 197). Indeed, so strong and dangerous is cosmic unrest that nothing would remain alive without natural healing, if left only to the external physician.

Paracelsus calls the next member in the chain of categories of being *ens spirituale,* our spiritual health and sickness. Here we are to think first of that power of the spirit which cannot only use the nature of the body, which is evidently so weak, but often enough even attempts to fight against nature. Paracelsus often also speaks of a "will" that enables human beings to intervene in *res naturales.* More important still, under this spiritual aspect we find the effects of *res non naturales* on natural things, the influence of that *nomos* on the *physis* which alone brings culture out of nature.

From this aspect sickness would not be a deviation from the norm of an elemental structure, a mere dislocation from a generally unstable symmetry, but the specific indication of a quite particular spirituality in critical situations of life. The *ens spirituale* should not therefore just be counted among Paracelsus's *nomina abstrusa;* rather, *spiritus* means the *creatio continua,* which as a productive force is also still at work in fallen creation. Here the "light of nature" becomes the master of our sensory capacity and also the master of our understanding (I, 325). From this bond, in the light of nature the universal demand arises to offer help in distress, to support all the needy as partners. Knowledge is only one form of action; insight remains bound up with an interest in life. Only here do human beings experience humanity as living beings and experience humanity in encounter.

The fifth and last sphere of existence, the *ens dei,* appears clearly demarcated over against the four profane categories. It is God himself who ultimately bestows health on us, allows sickness, and gives the means of healing. And just as God is the "physician of the great world," so now the physician is to become the "physician of the small world." As "the small world of God" the physician should seek the foundation for his healing art with that oldest physician, God. Only in this way does the physician become "the one who performs the works of God." Here the healing art gains that superior normative system of reference which cannot be given it by either science or society.

The Significance of the "Arcane" in Paracelsus

At the center of the history of sources and influence we found the role of the physician in this world of misery and distress, in which according to Paracelsus the physician is called physically to avert this distress. Hohenheim's theory of illness, the concept of a theoretical pathology, appeared to be directly bound up with this "medicine"—which means both the knowledge of healing and the means of healing. Only against this background can we understand the significance of the means of healing.

The cures in such a medicine, supported by natural philosophy and with a religious component, are aimed at the concept of a healing that could hardly be more comprehensive; we shall return to this in more detail. It is the *arcana* which support our body (III, 139) or secure the preservation of the body in health by driving out sickness (III, 140). In investigating natural forces one comes to the *arcana*, "and they are the mysteries from which the physician is to grow" (IX, 568). God has put these *arcana* in nature to help physicians to avert distress. However, the *arcana* do not display their natural powers spontaneously, but in communication through the *ars spagyrica*, that chemodynamic process which acts as the "art of Vulcan," as the "*archaeus*" in the body.

For Paracelsus, too, the alchemical process, just as in the earlier tradition, simply means a *modus praeparandi rerum naturalium*, a specific process for the preparation of natural materials. Here Paracelsus already marks himself off very clearly from the contemporary manipulations of the alchemists: "It is not the case as with those who want alchemy to produce gold, to produce silver. Here, rather, the request is: make *arcana* and direct these against sicknesses. One must start from that, that is the foundation" (VIII, 185). Thus the *arcanum* has "the power to change, to mutate, to renew, to restore" (III, 139). It is that specific power which the physician first brings into play with his art. "The *arcanum* is a mighty heaven in the hand of the physician" (I, 29).

As Paracelsus writes in his book on mountain sickness, God has given the physician "the knowledge to demonstrate good and evil in a thing, and has prescribed for him the Vulcan, through which art good and evil are divided from one another." Accordingly it is the "art of Vulcan" which separates poison from the good and thus prepares for the elixir. Produced by alchemy, this becomes the inner sustainer of men and women. Depending on the preparation and mixing, Paracelsus distinguishes between the *elixir balsami*, an *elixir salis*, the *elixir dulcedinis* and thus also an *elixir quintae essentiae*, through which, for example, the quintessence of the celandine or the balm is digested under the effect of the sun, so as then to come under the *magisterium* of wine. The effect of such a healing drink is further heightened by the *elixir subtilitatis,* in which the ingredients are subjected to many distillations, or also through the *elixir proprietatis,* in which Paracelsus tests the "very being" of a cure by prolonged distillation and digestion.

So Paracelsus can sum up by saying, "therefore nature is our own physician," but this is a nature that has not yet arrived at its goal, for first human beings must complete it, bring it from its *materia prima* through the *materia media, ad ultimam,* a whole world prepared for golden ripeness in the light of nature.

Thus in Paracelsus alchemy represents more a therapeutic process of healing that could best be described as physiological-pathological chemistry on a vitalistic basis. As the "third pillar" in the system of medicine it stands between astronomy and physics, as a symbol of the micro-macrocosmic process of material change and thus also of all transmutation and all individuation (see diagram).

Pillars of Medicine

	Philosophia	
Study of nature		Physiology
	Astronomia	
Study of time		Pathology
	Alchimia	
Material process		Therapy
	Physica	
Saving art		Medical ethics

Paracelsus thought out and planned his arcane theory of medicine for the future with great deliberation when he confessed: "What is it that the *medicus* repents of? Nothing! For he has spent his days with the *arcana* and has lived in God and in nature as a powerful master of the earthly light" (VIII, 321).

But there can be no doubt that already among the immediate successors of Paracelsus this term *arcanum* was developed further, surpassed, and distorted. The concrete *arcana* turned into the *mysterium magnum* of the *arcanum,* which could be interpreted only in spiritual terms and finally became an *arcanum sanctum.* Paracelsus's basic concept in natural philosophy was highly stylized and became a means of metaphysical manipulation.[3] The deutero-Paracelsian writings increasingly abandon their specific relationship to praxis and subsequently develop only purely speculative accents.

The Distortion of Paracelsus

Among the great personalities in the history of modern science whose works we suppose we know in critical editions, work and influence diverge most strikingly in Theophrastus of Hohenheim, called Paracelsus. So before we investigate the effects of this view of the world in the early period, we would do well to establish more clearly the traits and phases of the distortion of the *Corpus Paracelsicum*.

The First Editions of Important Individual Writings

In view of the abundance of Paracelsus's works which were printed in the sixteenth and seventeenth centuries, we should remember that during Paracelsus's lifetime, in all only sixteen different writings appeared under his name (between 1527 and 1538), including the smaller occasional writings like the *Intimatio* in Basel or the *Prognosticationes* at the turn of the year.

Immediately after Paracelsus's death in 1541 the collection of his writings began vigorously, in the first place in the search for usable prescriptions, which suggests that the earliest readers had pragmatic concerns. We may presume that at his death Paracelsus was supposed to have been in possession of medicines with mysterious effects. It is probable that as early as the sixteenth century a generation of physicians had grown up who could make biochemical use of Paracelsus's alchemical stimuli, and this indicates a series of usable medical formulas.[4] Nevertheless, it was only in the seventeenth century that Paracelsian medicines could be officially accepted.

The early history of the acceptance of this Paracelsian corpus need not be repeated in this context.[5] I need bring out only a few characteristic ideological features. Referring to the *Labyrinthus medicorum errantium*, which was already in print in 1553, the early Paracelsists oriented themselves on a twofold authority, embodied in the book of nature and Holy Scripture, a development in the history of ideas that continued into the eighteenth century. However, woven into the pragmatic concept a priori were also speculations from Neoplatonic tradition and religious mysticism, which were soon to give Hohenheim's system of medicine a predominantly speculative character. This is already very clear in the *Idea medicinae philosophicae* (The idea of a philosophical medicine) of Petrus Severinus, which appeared in The Hague in 1660.

The distortion of Hohenheim's influence presumably began already during his lifetime and was systematically encouraged soon after his death. The first editor of the *Opera Paracelsi*, Adam von Bodenstein, could still write in an early printing (1574): in Theophrastus of Hohenheim we find the whole corpus of medicine, the matter itself and the substance, and in *philosophia* and *medicina* the "only truth." This knowledge of the substance of medicine seems to have been lost already in the next generation. At the beginning of the seventeenth century Colberg would celebrate Paracelsus in his book *Das Platonisch-Hermetische Christentum* (1690) as the "pioneer of Platonic theology" and thus as a representative of Neoplatonism, to whom all contemporaries would refer as their teacher. Valentin Weigel speaks in 1618 of a *Theologia Paracelsi.*

In 1561 Conrad Gesner wrote to Cato von Krafftheim: "Theophrastus was certainly a wicked man and a magician, and he communicated with demons." Around the middle of the sixteenth century Paracelsus's reputation as a representative of black magic was already spreading. Thomas Erastus tersely wrote in 1572 that "Paracelsus was a magician," though he clearly distinguishes between two categories of magic: *operatrix mirabilium* (with *instrumenta* and *pharmakeia*) and *divinatrix* (with *praecatio, characteres* and *incantatio*).

In his *Testamentum Philippi Theophrasti Paracelsi* (1574), Michael Toxites, the "physician from Sterzingen," had regretfully to observe: "Much is published of Theophrastus which is not his! Why should one keep silent about that?" This skepticism resounds even more clearly in the *Wahrer Chymischer Weisheit Offenbarung* (1720) of Chymophilus, where we read: "So books of Theophrastus have been much falsified and many writings have been printed under his name which he never even thought of, far from their being the fruits of his work and ideas." Nicolaus Hunnius, who had published *Christian Consideration of the New Paracelsian and Weigelian Theology* in Wittenberg in 1622, acknowledges briefly and tersely: he regards all the matters that have been "brought into mystical philosophy" under the name of Paracelsus as inauthentic, because they did not correspond to his "Swiss-German style," so that "anyone who compares only a few lines can understand that both cannot have arisen from one author."

In view of this skepticism—and indeed uncertainty—we should remember, once again, what was printed during his lifetime: the *Intimatio,* a flysheet with an invitation to his Basel students (1527); the Guajak work and a further work on syphilis (1529/30); a tractate *Vom Bade Pfäfers* and the *Grosse Wundartzney* (1536); along with some *Practica* and *Prognosticationes,* occasional writings in the form of a calendar—all in all an extremely narrow textual foundation.

The Phase of the Great Collected Works

This sketch cannot set out to pursue the often tangled ways of the direct pupils and indirect successors of Paracelsus in chronological order or to investigate their regional branches; I shall deliberately limit myself to paradigmatic groups of themes in order to be able to mark out Hohenheim's following more clearly. Nevertheless it is important to recall the line of texts that primarily still gives a clear structure to the fabric of Paracelsism.

It was the Basel publisher Peter Perna who made a first attempt at a collected edition with a Latin edition in two volumes (*Operum latine redditorum*), of over 1,700 pages with twenty-six different works. Perna's business successor Konrad Waldkirch also published the *Cheirurgia Theophrasti Paracelsi* in 1585. A few years later, at the autumn fair of 1590, Johannes Huser, "Churfürstlich Cölnischer Rat und Medicus," was able to present the famous quarto edition in ten volumes (with about 4,800 pages). Another decade later Lazarus Zetzner in Strasbourg then published all the works of Paracelsus (medical and surgical as well as natural philosophical) in three large folio volumes (between 1603 and 1605).

Already at the end of the sixteenth century there was an increasing need to organize the terminology of Paracelsus's thought and language properly. So Hieronymus Reusner prefaced his edition *Etliche Tractate Philippi Theophrasti Paracelsi* (1582) with an explanation of the most important technical terms. Gerhard Dorn made a more systematic attempt at this with his *Lexicon Alchimiae sive dictionarium alchemisticum* (1612). The climax of these lexicographical introductions can be said to be the *Lexicon chymicum* (*Lexicon chymicum cum obscuriorum verborum, et rerum hermeticarum. Tum phrasium Paracelsicarum*) of Gulielmus Johnson (London, 1652).

The first comprehensive edition of Hohenheim's writings was therefore produced only at the end of the sixteenth century, by Johannes Huser, the Silesian physician and Princely Counsellor of Cologne, who had it printed in 1589/90 by Konrad Waldkirch in Basel. Huser explicitly mentions that here he relied on autographs in the library at Schloss Neuburg on the Danube, so we may assume this to be one of the first centers of Paracelsism.[6] In Neuburg the main figure was the librarian and book printer Hans Kilian, who went on to inspire and support the young Paracelsian trend at the court of Ottheinrich in Heidelberg, and above all the pragmatic alchemistic trend which was already associated with the name of Hohenheim. Here Paracelsus is regarded as the founder of a new science, as the hermetically enlightened *magus* and a *miraculum mundi*.[7]

Toward the end of the sixteenth century the thought of Paracelsus was first spread wider. Thus Gerhard Dorn unsuspectingly introduces parts of the pseudo-Paracelsian *Archidoxis magica* into his *Medicina coelestis sive de signis Zodiaci et mysteriis eorum* (1570). Large tracts of this astromedicine also found their way into Gerhard Dorn's *Dictionarium Theophrasti Paracelsi*

(1583). After barely a century of humanistic editions the real *Corpus Theophrasti* was no longer recognizable!

The Production of Forgeries

The distortion of Paracelsus's work became more evident with the printings in the second half of the sixteenth century, which merely made use of Paracelsus as a symbol; the language and content no longer had anything in common with the spirit of Hohenheim. This is true in exemplary fashion in the *Philosophia ad Athenienses*, which was printed in 1564. Here everything derives from the *mysterium magnum* and develops further in the alchemical process. It is precisely the structure of the thought of Theophrastus of Hohenheim, so corporeal in its transcendence, that I have attempted to describe as a concrete spirituality—that is, already completely concealed and extinguished in the "spiritualization of elemental matter."[8]

In my view the tractate *De natura rerum* (On the nature of things) must also be regarded as an explicit forgery. The first seven books of this makeshift work appeared in 1572, edited by Adam von Bodenstein, and the eighth and ninth books in 1584 from Bernhard Jobin in Strasbourg, edited by Lucas Bathodius. The ninth book, *De natura rerum*, was a particular influence on the later doctrines of signatures, that is, on Porta, Alsted, and many other physiognostics. It was from Paracelsus's *signatura rerum* that the Paracelsists created the system of a *signatura plantarum* (see the works of Porta, Croll, Schroeder, Hahnemann, Schlegel).

It is obvious that alongside printings, numerous manuscripts from the sixteenth and seventeenth centuries can also be shown to be forgeries. In passing, mention may be made of a manuscript at Wolfenbüttel (Cod. 51.3.Aug.), written shortly after 1600, which contains a *Thesaurinella naturae* (A little treasure of nature) with the subtitle *Libellus secretorum secretissimorum* (The little book of the most secret secrets) of Paracelsus, the mysteriarch, physician, philosopher, and Hermetic, in which is to be found a *mumia microcosmi*, spiritualistic *mumia, mumia* from an executed person and so on.[9]

A Vienna manuscript (Hofbibliothek 11 266) of the seventeenth century gives detailed instructions for the use of a magical bell, a "magical *arcanum*," a "secret *inventarium*," an experiment by Theophrastus in exorcism, and finally the water of paradise.[10] Also supposed to have been edited by Paracelsus are the *Magia veterum* (The magic of the ancients), with a "genial magic," an Olympian, Homeric, Sybilline, Pythagorean, Apolline, Egyptian, prophetic, and whole magic (Erlangen UB 1508).[11] Further manuscripts of the seventeenth and eighteenth centuries, including the *Magia Paracelsi* and so on, are in Copenhagen, London, Leiden, or in private collections.

A work appeared under the pseudonym of Basilius Valentinus that was soon to enjoy increasing popularity in alchemistic circles, especially because it referred back to an authority who was influential already before the lifetime of Paracelsus. Numerous individual works such as *Vom dem Grossen Stein der uralthen Weisen* (Of the great stone of the primeval sages), *Triumpf Wagen Antimonii* (Triumphal chariot of antimony, 1604), or *Offenbarung der veborgenen Handgriff* (Revelation of the hidden manipulations, 1624) are contained in *Chymische Schriften* (Chemical writings), which appeared in two volumes in 1700 in Hamburg. From the middle of the seventeenth century a flood of new impressions began with increasingly fantastic titles such as *Glücks-Rute zu Paracelsi Chymischem Schatz* (A wand to the discovery of Paracelsus's chemical treasure, 1679), *Paracelsi kleine Hand- und Denck-Bibel* (A portable Paracelsus Bible for thought, 1684), Paracelsus's *Geheimnüsse aller Geheimnüsse* (Mystery of all mysteries), or even *Paracelsische Rüst-Kammer der Gesundheit* (Paracelsus's armor of health, 1709), not to mention all the alchemical miracle books and lexica which are full of Paracelsian recipes.

Effects in the Early Modern Period

The influence of the world of Paracelsus's ideas is often woven into the history of ideas generally and also the political trends and religious movements of the seventeenth and eighteenth centuries.[12] Therefore different methods are available for an analysis of the many-sided and complicated writings of the successors and adversaries of Paracelsus: first the chronological arrangement of the most important representatives, then an account of the main trends (cosmological, chemiatrical, pharmacotechnical), and further a grouping by the decisive periods of historical development—not least attention to the particular types of regional coloring that may be found in individual works. Here I shall take a middle course, limiting myself to some paradigmatic aspects.

Any attempt to derive these complex speculations from a single principle will not go unchallenged; however, with the seventeenth century it becomes increasingly clear how—parting company with scholastic Galenism and in clear opposition to Aristotle—a line is built up which commits itself to the book of nature and thus to experience, as well as to Holy Scripture and thus to revelation, according to a synoptic guideline that attempts to do justice to the quite distinctive spirituality of the modern age.

In his tractate *Über die Zauberkräfte der Natur* (On the magical powers of nature, 1819), Karl von Eckartshausen still seeks to show "that there is perfect harmony between the spiritual and the physical." Here he finds it "quite remarkable that the truths of religion have a precise analogy with the great truths of nature." In this way nature shows us in all things "a physical savior or nature," just as religion has revealed to us "the divine savior of mankind." For Oetinger, in this sense magic was still "a power and knowledge analogous to the mysterious wisdom which God developed in creating the world." Therefore Oetinger calls magic "a knowledge of the friends of God" (*Die Theologie aus der Idee des Lebens abgeleitet* [Theology deducted from the idea of life], 185).

In what follows, I shall attempt to bring out three groups of characteristic representatives among the successors of Paracelsus, first seeking to distinguish a purely speculative Paracelsism from one with a more pragmatic trend, and then at a third level evaluating the elements and directions in a Paracelsian eclecticism.

The Beginnings of a Speculative Paracelsism

If we go more closely into the various trends of Paracelsism, in which the rational trend and a more empirical trend seem to dominate, in the last resort it emerges that all find their roots in an understanding of nature that bestows its own spirituality and religious character on the pure force of nature.

This similarly becomes clear from the "three bodies theory," which is attributed to Paracelsus. It states that the division of the microcosm occurs only in death.

> For in the death of a human being the two bodies separate, the heavenly and the earthly, i.e. the sacramental and the elemental. One flies up like an eagle and the other falls to earth like lead. The elemental body corrupts and becomes a foul corpse, is buried in the earth and no longer seen; the sacramental, that is, the heavenly and sidereal body, does not corrupt, is not buried, possesses no place; the same body appears to man, is seen after death. (XI, 361)

A fine, strong picture, but it should be noted that it comes from the book *De natura rerum*, the manuscript of which is not dated and the text of which cannot be certified. Moreover, for all the echoes of Paracelsian thought, the language is not that of Theophrastus of Hohenheim. For that reason Sudhoff already warned the reader not to take everything as valid currency![13] Here we have, rather, that "kabbalistic art" which is said to derive from the old magic, according to whose doctrine at death the three bodies separate and return to their origins: "the earthly body again to the *prima materia elementorum*, the soul to the *prima materia sacramentorum*, the spirit in turn to the *prima materia* of the chaos of air" (XI, 361).

6. A picture of Paracelsus from *In Cruce cum Sphaera*, 16th or early 17th century German, in the Collection of Alchemy Bibliography (MS. 230c).

An impressive example of this kind of speculative Paracelsism is the term *astrum*, which served as a popular model for Paracelsus's worldview and could also be extremely useful to us in distinguishing between the "authentic" and the "inauthentic" elements of Hohenheim's thought. Over against the Neoplatonic tradition, according to which the spiritual quintessence of humankind derives from the stars, in Paracelsus we find the clear and often repeated observation that astrology cannot say anything about human beings unless it incorporates the "inner heaven" into all prognostic considerations (VII, 466). From the stars as such only a "little spark" enters the sublunary sphere; it is quickly extinguished and cannot exercise any influence on human beings (IX, 241). These remarks stand in clear opposition to the *astronomia magna* which is constantly adduced; it is certainly wrongly attributed to Paracelsus, although as a "system of universal knowledge" it has become a thing of inestimable significance.[14]

The *astronomia magna* is divided into "four orders," which already stand in clear contradiction to Paracelsus's theory of disease. As *naturalis astronomia* it shows the influence of the firmament on the sidereal body; as *supera* it serves the new birth to a spiritual life (XII, 76); as *astronomia olympi novi* it shows the true faith; and as *astronomia inferiorum* it reveals the infernal powers (XII, 76). But the *astrologus* should and can recognize the *summum motorem naturae;* for the stars and human beings are "of equal capacity" (XII, 90). By means of the *signum signatum*, human beings will first learn the *virtutes* and thus arrive at real *inventiones* (XII, 99). In this way the magician becomes the ruler of nature: "Thus it is given to its natural saints, as magicians are called, to do violence to nature, its power and capacity" (XII, 130). Now the physician also gains this power over nature: "Where the astronomer ends, there the true physician begins, there the true philosopher begins" (XII, 77). But this also gives the physician control of all the mantic disciplines subordinated to *astronomia;* the physician is to investigate and control all that "lies secretly in nature" (XII, 185).

The parallel between macrocosm and microcosm nowhere seems so impressively "carried through in detail and exploited"[15] as in Paracelsus's *Astronomia*, which according to Pagel is one of the supporting pillars in the system of medicine. By contrast, in the *Labyrinthus* Paracelsus speaks only of the *Concordanz anatomiae* as a parallel to both fabrications, the *machina mundi* and the *physicum corporis* (XI, 183). It is hardly evident from this that Paracelsus alone is "close to the mystics," as Pagel thinks.[16] *Astronomia* is "the mother of all arts" only because it shows that life in all worldly things which then can be recognized in the light of nature. Even Pagel, who makes such efforts—though predominantly on the basis of inauthentic texts—to present Paracelsus as a nature mystic, has to concede that the specifically gnostic ideas derive predominantly from those "deutero-Paracelsian" writings that should be attributed to one of the later generations of speculative Paracelsism. Obviously the ideas about natural philosophy in Paracelsus's work as a whole must also be seen in their relationship to the theosophical and cosmological ideas of the Renaissance. However, in that case specific texts must always form the starting point and must be used critically. The intensive connections between Paracelsus's worldview on the one hand and the Neoplatonic traditions and a contemporary gnosticism on the other should not be overlooked. Walter Pagel in particular already drew attention to these interrelationships in 1962.[17]

Beyond question, links with traditional Hermeticism can be established wherever in Paracelsus there is talk of the parallel between the macrocosm and the microcosm, where the spiritual is played off against the earthly or the body against the soul, and where the invisible is said to be manifested in the visible. Such attempts are less convincing when the topic of discussion is a specific concept like the Neoplatonic concept of matter, the *logoi spermatikoi* of the gnostic tradition, the doctrine of the three principles or the mutual interpenetration of the light of nature and the light of grace.

By contrast, in more recent research into Paracelsus, historical attention has focused above all on the alchemical legacy of Neoplatonism in the thinking of Paracelsus. Here surprising insights have been gained into the therapeutic character of late medieval alchemy, a "medical alchemy" to which Paracelsus's theory of the arcane also made significant contributions. This could lead to Johann Heinrich Alsted's being able to include "alchemy" as a "part of medicine" in an encyclopedia as early as 1630.

It is more difficult to trace the alleged analogies to gnosticism where they are associated with historical figures; here careful comparisons ought to be made by means of specific texts. This is the case with Agrippa of Nettesheim and with Marsilio Ficino, but also with Hildegard of Bingen (1099–1180) or Arnald of Villanova (1235–1311) and not least with Nicholas of Cusa (1401–1464).

Here a methodological precept which Walter Pagel and Marianne Winder have used with Paracelsus is of special interest, a pattern of thought that is bound up with the question whether doctrines characteristic of the Renaissance naturalists (like Pico, Zorzi, and Agrippa) concerning the differences between "higher" and "lower" elements cannot also be applied to Paracelsus.[18] However, this reference loses significance if writings that are in all probability inauthentic (like *De vita longa*) are set alongside the "authentic" writings (like *Labyrinthus*).

With the sixteenth century, the *magia naturalis* increasingly abandoned its epistemological foundation and became a rapidly vulgarized *magia artificialis* which could as yet hardly adapt itself to the methods and progress of the natural sciences. Then the "mechanization of the world-picture" in the course of the seventeenth century fully demonstrated those regularities of nature that could no longer be harmonized with magical thought. Already in the seventeenth and eighteenth centuries the *magia naturalis* was regarded more as a quarry for esoteric societies.

The Basic Outlines of Pragmatic Paracelsism

Alongside the speculative tendencies of the Paracelsists of the sixteenth and seventeenth centuries is a more pragmatic feature, in which the positive or even polemical aspects emerge more clearly. There are evident attempts at a synthesis, though it does not seem possible to assign the individual representatives clearly to particular positions in each instance. Numerous sixteenth-century authors were already making efforts to arrive at a theoretical balance between the Galenists and the Paracelsists, for example, Daniel Sennert (1572–1637) in his work *De chymicorum cum Aristotelicis et Galenicis consensu et dissensu* (On agreements and disagreements of chemists with Aristotelians and Galenians); this was done above all by Johann Baptist van Helmont (1577–1644), deliberately taking forward the thought of Paracelsus.

Certainly there are still clear echoes of Hohenheim's basic concepts and aims in van Helmont's vitalistic pathology, and he also makes use of Paracelsian medical material in his prescriptions. Nevertheless, here we are already in a transitional period between the chemiatric trend and that iatrochemical trend which was very soon represented in exemplary form by Franz de la Boë, called Sylvius (1644–1672). Here at a very early stage— with the application of chemical-physical methods to biology and pathology—there developed a humoral pathology on a fermentative basis. But on all sides Paracelsus served as key witness, though hardly with justification, for this "new chemistry," which developed a "chemical philosophy" from simple "alchemy."[19]

As early as the seventeenth century the Arab physician Ibn Sallum could write a medical book, *Gāyat al-itqān*, in which he evaluated the "new chemistry" of Paracelsus. In it, after a general explanation of alchemy, we read: "But then came the German Paracelsus; he gave the art of chemistry a new aim and made it part of the art of medicine and in Latin called it Spagyria. That means 'collection and distribution of the differences.' This expression specifically applies to the art of chemical medicine."[20] "Barakalsus" is here already praised as "the supreme master of the new chemical medicine."

The purpose of the universal medicine that is of interest to us here is described by Johann Friedrich Helvetius, an alchemist of the seventeenth century, in an artistic dialogue between an *Elias Artista* and the *Medicus*. The question is why most people must prematurely "go from the most sweet light of this realm into the dark earth of the dying," and whether there is no means of "restoring health to the mortal body of man" and thus preserving life "to the fatal terminus," that is, death.

Here the alchemist praises the physician for that "medicinal nectar" which no "Galenic cure" and no "Paracelsian tincture" is in a position to provide. However, the *medicus* cannot believe in such a universal medicine because he is too well aware of the elementary structure of the organism and the four temperaments which derive from it, which determine all disease and therefore change every cure. Moreover, in any medical intervention one has to take account of a person's age, sex, particular constitution and disposition, "and many other circumstances," which all in turn must surpass the "effect of the universal medicine, however miraculous."

Over against this popular view of the physicians, the alchemist Elias can refer to the distinctive *modus operandi* of this universal medicine and the great difference between it and "particular medicament," which merely affects elements and temperaments. By contrast the "universal medicine" renews the nobler *spiritus vitales*, not the banal composition of juices; it is therefore in a special harmony and sympathy with the totality of the body, that *integritas* which in turn is none other than a picture of health. Now with the refreshing of the spirits of life the health which has been suppressed is again revived: therefore universal medicine is "the most splendid preservative," a guarantee of precaution and protection against all diseases.

In 1582 a tractate *Pandora* appeared from Samuel Apiario in Basel with this subtitle:

> That is the noblest gift of God, or the precious and wholesome philosophers' stone with which the philosophers of old including Theophrastus Paracelsus improved the base metals through the power of fire; and drove out all kind of damaging and unwholesome diseases, internal and external. A golden treasure, which has been saved from destruction, and is of use to all men, primarily the lovers of Paracelsian physic.[21]

Similarly, the *Arcana Paracelsi* are described in the *Rosarium novum olympicum et benedictum* of Benedictus Figulus (Basel, 1608) under the title *De lapide philosophorum* (On the Philosophers' Stone) (p. 23).

The pragmatic way in which the alchemical procedures of the Paracelsists are dealt with here can be demonstrated pragmatically by means of a further basic concept, the use of *magia* and *magica*. To the question What is magic? the following succinct answer is given: "It is that which can bring heavenly power into the medium and perform its operation in the same. The medium is the center, the center is man" (XII, 122). In this way, for example, it becomes possible to "introduce the *vires* of the firmament into man!"

Only "magic" teaches us that God does not want anything to remain hidden or secret. Rather, all things in nature are to become manifest and capable of being experienced (XII, 123). "Therefore so must magic be because of revelation." It alone reveals nature. "Many people judge the magic art and speak of it as a drunken and full dream, that is, they recognize its own deception and error. Who will follow them? Magic is a splendid thing and great in its works" (XII, 131). So anyone who wants to be "a medicus and an Apollo" cannot be taught by men (XII, 191). "For magic is only to be understood as a supreme physic, which acts only from the firmament and in the firmament, whether naturally or supernaturally" (XII, 135).

There seems to me to be a clear reference here to the Paracelsism that diverges from Paracelsus in the mention of the natural and supernatural firmament, of a tellurian and a celestial body, of the two lights of nature, and of an *opus magnum,* which ultimately seeks to fight for the liberation of the soul from its body. This picture certainly preserves the basic cosmological idea, but the theories of sympathy and antipathy in the universe are already being interpreted in the most varied ways. The criticism of Galen's humoral pathology is developed further; here on the one hand there are closer approximations to localized concepts, prompted by the theory of the three principles, and on the other hand far-reaching functionalistic dynamic consequences, floated by the Archaeus principle. It may be significant that a trend toward the pragmatic use of medical knowledge was connected with this. This is suggested not only by improvements in technological procedures and thus the effective exploitation of the *materia medica,* but also by application in individual therapeutic spheres, for example, in venereal diseases. This can clearly be seen in Joseph Duchesne's (Quercetanus) *De Signaturis Rerum* (1613).

Marsilio Ficino is also in line with this iatromagical concept; he interprets *magia naturalis* as the art of knowing the properties of natural things and making use of them in medicine or manticism. For Agrippa of Nettesheim in this sense magicians become *naturae accuratissime exploratores:* magic is a partial sphere of *philosophia naturalis.*[22]

Finally, with Oswald Croll's *Basilica chymica* (1609) we have an early standard work of chemiatry that was constantly supplemented and deepened. With reference to Paracelsus it stresses that all prescriptions must be tested "through fire," that is, experimentally. Oswald Croll (ca. 1560–ca.

1609) finally worked at the court of the emperor Rudolf II in Prague, where he wrote his *Basilica chymica*, a comprehensive textbook and handbook. The first part acknowledges the principles of Paracelsian medicine; the second part gives prescriptions; and the third part is a developed theory of signatures based on Hohenheim.

The new direction is clearer in Johannes Hartmann (1568–1631), professor of rhetoric and mathematics in Marburg, where in 1611 he was given the first chair of "chymiatry" and created a practical laboratory for the young doctors. His *Praxis chymiatrica* appeared in 1633, and in 1634 he wrote a commentary on Croll's *Basilica chymica*, thus making it for the first time a standard work of chemical prescriptions.

Then with the seventeenth century there began a deep conceptual distinction between the "cosmos" as the vision of an ordered totality and the "world" (*mundus*) as a universe to be experienced. Finally, in Francis Bacon's *Novum organum* the experiment, as a "deliberate experience," is clearly distinguished from any chance empirical observations; however, the guideline in the construction of the new experiential knowledge still remains nature with its purposeful action. Even in Vico the greater effectiveness of human nature is seen in this *magia naturalis*, a many-layered matrix of human designs, and thus the central focus of human formation, the field of all culture.

Paracelsian Eclecticism

Numerous followers of Paracelsus had already struggled at an early stage for a methodological and ideological balance by incorporating the elements of the new as much as possible into the proven traditions. Beyond all speculative outlines and the pragmatic stance is a group of eclectics who tried critically to combine the proven old with the innovations they had made. Here the "alchemical" trend—this time in the Paracelsian sense—not only forms the basis of the new medicine but also provides the key to the other natural sciences. Observation and attempt provide the basis for this; the stricter mathematical-experimental method is still largely left out of account.

Conrad Gesner (1516–1565), one of the last of the great universal scholars, certainly dissociated himself from the unsteady course of Theophrastus of Hohenheim but then went on to stress: "However, I hear that on all sides he cured many who were hopelessly ill and healed malignant tumors. He understood chemistry, with the help of which he prepared cordials, juices and oils—above all from antimony—and other wonderful medicines" (*Chirurgia* [Zurich, 1555] f. 408r).

The work of Hermann Conringius, *De caldo innato sive igne animali* (On innate warmth or animal fire [Helmestadii, 1647]), is somewhat more differentiated. It was followed shortly by the tractate *De hermetica Aegyptiorum vetere et Paracelsicorum nova medicina* (Helmestadii, 1648). After a look back to the *Hermetica medicina* of the Egyptians, the history of a medicine with an alchemical orientation and magical practice, Conring builds his *nova medicina* on the following four pillars: *theologia, naturalis philosophia, astrologia,* and *magia.* We find interesting comparisons with *Paracelsica medicina* and its characteristic theory of disease, according to which the five *entia* are seen as the specific causes of illness (see p. 195, de quinque entibus [ita appellat causas efficientes] morborum). Finally Conring arrives at a critical comparison between the hermetic cures (minerals, magical procedures) and the traditional cures (knowledge of plants).

For Johannes Otto Helbigius, too, with his *Introitus in veram et inauditam physicam* (Entry into a genuine and unheard-of physics [Heidelberg, 1680]), *physica,* as the total knowledge of nature and the knowledge of healing, is a kind of iatromagic in which the controversy with Paracelsus already has clearly rational features, as when we read: Chimia incepi; multum per medicam adjutus sum praxim. Here we already find the foretaste of the concept of a *chimia medica,* which is, however, still incorporated in a universal theory of the elements.

Paracelsus had said that each body consists of three things: "The names of these things, then, are sulphur, mercury and salt. These three are put together, and then it is called a *corpus.*" From this philosophical insight human beings have started on something the end of which is not yet in sight. For only now does the creative process make its way through the elements of the world and take its course to the consummation of nature. For this, fire is the prime element in nature, through its influence pouring fiery rays into the seeds of the air. Mixed with the seeds of the air, fire hurls itself into water which, as it were made pregnant, in turn sinks its own seeds in the earth.

With these principles, through the mixing of the elements and through such an elemental process, there finally arises that healing power of nature which is rooted in the idea of healing nature and comes to blossom and fruition in the art of healing. From this there arises the universal balsam and mercury of the world, which includes within itself the *tria principia* as salt, sulphur, and mercury. Sulphur is made of the seeds of heaven and air; salt of the seeds of water and earth. From salt and fire there comes into being, in an ultimate combination, the tincture which is also called "balsam" or "universal medicine."

Numerous other sixteenth- and seventeenth-century tractates belong in this strand of tradition. Mention need be made only of the *Coelum philosophicum seu De secretis naturae Liber* (The philosophical heaven, or Book of the secrets of nature) of Philippus Ulstadius from Nuremberg (Strasbourg, 1529), where with Pseudo-Geber there is mention of *magisterium* and how art can lead *ad sanitatem et ad naturam meliorum* (to the health and to the true nature of the best) (p. 58^r). As the *activa portio scientiae naturalis,* Wecker (1582) also promises the achievement of health, happiness, and power, when in his *Magia operatrix* he develops the whole technique of analogies in a magical picture of the world full of correspondences. Metals and minerals, like plants, are emanations of the elemental matter of the macrocosm and are therefore therapeutically akin. So black lead, the primal material of metal, is an emanation from the planet Saturn. Just as the suffering organism is a battlefield of cosmic forces, so it is healed by the same forces. In this connection mention should also be made of the *Magna Alchymia* (1536) of the controversial Paracelsist Leonhard Thurneysser zum Thurn (1531-1596), who managed to combine his theoretical knowledge of the work of Paracelsus with his own practical skills.[23] Thurneysser made use of largely quantitative methods in the expectation of discovering new and better medicines than were available to the Galenic *materia medica.*

Andreas Libavius (1550-1616) can be regarded as the most important representative of such a creative eclecticism; like Duchesne (1603) he defended with great energy not only the new remedies but the chemiatric method. With his *Alchimia* he produced a first handbook of the new chemiatric trend. In his *Alchymia triumphans* (1607) Libavius put forward the view that in the future a wise physician would follow neither the foolish paths of the Galenists nor the heightened mysticisms of the Paracelsists, but rather would rely on experience methodically marked out beforehand.

Mention should be made of one of Paracelsus's last followers—already in the middle of the eighteenth century—Samuel Richter, who called himself Renatus Sincerus, and above all of his *Theo-philosophia theoretico-practica,* which appeared in Breslau in 1711 and was included in the complete edition of his works in 1741. Renatus Sincerus stands wholly in the tradition of the "hermetic art," as is already clear from his first work *The True and Perfect Preparation of the Philosophical Stone* (1709).[24]

This art is practiced in the outside world by Vulcan and within the organism by Archaeus. Thus, Paracelsus writes, "nature must be made to show itself," namely, in human beings. Whereas the quest was previously more for an ordering of the structures of the living which was sought in both nature and history, so now there is increasingly a quest for the ordering of processes. This ordering is given us by the third pillar of medicine, alchemy, "nature in Vulcan," which, as Paracelsus said, must be the master of us all (IX, 44), our inner physician.

In his *Theo-philosophia theoretico-practica*, Renatus Sincerus, alias Samuel Richter, can still write in 1711: "The Archaeus is only the Medicus; if he does not help himself the medicament will be in vain." Now only in the fiery process does the medicament become a "pure tincture from paradise," a universal medicine, the "natural savior" which we have to form in the "philosopher's stone." Here too the ultimate concern is not with pragmatic procedures and remedies but with the anthropological medium which human beings must find in themselves. "By nature" therefore always means simply "Know thyself." This principle is described in more detail in chapter XII with the title "In what the origin of human sicknesses consists, and how they are generated in the human body. At the same time how the same can be removed by a physician both universally and also in particular."

The process of sickness appears to be analogous to birth, or more precisely, to be a series of monstrosities. The presupposition of the process of birth is the copulation in which two come together to "image," to impress themselves, in order for a third to arise. The other, a *contradictorium* or opposition, is understood to be feminine, and intercourse is a pulling and a struggling, a going under and a swallowing up, a compaction and coagulation, from which follows pregnancy. Birth, as the third item, is then union experienced as corporeality or "bodily fashioning," as "temperance." On the basis of such a primal biological experience, at the end of his *Theo-philosophia* Richter finally summons the reader: "To nature! To nature! Without its manifest guidance no one will arrive at the truth."

Critical Summary

In this inevitably sketchy survey, before I ventured on to Paracelsus's successors I deliberately started from an account of Paracelsus's world and anthropology as documented in the role of the physician, the system of medicine and the effect of the *arcana*. After that we first looked at the complicated cultural trends that are—quite wrongly—associated with the name of Paracelsism. Already at the end of the seventeenth century, as we saw, the question of the historical Paracelsus was no longer raised; it is the art of the *Paracelsicorum* which is everywhere dominant, just as around the turn of the century it is almost impossible to separate "Hermeticism" from its traditional origins.

We would therefore be well advised not to be too hasty in presenting an account of Paracelsus's thought and activity but to be more intensively concerned with any author who with more or less justification appeals to

Paracelsus. In the analysis of any text we should distinguish more clearly between "Paracelsus" and the Paracelsists than is done in the modern history of science. "Paracelsism" in the sense of a classification in the theory of science should be used only with the utmost reserve.

From Paracelsus there merely emanated an impulse to go on to apply chemical conceptions to the life process. These conceptions were largely rooted in an archaic medieval cosmology and provided a model that could be neither falsified nor rectified with the working methods of the time. Paracelsus in no way prepared for the methods and insights of the new natural science; rather, it was the ideas, the stimuli, the impulses associated with the name Paracelsus that were of further influence over subsequent centuries.

We may expect to find in the figure of Paracelsus neither a prototype of the "new science" nor an offshoot of authoritative medieval doctrines. Theophrastus of Hohenheim went his own way, and he could not be understood or explained by his "successors." On this point we can only agree with Walter Pagel when he says "Paracelsus stands before us as a cosmos of his own, to which there are no forerunners and no successors."[25]

What were transplanted into the eighteenth century and there developed further in a stormy fashion were above all the traditions of classical hermetics—alongside medicine and alchemy, not least also mysticism. Reference need be made only to Jacob Boehme, the Rosicrucians, theosophy, and other gnostic trends of completely independent spirituality—an extremely characteristic and uncommonly fascinating development, but one that cannot be dealt with here.

Translated by John Bowden

Notes

1. The life and work of Theophrastus von Hohenheim, who later called himself Paracelsus, have often been described. See Karl Sudhoff, *Paracelsus: Ein deutsches Lebensbild aus den Tagen der Renaissance* (Leipzig: Bibliograph. Institut, 1936); Ildefons Betschart, *Theophrastus Paracelsus: Der Mensch an der Zeitenwende* (Einsiedeln, 1942); Otto Zekert, *Paracelsus* (Stuttgart: Kohlhammer, 1968); H. Schipperges, *Paracelsus: Das Abenteuer einer sokratischen Existenz* (1983). Theophrastus Bombastus (Philippus Aureolus) von Hohenheim, ps. Paracelsus, was born in Einsiedeln (Switzerland) at the end of 1493 or at the beginning of 1494. He was the son of a physician and studied medicine in Ferrare. After having been granted the title of Doctor in 1515, he took part in various campaigns as a military physician. Between 1524 and 1527 he practiced in Salzburg and Strasbourg. In 1527 he was nominated Professor of Medicine at the university. But he was compelled to leave that town too, in 1528, because of the hostility of his colleagues. They reproached him for teaching in German (instead of Latin), and above all they were frightened by his courageous endeavors to reform medicine:

he publicly criticized the traditional ancient "authorities" (Hippocrates, Galen, Avicenna) and taught that a concrete, experimental study of the human body was more appropriate for the advancement of a genuine science. After leaving Basel, Paracelsus practiced in various towns in Germany and Switzerland until 1540. That year, he was offered by Bishop Ernst von Wittelsbach a position in Salzburg, which he accepted, but he died there shortly after, on September 2, 1541.

2. See W. F. Daems, "'Sal-Merkur-Sulfur' bei Paracelsus und das 'Buch der Heiligen Dreifaltigkeit,'" *Nova Acta Paracelsica* (1982) 189–207.

3. Kurt Goldammer, "Zur philosophischen und religiösen Sinngebung von Heilung und Heilsmittel bei Paracelsus," in *Perspektiven der Pharmaziegeschichte*, ed. Peter Dilg, 113–29.

4. See W. Schneider, *Mein Umgang mit Paracelsus*.

5. See K. Sudhoff, *Bibliographia Paracelsica;* W. Pagel, *Paracelsus: An Introduction to Philosophical Medicine in the Era of the Renaissance;* Allen G. Debus, "The Medico-Chemical World of the Paracelsians," in *Changing Perspectives in the History of Science*, ed. M. Teich and R. Young, 85–99; idem, *The Chemical Philosophy: Paracelsian Science and Medicine in the Sixteenth and Seventeenth Centuries*.

6. This is attested also by other sources; see Joachim Telle, "Killian, Ottheinrich and Paracelsus," *Heidelberger Jahrbücher* 18 (1974) 37–49.

7. Ibid., 49.

8. Kurt Goldammer, "Die Paracelsische Kosmologie und Materietheorie in ihrer wissenschaftsgeschichtlichen Stellung und Eigenart," *Medhis J* 6 (1971) 5–35.

9. See Karl Sudhoff, *Versuch einer Kritik der Echtheit der paracelsischen Schriften* 2:658f.

10. Ibid. 2:672f.

11. Ibid. 2:679f.

12. For England, see, e.g., Allen G. Debus, "The Paracelsian Compromise in Elizabethan England," *Ambix* 8 (1960) 71–97; P. R. Rattansi, "Paracelsus and the Puritan Revolution," *Ambix* 11 (1963) 24–32; etc.

13. Sudhoff, *Versuch einer Kritik der Echtheit*, XXIII.

14. Goldammer, "Die Paracelsische Kosmologie und Materietheorie in ihrer wissenschaftsgeschichtlichen Stellung und Eigenart," *Medhist J* 6 (1971) 5–35.

15. Walter Pagel, "Paracelsus als 'Naturmystiker,'" in *Epochen der Naturmystik*, ed. A. Faivre and R. C. Zimmermann, 52–104.

16. Ibid., 55.

17. Walter Pagel, *Das medizinische Weltbild des Paracelsus*.

18. Walter Pagel and Marianne Winder, "Die Konjunktion der himmlischen und irdischen Elemente in der Renaissancephilosophie und im echten Paracelsus," in *Paracelsus, Werk und Wirkung*, ed. S. Domandl, 187–204.

19. Allen G. Debus, *The Chemical Philosophy*.

20. Manfred Ullmann, *Die Medizin im Islam* (Leiden: Brill, 1970) 182–83.

21. Sudhoff, *Bibliographia Paracelsica*.

22. See Wolf-Dieter Müller-Jahncke, "Von Ficino zu Agrippa: Der Magia-Begriff des Renaissance-Humanismus in Überblick," in *Epochen der Naturmystik*, ed. F. Zimmermann, 24–51.

23. See Wolfgang Schneider, *Mein Umgang mit Paracelsus*.

24. See Rolf Christian Zimmermann, *Das Weltbild des jungen Goethe*, 105–28.

25. Walter Pagel, "Gedanken zur Paracelsus-Forschung und zu van Helmont," in *Paracelsus in der Tradition*, 18.

Bibliography

Sources

Agrippa, Henricus Cornelius. *De occulta philosophia. Libri Tres.* Cologne, 1533.

Boyle, Robert. *The Sceptical Chemist.* London, 1661.

Conring, Hermann. *De hermetica Aegyptiorum vetere et Paracelsicorum nova medicina.* Helmestadii, 1648.

Croll, Oswald. *Basilica Chymica.* 1609. Edited by J. Hartmann. Geneva, 1643.

Deutsches Theatrum Chemicum. Edited by Friedrich Roth-Scholz. 3 vols. Nuremberg, 1928–1732.

Duchesne, Joseph [Quercetanus]. *Liber de priscorum philosophorum verae medicinae materia . . . .* Leipzig, 1613.

——. *Traicté de la Matière: Preparation et excellente vertu de la Medecine balsamique des Anciens Philosophes.* Paris, 1626.

Erastus, Thomas. *Disputationum de medicina nova Paracelsi.* 2 vols. Basel, 1572.

——. *De Astrologia divinatrice Epistolae.* Basel, 1580.

Fludd, Robert. *Medicina catholica seu mysticum artis medicandi sacrarium.* Frankfurt, 1629.

——. *Utriusque Cosmi Metaphysica.* Oppenheim, 1617.

——. *Utriusque Mundi Historia.* Frankfurt, 1621.

Fontanus, Jacobus. "*Magiae Paracelsicae Detectio.*" In *Opera*, 313–25. Cologne, 1612.

Gesner, Conrad. *Bibliotheca universalis.* Zurich, 1545.

Helmont, Johannes Baptist van. *Ortus medicinae: Id est initia physicae inaudita.* Amsterdam, 1648. Lugduni, 1655.

Libavius, Andreas. *Alchemia.* Frankfurt, 1597.

Maier, Michael. *Atalanta Fugiens.* Oppenheim, 1618.

Manget, J. J., ed. *Bibliotheca chemica curiosa.* 2 vols. Geneva, 1702.

Pfaff, J. W. *Astrologie.* Nuremberg, 1816.

Sennert, Daniel. *De chymicorum cum Aristotelicis et Galenicis consensu ac dissensu.* Wittenberg, 1619.

Severinus, Petrus. *Idea Medicinae Philosophicae.* Basel, 1571.

Suavius, Leo [Jacques Gohory]. *Theophrasti Paracelsi philosophiae et medicinae utriusque universae compendium.* Basel, 1568.

Sylvius, Franciscus de la Boë. *Opera medica.* Amsterdam, 1680.

Tannstetter, Georg. *Artificium de applicatione Astrologiae ad Medicinam.* Edited by Otto Brunfels. Strassburg, 1531.

Theophrastus von Hohenheim [Paracelsus]. *Sämtliche Werke: 1. Abt. Medizinische, naturwissenschaftliche und philosophische Schriften.* Edited by Karl Sudhoff. 14 vols. Munich and Berlin, 1922–1933.

Virdung, Johannes. *Novae medicinae Methodus curandi morbos ex mathematica sententia.* Hagenau, 1533.

Wiegleb, Johann Christian. *Historisch-kritische Untersuchung der Alchemie, oder der eingebildeten Goldmacherkunst.* Weimar, 1777.

——. *Geschichte des Wachsthums und der Erfindungen in der Chemie der neuern Zeit.* Berlin and Stettin, 1790.

Studies

Achelis, Johann Daniel. *Die Überwindung der Alchemie in der Paracelsischen Medizin.* Sitzungsberichte der Heidelberger Akademie der Wissenschaften 1942. Heidelberg, 1943.

Boas, Marie. *Robert Boyle and Seventeenth-Century Chemistry.* Cambridge, 1958.

Daems, Willem Frans. "'Sal-Merkur-Sulfur' bei Paracelsus und das 'Buch der Heiligen Dreifaltigkeit.'" *Nova Acta Paracelsica* (1982) 189–207.

Debus, Allen G. *The Chemical Philosophy: Paracelsian Science and Medicine in the Sixteenth and Seventeenth Centuries.* 2 vols. New York, 1977.

——. *Chemistry, Alchemy, and the New Philosophy (1150–1700).* Aldershot, Hampshire, 1987.

——. *The English Paracelsians.* London, 1965.

——. *The French Paracelsians: The Chemical Challenge to Medical and Scientific Tradition in Early Modern France.* Cambridge University Press, 1991.

——. "The Medico-Chemical World of the Paracelsians." In *Changing Perspectives in the History of Science,* edited by M. Teich and R. Young, 85–99. London, 1973.

——. "The Paracelsian Compromise in Elizabethan England." *Ambix* 8 (1960) 71–97.

——. "The Paracelsians and the Chemists: The Chemical Dilemma in Renaissance Medicine." *Clio Medica* 7 (1972) 185–99.

——. "Solution Analyses Prior to Robert Boyle." *Chymia* 8 (1962) 41–61.

Dilge-Frank, Rosemarie, ed. *Kreatur und Kosmos: Internationale Beiträge zur Paracelsus Forschung.* Stuttgart, 1981.

Eis, Gerhard. *Vor und nach Paracelsus: Untersuchungen über Hohenheims Traditionsverbundenheit und Nachrichten über seine Anhänger.* Stuttgart, 1965.

Faivre, Antoine, and Christian Zimmermann, eds. *Epochen der Naturmystik: Hermetische Tradition im wissenschaftlichen Fortschritt.* Berlin, 1979.

Faivre, Antoine, and Fréderick Tristan, eds. *Lumière et cosmos: Courants occultes de la philosophie de la Nature.* Paris, 1981.

——. *Paracelse.* Paris, 1980.

Figala, Karin. *Die "Kompositionshierarchie" der Materie: Newtons quantitative Theorie und Interpretation der qualitativen Alchemie.* Habilitationschrift (typescript), Munich, 1977.

Fischer, Hans. "Die kosmologische Anthropologie des Paracelsus als Grundlage seiner Medizin." In *Verhandlungen der naturforschenden Gesellschaft Basel* 52 (1940–41) 267–317.

Freudenberg, F. *Paracelsus und Fludd: Die beiden grossen Okkultisten und Ärzte des 15. und 16. Jahrhunderts. Mit einer Auswahl aus ihren okkulten Schriften.* 2nd ed. Berlin, 1921.

García Ballester, Luis. *Historia social de la medicina en la España de los siglos XIII al XVI.* Madrid, 1976.

Garin, Eugenio. "Magia e astrologia nel pensiero del Rinascimento." *Medievo e Rinascimento* (1954).

Goldammer, Kurt. "Die Paracelsische Kosmologie und Materietheorie in ihrer wissenschaftsgeschichtlichen Stellung und Eigenart." *Medhist J* 6 (1971) 5–35.

——. *Sozialethische und sozialpolitische Schriften.* Tübingen, 1952.

——. "Zur philosophischen und religiösen Sinngebung von Heilung und Heilmittel bei Paracelsus." In *Perspektiven der Pharmaziegeschichte,* edited by Peter Dilg, 113–29. Graz, 1983.

Goltz, Dietlinde. "Alchemie und Aufklärung: Ein Beitrag zur Naturwissenschafts-geschichtsschreibung der Aufklärung." *Medhist J* 7 (1972) 31–48.

———. "Naturmystik und Naturwissenschaft um 1600." *Sudhoffs Archiv* 60 (1976) 45–83.

———. "Die Paracelsisten und die Sprache." *Sudhoffs Archiv für Geschichte der Medizin und Naturwissenschaft* 56 (1972) 337–52.

Hoykaas, Reijer. "Die chemische Verbindung bei Paracelsus." *Sudhoffs Archiv* 32 (1939) 166–75.

Jung, Carl Gustav. *Psychology and Alchemy*. London, 1953.

———. "Studies on Alchemistic Conceptions." In *Collected Works*, vol.13. London, 1957.

Kämmerer, Ernst Wilhelm. *Das Leib-Seele-Geist-Problem bei Paracelsus und einigen Autoren des 17. Jahrhunderts*. Wiesbaden, 1971.

Koelbing, H. M. "Paracelsus." *Schweizerische Rundschau für Medizin* 71 (1982) 1973–1976.

———. "Vom Paracelsus zur Labormedizin," *Schweizerische Zeitschrift für med.tech Laborfachpersonal* 8 (1981) 1–17.

Mahnke, Dietrich. *Unendliche Sphäre und Allmittelpunkt: Beiträge zur Genealogie der mathematischen Mystik*. Halle, 1937.

Mathias, P., ed. *Science and Society: 1600–1900*. Cambridge, 1972.

Müller, K., H. Schepers, and W. Totok, eds. *Magia Naturalis und die Entstehung der modernen Naturwissenschaften*. Studia Leibnitiana, Sonderheft 7. Wiesbaden, 1978.

Müller-Jahncke, Wolf-Dieter. *Astrologisch-magische Theorie und Praxis in der Heilkunde der frühen Neuzeit*. Habilitationsschrift, Marburg, 1982.

———. *Magie als Wissenschaft im frühen 16. Jahrhundert: Die Beziehungen zwischen Magie, Medizin und Pharmazie im Werk des Agrippa von Nettesheim (1486–1535)*. Marburg, 1973.

———. "Von Ficino zu Agrippa: Der Magia-Begriff des Renaissance-Humanismus im Überblick." In *Epochen der Naturmystik*, edited by A. Faivre and R. C. Zimmermann, 24–51. Berlin, 1979.

Multhauf, Robert. "Medical Chemistry and the Paracelsians." *Bulletin of the History of Medicine* 28 (1954) 101–26.

———. *The Origins of Chemistry*. London, 1966.

Pagel, Walter. *From Paracelsus to Van Helmont: Studies in Renaissance Medicine and Science*, ed. Marianne Winder. London, 1985.

———. *Johannes Baptist van Helmont: Einführung in die philosophische Medizin des Barock*. Berlin, 1930.

———. "Gedanken zur Paracelsus-Forschung und zu van Helmont." In *Paracelsus in der Tradition*, Salzburger Beiträge zur Paracelsusforschung 21 (1980) 11–19.

———. *Das medizinische Weltbild des Paracelsus: Seine Zusammenhänge mit Neuplatonismus und Gnosis*. Wiesbaden, 1962.

———. "The Paracelsian Elias Artista and the Alchemical Tradition." *Med.hist.J* 16 (1981) 6–19.

———. "Paracelsus als 'Naturmystiker.'" In *Epochen der Naturmystik*, edited by A. Faivre and R. C. Zimmermann, 52–104. Berlin, 1979.

———. "Paracelsus and the Neoplatonic and Gnostic Tradition." *Ambix* 8 (1960) 125–66.

———. *Paracelsus: An Introduction to Philosophical Medicine in the Era of the Renaissance*. Basel and New York, 1958.

———. *Religion and Neoplatonism in Renaissance Medicine*, ed. Marianne Winder. London, 1985.

———. *The Smiling Spleen: Paracelsianism in Storm and Stress*. Basel and Munich, 1984.

———, and Marianne Winder. "Die Konjunktion der himmlischen und irdischen Elemente in der Renaissancephilosophie und im echten Paracelsus." In *Paracelsus, Werk und Wirkung*, edited by Sepp Domandl, 187–204. Vienna, 1975.

Peuckert, Will-Erich. *Pansophie: Ein Versuch zur Geschichte der weissen und schwarzen Magie.* Berlin, 1956.

Plessner, Martin. *Vorsokratische Philosophie und griechische Alchemie in arabisch-lateinischer Überlieferung.* Studien zu Text und Inhalt der Turba Philosophorum. Wiesbaden, 1975.

Ploss, Emil Ernst, Heinz Roosen-Runge, Heinrich Schipperges, and Herwig Buntz. *Alchimia: Ideologie und Technologie.* Munich, 1970.

Rattansi, P. M. "Paracelsus and the Puritan Revolution." *Ambix* 11 (1963) 24–32.

Rudolph, Hartmut. "Kosmosspekulationen und Trinitätslehre. Ein Beitrag zur Beziehung zwischen Weltbild und Theologie bei Paracelsus." In *Paracelsus in der Tradition*, Salzburger Beiträge zur Paracelsusforschung 21, 32–47. Vienna, 1980.

Schipperges, Heinrich. "Arabische Medizin im lateinischen Mittelalter." In *Sitzungsberichte der Heidelberger Akademie der Wissenschaften. Mathemathisch-Naturwissenschaftliche Klasse 2.* Berlin, Heidelberg, and New York, 1976.

———. "Handschriftliche Funde zu den 'verdrängten Wissenschaften' in der frühen Neuzeit." *Berichte zur Wissenschaftsgeschichte* 4 (1981) 31–40.

———. *Kosmos Anthropos: Entwürfe zu einer Philosophie des Leibes.* Stuttgart, 1981.

———. "Magia et Scientia bei Paracelsus." *Sudhoffs Archiv* 60 (1976) 76–92.

———. *Paracelsus: Das Abenteuer einer sokratischen Existenz.* Freiburg, 1983.

———. *Paracelsus: Der Mensch im Licht der Natur.* Stuttgart, 1974.

———. "Vom Wesen des Arcanum im Weltbild des Paracelsus." In *Pharmazeutische Zeitung* 125 (1980) 706–12.

Schmitt, Wolfram. *Magie und Mantik bei Hans Hartlieb*, Salzburger Beiträge zur Paracelsusforschung 6. Vienna, 1966.

———. "Zur Literatur der Geheimwissenschaften im späten Mittelalter." In *Fachprosaforschung: Acht Vorträge zur mittelalterlichen Artesliteratur*, 167–83. Berlin, 1974.

Schneider, Wolfgang. "Die deutschen Pharmakopöen des 16. Jahrhunderts und Paracelsus." *Pharmazeutische Zeitung* 106 (1961) 1141–5.

———. "Grundlagen für Paracelsus' Arzneitherapie." *Sudhoffs Archiv* 49 (1965) 28–36.

———. *Mein Umgang mit Paracelsus und Paracelsisten: Beiträge zur Paracelsus-Forschung.* Frankfurt, 1982.

———. "Paracelsus und die Arzneimittel seiner Zeit." *Pharmazeutische Zeitung* 127 (1982) 1587–1591.

Sherlock, T. P. "The Chemical Work of Paracelsus." *Ambix* 3 (1948) 33–64.

Shumaker, Wayne. *The Occult Science in the Renaissance: A Study in Intellectual Patterns.* Berkeley, Los Angeles, and London, 1972.

Simili, Alessandro. "Astrologia, demonologia, pregiudizi terapeutici nella medicina legale e forense del Rinascimento." *Minerva Medica* 67 (1976) 3719–37.

Steinlein, Stephan. *Astrologie, Sexual-Krankheiten und Aberglaube in ihrem inneren Zusammenhänge.* 2 vols. Munich and Leipzig, 1915.

———. *Astrologie und Heilkunde: Ein vorläufiger Beitrag zur Kenntnis der "Entstehung" der Syphilis vor der Entdeckung Amerikas.* Munich, 1912.

Ströker, Elisabeth. *Denkwege der Chemie: Elemente ihrer Wissenschaftstheorie.* Freiburg and Munich, 1967.

———. *Theoriewandel in der Wissenschaftsgeschichte: Chemie im 18. Jahrhundert.* Frankfurt, 1982.

Sudhoff, Karl. *Bibliographia Paracelsica: Besprechung der unter Hohenheims Namen 1527–1883 erschienenen Druckschriften.* Berlin, 1894.

——. *Versuch einer Kritik der Echtheit der paracelsischen Schriften. I. Theil: Die unter Hohenheims Namen erschienenen Druckschriften.* Berlin, 1894. *II. Theil: Paracelsische Handschriften.* Berlin, 1899.

Teich, M., and R. Young, eds. *Changing Perspectives in the History of Science.* London, 1973.

Telle, Joachim. "Alchemie." *Theologische Realenzyklopädie* 2:199–227. 1977.

——. "Der Alchimist im Rosengarten." *Euphorion* 71 (1977) 283–305.

——. "Killian, Ottheinrich und Paracelsus." *Heidelberger Jahrbücher* 18 (1974) 37–49.

——. *Mythologie und Alchemie.* Beiträge zur Humanismusforschung 6 (1980) 135–54.

——. *Sol und Luna: Literar- und alchemiegeschichtliche Studien zu einem altdeutschen Bildgedicht.* Hürtgenwald, 1980.

——, ed. *Parerga Paracelsica: Paracelsus in Vergangenheit und Gegenwart.* Stuttgart, 1991.

Waltershausen, Bodo Sartorius von. *Paracelsus am Eingang der deutschen Bildungsgeschichte.* Leipzig, 1935.

Westfall, Richard S. "Newton and the Hermetic Tradition." In *Science, Medicine and Society in the Renaissance,* edited by Allen G. Debus, 2:183–98. New York, 1972.

Weyer, Jost. "Die Entwicklung der Chemie zu einer Wissenschaft zwischen 1540 und 1740." *Ber. Wiss. Gesch.* 1 (1978) 113–21.

Wilkinson, Ronald Sterne. "'Hermes Christianus': John Winthrop, Jr. and Chemical Medicine in Seventeenth-Century New England." In *Science, Medicine and Society in the Renaissance,* edited by Allen G. Debus, 2:221–41. New York, 1972.

Yates, Frances Amelia. *The Rosicrucian Enlightenment.* London, 1972.

Zimmermann, Rolf Christian. *Das Weltbild des jungen Goethe: Studien zur hermetischen Tradition des deutschen 18. Jahrhunderts, I. Elemente und Fundamente.* Munich, 1969.

6

Rosicrucianism: From the Seventeenth to the Twentieth Century

ROLAND EDIGHOFFER

T HE TWO LINKED symbols of the Rose and the Cross characteristically awaken all kinds of mysterious harmonies in the imagi-
nations of people, even those who do not refer to the Christian
cross. No doubt they correspond to those primordial images
inscribed in universal memory which C. G. Jung has called archetypes; no
doubt they constitute an essential sign of the harmony of opposites, of
totalization, of perfection, endowed with an evocative power comparable
to that of the Pythagorean *tetraktys* (the magical number 4) or the dynamic
union of Yang and Yin.

But the Rose-Cross also has a history, a precise geographical localization.
It has become concrete in texts—at first in manifestos and a novel, then in
a very large number of pseudepigraphic writings. The object of this study
is first to present the fundamental works, in the hope of resolving the
enigma they pose, then to indicate the possible sources of Rosicrucian
thought, and finally to display its developments up to our own time.

The First Rosicrucian Writings

In 1614 there appeared in Kassel, in Hesse, a 147–page collection containing
three texts: *Reform of the Universe, Fama Fraternitatis,* and *Short Reply to
the Esteemed Fraternity of the Rose-Cross,* signed by a certain Adam Hasel-
mayer. The first was only a retranslation of *Ragguagli di Parnaso,* a satirical
work by Traiano Boccalini published in Venice in 1612. It criticized the
vanity of pretentious reform projects in political and social affairs, and its
presence in the collection was probably designed simply to ward off criticism for sedition. Adam Haselmayer's missive proves that the *Fama* had
already been circulating in Europe since 1610 in manuscript form. Paracelsian

in inspiration, it invites the representatives of the Rose-Cross to manifest their boons to the world without further delay. The *Fama Fraternitatis* possesses two aspects. First, it presents in hagiographic tone the biography of the legendary hero Christian Rosencreuz, who was born in 1378, learned his science with the Arabs and Sabeans, and died in 1484 after having transmitted his knowledge to initiated brothers. Second, it contains an exposition of Rosicrucian doctrine, which rests on the notion of perfect harmony between the macrocosm and the microcosm. The refusal of the authors of the *Fama Fraternitatis* to admit the formula "hoc per philosophiam verum est, sed per theologiam falsum" expresses the globalist conception of the Rose-Cross, who considered Nature as the great book of marvels in which God might be apprehended. Thus is explained the optimistic affirmation of the *Fama,* which enthusiastically hails this period, now that it has become possible to know the "Son" of God more fully: this in fact is a reference to the *Filius macrocosmi,* the macrocosmic form of the savior, thanks to which creation escapes Satan's threats and recovers the primitive harmony. "Our philosophy is nothing new," proclaim the authors of the manifesto. It is in reality the heir of Christian kabbalism, marked by Pythagorean doctrine and directly influenced by Paracelsus, whose complete works were to be published only at the end of the sixteenth century. The celebrated philosopher-physician had magnified the human being—microcosm, temple of God, point of convergence of heaven and earth—and celebrated the immense human power of discovery and creation. Capable of commanding the stars, controlling events, and producing new beings, humanity was at the dawn of a new period of life on earth, a time in which the Spirit might breathe. Paracelsus heralded the arrival of one to come after him, who would possess and dispense knowledge. The mythical personage of Christian Rosencreuz was perhaps, in the eye of his creator, the symbol of that one.

According to the fiction of the *Fama Fraternitatis,* the tomb of the founder of the order had been discovered in 1604. That date corresponds to the appearance in the heavens of a new star, which the celebrated astronomer Johannes Kepler took to portend the appearance of a prophet charged with reestablishing religious unity and promoting a "rational Reformation." Echoing him, the *Fama* predicts the immanent appearance of a "general divine and human Reformation," which Haselmayer, the author of the *Response to the esteemed Fraternity of the Rose-Cross,* hails enthusiastically. He makes reference to the prophecy of the *Lion of the North,* who toured Europe in the sixteenth century and is erroneously identified with Paracelsus. This curious text mingles several themes found in the Rosicrucian myth: that of a hidden treasure, of an uncovered tomb, and of a mystagogue—the "Lion" to come from the north and vanquish the eagle and its *clericaille* after a merciless struggle and finally inaugurate a period of felicity in the world.

It is to this prophetic perspective that the second manifesto corresponds. It is called the *Confessio Fraternitatis*, for in it the Rose-Cross "confess" their ideas. The text of this manifesto was first published in 1615, in a Latin-German bilingual version, together with the *Fama Fraternitatis* and Hasel-mayer's *Response*. It exhibits noteworthy divergences in spirit from the *Fama*. It is an essentially ambiguous text, in the tradition of apocalyptic literature, which at once unveils and masks its message. The authors defend their revelation of the mysteries of the Rose-Cross, but impose the law of silence on anyone won over to them. They express their ideas but explain immediately that they are accessible only to those favored by God's grace. Whereas the *Fama* praised philosophy, the *Confessio* considers it to be moribund. On the other hand, it accords a favored place to the Bible, which it defines as "the compendium of the quintessence of the entire world," but which reveals its secrets only to those illuminated by the Holy Spirit. We recognize here the influence of Joachim of Floris; the *Miranda sextae aetatis* which the *Confessio* mentions recalls the age of the "Eternal Gospel," which according to the Calabrian monk was to begin at the end of the sixth millennium, when the sixth seal of the Apocalypse is fully opened and the "sixth candlestick" is lit. On the supposition that God reserves to the Rose-Cross the privilege of lighting it, its members could then be expected to enjoy all kinds of privileges—health, longevity, riches, omniscience, the gift of ubiquity, complete political power. The *Confessio* is therefore essentially of biblical and millenarian inspiration, and ignorant of the optimism of the *Fama Fraternitatis*.

The third fundamental writing of the Rose-Cross is again very different. Published in 1616, not in Kassel like the writings discussed above but in Strasbourg, the *Chemical Wedding* is unique in its literary genre, for it is presented as an autobiographical novel. Moreover, its hero, Christian Rosencreuz, does not have the characteristics here that he has in the *Fama* and the *Confessio*. He is not the founder of a venerated order, the possessor of immense powers and knowledge, to whom the infirm flock in the vast habitation of the "Holy Spirit," but a humble hermit, full of years, who has dwelt in his cavern in the side of a mountain in prayer and observation of the stars, and declares himself weak and ignorant. A few days before Easter he is visited by an angel with a letter for him, bearing a mysterious sign and containing an invitation to the "Wedding of the King." About this hier-ogamy, for which Christian has waited seven years and in which he is to participate, the experiences he is to have there, and his admission into two chivalric orders—though these are events of major importance for him—the

Fama Fraternitatis biography breathes not a word. We are thus forced to conclude that the main character of the *Fama* and the *Confessio* does not coincide with the hero of the *Chemical Wedding*.

Before undertaking his initiatic voyage Christian Rosencreuz would like to know if he is worthy to accept the invitation. The response is given in a dream which the author of the novel has borrowed from the elements of a sermon by St. Bernard. Confined with other people in a deep well into which a rope is thrown seven times, Christian Rosencreuz finally grasps it and pulls himself out. But he is wounded on the head and limps with both legs—a sign of moral lameness, as in the Bible (1 Kings 18:21). In this way the dream gives him to understand that he will be redeemed, saved by God's grace, and that since he carries within himself the stigmata of the sinner he cannot impute to himself the merit of having grasped the saving rope.

Christian sets out on the journey, ignorant of his itinerary. He arrives at an intersection shaded by three great cedars, trees that since Egyptian antiquity have symbolized human metamorphosis and are identified with Mercury, the *spiritus vegetativus*. A *Tabella Mercurialis*, hung from one of them, describes for the traveler the three possible ways to reach the wedding castle. In fact Mercury, or Hermes, is traditionally the mystagogue and psychopomp of alchemists, at once leader and seducer, and this explains his double appearance to Christian in the form of a white dove and a black crow. The first of these shows him the way. He is led next with the aid of a compass; he is *oriented*, that is, he seeks the *orient*, the spiritual east. His journey ends with the ascent of a "high mountain," a spiritual place *par excellence*, where the royal castle rises into the air, a symbol of the construction of the self. Christian arrives at sunset, a moment which tradition has always interpreted as a symbol of death and resurrection. The three portals through which he must then pass represent the spiritual passage from the profane night into illumination. At the threshold of initiation, the inscription on the first door is characteristic: *Procul hinc, procul ite profani!* ("Far from here, far from the profane!"). At each door Christian receives a golden badge engraved with initials, whose interpretation, written on the margin, is ambivalent, at once alchemical and spiritual. The pilgrim barely passes through the last door before it closes, as though to indicate the difficulties of a new birth. Other symbolic acts carried out there—the tonsure, a change of shoes—appear to be rites of passage.

Arriving at the castle, Christian is surprised to meet a great number of people of every social class, from emperors to would-be alchemists, who say they have been invited to the wedding. Their arrogance and bluster shock and trouble him until he understands that the decisive test has still not occurred. The next day, in fact, the guests are placed one by one on the scale of a massive golden balance, on the other end of whose beam are suspended seven weights corresponding to the virtues of faith, charity, concord, chastity, patience, humility, and sobriety. Christian's faith and moral "weight" are such that he does much better at the test than all his rivals and thus manifests his special election. The presumptuous are punished in various ways, from being sent back to being killed. The victors receive badges made of the Golden Fleece. Their admission into this order of chivalry signifies at once that they are embarked upon an adventure as perilous as the expedition of the Argonauts and that God will lend his assistance and save them by pure grace as at the time of Abraham's sacrifice (Genesis 22:9–14) or Gideon's prayer for the aid of Yahweh (Judges 6:36–40). From the collar of the Golden Fleece hangs a winged lion, whose significance may be clarified by reference to the *Atalanta Fugiens,* which was published in 1618 by Michael Maier, the friend of Robert Fludd and commentator on Rosicrucian thought. Emblem XVI in that work, entitled *De secretis Naturae,* depicts Nature as a winged lion, participating equally in the heavens and the earth. In this way we see the novel's fundamental ambivalence: it is at once spiritual and alchemical; it describes both the health of the creature and that of creation, and the restoration of harmony between the divine and the created order.

It is again a lion which, in a scene particularly dense in symbolic value, confirms this interpretation. He holds in his paws a drawn sword, breaks it, throws the pieces into a fountain, and gives forth a roar; a dove brings him an olive branch, which he swallows; a white unicorn, kneeling before him, manifests extreme joy. A text by Gerhard Dorn, the *Speculativa Philosophia,* published in 1602 in the *Theatrum chemicum,* clarifies the sense of this parable: God has decided in his mercy to destroy the sword of his anger, institute peace on earth, and pour out the dew of his grace. That grace is gathered in the mercurial fountain on which the lion is perched. The lion is not only the image of divine power, but also one of the representations of philosophical mercury. So it is not surprising that Christian sees him the next morning, bearing in his claws a placard on which these words are engraved:

I, Prince Hermes,
After so many injuries
With human cause,
Have become according to the secret of God
And with the assistance of art
A health-giving medicine,
I flow here
That whoever wishes may drink from me,

That whoever wishes may wash in me,
That whoever dares may trouble me:
Drink, Brothers, and live!

The meaning of this text becomes clear when we recall that Hermes is often called *varius ille Mercurius, duplex, versipellis,* that is, at once polymorphous and crafty. He is by turns good and evil, as chthonian power; he participates in the nature of Lucifer, of Lilith, of Melusine. There is therefore no question that there are diabolical aspects within him. But he is at the same time *homo philosophicus,* the second Adam, the image of the incarnation; he is the son of the macrocosm, that is, of nature. We may therefore conclude that he is a second son of God and in consequence a brother of Christ, and that he constitutes in Nature the counterpart of Christ in the divine revelation.

All of these symbols suggest a hermeneutic for this mysterious narrative. They are the epiphany of a new alliance, the reconciliation of spirit and matter; they are the announcement of a wedding that is not only spiritual but "chemical" in its miraculous realization of the *mysterium conjunctionis.* Two complementary indications contribute to the temporal dimension of this marvelous hierogamy. First, the new Golden Fleece delivered to Christian Rosencreuz and his companions comprises a badge on which the words of the prophet Isaiah may be read: "The light of the moon will be as the light of the sun, and the light of the sun will be sevenfold" (30:26). Second, a play presented in the presence of the princely couple unfolds in seven acts, recalling both the seven days of creation and also the hierogamy of the masculine heavens and the feminine earth. The *"Comoedi"* retraces the history of the church, "that unfortunate little prostitute who is despised," as Luther wrote in his treatise *The Liberty of the Christian.* Taken in by her uncle the king, the young orphan succumbs several times to the seductions of the evil one, until the son of the king, after a struggle in which he would seem to have lost his life, obtains the victory over the Moor and delivers her. After many episodes the seventh act at length describes the wedding, but we understand that it is celebrated only at the end of time, in the age of the Apocalypse, when the holy city descends from the heavens "prepared as a bride adorned for her husband" (Revelation 21:2).

The Golden Fleece and the *"Comoedi"* demonstrate that the events described in the novel are the actualization of an eschatological reality: they are already present through the medium of a symbolic system, but they are situated in a time that is metahistorical. Only the marvel of a mythic narrative could translate these ineffable truths and render them sensible, and it is in this way that we understand all the value and the richness of the scenes presented in the novel: Alchemy's pledge of allegiance to the Faith; the purification of the lustral fountain by the converted Hermes; the ascent to a superior level of spirituality by a flight of 365 steps, symbolizing the completion of a cosmic cycle. From that point the reader is conveyed with the eponymous hero to a *sacrificium*, in the proper and strong sense of the term: an initiatic path constituted by operations in which the boundaries between subject and object grow dim and disappear.

First is the visit to Venus, the true *catabase* of the hero in the depths of mother earth, in the room where Aphrodite sleeps entirely nude. The *virgo in centro terra*, symbol of *materia prima*, is in a mausoleum shaded by the *arbor philosophica*, whose mercurial fruits dissolve without ceasing. In the alchemical tradition, in which the adept is assimilated psychologically to the completed work, the obscure and unfathomable phase of the *nigredo* is full of perils and is not completed without loss for the operator. The author of the novel has very cleverly described these dangers under the form of carnal temptations, and it is Cupid who punishes Christian for having contemplated his mother nude, by pricking him on the hand with one of his arrows. This episode was suggested by the alchemical metaphor of the *telum passionis* sent by the "sagittarial Mercury."

This same philosophical Mercury is king; he is "thrice great," *triunus* or *ternarius*. As such he sits on three thrones. And since he is said to be a hermaphrodite we are not surprised to find him again in filigree in the tragic scene involving the decapitation of the three princely couples and their executioner. On the occasion of this sextuple execution Christian speaks of "blood marriages," thus showing once again that the drama is lived by him in its most profound reality, and that it is not a matter of the simple metaphorical interpretation of laboratory operations. The hero learns that this death is to be the germ of new life, on the condition that he and his companions participate in the mystery, said by the apostle Paul to concern Christ and the church (Ephesians 5:21). Elect and marked by the sign of the Golden Fleece, they will simultaneously "put on the new man" and ensure that creation "will be set free from the bondage to decay and obtain the glorious liberty of the children of God" (Romans 8:21).

The rest of the narrative is strange and at times disconcerting, but frequently filled with poetry and humor. On seven ships corresponding to the seven planets, the elect cross a sea where they are greeted by undines singing a hymn to love which is so beautiful that Goethe was to copy it almost word for word. The island where they land has the shape of a square, like the Jerusalem that is to descend from heaven. In the Tower of Olympus there are to take place the various operations of an alchemy that will disconcert the specialists of the time, like Brotoffer. After a preparatory

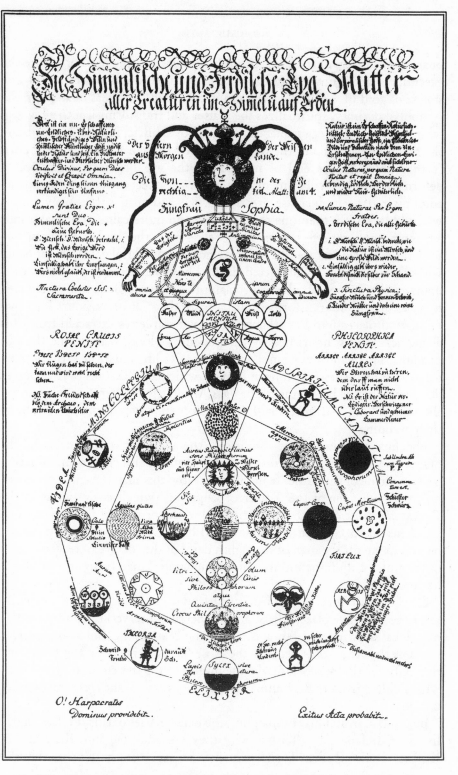

7. "The Heavenly and Earthly Eve" in Manuscript D.O.M.A. from *Codex Rosae Crucis*. Drawing executed probably between 1775 and 1780.

phase the cadavers of the three princely couples and the head of Maure the executioner are submitted to the *solutio,* and then the liquid is caught in a sphere of gold in which the *solificatio* is produced. The heat of the sun, the symbol of divinity, spiritualizes the matter and transforms it into a big egg, white as snow. The egg is placed in a kind of artificial incubator that bears the name Paracelsus and the date 1459, even though he was not yet born at that time. At the end of maturation the egg breaks and discloses a deformed bird that will immediately, under the effect of various nutriments administered to it, increase greatly in size and turn successively into a wicked black bird, then one that is white and more calm, and finally into a magnificent and perfectly tame peacock. This is the "bird of Hermes," the soul of the world, nature, the quintessence and universal germ, the phoenix whose metachromy is completed in the blue bird. Decapitated in its turn upon an altar whose attributes proclaim the renewal of all things, reduced to ashes, it will be transformed into a paste that Christian pours into two molds and places into the athanor. The two statuettes extracted from this alchemical uterus, nourished by the phoenix's blood, will assume the size of adults, a man and a woman. Each will receive life under the form of three tongues of flame descended from heaven, which are the souls of the couples decapitated at the beginning of the *opus.* When the regeneration is complete the young king and queen will be able, on the seventh day, to celebrate their wedding.

The final operation that "animates" the princely couple—that is, the operation that gives it an *anima,* a soul, a new life, also confers illumination on it in virtue of the flames from heaven. Now this major event is produced on the *eighth floor* of the Tower of Olympus, which corresponds in the *Corpus Hermeticum* to the ogdoatic level in the process of the ἄνοδος—that is, ascension to God. In the same way Philo, Origen, and certain church fathers spoke of "the man of the eighth day," of the "octave of resurrection," of the time of illumination in which "pneumatic" man brings to the world its redemption.

On the boat returning him from the island to the castle where the princely marriage is to take place, Christian Rosencreuz observes in wonder a splendid clock showing the minutes. Now the text of the *Fama Fraternitatis* explains that the *Rotae* kept by the Rose-Cross strike only the hours and that only the divine clock marks the minutes. It is therefore in *divine time,* which differs from that of humans, that the events of the *chemical wedding* unfold.

But Christian and his companions, the beneficiaries of this revelation, still live in mundane time. That is why they are admitted into the order of Knights of the Golden Stone, which is to say that the Christ, the true

Philosopher's Stone, arms them for the "good warfare of the faith," for the active and charitable life to which they promise to consecrate themselves as they flee the devil and all the seductions of the world.

At the end of the novel the young king, returned to life, accords special favors to Christian, who by divine grace alone has been an architect of this regeneration. But this election has not kept him from committing errors and transgressions, on account of which he is condemned to guard the portal of the castle without being allowed to enter it. The narrative ends with the fiction that the last pages have been lost, and the paradox of the hero who discovers for himself that he is expected at once to be a door-keeper for the rest of his days and however to return to his country home.

The paradox is not peculiar to Rosencreuz. It is common to each Christian, who lives at once in the world and beyond the world, in historical time and in that of redemption. But the experience which Christian Rosencreuz lives, since it is ogdoatic in nature, is at once superior and paradigmatic. The Knights of the Golden Stone have, by divine grace, known and experienced regenerating alchemy. Having become "friends of God," they can and must study the admirable mechanism of the universe. They are not blindly pretentious like those who glory in human omnipotence; it is God who by regenerating them opens their eyes to the marvels of Nature. And it is on account of the alchemy of their palingenesis that creation, freed from Satan's grasp, sees its mechanisms as if by miracle put back in motion in the universal harmony. This is why the mysterious castle where Christian has gone contains a planetarium, an astronomical clock, mines, and all kinds of workshops for the study of the sciences and the technological arts.

The mysterious symbol drawn on the letter, inviting Christian Rosencreuz to participate in the chemical wedding, proclaimed and synthesized this soteriological process. The author of the "hieroglyphic monad," John Dee (1527–1604), saw in it the representation of perfect unity, alpha and omega, the passage from the Trinity to the quaternity, the hierogamy of the creator with his creation. The young king, the "man of the eighth level," is the *homo philosophicus*, the second Adam, the *Adam Cadmon*, so often identified with the Christ. And Christian is named "Rosencreuz," for the quaternity of the cross appears frequently in Christian and mystical iconography beneath the circular form of a "rose." Heinrich Khunrath, one of the spiritual godfathers of the *Chemical Wedding*, saw in the *Monas catholica* generated from the rotation of the *quaternarium* an allegory of the Christ. So the *Chemical Wedding of Christian Rosencreuz* is at once the image of the second birth, of the liberation of Spirit concealed in Matter, and of the *matrimonium perpetuum* necessary to that redemption.

The Paternity of the First Rosicrucian Writings

The two early Rosicrucian manifestos, the *Fama Fraternitatis* and the *Confessio Fraternitatis*, like the novel about the chemical wedding, were published anonymously. But the extraordinary success of these writings, which were to arouse impassioned reactions across part of Europe, evidently provoked the curiosity of readers. Who could be hiding behind this mysterious enterprise? Very quickly suspicions centered on a young theologian of Württemberg. Johann Valentin Andreae (1586–1654) belonged to an important dynasty of Swabian Lutherans; his grandfather, Jakob Andreae, had helped draft the *Formula of Concord* (1580), a profession of faith resulting from an attempt at union between Lutherans and Calvinists. Committed to a career as pastor, the young Johann Valentin had to interrupt his studies on account of a political scandal in which he was implicated. In 1606 a libelous statement had circulated attacking a counselor of the duke of Württemberg. Suspected of being its author, Andreae was forced to go into exile. A few years later, his name cleared, he was to assume important ecclesiastical and diplomatic functions, but his pronounced taste for satire aroused powerful enmities against him. The Rosicrucian affair, in which he had participated, provided an auspicious setting for calumny, and Andreae was forced to take a position on this subject in a rather large number of his works.

In 1615, even though the *Fama* and the *Confessio Fraternitatis* were yet to appear, he opined in the *Herculis christiani luctae XXIV* that these writings contained "only obscure and affected discourse linked to the most baneful and shameful credulity." In 1619, when the attacks against him did not cease, he returned to the charge in the *De curiositatis pernicie syntagma ad singularitatis studiosos*, affirming that "the jesting of a certain rosaceous Fraternity" had been "at the same time the snare and the stumbling-block" of everyone eager for out-of-the-way knowledge. And the confusion of minds provoked by the Rosicrucian affair led him to publish in the same year a collection of twenty-five three-person comedies, which he called *Turris Babel*. The narrator is the *Fama* in person. The summary that she herself makes of the first manifesto demonstrates Andreae's critical attitude concerning the mirific promises of riches, longevity, health, wisdom, and success issued to all those won over to this fraternity, capable of banishing tyranny and constituting a happy and flourishing monarchy. From the *Confessio Fraternitatis* one can learn only that everything in it is spoken in a "superhuman" language. There follows a procession of the most celebrated of the innumerable texts published in the wake of the first manifestos: the *Echo of the Brotherhood (Echo der Fraternitët)* by Julius Sperber (1615); the

Silentium post clamores by Michael Maier (1617); the *Pandora sextae Aetatis* (1617) and *Speculum sophicum Rhodo-Stauroticum* (1618) by Theophilus Schweighart, alias Daniel Moegling; and the *Fortalitium scientiae* (1617) and the *Clypeum veritatis* (1618), both signed by Irenaeus Agnostus. Andreae brings all these works together under the common title *Urbis Utopiae phantasmata.* On the other hand, the *Chemical Wedding* is not mentioned in the *Turris Babel,* as though the author by this intentional omission were indicating to his readers his view that not everything about this fraternity is to be rejected. As for the character named *Conjectans,* he was probably invented by an "ingenious mind." According to *Poenitens,* this fiction "may be good in certain aspects." And *Resipiscens* declares in the presence of *Fama* that

> there is a worry which troubles me: that I have not established sufficiently careful distinctions among the writings which ... are revealed under the name of the Fraternity. The fact is that some of them are plainly games; some are very confused; some are evil; some have their trickery hidden; and finally some are pious and devout. All display a certain erudition, and in some it is even very great, but they all show evident imposture. Anyone who confuses all these writings or thinks they all issue from a single inspiration indubitably deceives himself. If in fact it were so, the world would be presented as good, the Christ would be rejected, what is vain would be praised, what is solid would be blamed, imposture would be esteemed, reason would be neglected, lies would be honored, and the truth scoffed at. Consequently if it is certain that I repudiate the Society of the Fraternity itself, on the other hand no one will ever make me renounce the true Christian Fraternity, the one which from beneath the cross exhales a perfume of roses and flees as far as it can the stain of wanderings and the vanities of the World; to the contrary, I aspire to enter that Fraternity with anyone who is pious, judicious, and sagacious.

Through the mouth of a *repenti,* something that is itself not without significance, Andreae therefore invites his readers to sort out the innumerable Rosicrucian productions, to separate the wheat from the tares, and to recognize the writings that are "pious and devout" and do not deny the existence of evil.

In the same year, 1619, Andreae published the *Reipublicae Christiano-politanae descriptio,* which seeks to represent the invisible city which the authentic Christians constitute among and within themselves. In the preface he summarizes the three stages of the fraternity of the Rose-Cross: first it offers wonderful and unusual revelations as nourishment to the *curiosi;* then it arouses the great hope of seeing religious, intellectual, and political life ameliorated; finally it adds the imitation of Christ.

These two references explain the sibylline and at times contradictory statements by Andreae concerning the Rosicrucian phenomenon. In the

Mythologia christiana (1619), for example, he has *Alethea,* or Truth, say sometimes that it is a dangerous and baneful game and sometimes that it should be seen as "a rather ingenious game which a masked person might like to play upon the literary scene, especially in an age infatuated with everything unusual." The contradiction is only apparent, insofar as Andreae subscribes only to part of the ideas set out in the first writings. A modern reader might be justified in asking why, under these conditions, Andreae did not clearly indicate what he wrote and what he rejected. This would be to misunderstand the situation of the times and the enormous professional and personal risks that would be run by a young pastor who had already been implicated in a delicate affair during his student years.

Andreae therefore preferred the most subtle and corrective method: since he approved only part of the *Fama* and the *Confessio,* he had two writings published that are parallel to them but rectify their meaning. To the *Fama Fraternitatis* there corresponds the *Chemical Wedding,* and what he keeps of the *Confessio* is cleverly included in the *Theca gladii spiritus.*

We have seen that the principal character, Christian Rosencreuz, is profoundly different in the *Fama* and in the *Chemical Wedding.* The humble anchorite of the latter novel is conscious of his weakness, his ignorance, his sinfulness. To the triumphal optimism of the *Fama* there is now opposed the necessity of regeneration of fallen creatures, which is brought about only by the grace of God. Nature is no longer apprehended by a philosophy, but by means of science and technical method made accessible to the regenerate. The fraternity of the Rose-Cross, whose members are initiates to a secret knowledge, gives way to the Knights of the Golden Stone, the symbol of the pantocratic Christ who comes to save both microcosm and macrocosm.

The *Theca gladii spiritus* appeared the same year with the same publisher, in Strasbourg, as the *Chemical Wedding.* The preface of this anonymous collection presented it as a volume of maxims recovered in the papers of Tobias Hess, a friend of Andreae who had died in 1614. Now the autobiography that Andreae composed in 1642 for the sake of his benefactor, Duke Augustus of Brunswick-Lunebourg, explains that both works are in fact from the hand of the Swabian theologian: "*plane mea,*" writes Andreae with reference to the *Theca.*

This affirmation is the more important as a careful reading of the text has made it possible, though only in the last few years, to establish that it is a kind of anthology of at least five works by Andreae, each published in its entirety between 1612 and 1618. Moreover, twenty-eight of the *Theca's* maxims are drawn from the *Confessio Fraternitatis.* I have been able to unearth the Latin edition of the *Confessio* and thus proceed to an accurate comparison with the corresponding Latin passages retained in the *Theca*. The following conclusions can be drawn: (1) All reference to the Rose-Cross and its founder is scrupulously avoided in the *Theca*. (2) There is no question here of an all-powerful fraternity, but of "humble" and "good" folk who have found favor with God. (3) Everything falling within the category of the miraculous has been suppressed. (4) The *Mirabilia sextae aetatis* and the allusions to a new Reformation have disappeared. (5) Communication with divine characters, in the Bible and in Nature, is reserved for those whom the grace of God has made "friends of the king" and who celebrate a wedding with the divine bridegroom. These expressions recall the spirit of the *Chemical Wedding*, but in the *Theca* they qualify not Christian Rosencreuz but Christian Cosmoxenus, to whom Andreae had dedicated a work published in 1612 under the title *De Christiani Cosmoxeni genitura, judicium,* from which more than thirty passages are reprinted in this anthology. He is a *Renatus;* he celebrates in permanence a *triplex matrimonium:* the soul with the body, and therefore with matter; orthodox faith with holy life; the soul-wife with the Christ, her husband. All of creation is thus at his service. This ideal state is accessible only to those who have known testing and penitence, and have become *cruce signati*. In the same way the Christian of the *Chemical Wedding*, at the end of the novel, no longer bears anything but a white banner with a red cross.

There was present in this comparison, for perspicacious readers, a subtle sign that the matter was closed, that the *Fama*—as the *De curiositatis pernicie syntagma* explains again in 1620—after having brought the people together, had sent them out again, since it had itself proclaimed in the *Turris Babel* that *"Peracta est fabula."*

Bringing down the curtain did not put an end to slander. All his life, Andreae was to be exposed to accusations and forced to defend himself. Again in 1632, when he was nominated as preacher to the court at Stuttgart, he was required to attest that he had never taken seriously the "fable" of the Rose-Cross.

What precisely had been his share of responsibility? He indicates its limits by the two corrections that the *Chemical Wedding* and the *Theca gladii spiritus* represent. Other clues, furnished by the biography, the correspondence, and the rest of the work, allow us to specify it more precisely.

There are two elements to consider: on the objective level, the religious, political, and cultural life at the beginning of the seventeenth century showed signs of crisis. The Lutheran Reformation had not kept its promises; a restrictive and polemical interpretation of the *sola fide* incited many pastors to neglect the essential and indeed quite Lutheran element of works born of faith and to allow a general laxity to become widespread. Moreover, the constitution of territorial churches led the state, to which Luther conceded no competence in matters religious, to develop caesaropapism. The princes, moreover, did all they could to extend their authority and impose absolutism everywhere, so that in a country like Württemberg, the homeland of Johann Valentin Andreae, the bourgeois parliament, which disposed of important prerogatives, notably in matters of finances, saw them suppressed one by one. The university and ecclesiastic oligarchy to which the Andreae family belonged lost a great deal of its influence. Duke Frederick I would henceforth decide everything and rule alone, assisted by his counselor, a turncoat jurist named Matthaeus Enzlin. A young student rebel named Johann Valentin Andreae was not willing to abide this situation. In 1606 he had a satire circulated against Enzlin, who, to be sure, demonstrated his aptness as a satiric subject but who consequently sent the young satirist into exile, rendering very problematic his hope of carrying out ecclesiastic functions in accordance with family tradition.

In the realm of sciences and technology considerable progress was made in mathematics, physics, chemistry, astronomy, and geography. The distrust of Aristotle and scholastic culture, the rediscovery of Pythagorean thought and the Neoplatonist vogue, and Huser's publication in 1591 of the complete works of Paracelsus profoundly altered the scientific landscape of the time. A new synthesis proved to be necessary between the data of faith and those of knowledge.

The young Andreae was led to reflect on these problems with Tobias Hess, whose acquaintance he had made in 1608. Eighteen years his senior, this very widely read man—at once jurist, physician, and theologian—developed a passion for the Kabbalah and came to be regarded as a "prince of utopia" and an organizer of secret societies. After his death, Andreae was to dedicate to his memory two important texts in which he had printed in italics the word *Fama*—as though to address a new sign to perspicacious readers.

And so the objective and subjective aspects of the genesis of Rosicrucian writings are joined. Uncertain about his future, wounded in his self-esteem, the young Andreae without doubt imagined a legendary, all-powerful character, one who rights wrongs and heralds a new age. The name of this hero, this Christian Hercules, was inspired both by the coat of arms of the Andreae family and by that of Luther, each of which bore the double motif of the rose and the cross. Moreover, the symbols of the rose and the cross have hermetic status: the rose is a synonym of the *anima* drawn from prime matter and conferring new life on the body, and the cross is the symbol of totality. One may therefore legitimately propose the hypothesis that the young Andreae invented the eponymous character, although Tobias Hess

8. Symbolical Rosicrucian Plate from an unpublished 18th-century manuscript and reproduced in *Codex Rosae Crucis*.

would have supplied the kabbalistic, Paracelsian, and Joachimite infrastructure of the original manifestos.

A passage from Andreae's autobiography alludes to different works "quarum nonnulla postea in lucem ab aliis protrusa" ("some of which have been edited afterwards by others"). It is not impossible that this willfully sibylline phrase refers to the publication in 1614 and 1615 of the *Fama* and the *Confessio Fraternitatis*, published against the wishes of Johann Valentin Andreae in Kassel on the presses of Wilhelm Wessel. Indeed, this publication could not have turned out worse for him—just when, totally rehabilitated, he had become a pastor and married the niece of a dignitary of the Lutheran Church. His double desire to exonerate himself and to use for this purpose means that diverged from any reference to or corrective for it might thus be explained.

By examining Wilhelm Wessel's privilege contract, signed in 1594, I have ascertained that he would have printed only texts that had received the endorsement of the landgrave of Hesse and would have observed orders of silence. There is therefore reason to think that the *Fama* and the *Confessio Fraternitatis* were published on the order of this prince, smitten with pansophism, who entertained alchemists and Paracelsians in his court.

The Sources of Rosicrucian Thought

According to the anthroposophist Walter Weber, Johann Valentin Andreae was only the editor of texts already preserved by an esoteric tradition. The contemporaries of Andreae had already put forward similar hypotheses. For Irenaeus Agnostus—whose pseudonym perhaps masks a friend of Andreae, the eminent jurist Christoph Besold, a devotee of gnosis and mysticism—the first representative of the order was Adam himself (*Clypeum veritatis*, 1618). Chapter 9 of the *Confessio* indeed indicates that the new and magical language of the Rose-Cross rejoined the one used by Adam, since it is taken from the characters inscribed by God in the great book of creation. A little less ambitiously, Michael Maier—who after having been Emperor Rudolph II's physician became the physician of the landgrave of Hesse—found the origins of the Rose-Cross in the Egypt of Thutmose III and made reference to the Osirian mysteries of death and resurrection. He also saw possible ancestors of the Rose-Cross in the adepts of the Eleusinian mysteries. Other filiations have been sought in the cult of Pythagoras, Hinduism and the gymnosophists, hermetic gnosis and the Sabeans, and so on.

Inquirers were thus led to think that the dawn of Rosicrucian writings at the beginning of the seventeenth century was the epiphany of a current of occult thought, the manifestation of a secret society that included various personalities of the Middle Ages and the Renaissance. Mention was made of the names of Dante Alighieri (1265–1321), Jerome Bosch (ca. 1450–1516), Cornelius Agrippa (1486–1535), Paracelsus (1493–1541), Giordano Bruno (1548–1600), and Heinrich Khunrath (1560–1605), as well as those of Aegidius Gutmann (1490–1584), Julius Sperber (d. 1616), and Simon Studion (b. 1543). Along with Khunrath, the last three persons certainly exercised a considerable influence on the formation of Rosicrucian ideas. Gutmann had edited, perhaps in 1575, a manuscript with the title *Offenbarung Göttlicher Majestät* whose thought is very close to the theories expounded in the *Fama Fraternitatis*. This text was published only in 1619 in Frankfurt am Main. Sperber had published in 1615 *Echo der von Gott hocherleuchteten Fraternität des löblichen Ordens R. C.,* whose manuscript went back at least to 1596. According to him, Adam had retained in his memory much knowledge received from God before the Fall. Through the mediation of Noah and the patriarchs, this gnosis was transmitted to Zoroaster, the Chaldeans, the Egyptians, and the sages of the Old Testament. Christ had kept the secret for a few of the elect, like Saint John the Evangelist and the apostle Paul. Among the later recipients of this gnosis Sperber mentions Saint Bernard, Cornelius Agrippa, Reuchlin, Guillaume Postel, and Pico della Mirandola. He himself had received in a vision the mission to announce a new age, the dawn of the age of the Holy Spirit of which Joachim of Floris had spoken. The preface of the *Echo der Fraternität,* edited after the publication of the *Fama* and the *Confessio,* accuses their authors of having "pillaged" the ideas expounded by Sperber. As for Studion, he announced in his massive manuscript entitled *Naometria,* that is, "measure of the temple," the coming of the new Jerusalem in 1590 and the establishment of a general Reformation by the *Cruce signati.*

We have seen that this expression was taken up by Andreae in the *Theca gladii spiritus.* In spite of this similarity, he kept his distance from all the proposals for godfather of the Rose-Cross that were being bruited. In the *Mythologia christiana* he characterizes Gutmann, Sperber, and Studion as "*insolitae eruditionis homines,*" and in the *Perigrini in Patria errores* he satirizes Pythagoras, the gnostics, the brahmanists, the gymnosophists, and the adepts of Orphism. But his a posteriori bantering does not prove that he had not in his youth taken a certain interest in all these ideas.

The Fate of Rosicrucian Ideas

The numerous occasions on which Andreae had felt forced to put things right show what waters had been stirred by the publication of the first Rosicrucian writings. Over two hundred texts for or against the Rose-Cross that were published between 1614 and 1620 have been counted—nine hundred up to the beginning of the eighteenth century. In France the storm broke only in 1623, when there appeared on the walls of Paris posters announcing the passage of "deputés du Collège principal des Frères de la Roze-Croix." The historian Gabriel Naudé (1600–1653) became interested in their ideas and discovered sources of them, among other places, in Paracelsus and in John Dee's *Monas hieroglyphica*. This English filiation has been brought out by Frances A. Yates in a remarkable study entitled *The Rosicrucian Enlightenment* (London and Boston: Routledge & Kegan Paul, 1972), in which she reports that the insignia of the order of the Jarretière bore a red cross with roses. According to her hypothesis, the ideas contained in the Rosicrucian manifestos were inspired by John Dee and would be crystallized at the moment when the Palatin Elector Frederick V, husband of Elisabeth, daughter of James I of England, accepted the crown of Bohemia.

In any case Rosicrucian ideas became acclimatized quickly and easily in the British soil. Robert Fludd (1574–1637), who introduced them, published from 1616 several treatises defending the Rose-Cross. Michael Maier's writings contributed to making the fraternity known in England. In 1652 Thomas Vaughan (1612–1666) brought out his translation of manifestos under the title *The Fame and Confession of the Fraternity R.C.*, and the English version of *Chymische Hochzeit, Chemical Wedding*, due to Ezechiel Foxcroft, was published in 1690. Elias Ashmole (1617–1682), great alchemist and admirer of Paracelsus, recopied by hand before their publication the translation of the *Fama* and the *Confessio*, accompanying them with an enthusiastic letter in Latin addressed "to the most illuminated Brothers of the Rose Cross." And in the preface to his *Theatrum chemicum britannicum*, a vast annotated collection of alchemical texts published in London in 1652, he made reference to Brother I. O., who according to the *Fama Fraternitatis* had gone to England to heal the Duke of Norfolk. Another English alchemist of this period, John Heydon (b. 1629), brought out between 1658 and 1665 eight works on the Rose-Cross. His *Holy Guide* of 1662 is in great part a Rosicrucian adaptation of the *New Atlantis* of Francis Bacon. Four years later there was published in Amsterdam a particularly sibylline work concerning Rosicrucian alchemy, *Chymica vannus*, whose author was English— if one believes the translator, who claimed nevertheless to have rendered the text from German into Latin.

This infatuation with Rosicrucian thought in England was due also to three people who had direct relations with Johann Valentin Andreae. Samuel Hartlib (1595–1662), originally of Danzig, came to live in Great Britain in 1628. He translated two Latin works by Andreae into English, the *Christianae societatis imago* and the *Christiani amoris dextera porrecta*, which, without any reference to the Rose-Cross, proposed an organization of Christian society into three religious and moral, economic and social, scientific and technological levels; then in 1641 he published a utopia entitled *A Description of the Famous Kingdom of Macaria*, inspired at once by Thomas More, Francis Bacon, and Andreae. The English theologian John Dury (1595–1680) had corresponded with Andreae in 1633 and revived his project *Societas christiana* in 1641 in his *Summary Discours concerning the work of peace ecclesiastical*. Finally, the Czech scientist Amos Comenius (1592–1670) had been an important mediator between Andreae and England. He dedicates an entire chapter of his work *Das Labyrinth der Welt* (1631) to the Rosicrucian hope, placing in the book, sometimes *in extenso*, passages from Andreae's works. Comenius dreamed of founding a universal college, made up of the elite of the entire world, which would gather in a collective labor the totality of knowledge. This erudition would benefit all people without distinctions of religion. These ideas existed in embryo in Rosicrucian fiction, and Andreae had transposed them into a more realistic context by proposing the organization of a *Societas christiana*, but his project remained limited to Lutheran Germany. With Comenius it took on planetary dimensions, and prefigured, several centuries in advance, the goals of UNESCO. The English civil war ruled out its realization in London. But the ideas sown by Comenius were to germinate in 1646 with the Invisible College, probably created at the instigation of Samuel Hartlib, and then in 1660 with the foundation of the Royal Society. The influence of Rosicrucian thought on the initiators of this body is undeniable, and some of its founders, like Elias Ashmole and Robert Moray, certainly belonged to Freemasonry. Thus were woven together the threads that linked these different elements. In the *London Magazine* of 1824 Thomas de Quincey affirmed that speculative freemasonry had issued from Rosicrucianism after the latter was planted in England. It was on British soil that the assimilation of Rosicrucian ideas with the medieval traditions of the masonic guild was to be effected; this conjunction was to take place between 1633 and 1646. In support of this assertion, Frances A. Yates cites a passage from a poem by Henri Adamson of Perth, published in Edinburgh in 1638:

For what we do presage is not in grosse,
For we be brethren of the Rosie Crosse:
We have the *Mason word* and second sight,
Things for to come we can foretell aright . . .

The links between philosophy of nature, the Rosicrucians, and the Royal Society should come as no surprise. Let us not forget that Robert Boyle, one of the founders of experimental physics, and Newton and the other scientists of the learned English Academy, were also interested in alchemy, and that in their eyes mathematical logic did not exclude reasoning by analogy. It is in this climate that a *high order of Freemasonry* was constituted, after the Grand Lodge of London in 1722–like a call, as it were, to the invisible masters of the Rose-Cross, who were objects of firm belief.

In 1630 Petrus Mormius said he had found, upon arriving in the French Dauphiné from Spain, an old man named Rose who had belonged to an order of the Golden and Rosy Cross. In 1654 an alchemical society was formed in Nurenberg; Leibniz, who was interested in the *Chemical Wedding,* belonged to it. At the end of the century Gottfried Arnold published his massive work *Unpartheyische Kirchen- und Ketzerhistorie,* delivering himself therein of an analysis of the first Rosicrucian writings. Interest in the fraternity grew still more in the eighteenth century. In 1714, just a century after the appearance of the *Fama Fraternitatis,* Sincerus Renatus, alias Samuel Richter, a Silesian pastor, secured the publication in Breslau of his *Die Wahrhaffte und vollkommene Bereitung Des Philosophischen Steins der Bruederschafft aus dem Orden Des Guelden- und Rosen-Cruetzes.* The end of the book is devoted to fifty-two rules of the order, and specifies that it is governed by an Imperator. In 1747 J. H. Schmidt, originally from Bohemia and the author of numerous writings published under the pseudonyms Elias Artista and Hermann Fictuld, asserted in his *Aureum vellus* that the Rosicrucian and hermetic tradition had been transmitted clandestinely until the creation of the fraternity of the Golden and Rosy Cross. In fact it consisted only of small scattered groups with no real link to Freemasonry. But there did exist a mutual fascination between the two: to the humanitarianism of Freemasonry, the Golden and Rosy Cross added its Christian coloration and the dynamic of its doctrine, focused on the conquest of the spiritual Golden Fleece. The idea that masonry possessed a Templar filiation, which was to fare so splendidly in the Stricte Observance Templière, was probably due to the Golden and Rosy Cross.

Still, the Golden and Rosy Cross had its own existence. Starting in 1757, masonic Rosicrucian circles developed in various German towns, blending the Templar legend with alchemy. In 1777 the Lodge of the Three Globes in Berlin, whose Grand Master was Duke Frederick Augustus of Brunswick, became the home of a new rite, the Order of the Golden and Rosy Cross of the Ancient System. Its founders were J. R. von Bischoffswerder (1714–1803) and J. C. Woellner (1732–1800). The former military officer and former pastor had secured the good graces of Prince Frederick Wilhelm (1744–1797), nephew and heir apparent of Frederick the Great, king of Prussia. When he ascended the throne in 1786 he named the former his minister of war, and the latter his minister of religion. In the meantime they had recruited Prince Frederick of Brunswick and arranged to have the national Mother Lodge of the Prussian States, that of the Three Globes, withdrawn from the Stricte Observance Templière, from which they had discharged a large number of members.

At the same time, the Stricte Observance was competing with them, discovering in Florence with the help of C. E. Waechter (1746–1825) a Rosicrucian filiation. Moreover, their order was the target of various attacks. The Golden and Rosy Cross of the Ancient System was accused of being in the service of the Jesuits (J. J. von Ecker und Eckhoffen, *Der Rosenkreuzer in seiner Bloesse*, 1782). At the convent of Wilhelmsbad (July–August 1782) the Golden and Rosy Cross of the Ancient System was quite simply rejected, in favor of the Chevaliers Bienfaisants de la Cité Sainte of Jean-Baptiste Willermoz of Lyon (1730–1824), and the Cohen teaching, of Martines de Pasqually (1710–1774). These snares and failures did not, to be sure, prevent the spread of the Golden and Rosy Cross of the Ancient System in Hungary, Poland, or Russia. But Austria had limited the activity of masonic lodges, and in Germany the order was discredited by its inability to keep the promises of its philosophy of nature. So in 1786 it was dissolved.

But, for all that, the Rosicrucian tradition within Freemasonry was not extinguished. In France a Council of the Knights of the East, founded in 1762, had established instructions for the seven grades of the adonhiramite rite. The seventh and highest was that of the Chevalier Rose-Croix. For its part, the Grand Lodge of Lyon cultivated an eighth grade, that of the Chevalier de l'Epée et de Rose-Croix. In 1763 Jean-Baptiste Willermoz created a Black Eagle Chapter, one of whose secret degrees was named Grand Maître de l'Aigle Noir Rose-Croix.

The Ancient and Accepted Scottish Rite today unites hundreds of thousands of freemasons around the world; it is one masonic rite among others, practiced in numerous masonic jurisdictions, including that of the Grand Orient in France. But it possesses, for our purposes, the peculiarity of having preserved as its eighteenth grade that of the Chevalier Rose-Croix, a grade associated with a ritual whose significance is perhaps not always well understood.

Among the current forms of Rosicrucian activity the most interesting is without doubt the Societas Rosicruciana in Anglia. Founded around 1865, it is a masonic body. Only freemasons may enter it. There also exists a Societas Rosicruciana in Scotia and a similar society in the United States. In France the Collège Bernard de Clairvaux is affiliated with the Societas Rosicruciana in Anglia. In 1887 an offshoot of this society appeared under the name of the Hermetic Order of the Golden Dawn. It had opened lodges in London, Bristol, Bradford, and Paris and counted among its members

Arthur Waite, the author of excellent works on the Rose-Cross and the alchemical tradition, and Aleister Crowley, a remarkable alpinist.

In 1888 the Ordre Kabbalistique de la Rose-Croix was created in France. Its founder, Stanislas de Guaïta (1861–1897), had been initiated into hermetic and masonic symbolism by Oswald Wirth. Functioning as a free university, the order awarded the grades of Bachelor, Licentiate, and Doctor in Kabbalah. Dr. Gérard Encausse, alias Papus (1865–1916), took part in the direction of the order.

In 1890 Josephin Péladan (1858–1918) organized an Ordre de la Rose-Croix catholique, whose mission was to keep alive within the church the esoteric tradition.

It was also in France, in Toulouse, that an American, Dr. H. Spencer Lewis (1883–1939), had a vision directing him to give renewed life from the United States to the Rosicrucian fraternity. The Anticus Mysticusque Ordo Rosae Crucis, founded in 1909, has its seat in California. Better known under the acronym AMORC, it remains today the source of an important activity in America and Europe.

The same is true of the Rosicrucian Fellowship, which was created in 1911 in Oceanside, south of Los Angeles, by Max Heindel (1865–1919), who dedicated himself to healing the sick, in addition to teaching his doctrine. Another group organized by Emerson M. Clymer, which has its seat in Beverley Hall, Pennsylvania, claims the Rose-Cross and concerns itself with medical care.

In the Netherlands the Lectorium Rosicrucianum, founded in Haarlem, explicitly harks back to the first Rosicrucian writings and to J. V. Andreae. It has published editions of the *Fama,* the *Confessio Fraternitatis,* the *Chemical Wedding,* and the *Christianopolis,* accompanied by commentaries characteristic of the organization's doctrine, written by J. van Rijcken-borgh. The Lectorium has affiliates in Europe, the United States, Brazil, Australia, and New Zealand.

Finally we mention the always very lively movement of anthroposophy. In 1917–1918 its founder, Rudolf Steiner (1861–1925), published in Munich an original study of the *Chemical Wedding.* His doctrine, impregnated with Hindu and Buddhist philosophy, goes far beyond the ideas of the initial Rose-Cross, but he considers the mission of the Rose-Cross to be that of "searching for a knowledge applicable to life and susceptible of ameliorating its conditions. . . . A scientific search which kept strictly to duly observed facts would supply the most solid proofs of Rosicrucian truths."

Like the Phoenix, the Rose-Cross is therefore always reborn under multiple avatars. Its persistence is not the result of chance. It demonstrates that the Rose-Cross is much more than the *"plaisanterie ingénieuse,"* the "*ludibrium*," of which J. V. Andreae spoke after the fact in depreciating its significance. The Rose-Cross is a "myth" with all the mysterious and incantatory value of the term with its rich and multilayered meaning—the presentation of a symbol, the epiphany of a profound reality, common to all people and present in all ages.

Translated by Stephen Voss

Bibliography

Arnold, Paul. *Histoire des Rose-Croix et les origines de la Franc-Maçonnerie*. Paris, 1955.

Brecht, Martin. "Johann Valentin Andreae. Weg und Programm eines Reformers zwischen Reformation und Moderne." In *Theologie an der Universität*, 270–343. Tübingen, 1977.

Edighoffer, Roland. "Johann Valentin Andreae: A propos du 400ᵉ anniversaire de sa naissance." *ARIES*, no. 5 (Paris, 1986).

———. *Les Rose-Croix*. Paris, 1982. 3rd ed. 1991.

———. *Rose-Croix et société idéale selon Johann Valentin Andreae*. 2 vols. Paris, 1982–87.

Faivre, Antoine. *L'ésotérisme au XVIIIème siècle*. Paris, 1973.

Frey-Jaun, Regine. *Die Berufung des Türhüters: Zur "Chymischen Hochzeit Christiani Rosenkreutz" von Johann Valentin Andreae (1586–1654)*. Bern, 1989.

Heindel, Max. *The Rosicrucian Cosmo-Conception*. Oceanside, 1909.

Jackson, A. C. F. "Rosicrucianism and its effect on Craft Masonry." *Ars Quatuor Coronatorum* 97 (Letchworth, 1985).

Kienast, Richard. "Johann Valentin Andreae und die vier echten Rosenkreutzer-Schriften." *Palaestra* 152 (Leipzig, 1926).

Lewis, H. Spencer. *Rosicrucian Questions and Answers with complete history of the Rosicrucian Order*. 6th ed. San Jose, 1959.

McIntosh, Christofer. *The Rosy Cross unveiled*. Wellingborough, 1980.

Maier, Michael. *Laws of the Fraternity of the Rosie Crosse (Themis Aurea)*. Preface by Manly P. Hall. Los Angeles, 1976.

Montgomery, John Warwick. *Cross and crucible: Johann Valentin Andreae (1585–1654), Phoenix of the Theologians*. La Haye, 1973.

Peuckert, Will-Erich. *Die Rosenkreutzer: Zur Geschichte einer Reformation*. Jena, 1928. Reedited by Rolf Christian Zimmermann, *Das Rosenkreuz*. Berlin, 1973.

Schick, Hans. *Das ältere Rosenkreuzertum*. Berlin, 1942. Reedited by Alain Godet, *Die geheime Geschichte der Rosenkreuzer*. Schwarzenburg, 1980.

Steiner, Rudolf. *Die Theosophie des Rosenkreuzers*. 5th ed. Dornach, 1967.

van Dülmen, Richard. *Die Utopie einer christlichen Gesellschaft: Johann Valentin Andreae, 1586–1654*. Stuttgart-Bad Cannstadt, 1978.

van Rijckenborgh, J. *Die Geheimnisse der Bruderschaft des Rosenkreuzes*. Haarlem, 1967–1980.

Waite, Arthur Edward. *The Brotherhood of the Rosy Cross*. London, 1924.

Yates, Francis A. *The Rosicrucian Enlightenment*. London, 1972.

7

Jacob Boehme
and His Followers

PIERRE DEGHAYE

Jacob Boehme and His Doctrine

J ACOB BOEHME was born in 1575 near Goerlitz, not far from the Bohemian border, in Silesia, a German provice won by the Reformation but also rich in spiritual heterodoxy and hermeticism. He came from a family of farmers but was not robust enough to farm; instead, in 1599 Boehme began to work as a cobbler in Goerlitz. The following year he had an illumination to which he ascribed great importance: while contemplating a pewter vessel he experienced himself as penetrating the mystery of nature. Later, in 1610, he had another illumination, and in 1612 wrote his first book, entitled *Aurora*. Boehme did not intend for his work to be published, but it was circulated privately nevertheless, much to the chagrin of Gregor Richter, the pastor of Goerlitz. From that time on, Boehme was considered a heretic. He was imprisoned and later released, but the ecclesiastical authorities prohibited him from further writing. Notwithstanding, after a few years he could no longer resist his inner voice, which he believed was the voice of the spirit, and he was compelled to write again. His friends, who considered him a genuine prophet, eagerly awaited further "messages" from his pen. Thus in 1618 he published his second work: *Beschreibung von den drey Prinzipien* (Description of the three principles). In 1613 he ceased work as a shoemaker and began to peddle clothing. Boehme traveled to many places, including Prague, and acquired many friends who believed in him and with whom he had very rewarding relationships. Part of his theosophical correspondence with those friends is published in *Theosophische Sendbriefe*. Between 1621 and 1623, Boehme wrote his most important works, in particular *De Signatura Rerum* and *Mysterium Magnum*. In 1624 his book *Der Weg zu Christo* (The way to Christ) was published. With the publication of this work, the antipathy which Gregor Richter felt for Boehme reached its zenith, but Richter died on April 24 of the same year. Boehme died shortly thereafter on November 17. Thanks to the intervention of an influential friend he was permitted a Christian burial.

Jacob Boehme seemed the most German of all spiritual figures of his time. He was called *philosophus teutonicus*, though he had not studied philosophy. Boehme said that he had been taught by God, and certain visions revealed his vocation to him; he had been called to be the "prophet of the dawn." The Spirit revealed truths of which scholars were ignorant. This instruction, however, was carried out with the aid of scripture. Boehme was a Lutheran, and the Bible, the daily bread of Christians, was at the center of the world he inhabited.

He was not totally unlettered. When he wrote his first book, *Aurora* (*Aurora, oder Die Morgenröte in Aufgang*), he had come under certain influences. He was more or less familiar with the philosophy of nature of the celebrated physician Paracelsus (1493–1541). The mayor of Goerlitz was a Paracelsian. He also seems to have read very early the writings then circulating under the name of Valentin Weigel (1533–1588), which were reviving the Christian mystical tradition in the face of an orthodoxy hostile to it.

Boehme had friends to whom he revealed sublime truths, even though they were lettered and lived better than he. But he also received something from them. Among the people who had real veneration for him, we name Karl Ender von Sercha, representing a nobility less orthodox than the people; Balthasar Walther, an enthusiastic student of the Kabbalah and alchemy who had traveled in the Orient in search of wisdom, whose search had in the end led to Jacob Boehme; and Tobias Kober, a Paracelsian physician. What exactly did they contribute to him? It is impossible to say, and yet we cannot doubt that it was real. If Jacob Boehme had been blessed with special gifts, nothing prevents us from saying that he was also instructed by human beings.

Nourished by his inspiration, scripture, and various other sources, Boehme forged a system that would be imitated but belonged to him alone. Although basing himself on the Bible, he began contradicting Lutheran orthodoxy. As we have already said, the religious authorities took note and Boehme was imprisoned as soon as they learned of his first work. To be sure, the author was not to remain in prison and would write still more, but until his death he would bring upon himself the censure of the church whose son he was. (It was entirely fitting that he was accorded a Christian burial.)

Transposing philosophy of nature to the level of the supreme knowledge proper to theology, Boehme made of it a *theosophy*. It was this theosophy that appeared incompatible with institutional theology based on dogma. In fact it is also a theology, that is, a science of God. But it is profoundly different from dogmatic theology, not only Lutheran but of any confession whatsoever. Theosophy represents another approach to God, and it is this that still interests us today.

According to Gershom G. Scholem, Jewish Kabbalah is a theosophy. For Henry Corbin, the eminent specialist in Islamic mysticism, the latter is also a theosophy. Boehme's system is a theosophy. What these three types of thought have in common is that their subject matter is God making himself known.

A text from Islamic tradition says that God is the hidden treasure who desires to be known and created the world to this end. Roughly the same thing can be said of the God of the Kabbalah and the God of Boehme. God is first of all a hidden God, and theosophy shows us how the hidden God becomes a revealed God. It is a theology of revelation.

According to the theologies we shall call traditional, in the broadest sense of the term, the end of revelation is only conceived from the perspective of the believer. For the theosopher, revelation exists first of all in God, even before human beings existed; human beings were created for the sake of revelation's fulfillment.

God makes himself known through humanity, but also, according to Boehme, God knows himself in humanity. Boehme does not hesitate to say that the Absolute does not know itself. Thus it is to himself that God is revealed as much as to the faithful.

The hidden God is the unknown divinity which does not know itself. This divinity aspires to be known not only by the creature but also by itself. The revealed God is the God who knows himself in humanity just as he is known by humanity. Theosophy describes the transition from the hidden God to the revealed God.

In order to render itself knowable, the divinity must assume an appearance whereby it will be visible. By analogy we conceive this appearance to be similar to the body, which is the visibility of the soul. The hidden God is the invisible God, which cannot itself be contemplated in its Glory. The revealed God is identified with this Glory made visible. This Glory is the body of light that the divinity assumes in order to become manifest, and it is in this radiant body that it contemplates itself.

In order to be known to creatures, the divinity must accommodate itself to them, must assume a created form. For Boehme, however, God knows himself in the same way that he is known by human beings. God knows himself through the method he uses to reveal himself to them. The theosopher shows us how the hidden God, invisible and without form, gives birth to a God which is manifest in a body.

For Boehme as for a kabbalist or an Islamic mystic, the form that the manifest God assumes is that of a human being. Is not every true form a human form? God is revealed only through the appearance of a human body. Without this appearance the divinity remains forever unknowable.

The human form is the symbol of all symbols. Theosophy is symbolic theology. In the spirit of theosophy, there is no real knowledge without a tangible support. Pure spirit can never be grasped. The God of Boehme can only know himself by assuming a tangible form. The God of theosophy is not the pure intelligible being of the philosophers.

God assuming human form in order to reveal himself to human beings— is this not the God of every Christian theology? In contrast to the Jewish kabbalist or the Islamic mystic, Boehme believes that Christ, the Son of God, was born in our flesh. Boehme is not a docetist, like the gnostics of the early Christian era, for whom the body assumed by the savior was only a façade. For Boehme, the earthly body of Christ was indeed real. However, God had made the human form his own before Christ was born from Mary's womb, even before our world was created. Now the primordial human form was not our body of bondage, the *forma servilis*. It was a body of light, the same one that the Christ born from Mary's womb was to possess under his earthly covering. It is in this radiant body that God truly manifests himself, and not in our covering of vile flesh. It is the body of the eternal Man which, when Christ was born on earth, was hidden under the appearance of his earthly body.

Before our world was created, God manifested himself in the form of the eternal Man who existed before earthly human beings. Since the latter did not yet exist, for whom did God render himself visible? The revealed God appears even before humanity is called to life in order to contemplate him. Does he not make himself visible only for himself? God could not reveal himself, even for his own contemplation, if there did not exist something other than him. In order to contemplate himself, God requires that a mirror be offered to him, in a form he has raised up, which, although inhabited by him, is distinct from him. This mirror must therefore exist before the birth of Adam. The mirror is the body of the angels. The revealed God appears the moment angels are there to contemplate him.

The God of Boehme is revealed only in his works. Theosophy speaks of God only in relation to his works. It understands the divinity only to the extent that the divinity is exteriorized, to the extent that it projects its action outside of itself. The works of God are the worlds that are called into existence. The only knowable God is the one who works under the eye of creation in order to manifest himself. To create and to manifest are one and the same thing. The hidden God creates nothing. He has no relation whatsoever with anything but himself. His solitude is absolute. By contrast, the revealed God manifests himself in accomplishing his works, not in the sphere of his pure interiority but rather outside of himself. The divine works are distinct from God, but they manifest the divinity. A divinity imagined as resting within itself, perfectly self-sufficient, could never be grasped.

* * *

The hidden treasure creates in order to be known. But the divine works, or creation, must be considered on two levels. Before creating our heaven, God brought into being a primordial heaven, that of the angels. This original heaven is at the same time a celestial earth. Heaven or earth, it is called "eternal nature." It is the true abode of God.

This eternal nature is distinct from our nature. Our nature came after it, and it infinitely surpasses ours. In the so-called traditional Christian theologies, that which is beyond our nature is called the supra-natural. For Boehme, this supra-nature is what is absolutely *outside of nature*. Supra-nature is the hidden divinity. Now between this supra-nature and our nature there is a higher nature that is the dwelling place of God. It is not perfect eternity; the word "eternal" must be understood in a relative sense. It is, however, *divine nature*, beyond which the divinity is totally inaccessible to humanity, and it is this nature that is the fullness of the divine works. It is distinct from God; nevertheless, it is his perfect mirror.

Thus the works of God are presented in two degrees. First God calls eternal nature into existence; then he creates our nature. These two degrees appear successively, but the two natures coexist. Eternal nature remains within the envelope of our nature. When the latter is destroyed, the former will be seen in all its glory, and then God will be fully manifest.

The supreme heaven for Boehme is a nature that is the abode of God. This dwelling is the body that God assumes in order to manifest himself. Nature is the body of God, but it must be understood that this is eternal nature. Our nature is not the true body of God.

The theosopher may speak of this primordial nature, but how can such discourse be sustained if this nature is different from our own? It is true that when one passes from one nature to another, a total break in levels occurs. The two natures are so completely separate that they can never meet. There is an analogy between them, however, without which we would have no idea of the higher world. Our world is a mirror sufficient to reflect the higher world for us, but which we must break in order to reach this world.

The difference in level is such that the two natures never touch. According to this ontological distinction, the dissimilitude is total. Nevertheless, the analogy between the two realms provides the basis for theosophical discourse.

The analogy between the two natures enables one to reflect the other, and it is thus that the path of knowledge is traced. Without denying that the separation between the two worlds is absolute, the commentator of Boehme can paraphrase a famous text of medieval Hermeticism, *The Emerald Tablet*—everything above is like what is below, and what is below is like what is above. This is why the creation of our world contributes to the purpose of the divine economy, which is the visibility of God. Still, it does not fulfill it in itself. Contemplation of our own nature shows the way. This is where one must begin, but by the end of the journey it is absolutely surpassed.

For Boehme, the world below is therefore our nature, but the world above is not supra-nature; it is another nature, situated between the Absolute and our visible heaven. It is another heaven. The celestial world possesses a higher *physis*. The philosophy of nature is transposed: it passes on to this nature, which is the proper sphere of divine manifestation.

This intermediate realm is not perfect eternity, but a human being cannot aspire to rise beyond it without falling into the sin of Lucifer. The God of theosophy, however, is commensurable with humanity. For we are not only the image of terrestrial nature. In the totality of our being, we embrace the two natures.

* * *

Of the two natures, one is prior to the other. Still, original nature is not created all of a piece in its perfection. It is not first of all the heaven of the angels. The theosopher shows us its genesis, which precedes that of our world. The creation of the angels is in fact the termination of an entire process of successive emanations at the end of which there is formed the luminous substance that will become their flesh. This radiant substance is heaven itself. The eternal heaven of which the bodies of angels are made is the precious material that develops over the course of a seven-part cycle described as the divine masterpiece.

Divine nature is perfect, therefore, only at the end of a movement, a becoming. Its perfection is that of the seventh day, and its rest is conceived of in relation to the previous movement. Without this preceding movement, how could simple rest be understood? On the one hand, theosophical discourse is based on the analogy between the world below and the world above. On the other hand, it is articulated through the becoming of which the appearance of the world from above is the conclusion. Movement is spoken of; rest is ineffable.

The nature that is called eternal is therefore the fruit of a seven-stage cycle, which is the week of creation transposed to the level of an utterly first origin. This perfect nature is already an end, but in relation to our world, which it antedates, it is a beginning. The cycle from which this perfect nature originated itself has a beginning. The supreme divinity or, as Boehme calls it, the *pure deity,* is absolute eternity. It has neither beginning nor end. It is the hidden divinity. The manifested God, however, has a beginning, which is his birth. The only God accessible to us, the true God of theosophy, is a God who is born. To be sure, all Christian theologies mention a God who is born. This God, which is the Son, is born both in perfect eternity from the bosom of the Father and on earth from the womb of Mary. For Boehme, there is no generation in perfect eternity. God is born only at the beginning of his works. But this birth precedes the coming of Christ into our world. God is born in the form of the Word expressed in eternal nature.

There is a perfect concomitance between the birth of God and the genesis of the eternal nature. The divine generation is mixed with the pains of birth; God is engendered in nature as in a womb. The start of the seven-stage cycle is a true gestation, which precedes the moment when God is, properly speaking, born. Parallel to this, however, nature is formed. It is the body through which God will be born. The primordial womb is no more than a dark abyss, and it is only when God is born that nature is a true body. The formation of this body is comprised within the birth of God.

The first origin of things occurs at the moment when the body that will be inhabited by God begins to be formed. This is the beginning of that nature which is called eternal. Pure eternity has no beginning. The eternity conferred on the divine nature is based on a beginning, and the seven-stage cycle that unfolds from this beginning is already the model for time. What Boehme calls eternity is in fact the archetype of human time. It is already a becoming, although perfect eternity is immutable.

Becoming is movement; perfect eternity is absolute repose. The relative eternity of nature is established on a beginning that Boehme also calls eternal. However, this commencement engenders a movement. It is a movement in seven successive degrees that presides over the generation of the Word. Repose is but the end of this movement, at the seventh degree of the primordial cycle. Another movement and another time will be born out of this repose. It will be the becoming of our earthly nature.

The first nature engenders the other nature, our own, which obscures it while at the same time manifesting it sufficiently to reflect it. This second nature will be destroyed and the primordial nature unveiled, manifesting God in all his Glory. Nevertheless, our nature is not a mere accident in the fulfillment of the divine economy. Divine manifestation is inconceivable without the sudden turn of events that, following the appearance of the supreme heaven and the angels, brings about the creation of our world and ourselves. Indeed, we are the beings in whom God will manifest himself fully, for we recapitulate the two natures.

Thus, in a distant origin, God is born. The birth of God at the beginning of all the ages is the Christian version of *theogony*. It is theogony reduced to a single God. Parallel to this theogony a cosmogony is realized. The nature that is to be the body of God will be an ordered world, a cosmos. Now this world is first formed in a state of disorder. It is first a chaos, an unformed world. The genesis of primordial nature is the passage from this chaos to a cosmos that will be the body of the manifested God.

The commentator on Boehme can return to the observation Scholem applies to the Kabbalah: theogony and cosmogony go hand in hand. This in no way signifies that Boehme's system, any more than that of the Kabbalah, is a form of *monism*. For Boehme, unity is conceived in differentiation. The unity between God and eternal nature will always be a union without a mingling. Boehme must not be made a pantheist for whom nature and God are one and the same; nothing could be further from his thought. But the worst nonsense would be for the theosopher to confound *our* nature and God.

At the level of the primordial cycle, there exists an absolute distinction between God and nature, even though nature is the covering of God. Besides, the two natures are separated, although the first, the divine, exists within the depths of the second, the earthly. Eternal nature is the kernel hidden within our apparent nature, and yet there cannot be the least confusion between the two. Depth is a synonym of transcendence. We imagine transcendence on the basis of height, but it exists no less in the depths. On the other hand, depths also exist in interiority. What is interior is transcendent in relation to what is exterior. So it is with the two natures, the one interior, the other exterior. The higher reality exists within things, under the appearance perceived by our earthly eyes. The inside is transcendent. That is why God, in being at our center, is no less transcendent than if we conceive of him in terms of an exteriority which distances him infinitely from us. For Boehme, divine transcendence remains an absolute. Even in relation to that nature which Boehme calls eternal, God's transcendence is perfect. Nature is his clothing. Let us not confuse clothing with the person who wears it.

We have given an initial idea of divine manifestation from its beginning until the creation of humanity, in whom it will be accomplished in its fullness. We will now set out the course it takes. We must first ask how one can speak of the divinity prior to this evolution, since in itself it is forever unknowable.

God is born along with nature. We may imagine a first moment, from which the birth of God is prepared. This is the period of gestation which begins at the first degree of the seven-part cycle. The gestation that precedes the birth of God is therefore contained within the cycle of primordial nature. The divine manifestation does not begin simply at the instant when God is born in his full radiance. The embryo is formed in four degrees, which correspond to the four months needed for the infant to begin its life in its mother's womb. During this first period God is invisible; God is not yet born. Still, the revelation begins with this negative manifestation. What the cycle of divine manifestation first reveals to us is a divinity that is still invisible. What will be completed in the seven-stage cycle is the transformation from the hidden to the revealed God.

The hidden God is a synonym for darkness, although certainly in himself he is not obscure at all. This deity, which is the Absolute, is totally inaccessible in itself. It is necessary to imagine the divinity in two ways that appear contradictory: on the one hand, in itself, as Absolute; on the other hand, revealing himself in his works. The divinity never reveals itself as Absolute. In its pure nakedness it cannot be grasped, like the *En-Soph*, the Infinite of the kabbalists. On the other hand, however, the divinity goes out from its absolute aspect in order to manifest itself. It is revealed in the light, in its Glory. It is first felt, however, as an obscure entity.

Revelation can be conceived of only in relation to a knowing subject. In the mind of this subject, revelation can only be the passage from darkness to light. The theosophy of Boehme is a theology of the light that shines forth from darkness, thus signifying that darkness precedes light. Dogmatic theologies speak first of all of the light that is synonymous with divine perfection. They mention darkness only in reference to the angel precipitated into it. Boehme puts darkness first. The first part of the seven-part cycle of divine manifestation is dark. In order for light to pour forth, it must shatter the darkness. Light is represented in the middle of the cycle, at the fourth degree.

The theosophy of Boehme is a dynamic theology which, rather than presenting us a priori with the God who is light, first suggests to us a God hidden in darkness, who then unveils himself to shine forth in his Glory.

Darkness does not merely signify the absence of God regarded in an abstract manner; it is experienced painfully. It represents the *anguish*

symbolized in the third degree of the seven-part cycle. Boehme has projected here the terror of the soul to whom God refuses himself and who
is terrified at the thought of the eternal pain to which it believes itself
condemned. This darkness is already hell; Boehme's God is born in hell. In
its obscure depths, eternal nature prefigures hell; it is its archetype. This
nature is the hell that will be objectivized after the fall of the angel. For
Boehme, hell antedates the devil.

Is hell within God? No, not if we consider the divinity in its absolute
aspect. But when we see it emerge from this Absolute in order to become
manifest, it is first identified with the dark abyss from which it will later
surge forth, resplendent in its Glory. God is engendered in a dark womb
that is the archetype of Gehenna.

Darkness means suffering. The birth of God in pain in the womb of eternal nature prefigures the resurrection of Christ after his passion. What
transpires on earth once Christ has come among us only objectivizes for
us the primordial event that unfolds in the seven-part cycle.

Christ died on the cross to expiate the sins of the world. Sin provokes
the wrath of God; Christ himself incurred this wrath. Darkness is identified
with the wrath of God which engenders the terror manifested in the third
degree of the cycle. The first phase of the seven reveals God only in his
wrathful aspect. The wrathful God is the hidden God; the manifested God
is the God of love. Darkness brings with it the experience of wrath; light
is synonymous with love. In truth, God is the God of love, but in order
for us to know him, God must be born. God does not appear a priori as
the God of love; he must manifest himself as such. His absence is felt as an
effect of his wrath.

God revealed is God manifested in his works. When we speak of God's
works, these must not be taken only as the created world, which is our
nature on earth. The works of God are accomplished essentially in the eternal nature which is prior to our universe. This eternal nature is an *emanated*
world which precedes our *created* world. In relation to the primordial
emanation, creation is a second act.

With regard to eternal nature, our earthly nature is judged negatively: it
is a world at the heart of which darkness predominates; it is doomed to
death. Eternal nature, however, includes within itself two aspects, which
alternate. It is perfect only when it is completed; it is luminous only when
light takes away darkness.

Eternal nature includes two *principles* that are at the origin of all things:
darkness and light. When our world is created, all things are formed from
these two principles. If the creation of our world is a second act, this is

because God has already produced darkness and light beforehand. Our world is not what exists before all else.

The two successive aspects of the emanated world give it the appearance of two primordial worlds, one dark, the other luminous. These two original worlds are the two kingdoms. They are also, above all, two modes of life. What the cycle of seven reveals is the birth of the true life, which is luminous. Now at its root life is dark. Before it is the light, life is a dark fire. The unfolding of the cycle causes this dark fire to give birth to light. Life is first of all a wrathful fire. Then later, when it has become true life, it is a gentle flame. This wrathful life, synonymous with unspeakable suffering, is a life that does not accept a body. The true life is that which is incarnated in a body of light. The Glory of God represents this body of light. It is this which is revealed when the primordial cycle is completed. Light is the subtle body of life.

Theosophy is a theology of revelation. Now the God who reveals himself is the God who incarnates himself. God revealed is the divine life manifested in a body of light. This is life become visible, since it is nothing but light. All life is first of all a dark life, which seeks itself. Then, when it finds itself, life is a luminous form. All life tends to become visible. The end of all life is an eye in which it will be fulfilled.

Theosophy is a theory of incarnation. Now life is incarnated on two levels. This is true for humanity, born first in a dark body and then in a luminous one. The two phases of the primordial cycle produce the archetypes of these two bodies. In its first degree, eternal nature is a body that is a symbol of extreme hardness and perfect opacity. Darkness is represented by matter that is so dense that it totally hides the light. Then once it is transformed, eternal nature becomes a body that is at once a symbol of stasis and of perfect fluidity. This body is identified with light and is represented at the seventh degree.

So God is enclosed in a body which hides him; then he leaves this covering as if leaving a dark womb, to take on another body that is perfectly transparent and radiant. Divine fullness is in this body, which will be that of the transfigured Christ. Before being manifested to humans, the Son is born in the body of light from primordial nature. What the theosopher is describing, according to the seven degrees of eternal nature, is the birth of the Son who is the true God. This birth is repeated when Christ is born from Mary's womb, and then in all human souls who are to become the dwelling place of divine fullness. The primordial cycle has an exemplary status and will be renewed to infinity.

* * *

9. N. van Werd, *Portrait of Jacob Böhme in a symbolic and theosophical setting* (1677: Amsterdam). Copperplate.

In its first phase, the seven-part cycle suggests only the absence of God, experienced as wrath. But God must surely be conceived of as animating this cycle, directing it in order to be engendered therein. We must imagine this God producing eternal nature. To do that he must preexist it. On the one hand, God is born at the same time as eternal nature; on the other hand, God calls this very nature into existence in order to be engendered. This presupposes that he exists first. It is this priority that is the sign of his transcendence.

Boehme emphasizes the transcendence of God in relation to eternal nature. It is necessary to consider this transcendence on two planes: that of the Absolute and that of Wisdom. Transcendence is conceived of first of all at the level of the supreme divinity. This pure deity is everywhere according to its infinity, but in fact it is nowhere. Boehme speaks of it as resting within itself; the Infinite, however, has no dwelling place, no abode. To say that it inhabits a space would be to impose a limit on it, whereas it is itself that space. To state that the Infinite is its own dwelling place would already be to limit it, and that would be contradictory.

Similarly, we assert that God is all. But the Infinite in itself is nothing. The Infinite of Boehme is Nothingness; it is not a fullness. In order to be realized as fullness, this pure deity must radiate into *some thing*, which will be its body. This thing will be the Being that blossoms forth from Nothingness. The pure deity, which Boehme calls the *Ungrund*, is the Nothingness that produces Being in order to become manifest. In its completion, eternal nature is the Being in which the divinity is incarnated in order to render itself visible. Thanks to its pure transcendence, the divinity is not Being. It calls Being into existence in order to clothe itself with it and to shine forth from its heart.

It is this passage from Nothingness to Being that takes place in the cycle of eternal nature. But how can it be explained that the Infinite, which has no beginning and no origin, which is signified by the word "*Ungrund*," comes to enclose itself in a nature that, though it may be called eternal, is not perfect eternity? On the one hand, Boehme speaks of the *Ungrund* as an Infinite that is perfectly self-sufficient. We are not to imagine the least relation between this Infinite and anything other than itself, any world created or emanated. The Deity rests within itself, in perfect solitude. On the other hand, Boehme says that this same Deity *goes out from itself* to produce eternal nature. How can these two aspects of divinity be reconciled?

The key to this mystery is Wisdom (Sophia). In its absolute transcendence divinity does not communicate itself, but it has a double that is its perfect mirror. This double is Wisdom. It is by means of Wisdom that God is known.

Wisdom is not supreme eternity; it has a beginning. According to scripture, it was created before the creation of our world. Divinity offers itself to be known in the form of Wisdom, which is the mediator between absolute eternity and the worlds that are called into existence.

Wisdom, the Divine Sophia, appears at the very beginning, beyond perfect eternity. It is not the supreme divinity; nevertheless it is its perfect mirror. Its virginity is the sign of its transcendence, which, although secondary, remains complete vis-à-vis nature, even when the latter is called eternal.

Wisdom represents divinity, which, while maintaining its transcendence, makes itself present, first in eternal nature and then in our earthly nature. Wisdom is the hypostasis of the divine presence. To know God is to grasp this presence which Wisdom personifies. The God of theosophy is the revealed—that is to say, the *present*—God. Wisdom is the thought of God that is incarnated at different levels. Its true incarnation will be realized in light. Wisdom is the spirit of light; light is its body. It is significant that for Boehme all thought is called to become incarnated. This is no mere metaphor. Wisdom is the thought of God. For Boehme, thought and will form a single whole, and will is expressed by desire. Wisdom is God's desire at the same time that it is his thought.

Can one ascribe desire to God? Is this not to subjugate God, for is not desire alienating? Is this not to afflict the divinity with a human weakness? First of all we must remember that Boehme speaks neither of desire nor even of will at the level of the supreme deity. Furthermore, the desire that awakens at the moment when Wisdom is born is a perfectly free desire; that is, it is dictated by a totally disinterested love, not by need. Wisdom is the love of God. It is the desire of love that aspires only to give itself, to communicate itself. Wisdom is the gift of God and also the joy that accompanies this gift.

The first manifestation of God is therefore in his desire to communicate himself. But to whom, to what, will God give himself? Nothing yet exists but him. God must produce the *something* that will be the receptacle of his presence, symbolized by Wisdom. It is then that God conceives his works in his Wisdom. Wisdom is God's design. It is the plan of his works. It will be their completion as well. The cycle of eternal nature is related at once to the plan and its realization. It is Wisdom that instigates it. It is Wisdom that operates in eternal nature without ever becoming mixed with it.

Wisdom produces eternal nature in order to clothe itself with it as with a body and to manifest itself in it. But it is also in and through his Wisdom that God conceives the plan of our earthly world and the humans who will inhabit it. All of God's works are related to Wisdom, which is their first cause and their final cause. Wisdom, however, does not create materially;

it is the Word that creates. The Word is the demiurge, God's laborer. The Word creates and is in contact with creation. It is identified with the divine works on their different planes. As for Wisdom, it invites existence, but does not create in the proper sense of the term.

Wisdom is the pure thought of God, which projects itself in an image. It is in this image that the divine works are formed through the direct action of the Word. A thought that projects itself in an image is an *imagination*. Wisdom is the imagination of God. It is through the divine imagination that the two natures are called into existence—the one emanated, the other created. God's thought, his desire, and his imagination are all one, for to desire is to imagine.

God divides himself, yielding a perfect image which is his Wisdom. Then Wisdom produces its own image, in the works of which it is the plan. To be sure, "image" here must not be understood in its modern sense. For Boehme, an image is not a mere reflection; it is not a *simulacrum*. It is in the image, the fruit of the divine thought, that the ultimate reality of things resides. For Boehme, everything tends to become visible. This means that the end of a thing is to produce a perfect image of itself. The image is the visibility of things that are completed according to their profound reality.

For Boehme as for Paracelsus, all thought becomes incarnated—both the best and the worst. This incarnation is realized in an image that *produces the real* and is identified with it. The theosophy of Boehme is a theory of the divine imagination. We have presented it as a theology of revelation. But the two are one and the same. The first act of divine revelation is completed when God imagines his works in his Wisdom. Then it is once again through divine imagination that these works, once brought into existence, are called to perfection. Finally, it is in accord with this perfection that God will fully reveal himself.

God desires to communicate himself. But God can be received only if he is desired. When God produces eternal nature in order to manifest himself therein, he places desire in it. The seven-stage cycle of primordial nature is the cycle of desire. All things are born through desire. As Boehme untiringly defines it, desire is energy condensed to be the substance of things. At different levels, *everything is desire*.

Emanated primordial nature is therefore endowed with its own desire, and by the strength of this desire it exists for itself. This conforms to the will of God, who calls things into existence in order to manifest himself in them. Now in existing for itself, nature separates itself from God. In order that God can fill it with his presence, this separation must be eliminated. The desire to exist for oneself is materialized in the form of a wall erected between the world God produces and God himself. For God's plan to be finally completed, this wall must fall. It must already have fallen at the level of eternal nature; in the same way it will have to fall on the plane of our earthly nature. Everything that takes place in the original world has the status of an archetype in relation to that which follows.

The first desire manifested in nature is a thing's desire to exist for itself. At the first degree of eternal nature, the energy it consists of is stabilized to form a body. The power exerted at the level of archetypes is such as to render this universal body extremely hard and completely opaque. With all its density, it is a wall of darkness. For Boehme, darkness is a wall in which a hole must be made so that light can pour forth. Thus the first body is broken in order that light may reign. Another body then forms, because God would not be manifested if he did not assume a body as his temple. This other body is light, which is perfect nature. Wisdom is the soul of this body, represented in the seventh degree of eternal nature.

What occurs before the creation of our world prefigures what will develop in the cycle realized by human beings. We are first of all in a body crystallized by the desire of our earthly nature to exist for itself. This body is a wall that hides the light. We must be born in another body in order for God to give himself to us. Then we will no longer desire to exist for ourselves, but only for God. We will then desire only one thing: to give ourselves to God so that God may give himself to us. We will then be the temple in which the Glory of God resides.

Let us return to eternal nature. Will is divided, for from the moment when this primordial nature is born, the will of God is distinct from another will which is expressed in an autonomous desire. These two wills confront each other from the beginning. Thus it is that all life, in its origin, is a battle that causes infinite suffering. Before it is harmonious, life is a terrible war. Then a turning point is reached, a conversion of nature. This is the vicissitude of desire. Instead of wanting to exist for itself, nature denies itself. Paradoxically, it is at the price of this denial that it will arrive at fullness of Being. There is no true Being but that which is the fruit of total renunciation.

The body represented in the final degree of the seven-part cycle is born of this conversion of desire. It is the body of the angels represented according to the dimension of the celestial macrocosm. The completion of eternal nature coincides with the first creation, which is that of the angels. The totality of this creation is the primordial heaven. The universal body is this heaven, which is the abode of God. The body of each angel is identified with this great body; this alone is heaven and the temple of God. Light is its substance, its flesh. This body which is the form of eternal nature is a human body. It is the figure of the eternal Man which exists prior to humans created on our earth. The human form is already that of Wisdom. It is manifested in the bodies of angels. The primordial heaven clothes it. The excellence of this heaven is in a perfect form—the human form. There is no perfection without form. The only true perfection is that which is incarnated in a body of light.

The body represents a limit in relation to the Infinite, and fullness can be conceived only within this boundary. The glorious universal body represents the full measure of Being produced by God beyond the Infinite. If this body shatters because the desire of nature impels it to make itself equal to the Infinite, there is a return to the darkness of the beginning.

This is what takes place with Lucifer. The most beautiful of all the angels, the one who realizes the full measure of creation, he is not satisfied with this splendor. Moved by the desire to affirm himself for himself, he wants to surpass himself. His own will exalts itself; he wants to make himself the equal of the supreme divinity. Lucifer wishes to be the Infinite. He claims to recreate himself by his own movement in order to be born still more beautiful. He returns to the dark root of life and plunges again into darkness, which then closes about him, enclosing him forever. The lesson of his fall is that Being must never return to the darkness from which it has issued.

In modern psychological terms, Lucifer's error is the return to the depths of the night—*regression*. Life is born in Gehenna and is its dark fire, but so that its fulfillment may be lasting it must find its measure in a body. It then becomes the light. It must live in this body of light, for the real dynamic of nature impels it from darkness and toward light. Escaping the fire which is consuming the cursed city, Lot's wife turns back instead of walking toward the light, and is transformed into a pillar of salt. Theosophy is not a mysticism of night; quite the contrary.

Lucifer is precipitated into the darkness which he is to objectivize, becoming the prince of the darkness which from then on is called hell. He remains imprisoned there and will not be delivered. Boehme rejected the theory of *apokatastasis:* he did not believe in the redemption of the devil and an end to hell.

For hell to cease to exist, darkness would have to be abolished. But light would no longer exist without darkness. That is why the duality of light and darkness persists throughout the time of divine manifestation. Light triumphs over darkness; this victory, which illustrates the seven-part cycle, is its exemplar. Darkness, however, remains latent like night hidden beneath day. Of course, if we say that light and darkness are co-eternal, we know that the eternity in question is relative. In fact, the two *principles* do not exist on the plane of perfect eternity. We are only reasoning within the perspective of the God manifested in his works. Boehme is not a dualist to the point of affirming the duality of two *principles* at the level of the Absolute.

* * *

The radiant angel lost his body of light and was thrown into darkness, but the light that was the substance of his body was not lost; it is indestructible. The fallen angel, nevertheless, occupied a space that was devastated and must be restored. This is the space of our world. It is Adam who is to take the place of the angel. The space abandoned after Lucifer's fall is to be the arena of our nature. It is now in humanity that Wisdom is to shine forth, at least for a time.

Our nature succeeds eternal nature. The abode of Lucifer has been burned up in the dark fire which the angel rekindled. God restores this dwelling place; nevertheless, the world to be created there is not the equal of the first. It is a lower nature.

Eternal nature includes two *principles,* light and darkness. Light triumphs over darkness, yet the night remains latent. But when it is unfolded, eternal nature shows itself in a fullness of light. Darkness is not abolished, but held in abeyance. Unless an upheaval occurs like the one caused by the angel's excess, only light is visible; it reigns alone. Darkness is imprisoned within itself.

Our earthly nature does not know this fullness of light. It participates in the supreme light thanks to our sun, but the latter is thereby diminished. Our light on earth alternates each day. It is this perpetual alternation of the two principles that constitutes the *third principle*—our universe. Thus the totality of divine works includes three principles, and so Boehme's second book (1619) is entitled *Of the Three Principles* (*Beschreibung von den drey Prinzipien Göttlichen Wesens*).

Eternal nature remains present at the heart of our world, but it is hidden by this world. For it to become visible in all its splendor again, our nature must first disappear. This is what occurs at the end of time, for our earth will be annihilated along with our heaven. A new earth will appear. This crystalline earth will in fact be the earth of light which preceded ours and was the fruit of the primordial cycle. Long hidden, first by Lucifer's fall and then by Adam's, this earth will once again become visible. The primordial earth blends with the heaven of the angels. It is made of the same crystal.

Our earth is ephemeral, but the humans who inhabit it are promised eternity. Adam will fall and must be redeemed, but as he is born he is a radiant being. Adam is born with a body of light that is the abode of Wisdom; in terms of this body, he is an angel. Adam has an angel's body, which represents eternal nature, but he has another body as well in which earthly nature is incarnated. Adam is more than the angels, since with his two bodies he embraces the totality of the divine manifestation. These two bodies include the three principles.

Human beings are superior to the angels since, once fallen, they are able to rise again. Angels are born only with bodies of light, and if they lose them they are plunged forever into darkness. After his fall, Adam is relegated not to pure darkness but to our earthly nature, which he already possesses to a greater degree than the other. He will have to leave this lower nature in order to accede to eternal nature, but the crucial point is that he has the possibility, at least through his posterity. Indeed, the light from above, invisible though it may be, is active in our light, whereas it is not active in the darkness of the infernal kingdom: the light shines in the darkness, but the darkness comprehends it not.

Adam sinned from the moment when he fell asleep. He was the victim of his imagination. Sleep, for an angel, is a sign of weakness. After giving in to sleep, Adam discovered his earthly body, which until then had been hidden by the brightness of his other body. Adam saw his animal body, and in gazing at it crystallized himself into nothing more than an image of it. It is through imagination that divine works are accomplished, and it is through imagination that humanity is lost. Imagination is led astray in sleep and in dreams. On the other hand, when our thoughts are good, our inner eye contemplates the light in an uninterrupted fashion and the light is in that eye. That is why the good angels never close their eyes.

In his angelic body, Adam was a virgin—that is, he was neither man nor woman. When he awoke from his sleep, however, Adam was no more than a half; he was only a male, and woman had been born. The duality of the sexes reveals the division which reigns in the third principle. However, humanity will be restored by the will of God; it is in humanity that the divine works are realized. This is why human beings were present in God's thoughts long before they were created; they had been chosen from the very first beginning.

Immediately following the Fall, God placed in Eve's womb a seed, called in the scriptures "the seed of the woman." It is the seed of light which is to bear fruit in the womb of Mary when the fecundating voice of the angel Gabriel resounds.

Humanity will be fully restored when Christ, the model of the human being inhabited by Wisdom, shines forth in his body of light after his resurrection. After Christ, bodies of light will be multiplied in the persons of all those who are converted. The body of Christ will embrace the totality of all these bodies, each of which in particular will be identified with him.

Each believer is first of all a human being born on earth according to the third principle. Though born terrestrial, the believer will be reborn celestial. Our second birth is the equivalent of the resurrection of Christ and is anticipated in the cycle of primordial nature. What takes place in this exemplary transformation at the threshold of time is already a death and a resurrection. The cycle of origins is simply repeated each time life blossoms forth following movement. All life is born only to die and be born a second time. The theosophy of Boehme is a theology of the second birth. This is what connects it with Christian mysticism, in which the focal subject is the birth of Christ in us.

True believers are born twice on earth. They are born first of their mothers after the flesh. Then they are born children of Wisdom after their bodies of light, which clothe them under their perishable covering even though they have not yet departed this earth. They incarnate in human beings what the apostle Paul calls "the inner person hidden in the depths of the heart," which is hidden, but visible to the eye of the spirit.

Clothed in this glorious body, the elect have a foretaste of the hereafter. Others, if not doomed to hell, will also be clothed by it, but only after the last judgment. On the other hand, those who are converted on earth to be born on high have already been judged. The true faithful undergo from their time on earth the test of God's wrath. They are purified by fire in their inner being and then incarnated in an angelic body. When we leave our mother's womb after the flesh, we have only a perishable body; we are not truly incarnate. It is after the faith that we are incarnated in a lasting manner. True life is manifested only in a body that is the incarnation of our faith. This body is our faith made visible, to be sure, to the eye of the spirit. And it is within the limits of this body that God offers himself to our understanding. We arrive at gnosis only through the flowering of our faith.

At the level of collective humanity the fullness of faith incarnate will be realized on earth during the last age of our world. Boehme is the prophet of this age, which he believes imminent. He already hears the trumpet call announcing it; it is the coming of the dawn. Boehme is not only the theosopher who unveils the mystery of origins; he is also the prophet of the dawn.

Boehme and His Spiritual Legacy

Germany and Holland

The first great disciple of Boehme after his death was a German who took refuge in Holland, Johann Georg Gichtel (1638–1710). We owe to Gichtel first of all an edition of Boehme's works (1682). Gichtel also developed his theosophy in numerous epistles, which were published in seven volumes under the title *Theosophia Practica*. During his life, Gichtel gathered around him a small family of kindred spirits. After his death, his disciple Johann Wilhelm Ueberfeld, a German who had likewise taken refuge in Holland and was his biographer and the editor of *Theosophia Practica*, founded an actual society, the Community of Brothers of the Angelic Life.

Gichtel was a visionary, but he interests us mainly because of the way he expounded Boehme's doctrine. He accentuated its tendency toward dualism, going so far as to defend Manicheism. Gichtel's dualist spirit is seen in his asceticism. Before turning to Boehme, Gichtel, a German Protestant born in Ratisbonne, a city where Reformed and Catholic lived side by side, had considered becoming a monk. It was not a true vocation, but it left in him a disdain for the flesh that pushed him so far as to renounce marriage. Like Boehme, Gichtel opposed celestial flesh to terrestrial flesh. He celebrated his wedding to Wisdom. But Boehme did not go so far as to prohibit marriage; he tolerated it because of the divine patience exercised until the day of judgment. Boehme himself was married and had children.

Gichtel bent Boehme's doctrine in the direction of dualism. He was faithful to the master, however, in rejecting the theory of apokatastasis, whose defenders took the universality of redemption to the letter, inferring the redemption of the devil and the end of hell.

Among the Germans who were "converted" to Boheme's ideas in Holland, we must mention the Silesian Quirinus Kuhlmann (1651-1689). He was initiated into Boehme's doctrine by the same man who had taught Gichtel, Friedrich Breckling (1629-1710), a German from the north. Kuhlmann was also influenced by Ludwig Friedrich Gifftheil (1595-1661), another German, a Swabian, living in Holland. Thus all these German lands—Bavaria (in the person of Gichtel), Silesia, Schleswig, and Swabia—were reunited in Holland in the name of Boehme.

Quirinus Kuhlmann was burned at the stake in Moscow. He was a militant millennialist, who saw in Boehme not only the prophet of the eternal gospel but also one called to establish it. Kuhlmann was a chiliast revolutionary. Gifftheil, under whose influence Kuhlmann had come, took him to be a new David. Nothing could have been more opposed to the spirit of Boehme than to seek to establish the reign of Christ on earth. Gichtel himself reprimanded these impatient prophets. Finally Kuhlmann dedicated a cult to the divine Sophia. On this point he would have been faithful to Boehme had he not established a dubious analogy between Sophia and a sister soul named Maria Anglicana. Any linking of Sophia with the earthly Eve would have horrified Boehme. For Gichtel it was the height of impiety.

* * *

10. Frontispiece: *Der Weg zu Christo* by Jacob Boehme, in Boehme's works edited by Johann Georg Gichtel (Amsterdam, 1682). Artist unknown.

We turn now to theologians who did not advertise themselves as disciples of Boehme but were influenced by him. The first is a French Protestant, a Huguenot, Pierre Poiret (1646–1719), born in Metz. His works were published in French, but he was a pastor in Germany and spent the last forty years of his life in Holland. It was in Amsterdam in 1687 that he published his most important work, *L'Oeconomie divine*.

Some major themes of Boehme's theosophy are found in Pierre Poiret. Thus, he understood that hell is at the root of the nature of the human soul. Like Boehme, he affirmed that in order to gain access to true life one must have lived through the anguish of hell. And the *mystical theology* that developed within German Protestantism, of which Poiret was a representative, rested on the idea of the second birth. The elect person privileged with a second birth has a foretaste of the eternal happiness to be granted after the last judgment. Now this type of "pre-eternity" makes one forget the beyond a little. This is a marked tendency in the spirituality of *Pietism*. To be sure, it does not lead one to confuse heaven and earth; nevertheless, the kingdom of God is located between the two. It is established on the one hand within the soul of each believer throughout every human epoch. It is further objectivized on the collective level in the reign of the elect during the last millennium. This reign in the twilight of time appears at the border between what is here on earth and what is beyond. Similarly, the world of the soul is an intermediary between the body and the spirit. It is the middle space between time and eternity; it is the privileged place of the mystical theology of which Pierre Poiret is an eminent representative. This is a logical development from Boehme's system.

On the other hand we are becoming further removed from Boehme. It was in the seventeenth century, in Germany and Holland, that mystical Christianity became systematized within Pietism. In Poiret as in Gottfried Arnold, of whom we shall speak later, mystical theology appears as an attempt at synthesis between different Christian traditions. Poiret was an indefatigable compiler, editing the works of Christian mystics. A veritable library of mystics was being created. Mystical theology is founded on this work, which seeks to achieve a genuine summation.

Different traditions mingled in this theology. First there is the confluence of medieval German mysticism and the theosophy of Boehme. Certainly the theosopher echoed the mystics of the past, but he also differed greatly from them. Thus, for Boehme, God offers himself to contemplation only within the limits of a form, whereas the mysticism of Tauler aimed at immersion in the ocean of divinity beyond all forms. Poiret more or less did away with these differences. He created an amalgam which risks making one forget the specificity of theosophy.

To these two currents is added a third, that of contemporaneous Roman Catholic mysticism. In his library of mystics Poiret devoted a large place to the Frenchwoman Madame Guyon (1648–1717), whose name evokes a heresy known as *quietism*, which was condemned by the Roman Catholic Church. This spirituality is for many people a *feminine* mysticism. As such it is different from the theosophy of Boehme. The theosopher celebrated the divine Sophia (Wisdom), but this did not prevent him from attributing to the female sex the nature of the dark fire. As for Gichtel, who also glorified Wisdom, we know what hatred he had for women.

Thus, Pierre Poiret was one of those through whom the theosophy of Boehme was transmitted, but he grounded it in a context that betrays the eclectic spirit of mystical theology.

Poiret was fascinated by a visionary whose writings he edited, Antoinette Bourignon (1616–1680), who was born in Lille and died in Holland. Though Bourignon had not read Boehme, she believed herself to be the Virgin whose coming at the twilight of time Boehme had announced. She came to be venerated as the Mother of the True Believers. When she died, Poiret declared the saint to be "the most divinized and pure soul who walked the earth since Jesus Christ." Here then is a "mystical" adventure to illustrate what was then called "Boehmenism."

Antoinette Bourignon may remind us of Gichtel, because she also considered marriage an abomination. But Gichtel's mysogyny did not permit him to feel any sympathy whatsoever for the type of feminine mysticism she represented. As for Poiret's veneration of this "saint," it displays the ambiguity of "Boehmenism." On the one hand, Poiret is an intelligent reader of Boehme's works. On the other hand, he becomes an enthusiast for a prophecy which is attributed to Boehme but which has nothing else in common either with the work of the theosopher or with his spirit.

Gottfried Arnold (1666–1714) does not present himself as a disciple of Boehme in the manner of Gichtel, but he contributed greatly to making Boehme accessible to his epoch. Arnold published a treatise in 1700 entitled *The Mystery of the Divine Sophia*, in which he echoed Boehme and Gichtel. He also published the latter's epistles.

Arnold's most famous work, however, is a monumental production entitled *Impartial History of Churches and Heretics* (1699). We may speak here of a Copernican revolution in religious historiography. In fact, when Arnold wrote his *History* he no longer followed criteria of orthodoxy, although he was himself a Lutheran pastor; instead, he reversed the roles. It is the visible churches that have fallen away from the faith, and the heretics who represent the true church. Arnold reversed the traditional study of heresy.

In this apology for heresy, the heretic *par excellence*, Jacob Boehme, occupies a place of honor. Arnold took pleasure in portraying the theosopher's agreement with scripture and the church fathers. Gottfried Arnold held that the only true church was the invisible church. Yet he was a pastor and did not leave the visible church. But this was not a contradiction according to him, since if the true children of God enjoy perfect freedom vis-à-vis external constraints, they submit to them, in a spirit of mortification. It is this submission to Babel that Boehme himself practiced while clerical authority was persecuting him. Boehme remained faithful to the visible church even though according to him one could gain salvation without having been baptized with a sacrament administered by human hands.

The true children of God observe the external rite in mortification. But they also do this for their neighbors, that is, all those who, unlike themselves, are not privileged with twice-born souls. For such people, the visible church is an institution that has its value. They need to be guided to acquire faith, and the rites serve as a support for them. It is necessary therefore to maintain religion. That is why Arnold attacked separatists who left the church out of impatience.

This distinction between true children of God and other Christians proves to be of capital importance within Pietism, as it already had been with Boehme. Even more than Sophianic mysticism, it is the duality between the invisible church and the visible churches, on the one hand, and, on the other, that between true children of God and common Christians, which places Arnold in the current of thought that began with Boehme.

This same duality is found in Count Nikolaus Zinzendorf (1700–1760), the founder of the Herrnhut community, of which the Moravian Church, still very much alive in America, is an offshoot. The duality mirrors an invisible separation: the true children of God remain faithful to the visible church even while they are elsewhere. The twice-born faithful are members of two churches—one visible, the other invisible. As for other believers, they belong only to the visible temple.

From its beginning, the Assembly of Brothers (*Brüdergemeine*) conceived of itself as the communion of the true children of God. It was absolutely distinct from the communion of ordinary believers within the visible church. According to the Spirit which presided over its creation, it located itself above confessions. The religion of the Brothers, a *religion of the heart*, was the only true religion. It did not mingle with any of the visible religions, however reformed they might be.

Nevertheless, the Brothers maintained their practice within the visible church, imitating Jesus, who meticulously performed the rites of the synagogue. They were part of two churches. Through their body of light, that of the Inner Person, they were members of the body of Christ. This body made up the only true church on earth, invisible to the eyes of the flesh. The Brothers, however, belonged to one of the visible churches through the perishable body which they had not yet left behind. With regard to this body, they were not distinguishable from other believers.

The visible church, even when Christian, is the synagogue. The church, the only true church, is the communion of those who by the privilege of their second birth have become *participants in the divine nature*, according to the words of scripture (2 Peter 1:4).

According to our earthly body, we are citizens of this world and are always under the law, like the Jews of the Old Testament. The visible religions are themselves, without exception, expressions of the law, which is abrogated only for true believers and then only at the level of the Inner Person. Thus, the rule of law and that of the Gospels operate simultaneously until the consummation of time.

The law exists relative to sin. It is the manifestation of divine wrath. For Zinzendorf as for Boehme, there are two faces to the divinity. God manifests himself through his love and through his wrath. Love is synonymous with light, while wrath is identified with the dark principle. The law is at once the expression of divine wrath and divine patience. It was instituted for human good, but at the same time is the sign of human downfall. Thus it was, for Zinzendorf, that religions practiced in visible churches existed as a result of divine patience. They prepare for conversion. To be sure, one day this patience will end; this will be the Day of Wrath, the fall of Babel. For Zinzendorf, Babel was not only Rome; it was the totality of all visible churches.

On this point Zinzendorf is in agreement with Boehme. He similarly echoes the theosopher when he describes the Lamb, the Christ, offered to the wrath of the Father. This wrath is the *devouring fire* of which Boehme speaks in the vocabulary of scripture. Zinzendorf expresses himself in Boehme's style when he defines the blood of Jesus in alchemical terms. This blood is the *universal tincture* which purifies and regenerates. It is the fire that annihilates corrupt matter; it is the light that gives life.

Zinzendorf did not claim to be a disciple of Boehme. On the contrary, he protested his orthodoxy. Nevertheless, the main ideas of Boehme reappeared in his theological discourse. He was without doubt influenced by an avowed disciple of Boehme, to whom we shall now turn. Although it is true that the two men had a falling out, the hypothesis of an influence nevertheless appears completely legitimate.

* * *

Friedrich Christoph Oetinger (1702–1782) was a dignitary of the Lutheran Church of Württemberg and one of the great figures of Swabian Pietism. Oetinger declared himself a disciple of Boehme, who represented in his eyes an age of revelation. Oetinger viewed himself as living in a later age, but the theosophy of Boehme had not for all that passed away. On the contrary, it had not yet been fully discovered, and there remained the task of making clear what Boehme had expressed in an obscure fashion. It was this task that Oetinger set about to accomplish.

But Oetinger was not a disciple of Boehme alone. He absorbed the heritage of the Kabbalah, upon which he made a commentary, in its christianized form, harmonizing it with Boehme's theosophy. It is this conjunction of the theosophy of Boehme and Christian Kabbalah that constitutes the uniqueness of Oetinger's writings. We have an illustration of it in his most important work, the commentary on a kabbalistic painting commissioned in the seventeenth century by a princess of Württemberg for a small church in the Black Forest—*Oeffentliches Denckmahl der Lehr-Tafel . . .* (1763).

Boehme places at the origin of eternal nature a massive power of contraction which produces bodies and gives them an extreme hardness. Immediately thereafter an opposite force appears, which causes them to break apart. These two forces confront each other, resulting in a terrible vortex, which is the dark life. Nature is originally torn apart by this struggle, a cause for infinite suffering. It must cease for light to pour forth by the action of gentleness. When it does, nature will be harmonious. Darkness is dissonance; light is synonymous with harmony and a blessed life.

There are therefore two phases in the cycle of archetypal nature, which Boehme calls eternal nature. The first is dark. It is the time of merciless combat; the two forces facing each other appear irreconcilable. It is only in the second phase that violence is conquered by gentleness, and then the light streams forth.

Oetinger modified Boehme's system. He saw clearly at the origin of nature an opposition between two forces, but they are opposites, which are balanced at the outset. Swabia is accustomed to reconciling opposites. For Oetinger, this reconciliation is brought about through an alternation between two poles. The opposition between opposites is described as a type of *polarity*—in fact, a bi-polarity. Goethe will echo Oetinger when he sees in polarity, thus defined, the phenomenon upon which all life rests.

Oetinger was a scientist who embraced the knowledge of his time. He outlined a *theology of electricity*. The fire that is the reality of life is electricity, which is governed by polarity. Thus Oetinger stressed the resolution of opposites. In reading his works one often forgets the terrible confrontation which for Boehme was the drama of life at its creation. Oetinger softens the memory of hell, the universal suffering at the root of Being.

For Boehme, not only does hell lie at the origin of all life; it remains even when light has triumphed. Of course, when God fills everything with his Glory, hell is only latent, buried under the light. Nevertheless, it continues to exist; it is the night hidden under the day. For Boehme, there cannot be light without darkness, and darkness is the archetype of hell.

Boehme wrote that in order to conceive of the absence of darkness, one must rise to the level of the *pure deity*, although at this plane of the Absolute, light no longer exists. This Absolute does not manifest itself; it does not create. To the extent that God manifests himself in his works, light and darkness appear co-eternal. Oetinger delicately shades his conception of darkness. He examines it in its different degrees. Darkness is no longer necessarily synonymous with hell; it even appears under a positive aspect. Hell itself is no longer eternal. In other words, Oetinger admits the thesis of apokatastasis and on this point is not faithful to Boehme.

By contrast, Oetinger is the perfect disciple when he makes the incarnation of the Spirit the goal of all divine manifestation. God is incarnated in a body of light, which is his Glory. Of course, this body is not our covering of vile flesh; nevertheless, it is a body. The Spirit makes itself body, and body is sublimated until it becomes Spirit. It is thus that God manifests himself in his works by his Spirit.

Oetinger was a man of the eighteenth century. He reacted against a philosophy, inherited from Leibniz, that made of God an abstract entity. Idealist philosophy seemed to him to empty the Christian revelation of its substance and make of it a great metaphor. Faced with this idealism, Oetinger insisted on the materiality of the divine manifestation, although he was not in any way a materialist in the modern sense of the word.

The *sacred philosophy* of Oetinger is presented as both a physics and a chemistry. Theology becomes a science of divine nature. Of course, this nature is not the one studied according to the laws of modern science. It is a nature known to be full of God, without for all that being confused with God. Divine nature is the ground wherein God unfolds himself in his works. God dominates it and penetrates it. Oetinger is no pantheist, but for him God is present in all things. Like Boehme's, his theosophy is a theology of the divine presence. The transcendent divinity becomes immanent and is incarnated in that light which is sublimated Being.

Before leaving the eighteenth century, we shall return briefly to Germany; we must mention a work that popularized the theosophy of Boehme, the *Theo-Philosophia Theoretico-Practica,* published in 1711 in Breslau and republished in 1741. Its author is a certain Sincerus Renatus, whose real name was Samuel Richter. The work is written in a language imitative of Boehme's. Although lacking originality, the work is of interest to the historian because it documents eighteenth-century Hermeticism. It displays Boehme as well as Paracelsus integrated into the hermetic tradition. The theosophy of Boehme became a component of the wisdom that flourished in Rosicrucian and Masonic circles.

The idea of this tradition was reinforced by the very people who decried it. Thus in 1690 a Lutheran professor of theology, Ehregott Daniel Colberg, published a work entitled *Platonic-Hermetic Christianity* (*Das Platonisch-Hermetische Christentum*), by which he meant a theology of *fanatics* among whom he lumped together indifferently descendants of Boehme and Paracelsus, Rosicrucians, quietists, Quakers, Baptists, and so on.

In enumerating all these sects, Colberg gives the impression of a very diverse group, but at the same time he attributes a common doctrine to them. He fights against them and yet seems to proceed from a profound aspiration present among them: the search for a *philosophia perennis,* which motivated many eighteenth-century minds, particularly within Freemasonry but in general within that truly diverse crowd designated by the name of Pietism. All things considered, Freemasonry and religion were intimately mingled during this period in Germany. The eternal philosophy allowed confessional barriers to break and then allowed them to rejoin in a kind of higher Christianity. This dream of universality was based on the idea of a tradition developed over the course of centuries which in its depths crosses the boundaries of different communities. This tradition, more or less hidden, must be rediscovered. It is to this search that Arnold dedicated himself when he retraced the history of Christianity. From another side, an orthodox theologian like Colberg demonstrates its existence even as he combats it.

Colberg denounces the *paganism* of this philosophy, with which Boehme's theosophy was now identified. It is true that Boehme elevated the philosophy of nature to the rank of a theology, which may seem "pagan." But in return, in the Germanic world, Hermeticism was christianized to the point where it was impossible to separate it from the religious context. This was already true for Paracelsus, and it is obvious in Boehme. All of German Hermeticism was imbued with a Christian spirit. Was not the Jewish Kabbalah christianized?

We have mentioned the *Theo-Philosophia Theoretico-Practica* to attest to the permanence of Boehme at the heart of this tradition in the midst of the Age of Enlightenment.

* * *

Having spoken of Oetinger, we now recall the figure of Johann Michel Hahn (1758–1819), who was his heir. He was also from Swabia, fertile ground for theosophers. Hahn founded a community that still exists in the twentieth century. Johann Michel Hahn did not invoke Boehme's name, and yet the spirit of Boehme's theosophy was communicated to him via Oetinger. The symbols he uses are significant. Like Oetinger, but also like Boehme, he speaks of theology in terms of chemistry. In a certain sense he materializes the spiritual life. On the other hand, Hahn imitates Oetinger in a way that distances him from Boehme: he espouses the famous theory of the restitution of all things (*Wiederbringung aller Dinge*), otherwise known as apokatastasis.

Despite these differences, Johann Michel Hahn is interesting because he enabled the survival of a Pietism colored by theosophy. He inhabited the region of Württemberg, in which mystical theology found a way to prosper without a violent rupture with the Lutheran Church. On that account spiritual life there was so much the richer.

The last great disciple of Boehme in Germany was Franz von Baader (1765–1841). Of course, Boehme had still other followers, but they were contemplatives living in anonymity, the peaceful sort known, from an expression in the Thirty-fifth Psalm, as "the quiet in the land"—in Luther's translation "*die Stillen im Lande*." A very small group among them piously guarded the manuscripts of Boehme's works that were brought back from Holland in the eighteenth century when the friends of Gichtel were dispersed. Thus the manuscripts could be rediscovered and finally published by Werner Buddecke in 1966.

Baader was the last disciple known by his work, which is considerable. In his writings he comments on Boehme almost continuously. In this regard, a title particularly worth mentioning is the *Fermenta cognitionis* (1822–1824). Baader was not a Protestant; he was a Bavarian Catholic. Converted to Boehme, he still did not renounce his Catholicism. It is curious to see Oetinger, a Lutheran pastor, followed after a brief interval by Baader, a Catholic thinker, upon the terrain of theosophy. This argues for the universality of theosophical thought.

Oetinger clarifies *sacred philosophy*, opposing it to the *profane* philosophy of Enlightenment illumination, especially that inherited from Leibniz. Baader builds his theosophical system by refuting in particular the two great philosophers who were his contemporaries, G. W. F. Hegel (1770–1831) and Friedrich Schelling (1775–1854). It has been said that the thought of Boehme and Oetinger influenced these two philosophers. If they had been thus influenced, however, would this not have caused Baader to join them rather than oppose them? Let us remember that Schelling and

Hegel were from Swabia, as was Oetinger. They all came, therefore, from the same milieu. Moreover, Baader had close contacts with Schelling.

In his *Lessons on the History of Philosophy*, Hegel devoted an entire chapter to Boehme and said a great deal about the theosopher. Furthermore, there is in Boehme an opposition between yes and no and then a passing beyond them which seems to prefigure the dialectic of Hegel. There is therefore a temptation to see, in the humble person of the cobbler from Goerlitz, the ancestor of modern philosophy. In truth, the spirit of Boehme was something else entirely.

For Hegel the dialectic of yes and no is a response to a problem of logic. Hegel attempts to define the absolute concept, and he locates it at the end of a contradiction. With Boehme, the perspective is nothing like this. What Boehme projects into his theosophy is a specifically *religious* experience. In order to understand Boehme's theosophy properly one must place it in its religious context. Therein lies all the difference between the spirit of Boehme, which is deeply religious, and idealist philosophy, which depends on modern thought freed from a God with absolute dominion over souls. Baader felt this difference deeply; that is why his testimony is so invaluable.

If Hegel was inspired by Boehme, Boehme does not prefigure Hegel. But what of Schelling? This other great philosopher of modern idealism read not only the works of Oetinger but also those of Boehme. It was Schelling who invited his contemporaries to see in Boehme the great precursor of modern philosophy. Schelling seems close to Boehme and Oetinger. His philosophy is first of all a philosophy of nature, and it appears from the beginning to be allied to theosophy, which is essentially a science of the divine nature. There are similarities between Schelling and Boehme, but the spirit is different.

Baader himself was influenced by Schelling. That is why, until a certain period, historians of philosophy viewed him as a minor disciple of Schelling. Yet this was not the case, for Baader forcefully emphasized everything separating modern philosophy of nature from theosophy. It is this dispute, carried on during the period of German romanticism, that gives interest to the work of Baader. It revolves around Boehme.

Like Oetinger, but at a later time, Baader opposes theosophy to modern philosophy. The latter is a profane philosophy, whereas theosophy, as defined by Oetinger, is a sacred philosophy.

Baader blames René Descartes first of all; he charges him with the original sin of modern philosophy—dualism between spirit and body. The dualism that theosophy deals with is something else; it separates not only the spirit and the body but also the two bodies, the two natures—the one corruptible, the other incorruptible. The theosopher unites spirit and body with the notion of the spiritual body. The spirit cannot manifest itself without being clothed in a body. Of course this is the body of light.

Baader also criticizes Immanuel Kant. Contrary to the philosopher, the theosopher proclaims the primacy of religion in relation to practical reason. For the philosopher, human beings are autonomous. They derive from themselves the laws they obey. On the contrary, the theosopher rehabilitates the idea of transcendence. Human beings can find fulfillment only by a gift of God. Theosophy is a theology of divine grace which becomes the substance of the human being it renews. Everything comes to us from God.

Oetinger blames the idealism that denies nature. Baader calls this idealism *supra-naturalism*. It is illustrated in the systems of Johann Fichte and Hegel.

Baader retained the great lesson of the theosophy of Boehme. It is the devil who denies the body. The devil is an idealist. Lucifer wanted to rise above nature, however perfect, and he fell below it. Idealism is the sin of pride. It is the sin of every created being who, like Goethe's Faust, claims to be equal to the Infinite. Baader blames those who believe they can rise above all of nature. However, he criticizes as well the *naturalism* that he attributes to Schelling, whereas Oetinger takes aim principally at idealism, the enemy of every perceivable form. Baader defines theosophy by its relation to the two opposing poles of contemporary philosophy—the one represented by Hegel, the other by Schelling. Hegel, he thinks, denies nature. Schelling exalts it, but at the expense of spirit.

Baader reproaches Schelling for not clearly distinguishing between corruptible nature and the incorruptible nature that Boehme calls eternal. It is at the level of this eternal nature that spirit and body are reconciled. Even so, they do not commingle but are perfectly united. In the imagery of Boehme's theosophy, Baader's system is a theory of spiritual incarnation. Christ, who is the Word, is the key to it. Theosophy is a *Christosophy*. Modern philosophy forgets Christ. Like the ancient heretics called docetists, it denies the very idea of incarnation at any level.

As a theosopher, Baader rejects the pantheism which derives from Benedict Spinoza. Under its different aspects pantheism leads to a monism which effaces the distinction between God and the world. Against every pantheism Baader opposes the distinction established by Boehme between the supreme deity, the Absolute, and the God who manifests himself, that is, the Word. It is the latter who produces nature and lives in it. The Word clothes itself with nature, which is its work, while the perfect transcendence of the pure deity remains untouched. Immanence in no way diminishes transcendence. God is no less transcendent for being in us.

Thus Baader draws from Boehme's theosophy his arguments against modern philosophy. From this perspective he explicates the doctrine of the master while remaining faithful to him. Nevertheless, on one point he betrays Boehme, as does Oetinger: he denies eternal suffering. For Baader, hell is but a purgatory, that is, a means of purification. This means that everyone, without exception, will be saved, and hell will come to an end. It is significant that the later disciples of Boehme did not follow him on this point.

Confronted by the philosophers of his time, Baader insists on the *substantial* reality of evil. For him, evil is incarnated in Satan. Evil is not simply the absence of good; it is the objectivization of darkness, which is a principle, light being another principle. Baader insists on the substantial reality of the dark principle, but at the same time he rejects the eternity which Boehme attributes to it. Baader rejects Boehme's idea of an eternal hell as well as Kant's idea of radical evil.

The main interest of Baader's work derives essentially from its context. Reading Baader, we see how theosophy is affirmed in a time of idealist philosophy.

England

The transmission of Boehme's teachings in England was realized first of all by the publication of his works in English (1645–1662) by John Sparrow (1615–1665) and his collaborators, John Ellistone, Humphrey Blunden, and Charles Hotham. This edition was to be republished in the following century.

These admirers of Boehme were Anglicans and remained so. They were Boehmenists without, however, considering themselves dissidents. Serge Hutin, who has devoted a work to the English disciples of Boehme, speaks of "Anglican Boehmenism." According to him, John Sparrow and his friends intended to renew their church's faith by means of theosophy. We observe that through one member of this group, Charles Hotham, Boehme's theosophy came to be known at Cambridge University.

Organized Boehmenism is tied to the name of John Pordage (1608–1681). It was around Pordage and his wife that the enthusiasts gathered. They called themselves "behemists" (in England the name was written "Behme"). Thus a sect was born whose members sought sanctification through the inspiration of Boehme.

There were points in common between the English Boehmenists and the adepts gathered around Gichtel in Holland. To begin with, visions held great importance for them. Pordage was a visionary. This vicar of an Anglican church converted to Boehme under cover of a series of visions. Then Pordage, although married, had the same conception of purity as Gichtel:

the English Boehmenists did not allow themselves sexual relations. They refused to procreate, the only birth of value being the virgin birth, that of the soul engendered by the divine Sophia.

Pordage had to abandon his ministry, because in his case Boehmenism involved dissidence. Pordage wrote *Treatise on Eternal Nature and Its Seven Forms*, which appeared in London in 1681. The "nature" is Boehme's and follows the septenary cycle. Among Pordage's essential writings, his *Theologia Mystica* must be mentioned. It was published in London in 1683.

The small brotherhood of which Pordage was the head expanded to become the Philadelphian Society. The heart of the society was Jane Lead (1623-1704), a visionary widow with whom Pordage contracted a spiritual union (Mrs. Pordage died in 1668). Jane Lead did not owe everything to her visions; she had read Boehme, but her visions were the principal source of her writings.

The Philadelphian Society ceased to exist after the death of Jane Lead. The branches of the society established in Germany and Holland did not survive very long thereafter. In the eyes of Jane Lead, this brotherhood represented a new church. It was already the New Jerusalem, which signified the abolition of the other churches. The Philadelphians had separated from the Anglican Church. This visible separation was no longer in Boehme's spirit. Nor could they invoke Boehme's name in giving an institutional form to the mystical life. That is why Gichtel himself was hostile to all the sects established under the pretext of renewal.

In comparison with Boehme, Jane Lead and John Pordage exalt the feminine aspect of God in the name of the divine Sophia. The terrestrial Eve is denigrated; the celestial Eve is glorified. This also distances us from Boehme, who tolerates earthly woman because God exercises his patience vis-à-vis everything mortal, but who does not believe that woman is transported to heaven as she is. Renewed, the creature is no longer man or woman. As for the divine Sophia, she transcends the sexes absolutely; this is what her virginity signifies. To be virgin is to be neither man nor woman. The Wisdom Boehme speaks of is not a celestial Eve. Finally, Jane Lead saw Lucifer as saved by Christ. Gichtel criticized her on this point and based his criticism on his discipleship to Boehme.

As for the English Philadelphians and their practical actions, they gave material support to the followers of Boehme who had left Germany for Pennsylvania, where they established a small community. Although the community proved to be ephemeral, the influence of these Boehmenists survived.

We turn now to someone who did not place himself above others, who was not a visionary but who read Boehme with passion and commented on his work with great seriousness. Dionysius Andreas Freher (1649–1728) was a German who spent some years in Holland, where he was an intimate of Gichtel. Later he left for England, attracted by the Philadelphians. He was disappointed by Jane Lead, but settled in London, where he was to die.

Among the writings of Freher is a commentary on the theosophy of Boehme in eight volumes entitled *Serial Elucidation of the Principles of Philosophy and Theology* (1699–1712). As Serge Hutin remarks, to exposit the work of Freher is to repeat Boehme. But Freher also explains Boehme, and the merit of his commentary lies in the intelligence of its method and in its clarity. In contrast to the enthusiastic Boehmenists, this follower of Boehme, who was not a visionary but knew how to read the texts, shows clearly that Lucifer could not possibly be saved. He scrupulously restores the thought of Boehme. Freher does not interpret mystical experience by emphasizing visions. Along with Boehme, he places it entirely within the context of the second birth. (In 1951 an excellent study of Freher was published in New York by Charles A. Muses.)

After 1710, organized Boehmenism no longer existed in England. A great admirer of Boehme appeared, however, in the person of William Law (1686–1761). A theologian of considerable merit and possessed of a rigorous piety, William Law exerted great influence within the Anglican Church. He was excluded from it because he had refused to swear allegiance to the Hanover dynasty, but he always considered himself a pastor. It has been said that Law was literally *converted* to Boehme. He undertook to read his texts. He made use of Freher's commentary, and then commented on Boehme himself.

Law thoroughly grasped an essential aspect of Boehme's thought: theosophy stems from reflection on the problem of evil. From where does evil come? Boehme wants to show that it is not God who is the cause of evil. God does not will our damnation. It is not possible that God wills to lose this or that one among us; this is what Boehme maintains with great power against the supporters of predestination. Like Boehme, Law insists on our free will, capable, with the aid of grace, both of turning toward God and of turning away from God. Unlike Boehme, however, Law espoused the doctrine of universal redemption, apokatastasis. For him, the universality of redemption must be taken literally. Thus the devil will be redeemed and hell will end.

Despite this contradiction, Law claimed to be a disciple of Boehme. Among the English, he was the last. After him, William Blake (1757–1827), the poet, painter, and visionary, read Boehme's writings in the English translation republished in the eighteenth century. Blake appears to be imitating Boehme when he declares that all life is based on an opposition between contraries, between attraction and repulsion, love and hate, good and evil. Boehme does say that without evil good would not exist. But for Blake, as Serge Hutin emphasizes in his work on the English disciples of Boehme, the dialect of contraries ends with an inversion of values. Blake celebrates the beauty of the devil. How then can he be linked to Boehme? Boehme's hatred of the devil places him at the opposite extreme of all modernity complacent with regard to the night.

France

The spiritual legacy of Boehme in France can be summed up in a single name—Louis-Claude de Saint-Martin (1743–1803). Because he wrote anonymously, Saint-Martin was the Unknown Philosopher. Before learning of Boehme and coming to venerate him, Saint-Martin had belonged to Freemasonry. He was a member of the Order of Elus Coëns, whose Grand Master was Martinès de Pasqually. What had he sought in a Masonic order? Initiation, in the full sense of the term. The entire life of Saint-Martin was a search for truth. Masonic initiation, completed through all the Masonic degrees, was to enable recovery of the faculties which Adam had possessed before his fall.

Truth comes from God. It is not by our own means, by simple human reason, that we can attain to the knowledge to which we aspire most profoundly. But how can we obtain from God the illumination which the "man of desire"—to use Saint-Martin's words—calls for in all his prayers? Certain members of the Elus Coëns, those of Lyon, gave themselves over to theurgical practices. In order to reach God, one went by way of spirits. Saint-Martin turned to these adepts but was disappointed. He left the order of the Elus Coëns. Nevertheless, his name remains inscribed in Masonic tradition. Even now in France it is through him and among the descendants of Templar Masonry that an interest in Boehme manifests itself.

On a trip to Strasbourg, Saint-Martin discovered Boehme. He was initiated by Rodolphe Salzmann, a Freemason theosopher, and a certain Madame de Boecklin, with whom he entered into a spiritual friendship. Saint-Martin read Boehme using English translations republished in the eighteenth century, which William Law is believed to have edited. This Frenchman also learned German in order to plunge into the original texts. Better still, Saint-Martin set himself to translating Boehme. His translations were published and are still reprinted today. Despite criticisms that can be made here and there, they have shown a real charisma. (When we take into consideration the difficulty of Boehme's German, we might easily believe that the translator must have benefited from a state of grace in order to become initiated so rapidly.)

While translating Boehme, Saint-Martin carried on a very interesting correspondence with a Swiss theosopher, Niklaus Anton Kirchberger, baron of Liebisdorf. Not only did Kirchberger help him decipher Boehme's texts; he also exchanged ideas concerning their essence.

In Boehme, Saint-Martin seems to have found the definition of that which was dearest to his heart: human regeneration. If we are not renewed in our essence, we will not attain true understanding. We must be born again. According to Boehme, this second birth is magical, although this magic has nothing to do with the theurgy from which Saint-Martin had turned away. It is Wisdom, the symbol of absolute purity, which enables us to be born to true life, whereas the spirits we claim to subdue in order to gain knowledge evolve in a sphere where the impure mingles with the divine. It is from this *astral* realm that Saint-Martin had turned away. He freed himself from it in order to follow the inner way in all its rigor.

Boehme and Saint-Martin had different minds, but the Frenchman did grasp the essence of Boehme's theosophy, as shown in the pages he devoted to him in one of his great works, *Le ministère de l'Homme Esprit* (1802).

It is fascinating to follow this encounter between an eighteenth-century Frenchman, who wrote according to the particular genius of his language, and this German of another age and an entirely other world, who was called the *philosophus teutonicus*. It is a subject for study that is not soon exhausted.

Translated by Katherine O'Brien and Stephen Voss

Bibliography

Sources

The best complete German edition of Boehme's works is *Sämtliche Werke*, ed. Will-Erich Peuckert (Stuttgart, 1955–1961; reprint of the 1730 edition in 11 vols.). For a full bibliography, see Werner Buddecke, *Die Jakob Boehme Ausgaben*, vol. 1, German editions; vol. 2, translations (Göttingen: L. Häntzschel, 1937, 1957). In English, various works are available, e.g., *The Way to Christ*, translation and introduction by Peter Erb, preface by Winfried Zeller, Classics of Western Spirituality (New York and Toronto: Paulist Press, 1978); and *Six Theosophic Points and other Writings*, with an introductory essay by Nicolas Berdiaev (Ann Arbor: University of Michigan Press, Ann Arbor Paperbacks, 1971).

Baader's collected works have been reprinted at Aalen (Scientia Verlag), 1963, after the edition of 1851–1860 presented by Franz Hoffmann (16 vols.).

See also Friedrich Christoph Oetinger, *Biblisches und emblematisches Wörterbuch* (1776 [s.l.]; reprinted, Hildesheim: Georg Olms Verlag, 1969) with a foreword by

Dmitrij Tschizewskii. On Oetinger's *Lehrtafel der Prinzessin Antonia* (Tübingen, 1763), see the new edition by Reinhard Breymayer and Friedrich Häussermann (2 vols.; Berlin and New York: Walter de Gruyter, 1977). For other works by Oetinger, see *Etwas Ganzes vom Evangelium,* compiled by Guntram Spindler (Metzingen, 1982).

Studies

Deghaye, Pierre. *La Naissance de Dieu ou La Doctrine de Jacob Boehme.* Spiritualités vivantes. Paris: Albin Michel, 1985.

Faivre, Antoine. "Ame du monde et divine Sophia chez Franz von Baader." In *Sophia et l'Ame du monde.* 243–88. Cahiers de l'Hermétisme. Paris: Albin Michel, 1983.

———. "Ténèbre, éclair et lumière chez Franz von Baader." In *Lumière et Cosmos,* 265–306. Cahiers de l'Hermétisme. Paris: Albin Michel, 1981.

Gorceix, Bernard. *Johann Georg Gichtel, théosophe d'Amsterdam.* Paris, 1975.

Hutin, Serge. *Les disciples anglais de Jacob Boehme.* Paris: Denoël, 1960.

Muses, Charles A. *Illumination on Jacob Boehme: The Work of Dionysius Andreas Freher.* New York: Columbia University, King's Crown Press, 1951.

Susini, Eugène. *Franz von Baader et le Romantisme mystique.* 2 vols. Paris: Vrin, 1942.

Wehr, Gerhard. *Jakob Böhme in Selbstzeugnissen und Bilddokumenten.* Series "ro-ro-ro." Reinbek: Rowohlf Verlag, 1971. Translated into French in the collective volume on Jacob Boehme, edited by A. Faivre and F. Tristan, *Jacob Boehme,* Cahiers de l'Hermétisme. (Paris: Albin Michel, 1977). Gerhard Wehr is the author of numerous other works in German on Boehme.

8

Freemasonry and Esotericism

Edmond Mazet

EFORE DEALING with Freemasonry as an "esoteric" movement, it is necessary to determine in what sense it can be termed esoteric. The most usual meaning of "esoteric" is "secret" or "reserved for the few," and certainly Freemasonry is esoteric in this sense. It is a society of selected men, who are admitted to it through secret ceremonies, in the course of which they receive secret means of recognition which they swear not to reveal to people who have not been admitted in the proper manner. But etymologically "esoteric" means "inner" and can be opposed to "exoteric" or "outer." These two terms apply, for instance, to the teachings of a master who freely delivers to the public the exoteric part of his doctrine and keeps the esoteric part for a few selected disciples. The established religions themselves are held, in various circles, to have an exoteric meaning accessible to the whole congregation, and an esoteric one, the knowledge of which can be attained only through exceptional spiritual insight, a special grace from God and/or admission to a proper brotherhood endowed with the means of leading its members to such knowledge.

Freemasonry may also be termed esoteric in a sense connected with this second use. It conveys to its members, through ceremonies and symbols, a body of moral, religious, and spiritual teachings. A classical English masonic lecture defines Freemasonry as "a peculiar system of morality, veiled in allegory and illustrated by symbols." But it can hardly be said that all freemasons agree on the precise content of these teachings, and to what extent they are esoteric. All freemasons agree on a set of basic principles, and all masonic initiation ceremonies have a common basic core; but there is much variation in the details of rituals and symbols, and much more in their interpretation. Some freemasons are reluctant to admit that Freemasonry contains anything other than a moral and religious teaching common to all theistic religions and would wholly discard the term "esoteric" in the second sense as applied to it. Other freemasons, on the contrary, insist on the esoteric character of masonic teachings; but in many cases their interpretations of masonic rituals and symbols merely consist in finding in them elements of esoteric doctrines which are by no means specifically masonic, such as Kabbalah or alchemy.

We are therefore led to ask the following questions. Has Freemasonry an esoteric content at all? Has it an esoteric content, and more generally a spiritual content, of its own? What are its relations with morals and religion, and to various specific esoteric doctrines?

The basic principles of Freemasonry give some rather limited and partial answers to these questions. Freemasonry is definitely not a religion, but its members must be religious men. They may belong to different religions, and they must be tolerant of others' opinions. It is forbidden to discuss religious matters during masonic work. They must all believe in God, the Great Architect of the Universe, and in the immortality of the soul. They must also believe that God reveals himself to humanity in the volume of the sacred law, which is for each of them the sacred book of his own faith, on which he takes the oath that binds him to the order. He must regard all men as brethren, since they are creatures of the same God, and from this principle all masonic morals are derived, especially the practice of charity, which is the main feature of the exoteric side of the society.

As for the esoteric character of Freemasonry in the second sense, the basic principles say nothing explicit about it, and no universally recognized masonic authority has committed itself to assert or deny it, still less to define a precise esoteric content. Therefore it remains a matter of private interpretation among freemasons. For instance, the way the basic principles deal with differences of religions suggests an underlying belief in a transcendental truth of which the various religions would be different expressions in different historical and cultural contexts. Such a belief is generally recognized as part of the metaphysical foundations of the distinction between the exoteric and the esoteric sides of religions. Then the esoteric character of Masonry would consist in leading its members, each through proper understanding of his own faith, to this transcendental truth. Indeed, such a view is professed by many freemasons, but on the other hand those who are unwilling to acknowledge the esoteric character of the society may argue that the attitude toward religions involved in the basic principles simply means that Freemasonry is interested only in those few simple truths which are common to all religions, without searching for any inner or higher meaning beyond them.

Thus, the answers we shall try to give to the questions we have asked, however tentative, will necessarily reflect the private opinions of the author, as well as the problematic and views of the masonic circles (mainly French) with which he is best acquainted.

In my opinion, the only correct approach to our questions is a historical one. One of the main features of Freemasonry is to be a traditional society. Its ceremonies, symbols, secrets, rules, and customs are faithfully transmitted "from generation to generation." Since all such things are intended to convey to the mason the teachings of the order, the teachings themselves must be part of the tradition—in fact the most essential part. But a survey of masonic history through the three last centuries shows that the fixing of formal tradition in Freemasonry is rather recent and is mainly due to the existence of strong and united Grand Lodges, able to maintain the observance of fixed rules and customs each in its own jurisdiction. In the eighteenth century, when Grand Lodges were weaker or when different and rival Grand Lodges existed in the same country, and in older days when there were no Grand Lodges at all, masonic customs were much more likely to undergo changes that in the course of time might become important. There was an evolution of masonic tradition, and not the mere transmission of the tradition unaltered. In the late eighteenth and early nineteenth century, different masonic authorities undertook to stop the process and to fix the evolution. This resulted in the different streams of masonic tradition existing today.

Such an evolution of masonic formal tradition necessarily affected the perception of the teachings it was intended to convey and generated new interpretations which, in turn, would suggest further modification of the formal tradition. Because of lack of evidence, we do not know precisely how or when this process began, but we can say that the transition from "operative" (i.e., craft) to "speculative" Masonry was certainly a most crucial step.[1] Freemasonry as we know it today is derived from a medieval organization of craft masons, which was gradually invaded by persons of quite different social status. The craft masons were eventually excluded from it— or rather excluded themselves. Therefore masonic tradition was originally a craft tradition which underwent a tremendous change of social makeup. The gentry, which now formed the membership of the society, did not drop the tradition at the formal level, although in some cases they blurred it by ignorance and misunderstanding. They could not interpret it in the same way as the operatives did. They brought with them their own cultural background and started an evolutionary process that was still more important than that which merely resulted from more or less random variations in the formal tradition.

This is the reason why, although we have to deal with Freemasonry as a "modern" esoteric movement, we shall begin with a few words about medieval Operative Masonry, in order to appreciate correctly the state of affairs in the beginning of the modern or "speculative" period, which is crucial for understanding the character of modern Freemasonry as an esoteric movement.

Medieval Operative Masonry

We shall center on the information yielded by the two medieval manuscripts belonging to the large family of masonic documents known as the *Old Charges:* the *Regius* manuscript and the *Cooke* manuscript (respectively end of the fourteenth and beginning of the fifteenth century).[2] The reason for this choice is that these documents provide an almost continuous link between medieval Operative Masonry and modern Speculative Masonry. Indeed, much of the content of the two medieval manuscripts reappears in the *Old Charges* of the seventeenth century, and even in *Anderson's Constitutions* of 1723 (Anderson knew the *Cooke* manuscript and used it as a source).

The craft of masonry in the Middle Ages was not organized in the form of municipal guilds[3] as most crafts were. But according to the *Regius* and *Cooke* manuscripts, they had a particular form of organization, consisting of annual or triannual provincial assemblies. At such assemblies new fellows of the craft were admitted; they were instructed in the regulations of the craft and swore to observe the same, while masons who had committed faults were tried and punished. The manuscripts yield the regulations in form of "articles" and "points" with a legend explaining their origin. According to the simplest and oldest form of the legend, the regulations had first been given to the masons by Euclid, who founded the craft in Egypt, and had later been confirmed in England by King Athelstan. A more elaborate version, which appears in the *Cooke,* displayed a history of the craft from antediluvian times.

Although an obligation of secrecy is mentioned—the object of which is only vaguely defined as the "counsel" of masons—there is no clear evidence of an esoteric character in the strict technical sense (communication of secret means of recognition). As for the problem of the esoteric doctrinal content, or at least of the spiritual content of medieval Operative Masonry, the most interesting feature to be noted is the importance of the relations between masons and clerics, and interference of the clergy in the affairs of the craft. Both manuscripts were clearly written by clerics. They contain (especially the *Regius*) a set of moral and religious instructions that express the clerics' concern to moralize and catechize the masons. The mention of the seven liberal sciences tries to fill the gap between the empirical knowledge of the masons and the scholarly knowledge of the clerics; the legends combine elements of a craft folklore that probably originated in important ecclesiastical building yards, with purely clerical notions such as the foundation of the craft by Euclid. The history of the craft displayed in the *Cooke* is a typical piece of monastic scholarship of the time.

Adding to the evidence of the manuscripts the fact that the masons had to work out, under the direction and control of the clerics, the carved ornamentation of the churches, which was mainly a plastic expression of clerical lore and teaching, it is not difficult to guess what the spiritual content of medieval Operative Masonry must have been. It could only have been thoroughly Christian and certainly reflected the teachings of the clerics; that is to say, it was founded on the Bible and biblical exegesis, which the masons knew not from reading the book or commentaries on it, but from hearing the clerics' sermons about them and carving historical or symbolic scenes taken from them.

Some masonic symbols are derived from medieval iconography, for instance, the triad of the sun, the moon, and the Master Mason or Master of the Lodge (to be understood in a mystical sense). This is clearly derived from the well-known representations of Christ between the two luminaries. Another example is a symbol that was known to early speculative Freemasonry as the "broached thurnell" and is still to be seen in French lodges as the "pierre cubique à pointe." Although it cannot be traced continuously through the operative period, there is little doubt that it goes back to a set of illuminations in eleventh-century manuscripts of Beatus's commentary on Revelation, in which it appears as a representation of the ark of the covenant and as a symbol of the church. It is interesting to note that the freemasons of the eighteenth century had lost all memory of this origin and meaning.

It is only in this context that one can reasonably imagine what the esoteric content (if any) of medieval Operative Masonry may have been. It can only have consisted of such speculation about the Bible as took place among the clerics themselves, of research into the arcana of the holy book and of the Christian religion. Everything that was not of Christian origin must have been, at least formally and superficially, christianized. The medieval manuscripts give no evidence of such esotericism. However, a later document, the *Graham* manuscript (dated 1726, but the content of which is, at least in part, probably much older), gives perhaps some insight, though obscure, into the practices and speculations of medieval Masonry.[4] The text mentions an exorcism ritual which masons are supposed to perform when undertaking a building, in order that their work may not be shaken by infernal spirits. The ritual makes use of "foundation words" which form the "primitive [secrets?]" of Masonry. It may go back to a pagan origin but appears here in the Christian form of an invocation to the Holy Trinity. Moreover, the text insists strongly on its Christian orthodoxy. Later, the text explains how the secrets of Masonry were "ordered" at the building of Solomon's Temple:

> So, all being finished, then were the secrets of Freemasonry ordered aright as is now and will be to the end of the world for such as do rightly understand it—in 3 parts in reference to the blessed Trinity who made all things, yet in 13 branches in reference to Christ and his 12 apostles, which is as follows: one word for a divine, six for the clergy[5] and 6 for the fellow craft.

The modern reader is not in a very good position to "rightly understand it"! However, the text clearly reveals the existence of an underlying doctrine of the power of words and numbers in connection with the inner life of the Godhead and the occurrence of numbers in scripture—that is to say, something very similar to classical kabbalistic speculation, though in a purely Christian context.

The Transition from Operative to Speculative Masonry

The Reformation, and especially the dissolution of the monasteries, must have had important consequences for Masonry. Unfortunately, no document allows us to follow the masonic history of this period. After the *Regius* and *Cooke* manuscripts, no documents of the *Old Charges* family appear before 1583. One thing, however, is certain: the link between Masonry and the clergy that had existed in the Middle Ages was broken. In Scotland, the lodges came in 1598 under the control of the royal power, which did not prevent them from looking for protectors in the nobility. This was probably the origin of the admission to the lodges of persons not belonging to the craft, a process that was to develop so much through the seventeenth century. The Scottish lodges were bound by the *Schaw Statutes* of 1599 to keep records of their meetings—a fact that allows us to follow the details of the process, at least from the administrative viewpoint. Clearly the lodges had difficulties maintaining a sufficient membership by recruiting only operative members, and since the door had been opened to nonoperatives they were more and more tempted to increase their membership (and income) in this way. Less clear are the reasons why so many nonoperatives were eager to enter the lodges. One reason at least can easily be seen—curiosity. It was known (from at least 1637 on) that masons had secrets. More precisely, people who had been admitted to the society were

said to have the "Mason's word." It is from this period that the esoteric character of Freemasonry in the narrow sense is proved with certainty by
evidence of the day. The Scottish minute-books—that is, the registers in
which the lodges kept the minutes or accounts of their meetings—show that
the process did not proceed everywhere at the same pace; nor did it always
develop regularly. Sometimes the operatives became impatient with the
presence of nonoperatives and managed to expel them. Sometimes they
abandoned the lodge to them. In the long run, however, Scottish lodges
evolved from purely operative to purely nonoperative membership.

In England the process cannot be followed as in Scotland, since the lodges
appear to have kept no records of their proceedings—at least no such
records have ever been discovered. But the great number and activity of
English lodges in the seventeenth century are shown indirectly by the
numerous *Old Charges* manuscripts from this period. Apart from the *Old
Charges,* the only contemporary evidence consists of casual mentions of
Freemasonry in nonmasonic writings,[6] and of the two famous entries of
1646 and 1682 in Elias Ashmole's diary, mentioning his initiation in a lodge
of Warrington (Lancashire) and his attendance at a lodge meeting in London.
Such evidence gives us no insight into the inner life of lodges, but it is
sufficient to ascertain the existence, in the 1680s at least and probably much
earlier in the century, of a Society of Freemasons that was quite distinct
from any operative organization, though keeping strong links with the
craft. The case of the lodge that Elias Ashmole visited in 1682 is particularly
interesting. It was inside the operative London Masons Company but
distinct from it. While it received nonoperatives such as Ashmole, not all
members of the company were members of the lodge, which thus appears
as a kind of inner circle in the operative society.

It may be noted that already in the seventeenth century, in Scotland as
well as in England, the secrecy in which the masons wrapped themselves
and their proceedings aroused popular comment and suspicion. They were
supposed to have magical powers, or even to make a covenant with the
devil; and a London leaflet of 1698 plainly denounces them as a "devilish
sect" and as being "the Anti-Christ," thus foreshadowing what was later to
be the fate of Freemasonry in some countries. Some texts more gently—and
sometimes humorously—associate Freemasonry with the "Brotherhood of
the Rosy-Cross" and/or the "Hermetic Adepti." There is, however, no
evidence of any real connection at that time between Masonry and Rosicrucianism or alchemy. A text of 1676 also associates Freemasonry with the
"Modern Green Ribbon'd Caball" and, though the latter society is clearly
fanciful, its name probably contains an allusion to Kabbalah, which would
be nearer to the mark, as we shall see later. Anyway, these texts show that

Freemasonry was held in some circles to be a society teaching an esoteric doctrine.

What can we say in fact about the spiritual content of this seventeenth-century Masonry? The documents of the seventeenth century proper are of limited help here, but some documents of the beginning of the following century and even of the first years of the Grand Lodge period (from 1717 on) give us complementary evidence, since they can be safely assumed to be copies of older documents or to reflect a situation which continued that of the preceding century.[7]

The first point is the persistence of the Christian character of the order. The *Old Charges* of the seventeenth century maintain that the mason's duty is to be faithful to God and his Holy Church. Many of them begin with an invocation to the Holy Trinity. Moreover, Scottish rituals of the end of the century show that the masons' oath was taken not only on the Bible but more precisely on the Gospel of St. John. That custom must have been observed in England, too, at least in the first years of the Grand Lodge period, since it passed on to the Continent in the 1720s.

The later texts show the interest of masons in the person of Christ, not to say their devotion toward him. For instance, the *Graham* manuscript (1726), dealing with the clothing and posture of the candidate on taking his oath, explains them by reference to the double nature of Christ, implying that by faithfully imitating his Master, the Christian may become a participant in his divinity:

> I was neither sitting, standing . . . , naked nor clothed, shod nor barefoot.
> — A reason for such posture?
> — In regard one God one man make a very Christ, so one object being half naked half clothed, half shod half barefoot, half kneeling half standing, being half of all, was none of the whole, this shows a humble and obedient heart for to be a faithful follower of that just Jesus.

At least part of this Christ-centered spirituality certainly came from medieval tradition. This is the case, for instance, with the passages that interpret the Great Architect of the Universe not merely as God but more precisely as Christ, as in Samuel Prichard's *Masonry Dissected* (1730): "The Grand Architect and contriver of the Universe, or He that was taken up to the top of the pinnacle of the Holy Temple." Indeed, in medieval iconography the creator was always presented as Christ, while from the sixteenth century on he was presented as the Father. Another most striking instance of a piece of medieval tradition appearing in an eighteenth-century text is provided by the "Questions concerning the Temple" which form part of the *Dumfries n° 4* manuscript (ca. 1710). Solomon's Temple and all its furniture are interpreted in reference to Christ and to diverse attributes of Christ, which is perfectly in the line of medieval exegesis interpreting the Old Testament by reference to the New.

All these items appear in eighteenth-century texts as elements of a heritage which by that time was passing into oblivion among British masons. This is shown by the fact that nothing of it reappears in later British texts nor in continental Masonry. But they show that during the period of transition from Operative to Speculative Masonry, the order remained in possession of such a heritage, which was handed down to it by medieval Masonry through the changes of the Reformation period.

Yet in the same texts we observe the appearance of speculative elements of a new kind, which are most unlikely to be part of the medieval heritage but were much more probably introduced into Masonry by the nonoperatives in the post-Reformation period. They are no longer Christian, but point to an interest in Jewish esoterism. Since the Jews were certainly not admitted into Masonry in the seventeenth century, such speculative elements must have been introduced by adepts of the Christian Kabbalah movement. The example of Elias Ashmole (though in his case Kabbalah was not his main field of interest) shows that persons interested in all kinds of esoteric knowledge entered Masonry. There is no doubt that they were led to do so by the notion that Masonry had secrets and by the hope of finding such knowledge there as appealed to them. They were apt to develop along their own lines of interest the elements of the medieval heritage which seemed to answer their hope and to enrich thereby the speculative content of Freemasonry. Such elements seem indeed to have been present, so that the process we are describing was a rather natural development.

The most obvious outcome of this process is the multiplication of Hebrew words that appear, though often in corrupted form, in several texts of the 1720s. One of them, A Mason's Examination (1723), has even the word RoSheM (wrongly written RoSeM) in Hebrew letters. On the other hand, definite kabbalistic items remain rare. The most striking one seems to be the following passage of The Whole Institution of Freemasons opened (1725): "Yet for all this I want the primitive word, I answer it was God in six Terminations, to wit I am." This is in my view a clear allusion to the six permutations of the trigrammaton YHW, by which, according to the Sepher Yetsirah (1.8), God has sealed the six directions of space, and which are identical with the six last Sephiroth Belimah.

If, as I believe, those introducing such pieces of Jewish esoterism in Freemasonry were Christian kabbalists, they certainly did not mean to substitute them for the older Christian speculation, but rather to shed a new light on it thereby. The situation, however, changed in the eighteenth century. Partly under the spontaneous trend of the century and partly under the urge to facilitate the admission of non-Christians into Freemasonry, the Christian character of the order gradually faded away (though not everywhere completely), giving place to more and more non-Christian speculation, which could freely develop within the frame of a Masonry almost completely drained of its earlier spiritual content.

The Beginning of the Grand Lodge Period

The foundation of the first Grand Lodge in 1717 was not so radical an innovation as is commonly thought. By the Middle Ages, the assembly described by the *Regius* and *Cooke* manuscripts brought together masons from different boroughs and construction yards—that is, from different lodges. In Scotland, the *Schaw Statutes* of 1599 acknowledge the jurisdiction of the lodges in Edinburgh, Kilwinning and Stirling over the lodges in their respective regions, thus giving them (or rather confirming to them) a status, so to speak, of provincial Grand Lodges. Therefore, Operative Masonry did not lack central organization, at least on a local level. According to *Anderson's Constitutions* of 1723, the Grand Lodge itself, in its first years, claimed jurisdiction only "in and about London and Westminster" and seems to have regarded itself, in the beginning, as the continuation of the old provincial assembly (though with more frequent meetings and much more complex organization), as Anderson suggests when he writes ". . . this fair metropolis flourishes, as well as other parts, with several worthy particular lodges, that have a quarterly communication, and an annual grand assembly, wherein the forms and usages of the most ancient and worshipful Fraternity are wisely propagated."[8] More generally Anderson insisted on the continuity between the newly founded Grand Lodge and Operative Masonry; and Desaguliers, in his dedication to the duke of Montague, deals with the *Constitutions* as being merely a new redaction of the *Old Charges,* amended of their historical and chronological errors.

But the spirit of the new "Speculative" Freemasonry, of which Anderson's *Constitutions* are the acknowledged charter, turns out to be quite different from the spirit of medieval Masonry. It insists on notions that are completely unknown to the latter, namely, religious toleration and the setting up of friendly relations among men of different denominations by uniting them in "that religion in which all men agree."

Religious toleration was not by itself completely new in Freemasonry. It was practiced at least in some seventeenth-century lodges, as is shown by the instance of the lodge that in 1646 admitted Elias Ashmole along with his cousin, Colonel Henry Mainwaring. Ashmole belonged to the Church of England, while his cousin was a Puritan. Moreover, the two men had fought on opposite sides in the civil war. The lodge nevertheless received both of them on the same evening; but such religious toleration was restricted to Christians. The controversies that arose in the mid-eighteenth century about the admission of Jews show that this was something new by that time. What is more, as we have seen, it did not prevent the lodges from cultivating an essentially Christian speculation. It is quite possible, not to say quite likely, that in 1723 Anderson had nothing more in mind than the reconciliation of the different Christian denominations which had so cruelly fought against one another in the two previous centuries. But, though he casually mentions Christ as "God's Messiah, the great architect of the Church," his definition of "that religion in which all men agree" is purely moral and contains nothing specifically Christian: "that is to be good men and true, or men of honor and honesty."

In the 1738 edition of the *Constitutions,* the possibility of admitting non-Christians into Freemasonry is clearly implied:

> In ancient times, the *christian masons* were charged to comply with the *christian* usages of each country where they travelled or worked; but Masonry being found in all nations, even of divers religions, they are now only charged to adhere to that religion in which all men agree (leaving each brother to his own particular opinions), that is, to be good men and true, men of honor and honesty, by whatever names, religions or persuasions they may be distinguished.[9]

As is well known, Anderson excludes from Masonry the "stupid atheist" and the "irreligious libertine." The Mason must observe the moral law "as a true Noachida" (this is supposed to have been "the first name of Masons, according to some old traditions"), and all men agree on "the three great articles of Noah." Unfortunately Anderson does not quote these articles explicitly. Since all humanity after the Flood is descended from Noah, the term Noachida implies by itself no restriction at all. On the other hand, only true Noachidae, that is, men who observe the articles of Noah, may be admitted to Masonry. Whatever the articles may be, the reference to Noah can mean but little to a man without a biblical background, so that it may be suggested that Anderson contemplated only the admission to Freemasonry of Christians, Jews, and Muslims. Indeed in 1738 admissions of Jews had already occurred,[10] and Muslims were soon to follow. For persons belonging to other non-Christian religions the question was rather unlikely to arise in those days.

The admission of Christians of different professions was never questioned, probably because it had been a well-established custom since the

11. Copperplate in *Protokoll über den Spiritus Familiaris Gablidone* (Vienna?, 1787). This picture is signed A. Roehmel and J. G. Klinger.

seventeenth century.[11] On the contrary, the admission of non-Christians did not proceed without problems, especially in continental Europe, where the earliest constitutional texts of Freemasonry explicitly restrict admittance to Christians. In the first constitutions of French Masonry, the *Devoirs enjoints aux Maçons libres* (1735), Anderson's "religion in which all men agree" is replaced by "la religion dont tout chrétien convient." A similar text that was brought from Paris to Stockholm in 1737 by the baron of Scheffer, founder of Swedish Freemasonry, says that masons are no longer examined on their particular opinions, provided that they are Christians. The attitude of French masonic authorities was soon to change completely, but the opposition to non-Christians remained strong in Germany and Sweden, where it was to last almost up to our own time.

The main objection to admitting non-Christians consisted in the fact that the candidate, on his initiation, traditionally took his oath on the Gospel of St. John, so that he had to be Christian in order that his oath should bind him. In fact, different lodges followed different practices. In France in the 1780s many lodges had dropped not only the Gospel but also the Bible, and the candidates initiated into such lodges took their oath on the book of regulations of the lodge. Other lodges firmly maintained the custom of taking the oath on the Gospel, and consequently refused to admit non-Christians. As late as 1791, an assembly of several lodges in Bordeaux concluded:

> The Jews are not admitted to our mysteries. Our lodges are dedicated to Saint John the Baptist, forerunner of the Messiah, and the Jews acknowledge neither the divinity of the Messiah nor the mission of Saint John the Baptist. It is on the Gospel of Saint John that we take our oath, and that Holy Book, object of our eternal worship, is for the Jews a work of mere darkness and lies.[12]

In 1786 a Muslim brother from Algiers complained to the Grand Orient of France that a lodge in Nantes had refused to receive him as a visitor because of the difference of religion, and the Grand Orient gave him a warrant in order that such misadventure might not happen to him again.[13]

Being adepts of the philosophy of the Enlightenment, the leading members of the order in France favored the admission of non-Christians. In 1785 the Grand Orient approved an official ritual that was to be used in all lodges of its jurisdiction. This ritual, the promoters of which were by no means atheists, maintained the invocation to the Great Architect of the Universe. The oath was, however, no longer to be taken on the Gospel, nor on the Bible, but on the general regulations. In the same years the Rectified Scottish Rite was founded, a rite still practiced today in Belgium, France, and Switzerland. Its founders reacted against the dechristianizing trend and insisted on the Christian character of the order, asserting in the *Code des Loges Réunies et Rectifiées de France* (1778) that no man can be admitted a Freemason if he does not profess the Christian religion—and further that the oath had to be taken on the Gospel of St. John.

Of course, insistence on this point was not motivated merely by the desire to maintain an old custom, but more deeply by the intrinsic importance that the brethren saw in the Gospel of St. John as a basic source of their spiritual life. The brethren of Bordeaux in 1791 called it, as we have seen, the "object of our eternal worship," and a text of the Rectified Scottish Rite, written in 1809 but undoubtedly reflecting the thought of the founders of the rite in the years before the French Revolution, mentions it as the book in which "that beloved disciple, enlightened by a divine light, has asserted with so much sublimity the divinity of the Word incarnate."[14] The French Freemasons knew nothing of the Christian speculation of seventeenth-century English Masonry, but by meditating on the Book, some of them found their way to a somewhat similar spirituality, which they regarded as an essential part of masonic tradition. The fact that all lodges bear the name of Saint John helped to comfort them in this thought, as is shown by the Bordeaux resolution previously quoted.[15]

Thus, the opening of the order to non-Christians and its subsequent dechristianization were felt by some of the brethren as a break in masonic tradition. And a break it was, indeed. But it was bound to happen as soon as Masonry was no longer a society of craftsmen but, as Anderson put it, of "noblemen and gentlemen of the best rank, with clergymen and learned scholars," that is, of persons belonging to social classes that were pervaded to a large extent by the liberal ideas of the century.

Indeed, some masonic authors think that these men created a completely new institution and that speculative Freemasonry as it has been constituted since 1717 has no real connection with Operative Masonry. Against the traditional thesis of a continuous transformation of operative lodges into speculative ones through the admission of nonoperative members, Eric Ward, the main supporter of this thesis, writes that "in England . . . lodges began to appear which from their inception were independent of the mason trade." More precisely:

> During the seventeenth century—and as far as we know it was in England alone—groups of men of diverse occupations organized themselves into small autonomous societies or lodges whose connection with the building trade was no more than nominal. In some instances some of their members were masons by trade, but that was incidental to the activities of the lodges which were broadly speaking philosophical and social. In short these bodies were the primitive prototypes of speculative mason lodges of the present days.

They borrowed ritual and legendary material from Operative Masonry in order "to give the Society the appearance of having a direct historical linkage with the English stone masons of the middle-ages," satisfying thereby a "quest for antiquity."[16]

If this thesis were true, we should not speak of a break in masonic tradition. We should rather say that operative tradition was completely foreign to speculative Freemasonry as it was created in the seventeenth century and constituted in 1717. But in my view the thesis, although containing elements of truth, is an oversimplification of the reality. It is true that the Society of Freemasons in the seventeenth century was quite distinct from any operative organization, but "distinct" does not mean "independent," still less independent "from inception." There is no evidence at all on the origin of the rare English lodges that we know in the seventeenth century, so that we do not know whether they were creations *ex nihilo* or had evolved from operative lodges. But the fact that the existence of the process of evolution is well established in Scotland gives likelihood to its existence in England too, even if the communications between the two countries remained difficult. Moreover, I do not see clearly how newly created speculative lodges could have borrowed elements of operative tradition, except by contact with operative lodges or with speculative lodges evolved from operative ones. I am not unwilling to admit the possible existence of newly created speculative lodges, but I think the truth is that both processes coexisted and converged, so that on the whole the traditional thesis of a continuous link between Operative Masonry and seventeenth-century English Speculative Masonry seems to me to be more adequate.

On the other hand, even if the unorthodox thesis were true, I would say that the claim to continuity could not be so easily ruled out. By borrowing so many ritual, legendary, and spiritual elements from Operative Masonry and by incorporating them so integrally into its system, seventeenth-century Speculative Masonry assumed in some sense an operative tradition, which really became its heritage even if it had not been such before! I therefore maintain that in any case the opening of the order to non-Christians and its dechristianization were really a break in a tradition which could rightly claim to be rooted in medieval spirituality. I do not intend to discuss the legitimacy of this break here, but I will explore its consequences for the development of the "modern esoteric" character of Freemasonry.

Freemasonry in Search of Its Own Meaning

For many of its members, especially in English-speaking countries, Freemasonry is a "philosophical and social" association, based on a few simple and presumably universal religious principles, inculcating in its members good morals, friendship, and charity. As we said earlier, masonic authorities, though leaving individual masons free to pursue further spiritual research, do not commit themselves to asserting that Masonry is more than that, and many masons would be reluctant to admit it. This minimal definition of Masonry undoubtedly offers a noble and exalted ideal—and, we must add, a rather austere one. It is quite apt to satisfy men of a certain spiritual outlook, but it may not suffice for all the different kinds of persons that Masonry brings together in its lodges, some of whom may have more mystical aspirations.

Such men are naturally led to look for a more specific, and less obvious, speculative content in Masonry—a content that will demand a special effort and insight to be discovered and may therefore be termed "esoteric." There have always been men of this kind in Masonry, and they have greatly contributed, for more than 250 years, to fashioning the different esoteric aspects of the order. Some of them, starting from the remains of Christian tradition that persisted in the ritual, developed a Christian speculation, and even a Christian mysticism, which they had not found in the official, "exoteric" teachings of their respective churches. As we have seen, this was in the oldest masonic tradition, but it seemed to conflict with the universalist tendency newly introduced in the order, and it certainly conflicted with the general ideological trend of the eighteenth and nineteenth centuries. Others were adepts of the intellectual and esoteric movements that flourished in the surrounding environment, such as illuminism and occultism, and they were prone to find in Masonry what already appealed to them in the outer world. They were encouraged to do so by the esoteric character of Masonry, in the narrow sense—that is, by the secrecy of its ceremonies—and also by the fact that the ceremonies themselves, being symbolic, seemed to them mysterious. In fact, Freemasonry, having kept the formal tradition inherited from older times, but having lost, through its transplantation into another social and intellectual environment, its primitive spiritual content, appeared to many as an empty frame which could be filled with virtually anything.

The questions the Masons asked themselves in the eighteenth century, concerning the meaning of masonic secrets and ceremonies, have been well expounded by Joseph de Maistre in his *Memoir to the Duke of Brunswick* (1782), a text written on the occasion of the Convent of Wilhelmsbad, which had been summoned to elucidate the historical and spiritual foundations of the masonic order of the Strict Observance:

There is perhaps not a single mason, if somewhat able to think, who has not asked himself within one hour of his reception "What is the origin of all that

I see? Whence come these strange ceremonies, this pomp, these grand words, etc. . . .?" But after having lived for some time in the Order, one asks other questions: "What is the origin of these mysteries which veil nothing, of these types which represent nothing? Lo! Men of all countries will meet (and perhaps have done so for several centuries) to rank on two lines, swear never to reveal a secret which does not exist, put their right hand to their left shoulder, draw it to the right one, and sit down to table. Can't they talk nonsense, eat and drink to excess, without discoursing about Hiram and Solomon's Temple, the Blazing Star, etc., etc., . . . ?"[17]

In fact, many masons did not seriously try to obtain answers. From time to time, they enjoyed spending a merry evening with good friends, "sitting down to table," and singing masonic songs. They were satisfied with this convivial side of Masonry. Others found in Masonry satisfactions of vanity, especially when the so-called higher degrees began to develop. It even happened that unscrupulous persons made money by conferring irregular initiations and fake degrees upon credulous people. Thus, Masonry too often appeared as something at best frivolous and at worst dishonest. This unfortunate situation was undoubtedly furthered by an apparent lack of meaning. The result was that persons of high moral standards who entered Masonry might feel rather disappointed. But those who had sincerely expected to find spiritual teachings were all the more anxious to discover the true meaning of Masonry and eventually to restore it, if possible, in its primitive glory. A striking example of this attitude is provided by Jean Baptiste Willermoz (1730–1824), a famous mason of Lyons and one of the founders of the Rectified Scottish Rite. He was initiated in Lyons at the age of twenty and was soon "accoutred in all possible ribbons and colors" as he himself records in a letter. His biographer Alice Joly notes that "he writes disdainfully about this lodge and these old days, and describes himself as having been disgusted with the frivolity and indiscipline which pervaded Freemasonry."[18] He was even tempted to leave Masonry, but as he writes in another letter, he was "convinced on entering the Order that Masonry veiled rare and important truths, and this opinion became [his] compass."[19] For seventeen years he would search for these rare and important truths, and when he thought he had found them he wrote this significant sentence: "We judge with a very different look from the ordinary masons' the emblems which the symbolic lodges offer to us."[20] He was sure he had found the true meaning of Masonry. From thence he endeavored to reform Masonry in such a way that it might efficiently convey this meaning to its adepts. In fact, this meaning, which consisted of a Christian esoteric doctrine, was explicitly taught only to those who had reached the highest degree of the system. In the lower degrees it was veiled in symbols, but the symbols were commented on in a way which was intended to turn more and more precisely the thoughts of the perspicacious mason toward the proper interpretation.

It is interesting to note that Willermoz did not find his "rare and important truths" in Masonry itself, but in a parallel order into which he was admitted in 1767, the Order of the Elus Coëns, which had been founded in the 1750s by Martinez de Pasqually, a man of rather mysterious origin.[21] Martinez taught an esoteric doctrine which Willermoz confidently held to be the deepest meaning of the Christian religion, but which seems rather to have been an approximately christianized version of a later stream of Jewish Kabbalah. Within one year of his reception Willermoz had reached the highest degree of this order, and he felt he was in possession of the true meaning of Masonry. Then only he could turn back to the latter and start the reformation process that gave birth to the Rectified Scottish Rite.

Indeed, many developments in Masonry arose from the need to answer the questions concerning its meaning, origin, and aim. A very early and conspicuous one is the development of the so-called higher degrees (as distinct from the three older degrees of Apprentice, Fellow-Craft, and Master Mason, which in the eighteenth century were called "symbolic degrees"). The development of degrees originated in France about 1740 but quickly spread to the rest of Europe and to America. Its success is partly due to vanity and, as Willermoz put it, to the taste for "ribbons and colors," but more deeply to the disappointment felt by many masons about the secrets which they had expected to learn, about "these mysteries which veil nothing" and this "secret which does not exist." The brethren who had failed to receive in one degree the expected revelations could always hope to obtain them in the next one. So the degrees became more and more numerous, and the systems more and more complicated. A need was felt to bring order into this proliferating mass of degrees, and it led to the formation of systems in which a fixed number of degrees, each of them having been selected among many variants, were organized into a pyramid which was to be climbed by the mason from the lowest (Apprentice) to the highest one.

The "higher degrees" are no longer considered today to be part of Freemasonry proper, but the situation was different in the eighteenth century. The higher degrees were then regarded in many countries as the natural continuation of the "symbolic" ones, especially when both kinds of degrees were incorporated into pyramidal systems. Which authorities were entitled to govern the higher degrees was not clear. Many lodges practiced upon their own private authority such degrees as they pleased, only maintaining a formal distinction from the symbolic degrees by styling themselves "perfect lodges" or "chapters" when meeting in the higher degrees. On the other hand, specific bodies arose, beside the Grand Lodges and distinct from them, claiming authority on specific systems. Some of them limited their claim to the higher degrees, but in some instances such bodies extended their authority over the symbolic degrees by creating symbolic lodges or taking such lodges under control. In France such was the case with the Scottish Mother Lodge of Marseilles and of the Mother Lodge of the Philosophical Scottish Rite, both of which successfully maintained their independence from the Grand Orient until the end of the reign of Napoleon. In Germany such was the case with several Grand Lodges or Mother Lodges, each of which governed its own symbolic lodges and its peculiar system of higher degrees, and of the order of the Strict Observance, which in its higher degrees was a Templar order. The latter even managed to extend its jurisdiction over foreign lodges, in almost all continental European countries, by "rectifying" them.[22] Even in England, while the Grand Lodge of 1717 stood firmly against all kinds of higher degrees, the "Antients" Grand Lodge (founded in 1751) conferred the Royal Arch as a fourth degree.

In the eighteenth century it seemed natural to most masons that pyramidal systems starting from the Apprentice degree should be governed from top to bottom by unique authorities. On the other hand, a clear difference was felt between the symbolic degrees and the higher ones: the former were essentially the same in all systems, while the latter were different. The formula "essentially the same" as applied to the symbolic degrees appears, for instance, in the compact of 1776 between the Grand Orient of France and the French branch of the Strict Observance, in which these degrees are called "the fundamental degrees of Masonry." In this compact the Grand Orient acknowledged the authority of the Strict Observance on the lodges which this German (and international) masonic body had created or "rectified" in France. At the same time, the Grand Orient was elaborating its own system of higher degrees, and when that work was completed in 1786, the Grand Orient assumed the government of the higher degrees under the denomination of General Grand Chapter. This is an instance of the fact that the principle of systems governed from top to bottom by unique authorities tended to be accepted by the main masonic bodies of the time.

However, there was a growing feeling that rivalry between such systems caused division among masons and that the unity of Freemasonry was to be found only in the three fundamental degrees that were common to all systems. This feeling was eventually to prevail. In the Articles of Union, promulgated in 1813 when the two English Grand Lodges of the "Moderns"

(1717) and of the "Antients" (1751) came together to form the United Grand Lodge of England, it was stated for the first time that "pure ancient Masonry consists of three degrees and no more; viz. those of the Entered Apprentice, the Fellow-Craft and the Master-Mason." This principle has been generally accepted world wide by regular Grand Lodges, so that the higher degrees are now regarded as something distinct from Masonry and are governed by distinct authorities such as Supreme Councils and Grand Chapters.

Nevertheless, the higher degrees have always been closely connected with Masonry, since their members are recruited exclusively among masons, and they have played an important part in the formation of modern masonic esoterism in two ways: (1) Older kinds of masonic speculation that had fallen in disuse in the symbolic lodges—such Christian and kabbalistic speculations as were cultivated in seventeenth-century lodges—started afresh in the higher degrees. (2) It is mainly through the higher degrees that new speculative elements, such as alchemy or chivalric legends, were introduced into Masonry.

The kabbalistic speculations are probably those which are the most closely related to similar speculations in the seventeenth century. They center on the meditation and invocation of divine names and are to be found mainly in the Royal Arch, which, as we have said, was conferred in eighteenth-century England as a fourth degree, and in various "Scottish" degrees on the Continent.[23] These degrees are strongly rooted in biblical tradition, and the happy combination of the kabbalistic elements with eschatological themes gives them great spiritual richness. The kabbalistic speculations received further development in the nineteenth century when the occultist movement aroused a new interest in Kabbalah. But these later developments are, in my view at least, rather negative because this new kabbalistic trend was much more interested in the magical side of Kabbalah than in the authentically spiritual one.

As for the Christian speculations, the link with the seventeenth century is perhaps more formal: it consists of the importance still accorded to the name and the Gospel of Saint John, but that belongs essentially to symbolic Masonry. The many Christian degrees that appeared in the eighteenth century seem to be new creations rather than continuations of the seventeenth-century tradition. In some cases the distinction between them and symbolic Masonry is marked by the fact that they have Saint Andrew as their patron rather than Saint John, which is absolutely unprecedented in Masonry.

There is a large variety of such degrees, and they develop rather different lines of teaching, presumably according to the spiritual outlook of their creators—who in almost all cases are unknown to us. Quite often their Christian content is mixed with a component of different origin. In some cases this does not fundamentally affect their Christian character. Let us consider, for instance, the degree of Scotch Master of Saint Andrew, fourth degree of the Rectified Scottish Rite. In this case, its author is known—Jean Baptiste Willermoz, whom we have previously mentioned. What we know of him allows us to infer what teaching he intended to include in that degree. So we can say that in the background stands the esoteric doctrine of Martinez de Pasqually, but since this was merely for Willermoz the spark that illuminated for him the depth of Christian revelation, we may say that the ultimate meaning of the degree is really Christian. Not so clear is the case with the most famous of the formally Christian degrees, that of Rose-Croix, which is essentially ambiguous. Here the mingling of Christian and extra-Christian elements is much more subtle, so that the degree can be said properly to have a double meaning—one more obvious, referring to the events of the passion and resurrection of Christ; and the other more hidden, which is hermetic and refers to the successive phases of the Opus Magnum, of which the former were classical figures among alchemists. Here, each brother—and each chapter—may interpret and work the degree as a purely Christian one or as a hermetic one, according to his or its own spiritual interests.

There is no evidence of alchemy as part of the speculative content of seventeenth-century Masonry.[24] The fact that nothing alchemical appears in subsequent English Masonry suggests that the introduction of alchemy took place on the Continent in the eighteenth century. There it had an immense success. Alchemy was more or less viewed as the quintessence of all esoteric knowledge, so it was all too natural to think that it was the real secret of Masonry. It flourished in degrees such as that of Rose-Croix and in systems whose names contained an explicit reference to Hermetism, such as the Hermetic Rite or the Philosophical Scottish Rite (Philosophical being here a synonym of Hermetic). In the latter the highest degree was the degree of Wisdom, and the brethren who possessed it were said to be "dressed in the three colors," which clearly meant that they were supposed to have performed the three phases of the Opus Magnum.

From the higher degrees Alchemy gradually descended into symbolic Masonry. Rituals of the late eighteenth and of the nineteenth centuries give evidence of this descent. The ritual approved in 1785 by the Grand Orient of France ordered that little vessels containing salt and sulphur should be placed in the room where the candidate waited for his initiation. This was clearly intended to direct the candidate's thoughts toward an alchemical interpretation of the ceremonies which he was to undergo—even if sulphur and mercury would have been more significant. It is possible to follow the gradual introduction of alchemical symbolism in the ceremonies themselves. In the second half of the eighteenth century, "proofs" by water and fire had appeared in the initiation ceremony as performed in France. At first these proofs had no alchemical meaning at all; they were mere purifications, clearly inspired by the two baptisms mentioned in the Gospels—one with water, the other with the Holy Ghost and fire. In the 1785 ritual of the Grand Orient they are given no other explicit meaning in the course of the ceremony; however, they are announced to the waiting candidate as purifications "by the elements." This last notion was developed in the Rectified Scottish Rite by the addition of earth. Here the intended meaning was not alchemical—the founders of that Rite being hostile to alchemy—it rather referred to the imprisonment of the fallen Man in matter, in the context of Martinez de Pasqually's theory of matter, in which there are only three elements. The brethren who ignored the martinezist doctrine were bound to interpret these proofs in an alchemical sense. Then, in the beginning of the nineteenth century, the Ancient and Accepted Scottish Rite was introduced in France. At first it was a mere system of higher degrees, as it still is in most countries. But the Supreme Council which governed it, and had also its own symbolic lodges, created a new ritual for the three first degrees in order to distinguish these lodges. This ritual, which has become very popular in France and has spread to some neighboring countries, is also known there as the Ancient and Accepted Scottish Rite. It is in the context of this ritual that the alchemical meaning of the proofs by the elements has received its most complete development. A proof by air has been added, and the sojourn of the candidate in the "cabinet de réflexion" (which is supposed to be underground) is interpreted as a proof by earth, so that the four elements are present. This is a striking example of the way formal tradition and esoteric teaching interact in their development.

As a last example, let us consider the chivalric legends. These legends provided answers not so much to the question of the meaning of Masonry as to that of its origin—though the two questions cannot be completely separated.

The chivalric legends are generally regarded as having arisen from the two famous speeches of Chevalier Ramsay in 1736 and 1737. In fact, references to the crusaders appear before Ramsay, but his speeches certainly gave a decisive impulse to the development of the legends. Ramsay considered his account of the origin of Masonry as the true historical one, as opposed to the "old traditions" about Noah, Solomon, and so on, which he clearly regarded as legendary. According to him, Masonry was founded in the time of the crusades by "several princes, lords and freemen" who "joined together and made a vow to restore the temples of the Christians in the Holy Land and endeavour to bring their architecture to its primitive institution." It is to distinguish themselves from the Saracens that these men would have adopted the secret means of recognition of Masonry. Ramsay adds: "Some time later, our Order became intimately united with the Knights of Saint John of Jerusalem," and this, in his opinion, explains why all masonic lodges bear the name of Saint John.

Ramsay's intention seems to have been only to provide a model of what he thought Masonry should be—that is, a society that would "unite the Christians of all nations in one brotherhood." But his speeches had an outcome that he had probably not foreseen. They inspired the creation of many chivalric degrees, some of them on the theme of the building of the second Temple, which, he had said, had been taken as a model by the crusaders (these were the degrees of the type "knight of the east"), some others on the very theme of the crusades (degrees of the type "knight of the west").

Especially important are the Templar legend and the Templar degrees. Ramsay himself had mentioned the Knights of Saint John of Jerusalem rather than the Templars. But the latter, since their order no longer existed, offered much more freedom to the speculation. The Templar legend seems to have originated in Germany,[25] and it was systematically developed by the order of the Strict Observance, which claimed to be nothing else than the Order of the Temple, having secretly survived after its trial and its suppression by Pope Clement V. Masonry was supposed to be a creation of the Templars, a mere disguise under which they perpetuated their existence.

The Templar legend has a strong link with the esoteric content of Masonry, because the Templars were supposed to have possessed a secret knowledge. This belief was favored by the mysterious ceremonies that were alluded to in their trial and by the historical fact that their dwelling place in Jerusalem was on the very site of Solomon's Temple. They were assumed to have found or received in one way or other the secrets of the initiates of Solomon's time, and to have transmitted them to Masonry. The Templar legend thereby provided an answer not only to the question of the origin of Masonry, but eventually to that of its content and meaning. The Strict Observance has disappeared, but it has bequeathed its chivalric character to the Rectified Scottish Rite, though the latter no longer claims the Templar succession in so material a sense as the former did. Other Templar systems, which appeared a little later, are still alive and prosperous, in close connection with Masonry, especially in scandinavian countries with the Swedish system, and in English-speaking countries with the order of the Knights Templar.

12. Esmond Jerries, *First Masonic Grade in Modern Rite*
(n.d.: Deutsches Freimaurer-Museum, Bayreuth).

The Templar degrees have had little influence on the ritual and symbolism of the properly masonic degrees, but the notion of the Templar origin of Masonry and of its content has had much success in the lodges, and has left a durable mark on masonic spirituality. Even if most masons no longer literally adhere to the Templar claim, for many of them Masonry does have a chivalric dimension, and that must be reckoned among the aspects of Masonry as an esoteric movement.

* * *

We can now answer the questions we asked in the beginning of this paper. Masonry does have an esoteric content. But in the present state of things, as far as we are concerned with explicit esoteric teachings, this content appears to be rather unspecific, being made to a large extent of elements borrowed from various esoteric traditions; or, more exactly, its specificity seems to lie in the fact that is has developed through the assimilation of so many elements of different origins. Masonry has functioned, during the two last centuries, as a kind of melting pot of different traditions.

The reason for that has been, I trust, clearly shown: Masonry *once had* an esoteric content of its own, but it was to a large extent forgotten. This came about when, having opened its lodges to members of the enlightened classes, Masonry became conscious of having a vocation for universalism. The Western world was then emerging from a period of self assertion, during which time it had been firmly convinced of the superiority of its spiritual traditions and values, into a new period in which it discovered the relativity of such things and felt a keen interest in the traditions and values of foreign cultures. In this context the old medieval operative heritage, and even the seventeenth-century heritage, deeply rooted as it was in the tradition of the previous period, was bound to appear as an obstacle to universalism. Therefore it had to be discarded or—as for what was retained of it— to be reinterpreted in a different way, more open to the intellectual tendencies of the time.

Today this universalist vocation, which Masonry assigned to itself in the beginning of the Grand Lodge period, has been accomplished in a fairly satisfactory way. Freemasonry has become a worldwide association of men of all races, languages, religions, and cultures, united by their common adhesion to religious and moral principles that appear to all of them as common and essential teachings of their respective religions. The loss of the original and specific esoteric content of Masonry was merely the price paid for its accession to such universalism.

This entailed the development of a new esoteric content, mainly through borrowing from other traditions, a process that has been described in the previous chapters. In the twentieth century this process has developed still further, through the increasing interest of many Western masons in Eastern religions and esoteric doctrines, in which they are tempted to find the meaning of masonic mysteries.

When doing so, these masons of our time do not differ very much from their predecessors, who found in Masonry the kind of esoteric teachings in which they were interested in the outer world. Undoubtedly the present success of Eastern doctrines among masons reflects to a large extent the general interest of the Western world in Eastern spirituality. A special mention must be made of the influence of René Guénon (1886–1951). Guénon was not merely an instance among others of this tendency of the modern Western world; he rather anticipated it, and his work had a profound echo both in and outside of Freemasonry. Many masons who look toward the east to find the meaning of Masonry refer to him. This is due to the fact that Guénon founded his doctrine of tradition and initiation on the metaphysics of the Vedanta, and in many instances interpreted masonic symbols in the light of Eastern teachings; however, Guénon did not deny the existence of a specific Western tradition. He expounded that there exists a unique and universal Primeval Tradition which humanity possessed in plenitude in the beginning of our cycle of time, and from which are derived the various particular traditions that have existed and exist in known history. So there existed a Western tradition as well as an Eastern one, each of them providing a specific way to spiritual realization of the Self, which is, according to Guénon, the aim of initiation. But in the last centuries of our age, Western tradition has been almost completely obscured by the growth of anti-traditional ways of thought, while Eastern tradition has been better preserved. Guénon considered Masonry as an authentic vehicle of Western tradition, but the confusion now prevailing in the West has affected Masonry itself and obscured its esoteric teaching.[26]

This is not the place to discuss Guénon's doctrine, which is treated elsewhere in this volume; but its importance with respect to Masonry must be acknowledged. It goes far beyond the introduction of Eastern doctrines into masonic speculation, which would have come about anyway. Guénon's importance lies in the fact that he has given precise definitions of notions such as exoterism and esoterism, tradition and initiation, in the frame of a general and synthetic theory.[27] He thereby offers to masons a logically consistent frame in which to think the problems and perspectives of their order, and this is the true reason of his success among them, even among those who put the accent on the Western-traditional, and especially Christian, aspect of Masonry. The definitions, as well as the theory as a whole, may be accepted or not, but they cannot be ignored. They have given a new and decisive impulse to masonic thought about the nature, foundations, and aim of the order.

Let us conclude by giving some hints about the perspectives of Masonry as the present writer sees them. And first let us dismiss an illusion that could arise from the description of Masonry as a melting pot of traditions. One might be tempted to think that out of this melting pot will emerge the religion of the third millennium or something like that. This is not the case, for it is contrary to the true vocation of Masonry. As we have said, all masonic authorities agree on the fact that Masonry is not a religion, need not become one or promote one. But it has to initiate in each of its members a process of spiritual development and to give him the tools that are necessary to further this process.

The traditional teachings are part of these tools, and from this standpoint it is to be feared that the loss of the original masonic esoterism, operative and Christian, weakened the efficiency of masonic initiation as a spiritual process. The subsequent introduction of bits of esoterism from different origins was a doubtful remedy. Although it provided Masonry with a rich and interesting symbolism of a new kind, it was made in so disorderly a way that it brought about much confusion and dispersion of mind. Of course, this does not mean that everything must be rejected of this later masonic esoterism, nor that Masonry should try to revive the state of things that prevailed before the Grand Lodges. This at any rate would be impossible after so many centuries and also because of the lack of primary material to facilitate this revival. But Masonry could, and in my view should, give a larger place in its teachings to what can be retrieved of its original esoterism, and there is indeed a tendency to do so in some masonic circles. This original esoterism, being deeply rooted in a particular tradition, was once felt for this reason as an obstacle to universalism, but it should no longer be regarded as such today. As the modern world is growing more and more uniform, humanity is growing more and more conscious of the value of specificity and of the fact that the suppression of differences or the disorderly mixing up of traditions is not a good way to universality. Rather, universality should be reached through deeper understanding of specific traditions, and this principle applies to Masonry.

All this concerns the level of the explicit teachings that are given to the masons as a help and a guidance in their spiritual progress. But it must not be forgotten that beyond the explicit teachings there are the implicit ones which are contained in ceremonies and symbols offered to masons for silent meditation. Here lies the ultimate esoterism of Masonry, for the ultimate esoterism is unspeakable. Here lies the essence of masonic initiation.

Notes

1. "Operative Masonry" and "Speculative Masonry" are terms commonly used among masons and in masonic literature. By Operative Masonry is meant the building trade. Speculative Masonry is Freemasonry regarded as a society of men who are no longer necessarily masons by trade but are mainly concerned with the practice of charity and/or philosophical and spiritual research, in a traditional frame inherited from Operative Masonry. Connected terms, such as "Operative/Speculative masons" and "operative/speculative lodges" are also commonly used.

2. See Douglas Knoop, G. P. Jones, and Douglas Hamer, *The Two Earliest Masonic Manuscripts.*

3. See Douglas Knoop and G. P. Jones, *The Medieval Mason.*

4. See Douglas Knoop, G. P. Jones, and Douglas Hamer, *Early Masonic Catechisms.*

5. This mention of the clergy in close connection with the craft is the reason why I think that this part of the text goes back at least to the pre-Reformation period, though the present manuscript is much later.

6. See Douglas Knoop, G. P. Jones, and Douglas Hamer, *Early Masonic Pamphlets.*

7. These texts are published in Knoop, Jones, and Hamer, *Early Masonic Catechisms.*

8. James Anderson, *The Constitutions of the Free-Masons.*

9. James Anderson, *The New Book of Constitutions of the Ancient and Honourable Fraternity of Free and Accepted Masons.* The emphases are Anderson's. They clearly imply the existence of non-Christian masons beside the Christian ones.

10. John M. Shaftesley, "Jews in English Freemasonry in the 18th and 19th centuries," *Ars Quatuor Coronatorum* 92 (1979) 38, 42. There were Muslim masons in the 1780s, as we shall soon see, but the first ones were probably members of the lodges that were founded in the harbors of the Levant at a date that was certainly earlier, even if it cannot be precisely determined.

11. When Freemasonry was introduced in Roman Catholic countries, it kept its multidenominational character, and this was one of the main causes of its condemnation by Pope Clement XII in 1738.

12. Quoted in Jean Baylot, *Dossier français de la Franc-Maçonnerie régulière,* 81.

13. General assemblies of the Grand Orient of France, 168th meeting, 4-7-1786. Bibliothèque Nationale de Paris, FM1 16.

14. Manuscript 5922, Bibliothèque de la Ville de Lyon.

15. In fact the brethren of Bordeaux interpreted the name of the lodges as referring to Saint John the Baptist, but the two Saint Johns are always associated together in masonic tradition.

16. Eric Ward, "The Birth of Freemasonry," *Ars Quatuor Coronatorum* 91 (1978) 77–100.

17. Joseph de Maistre, *La Franc-Maçonnerie, mémoire inédit au duc de Brunswick,* 55.

18. Alice Joly, *Un mystique lyonnais et les secrets de la Franc-Maçonnerie.*

19. Letter to Landgrave Charles of Hesse, 10-12-1781, quoted in René Le Forestier, *La Franc-Maçonnerie templière et occultiste aux XVIIIème et XIXème siècles,* 278.

20. Letter to the Baron of Landsperg, 11-25-1772, published in Steel-Maret, *Archives secrètes de la Franc-Maçonnerie,* 141–42.

21. According to some documents Martinez was born in Grenoble about 1727 and his father was born in Alicante, but the evidence is not quite conclusive.

22. The French branch of the Strict Observance gave birth to the Rectified Scottish Rite.

23. The appellation "Scottish" is merely conventional, and the degrees under consideration have nothing to do with Scotland.

24. This is rather surprising, considering the success of alchemy and Rosicrucianism in seventeenth-century England. Indeed, some nonmasonic texts allude to a connection between Masonry and Rosicrucianism, but nothing of the kind is to be found in masonic texts proper.

25. Le Forestier, *La Franc-Maçonnerie templière et occultiste*, 64ff.

26. See especially René Guénon, *Le règne de la quantité et les signes des temps; La crise du monde moderne*.

27. See René Guénon, *Aperçus sur l'initiation*.

Bibliography

Sources

Anderson, James. *The Constitutions of the Free-Masons, containing the History, Charges, Regulations etc. of that most Ancient and Right Worshipful Fraternity.* London, 1723.

――. *The New Book of Constitutions of the Ancient and Honourable Fraternity of Free and Accepted Masons, containing their History, Charges, Regulations, etc.* London, 1738.

Maistre, Joseph de. *La Franc-Maçonnerie, mémoire inédit au duc de Brunswick.* 1782. Publié avec une introduction par Emile Dermenghem. Editions d'aujourd'hui, 1980.

Steel-Maret. *Archives secrétes de la Franc-Maçonnerie.* Lyon, 1893.

Studies

Ars Quatuor Coronatorum. Transactions of Quatuor Coronati Lodge no. 2076, London.

Baylot, Jean. *Dossier français de la Franc-Maçonnerie régulière.* Paris: Vitiano, 1965.

Faivre, Antoine. *L'ésotérisme au XVIIIème siècle en France et en Allemagne.* Paris: Seghers, 1973.

Guénon, René. *Aperçus sur l'initiation.* Revised edition. Paris: Villain et Belhomme, 1975.

――. *La crise du monde moderne.* Paris: Gallimard, 1946.

――. *Le règne de la quantité et les signes des temps.* Paris: Gallimard, 1945.

Joly, Alice. *Un mystique lyonnais et les secrets de la Franc-Maçonnerie.* Mâcon: Protat, 1938.

Knoop, Douglas, and G. P. Jones. *The Mediaeval Mason.* 3rd ed. Manchester: Manchester University Press; New York: Barnes & Noble Inc., 1967.

Knoop, Douglas, G. P. Jones, and Douglas Hamer. *Early Masonic Catechisms.* 2nd ed. London: Quatuor Coronati Lodge no. 2076, 1975.

――. *Early Masonic Pamphlets.* London: Q.C. correspondence circle Ltd. in association with Quatuor Coronati Lodge, 1978.

――. *The Two Earliest Masonic Manuscripts.* Manchester: Manchester University Press, 1938.

Le Forestier, René. *La Franc-Maçonnerie templière et occultiste aux XVIIIème et XIXème siècles.* Edited by A. Faivre. Paris: Aubier-Montaigne and Louvain: Nauwelaerts, 1970. Reprint, Paris: La Table d'Emeraude, 1987.

9

The Primitive Characteristics of Nineteenth-Century Esotericism

JEAN-PIERRE LAURANT

THE WORDS "ESOTERICISM" and "occultism" and their cognates appeared, as derivatives of the corresponding adjectives, in the second quarter of the century. They surfaced first in French—"*ésotérisme*" in 1828, in Jacques Matter's *Histoire critique du gnosticisme* (Paris: Levrault), within a Protestant environment in Strasbourg in contact with German Illuminism. They turned up next in English—"esoterism" in 1835 (Maurice, *Letter to Acland:* Oxford English Dictionary) and "esotericism" in 1846 (*Christian Observer*, OED). The dictionaries of the chief European languages quickly followed suit.

"Occult" and "occultism" arose in parallel fashion from older usages. The English words appear in 1545 (OED);[1] "*occolto*" belongs to the philosophical vocabulary of the Italian Renaissance, Giordano Bruno (1548–1600) in particular;[2] and Henry Cornelius Agrippa's celebrated *De occulta philosophia* (1533) summarizes under this title the teaching of the "occult sciences." The French noun "*occultisme*" is recorded in Richard de Radonvillier's *Dictionnaire des mots nouveaux* in 1842, confirming one of its usages.

These transformations were the marks of a desire to substitute an autonomous system of thought or explanation of the world for a type of outlook attached to a preexisting discipline—theological exegesis, astrological or alchemical scientific speculation, and so on. But at the same time they expressed the desire to recover a lost ancient tradition, a *prisca theologia* or *philosophia perennis,* as the dying Middle Ages and Renaissance had dreamed of doing. There was at once a resurgent reach for the immemorial and an aspiration to complete an age of progress. Again, Edward A. Tiryakian's analysis may be applied to the nineteenth century; on his analysis "esotericism" designates "religio-philosophic belief systems which underlie occult techniques and practices; that is, it refers to the more comprehensive cognitive mappings of nature and the cosmos . . . which mappings constitute a stock of knowledge that provides the ground for occult procedures."[3]

In various degrees the movement had an impact throughout Western culture, already stamped by the shock of the French Revolution, which had profoundly altered the direction and significance that the eighteenth-century Enlightenment, for example, might have taken. The shock had been felt in France in particular, where people were debating what status to give reason and what place to accord traditions. How was it possible to reintegrate into society the spiritual power that Montesquieu had forgotten in *L'Esprit des lois,* a power that people had attempted in vain to root out between 1792 and the Napoleonic Concordat, an internal force like the external one at the frontiers where the victories of revolutionary imperial armies had swept away the traditional structures of society?

The Catholic Church rejected entirely a society that was born of the terror and dechristianization and was bent on a path of secularization. It had to face an ineluctable modernity and found it impossible to restore the old order. Hence the search for new ways and the allure of esotericism.

In the camp of the "spiritualists," the adherents of modernity attributed the population's failure to become emancipated to insufficient education. Because the times were not ripe, it seemed proper to hide the liberating light under a bushel. Since the Catholic Church identified itself with the old order, and since the reason of the *philosophes* by itself was impotent, they sought a way out in "the new religion," or more precisely in the religion of a new period, which was to be the heir of the persecuted ancient traditions that were preserved in occult sanctuaries. The secrecy and the style of secret societies accompanied the rise of the democratic age, particularly in Italy and France.

On the one hand, the Freemasonry which in the eighteenth century had crystallized aspirations for renewal no longer played the same role in the next century. Abbé Barruel's denunciation in his famous *Mémoires pour servir à l'histoire du jacobinisme* (London, 1798; Hamburg, 1799), in spite of its implausibility, rendered the institution suspect in the eyes of Catholics. Count Joseph de Maistre (1753–1821), the ambassador from the king of Piedmont to Russia and a fervent architect of Christian renewal, had to take great precautions in order to justify his membership in the order. He found it necessary to distinguish good Illuminism, which could only be Christian, from that which had made its bed with rationalism and the Revolution. In France Masonry had first served the empire, then the restored Bourbons ready to rally to the side of Napoleon III, and finally the Republic. Those who contested the established order withdrew from it, as did their Italian counterparts, to the benefit of the marginal rites and secret societies which from time to time emerged from the old trade guilds like the Carbonari.

Esotericism was therefore to develop, especially in continental Europe, in environments in rupture with the great institutions—politico-mystical groups and sects, utopian socialists, friends of Lamennais after his rejection by Rome, partisans of the republican Mazzini or Garibaldi in Italy. On the other hand, the partisans of theocracy were happy to rely on visions and prophecies of an esoteric character (both orthodox and heterodox) and on the heritage of Christian theosophy in the Germanic world in their attempts to change the course of history.

The ground had been prepared by the return of religious feeling which animated the resistance to attacks upon the revolution in Europe and accompanied the fall of the empire. The movement asserted itself within the ferment of ideas in the "People's Spring" of 1848. It realized an extraordinary success around the 1880s in England, the United States, and France; in the latter country it sought, under cover of anticlerical struggles within the Republic, to transform itself into an official church. It spread to Germany a little later. But all those who participated in it were bound together: they sought beyond frontiers and seas a legitimacy which they were not always assured.

History, theology, and the sciences, as well as literature and the arts, were to be touched in various ways by esoteric thought and occultism.

The Birth of Twins

Jacques Etienne Marconis de Nègre (1795–1868), the son of an Italian officer in the Napoleonic army, was cofounder of the so-called Memphis Egyptian Masonry, which spread into Italy, into England after 1850, and to the United States in 1856 under the leadership of Harry J. Seymour. He defined the notion of esotericism in this way: "A Greek philosopher, after passing through Egypt and visiting the main sanctuaries of science, reported . . . that one of the main points of the doctrine of the priests of Egypt was the division . . . into exotericism or external science and esotericism or internal science."[4] He was immediately followed by the socialist writer Pierre Leroux (1797–1871), a friend of George Sand, in De l'humanité (1840). Esoteric argument is used in a debate over an afterlife different from the metempsychosis which "Plato allowed himself to teach," although his master Pythagoras, who had nothing to do with the masses, "himself had . . . esotericism, the secret school, the religious and political sect, a kind of superior caste, raised to comprehension by initiation, having as its mission moralizing, teaching, and the governance of common people." Le Dictionnaire universel of Maurice Lachâtre (1814–1900) confirmed in 1852 the links with utopian socialism: a number of the followers of Saint-Simon sought to make of their doctrine a kind of esotericism.

"Abbé" Louis Constant (1810–1875) made the word *"occultisme"* famous, with a sense akin to that of the word just characterized, on the occasion of his own transformation into a magus under the name Eliphas Levi: "We have dared to dig into the old sanctuaries of occultism."[5] His discoveries were meant to end the monstrosity of a world without God, by revealing the unity of universal dogma in the secret doctrines of the Hebrews, Egyptians, and Chaldeans, following here J. de Maistre, who had demonstrated that Newton was reducible to Pythagoras. The theosophist Alfred P. Sinnett made use of the English "occultism" in *Occult World* in 1881, locating its sanctuaries in the Orient, mainly India.

In connection with both *"ésotérisme"* and *"occultisme,"* the pair secret/ revelation rested on needs that were characteristic of the time. Esotericism was a response to history.

Putting the Occult Sciences into a System

This approach to knowledge was inspired by the Renaissance, but it sought to constitute itself a system appropriate to its own time. Following Kant, the universality of reason was affirmed; but its limits were ignored, for the approach held in low esteem both Aristotelian distinctions and the medieval division between the book of nature and the book of revelation. Reacting to the explosion of knowledge and of religious, intellectual, and political authorities, the occult sciences aspired to transfigure the world by submitting revelation to criticism—not to deny it, which had been the fatal error of eighteenth-century ideologues, but to render it obvious.

Popular orthodox traditions and Celtic legends supplied the material for the *Myvyrian Archaeology of Wales: An Anthology of Welsh Literature* by Owen Jones (1741–1814).[6] In it there were mingled divination, astrology, magical medical recipes, philters, and legends, as there also were in the *Dictionnaire des sciences occultes* by Collin de Plancy (1846). The reworking of these prescientific—in Auguste Comte's sense, in his law of three stages— intuitions would give them their reality.

The intermediate powers—spirits, angels, and demons—and obscure forces of the ancients which Dom Calmet (1672–1757) had restored to honor, like the animal magnetism of Mesmer (1734–1815) at the end of the eighteenth century, played a large role in the elaboration of these theories. In the first place spiritualism, whose manifestations began in Hydesville, New York, in 1847, revived the debate over the structure of the cosmos and the plurality of worlds. The practice spread rapidly into all of Europe, accompanied by theories of the evolution of souls. Emma Hardinge-Britten (d. 1890) wrote in *Modern American Spiritualism* (1870) that its phenomena had been aroused by living men who had been initiated into secret techniques by a mysterious Hermetic Brotherhood of Luxor, of which she herself was a member. The novel *Zanoni* (1842) by Edward Bulwer-Lytton (1802–1873) echoed these practices and realized an enormous success. The Parisian magus Eliphas Levi met its author in London in 1854 and 1861, where he devoted himself to the evocation of Apollonius of Tyana, along with an exchange of initiations. Nor was there any lack of scientific guarantors, such as Ferdinand Denis (1798–1890), a traveler in the style of Humboldt, great connoisseur of ancient manuscripts at the Bibliothèque Sainte-Geneviève in Paris, which he directed, and patron of romantic writers who gave their thought a mystical and "missionary" turn. Denis justified occult sciences[7] by the social function of all knowledge and argued that the solitary inquirer, persecuted because of general incomprehension, had to take shelter within secrecy. He argued that a different kind of knowledge could be transmitted from ancient initiations through the sects of the Middle Ages to modern societies.

In addition, occultist attempts at synthesis of the sciences and religion abounded from one end of the century to the other. In the first years of the nineteenth century, the Polish mathematician Hoene Wronski (1776–1853) worked out a universal law of creation, based on the final causation or teleology of numbers, to explain the historical evolution of the world. His speculations, which the Academy of Sciences in Paris at first received favorably, were accompanied by technical achievements like the invention of chain-treaded tractors.

At century's end occultists like Alexandre Saint-Yves d'Alveydre (1842–1909) revived the idea of synarchy, a political, intellectual, and social system in which all forces are balanced in a restored spiritual harmony. *L'Archéomètre,* published after his death, established universal correspondences of colors, sounds, and geometrical shapes on the basis of the recovered primordial language Vatan. A disciple, F. C. Barlet (1831–1921), defended his theses on the basis of new sciences, like sociology, which seemed capable of recovering "spirit" (*Principes de sociologie synthétique,* 1894). He attempted as well to apply Saint-Yves' theses to domains which lay beyond the rational positivism of the "hard sciences." To this end he posited in *L'Art de demain* (1897) laws governing the evolution of painting and sculpture, on the basis of a spiritualist philosophy of history involving a prefiguration of forms manifested subtly in the astral world.

Christian Renewal and the Return to Tradition

Christian renewal was visible from the beginning of the century, with the success of pietism, for example, and Bible societies, whose development had been favored by the English as an antidote to the revolutionary spirit. German theosophy, so dazzling in the eighteenth century, bent its debates and positions in this direction. For example, Bern's Friedrich Herbort (1764–1843) and Strasbourg's Friedrich Saltzmann (1749–1821) bore witness to the concern to act within the very bosom of the churches (in Herbort's case, the *Société Chrétienne*), constituting an inner circle where it was possible to grapple with speculations inspired by Jacob Boehme (1575–1624) or Karl von Eckartshausen (1752–1803) on the divine unity and the creation and transmigration of souls. Franz von Baader (1765–1841), whose work essentially involves the conception of a modern Christian gnosis, after the fracture of the Enlightenment,[8] produced the bulk of his theosophical writings between 1815 and 1822. Relying on the teaching of Louis-Claude de Saint-Martin and Jacob Boehme, he attempted to integrate faith and science by means of a system based on correspondences, a *Naturphilosophie* linking God, world, and man. It is in the heart of the latter that the model of the heavenly Jerusalem is built, the spiritual city that is to reign over the earth. The same concern for regeneration inspired Ivan Lopoukhine (1756–1816) in *Quelques traits de l'Eglise intérieure* (1798), which was immediately translated into French and then German by Jung Stilling (1740–1817), another theosophist, who insisted on the eschatological and millenarian aspect of postrevolutionary Christianity. Joseph de Maistre also reflected on this fracture in *Les Soirées de Saint-Petersbourg*, written during his sojourn in Russia between 1802 and 1817.[9] Maistre rehabilitated the notions of revelation and the primacy of spiritual power in a true remythification of history, which he called an "*événement immense*" which gave past suffering its spiritual significance. The entire romantic movement was impregnated with these ideas. Chateaubriand, for example, pirated the ideas of Pierre-Simon Ballanche (1776–1847), whose *La Ville des expiations* and *Essais de palingénésie sociale* (1827) called for a reconciliation in the New Jerusalem. Ballanche influenced the first socialists, the followers of Saint-Simon and the Catholic disciples of Fourier, who turned toward esotericism. The Fourier communities, sometimes inspired as well by the thought of Swedenborg (1688–1772), spread to the United States and Russia.

The comparative study of non-Christian traditions and the symbols of ancient and oriental religions, which had gained currency with the publication of *Symbolik und Mythologie der alten Voelker, besonders der Griechen* by Friedrich Creuzer (1771–1858), professor at the University of

Heidelberg, was meant to supply a confirmation of Holy Scripture, by tracing a path back to the primordial revelation.[10] This entire unitary procedure in opposition to naturalism and Rousseau's position was sustained by the idea of an original revelation.

After advances in historical criticism had shaken these theories, and Rome's condemnation of traditionalism had been followed by a return to Thomas Aquinas, they were salvaged in part by "symbolizers," who applied to Christian art and liturgy ideas that official theologians now preferred to ignore, and in part by esotericists. "Learned canons of the cathedrals" like J. S. Devoucoux à Autun (1804–1870), bishop of Evreux in 1858, found the key to religious architecture in kabbalistic number speculations—techniques which the freemasons had inherited and whose monopoly over the occult sciences had to be overcome. The influence of this current on literature was considerable (see Huysmans, *La Cathédrale,* 1898).

If millenarianism had marked theosophy, it was prophecy—present at the start of the nineteenth century with Mme. de Kruedener (1764–1824), the inspiration of Czar Alexander I at the Congress of Vienna—that imbued occult theories. It staked its legitimacy on certain passages from Paul's epistles (1 Thessalonians 5:19–21 and Ephesians 4:11) and aspired to serve as spiritual guide in political and even scientific matters. In France, a laborer, Martin de Gallardon, had shifted the question of legitimacy in the direction of mysticism by affirming the survival of Louis XVII, the child martyr of the temple. In Germany, the clairvoyant of Dulmen, Anne Catherine Emmerich (1774–1823), described the life and passion of Christ with a profusion of details intended to silence textual criticism, but her description of the resurrection owed much to theories of the astral body. Clemens Brentano, whose interest in occultism was common knowledge, made sure that these visions were written up.

Pierre-Michel Vintras (1807–1875), who was favored by visions of the Virgin and founded a sect, is a good example of this amalgam. The Abbé Charvoz, a theologian, collected his narratives in a *Livre d'or* (1849), which attracted numerous disciples endowed with the mission of announcing the time of the transfigured woman, who was identified with the Holy Spirit. Vintras had recognized in Naundorff, Louis XVII, the Great Monarch sought by the nations, the "arm" of the regeneration of peoples. Vintras was imprisoned and persecuted, but his work survived him, and the "Vintrasian Cloister" of Lyon, which was accused of satanism, helped to generate a debate at the end of the century between the occultists Stanislas de Guaïta (1861–1897), Papus (1865–1916), and Huysmans. They all sought in the fulfillment of prophecies rational proofs of a counterhistory that could be set against "science without God"; they sought in their cyclical and even kabbalistic exegesis an application to modern times.

Occultism Institutionalized (1870–1907)

The great hopes for progress and unity among the peoples of the world, which had inspired such events as the Universal Exposition of 1855, were slowly effaced. The Eiffel Tower—a work of the iron age—marked the 1889 Exposition, and the emperor of Germany was not received in Paris. The spirit of the century nevertheless survived, projected into an ideal Orient to support the awaited new religion; and this position appeared justified by the successes of European expansion in the world. Madame Blavatsky (1831–1891) , founder of the Theosophical Society in 1875 in New York, recruited members for an "esoteric Buddhism" transmitted by mysterious Tibetan masters. The movement experienced striking success in the United States, France, England, and the Netherlands until it encountered the problems inherent in all institutionalization. It was in addition suspected of serving British interests in India and anticlerical politics in France. It also collided with the religious mentality of certain of its adherents, like Lady Caithness (1832–1895) of Paris, who directed a Christian "inner circle" within the society and in 1886 founded a prophetic journal, *L'Aurore du jour nouveau,* inspired by J. Boehme and Swedenborg, which proclaimed the reign of woman (Lady Caithness announced herself in communication with Queen Mary Stuart). She surrounded herself with occultists, marginal priests, and liberal Protestants, and spent a fortune in her private hotel. Her ideas had been drawn in good part from Anna Kingsford (1846–1888), the author of *The Perfect Way* (1882), who developed a feminine theology of the Holy Spirit and resigned from the Theosophical Society in 1882 to organize the Hermetic Society in London, which had a considerable influence in the Anglo-Saxon world.

Difficulties of the same order had set the Theosophical Society against one of its German members, Dr. Franz Hartmann (1838–1912) , who called himself heir to an ancient Rosicrucian fraternity. As for the departure of Rudolf Steiner (1816–1925) in 1913, this was provoked by the syncretist attempt to create a new messiah in the person of Krishnamurti (1895–1986), the son of an Indian from Madras and a member of the Theosophical Society, who under the name "Alcyon" was to be the instructor of the world for the new cycle. Steiner then founded the anthroposophical movement.

In fact the occultist organizations that flourished from the 1880s on frequently reacted against the Theosophical Society even while they remained mingled with its history. Their origins are complex. First of all, the Hermetic Brotherhood of Luxor publicly manifested its existence in the United States around 1870 through the medium of Paschal B. Randolph (1825–1875) whose sexual magic later inspired a number of esoteric groups. The Brotherhood proclaimed itself the heir of ancient initiations, and its organ in Glasgow, *The Occult Magazine,* fought the Theosophical Society in 1885. Two of its members, Peter Davidson (1837–1915), founder of an initiatic agricultural colony in Loudsville, Georgia, and the enigmatic Max Théon (1848?–1926), had a profound impact on occultist movements, particularly by way of Barlet. The "cosmic philosophy" of Théon, which issued successively from London, Paris, and Tlemcen, Algeria, transmitted a very strange initiatic teaching which captivated Myra Alfassa, the "mother" of Sri Aurobindo's ashram at Pondichery.

In England a group of masons, including William Wynn Westcott (1848–1925) and Samuel Liddle MacGregor Mathers (1854–1918), members of the Societas Rosicruciana in Anglia (founded in 1866), claimed to find in an encoded manuscript communicated by a German initiate (Anna Sprengel, whose supposed correspondence with Westcott constitutes the only proof of its existence) the key to the enigmas of the work of the Abbot Trithemius (1462–1516). They thereupon created a hermetic order, The Golden Dawn in the Outer (1888–1896), which practiced ceremonial magic. Papus (Gérard Encausse, 1865–1916) himself had also broken with the Theosophical Society, to create in 1888 a journal, *L'Initiation,* and a hermetic school designed to defend a Christian esotericism far removed both from the strict dogmatism of the church and from an orientalism too foreign to the Western tradition. The journal combined with the study of the usual occult sciences an experimental spiritualism which sought to retain the occultists' work on the unconscious and hypnotism (relying in particular on the experiments of William Crookes), as well as articles on the legends and popular or prophetic magical practices in which the beginning of the century had taken such delight. *L'Initiation* was placed on the Index in 1891, the date of Papus' founding of the Supreme Council of the Martinist Order. This order claimed inclusion in an initiatic filiation connected with Louis-Claude de Saint-Martin (1743–1803). Occultists like Barlet associated with writers like Paul Adam, Maurice Barrès, and Péladan, the latter gaining recognition with *Le vice suprême* (1884). Their engagement in the great debates over ideas and the society of the time multiplied occasions for conflicts and schisms.

The enterprise that made the greatest impact was that of "Sar" Joséphin Péladan, who broke in 1891 with the kabbalistic Order of the Rose-Cross (organized on the fringe of the Martinist Order by the occultist writer Stanislas de Guaïta) to proclaim himself Grand Master of a Catholic Rose-

Cross. Péladan united in his person the powers of priest and scientist, taking as precedent the Chaldean magi whose role he defined in *L'occulte catholique* (1899). From 1892 on he gained particular renown through the salons of the Rose-Cross, which were put to the service of an idealistic and mystical art that sought to revive a sacred art, an *"Art-Dieu"* as Péladan called it, which drew greatly upon the conception of the symbol at the beginning of the century. The painters Armand Point, Alexandre Séon, and Georges Rouault had expositions there, and Erik Satie composed the Rose-Cross's carillon music.

The Separation of Occultism from Esotericism (1905–1914)

A separation of occultism from esotericism followed the separation of church from state in France in 1905. Rome was soon to condemn the modernism behind which Christian occultists were taking cover in search of unity with other confessions and oriental traditions. Ideological confrontation of one bloc against another accompanied the rise of nationalism. The socialist mystique, postponed to a distant utopia, had ceded its place to Marx's theories on violence; and harmony among peoples looked ridiculous in the face of the *Realpolitik* which prevailed after the 1870s. Occultist literature was transformed from universalism into patriotic discourse: Papus predicted the victory of the Russians over the Japanese, and Theodor Reuss (1855–1923), the Grand Master of the Ordo Templi Orientis (which Aleister Crowley [1875–1947] was to inherit), spied for the imperial police on the German socialists who were refugees in London.

Moreover, doubts had arisen over the very object of occultism, in the quarters which had been most favorable to it. What remained of the astral body and spiritualist doctrines in the face of scientific work on the unconscious? Finally, the gulf between science and faith had grown wider, and occultism now appeared a further obstacle to settling the problem. The magicians of the Golden Dawn and their Parisian colleagues seemed trivial indeed.

Thus esoteric thought progressively abandoned the trappings of the occult, effecting a return to the texts and casting a critical eye on initiatic affiliations. When Paul Vulliaud (1875–1950) founded a new journal in Paris, *Les Entretiens idealistes* (1906–1914), to defend sacred art against Manet and Huysmans against Zola's realism, he took issue with Péladan's interpretations, which depicted Leonardo da Vinci as an individual genius who had gained initiation, and displayed instead the continuity of symbolic traditions in the work of the master (*La Dernière leçon de Léonard de Vinci*, 1904). His efforts to ground the legitimacy of Christian esotericism on authentic post-Renaissance texts rested on a serious critique, which he then extended to his kabbalistic studies.

The history of the movement ends with René Guénon (1886–1951), who, in the years before the war, carried out a comparison of most of the occultist initiations, in order to denounce the artificial character and "transposed materialism" which undergirded their theories. Over against them he set a "metaphysical tradition," in radical opposition to the "modern world."

The final survivors of romanticism disappeared with the onslaught of the general war.

Translated by Stephen Voss

Notes

1. The word "*occulte*" appears in French in 1120 in the *Psautier d'Oxford*. In 1633 it is enriched, according to the *Oxford Dictionary*, with a new meaning related to ancient knowledge and the secrets of antiquity and the Middle Ages.

2. See Michele Ciliberto, *Lessico di Giordano Bruno* (Rome: Edizioni dell'Ateneo, 1979), notably in *Cena de le ceneri*, 1584.

3. Edward A. Tiryakian, "Toward the Sociology of Esoteric Culture," *American Journal of Sociology* 78 (November 1972) 498.

4. J. E. Marconis de Nègre and E. N. Mouttet, *Le Hiérophante, développements complets des mystères maçonniques* (Vallée de Paris, 5839 [1839]).

5. L. Constant, *Dogme et rituel de la haute magie* (Paris: Baillière, 1856) 3.

6. London: S. Rousseau, 1801–1807.

7. "Sciences occultes," *Encyclopédie Paul Lacroix, Le Moyen-Age et la Renaissance*, vol. 4, part 2 (Paris, 1851).

8. See *Philosophische Schriften und Aufsaetze* (Münster: Theissing, 1831–32); *Der moergenlaendische und abendlaendische Katholicismus* (Stuttgart: H. Koehler, 1841).

9. Published upon his death in Paris in 1921.

10. Leipzig and Darmstadt: Karl W. Leske, 1810–12. Three editions followed, with considerable success in Germany up to 1824.

Bibliography

Eliade, Mircea. *Occultism, Witchcraft and Cultural Fashions*. Chicago and London: University of Chicago Press, 1976.

Faivre, Antoine. *Accès de l'ésotérisme occidental*. Paris: Gallimard, 1986.

Guénon, René. *L'Erreur spirite*. Paris: Rivière, 1921.

Howe, Ellic. *The Magicians of the Golden Dawn*. London: Routledge & Kegan Paul, 1972.

James, Marie-France. *Esotérisme, occultisme, franc-maçonnerie et christianisme, aux XIXᵉ & XXᵉ siècles*. Paris: N.E.L., 1981.

Laurant, Jean-Pierre. *L'Esotérisme chrétien en France au XIXᵉ siècle*. Paris: L'Age d'Homme, 1992.

Moeller, Helmut, and E. Howe. *Merlin Peregrinus, vom Untergrund des Abendlandes*. Würburg: J. Königshausen, 1986.

Viatte, Auguste. *Les Sources occultes du romantisme*. 2 vols. Paris: Champion, 1928.

Webb, James. *The Occult Underground*. La Salle, IL: Open Court Publishing Company, 1974.

10

Rudolf Steiner
and Anthroposophy

ROBERT A. McDERMOTT

RUDOLF STEINER (1861–1925), spiritual and esoteric teacher and founder of Anthroposophy, or Spiritual Science, made substantial contributions to philosophy, sciences, social sciences, arts, and education. He wrote approximately forty books, beginning in 1891 with *Truth and Knowledge,* his philosophy doctoral dissertation, and ending in 1924, the year before his death, with his autobiography. He delivered more than six thousand lectures, which have been published in three hundred volumes. Steiner is perhaps best known for the Waldorf School Movement, consisting of more than five hundred schools in thirty-five countries which continue to draw guidance from his hundreds of lectures on child development, curriculum, and pedagogy.

Rudolf Steiner was an esoteric teacher in the Rosicrucian-Christian tradition who delineated a comprehensive and detailed account of the evolution of consciousness as a background to his plea for the transformation of thinking, feeling, and willing in the present century. He considered the purpose of evolution of human consciousness, for which he regarded the incarnation of the Christ as the central event, to be the attainment of human love and freedom. His written works and lectures seek to establish that humanity lost its previous access to the inner reality of the self and the external world. He offers a method by which to develop a warm and will-filled overcoming of the alienation that he considered to be characteristic of modern Western consciousness.

Steiner's practical contributions—including the Waldorf School Movement; biodynamic farming; contributions in the arts, sciences, medicine, and social life; as well as esoteric research concerning karma and rebirth—are the fruits of a clairvoyant capability that was both innate and subsequently further developed. Through his foundation books, *Philosophy of Freedom* (1894), *Knowledge of the Higher Worlds and Its Attainment* (1904), and *Occult Science: An Outline* (1909), Steiner offers a spiritual discipline by which others can strive to develop higher capacities. All of these works serve the same essential task of Steiner's Anthroposophy, or Spiritual Science, namely, the attempt to gain a loving and creative knowledge of the spiritual in the individual and the spiritual in the universe, and the relation between them. His spiritual and esoteric teachings claim to be both life-affirming and life-knowing.

Just a few months before his death, in a series of letters written for members of the Anthroposophical Society and published as *Anthroposophic Leading Thoughts,* Steiner wrote his own description of Anthroposophy:

> Anthroposophy is a path of knowledge, to guide the spiritual in the human being to the spiritual in the universe. It arises in the human being as a need of the heart, of the life of feeling; and it can be justified only inasmuch as it can satisfy this inner need. Only those can acknowledge Anthroposophy who find in it what they themselves in their inner lives feel impelled to seek. Only they can be Anthroposophists who feel certain questions on the nature of the human being and the universe as an elemental need of life, just as one feels hunger and thirst.
>
> Anthroposophy communicates knowledge that is gained in a spiritual way. Yet it only does so because everyday life, and the science founded on sense-perception and intellectual activity, lead to a barrier along life's way—a limit where the life of the soul in the human being would die if it could go no further. Everyday life and science do not lead to this limit in such a way as to compel the human being to stop short at it. For at the very frontier where the knowledge derived from sense-perception ceases, there is opened through the human soul itself the further outlook into the spiritual world. (p. 13)

Anthroposophy refers to a way of knowing the essentially human, or essential human wisdom; at the same time the term refers to the knowledge attained by the higher (or more spiritually active) self. Steiner's aim is to enable human beings to develop their spiritual faculties and thereby to develop a knowledge of the spiritual in the cosmos. According to Steiner, this achievement is possible by a kind of thinking which he describes synonymously as active, loving, spiritual, and free. He tries to show that this new mode of spiritual thinking is at the core of great advances in science, art, and religion. He intends his ideal of spiritually active thinking as a call to the heart, to the affective and artistic. He develops his concept and method of spiritual "living" thinking as a contrast to ordinary intellectuality.

Steiner tried to show how spiritual thinking leads to an experience of freedom. He entitled his first major work *Die Philosophie der Freiheit,* which has been translated accurately both as *The Philosophy of Freedom* and as *The Philosophy of Spiritual Activity.* For Steiner, these are synonymous: To be free is to be capable of thinking one's own thoughts—not the thoughts merely of the body, or of society, but thoughts generated by one's deepest, most original, most essential and spiritual self, one's individuality.

Steiner emphasized repeatedly that our faulty (nonspiritual, unfree) thinking is due to alienation, both innate and imposed, from other human beings and from cosmic rhythms. This same metaphysical isolation leads to a faulty image of human beings, particularly of children, the aged, the ill, and the disabled. Concerning all of these special populations Steiner offered analyses and methods of care. He sought to show how the thinking characteristic of the past three centuries has led to a disregard for the life of feeling. He sought to critique and replace scientific-rationalistic thinking, which excludes the entire affective dimension of life, including the religious and the artistic. His method of Spiritual Science aims to restore the affective not merely to the rational-intellectual in general, but particularly to the sciences.

Rudolf Steiner's Life and Work

Rudolf Steiner was born on February 27, 1861, at Kraljevec on the Murr Island in Croatia, within the Austrian Empire. His parents, both born in southern Hungary, were Johann Steiner (1829–1910), an employee of the Southern Austrian Railway, and Franziska Blie Steiner (1834–1918). He spent his early childhood, ages two to seven, at Pottschach, a station on the Southern Austrian Railway, attended a scientific high school until age eighteen, and graduated from a polytechnic college in Vienna.

As a college student, Steiner was employed as a tutor to a family of boys, the youngest of whom, Otto Specht, had virtually been abandoned because of his "hydrocephalitic tendencies." After two years of patient work, Steiner brought the boy not only into normal family life but educated him to a par with those of his age and equipped him for productive life; he eventually became a physician.

Through his professor, Karl Julius Schroer, Steiner began to edit, at age twenty-two, *Goethe's Natural Scientific Writings* for the Josef Küreschner's edition. At age twenty-five he wrote *A Theory of Knowledge Implicit in Goethe's World Conception*. In 1891 he received his doctorate in philosophy from the University of Rostock, and a year later he published his dissertation under the title *Truth and Knowledge*. In 1894 he published his primary work in philosophy, *The Philosopy of Freedom*, followed immediately by *Friederich Nietzsche: Battler Against his Time* and *Goethe's Conception of the World*.

Presumably, if karma, or destiny, is to be taken at all seriously, from the beginning of his life Steiner was on his way to being an initiate—that is, one sent by the spiritual world to undertake an important work for humanity. As a boy, Steiner felt that he could not speak to anyone concerning an aunt who, immediately after committing suicide, appeared to him and sought his help. When his elementary school teacher gave him a geometry book, Steiner found that the pure geometric forms were rather like the world of spiritual forms with which he was already familiar. This discovery of geometry was one of the great experiences in his early life, for it provided reassurance that the world of spirit was a shareable experience and a communicable mode of knowledge.

In a brief autobiographical sketch called "The Barr Document," which he wrote in 1906, Steiner acknowledges but does not identify his master:

> I did not at once meet the M. [master], but first someone sent by him who was completely initiated into the mysteries of the effects of all plants and their connection with the universe and with man's nature. For him, converse with the spirits of nature was a matter of course, which he described without enthusiasm, thereby awakening enthusiasm all the more. (*Essential Steiner*, 14)

This intermediary was an herb gatherer named Felix Koguzski. He gave Steiner his first opportunity to share with another human being the reality of the spiritual world manifest in nature, which had been an integral part of his experience from his earliest years. After this meeting with the herb gatherer, Steiner's spiritual master, or initiator, apparently gave him several tasks, including the immeasurably difficult task of reversing the plunge of Western thought and culture into materialism and the more specific task of restoring to the West the double concept of karma and rebirth.

Steiner was also led to the idealist philosophy of Fichte, whose concept of the "I" he used as a basis for his doctoral dissertation. From his earliest philosophical writings, however, it was clear that Steiner would not rest in the idealist philosophy of Fichte and Hegel; he complemented this idealism with the natural philosophy of Goethe and with his own esoteric empiricism. This typifies Steiner's habit of synthesizing mind and spiritual path: he sympathized with diverse and competing positions in such a way as to save and reconcile the positive contributions of each. By his thought and action he repeatedly brought together perspectives that are ordinarily kept apart. His life as much as his thought can be seen as an attempt to embody the reconciliation of polarities, whether science and art, matter and spirit, individualism and community.

Until 1899 Steiner's life appeared academically quite promising, and perhaps even brilliant, but not yet publicly esoteric. It was not until age thirty-nine that he publicly manifested occult, clairvoyant capacities. It was at this time, as he later reported in his autobiography, that he entered a deep spiritual struggle and then experienced the mystery of Christian redemption. As a result of this life-transforming experience his Spiritual Science was thereafter bathed in a Christian light.

Despite the increasingly significant role that he ascribed to the Christ, Steiner continued to lecture to large audiences of Theosophists. From 1902 to 1909 he served as general secretary of the German branch of the Theosophical Society, but he had not actually joined the society. In 1909, during the Theosophical Congress at Budapest, Steiner formally separated from the Theosophical Society. His increasingly Western, and specifically Christian, orientation would undoubtedly have led him to separate from the Theosophical Society eventually, but in fact from his point of view this break was forced upon him when C. W. Leadbeater and Annie Besant announced that J. Krishnamurti, who was then sixteen years old, was the vehicle of a coming world teacher. Leadbeater himself apparently believed that his student Krishnamurti was the reincarnated Christ.

From 1904 to 1909 Steiner wrote three of his foundation books—*Knowledge of the Higher Worlds and Its Attainment* (1904), *Theosophy* (1904), and *Occult Science: An Outline* (1909)—and lectured on a wide variety of themes within the history of Western esotericism. Beginning in 1909, he delivered many lectures on the events depicted in the Christian Gospels.

In 1913, in Berlin, Steiner's followers, including mainly those who had worked with him in the Theosophical branches and those who had heard his hundreds of lectures throughout Europe, formed the Anthroposophical Society. Technically, Steiner neither founded nor joined the society that his followers formed at this time, but ten years later, during Christmas week of 1923, Steiner refounded the General Anthroposophical Society and assumed its leadership. In the same year, 1913, Steiner laid the foundation stone for the Goetheanum, an enormous wood structure which he designed to be built on an imposing hill in Dornach, near Basel, Switzerland. Since that time the Goetheanum has served as the public and esoteric center for the worldwide work of the Anthroposophical Society.

Steiner chose the name Goetheanum in order to honor Goethe's understanding of the aesthetic principle that form follows function, the same principle that governed Steiner's architectural design. This architecturally influential double-cupola structure, made of woods from all over Europe and North America, with the most spiritually enlightened forms, was under construction for a full decade (including the years of the First World War when workers from seventeen nations, including France, Germany, and England, lived and worked together on top of a hill in Switzerland within hearing distance of the battles raging around them). The Goetheanum was just completed when it was burned to the ground by an arsonist on New Year's Eve, 1922.

In 1899 Steiner married Anna Eunike, widowed mother of the five children for whom Steiner had been a resident tutor. Steiner had his own section of Frau Eunike's house for his work and for meetings with colleagues. When asked about this relationship, which was clearly a marriage of convenience lasting approximately three years, he dismissed the inquiry with a typically Victorian explanation that "private relations are not something to be publicized." Anna Eunike died in 1911.

Steiner married Marie von Sievers immediately after she crossed the border from Germany into Switzerland in 1914, at the outbreak of the First World War. For more than a decade von Sievers had been his assistant in the German branch of the Theosophical Society. While we remain uninformed about their marriage as such, it is clear that Marie Steiner shared every detail of Steiner's work on behalf of Anthroposophy. She was particularly influential in her collaboration with Steiner for the spiritual-esoteric renewal of the arts.

It seems that Steiner's deepest personal relationship, one which he believed had extended through previous lifetimes, was with Ita Wegman, a Dutch physician with whom Steiner collaborated on medical research for more than two decades, some of the results of which are published in their book *Fundamentals of Therapy: An Extension of the Art of Healing through Spiritual Knowledge*.

With the sole exception of his teaching concerning karma and rebirth, Rudolf Steiner's entire life's work was in response to other people's requests for help. Except for a series of lectures that he delivered to followers who had joined the School of Spiritual Science, an esoteric membership at the core of the Anthroposophical Society dedicated to spiritual scientific research, Steiner gave all of his innovative ideas and methodologies openly and in a way that was intended to be shared by anyone interested in them.

In response to a request from a dancer for a new art form, Steiner developed an art of movement called eurythmy. Superficially resembling forms of dancing and gliding, with distinctive movements, eurythmy can be expressed as speech and music made visible. Like all true art forms, eurythmy is spiritually restorative. Specifically, it is a way of forming and strengthening the performer's subtle body; an etheric aspect to the human being which surrounds and pervades the physical body. Steiner developed eurythmy for three distinct uses: as a performance art, in curative work, and for pedagogical use in Waldorf schools and other schools. In addition to eurythmy, which he created as a new art form, Rudolf Steiner also gave new methods and creative innovations to a variety of traditional art forms, including sculpture, architecture, painting, and music.

From 1910 to 1913 Steiner wrote four mystery dramas so that modern Western audiences could experience in dramatic form the karma of paradigmatic individual lives over several incarnations. First performed in Munich, these dramas continue to be performed in the Goetheanum, with its enormous auditorium and stage, which Steiner designed especially for performances of eurythmy and mystery dramas.

Steiner taught that the etheric, or life-body, can be nourished and made healthy by sculpture and eurythmy; the soul or astral body is strengthened by painting, and the "I" or individual spirit is actualized by language. He left important insights for these and other arts as necessary healing for the destructive power of materialistic consciousness. He hoped that the Goetheanum, in which virtually all of the arts were developed to their full powers, would serve to give future generations of spiritually searching visitors some clues as to the health-giving capacity of spiritually-based artistry. Rudolf Steiner's own health suffered a devastating blow when the first Goetheanum was totally destroyed by fire.

The economic and social ills of the decade surrounding the First World War led Steiner to develop an elaborate social, political, and economic philosophy called the threefold social order. He based this ideal commonwealth on the threefold nature of the individual and society, according to which rights and responsibilities fall into three distinct but related groups: the economic, the rights or political, and the cultural. Among the many significant implications of this division is the separation of the cultural sphere (including religion, education, and the arts, and all other expressions of individual freedom and creativity) from both the rights and the political spheres.

In 1919, in response to the plea from Emil Molt, owner of the Waldorf Astoria Tobacco Factory in Stuttgart, for help in educating the children of his employees, Steiner developed a novel educational experiment based on anthroposophic wisdom concerning the inner life and development of the child. The Waldorf schools are especially significant for reconciling sciences and the arts on the basis of a single source and methodology—active, heartfelt thinking. This model school became the foundation for the Waldorf School Movement, which now includes five hundred schools around the world, including ninety in North America. The Waldorf schools, which constitute the largest nonsectarian private school movement in the world, are characterized by the attempt to integrate the works of head, heart, and hand (or disciplined cultivation of thinking, feeling, and willing), and the aim of educating the total child in freedom and responsibility for nature, for the individual, and for the global human community.

In response to requests from doctors for a course of lectures on homeopathic and anthroposophic healing, Steiner classified numerous herbs and other natural substances with their various healing powers. There are now more than two thousand physicians who enjoy the advantage of a double training and methodology—standard medical diagnostic and prescriptive treatment as well as a capacity for insight and an image of the human being based on the teachings and discipline of Anthroposophy.

Answering the plea of farmers, Steiner lectured extensively on a method of agriculture based on his supersensible knowledge of the soul-spiritual forces operative in the earth, plant, and animal worlds. This method of farming, called biodynamic, is an increasingly important agricultural alternative to chemically dominated farming in Europe and North America, as well as in New Zealand and Australia.

In an act that is not strictly within Anthroposophy, Steiner responded to the requests of ministers and theology students who asked him for help in their effort to renew Christian life and liturgy. He inspired and helped fashion an institutional and ecclesiastical structure called the Christian Community, also called the Movement for Religious Renewal. For this community, he disclosed seven sacraments, including a liturgy called the Act of Consecration of Man, a ritual not unlike the Roman Catholic Mass. In contrast to Spiritual Science, whereby human beings strive essentially on their own to experience the spiritual ascent, the Act of Consecration of Man allows the participant to experience a descent of the divine into the assembled community.

In response to the needs of individuals who felt themselves called to practice supersensible, heart-filled thinking, Steiner formed the Anthroposophic Society and Anthroposophic Movement as ways of providing increased opportunities for collaboration and mutual support.

Perhaps Steiner's most significant contribution to contemporary humanity is his providing a method for the acquisition of spiritually clear knowledge as a precondition for human freedom in thought and action. Through his contributions to thought and culture, and the methods he bequeathed, Rudolf Steiner remains one of the most important exemplars of esoteric knowledge in the modern West. Although there are many clairvoyants throughout the world, Steiner is distinctive, and perhaps unique, in the degree to which he understood his clairvoyance, disciplined it, applied it to numerous fields of knowledge and culture, and, most important, published directions for people born with ordinary consciousness to begin to develop a modicum of spiritual intuition.

Rudolf Steiner was not only endowed with a capacity for imagination, inspiration, and intuition; he carefully explained how such modes of knowing can be cultivated. He emphasized that the cultivation of spiritual knowledge is difficult because it runs against a deep cultural and intellectual prejudice. He tried to show that neither ordinary ways of knowing nor knowledge by faith would bring Western culture out of its present impasse. What is needed, according to Steiner, is a knowing that is individual yet objective, spiritual yet reliable.

The spiritual knowledge scattered throughout Steiner's hundreds of volumes includes disclosures—some of them quite startling—concerning such topics as evolution of the sun, moon, and planets, especially the earth, and the etheric or formative forces working in the plant and animal worlds. He describes the role of great spiritual beings such as Krishna, Buddha, and the Christ, and angelic beings such as the tempters, Lucifer and Ahriman, and the archangel Michael (whom Steiner regards as the regent of the current age). This vision also includes descriptions of the salient characteristics of Western civilization, which Steiner places in a detailed evolutionary sequence, including historically significant and paradigmatic individuals such as the pharaohs of ancient Egypt, the patriarchs and prophets of Israel, Zoroaster, Plato, and Aristotle, as well as Christ and a series of influential Christian personalities. He particularly emphasizes the descent of the spiritual, Sun-Being, Christ into history through the agency of Jesus and several predecessors. He uses the phrase "the Mystery of Golgotha" to refer to the redemptive world-transformative presence of the Christ in Jesus of Nazareth.

When discussing his experience of the Mystery of Golgotha, first disclosed in his *Christianity as Mystical Fact* (1902) and developed in many subsequent lectures and writings on the events depicted in the New Testament, Steiner explained that his understanding was based entirely on direct vision. He consulted standard scriptural sources and scholarly interpretations only as a way of relating his own spiritual insight to conventional scholarly interpretations. In his autobiography Steiner writes as follows:

> I never found the Christianity I sought in any of the existing denominations. I found it necessary to enter into a direct and living experience of Christianity—and indeed into the world of spirit itself after severe inner struggles during the time of testing. (p. 318)
> During the period when my statements about Christianity seemingly contradict my later ones, a conscious knowledge of true Christianity began to dawn within me. Around the turn of the century this knowledge grew deeper. The inner test described above occurred shortly before the turn of the century. This experience culminated in my standing in the spiritual

presence of the mystery of Golgotha in a most profound and solemn festival of knowledge. (p. 319)

Steiner never claimed certitude for his clairvoyant findings nor dismissed ordinary texts and interpretations when they were inconsistent with his spiritually based research. On some points, he revised and supplemented his earlier research. In his 1925 preface to *Occult Science,* written just a few months before his death, he acknowledged that he had been able to include in *Occult Science,* written in 1909, material that had not been available to him just five years earlier when he wrote *Theosophy.* He explained that at the time when *Theosophy* was written, the facts of cosmic evolution were not present then to the same extent: "I was indeed aware of them in many details, but the picture as a whole was lacking."

Steiner's spiritual-scientific research continued to be work in progress. He refined and deepened his findings throughout his life, and he sought collaborators who could penetrate as deeply as he the secrets of humanity and the universe. A very short list of individuals who appear to have developed impressive capacities by working with Steiner's methods includes George Adams, Owen Barfield, D. N. Dunlop, Michaela Glueckler, Eugen Kolisko, Karl Konig, Georg Kuhlewind, Ernst Lehrs, Edith Maryon, Hermann Popplebaum, Ehrenfried Pfeiffer, Sergei Prokofieff, Albert Steffen, Walter Johannes Stein, Karl Unger, Marie Steiner, Gunther Wachsmuth, Ita Wegman, and F. W. Zeylmans von Emmichoven.

Although he sought collaboration and expected subsequent generations of spiritual scientific researchers to improve on his findings, he was not willing to regard materials developed at the more usual intellectual level as a more reliable source of knowledge than that which he gleaned clairvoyantly from the spiritual world. Steiner explains the relationship between clairvoyance and intellectual insight by the evolutionary scheme within which he understands not only these terms but the complex destiny of civilizations and souls, the modes of human consciousness, and the law of karma which governs all of these.

This summary of Steiner's thought gives prominence to his life and works, his account of evolution of consciousness, and his spiritual-scientific epistemology, but a complete—or at least more adequate—presentation would include an account of Steiner's sophisticated and highly detailed teaching concerning karma and rebirth. At the core of this teaching is Steiner's claim that the human being has two closely related life histories— waking and sleeping. The beginning of sleep represents a kind of death to the waking biography, just as the beginning of waking consciousness is a kind of death to the sleeping biography. The activity of the soul after its earthly life parallels the activity of the soul during sleep. In sleep, the astral or soul life as well as the spirit leave the remainder of the sleeping individual—the physical and etheric bodies—and return to the spiritual world for the period of sleep. After death, the sleep biography is relived in an ingenious reversal of the individual's earthly life.

At death, only the physical body dies immediately. The etheric body, which has recorded the essential qualities of a person's lifetime, presents a detailed summary of this life to the astral body. Presumably, this is the phenomenon described in the "Near Death" research. After it absorbs the panoramic report of the etheric body, the astral body remains in existence for approximately one-third the duration of a person's lifetime. During this time, the astral body, in which is embedded the individual's desires and emotions, continues to seek the kinds of satisfaction it enjoyed on earth; to the extent that it clings to physical and selfish satisfaction, it can only be frustrated. In the second phase of this process, the spirit of the individual relives its entire past life from death to birth, all the while receiving the consequences of its earthly actions as they were experienced by the objects of those actions. The recipients rain down the appropriate sympathies and antipathies as learning experiences preparatory for the individual's next life.

The law, or spiritual fact, of karma refers to the complex process by which the enduring qualities of each action, and a full lifetime, fashion the possibilities and the tasks of the next moment—and the next lifetime. On the basis of the previous life experience, as summarized and reexperienced between death and rebirth, the individual Self, or "I," chooses personal and environmental conditions of its next life. It is the karmic condition of the individual which largely determines the components of the next life, including the "choice" of parents, body, disposition, and capacities, as well as important influences and tasks. One's tasks are significantly affected by each person's karmic choice, just as one's karmic contributions help to fashion, for well or ill, the character of each culture.

Evolution of Consciousness

Even a brief outline of Steiner's disclosures concerning the evolution of consciousness would include the course of cosmic history from ages preceding the formation of the earth as we know it, the formation of the human body, the comings and goings of civilizations, and some previsions of the overall direction of cosmic and human evolution.

In broad outline, Steiner's account of the evolution of consciousness, particularly during the past three millennia of Western civilization, focuses on the steady decrease in human spiritual-intuitive thinking and a corresponding

13. Rudolf Steiner.

increase in the capacity for and reliance on human intellect. Steiner paints this evolutionary drama on an enormous canvas—including the evolution of the planets and of plant and animal life, and the early evolution of humanity through life on the continent of Atlantis, up to the extraordinary cultural and material changes of the nineteenth and twentieth centuries. His account of ancient events, including the emergence and disappearance of civilizations, represents the results of his ability to "read" (which can also be understood as a supersensible seeing) the essential events recorded in, or by, what is known in the esoteric tradition as an astral or akashic record, or world memory. As Steiner read this akashic record, or simply the akasha, he found that the civilization known as Atlantis came to destruction in approximately the tenth millennium B.C.

Subsequent to the destruction of Atlantis, through the agency of exceptional beings called the seven *rishis* (spiritual masters), the wisdom achieved during the Atlantean civilization was transmitted to "ancient India," which Steiner refers to as the first post-Atlantean epoch, the mode of consciousness which prevailed during the eighth to the sixth millennium. "Ancient India" refers to a period more than seven thousand years earlier than the period of Indian civilization when the ritual and mystical texts of the Vedas and Upanishads were composed. These texts were preserved by mnemonic chanting until the present time. Steiner regarded this well-known historical period of Indian civilization as a crystallization of the earlier, "ancient Indian" consciousness.

The consciousness of the second post-Atlantean epoch, from the sixth to the third millennium, was typified by "ancient Persia." As with "ancient India," Steiner's term "ancient Persia" refers to the original source of the Persian civilization, which flourished throughout the first millennium B.C. Steiner identifies the third post-Atlantean epoch, from the third millennium to the eighth century B.C., with Babylonian, Chaldean, and Egyptian civilizations. Unlike the first and second post-Atlantean epochs (from the eighth to the third millennium B.C.), which refer to modes of consciousness to which we have scant access by ordinary historical research, the third post-Atlantean epoch refers to historical civilizations for which we have extensive records.

The paucity of historical data makes it difficult to evaluate Steiner's rendering of the first two post-Atlantean epochs (the six thousand years from the end of Atlantis to the late Egyptian and early Hebraic civilizations in the middle of the second millennium B.C.), and his interpretation can be properly corroborated or revised only by someone with a comparable capacity for historical intuition. His accounts of the third, fourth, and fifth epochs, however, are subject to exoteric historical review.

Readers who are new to Steiner's vast and sometimes astonishing writings might find it difficult to know how to assess the implications, as well as the veracity of these accounts of events from millennia and centuries long past. The key to such complexity is almost always to be found in his overall program—to explain how modern Western consciousness lost the clairvoyance it possessed in early post-Atlantean epochs, and how this loss can be turned into a gain by developing a clairvoyance that is simultaneously scientific and spiritual. Unlike many New Age enthusiasts and others who long for a return to an ancient clairvoyance (referred to variously as primal, primordial, mythic, and archaic consciousness), Steiner traces the loss of ancient clairvoyance without regret: It is precisely this loss which made possible the development of the rational intellect and scientific objectivity. The cause for regret, according to Steiner, lies in the failure of modern Western (rational or scientific) consciousness to develop a new thinking capability which is at once scientific and spiritual.

The transition from direct spiritual intuition to reliance on intellect occurred most dramatically by the agency of the Greeks, at the beginning of the fourth post-Atlantean epoch. This epoch, for which Steiner considers the Greco-Roman-Christian consciousness to be paradigmatic, extends approximately from the eighth century B.C. to the fifteenth century A.D. It is during these two millennia, particularly because of innovations wrought by classical Greece, that human consciousness in the West can be seen to have developed a new paradigm: the mythic was gradually replaced by the intellectual.

The present century—which is, after all, Steiner's primary concern—is characterized by an intellectual paradigm that is deadening and in desperate need of revitalization by a new version of what has been lost during the past several millennia, namely, spiritually grounded, imaginative, inspirational, and intuitive capacity. The distinctive mode of consciousness of the present age, which is the fifth post-Atlantean epoch, dates to the fifteenth century and can be expected to continue developing this kind of consciousness until the thirty-fifth century. The sixth and seventh epochs in this seven-part cycle are, of course, far in the future, though Steiner also gives some notes on broad possibilities within those two periods.

Perhaps because the present is approximately the right distance from which to see its beginning, development, and end, the fourth post-Atlantean epoch would seem to offer us the best opportunity for grasping the significance—and evaluating the veracity—of Steiner's interpretation of these seven epochs. The most important potential contribution of Steiner's account is simply that it might enable us to understand how and why we have come to think, feel, and will as we do, and how modern Western consciousness differs from other modes of consciousness, both ancient and contemporary. Most of the distinctive features of modern Western consciousness came into being during the fourth post-Atlantean epoch—that is, during the centuries that mark the transition from Greco-Roman to Christian thought and culture. Greek thought, epitomized by Socrates, Plato, and Aristotle, represents a remarkable transition from the old clairvoyance represented by the gods of ancient Greek religion, to the possibility of rational, intellectual thinking represented by Socratic inquiry, Platonic dialectic, and Aristotelian logic.

At the time when this transition was taking place, but still uncertain of success, Steiner says the Logos, or Christ-Being, incarnated and rescued human evolution from the ever-increasing control of the material world. The Christ released a spiritual power, well summarized in the Gospel of St. John, which made possible a more creative and individualized thinking capability. Steiner saw the incarnation of Christ as the instrument of a potentially universal transformation, one that aims to reunite the spiritual and physical. According to Steiner's research, the Christ, or Logos, was from the beginning and continues to be the source of cosmic and human evolution. By entering the body of Jesus of Nazareth, the logos brought into the earth a spiritual impulse that can help lead humanity to greater freedom and love.

Steiner's teachings are permeated by the Christ impulse but are not constrained by Christian dogma or the ideal of faith. Rather, he teaches that in the present age the Christ impulse should champion the ideal and practice of human freedom in thinking and action. More than any of the myriad insights and impulses, Steiner's work on behalf of human freedom is his most distinctive and significant contribution.

According to Steiner, the Christ—the Logos or Word—was not comprehended by the darkness into which it entered, but the spiritual impulse which it brought into matter made possible the kind of thinking for which the Western world is justly prized and imitated. Steiner does not pit spiritual perception against science and intelligence, but rather sees the cool thinking of science as a necessary and essentially positive development in human evolution. These two competing, and yet complementary, capabilities—the intellectual and the intuitive—are both necessary for human progress and survival in the present age.

The task of the modern age, then, is to bring to bear on the physical world a new kind of spiritual seeing-thinking capability. Steiner urges the development of spiritual perception by the cultivation of the cognitive powers appropriate for the present stage of cultural and psychic evolution— imagination, inspiration, and intuition. Compared to these more spiritual and creative modes of thinking, our usual ways of thinking tend to be determined by impersonal forces, such as culturally engendered habits or physical impulses. Steiner refers to our ordinary thinking as a dead-thinking; he could as readily use Plato's allegory and refer to modern Western thinking as cavelike. The modern thinking person is capable of rationality but generally not capable of clairvoyance characteristic of past epochs. But by disciplined effort, the modern person can learn clairvoyant imagination, or imaginal thinking.

Although it may be regrettable that humanity had to lose its capacity for clairvoyance, and the intimate relation with the external world that was apparently commonplace in the ancient world, these losses made possible the development of scientific intelligence and a degree of individual freedom unimagined by primal consciousness. This loss of clairvoyance also led to the human estrangement and alienation characteristic of modern Western experience. The separation of mind from nature, as formulated by Descartes in the seventeenth century, is the birthright and fundamental life problem of the modern Western individual. The solution to this inescapable problem lies in a new kind of clairvoyance based on an intensely active spiritual thinking. The nature and function of this kind of thinking constitute the essence—the spiritual methodology or discipline—of Anthroposophy.

The Discipline of Spiritual Science

Steiner's teaching can be treated under two headings: its content—the results of his spiritual scientific research; and its practice—the path by which others can attempt to develop a comparable capability. As a path, or spiritual discipline, Anthroposophy includes a detailed method for schooling of consciousness leading to the attainment of spiritual knowledge and the gradual transformation of the individual practitioner. Because many Anthroposophists are understandably so in awe of the fruits of Steiner's spiritual scientific research, there is a tendency to emphasize the study of Steiner's writings at the expense of cultivating spiritual cognition. Even in his own day this mistaken emphasis caused Steiner considerable frustration and sadness, and it obviously limited the effectiveness of Anthroposophy as a spiritual-esoteric teaching and movement. He intended his research into the spiritual world to be exemplary of his method and to show the need for solutions on a higher level of insight than that on which arguments ordinarily swirl.

Anthroposophy represents a method of spiritual growth and transformation that aims to create an ideal harmony between thinking, feeling, and willing. Steiner recommends rather simple exercises that both cultivate these three components of human life and serve as a basis for the more advanced work of Spiritual Science. As virtually all spiritual teachers insist, spiritual or esoteric exercises can actually be harmful when undertaken by an individual whose exoteric (ordinary, observable) personality and character are ill-formed. Enthusiasts for yoga, for example, sometimes forget that the first two of the eight steps in Patanjali's *Yoga Sutras* set out the moral preconditions for progress in physical and spiritual exercises.

Steiner offers six preconditions for spiritual-esoteric progress:

1. Practice concentrating: gain control of one's thoughts for a few minutes faithfully every day.
2. Practice controlling the will: perform one or more positive but relatively insignificant tasks the same time of day, each day.
3. Practice equanimity: learn to stabilize fluctuations of pleasure and pain, joy and sorrow.
4. Practice seeking the positive in all things and events; resist antipathetic criticism.
5. Practice openness to new experiences and ideas.
6. Practice repeating and harmonizing the first five exercises.

These exercises are intended as an aid to establishing the conditions necessary for esoteric research. The first three of these six preconditions refer to the three strands of spiritual discipline needed for modern Western consciousness—namely, thinking, willing, and feeling.

The essential principles of Steiner's Spiritual Science or Anthroposophy (the wisdom of humanity, or wisdom based on human spiritual capacities) are based primarily on three works treating esoteric epistemology and methodology: *The Philosophy of Freedom* (1894), *Knowledge of the Higher Worlds and Its Attainment* (1904), and *Occult Science: An Outline* (1909). Each of these volumes, in different ways, reveals Steiner's case for the possibility of, and approach to, spiritual or esoteric knowledge. In order to understand his teaching on the acquisition of spiritual knowledge, one must first bear in mind that esoteric knowledge is accessible.

In his *Philosophy of Freedom,* Steiner sought to establish the theoretical and experiential possibility of access to spiritual or esoteric knowledge. Because the book is not particularly rewarding to the usual intellectual method of reading a philosophy text, it is not unusual for readers to find it disappointing. By this book, Steiner tried to show the causes of alienated thinking and the possibility of thinking in a new, more creative, more integrating way. The problem for most readers of *Philosophy of Freedom* is that they are caught by the very problem that Steiner is trying to expose and overcome—impoverished or conventional (nonintuitive) thinking. The book calls for an experience that is possible only for those who are able and willing to attempt a different way, or different level, of thinking. The book is intended to be its own verification—or, lacking the reader's willingness and ability, its own refutation. The result of working conscientiously through Steiner's *Philosophy of Freedom* is none other than what the book's title suggests—to think freely, to intuit ideas and ideals that live in the spiritual world of which the free thinker is a creative member.

Knowledge of the Higher Worlds and Its Attainment is intended as a kind of handbook for the development of clairvoyance or supersensible perception, the possible attainment of which Steiner insists on in the opening paragraph:

> There slumber in every human being faculties by means of which individuals can acquire for themselves a knowledge of higher worlds. Mystics, Gnostics, Theosophists, all speak of a world of soul and spirit which for them is just as real as the world we see with our physical eyes and touch with our physical hands. At every moment the listener may say: That, of which they speak, I too can learn, if I develop within myself certain powers which today still slumber within me. There remains only one question—how to set to work to develop such faculties. For this purpose, they alone can give advice who already possess such powers. As long as the human race has existed there has always been a method of training, in the course of which individuals possessing these higher faculties gave instruction to others who are in search of them. Such training, and the instruction received therefrom, is called occult (esoteric) teaching or spiritual science. (pp. 1–2)

Secret, esoteric, or occult knowledge is available to anyone who seeks it by a method guaranteed by a genuine spiritual school and teachers genuinely disciplined in the methods of that school. Steiner also offers two corollaries to this basic point: First, anyone who is eager to receive such knowledge and willing to meet the requirements of the discipline, ought to be accepted by a teacher or a school irrespective of that person's social, economic, or cultural resources. Similarly, as a second corollary, teachers should avoid making this knowledge available to those who are ill-prepared either in aspiration or ability.

Steiner emphasizes the continuity and the differences between levels of knowledge, for example, from perception to imagination, to inspiration, to intuition. Whereas almost everyone has at least a modicum of imagination, fewer are capable of inspired feeling, and fewer still of intuition. In the early post-Atlantean epochs, every human being had powers of imagination—that is, the capacity to know images, or pictures, of spiritual realities—which the typical modern Western individual can neither understand nor imitate. Increasingly, our society, and particularly our educational system, insists that because spiritual or intuitive knowing of images is not possible by ordinary thinking, such a capacity is not now and never was possible.

In direct opposition to this reductionist perspective, Steiner argues that because Moses and Homer, for example, lived in the consciousness of their time (specifically, the third post-Atlantean epoch), Moses presumably did, and in any case would have been able to, hear the voice of Yahweh, as Homer would have been able to see and hear the gods. And because they were exceptional individuals, they were able to express their respective hearing-seeing-knowing in a way that we can still reexperience and appreciate.

Steiner is not recommending that we return to the consciousness of Moses or Homer, but rather that we develop a capacity for a kind of knowing that is more awake and more appropriate for a person who lives in and through modern Western consciousness. Using the first two of Steiner's preconditions for spiritual-esoteric progress (practicing concentration and control of the will), it would be helpful to gain control of one's thinking sufficiently to think new kinds of thoughts, lovingly to think with Moses or Homer, or Plato or Jesus. This discipline could enable practitioners to enter the consciousness of individuals and cultures entirely different from their own. Steiner recognized that the widespread inability to experience the thinking, feeling, and willing of others would seem to be at the root of racial, gender, and generational misunderstandings and violence, and he offered a discipline by which to overcome the alienation that afflicts modern Western culture.

The difficulty, which Steiner also discussed repeatedly, is that modern Western individuals lack even the imagination to recognize the ways in which they are alien to other modes of human consciousness, past and present. This modern Western way of alienated thinking has resulted in the separation of the individual from nature and from the cosmos as living realities.

The alienation between our own inner self and the inner life of all else — God or gods, spirits, Buddha and Krishna, light, living forms, true ideals — is so well established as normal that the modern Western person ordinarily cannot experience this alienation for what it is. To develop the capacity for nonalienating (i.e., loving) thinking requires a significant commitment to a very demanding discipline. Not the least of the problems or dangers is simply that it is not unusual for individuals to develop a degree of clairvoyance in advance of their moral and psychological development.

The steps to esoteric knowledge follow a systematic progression — not unlike the six levels of knowledge in classical Yoga and Vedanta, the ladder of knowledge in Plato, or the levels of spiritual knowledge in Christian mysticism. As Steiner describes it, this progression runs from intellectual knowledge up through imagination, inspiration, and intuition. Each of these levels of higher knowledge in Steiner's epistemology corresponds to a part of the human being: imagination is a capacity developed by, and in the realm of, the life principle (also called etheric, or formative, principle); inspiration corresponds to the astral (or soul) principle; and intuition corresponds to the "I," or the spiritual self.

In this respect, the knowledge peculiarly available to modern Western people is a knowledge that is still less clairvoyant than ancient spiritual knowledge, but since it is based on the "I," the part of the self made possible by the impulse of Christ, it holds out the possibility of the richest combination, namely, universal spiritual knowledge grasped by a genuinely individual knowing "I."

Spiritual or meditative thinking applied to nature finds its fullest expression, prior to Steiner, in the writings of Goethe, who pioneered the work of observing the metamorphosis of plant forms. Goethe conducted thousands of investigations into the world of the plant and thereby began to develop living or imaginative thinking. Goethe entered so deeply and sympathetically into the life of the plant he was observing that he was able to see-think the plant's essential or formative idea. Goethe's highly conscious receptivity to the inner reality of what he termed the *Urpflanze*, or fundamental creating principle of the plant, is an example of what Steiner means by a path of knowing "to guide the spiritual in the individual to the spiritual in the universe."

While Steiner shared Goethe's interest in plants, and indeed shared virtually all of Goethe's interests, it was not in relation to plants that he sought to give imaginative thinking its most important role. Rather, he sought to show that this kind of inner penetration of the natural world would reveal to the observer a capacity for thinking that is self-referential or self-confirming. Steiner contended that individuals conducting such exercises as Goethe conducted on plants—though it need not be on plants and in fact could work equally well on any object or on the process of thinking itself—would eventually begin to notice their own new or more highly developed capacity for the intuitive seeing-knowing of the interior.

As Steiner is at pains to show repeatedly, science and art are equally fruitful areas by which to develop this spiritual-thinking capacity. The result will be twofold: a spiritual knowledge or esoteric insight and a heightened faculty or capability for spiritual-scientific thinking which can be used in all areas of inquiry. Like other great spiritual esoteric figures, Steiner was able to manifest his spiritual powers in the widest possible range of enterprises, from natural science to the arts, philosophy, and history. Meditative or imaginative thinking according to the method of Anthroposophy can enable one to acquire higher ways of knowing as well as a more fruitful relationship to one's self, to the rest of humanity, and to the universe.

The Anthroposophical Society

By the time of the Christmas Foundation Meeting in 1923, Steiner's followers had spent ten years implementing his insights, and to a lesser extent their own, but the results had proved uneven at best. In some respects, Steiner's life work was nearly in ruins: both the Goetheanum, which had been totally destroyed by fire, and the Anthroposophists themselves, who were given to dissension and dependency on Rudolf Steiner, seemed to suggest that the task of bringing Anthroposophy into the world was proving to be more difficult than its founder had anticipated.

At the Christmas Foundation Meeting, Rudolf Steiner founded a public society, the members of which had simply to affirm the value of the kind of spiritual scientific research conducted at or by the Goetheanum, that is, the individuals practicing the spiritual scientific research that Rudolf Steiner recommended. Soon afterward he also founded an esoteric School of Spiritual Science. The General Anthroposophical Society is an esoteric community continuous with the Christian esoteric tradition, but is distinctively modern in its emphasis on individuality and freedom. Steiner regarded the School of Spiritual Science as a source and guide of esoteric teaching; and it is an esoteric community which has its source and inspiration in or from the spiritual world. Members of this esoteric school are expected to be in the process of transforming spiritual scientific content into a living soul mood, one that expresses warm and loving truths concerning the full range of human concerns.

Steiner created a medical section of the School of Spiritual Science, and intended to create other sections, for individuals who were prepared to work out of the esoteric core of Anthroposophy. The other six sections included: general Anthroposophy and pedagogy, arts of speech and music, visual arts, letters, mathematics and astronomy, natural science. In recent years, additional sections have been included for work in pedagogy, social sciences, nutrition and agriculture, and the spiritual striving of youth. At the end of this century, nearly seventy years after the founding of the General Anthroposophical Society and the School of Spiritual Science, spiritual research continues in a host of disciplines and on a wide range of critical issues, including cancer, soil research, early childhood and aging, new forms of banking, and others.

One of the most pressing problems facing the Anthroposophical Society and Anthroposophists is simply the nearly overwhelming impact of Steiner's vast knowledge. It remains to be seen whether Anthroposophists will pay sufficient attention to Steiner's recommendations concerning spiritual work—particularly meditation, without which his research will become a resting place rather than, as he intended, a base for future research. The obvious significance of the Waldorf School Movement, as well as spiritual scientific research in sciences, social sciences, and arts would seem to suggest that Anthroposophy will yet make an important contribution to cultural renewal.

Guide to Reading

Steiner's writings in German consist of three hundred volumes, approximately two hundred of which have been translated into English. Many of these works are collections of his six thousand lectures. His followers frequently suggest that the most effective way to study Steiner and Anthroposophy is to begin with one of the three foundation books. In the first of these works, *Knowledge of the Higher World and Its Attainment*, published in 1904, Steiner expounds his method for schooling consciousness and offers advice on how to progress along this line.

In *Theosophy*, the second foundation book, also published in 1904, Steiner articulates an image of the human being as well as an explanation of karma and rebirth. He entitled this work *Theosophy* in an effort, thus far unsuccessful, to rescue this term from the Blavatsky version of Theosophy and to render it a more general term for spiritual or divine wisdom as taught by Gnostics, mystics, alchemists, and a long line of European Christian esoteric thinkers.

The third major work, *Occult Science: An Outline* (1909), is a full summary of the main points in Steiner's Anthroposophic teaching. In this work, which should be entitled "esoteric knowledge," Steiner offers a theory of human nature, an analysis of sleep and death, a lengthy section on the evolution of humanity and the world, and a chapter entitled "Knowledge of Higher Worlds–Concerning Initiation."

The Anthroposophic Press (Hudson, New York 12534) publishes an annotated catalogue of more than one thousand books by and about Rudolf Steiner, Anthroposophy, and practical works such as the Waldorf approach to education, biodynamic farming, the Camphill Movement, and the Christian Community. The headquarters of the Anthroposophical Society in America is located at 529 West Grant Place, Chicago, Illinois 60614; the General Anthroposophical Society is located at Goetheanumun, CH-4143 Dornach, Switzerland.

Bibliography

Easton, Stewart C. *Man and World in the Light of Anthroposophy.* New York: Anthroposophic Press, Inc., 1975.

——. *Rudolf Steiner: Herald of a New Epoch.* New York: Anthroposophic Press, Inc., 1980.

McDermott, Robert, ed. *The Essential Steiner.* San Francisco: Harper & Row, 1984.

Prokofieff, Sergei. *Rudolf Steiner and the Founding of the New Mysteries.* Trans. from Russian by Paul King. London: Rudolf Steiner Press, 1986.

Steiner, Rudolf. *Anthroposophical Leading Thoughts: Anthroposophy as a Path of Knowledge; The Michael Mystery.* Trans. George and Mary Adams. London: Rudolf Steiner Press, 1973. Orig. *Anthroposophische Leitsatze: Der Erkenntnisweg der Anthroposophie: Das Michael Mysterium,* 1924.

——. *The Boundaries of Natural Science.* Trans. Frederick Amrine and Konrad Oberhuber. Foreword by Saul Bellow. New York: Anthroposophic Press, 1983. Orig. *Grenzen der Naturerkenntnis.* 1920.

——. *Four Mystery Dramas.* Trans. Ruth and Hans Pusch. North Vancouver, Canada: Steiner Book Centre, Inc., 1973. Includes *The Portal of Initiation (Die Pforte der Einweihung), The Soul's Probation (Die Prüfung der Seele), The Guardian of the Threshold (Der Huter der Schwelle), The Soul's Awakening (Der Seelen Erwachen).* 1910–1913.

——. *Knowledge of the Higher Worlds and Its Attainment.* Trans. George Metaxa. New York: Anthroposophic Press, Inc., 1947. Orig. *Wie erlangt man Erkenntnisse der hoheren Welten?* 1904.

——. *Occult Science–An Outline.* Trans. George and Mary Adams. London: Rudolf Steiner Press, 1969. Orig. *Die Geheimwissenschaft im Umriss.* 1909.

——. *The Philosophy of Spiritual Activity.* Trans. William Lindeman. New York: Anthroposophic Press, 1986. Orig. *Die Philosophie der Freiheit.* 1894.

——. *The Riddles of Philosophy, Presented in an Outline of its History.* New York: Anthroposophic Press, 1973. Orig. *Die Rätsel der Philosophie.* 1914.

——. *Rudolf Steiner, An Autobiography.* Trans. Rita Stebbing. New York: Rudolf Steiner Publications, 1977. Orig. *Mein Lebensgang.* 1924.

——. *Theosophy: An Introduction to the Supersensible Knowledge of the World and the Destination of Man.* Trans. M. Cotterell and A. P. Sheperd. London: Rudolf Steiner Press, 1973. Orig. *Theosophie: Einführung in übersinnliche Welterkenntnis und Menschenbestimmung.* 1904.

Steiner, Rudolf, and Ita Wegman. *Fundamentals of Therapy: An Extension of the Art of Healing through Spiritual Knowledge.* Trans. George Adams. New York, 1967. Orig. 1928.

11

Theosophy and
The Theosophical Society

EMILY B. SELLON AND RENÉE WEBER

T HEOSOPHY HAS BEEN described as a knowledge of nature more
profound than that obtained from empirical science and embodied in an esoteric tradition of which the various historical
religions are only the exoteric expression. The word itself (from
theos, "God," and *sophia*, "wisdom") means "wisdom concerning God or
things divine" and carries the implication that such wisdom is accessible to
the human soul through direct intuition of a supersensible reality.

In the West, theosophy may be said to have originated in Pythagorean
Greece and to have been elaborated by such figures as Plato, Ammonius
Saccus, and Plotinus, as well as through the Neoplatonic movement of
Alexandria. It has affinities with kabbalistic and gnostic traditions and is a
central doctrine in Islamic Sufism, as taught by such masters as Ghazzāli
and Ibn 'Arabi. In Europe, it reappeared from time to time under different
guises: in hermetic and alchemical doctrines and in fraternal organizations
like the Rosicrucians and the Freemasons. In the modern period, the term
theosophy is most legitimately associated with such figures as Meister
Eckhart, Giordano Bruno, Emanuel Swedenborg, and Jacob Boehme.

This esoteric tradition was, of course, not known under the name of
theosophy in the East; but its major features are central to the classic
literature of Hinduism, and its perspective is evident both in the worldview
of Mahayana Buddhism and in the process philosophy of Taoism and the
I Ching.

This claim to universality is supported by the fact that the theosophical
worldview, no matter how expressed, rests on a metaphysical foundation
that is reached through insight into the essences of things as they are, rather
than through intellectual reasoning. Furthermore, the pursuit of this
insight holds out the possibility of the perfecting of the human soul and
embraces a tradition of enlightened masters whose chosen task is to lead

humanity toward a selfsame realization. Metaphysical truths, while themselves nonrational, are to be developed in a rational way, as "teachings," but their purpose is not to elaborate or proselytize a particular philosophical system or dogma. Rather, they are designed to encourage seekers to explore the nature and meaning of existence, to test the validity of their values in experience, and thereby to accomplish not only their own self-transformation but the spiritualization of humanity.

H. P. Blavatsky and
the Modern Theosophical Movement

After a considerable period of obscuration in the West, theosophy was revived at the end of the nineteenth century. Today, whatever their affiliation, virtually all theosophists agree that the modern theosophical movement stems primarily from the life and work of Helena Petrovna Blavatsky (1831–1891). H.P.B., as her followers call her, was—and continues to be—a mysterious, enigmatic, and controversial figure. Her life was highly picturesque, filled with extraordinary events and encounters, and her magnetic, tempestuous personality made her continuously interesting and challenging to her contemporaries.

Born in 1831 into an aristocratic Russian family, she married young, only to leave her husband within a very short time in order to embark on a series of journeys which took her into Egypt, India, Tibet, and the Americas—all at a time when few women traveled alone. She was in fact a notable example of the "liberated woman," pursuing her interests even though they defied the conventions and restrictions of her day. This attitude, together with her unorthodox philosophical views, brought her into continuous conflict with the mores of Victorian culture.

From earliest childhood she displayed remarkable psychic powers, including the paranormal perception of "presences." One such figure which appeared to her was to change her life: the Indian Master she called "M," to whose teaching she totally committed her life. But throughout the early years of her life she appeared to be searching for her mission and developing her psychic gifts.

It was not until her 1873 meeting in New York with Henry Steele Olcott (1832–1907), a well-known lawyer and journalist, that her long-sought mission began to take shape. The meeting came about during their mutual investigations of some of the spiritualist phenomena that were arousing widespread attention at that time. They both wrote many articles related to these phenomena in the New York daily press, thereby attracting the attention of others who were drawn to the esoteric tradition. So strong an interest was aroused that a small group began to form itself around H.P.B. This was the genesis of the Theosophical Society, which was founded in New York City on November 17, 1875, with Olcott as President and Blavatsky as Secretary; its members included William Quan Judge, George Henry Felt, and C. C. Massey. Although small in numbers, the movement spread rapidly, and within a few years branches were established in Great Britain, Greece, Germany, Russia, France, and India, attracting such notables as Thomas Edison, Alfred Russel Wallace, Sir William Crookes, and Camille Flammarion.

The stated objects of the fledgling society at first embraced a variety of esoteric and spiritual goals, notably those of tolerance and respect for Eastern religious traditions and the condemnation of the prevailing materialistic science and dogmatic Christian theology—which brought charges of an anti-Christian bias against the society. A colorful account of the early days of the movement in New York, with attendant "occult phenomena," can be found in Olcott's *Old Diary Leaves*.[1]

Theosophy in India

In an effort to broaden the scope of the Theosophical Society, Blavatsky and Olcott left for India in 1878. There they aroused immediate interest, not only among Indians but also among some influential Anglo-Indians, notably A. P. Sinnett, who was editor of a widely read journal, *The Pioneer*, and A. O. Hume, an important member of the Civil Service. It was to these two that the famous *Mahatma Letters to A. P. Sinnet* (1923) were written, the originals of which are preserved in the British Museum in London.

From the first, Blavatsky had vowed that the true founders of the theosophical movement were two mysterious Indian personages living in the remote Himalayas, whom she later identified as the Mahatmas (or Masters) K. H. (Kuthumi) and M. (Morya). Their teachings were conveyed to Sinnett and Hume through a series of letters said to have been transmitted phenomenally through the instrumentation of Blavatsky and other chelas (accepted pupils) of the two Mahatmas. Belief in the continuing presence of these Mahatmas has played a central role in the life of H.P.B. and in the modern theosophical movement.

Throughout her life, Blavatsky wrote prolifically, restating the ancient wisdom tradition in terms she and her teachers felt would be understandable in the light of contemporary knowledge. The public was fascinated with her unusual material: her first major work, *Isis Unveiled* (1877), sold out in nine days. During the remaining years of her life she wrote numerous articles for the journals she founded, *Lucifer* and *The Theosophist*, as well as two important works, *The Key to Theosophy* (1889) and a devotional classic, *The Voice of the Silence* (1889). In all, her miscellaneous writings, now issued in a chronological series entitled *Collected Writings,* comprise twelve volumes. *The Secret Doctrine* (1888), which is indubitably her masterwork, remains to this day the foundation of subsequent theosophical thought.

Everywhere in these works the author showed herself knowledgeable in a wide variety of subjects which, given her lack of formal education, she could not easily have mastered. Her profuse references to science, mythology, philosophy, and comparative religion, in fact, led to charges of plagiarism. Blavatsky herself repeatedly stated that the occult doctrines she propounded were not original to her and that she was but a passive transmitter of teachings received verbatim from her Tibetan teachers—who used whatever English words seemed most fitting, including those borrowed from other works, since to them the concepts, not the words, were important. She described her method of writing in a letter to her sister, Vera, as proceeding from what was "shown" her: images, visions, and even whole pages of manuscript appeared before her and she copied them without questioning their source. This method of writing may in part account for the extreme rapidity with which she was able to produce such lengthy handwritten manuscripts.

Accusations and Attacks:
The Coulomb Affair

Accusations of plagiarism were not the only attacks made upon H.P.B. In India, she and Olcott made many friends and adherents to theosophy within the Indian community. At a time when there were virtually no social contacts between Westerners and the native population, they fraternized freely with members of different castes. Moreover, the magazine they founded, *The Theosophist,* was a strong voice in upholding the values of Hindu culture, even though it also condemned such practices as child marriage and caste stratifications and urged the importance of Western education. While Blavatsky's respect for Indian religion won her the support of Indian scholars, it aroused the antagonism of the Christian missionaries, who were a powerful group in India at that time.

This antagonism came to a head in what has been called the Coulomb affair. The Theosophical Society had set up its headquarters in Adyar, near Madras in southern India, where Blavatsky and Olcott had taken up residence. Among the members of the staff of the society were a Mr. and Mrs. Coulomb, whom Blavatsky had trusted enough to put in charge of her

14. Illustration from Heinrich Khunrath, *Amphitheatrum Sapientiae Aeternae* (Hanau, 1609).

rooms while she was absent in Europe. However, a series of incidents aroused the Coulombs' animosity, and in 1884 they published an article in the *Christian College Monthly* denouncing the transmission of the Mahatma letters as a fraud. This created such an uproar of charges and countercharges that the Society for Psychical Research sent Richard Hodgson, a young Cambridge-trained lawyer, to Madras to investigate. The subsequent verdict, known as the Hodgson Report, went against Blavatsky, but in 1968 and again in 1986 the case was reexamined by the Society for Psychical Research and declared "not proven."[2]

Although the Indian members of the society remained loyal, this controversy had a devastating effect upon Blavatsky, and in March 1885 she left India, settled in London, and began work on *The Secret Doctrine*. Of this encyclopedic work, she herself said, "the teachings . . . contained in these volumes do not belong to the Hindu, the Zoroastrian, the Chaldean or the Egyptian religion, nor to Buddhism, Islam, Judaism, or Christianity exclusively. The secret doctrine is the essence of all these." Mme. Blavatsky died in London in 1891.

The Schism within the Society

Meanwhile, the Theosophical Society was flourishing in America under the leadership of one of its principal founders, Wm. Q. Judge (1851–1896), a member of the New York Bar. After the departure of Olcott and Blavatsky for India, Judge became general secretary and president of what became known as the American Section of the Theosophical Society. Mr. Judge was a fine organizer and administrator, as well as speaker and writer, and the society grew rapidly under his aegis. Concurrently, Olcott, as president of the society, traveled widely throughout India, gaining new members and branches and organizing the society's work. In 1880 he went to Ceylon (Sri Lanka), where, almost single-handedly, he revived the Buddhist religion (which had declined almost to the point of extinction under the influence of the Christian missionaries) and established Buddhist schools and colleges. This is a contribution for which he is still honored in Sri Lanka.

One of the most outstanding persons who joined the society in its early days was the Irish-born Annie Besant (1847–1933), who was well-known in England as a member of the socialist Fabian Society and an ardent voice in support of child labor reform. Mrs. Besant was adopted as a friend and confidante by Blavatsky and quickly became an influential leader within the movement. Upon Blavatsky's death, a deep controversy arose over whether it should be Judge or Besant who would assume H.P.B.'s role as the principal articulator of theosophical doctrine. This led to a schism within the society in 1894. Seventy-five of the American Branches seceded from the parent society and formed a new organization under the leadership of Judge. His death within a year, however, left the new American Society without a leader. Into this vacancy stepped a comparative newcomer, Katherine Tingley (1847–1929), an American woman who was to lead this branch of the theosophical movement for more than three decades. Her outstanding contribution was the founding of a theosophical community at Point Loma, California, where she instituted a number of experimental educational and agricultural programs.

A third group was formed in Los Angeles in 1909 under the leadership of Robert Crosbie (1849–1919), who had been a member of the Point Loma Society. Crosbie formed a group of people who were dissatisfied with the increasing emphasis in the Theosophical Society (Adyar) upon the writings of such contemporary writers as Besant and Leadbeater. He wished to concentrate on the original teachings of Blavatsky and Judge. This was the genesis of the United Lodge of Theosophists, a group which still minimizes formal organization and the role of so-called leaders.

To the contemporary sensibility, it is striking that women have been so prominent in the history of the theosophical movement, beginning with Blavatsky and followed by Katherine Tingley, whose innovative ideas persist in many ecological and educational concepts current today. Annie Besant is equally notable. Becoming president of the Theosophical Society (Adyar) after the death of Olcott, she quickly involved herself in social and educational causes, establishing many schools for Indian children, including girls, as well as institutions of higher learning such as the Central Hindu College, now the Benares Hindu University. A powerful speaker and writer, she founded the influential newspaper *New India* and was so eloquent in the cause of Indian self-government that she was interned by the British authorities. She was elected President of the Indian National Congress, where she was closely associated with Mahatma Gandhi, although she later split with him about the direction of the independence movement, since she favored Indian Home Rule rather than complete independence.

A close associate and co-author of Mrs. Besant was an English clergyman, C. W. Leadbeater (1847–1934), one of the most influential of the "second generation" of theosophical writers. Leadbeater's books all reflect his own perception of theosophy, stemming from what he described as his clairvoyant investigations. One of the most controversial consequences of this clairvoyance was his discovery of a poor young Indian boy, J. Krishnamurti (1895–1986), who he prophesied would become a spiritual world-teacher of exceptional power. Although Krishnamurti was nurtured by theosophists—

especially Annie Besant—throughout his formative years, he repudiated the affiliation in 1927.

The Theosophical Society Today

The Theosophical Society, whose international headquarters are at Adyar, Madras, India, now has a membership of around thirty-five thousand, with national sections in thirty-seven countries. The second largest group is the Theosophical Society International (now in Pasadena—formerly in Point Loma), which has a worldwide membership of about fifteen hundred with headquarters in Altadena, California. The United Lodge of Theosophists has about twelve hundred associates and almost two dozen lodges world-wide. All three organizations are active in the republication of the works of Blavatsky and other early writers. In addition, the Theosophical Publishing House, an enterprise of the Theosophical Society in America (Adyar) issues new works in paperback under the name Quest Books, and publishes Quest, a quarterly journal for the general public.

Despite individual differences in the interpretation of theosophical doctrines, all theosophists support a fundamental proposition: the oneness of all beings. This has been formulated as the First Object of The Theosophical Society (Adyar):

1. *To form a nucleus of the universal brotherhood of humanity, wthout distinction of race, creed, sex, caste, or color.*

This strong proclamation of inherent human worth regardless of differences dates back to the early 1900s, a time when these values were widely rejected and even actively opposed by the dominant culture.

To this mandate two additional Objects have been added which, although important goals, do not command the same undeviating allegiance from all members:

2. *To encourage the study of comparative religion, philosophy and science.*
3. *To investigate unexplained laws of nature and the powers latent in man.*

In addition to these Objects, the Theosophical Society (Adyar) has adopted a motto which sums up its essential outlook: "There is no religion higher than truth."

Fundamental Principles of Theosophy

The metaphysics upon which the theosophical worldview rests is embodied in the classical literature mentioned above, but was enunciated most comprehensively in Blavatsky's definitive work, *The Secret Doctrine*.

In the Proem to that work, the theosophical metaphysics is said to be based on three fundamental propositions:

1. *An omnipresent, eternal, boundless and immutable Principle on which all speculation is impossible, since it transcends human conception.* It is "unthinkable and unspeakable" and can only be pointed to; therefore it is usually referred to as the Absolute or as Parabrahman, the "Secondless Reality."

This Reality, although itself absolute negation (not this, not that), is nevertheless the infinite and eternal source of all that was, is, or ever shall be. It is the field of absolute consciousness, the essence beyond all conditioned existence, but of which conscious existence is the conditioned symbol. From the point of view of existent being, this absoluteness is perceived in the contrast of subject and object, inwardness and outwardness, spirit and matter. The universe seems to be pervaded by these pairs of opposites, but theosophy holds that they are not independent realities but rather polar aspects of the one unity in which they are synthesized. The tension that arises in the indivisible fabric of the One through the pull of this inward/outward complementarity creates a "bridge" between them—the magnetic attraction and interaction between the two poles of being, without which both would disappear. The indissoluble relationship between spirit or consciousness and matter constitutes both the ground and the vindication of theosophical non-dualism.

2. *The eternity of the universe in toto as a boundless plane, periodically the playground of numberless universes incessantly manifesting and disappearing in a regular tidal ebb and flow.* The cyclicism that is apparent in the universal sequence of birth, maturation, senescence, and death, as well as in the regular alternations of day and night, activity and rest, is held to be a basic law of nature. Change may superficially appear to be random and chaotic, but theosophists see it as an inescapable aspect of the universal order.

3. *The fundamental identity of all souls with the universal Oversoul, the latter being itself an aspect of the unknown Root. Furthermore, there is an obligatory pilgrimage for every soul through the grand cycle of incarnation, in accordance with the karmic law of action and response.* Since there is no possibility of independent conscious existence without individuality, the soul must acquire selfhood, first by natural impulse and then by self-induced and self-devised efforts, ascending through all the degrees of intelligence, from mineral and plant up to the holiest archangel. The doctrine holds that there are no special privileges or gifts in humans, save those won through personal effort and merit throughout a long series of experiences in incarnate life.

Theosophical Epistemology

Historically, esotericism has been taught in mystery schools which carefully chose their candidates not only for their spiritual qualifications but also for their ability to keep silent and thereby protect the teachings from popular debasement. The teachings themselves were often enigmatic. Works like *The Secret Doctrine* are so full of ambiguities, digressions, and overlapping symbologies that they bewilder and frustrate the casual reader. The use of paradox and symbolic language as a valid method for conveying truth is, however, central to the theosophical epistemology, which regards the awakening of intuition (*buddhi*) as essential to spiritual growth. For example, it is taught that the divine Reality lies beyond the reach of thought, but also that it can be known since it is present in each of us. Such knowing is nonrational but is to be reached by rational means; therefore the mind must be doubted, but also purified and made transparent to reality. Consequently, seekers receive only oblique guidance and must learn for themselves how to exercise discrimination and judgment in the midst of a profusion of ideas and images that are open to many different interpretations.

Another aim of this method is to encourage the student to avoid blind belief, to query all statements, and to be prepared to abandon opinion in favor of a more liberating idea. As noted, theosophy claims no dogma; it takes seriously Buddhism's admonition to accept no statement that anyone has made (even if the Buddha himself has said it) unless it accords with one's own reason. In short, the pursuit of truth is held to be more valuable than its possession, for in the phenomenal world, what we accept as truth is always problematic. Thus our ideas need constant reevaluation, not only in light of the growth of knowledge but also in terms of our own growth in understanding; for in the final analysis the self within us, being divine, must be our highest guru.

Cosmic Mind

The main task of any metaphysics is to relate the noumenal Reality to its consequences in the phenomenal world. Theosophy regards change and process as the indispensable instruments whereby the Real becomes actualized in the world and thus can be realized. This process is without finality, but it is teleological in character, its *telos* being embedded in the drive of conscious life to fulfill itself and thus realize its divine essence.

Since consciousness or spirit is the first expression of the Real, its objectification in the world requires a "garment" or vesture: in other words,

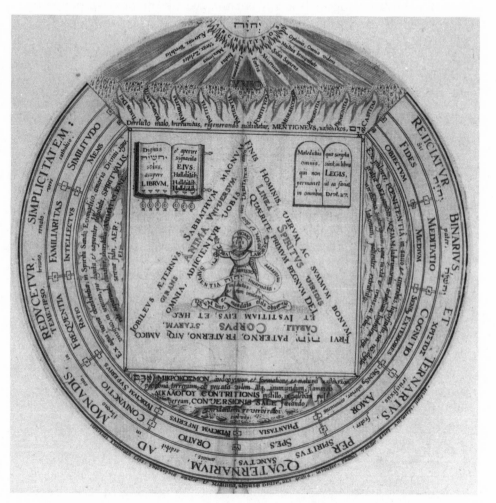

15. Illustration from Heinrich Khunrath, *Amphitheatrum Sapientiae Aeternae* (Hanau, 1609).

appropriate material structures. The agency of this accomplishment is the divine Mind, Nous, or Mahat, working from within the very heart of matter to create forms consonant with its essential nature, which is defined in Platonic terms as the Good, the True, and the Beautiful. Thus the universe is seen as both intelligent (since it is animated by the creative power or *Logos* of the divine Intelligence) and intelligible (since its intrinsic order and coherence open it to human understanding). The theosophist has no difficulty in reconciling the timeless, static character of the archetypal world with the dynamism of evolutionary change, since the former represents aspects of the ideal Reality, and the latter furnishes the means for actualizing them in the world.

The fundamental unity and coherence of the universe are displayed most impressively in the order that pervades all of nature, not only in the uniformity of physical laws but also in the musical and mathematical proportions of all natural forms, from crystals and plants to spiral galaxies. This Pythagorean/Platonic conception of an underlying harmonic order is revealed in the persistent geometry of dynamic form, visual testimony to the passage from indivisible unity to unity-in-multiplicity.

Evolutionary Theory

The theosophical doctrine of emanation, whereby the appearance of diversified physical forms is preceded by an involution of consciousness into matter, rejects the mechanical or physicalist view of development in favor of a process of unfoldment "from within without." This begins at the very moment the universe is born—or is aroused once more into activity, as the theosophist would say, following a dormant period or *pralaya*. At this moment, the undivided unity is broken and time begins. Thus seen, involution is the movement from unity to diversity; evolution is the realization of unity in the midst of diversity.

This vision of the world process, epitomized in the hermetic doctrine "as above, so below," sees it as initiated by spiritual intelligences, or *logoi*, which have appeared in the great religious traditions as angels, rishis, devas, elohim, seraphim, and the like. These embodiments or personifications of the creative power of the divine Intelligence become the agents of its action, which never ceases so long as the universe persists.

Looked at from a perspective of this kind, the continuity of nature itself is witness to the role of consciousness or mind in self-organization at every level. For theosophists, evolution of biological forms is primarily a growth of consciousness corresponding to a particular level of existence: one continuous learning process, from mineral to plant to animal to human (and beyond to the suprahuman). Evolution does not cease with achievement of the human condition, but becomes internalized as the search for union with the true, spiritual Self. The goal of evolution, which is self-development, self-realization, and self-transcendence, is therefore inherent in its processes.

The Hierarchy of Being

Theosophy sees the physical world as a domain which, far from being the only sphere of life, is interpenetrated by a hierarchy of other fields, or levels of organization, all of which are essential to life. These have been systematized in various ways, but always with an internal relationship akin to the Pythagorean harmonic system. The manner in which the one becomes three (while remaining itself one) unfolds by natural progression into seven (a, b, c, ab, ac, bc, abc). This process of organic development proliferates to produce a hierarchical system of interpenetrating domains which have been conceptualized in ways suggestive of modern fields, in that each represents a continuous condition throughout space. These range in degree of subtlety from the most spiritual to the most material, but they are all simultaneously present in the world. Theosophists maintain that spirit is never entirely "pure," that is, completely dissociated from matter, in the phenomenal worlds. Similarly, matter is never without its indwelling consciousness or spirit, even in its most elementary condition.

Concurring in the Advaita Vedanta view that *atman*, or the supreme self in the individual, is identical with Brahman, the universal self, theosophy holds that universal consciousness, which is the essence of all life, constitutes the point of individual consciousness or ultimate being in every soul. Since humanity is inseparable from the cosmic process, the sevenfold hierarchy of universal domains—or fields—of consciousness and matter/energy have in human beings a complementary hierarchy of principles. These, which are referred to as vehicles or bodies, may be thought of as localizations in a universal field.

This sevenfold nature is described as follows: At the innermost level, the *atma* (that is, *atman* reflected in the individual soul) is the principle of action or true being, characterized by intentionality or the will-to-be; next *buddhi*, or insight, is characterized by intuition or direct knowledge, since it is the first vesture of the self. Together, they form the *monad* or spiritual soul, which overshadows all living beings. The third principle, *manas*, or mind, is twofold both in character and function: one aspect is unitive and synthesizing, being reflective of the two higher principles; the second is discursive, analytical, and information-gathering, being turned outward to the external world, As such, it is closely linked with the next level, that of feeling and desire, and with the vital or life-function aspect of the physical body, sometimes called *pranic* or etheric.

The physical is held to be the necessary instrument of all these higher functions, for the *atma,* or true self, can only express itself in the world by means of a physical vesture (*upadhi*) in which its powers of intentionality, inspiration, reason, and compassion can be focused, in order to create a life reflective of these values. Accordingly, theosophy does not see itself as other-worldly, concerned only with supramundane realities, but as a practical doctrine aimed at the integration and self-transformation of human beings.

The Role of Humanity

In *The Secret Doctrine,* the statement is made that "everything in nature tends to become man." This apparent anthropomorphism signals a perception that, in the human person, the mind of nature has reached a critical point in evolution—what might be called a transcendence, since it marks a wholly new development in self-conscious life. The mind that can initiate self-reflexive action gives control, permits novelty and invention, discriminates and exercises choice, and thereby offers the possibility of individual freedom. Theosophists concur with the Eastern view, however, that the mind also separates us from reality, misleads us by its conditioning, and is easily captured by desire as well as deluded by egotism. Since the twofold nature of the mind makes it both liberating and limiting, the human person must learn to integrate its functions in service to the spiritual Self—a task that is far from complete.

From the theosophical point of view, humans have inhabited earth for a very long time. One of the more controversial aspects of *The Secret Doctrine* is its insistence that the history of humankind spans epochs of time whose duration is equivalent to the *yugas* of the Hindu system. Modern paleontology, unlike nineteenth-century science, recognizes that the human race developed from direct ancestors as far back as three million years, a period that begins to approach Blavatsky's claim. But no evidence has ever been uncovered to substantiate her statement that humans evolved cultures in the past that periodically rose, fell, and then disappeared, leaving no record apart from worldwide legendary accounts of floods and inundations, as in the myth of Atlantis. All of these Blavatsky holds to have been based on fact. Her detailed account of so-called earlier races (which represent developmental stages rather than anthropological types), through which all human souls have evolved via repeated incarnation, remains an interesting but unproven hypothesis.

Theosophical evolutionary theory holds that human beings have not yet fully realized their humanity and will continue to evolve into a future of almost limitless spiritual unfoldment. The role models for such growth are the great religious figures, such as the Buddha, the Christ, Moses, and Lao Tzu, as well as the hierarchy of saints and sages throughout history, all of whom foreshadowed in their lives what humanity as a whole will one day attain. These figures are not regarded as miraculous or isolated from humanity but rather as spiritual guides and exemplars, whose compassion for "the great orphan, humanity" causes them to emerge periodically as the teachers of human beings, as in the Bodhisattva tradition of Mahayana Buddhism. It is to members of this spiritual brotherhood, the Mahatmas or Masters, that theosophists feel they owe their doctrines.

Karma and Reincarnation

Closely associated with the idea of progressive self-unfoldment and enlightenment are the concepts of karma and reincarnation, which may be regarded as the mechanism whereby the process of inner development is achieved. Karma, the law of universal causation, is neither fatalism nor a rigid determinism; it teaches that we are what we have made of ourselves and that we are responsible for this condition. Thus autonomy and opportunity are the basic meaning of karma. This implies a sense of cosmic balance: of action and reaction, the equilibration of forces, and the maintenance of dynamic harmony. Karma is thus the principle of universal justice.

Reincarnation is a concept ancillary to karma, as in much of Hinduism and Buddhism. Since stored-up seeds of past karmic impulses and patterns cannot all be worked out in a single lifetime, multiple and repeated incarnations are necessary in order that these seeds can bear fruit. Life is like a school that teaches us the spiritual and other lessons we need to learn; when these lessons have been absorbed, as in the enlightened individual, incarnation is held to be voluntary rather than enforced, a position akin to that of Mahayana and Tibetan Buddhism.

Theosophy and Religion

Perhaps the major contribution of the theosophical movement in modern times has been the breaking down of Western misconceptions and prejudices about Eastern religious traditions. In harmony with the Second Object of the society, theosophists in Europe and America consistently presented a more authentic perception of these traditions, which had heretofore been largely dismissed as inferior to Western religious thought. With the exception of such isolated figures as Emerson, Thoreau, and the New England transcendentalists, nineteenth-century intellectuals paid little attention to Hindu and Buddhist spirituality. The grandeur of these traditions was so trivialized that they were not taken seriously as ontologies to be placed alongside Western claims about reality. It was not until the late nineteenth century, after the advent of the theosophical movement, that interest in Eastern thought was stimulated, and its flow into the West from many directions became accelerated. This cumulative process has continued and intensified in this century, so that today there is widespread interest and respect for all the-major religious traditions of the East. Wherever the final credit for this achievement may be due, it is a fulfillment of the Second Object for which the Theosophical Society stands.

Theosophy and Science

The impulse toward ecumenism is intrinsic but not unique to the theosophical movement. What is more unusual in spiritually oriented worldviews is a radical perception of the fundamental Reality as the basis of the natural world. At the time *The Secret Doctrine* was written, science was uniformly deterministic and mechanistic, in ways which the twentieth century has thoroughly discredited. Anticipating the conclusions of Einsteinian relativity and field theory, as well as quantum mechanics, Blavatsky proposed a universe in which billiard-ball atoms and push-pull forces were replaced by space, time, motion, and energy, yielding a picture of a dynamic universe far in advance of her time.

Perhaps her most revolutionary concepts were concerned with the unity and universality of consciousness and the perception of mind and matter as parallel streams of development arising from a common ground. Life and mind, which were dismissed contemptuously as epiphenomena in Blavatsky's day, are now perceived by a few scientists like David Bohm and George Wald as inherent in nature. A contemporary statement that "life appears no longer as a phenomenon unfolding in the universe—the universe becomes increasingly alive,"[3] is close to Blavatsky's conception of life as incipient in the universe, ready to arise spontaneously given sufficient time and suitable conditions.

Theosophy and Art

To a student of early twentieth-century art, it is evident that theosophical ideas exerted an important influence on the development of abstract expressionism, particularly in the work of Kandinsky, Mondrian, and Klee.

Kandinsky himself wrote of his work as embodying key theosophical principles, especially the non-dualist view that mind and matter are not radically different, but rather "relative modifications of one or the other."[4] In his application of this view, Kandinsky owed much to the work of C. W. Leadbeater, whose clairvoyant investigations into the dynamic energy patterns created by thought and emotion were published in 1901.[5] Mondrian joined the Dutch branch of the Theosophical Society in 1909, and in this period drew on Blavatsky and the work of Rudolf Steiner for his aesthetic. Major works of this period (such as "Evolution") contain elements that are quite specifically theosophical.

Theosophy also had a vital influence in the Irish literary renaissance of the late nineteenth and the early twentieth centuries, particularly as seen in the works of George Russell (A.E.), William Butler Yeats, Charles Johnston, and, more indirectly, James Joyce.

Ethical Consequences

Like all cosmogonic systems, theosophy may appear speculative and abstracted from the world of experience. Yet because that world is derived from the divine Reality, it holds that the spiritual is ever-present and accessible in the immediacy of everyday life. Since it stresses that the task for humanity is to become aware of its innate spirituality, to give it sovereignty in life, and to use it as the basis for action, it is not enough to grasp the essentials of the theosophical worldview intellectually. Principles must be practiced in daily life, used as the grounds for choice, and pursued for their ethical consequences in all human relationships.

Brotherhood is held to be a fact in nature, not a matter derived from human speculation or value judgment. It therefore becomes a criterion against which all human morality is measured. The interpretation of the meaning of brotherhood and its applications in personal life, however, are held to be a matter of individual responsibility. Personal choice, therefore, is to be based on dedication to the unity of all life as a principle of action and is to be achieved through steady effort to discover the roots of our own motivation. The idea that human growth is ongoing, and that human spiritual development lies in one's own hands, leads to a deepening sense of responsibility for the state of the world which is our human creation.

A succinct statement of the ethical consequences embodied in the theosophical worldview has been formulated as follows (The Theosophical Society in America):

The Theosophical Worldview

The Theosophical Society, while reserving for each member full freedom to interpret those teachings known as theosophy, is dedicated to preserving and realizing the ageless wisdom, which embodies both a worldview and a vision of human self-transformation.

This tradition is founded upon certain fundamental propositions:

1. The universe and all that exists within it are one interrelated and inter-dependent whole.

2. Every existent being—from atom to galaxy—is rooted in the same universal, life-creating Reality. This Reality is all-pervasive, but it can never be summed up in its parts, since it transcends all expressions. It reveals itself in the purposeful, ordered and meaningful processes of nature as well as in the deepest recesses of the mind and spirit.

3. Recognition of the unique value of every living being expresses itself in reverence for life, compassion for all, sympathy with the need of all indi-viduals to find truth for themselves, and respect for all religious traditions. The ways in which these ideals become realities in individual life are both the privileged choice and the responsible act of every human being.

Central to the concerns of theosophy is the desire to promote understand-ing and brotherhood among people of all races, nationalities, philosophies, and religions. Therefore, all people, whatever their race, creed, sex, caste, or color, are invited to participate equally in the life and work of the Society. The Theosophical society imposes no dogmas, but points toward the source of unity beyond all differences. Devotion to truth, love for all living beings, and commitment to a life of active altruism are the marks of the true theosophist.

Notes

1. H. S. Olcott, *Old Diary Leaves*, 6 vols. (Adyar: Theosophical Publishing House, 1974); see especially vols. 1 and 2.

2. The Hodgson verdict was issued as the *Report of the Committee appointed to investigate Phenomena connected with the Theosophical Society*, Society for Psychical Research, *Proceedings*, Vol. III, Part IX, December 1885. However, in 1968 the issue was revived, and in 1986 Hodgson's research was found to have been flawed, and the case against Blavatsky declared "not proven." See Vernon Harrison, "J'Accuse: an Examina-tion of the Hodgson Report of 1885," *Journal of the Society for Psychical Research* 53 no. 803 (April 1986).

3. Erich Jantsch, *The Self-Organizing Universe* (New York: Pergamon, 1980) 9.

4. Wassily Kandinsky, *Concerning the Spiritual in Art* (New York: Dover, 1977).

5. Annie Besant and C. W. Leadbeater, *Thought-Forms* (Adyar: Theosophical Publishing House, 1925).

Bibliography

Barker, A. Trevor, ed. *The Mahatma Letters to A. P. Sinnett.* London: T. Fisher Unwin, 1923. 3rd revised edition edited by Christmas Humphreys and Elsie Benjamin. Adyar: Theosophical Publishing House, 1962.

Besant, Annie. *The Ancient Wisdom: An Outline of Theosophical Teachings.* 1924. Adyar: Theosophical Publishing House, 1972.

Blavatsky, Helena P. *Isis Unveiled: A Master-Key to the Mysteries of Ancient and Modern Science and Theology.* 2 vols. New York: J. W. Bouton, 1877. Pasadena, CA: Theosophical Press, 1972.

————. *The Key to Theosophy.* London: Theosophical Publishing Society, 1889. Reprint, London: Theosophical Publishing House, 1968.

————. *The Secret Doctrine: The Synthesis of Science, Religion, and Philosophy.* 2 vols. London: Theosophical Publishing Co., 1888. 2 vol. edition with historical introduction, edited by Boris de Zirkoff. Adyar: Theosophical Publishing House, 1978.

————. *The Voice of the Silence, Being Chosen Fragments from the "Book of the Golden Precepts."* London: Theosophical Publishing Society, 1888. Reprint, Wheaton, IL: Theosophical Publishing House, 1992.

Campbell, Bruce F. *Ancient Wisdom Revived, a History of the Theosophical Movement.* Berkeley, CA: University of California Press, 1980.

Cranston, Sylvia. *H.P.B., The Extraordinary Life and Influence of Helena Blavatsky, Founder of the Modern Theosophical Movement.* New York: Tarcher/Putnam, 1993.

Ellwood, Robert S. *Theosophy, a Modern Expression of the Wisdom of the Ages.* Wheaton, IL: Quest Books, 1986.

Gomes, Michael. *The Dawning of the Theosophical Movement.* Wheaton, IL: Theosophical Publishing House, 1987.

Jinarajadasa, C., ed. *The Golden Book of the Theosophical Society.* Adyar, Madras, India: Theosophical Publishing House, 1925.

Judge, William Quan. *The Ocean of Theosophy.* 1893. Pasadena, CA: Theosophical University Press, 1964.

Nicholson, Shirley. *Ancient Wisdom, Modern Insight.* Wheaton, IL: Quest Books, 1985.

Santucci, James A. *Theosophy and the Theosophical Society.* Department of Religious Studies Seminar Paper Series 39. Fullerton, CA: California State University, 1984.

Sinnett, A. P. *Incidents in the Life of Madame Blavatsky, Compiled from Information Supplied by her Relatives and Friends.* London: George Redway, 1886. Reprint, London: Theosophical Publishing Society, 1913 (abridged).

Theosophical History: A Quarterly Journal of Research, founded by Leslie Price in 1985; chief editor James A. Santucci, who is also the editor of the Theosophical History Center Publications, which has published eleven books to date, including Joscelyn Godwin's important *The Beginnings of Theosophy in France* (Fullerton, CA: California State University, 1989).

Theosophical Movement. Part I, 1875–1925. New York: E. P. Dutton, 1951. Part II, 1875–1950. Los Angeles: Cunningham, 1951.

12

René Guénon and the Traditionalist School

JEAN BORELLA

René Guénon and the Doctrine of the Traditional Metaphysics

His Life

Childhood and Adolescence (1886–1905)

RENÉ-JEAN JOSEPH GUÉNON was born in 1886 in Blois, Anjou, in the pleasant valley of the Loire. The young René was an only child of fragile health. He was baptized very early and lived a sheltered childhood. His maternal aunt, Mme Duru, a childless school teacher in Blois, gave her affection to her nephew, teaching him to read and write.

It was not until October 1898 that Guénon entered Notre Dame des Aydes, a religious school in Blois. He did well there but left in 1901 after a disagreement with one of his teachers, and in January 1902 he entered the Augustin Thierry school as a student of rhetoric. Guénon obtained his baccalaureate in philosophy in 1903, then in mathematics in 1904, and he showed himself to be gifted in both disciplines.

Arriving in Paris in October 1904, Guénon enrolled in a special mathematics class in the Rollin school to prepare for a license and perhaps for the Ecole Polytechnique, but he soon found the promiscuity of the boarding school to be intolerable and he was, in the end, unable to keep up with the work imposed upon him. A second year only served to confirm his disposition, but, more important, Guénon heard another call and his life suddenly took a new turn. Abandoning his pursuit of a scientific career, he left the noisy Latin Quarter for the calm of the Ile Saint-Louis and undertook, at the end of 1906, a search for the "lost word," which would lead him to several crucial encounters.

Doctrinal Education (1906–1912)

The "mysteries" of Guénon's life over which many biographers have puzzled seem to have arisen between 1906 and 1912 in relation to two developments: (1) Guénon became a member of several allegedly (or legitimately) initiatory movements in an effort to verify their authenticity, and (2) he encountered authentic Eastern masters who transmitted the knowledge of their respective traditions to him. We will briefly investigate these two points.

In 1906, when Guénon was twenty, he attended courses at the Ecole Hermétique, which formed the outer "antenna" of the occultist movement then directed by Papus (Dr. Gérard Encausse). Guénon was admitted into all the organizations controlled by Papus, including the Ordre Martiniste (which refers to Martinez de Pasqually). He eventually rejected certain of Papus' beliefs (spiritism, reincarnation), and in 1908 Guénon, encouraged by Martinist friends, assumed control of the short-lived Ordre du Temple Renové (O.T.R.), which was dissolved by Guénon at the end of 1911. The minutes of the O.T.R. meetings, revealed by Jean-Pierre Laurant,[1] contain as untitled drafts, virtually all of the topics of Guénon's future work. We have what is no doubt one of the originals of this enigmatic work. But these minutes are themselves merely traces of subjects proposed by Guénon.

Guénon's affiliation with the O.T.R. precipitated an agitated break with occultism in 1909. This break also prompted Guénon to leave certain suspect masonic-occultist organizations and to solicit admission to the Theban lodge, which was under the firm authority of the Grand Lodge of France (Ancient and Accepted Scottish Rite). Finally, still in 1909, Guénon entered the Eglise Gnostique (founded by J. Doinel in 1889), which claimed to be the authentic reestablishment of historical Catharism. He became holy bishop and took the name Palingenius. On the initiative of Synesius, patriarch of this church, he began a review, *La Gnose*, which he directed until he ended the magazine in 1912. This review served as a vehicle for Guénon's earliest work.

Taking into account Guénon's later work, which reveals him as an implacable adversary of all pseudo-initiation (occultism, theosophism, neognosticism, and so on), the only possible reason for these multiple affiliations is that Guénon was in fact seeking to verify claims of authenticity while struggling against the parodies of genuine esotericism.[2] This hypothesis assumes that Guénon possessed the doctrinal criteria for discriminating and, moreover, the awareness of a personal mission. In regard to doctrine a great deal is revealed in the articles published by Guénon in *La Gnose* from November 1909 to February 1912. These works contain the essentials of two later works—*Le Symbolisme de la Croix* and *L'Homme et son Devenir selon le*

Vedânta. The linguistic and metaphysical knowledge that these investigations required could not have been acquired in less than one or two years;[3] thus their acquisition may be assumed to have taken place before 1909. This knowledge concerned essentially Hinduism, Taoism, and Islam;[4] and its acquisition, according to the firm evidence of Guénon himself, was accomplished by direct contact with authentic representatives of these traditions rather than through written work.

Since, according to Guénon, Hinduism serves as the standard and central tradition for present humanity, it is reasonable to assume that Guénon was educated by Hindus. Careful study of Guénon's work shows that these teachers represented the "orthodox" and traditional Vedānta of Shankara, which is found in the "scholastic" synthesis of later commentators—most notably Vijnāna Bhikshu (sixteenth century), who integrates aspects of traditional cosmology (*sāmkhya*) into the metaphysics. It is a Vedānta not of the erudite historian, but the very one found in Vedantine schools. This is a point of fundamental importance.

As for the Taoist influence, through his affiliation with the Ecole Hermétique and the Eglise Gnostique, Guénon became acquainted with two Frenchmen, Léon Champrenaud (1870–1925) and Albert de Pouvourville (1862–1939). The latter of these two played an especially important role in the formation of Guenon's thought. Albert de Pouvourville had been a colonial officer in Tonkin and had received, in China, a Taoist initiation, with the name Matgioi, which means "day's eye." In 1907 he published *La Voie rationnelle*, a translation of the *Tao Tē Ching*. Guénon had further contact with the native tradition through a Chinese Taoist (the son of Matgioi's master, who had come to France to assist Matgioi in the translation of the *Tao Tē Ching*),[5] from whom, in the words of Paul Chacornac, "Guénon received more than had Albert de Pouvourville."[6]

It is likely that in each of these encounters the doctrinal knowledge received by Guénon was accompanied by the transmission of an initiatory rite[7]—a likelihood that applies equally to his encounter with the East under the sign of Islam. In 1912 he became connected with the *tarīqah* of Sheikh Elish Abder-Rahman el-Kebir, an illustrious sage of Cairo, to whom he dedicated *Le Symbolisme de la Croix*. The "blessing" was given to Guénon on behalf of his master by Abdul Hādi (a Swedish painter and contributor to *La Gnose* with the given name Ivan Aguéli). The reason for the pursuit of Islam was Guénon's search for an authentically initiatory tradition. In 1912, however, Guénon made a definite break with pseudo-esotericism, its organizations, and its reviews. Henceforth, the standard and the function of his work are established according to their own unique nature.

The Metaphysician of the Ile Saint-Louis (1912–1920)

That 1912 marked a turning point in Guénon's life is indicated not only by his association with Islam and the resulting break with former affiliations but also by his marriage to Berthe Loury, an assistant to Mme Duru, Guénon's childhood tutor. The Guénons soon welcomed Mme Duru herself and a four-year-old niece, Françoise, into their household. The metaphysician lived in the midst of this triple feminine affection for ten years. Because he needed to earn his living, and having been exempted from military service because of his health, Guénon received a bachelor's degree of arts (in order to teach philosophy) from the Sorbonne in 1915, then his maîtrise with a thesis on the meaning of Leibniz's infinitesimal calculus. This work would furnish the material for *Les Principes du Calcul infinitésimal* (1945). He took a state teaching exam in 1919 but failed the oral examination. Finally, in 1921 he wished to present his first book, *Introduction générale à l'étude des doctrines hindoues* as a state dissertation but was stymied by the orientalist Sylvain Lévi. Nevertheless, his degrees allowed him to teach in various institutions from 1915 to 1929 with few interruptions.

During this period Guénon wrote a great deal: works commanded by contemporary circumstance (*Le Théosophisme, La Crise du Monde moderne, Autorité spirituelle et pouvoir temporel,* etc.), but also "timeless" accounts of traditional metaphysics (*L'homme et son Devenir selon le Vedânta, Le Roi du monde, L'esotérisme de Dante*). He contributed to numerous reviews,[8] frequented diverse circles, was appreciated by Léon Daudet and by certain monarchist intellectuals, and drew near to Jacques Maritain and the neo-Thomists; finally, however, Guénon came up against utter hostility.

From 1925 to 1927 he submitted several articles to *Le Voile d'Isis,* a review directed by P. Chacornac. In 1928 Guénon became its main contributor and was able to exercise complete doctrinal authority over it. Every month until his death he published an article on metaphysics, a study on a particular point (generally on symbolism), a review of periodicals, and a review of books—a truly colossal undertaking if his abundant correspondence (he always answered letters) is taken into account. This review also became the instrument of his struggle against all forms of pseudo-esotericism and diabolical counter-initiation. Much of his time was taken up with this task, in which he showed himself to be a formidable polemist. In 1936, *Le Voile d'Isis* took the name *Etudes Traditionnelles,* which it has kept to the present day.

Yet once again Guénon's life took a dramatic turn: he lost his wife in January 1928 and his aunt in October. In 1929 his niece left him and returned to her family. He was left alone without attachments and deeply disconcerted. His departure for the East was near.

In the Shadow of the Pyramids (1930–1951)

In September 1929, Guénon met Marie Dina, the widow of an Egyptian engineer and daughter of Shillito, the Canadian railway baron. She admired Guénon's work and offered to create a publishing house (Véga) that would publish all his books and all the translations of Sufi texts that he could produce. It was in order to find these texts that they left together on March 5, 1930, for Cairo. The trip was supposed to last three months, but this proved not enough time for the task. Guénon stayed on in Cairo, while Mme Dina returned to France and, in the end, partly abandoned the project. Alone and without funds—he could hardly afford stamps for his correspondence—Guénon lived two lean years, during which he became more and more assimilated into the Arab culture. He decided definitely against returning to France (in 1949 he became an Egyptian citizen). It was during these two years that two of his most important works were published by Véga: *Le Symbolism de la Croix* (1931) and *Les Etats multiples de l'être* (1932), the manuscripts of which had been written before his departure.

Henceforth, Guénon's life was entirely Muslim. He spoke Arabic without an accent, frequented El-Azhar University, and wrote articles for the Egyptian review *El-Maarifah*. In 1934 he married Fatima, the eldest daughter of an Egyptian friend, Sheikh Muhammad Ibrahim. She would give him two daughters and two sons, the last son born after Guénon's death.

Now in the calm of his abode in Cairo, Guénon could make use of the full breadth of his skills in his writing. His doctrinal "presence" became more widespread. The translation of his books, which began in Italian in 1927, then English in 1928, extended to German, Spanish, Portuguese, and even Tibetan. The number of his correspondents also continued to grow: he wrote fifty letters a week! Writers and intellectuals read and discussed him, and, although not widely known, he already had considerable influence in Europe.

Such a life-style could not help but harm his health. On Sunday, January 6, 1951, Guénon, nearing death, sat up in bed and called out repeatedly, "*al-nafs khalās,*" "my soul is departing." Then, around 11:00 P.M., having twice repeated "*Allāh,*" he died.

* * *

The Work and the Doctrine

The Place of the Work

A work has style as well as content. Guénon's style seems to have allowed him to escape ordinary classifications, but there were many criticisms of his work. Although his work was much discussed and widely recognized, it was also scorned by the university critics who, in France, lay down the law. Guénon was criticized as "not a serious author"; his works were described as "second-hand"; his documentation, "third-rate"; his references, often missing or "unverifiable." His work was described as nothing more than a new form of occultism or illuminism, of which there exist many examples in European history, and in which he illustrates the most classic themes: dogmatic claims of a mysterious science unknown to the masses, belief in an original tradition or revelation beyond all religions, an overuse of hermeneutics that endows the least symbol with metaphysical meaning, a view of history secretly manipulated by occult groups—in short, everything to satisfy the public taste for the supernatural. As for Guénon's traits—the radical rejection of the modern world, the abstract stiffness of his language, and so on—in these the modern critic will see the well-known symptoms of paranoia.

Now it is necessary to admit that certain of these criticisms are not without foundation, and our appreciation of Guénon's ideas should not prohibit us from being fair to the objections of certain of his adversaries. Thus one can see that sudden attacks by Guénon against the orientalists, or his arguments for such and such, in *Le Voile d'Isis,* then in the *Etudes Traditionelles,* have a somewhat obsessional aspect: Guénon did seem very often inclined to suspect evil or conspiratorial intentions everywhere. The case of the *Introduction générale à l'étude des doctrines hindoues,* a work that Guénon wished to present as his doctoral report, is in this regard significant. This book, whatever its value, did not comply at all with the requirements of the university authorities for material of historical erudition, requirements which constitute the "rule of the genre" and which one cannot logically avoid when soliciting approval of these same authorities. When, in addition, Guénon declared peremptorily that, for all this "erudition," there did not result the slightest comprehension of the true idea within academia, then the rejection of Sylvain Lévi is very easily explained, and it is not at all necessary to invoke partisan motives.

Guénon marked his distance from official orientalism without establishing singular infallibility for himself, though in matters of principle, he was most often right. But if a pure metaphysician is not concerned with rules and requirements, it is not the same for a hermeneutist of religions who is faced with facts to interpret. The interpreter of religions must at first make inquiry by means of extensive documentation—this Guénon did not always do. The interpreter of religions should, moreover, possess an intellectual affinity for the subject; otherwise the interior essence of the religion being considered will escape him or her. That is what happened with Buddhism, which Guénon, a disciple of Shankara, at first rejected as heterodox, before Coomaraswamy convinced him of his error. In the same way, a profound comprehension of the Christian "form" always escaped Guénon. He was certainly capable of explaining elements of the Christian faith such as scriptural or liturgical symbols, and he offered remarkable, sometimes definitive, interpretations; but he was not in a position to accept the paradox of a religion that, by nature, ignores the institutional distinction of esoterism and exoterism and whose function is to proclaim the greatest mysteries in the public place.

These points notwithstanding, it is enough to enter into Guénon's writing to be captured by the manifest clarity and transcendent limpidity of a mind in perfect mastery of itself. Of course, the work has its limits, its imperfections, even its errors—this is the lot of every human endeavor. But no one can read Guénon without experiencing the quite extraordinary feeling that all which human reason had more or less obscurely dreamed, all that the great sages in times past had taught but which seemed lost, all that glistened in the deceiving forms of a multiple occult tradition—all this finally finds an order and becomes possibly true. From this point of view, the work produces a kind of "miracle"; it breaks down the fundamental incredulity of modern readers; it awakens in them a forgotten intelligence.

The means it uses for this are of an adamantine simplicity. Guénon calls on only the intrinsic evidence of the truth, and this is why he could say that his writings did not require references:

> No tradition has "come to our knowledge" by "writers," above all by modern Western ones. . . . Their works have only provided us with a convenient occasion to present it, which is quite different. For we are under no obligation to inform the public of our "sources" and besides, these do not entail any "references."[9]

A provocative statement, certainly, and partly inaccurate, for when it is a question of Holy Scripture or historical research, Guénon almost always provides references. But besides the assertion that he had direct access to certain sources, he also means that, *by definition*, metaphysical doctrine possesses its truth within itself, that it does not depend at all on a reference to any authority but only on the assent of the intelligence that becomes

aware of it. Moreover, a direct teaching given by an authentic representative to a qualified mind communicates a deeper comprehension of the
religion or tradition than any scientific study. This is why Guénon's sources
"do not require references."[10]

As to the truth of Guénon's work, there exists also an indirect criterion—
its "hermeneutic fecundity." If a work such as that on the Vedanta, in spite
of the (apparent) poverty of its documentation, provides us with a synoptic
intelligence whose essence no later investigation will contradict and no
other work communicates so clearly; when one notices, as we ourselves
have, that this hermeneutic fecundity extends in the end to all the traditional doctrines, even to those Guénon did not speak about, and that he
furnishes us with the keys to understand the metaphysics and symbolism
of numerous religions, it becomes extremely difficult to doubt the essential
truth (in spite of minor errors) of what he has taught us.

Finally, it must be added that Guénon possessed a kind of didactic genius.
The least of his writings is always composed like a systematic treatise and
in such a clear, decisive way that the content impregnates itself quasi-
automatically in the memory. Few writings in the world have such an
instructive power. Guénon excels in forming definitions and in establishing
a vocabulary so precise and so attuned to the meanings of what he wished
to express, that it is almost impossible not to use it once it has become
known. In this sense, Guénon is indeed a "founder." He establishes the
language of sacred metaphysics with a rigor, a breadth, and an intrinsic certainty such that he compels recognition as a standard of comparison for the
twentieth century. Such is Guénon's essential and paradoxical contribution:
to give to the universal esoteric gnosis—which had passed for an obscure
collection of "poetic" confusion—the most crystalline and mathematical
form, even if at the expense of its "musical" aspects.

The Governing Ideas

The Notion of Traditional Metaphysics

Rather than offer details about the content of Guénon's works, which
would necessitate useless repetition, we find it preferable to give a synthetic
presentation of the doctrine,[11] which forms itself around five fundamental
themes: an initial theme of intellectual reform and criticism of the modern
world; three central themes, each constituting a particular synthesis of the
other two—metaphysics, tradition, and symbolism; and a concluding theme
of accomplishment, of spiritual realization. All together they can be
represented by the following diagram:

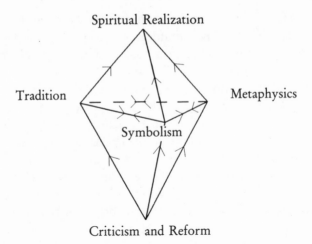

Yet before studying each of these themes by itself, it would be best to examine the connection Guénon makes between metaphysics and tradition, not only because the idea of traditional metaphysics (which is connected to the idea of sacred intellectuality) constitutes the essential standard of all Guénon's work but also because this idea is completely unknown in the present Western world.

If we accept the term metaphysics, whatever its etymological derivation, as designating the knowledge of what is "supra-physical," that is to say, "super-natural" in the highest sense of the term, we can understand how it can be adequately applied to the "supreme science." But in the way it has been described among the Greeks or Christians, especially from the scholastics on, metaphysics seems to present itself as coming from natural reason, functioning according to its own system from information gathered by perceptible knowledge and by reference to history. In this case, it has nothing to do with any tradition, except in the derivative and secondary sense of a human tradition (for example, the Platonic tradition). It is not a tradition in the real sense of a teaching connected with a revelation (generally scriptural) of which it comprises the authorized intellectual commentary which is set forth and fixed in a standard corpus.[12]

Yet Guénon views metaphysics not as a profane exercise of the reason freely speculating about empirical data but as a received doctrine,[13] intrinsically sacred and always surrounded by a traditional form. There is not one of his works, even the most all-embracing or abstract (*Les Etats multiples de l'être*), where Guénon is not careful to back up his metaphysical affirmations by calling on specific, recognized, traditional facts (Hindu, Chinese, Islamic, Christian, etc.). Often, when asked by a correspondent for information on a point of doctrine or cosmology, he would explain that he could not answer for want of traditional evidence.

Such a doctrine is well known in the West; it is given the name "theology." Thomas Aquinas called it *sacra doctrina*. But one often forgets (or denies) that such a doctrine demands an equally nonprofane type of intelligence. There are those who have even gone so far as to claim that an atheist who accepted the articles of faith in jest could become a good theologian. Quite otherwise is metaphysical knowledge, which depends on an intrinsically sacred intellectuality, that is, an actual participation in the knowledge by which God knows himself. By virtue of this supreme noetic identity between human essence and divine essence, when a mind opens to the light of revelation, it accesses in a way its own transcendent content, which is pure inspiration, intellectual intuition, the "eye of the heart."

Criticism of the Modern World as Metaphysical Preparation

The knowledge of which Guénon speaks requires from modern minds a veritable intellectual conversion that expresses itself as a radical change in one's mental bearings. Guénon sets forth a penetrating criticism of modernity in several works in which he attacked the errors and illusions of the profane world as well as the deceptions and parodies of pseudo-religions.[14] There does not exist in the literature of the twentieth century such a total and profound indictment of the ideologies of our times.

Guénon denounces the idea of *progress,* which is purely and simply denied, except on the level of material power. For him there is not one sector of thought and human activity that does not show a veritable regression. He demonstrates how this idea of progress directs, as a real influence, all our reactions and judgments, as if it is simply enough to follow an epoch in time to be superior to it. He also attacks the superstition of science, which he says is no more than "ignorant knowledge."[15] Not that the real results of science are disputed (Guénon's competence in mathematics and classical physics was very extensive), but only their claim to be the only form of authentic knowledge. Science too often becomes an idol, causing a real cultural terrorism to reign. Guénon mistrusted all concordism, and he had only contempt for those who looked for confirmation of the Holy Scriptures in the so-called discoveries of physicists.[16] He also struggled against what he admirably called "the illusion of ordinary life,"[17] which is, in fact, one of the most powerful obstacles to the reception and practice of traditional doctrine. This illusion consists in the belief that human existence is a closed domain, rigorously neutral and autonomous, where we have nothing else to do but produce, consume, play, and avoid harm; and where religion constitutes an exterior domain that one has the perfect right to ignore. Furthermore, this is an illusion that is reinforced by everything in our present society—a society that is characterized by the overvaluation of work and the closely related cult of leisure and television. Finally, we point out the clear analyses by which Guénon shows the natural alliance between sentimental moralism and industrial rationalism, an alliance that gave rise politically to the democratic ideology of the French Revolution and sociologically to the capitalist ideology of Anglo-Saxon civilization.

As for religious imposture and parodies of esotericism, Guénon took no less trouble to denounce them in his two largest books, *Le Théosophisme* and *L'Erreur spirite*. The term "theosophism" is, moreover, a neologism of a derogatory nature. The stakes are all the more important as the theosophist religion, invented by Mme Blavatsky and Annie Besant, claims for itself two principal themes of Guénon's work—Hinduism and esotericism—and presents them in a completely distorted way, thus contributing to the increase in confusion of thought and making any true conversion impossible. The enormous documentation used by Guénon in his work on theosophism was furnished to him in part by Hindus. This being so, he could rectify many errors, the most important being the false interpretation of reincarnation. He takes up this question in *L'Erreur spirite* as he provided information on satanism and on the nature of the subtle (or psychic) world and its distinction from the spiritual world—information that is found nowhere else.

The two keys to this metaphysical preparation consist of a double contrast: geographical, between the East and the West; and historical, between the traditional and modern worlds. All becomes clear if we accept that we are at the end of the *Kali* age (the *Kali-Yuga* or "age of troubles"); when the lowest possibilities of the cycle must be realized. In other words, the modern West is characterized by the denial or the forgetting of tradition and by the ignorance or lack of understanding of metaphysical doctrine.

Tradition and Cyclology

Guénon confers on the word "tradition" (from *tradere*, "deliver," "transmit") its strictest meaning: tradition is what humanity has not invented but received, and which thus finds its starting point, in the final analysis, in the superhuman origin of all things. This tradition is identical to the *Logos* of humanity; it is the expression of its law and the standard of its earthly existence. Thus, *normal* life is what takes place according to this standard—

by which all moments, all acts, all works are accomplished according to its rule and in its light.

This tradition was given to humanity at the beginning of time: it constitutes the primordial tradition which manifested itself in the "arctic cradle" of humanity, that is, in the "earthly paradise." Afterwards it took on multiple forms—which are all the world's religions given by God's revelation—according to the times and mentalities; but, despite this diversity, there remains the essential unity of the truth. To our knowledge, no thinker before Guénon, Western or Eastern, had brought the "transcendent unity of religions" (according to the expression of F. Schuon) so ruthlessly and clearly to light.

The idea of tradition, so understood, is the distinctive, essential mark of all non-modern civilizations. This does not imply, however, anything static, and it is combined with another doctrine, that of cosmic cycles through which the law of evolution governs not only human history but also the universal manifestation—which undergoes periodic phases of reabsorption. From this point of view, tradition is what remains after all passes on and is lost. Guénon insists that the cyclic doctrine excludes all identical repetition, since it simply expresses the fact of a successive "using up," in a "descending" direction, of such possibilities initially existing in the beginning—a "using up" that according to each cycle passes through qualitatively analogical phases. Each great cycle comprises secondary cycles, the succession of the four ages of gold, silver, bronze, and iron of the Hesiodic and Platonic tradition. According to all the revealed traditions, we are presently at the end of the age of iron—or of "troubles" (*Kali-Yuga*) according to Hindu terminology—when the spiritual darkening attains its limit. But finally, when the lower possibilities are completely exhausted, order is restored, tradition is reestablished, and truth illuminates all hearts.

The Metaphysics: The Degrees of Reality

Considered in its largest sense, metaphysics is the science of degrees of universal reality, degrees that together constitute precisely the content of the teaching (more or less developed) of any tradition. In a stricter sense, it pertains only to the metaphysics which belongs to the order of the Principle, the remainder arising more specifically whether from cosmology (point of view of the macrocosm) or from anthropology (point of view of the microcosm).

Metaphysical categories.   These are logical and ontological. Logically, when considering the degrees of reality starting from what is human, the first distinction to be made, according to Guénon, is that between the individual and the universal: since the human person is an individual being, everything that is beyond the human person is nonindividual or universal. The individual encompasses the general (humanity) and the particular (the individual), the latter going from the collective (a number of persons) to the singular (one individual). Thus the following table:

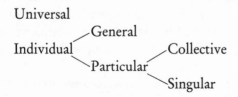

Universal
Individual ─ General
           ─ Particular ─ Collective
                        ─ Singular

Ontologically, considering the degrees of reality themselves, the universal encompasses both informal manifestation and the nonmanifested. The individual encompasses formal manifestation, which includes the subtle or psychic world and the corporeal or gross world. Thus the following table:

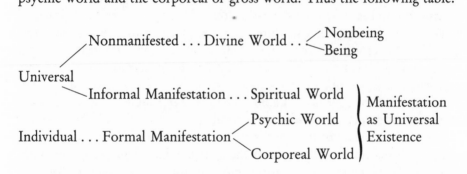

Universal ─ Nonmanifested . . . Divine World . . . ─ Nonbeing
                                                   ─ Being
          ─ Informal Manifestation . . . Spiritual World ⎫
                                                         ⎬ Manifestation
                                    ─ Psychic World   ⎬ as Universal
Individual . . . Formal Manifestation ─   ⎬ Existence
                                    ─ Corporeal World   ⎭

The Nonmanifested or metacosm. In the strictest sense of the term, metaphysics "begins" beyond Being (or causal ontological determination symbolized by the number 1). This is the nondualistic (*advaita-vada*) point of view. The highest superontological principle, symbolized by zero, is designated as the Infinite, that is, what is limited by nothing, by no specific nature or essence, and which therefore encompasses everything and knows no contradiction. The Infinite so understood cannot be directly conceived of "in itself." We can only indirectly conceive of it as *what can be absolutely everything*, to which Guénon gives the name "universal Possibility." It is not a matter here of a simple human point of view, but of an objectively based "aspect" of the Infinite. The universal Possibility embodies both ontological possibility (or "Being") and superontological possibility (or "Non-Being").[18] In the final analysis, it is none other than the Infinite itself which alone is

6. René Guénon.

absolutely real—from which arises the metaphysical identification between the possible and the real.

By its self-determination, Being is the principal "affirmation" of Non-Being. It is thus the synthetic cause of all creatures' secondary determinations or archetypes and contains them in itself as possibilities of manifestation.

Universal manifestation or macrocosm. Guénon, speaking the language of India, more readily describes the cosmogonic process as a manifestation than as a creation, which emphasizes the essential or exemplary continuity of the cosmos with the Principle rather than its existential discontinuity. At the level of the nonmanifested, this process results in the bipolarization of Being in a determinative or active Principle and in a receptive or passive Principle (in Hinduism *Purusha* and *Prakriti* respectively). All manifestation is produced by the (nonactive) action of *Purusha* (the determinant Principle, Spirit) upon *Prakriti* (the determined Principle, primordial Nature). In this way, the innumerable possibilities of creation contained in an undifferentiated and unified form in causal Being are actualized in distinct and different forms. *Purusha* and *Prakriti* remain nonmanifested in themselves, but they constitute the double primordial condition of every manifested being and exist analogically in each of them as its essential or intelligible pole and its substantial or "material" pole.

Universal manifestation is made, on the one hand, of limiting conditions, and, on the other, of beings determined by these conditions. A certain group of conditions defines a "world" or *degree of reality*, representable by a horizontal plane. A being finds itself invested with conditions proper to the degree of reality it currently is crossing and which determine the *modalities* of that being. Since these degrees, without counting the ontological and superontological, are of an innumerable multitude, one can speak of "multiple states of being" all of which subsist in a permanent actuality, their continuity being representable by a vertical line emanating from the Principle.

As to the degrees of universal manifestation, Guénon, following the Hindu doctrine, groups them in three worlds (*Tribhuvana*): the informal world, or world of the *devas* (Hindu "gods" corresponding, says Guénon, to the angels of Abrahamic monotheism), the subtle or animic world, and the corporeal or gross world. This cosmic tripartition results in the differentiated actualization of the three "qualitative tendencies" (*sattwa*, or ascending tendency; *rajas*, or expansive tendency; *tamas*, or descending tendency) contained in *Prakriti* as an undifferentiated equilibrium. Everything that exists participates in all three at once, but does so by way of the prevailing tendency which establishes an adherence to this or that world. In fact, this schematic presentation masks the nuances of a highly complex doctrine in which the informal or spiritual world in particular can be in a way "annexed" by the divine metacosm. The corporeal world is defined by five conditions (space, time, number, life, and form). The psychic world is conditioned by duration, life, and form. The spiritual world is superformal and is characterized not by a formal and individualizing withdrawal within itself; rather, it is a manifestation of the unity of Being—a world of essences distinguished by their pure quality and thus not allowing any division in their unity.

Human being or microcosm. If we now view things from the point of view of a being, thus microcosmically, the vertical which unites all the states of this being in their centers and which connects them to the Principle precisely constitutes its self (*personalitas*), which must be carefully distinguished from individuality (*individualitas*) that has only to do with the present human state (psycho-corporeal). This self which unifies all the states of being and connects them to their principle, is none other than the primordial determination of the Principle *relative* to that particular being. It is the metaphysical "place" where the being, through the multiplicity of its states, is truly itself, that is, the "Self" (*Atman*). The "supreme Self" is the Over-Being, the absolute and infinite Reality. Outside of this supreme identity, all the rest is *Māyā*, illusion, and divine play.

The individual being must ascend along this vertical—become what one is in oneself, that is, realize one's own archetype, and even beyond to the supreme and unconditioned Self as a "fusion without confusion." But for this one must bring into play, ritually activate, all the symbolic correspondences uniting together the different planes of reality, thus accomplishing the oneness of existence.

Universal Symbolism

Symbolism is indeed not only a means of knowledge; it is still more deeply a means of spiritual realization. Based on the nature of things, it truly connects the sensible and corporeal being with higher states and, in the end, with the Principle. Its meaning must thus be known.

Guénon dedicated a large part of his work to the science of symbols, and there is perhaps no other sphere where he gives such a feeling of mastery.[19] There is none either where the unity of sacred forms appears more keenly, as though it were palpable. This unity of sacred forms verifies the doctrinal content not only of the different revelations but also of the Holy Scriptures, traditional art forms, rites, and finally the entire cosmos. To read so many astonishingly exact treatises on the interpretation of symbols, one comes to the point of wondering where Guénon culled this knowledge. We could not give here the least idea of his extreme conceptual rigor any more than his precision, without examining it in the smallest of details. We will only say that there arises from it a real change in our perception of sensible realities that naturally acquire a kind of intelligible transparence. The world reveals itself like a spark from the *Logos*.

Yet symbolism plays in this regard a discriminating role, for all men are not capable of perceiving this transparence. They have eyes, but see not, or see only the exterior aspect of things—the scriptures, the rites, the sacred forms—and cannot penetrate their inner meaning. The existence of symbolism thus bears witness to the distinction between an exoteric teaching, which indicates all that is relatively outer in a tradition that is public and evident to all, and an esoteric teaching, which concerns the knowledge of what is most inner and is necessarily reserved, by the force of circumstances, for those who can grasp the hidden meaning behind appearances. The distinction between esotericism and exotericism is a major distinction in Guénon's thought.

It remains to be said that the metaphysical conception of symbolism he laid out is doubtless the only one that (intelligibly and without any diminution) allows one to take in all the sacred scriptures and thus escape the destructive deviations of modernism.

Spiritual Realization

Tradition, metaphysics, and symbolism have but a single aim: to lead one to the attainment of one's true destiny, namely, one's real unification with one's own essence: "become what you are," which assumes that now we are not and that modern individuals "remain outside" of their essences, which is precisely the meaning of the word existence (from *ex-sistere*, "remain out of"). Guénon called this process metaphysical or spiritual realization. This realization, which consists of a true awareness of the reality of the Spirit, brings about a radical transformation of the human being and is thus possible only by the grace of a spiritual influence coming from above and communicated by a rite of nonhuman origin. Outside of a real connection to an authentic religion and the receiving of such a rite, it is not possible to obtain any actual spiritual result, that is, to pass beyond the human level. But, on the other hand, the rite should be adapted to the spiritual possibilities of the one who receives it. Now, human beings do not exhibit an equal capacity for reaching the end of their realization which is their

supreme unity with the Principle—each according to his or her own archetype. It is thus necessary that rites of a different nature exist, according to
the ends they allow one to attain.

For the human being, two ends are conceivable: perfection of the human
state and perfection of the divine state, for in each person there is something of God. All religions proffer the first end, which Guénon calls by the
term "salvation." They appeal to all to save the whole person. But to attain
the second end, which India calls "deliverance," a special rite is necessary,
given only to those who are "qualified," and which Guénon calls an
initiatory rite (from *initium*, "beginning"), because it inaugurates the beginning of the spiritual path and it confers the germ of deification. The bringing into play of this spiritual influence necessitates the use of appropriate
techniques, which constitute the *method* properly so-called, in contrast to
the doctrine. For Guénon, every complete tradition should include these
two kinds of rites: initiatory and exoteric.[20] The method varies with the
path followed, which is itself adapted to the diversity of individual natures.
This diversity can be reduced to the ways of action, love, and knowledge.

* * *

In its broad outline, such is the doctrine that Guénon was able to set out
with a rare authority. Even if it remains fragmentary and sometimes
excessive, his work constitutes, as Frithjof Schuon said, "the great traditionalist metaphysic and esotericist message of the 20th century." We can summarize it in the following text:

> All the opposing energies will finally shatter against the unique force of the
> truth, like clouds dissipating before the sun, even if they have succeeded in
> momentarily hiding it from our gaze. The destructive action of time will
> only allow what is greater than time to subsist: it will devour all those who
> have limited their horizon to the changing world, all those who have made
> a religion of the contingent and transitory, and "he who sacrifices to a god
> will become food for that god"; but what can time do against those who carry
> within themselves the awareness of eternity?[21]

Ananda K. Coomaraswamy and the Treasure
of the Traditional Literatures

The son of a Hindu jurist and an English mother, Coomaraswamy was
born in Colombo on August 22, 1877. A man of universal knowledge, he
turned first to the sciences (chiefly mineralology) and then, after a failure
in social action, gave himself over to the history of art (mainly Islamic art

and the art of the Middle East). In that capacity he joined the Boston Museum of Fine Arts, where he remained until his sudden death on September 9, 1947.

His work is immense. A first bibliographical survey shows 627 published books and articles. An exceptional polyglot—he knew more than a dozen languages—and having vertiginous erudition able to satisfy the most demanding scholar, he excelled in gathering the most distant and appropriate texts on each of his chosen themes: from the Nordic *Eddas* to the Buddhist *tantras* through the Neoplatonists and the rheno-Flemish mystics. Having become acquainted with Guénon's works about 1930, he received the notions of traditional orthodoxy and the unity of religions, which he found evidence of everywhere. His exceptional quality of intellectual openness and his inexhaustible knowledge allow the sacred cultures of the world to resonate as if in symphonic dialogue. Moreover—and this is his principal care—Coomaraswamy transmits a documentation otherwise impossible to find.

Besides books on art such as *The Dance of Śiva* (1918), *La Sculpture de Bodhgayâ* (1935), and others, Coomaraswamy published books on metaphysics and the history of religions and articles of which some have been collected in volumes after his death. We mention *The Transformation of Nature in Art* (New York, 1934); *Elements of Buddhist Iconography* (1935); *Christian and Oriental Philosophy of Art* (New York, 1943); *Hinduism and Buddhism* (New York, 1943); *Figures of Speech or Figures of Thought* (New York, 1946); *The Religious Basis of Forms of Indian Society* (1946); *Am I My Brother's Keeper* (1947); *Time and Eternity* (Ascona, Switzerland, 1947); *The Living Thoughts of Gotama the Buddha* (1949); and *Selected Papers* (2 vols.; 1978).

Frithjof Schuon and the Realization of the Perennial Wisdom

Together with Guénon's work, that of Schuon constitutes the most typical message of the current that reveals the traditional and universal metaphysics in the twentieth century. Like Guénon, Schuon must be considered a leader of a school, the school of perennial wisdom (*Sophia Perennis*). Moreover, it is impossible to review here all the authors who bear witness to this wisdom—authors from every continent, representing the principal languages of the world. We must restrict ourselves to an extremely limited choice of several spokesmen as the most representative and influential of this spiritual current. These are but examples and in no way exclude other possible choices, and this school never ceases to inspire new testimony.

Frithjof Schuon

Different in form from Guénon's work, that of Schuon is more open to the intelligence of beauty. Frithjof Schuon was born in Basel, Switzerland, on June 18, 1907, of a southern German father and an Alsatian mother. The elder Schuon was a great concert violinist and teacher at the Basel Conservatory of Music. His death forced Mme Schuon to settle in Mulhouse in 1920. Here her two sons (one of whom would follow the way of Christian monasticism) received a French education. At the age of sixteen Frithjof left school in order to become a designer, which would permit him to develop his remarkable talent for painting. At the same time he read the philosophers of the East and West, notably, Plato, Meister Eckhart, and the *Bhagavadgītā*. At the museum of Basel, contemplation of a magnificent Buddha had already revealed to Schuon the sacred plenitude of the Orient. At seventeen he became familiar with the work of Guénon, which confirmed him in his rejection of the modern world and crystallized his metaphysical intuition.

After his military service in France, he came to Paris, where he worked as a designer and perfected his knowledge of Arabic. On two occasions, in 1932 and 1935, prolonged journeys in Africa allowed him to become familiar with the Islamic traditions. In 1938, and then again in 1939 during a voyage cut short by the war, he met with Guénon in Cairo. As a French soldier, he was imprisoned by the German army, but he escaped by way of Switzerland, from which he later received citizenship. In 1949 he married Catherine Feer, the daughter of a Swiss diplomat. Schuon's voyages (Morocco, Spain, Turkey, North America, etc.) allowed him to experience the multiple forms of the sacred, including the sense of virgin nature that he found above all in the tradition of the Native Americans, principally the Sioux, with whom he had considerable contact (1959 and 1963) and who formally received him and his wife into their tribe. (In 1987 Schuon also became a member of Thomas Yellowtail's family. Yellowtail is presently the greatest medicine man of the Crow Indians and for many years fulfilled the function of Sun Dance Chief.)

The published works of Schuon—without counting his pictorial work—include at the present time twenty-one books written in French (and already translated in nine languages) plus three works drafted in German, of which two are collections of poems. A considerable body of work has resulted from his collaboration with *Etudes Traditionnelles* since 1933, the English review *Studies in Comparative Religion* since 1963, and the French review *Connaissance des Religions* since 1985; many of these articles have been reprinted in the books mentioned above.[22] With certain exceptions, his publications do not constitute systematic treatises and are not given over to only one subject. His purpose, essentially, is not to transmit factual information on this or that point of traditional doctrine (although it becomes evident, in reading over his work, that he presents a considerable amount of scholarly data). Such information, certainly indispensable, can in fact be accompanied by a veritable spiritual unconsciousness when it is reduced to erudition or sterile theorizing. All of Schuon's effort, on the contrary, aims to awaken in his reader the living consciousness of what is God and what is humanity and the responsibility that derives from this for the latter vis-à-vis the former.

To be a human being, this master teaches us, is to be a bearer of an intelligence endowed with objectivity, that is, to be able to grasp things *in themselves,* in their absoluteness, and thus to be conscious, in the end, of the Absolute such as it is. By itself, in its intrinsic properties, intelligence is a theophany. Now consciousness of the Absolute necessarily implies consciousness of what is relative, not in the sense of an unreality or nothingness but of a lesser reality. Then again, since the supreme Principle is the Absolute Reality, it must encompass in itself all reality, albeit only relative. This encompassing constitutes the "infinite dimension" of the Principle, what Schuon sometimes calls the infinite Possibility. Finally, the "properties" of the infinite Possibility, being the Absolute itself, are necessarily perfect and constitute the Perfection of Sovereign Good (*Summum Bonum,* τὰ ἀγαθόν). These are the three "notes" of the supreme and superontological Principle: Absoluteness, Infinitude, Perfection or Sovereign Good.

Particularly in his later works, Schuon specifies the Perfection of the Sovereign Good (τὰ ἀγαθόν). This idea refers to the Platonic tradition and to Augustine; it should not be considered a "third aspect" of the Principle. It designates the Principle itself, in its essence, pure and incorruptible, and this is the Absolute and the Infinite. This corresponds effectively to a "polarization" in the heart of the Sovereign Good. In terminology Schuon differs considerably from Guénon. Their doctrinal styles are very different: Guénon builds an axiomatic (hence invariable) speculation, whereas Schuon, "polisher" of metaphysical icons, varies his point of view.

Yet the Sovereign Good does not polarize only according to "aspects" or "dimensions" but also radiates according to "hypostatic degrees," which, even in the middle of the divine metacosm, prefigures in a way the degrees of manifestation: these are the Over-Being, the created Being, and the Spirit, "the divine center of the whole cosmos."[23]

Such is the general metaphysical framework that Schuon presents us with, mainly in his later works.[24] But if the intellect is naturally metaphysical or "supernatural," it is not exactly the same with affectivity and will, which also make up the human being. Now, it is the whole person that must discriminate between the real and the illusory—and thereby unite with the one Reality. A true and deifying gnosis cannot be had without love and without virtue, which comes down to saying that God cannot be known if one is without knowledge of the essence and forms of humanity, the Beauty and theophanic transparence of the world (and objects); and finally, the saving power of divine revelation. Here we have the three major axes of Schuon's work. As for the first axis, not only does Schuon provide numerous analyses of human feelings, the alchemy of the animic substance, etc., but he also establishes the foundation of a science of spiritual temperaments in function of "natural castes and races"—studies which bear witness to an acute sense of ethnic qualities and to a great wealth of observation.[25]

The second axis, relating to the beauty of sacred art as well as of virgin nature, yields us definitive works on the principles of universal art: a direct and metaphysical understanding of the most varied styles, of the symbolism of colors, and of animal and vegetable forms, in addition to reflections on space, time, and form and on numbers and their theophanic capabilities.[26]

Finally, concerning the divine revelations, Schuon has never ceased pondering over and thoroughly investigating them in order to understand not only their "transcendent unity" (the title of his first and most famous French book) but also their place and metaphysical meaning—in other words, the divine intention that presides over their appearance. The Vedanta of Shankara, the Native American tradition (to which he has given a metaphysical synthesis), Islam and Sufism (in *L'oeil du Coeur* he translated texts until then unpublished in the West), Chinese and Japanese Buddhism (above all, the mystery of the Bodhisattva and the way of *nembutsu*), Shinto, Christianity—these are so many forms of the Spirit, of the "languages of the Self," the intelligence of which Schuon transmits to us.

The writings of Frithjof Schuon concerning the religious phenomenon are not limited to giving to us the keys to his thorough comprehension and to communicating the flavor of each of its forms. This work, which results from the genius, visual and pictorial, of this thinker and which offers us so many spiritual portraits of different religions and sacred traditions, accompanies another search, of a more intellectual nature, aiming at elaborating a defense of religion in general. Schuon is, in effect, essentially preoccupied with the drama of contemporary humanity. The only remedy for our present suffering is found in religion, but the entire modern world diverts us from our return. We die of thirst beside a spring because we are persuaded that it has been poisoned. It is necessary then to indicate (and to demonstrate, because Schuon is always logical) that religion has a rational vitality and at first to resolve, as much as it is possible, the scandal that constitutes the existence of evil. This is what Schuon works for, and this question has, for him, so much depth that he returns to it in each of his books. All things considered, it is his concern for human happiness that leads him to entertain the major questions of our religions condition.[27]

Such appears to us to be Schuon's fundamental message, the purpose of which is to extend the message of Guénon and, rectifying it, to render its normal accomplishment possible in spiritual realization. We turn now to five other distinguished authors of the school of perennial wisdom.

Titus Burckhardt

Born in Florence in 1908 of German stock,[28] Titus Burckhardt acquired world renown with his numerous monographs on the sacred art of different civilizations.[29] But he is also considered one of the foremost European metaphysicians and one of the greatest authorities of Sunni Sufism. Of an unsurpassed clarity, his works make up the most reliable introduction in this field. Also of great importance are his studies of alchemy and of traditional cosmology. We mention *De l'Homme Universel*, a translation of *Al-Insan Al-Kamil*, which is a treatise from Abd Al-Karîm Al-Jîlî (Lyon, 1953); *Introduction aux Doctrines Esotériques de l'Islam* (Lyon, 1955); *La Sagesses des Prophètes*, a partial translation of *Fucûc Al-Hikam*, a treatise from Muhyi-d-dîn ibn 'Arabî (Paris, 1955); *Principes et Méthodes de l'Art Sacré* (Lyon, 1958); *Alchemie: Sinn und Weltbild* (Freiburg im Breisgau, 1960).

After a life dedicated to the publication of art (editions Urs Graf in Switzerland) and, from 1972 to 1977, to the safeguarding of the architectural and cultural patrimony of the city of Fez, as well as the traditional arts of Morocco (in the setting of a mission which UNESCO had entrusted to him), Titus Burckhardt died in January 1984.

Martin Lings

A curator of Arabic manuscripts and prints in the British Museum (London) and a professor for twelve years at the University of Cairo—where he knew Guénon—Martin Lings devoted the essential part of his work to making Islamic esotericism known to the West. Among his best-known works, where the most extensive Islamic science comes together with a great serenity of tone and a keen poetic and spiritual sensibility, we mention *A Moslem Saint of the Twentieth Century* (London, 1961), where Lings presents one of the purest figures of esoteric Islam, the Shayh Ahmad al-Alawî; *Ancient Beliefs and Modern Superstitions* (London, 1964), which presents a particularly strong denunciation of the idolatry of science; *What is Sufism?* (London,

1975), a brilliant synthesis and striking evocation of the spiritual climate of Sufism; and finally *Muhammad, his Life Based on the Earliest Sources* (London, 1983), a veritable encyclopedia on the Prophet, where the oldest and most traditional documents are used and translated for the first time in the West.

Marco Pallis

This writer and scholar was born in Liverpool in 1895 of Greek parents. His highly cultivated father had passed twenty years of his life in India. Marco Pallis was attracted by the East, having experienced the strong influence of Guénon, and later of Schuon; he undertook an expedition in the Himalayas in 1933, which he renewed in 1936, in 1947, and again in 1948. Gifted not only for the most rugged mountain climbing but also for Eastern languages, botany, and music, Pallis is now considered one of the best Tibetan scholars in the West. Besides his famous *Peaks and Lamas* (London, 1953), we mention his last work, which exhibits all the characteristics of a spiritual testament and contains highly inspired pages in a language of noble simplicity—*A Buddhist Spectrum* (London, 1980). He died in 1989.

Leo Schaya

Born in Basel in 1916, of a family rooted in the purest Jewish tradition, Leo Schaya studied the works of Guénon and Schuon very early. Having investigated the doctrines of both India and Islam (especially during a journey to the East), he wrote what is today considered the most lucid metaphysical synthesis of the sephirothic doctrine: *L'Homme et l'Absolu selon la Kabbale* (Paris, 1958, 1977, 1988); it has been translated into German, English, Italian, Spanish, and other languages. In *La Doctrine Soufique de l'Unité* (Paris, 1962), he studies what Islamic esotericism calls *waḥdat al-wujūd*, the universal "unity of Being," with its inevitable spiritual implications. *La Création en Dieu, à la Lumière du Judaisme, du Christianisme et de l'Islam* (Paris, 1983) at once demonstrates that the metaphysical notion of the creation *ex Deo* and *in Deo* must take the place of the irrelevant (according to him) theological notion of *creatio ex nihilo*. It then presents a very thorough commentary on the first chapters of Genesis. Finally, this book reveals that the cosmogony of Moses includes a complete prophetic teaching on the spiritual destiny of created beings, a destiny that occupies a large part of this book. Leo Schaya died in May 1986, and *La Naissance à l'Esprit* was published posthumously in 1987.

Seyyed Hossein Nasr

This great Iranian intellectual, presently a professor of philosophy and islamology in the United States, is perhaps closer to Schuon's work than Guénon's. Among his many works we note *Three Muslim Sages* (Cambridge, 1964), *Islamic Studies* (Beirut, 1966), *Ideals and Realities of Islam* (London, 1967), *The Encounter of Man and Nature: The Spiritual Crisis of Modern Man* (London, 1968), *Science and Civilization in Islam* (Cambridge, 1968), *Islam and the Plight of Modern Man* (London and New York, 1975), and *Knowledge and the Sacred* (the 1981 Gifford Lectures).

Notes

1. *Le sens caché dans l'oeuvre de René Guénon,* L'Age d'Homme (Lausanne, 1975) 46–49.

2. According to the testimony of Noële Maurice-Denis Boulet ("L'ésotériste René Guénon, Souvenirs et jugements," *Le Pensée catholique* 77 [1962] 23), Guénon had told him that he joined the neo-gnostics "only to destroy them."

3. Guénon was endowed with an exceptional memory and a great linguistic ability. Besides Greek, Latin, Hebrew, English, Italian, and, it is said, Spanish, Russian, and Polish (Paul Chacornac, *La vie simple de René Guénon: Editions Traditionnelles* [Paris, 1958] 85), he read and wrote Arabic perfectly (he wrote several articles in this language). He also knew Sanskrit rather well and some Chinese.

4. Chacornac, *La vie simple,* 42. This little book, written by a friend of Guénon, remains the classic reference work on the subject.

5. On Albert de Pouvourville, see J. P. Laurant, *Matgioi: Un aventurier taoist* (Paris: Dervy-Livres, 1982) 114.

6. Chacornac, *La vie simple,* 43.

7. Frithjof Schuon, who knew Guénon personally, told us that he "had received four initiations: Hindu, Masonic, Taoist, and Sufi."

8. In the Catholic review *Regnabit* he published, from 1925 to 1927, a series of articles on symbolism.

9. This text is from 1932; Guénon was responding to criticism from a Jesuit. See *Comptes-Rendus* (1973) 130.

10. The French Indianist Louis Renou declares that Guénon "is the author of a second-hand work on the *Vedānta* of Shankara" (*Les Littératures de l'Inde* [Presses Universitaires de France, 1951] 118)—to which one of our friends responded: "second-hand, perhaps, but from a first-rate mind!" In fact, this work is also a first-hand work. The eminent Indianist Olivier Lacombe has personally affirmed to us that Guénon's essays on the Vedānta are free of any errors.

11. What follows is a description, as objective as we can make it, and not a critical appreciation.

12. Such is the case, for example, of the Vedānta, which makes up a standard corpus of 555 aphorisms, entitled *Brahma-sutra* (or *Vedānta-sutra*) and is attributed to Bādarāyana.

13. The word "Kabbalah," which is used to designate the metaphysical commentary

on the Torah, means in fact "reception." See Leo Schaya, *L'Homme et l'Absolu selon la Kabbale* (Paris: Dervy, 1977).

14. Guénon, *Orient et Occident; La Crise du Monde moderne; La Règne de la Quantité et les Signes des Temps* (one of his best books); *Le Théosophisme: Histoire d'une pseudo-religion; L'Erreur spirite* (a projected *Erreur occultiste* was not written).

15. Guénon, *Orient et Occident*, chap. 2. The expression comes from a Hindu.

16. No doubt he would have seen only confusion and illusion in such works as those of F. Capra or the "Cordoba Conference."

17. Guénon, *La Règne de la Quantité*, chap. 15.

18. The superontological possibility includes all the possibilities of nonmanifestation, namely, Being (which is never manifested although it causally synthesizes the possibilities of manifestation in itself) and what is beyond Being. The transontological is symbolized by emptiness, silence, and darkness.

19. Most of the articles have been collected in the posthumous collection *Symboles fondamentaux de la Science sacrée*.

20. Is Christianity, whose only rites are the sacraments offered to all Christians, a complete tradition? For Guénon, it was but is no longer. As for us, and without going into a debate which would be out of place here, we are in complete agreement with F. Schuon's point of view on the continuing initiatory character of the Christian baptism, it being understood that this character develops the fullness of its deifying quality only by being brought into play by a spiritual realization.

21. Guénon, *Etudes sur l'Hindouisme*, 25–26.

22. S. H. Nasr has edited a large volume, *The Essential Writing of Frithjof Schuon* (Amity House), and T. Beguelin has edited a short book that is a selection of maxims and spiritual teachings, *Les perles du pélerin* (Paris: Seuil, 1990).

23. This doctrine allows for a metaphysical interpretation of the trinitarian mystery that Schuon has set out on several occasions.

24. Schuon, *Logique et Transcendance; Forme et substance dans les religions; L'Ésotérisme comme Principe et comme Voie; Du Divin à l'Humain; Sur les traces de la Religion pérenne; Résumé de Métaphysique intégrale*.

25. Schuon, *Le Stations de la Sagesse; Castes et Races; Regards sur les Mondes anciens; Avoir un Centre; Les Racines de la condition humaine*.

26. Schuon, *Perspectives spirituelles et faits humains; Sentiers de Gnose; The Feathered Sun: Plains Indians in Art and Philosophy*.

27. Schuon, *L'Unité Transcendante des Religions; L'Oeil du Coeur; Comprendre l'Islam; Le Soufisme, voile et quintessence;* the preface of *Rites secrets des Indiens sioux; Images de l'Esprit, Christianisme/Islam; Approches du phénomène religieux*.

28. He is kin to the great historian of the Renaissance Jakob Burckhardt, and his father was the sculptor Carl Burckhardt.

29. Many of these studies written in German still await translation into French or English. We note, among others, *Land am Rande der Zeit* (1941), a work dedicated to Morocco; *Siena, Stadt der Jungfrau* (1958); *Fes, Stadt des Islam* (1960); *Chartres und die Geburt der Kathedrale* (1962); *Art of Islam* (London, 1976; written in French but published in English, this work is unanimously considered a masterpiece).

Bibliography

Works of René Guénon

The dates given are either the date of the first publication or that of the new edition when it represents a change in relation to the first. Successive editions are not indicated. Only the name of the current publisher is given.

Introduction générale à l'étude des doctrines hindoues. 1921. Véga, 1952. Eng. trans. *Introduction to the study of the Hindu Doctrines.* 1945.
Le Théosophisme: Histoire d'une pseudo-religion. 1921. Editions Traditionnelles, 1965.
L'Erreur spirite. 1923. Editions Traditionnelles.
Orient et Occident. 1924. Véga. Eng. trans. *East and West.* 1941.
L'Homme et son Devenir selon le Vedânta. 1925. Editions Traditionnelles, 1952. Eng. trans. *Man and his Becoming according to the Vedânta.* 1945.
L'ésotérisme de Dante. 1925. Paris: Gallimard.
Le Roi du monde. 1927. Paris: Gallimard. Eng. trans. *The Lord of the World.* 1983.
La Crise du Monde moderne. 1927. Paris: Gallimard. Eng. trans. *The Crisis of the Modern World.* 1942. 1945.
Autorité spirituelle et pouvoir temporel. 1929. Véga.
Saint Bernard. 1929. Editions Traditionnelles.
Le Symbolisme de la Croix. Véga, 1931. Eng. trans. *Symbolism of the Cross.* 1958.
Les États multiples de l'être. Véga, 1932. Eng. trans. *The Multiple States of Being.* 1984.
La Métaphysique orientale. Editions Traditionneles, 1939.
Le Règne de la Quantité et les Signes des Tempes. Paris: Gallimard, 1945. Eng. trans. *The Reign of Quantity.* 1953.
Les Principes du Calcul infinitésimal. Paris: Gallimard, 1946.
Aperçus sur l'Initiation. Editions Traditionneles, 1946.
La Grande Triade. 1946. Paris: Gallimard. Eng. trans. *The Great Triad.* 1992.

Posthumous works (collected from articles already published)

Initiation et Réalisation spirituelle. Editions Traditionnelles, 1952.
Aperçus sur l'ésotérisme chrétien. Editions Traditionnelles, 1954.
Symboles fondamentaux de la Science sacrée. Paris: Gallimard, 1962. Eng. trans. *The Fundamental Symbols of Sacred Sciences.* Forthcoming.
Etudes sur la Franc-Maçonnerie et le Compagnonnage. 2 vols. Editions Traditionnelles, 1964.
Etudes sur l'Hindouisme. Editions Traditionnelles, 1968.
Formes traditionnelles et Cycles cosmiques. Paris: Gallimard, 1970.
Aperçus sur l'ésotérisme islamique et le Taoïsme. Paris: Gallimard, 1973.
Comptes-Rendus. Editions Traditionnelles, 1973.
Mélanges. Paris: Gallimard, 1976.

Studies about Guénon

1. Articles from reviews and periodicals

Etudes Traditionnelles, 1951, triple no. 293, 294, 295.
France-Asie, janvier 1953, no. 80.
La Pensée catholique, 1962, nos. 77, 78–79, 80.
Le Symbolisme, janvier-fevrier 1965, no. 368.
Planète Plus, avril 1970, no. 15.
Les Cahiers de l'Homme-Esprit, 1974, no. 3.
Narthex, mars-août 1978, nos. 21, 22, 23.
Dossiers "H." Editions L'Age d'Homme. Lausanne, 1983.
Les Cahiers de l'Herne. Paris, 1983.

2. Studies, biographies, etc.

Andruzac, Christophe. *René Guénon: La contemplation métaphysique et l'expérience du mystique.* Dervy, 1980.
Asfar, Gabriel. *René Guénon: A chapter of French symbolist thought in the twentieth century.* Dactylographié. Princeton University, Department of Romance Languages and Literatures, 1972.
Chacornac, Paul. *La vie simple de René Guénon.* Editions Traditionnelles, 1958, 1982.
Cologne, Daniel. *Julius Evola, René Guénon et le christianisme.* Ed. Vatré, 1978.
Desilets, André. *René Guénon, Index, bibliographie.* Québec: Les Presses de l'Université Laval, 1977.
James, Marie-France. *Esotérisme et christianisme autour de René Guénon.* Nouvelles Editions Latines, 1981.
Laurant, Jean-Pierre. *Le sens caché dans l'oeuvre de René Guénon.* Editions L'Age d'Homme, 1975.
Meroz, Lucien. *René Guénon ou la sagesse initiatique.* Plon, 1962.
René Guénon et l'actualité de la pensée traditionnelle. Actes du Colloque international de Cerisy-La-Salle (13–20 July 1973). Ed. du Baucens, 1977.
Serant, Paul. *René Guénon.* La Colombe, 1953. Le Courrier du Livre, 1977.
Tourniac, Jean. *Propos sur René Guénon.* Dervy, 1973.
Waterfield, Robin. *René Guénon and the Future of the West.* Crucible, G.B., 1987.

Works of Frithjof Schuon

Leitgedanken zur Urbesinnung. Orell Fussli Verlag, 1935.
De l'Unité transcendante des Religions. Paris: Gallimard, 1948. Paris: Seuil, 1968. Eng. trans. *The Transcendent Unity of Religions.* 1984.
L'Oeil du Coeur. Paris: Gallimard, 1950. Dervy, 1974.
Perspectives spirituelles et faits humains. Cahiers du Sud, 1953. Editions Maisonneuve et Larose, 1989. Eng. trans. *Spiritual Perspectives and Human Facts.* 1987.
Sentiers de Gnose. La Colombe, 1957. La Place Royale, 1987. Eng. trans. *The Sword of Gnosis* (principal contributor). 1974.
Castes et Races, suivi de *Principes et critères de l'Art universel.* Derain, 1957. Milan, Arche, 1979. Eng. trans. *Castes and Races.* 1982.
Les Stations de la Sagesse. Buchet-Chastel, 1958. Eng. trans. *Stations of Wisdom.* 1980.
Images de l'Esprit. Flammarion, 1961.
Comprendre l'Islam. Paris: Gallimard, 1961. Paris: Seuil, 1977. Eng. trans. *Understanding Islam.* 1972.
Regards sur les mondes anciens. Editions Traditionnelles, 1968. Eng. trans. *Light on the Ancient Worlds.* 1984.
Logique et Transcendance. Editions Traditionnelles, 1970. Eng. trans. *Logic and Transcendence.* 1975.
Forme et substance dans les religions. Dervy, 1975.
L'Ésotérisme comme principe et comme voie. Dervy, 1978. Eng. trans. *Esoterism as Principle and as Way.* 1981.
Le Soufisme, voile et quintessence. Dervy, 1980. Eng. trans. *Sufism: Veil and Quintessence.* 1981.
Du divin à l'humain. Courrier du Livre, 1981. Eng. trans. *From the Divine to the Human.* 1982.

Christianisme/Islam—Visions d'oecuménisme ésotérique. Milan: Arché, 1981. Eng. trans *Christianity/Islam: Essays on Esoteric Ecumenism.* 1985.
Sur les traces de la Religion perenne. Courrier du Livre, 1982. Eng. trans. *Survey of Metaphysics and Esoterism.* 1986.
Approches du phénomène religieux. Le Courrier du Livre, 1984.
Résumé de Métaphysique intégrale. Le Courrier du Livre, 1985.
Avoir un centre. Editions Maisonneuve et Larose, 1988. Eng. trans. *To Have a Center.* 1990.
Racines de la condition humaine. La Table Ronde, 1990. Eng. trans. *Roots of the Human Condition.* Forthcoming.
The Feathered Sun—Plains Indians in Art and Philosophy. World Wisdom Books, 1990.
Le jeu des masques. Editions L'Age d'Homme, 1992.

Collections of texts and anthologies

The Essential Writings of Frithjof Schuon. Edited by S. H. Nasr. World Wisdom books, 1986.
Les perles du pélerin. Edited by T. Béguelin. Paris: Seuil, 1990. Eng. trans. *Pearls of the Pilgrim.* Forthcoming.

Collections of poems

Tage- und Nächtebuch. Bern: Urs-Graf-Verlag, 1947.
Sulamith. Bern: Urs-Graf-Verlag, 1947.

Study

Religion of the Heart: Essays presented to Frithjof Schuon on his eightieth birthday. Edited by Seyyed Hossein Nasr and William Stoddart. Washington: Foundation for Traditional Studies, 1991.

13

G. I. Gurdjieff
and His School

JACOB NEEDLEMAN

LTHOUGH THERE IS an increasing recognition of the importance
of G. I. Gurdjieff in the spiritual landscape of the twentieth
century, his name continues to evoke a variety of reactions
throughout the world, ranging from awe and reverence to suspicion and hostility. It will no doubt be some time before a general cultural
consensus appears, and in this brief account we shall attempt only to survey
those aspects of his life and teaching that are of signal importance for
anyone approaching this influential spiritual teacher for the first time.

The Early Years

Of Gurdjieff's early life we know only what he has revealed in the autobiographical portions of his own writings, mainly *Meetings with Remarkable Men*. Although there is no reason to doubt the accuracy of his account,
the fact remains that the principal aim of Gurdjieff's writings was not to
provide historical information but to serve as a call to awakening and as a
continuing source of guidance for the inner search that is the *raison d'être*
of his teaching. Pending further discussion of the nature of this search, we
can say only that his writings are cast in forms that are directed not only
to the intellectual function but also to the emotional and even subconscious
sensitivities that, all together, make up the whole of the human psyche. His
writings therefore demand and support the search for a finer quality of self-
attention on the part of the reader, failing which the thought contained in
them is unverifiable at its deeper levels.

Gurdjieff was born probably in 1866 of a Greek father and an Armenian
mother in Alexandropol (now Gumri), Armenia, a region where Eastern
and Western cultures mixed and often clashed. The environment of his
childhood and early adolescence, while suggesting a near-biblical patriarchal

culture, is also marked by elements not usually associated with these cultural traditions. The portrait Gurdjieff draws of his father, a well-known *ashokh,* or bard, suggests some form of participation in an oral tradition stretching back to mankind's distant past. At the same time, Gurdjieff speaks of having been exposed to all the forms of modern knowledge, especially experimental science, which he explored with an impassioned diligence. The influence of his father and certain of his early teachers contrasts very sharply with the forces of modernity that he experienced as a child. This contrast, however, is not easily describable. The difference is not simply that of ancient versus modern worldviews or patterns of behavior, though it certainly includes that. The impression, rather, is that these "remarkable men" of his early years manifested a certain quality of personal presence or *being.* That the vital difference between human beings is a matter of their level of being became one of the fundamental elements in Gurdjieff's teaching and is not reducible to conventional psychological, behavioral, or cultural typologies.

Meetings with Remarkable Men shows us the youthful Gurdjieff journeying to monasteries and schools of awakening in remote parts of Central Asia and the Middle East, searching for knowledge about man that neither traditional religion nor modern science by itself could offer him. The clues to what Gurdjieff actually found on these journeys are subtly distributed throughout the narrative, rather than laid out in doctrinal form. Discursive statements of ideas are relatively rare in the book, and where they are given it is with a deceptive simplicity that serves to turn the reader back to the teachings woven in the narrative portions of the text. Repeated readings of *Meetings with Remarkable Men* yield the realization that Gurdjieff meant to draw our attention to the search itself and that what he intended to bring to the West was not only a new statement of what has been called "the primordial tradition," but the knowledge of *how* modern man might conduct his own search within the conditions of twentieth-century life. For Gurdjieff, as we shall see, the search itself, when rightly conducted, emerges as the principal spiritualizing force in human life, what one observer has termed "a transforming search," rather than "a search for transformation."[1]

Gurdjieff began his work as a teacher in Russia around 1912, on the eve of the civil war that led to the Russian Revolution. In 1914 he was joined by the philosopher P. D. Ouspensky and soon after by the well-known Russian composer Thomas de Hartmann. Ouspensky was later to produce *In Search of the Miraculous,* by far the best account of Gurdjieff's teaching written by a pupil or anyone other than Gurdjieff, while de Hartmann, working in a unique collaboration with Gurdjieff, would produce what has come to be called the "Gurdjieff/de Hartmann music," the qualities of

17. Gurdjieff.

which will be discussed below. Soon after, as the Revolution drew near and the coming breakdown of civil order began to announce itself, Gurdjieff and a small band of dedicated pupils, including Thomas and Olga de Hartmann, made perilous journeys to the Crimea and Tiflis. There they were joined by Alexandre and Jeanne de Salzmann, the former a well-known artist and theatrical designer and the latter a teacher of the Dalcroze system of rhythmic dance who was later to emerge as Gurdjieff's greatest pupil and the principal guide under whom his teaching continued to be passed on after his death in 1949. It was in Tiflis, in 1919, that Gurdjieff established the first version of his Institute for the Harmonious Development of Man.

The account by Ouspensky and notes by other pupils published in 1973 under the title *Views from the Real World* show that in the Moscow period, before the journey out of Russia, Gurdjieff tirelessly articulated a vast body of ideas about man and the cosmos. It is appropriate here to interrupt the historical narrative in order to summarize these formulations, which played an important role in the subsequent development of his teaching, even as Gurdjieff changed the outer forms and certain inner emphases in his direct work with pupils. Also, to a limited extent, these ideas throw light on developments that came later, some of which have given rise to unnecessary confusion in the minds of outside observers. One caveat, however, is necessary. If in his writings Gurdjieff never sought merely to spread out a philosophical system, all the more in his direct work with pupils did he mercilessly resist the role of guru, preacher, or schoolteacher. *In Search of the Miraculous* shows, with considerable force, that Gurdjieff always gave his ideas to his pupils under conditions designed to break through the crust of emotional and intellectual associations which, he taught, shut out the small voice of conscience in man. The exquisite and often awesome precision with which he was able to break through that crust—ways of behaving with his pupils that were, in turn, shocking, mysterious, frightening, magical, delicately gentle, and omniscient—remains one of the principal factors around which both the Gurdjieff legend and the misunderstandings about him have arisen, as well as being the element most written about by those who came in touch with him and most imitated in the current age of "new religions."

The Gurdjieff Ideas

It is true enough to say that Gurdjieff's system of ideas is complex and all-encompassing, but one must immediately add that their formulation is designed to point man toward a central and simple power of apprehension which Gurdjieff taught is merely latent within the human mind and which is the only power by which man can actually understand himself in relation to the universe. In this sense, the distinction between doctrine and method, which is fairly clear in most of the older spiritual traditions, does not yet entirely obtain in the Gurdjieff teaching. The formulations of the ideas are themselves meant to have a special action on the sense of self and may therefore be regarded as part of the practical method. This characteristic of the Gurdjieff teaching reflects what Gurdjieff perceived as the center of gravity of modern man's subjectivity—the fact that modern civilization is lopsidedly oriented around the thinking function. Modern man's illusory feeling of "I" is built up around his thoughts and therefore, in accordance with the level of the pupil, the ideas themselves are meant to affect this false sense of self. For Gurdjieff the deeply penetrating influence of scientific thought in modern life was not something merely to be deplored, but to be understood as the channel through which the eternal Truth must first find its way toward the human heart.

Man, Gurdjieff taught, is an undeveloped creation. He is not really man, considered as a cosmically unique being whose intelligence and power of action mirror the energies of the source of life itself. On the contrary, man as we encounter him is an automaton. His thoughts, feelings, and deeds are little more than mechanical reactions to external and internal stimuli. He cannot *do* anything. In and around him, everything *happens* without the participation of his own authentic consciousness. But human beings are ignorant of this state of affairs because of the pervasive influence of culture and education, which engrave in them the illusion of autonomous conscious selves. In short, man is asleep. There is no authentic *I am* in his presence, but only an egoism which masquerades as the authentic self, and whose machinations poorly imitate the normal human functions of thought, feeling, and will.

Many factors reinforce this sleep. Each of the reactions that proceed in one's presence is accompanied by a deceptive sense of I—man is many I's, each imagining itself to be the whole, and each buffered off from awareness of the others. Each of these many I's represents a process whereby the subtle energy of consciousness is absorbed and degraded, a process that Gurdjieff termed "identification." Man identifies—that is, squanders his conscious energy, with every passing thought, impulse, and sensation. This state of affairs takes the form of a continuous self-deception and a continuous procession of egoistic emotions, such as anger, self-pity, sentimentality, and fear which are of such a pervasively painful nature that man is constantly driven to ameliorate this condition through the endless pursuit of social recognition, sensory pleasure, or the vague and unrealizable goal of "happiness."

According to Gurdjieff, the human condition cannot be understood apart from considering humanity within the function of organic life on earth. The human being is constructed to transform energies of a specific nature, and neither his potential inner development nor his present actual predicament is understandable apart from this function. Thus, in the teaching of Gurdjieff, psychology is inextricably connected with cosmology and metaphysics and even, in a certain sense, biology. The diagram known as "the Ray of Creation" provides one of the conceptual keys to approaching this interconnection between humanity and the universal order, and as such invites repeated study from a variety of angles and stages of understanding.

In this diagram, the fundamental data about the universe gathered by science, and specifically the principal cosmic entities that modern astronomical observation has marked out, are arranged in a manner coherent with ancient metaphysical principles about humanity's actual place in the scheme of creation. The reader is referred to chapters 5, 7, and 9 in *In Search of the Miraculous* for an explanation of this diagram, but the point to be emphasized here is that, at the deepest level, the human mind and heart are enmeshed in a concatenation of causal influences of enormous scale and design. A study of the Ray of Creation makes it clear that the aspects of human nature through which one typically attempts to improve one's lot are without any force whatever within the network of universal influences that act upon man on earth. In this consists man's fundamental illusion, an illusion only intensified by the technological achievements of modern science. Man is simply unable to draw upon the conscious energies passing through him, which, in the cosmic scheme, are those possessing the actual power of causal efficacy. Man does not and cannot participate consciously in the great universal order, but instead is tossed about *en masse* for purposes limited to the functions of organic life on earth as a whole. Even in this relatively limited sphere—limited, that is, when compared to man's latent destiny—mankind has become progressively incapable of fulfilling its function, a point that Gurdjieff strongly emphasized in his own writings. This aspect of the idea of the Ray of Creation—namely, that the "fate of the earth" is somehow bound up with the possibility of the inner evolution of individual men and women—resonates with the contemporary sense of impending planetary disasters.

How are human beings to change this state of affairs and begin drawing on the universal conscious energies which they are built to absorb but which now pass through them untransformed? How is humanity to assume its proper place in the great chain of being? Gurdjieff's answer to these questions actually circumscribes the central purpose of his teaching—namely, that human life on earth may now stand at a major transitional point

ABSOLUTE	(1)	do
ALL WORLDS	(3)	si
ALL SUNS	(6)	la
SUN	(12)	sol
ALL PLANETS	(24)	fa
EARTH	(48)	mi
MOON	(96)	re
ABSOLUTE	▽	do

18. "The Ray of Creation" in the teaching of Gurdjieff: The Absolute is the fundamental source of all creation. From the Absolute the process of cosmic creation branches and descends (involves) according to an ordered sequence of increasing complexity and density, following the law of the octave. The universe as a whole comprises countless such branchings from the Absolute; this particular diagram represents the "ray" containing our planet earth.

comparable perhaps to the fall of the great civilizations of the past and that development of the whole being of man (rather than one or another of the separate human functions) is the only thing that can permit man to pass through this transition in a manner worthy of human destiny.

But whereas the descent of humanity takes place *en masse,* ascent or evolution is possible only within the individual. *In Search of the Miraculous* presents a series of diagrams dealing with the same energies and laws as the Ray of Creation, not only as a cosmic ladder of descent but also in their evolutionary aspect *within the individual.* In these diagrams, known collectively as the Food Diagram, Ouspensky explains in some detail how Gurdjieff regarded the energy transactions within the individual human organism. As in the Ray of Creation, the Food Diagram arranges the data of modern science, in this case the science of physiology, in a manner that subsumes these data naturally within the immensely vast scale of ancient metaphysical and cosmological principles. Again, the reader is referred to Ouspensky's book, the point being that humanity can begin to occupy its proper place within the chain of being only through an inner work with the specific intrapsychic energies that correspond to the higher energies in the cosmic order and which within the individual human being may be subsumed under the general term *attention.* The many levels of attention possible for man, up to and including an attention that in traditional teachings has been termed Spirit, are here ranged along a dynamic, vertical continuum that reaches from the level of biological sustenance which humans require for their physical bodies up to the incomparably finer sustenance that they require for the inner growth of the soul. This finer sustenance is termed "the food of impressions," a deceptively matter-of-fact phrase that eventually defines man's unique cosmic obligation and potentiality of constantly and in everything working for the development within himself of the divine attributes of devotion to the Good and objective understanding of the Real.

The Ray of Creation and the Food Diagram, extraordinary though they are, are only a small part of the body of ideas contained in *In Search of the Miraculous.* They are cited here as examples of how Gurdjieff not only restated the ancient, perennial teachings in a language adapted to the modern mind but also brought to these ancient principles something of such colossal originality that those who followed him detected in his teaching the signs of what in Western terminology may be designated a new revelation.

However, as was indicated above, the organic interconnection of the ideas in *In Search of the Miraculous* is communicated not principally through conceptual argument but as a gradual unfolding which Ouspensky experienced to the extent that there arose within him that agency of inner unity which Gurdjieff called "the real I," the activation of which required of

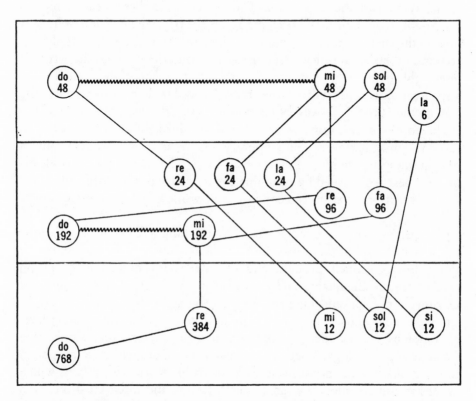

19. "The Food Diagram" in the teaching of Gurdjieff: the culmination of a series of diagrams illustrating the manner in which different qualities of energy are assimilated and evolve (following the law of the octave) in the human organism. This diagram represents the energy transactions in a moment of authentic consciousness.

Ouspensky a rigorous and ego-shattering inner work under the guidance of Gurdjieff and the group conditions he created for his pupils. Each of the great ideas in the book leads to the others. The Ray of Creation and the Food Diagram are inseparable from Gurdjieff's teaching about the fundamental law of three forces and the law of the sevenfold development of energy (the Law of Octaves), and the interrelation of these laws as expressed in the symbol of the *enneagram*. The reflection of these ideas in man is inseparable from Gurdjieff's teaching about the tripartite division of human nature, the three "centers" of mind, feeling, and body, and the astonishing account of how Gurdjieff structured the conditions of group work is inseparable from the idea of his work as a manifestation of the Fourth Way, a spiritual path distinct from the traditionally familiar paths termed "the way of the fakir," "the way of the monk," and "the way of the yogi."

The notion of the Fourth Way is one of the Gurdjieff ideas that have captured the imagination of contemporary people and have brought quite a new meaning to the idea of esotericism itself. The meaning of this idea is perhaps best approached by resuming the narrative of Gurdjieff's life, with special attention given to the conditions of work which he created for his pupils.

Gurdjieff's own written statement of his teaching will be discussed below. But first it should be reemphasized that the diagnosis of the human condition which Gurdjieff brought and the means for human regeneration revolve around the quality and level of man's *being*. This central aspect of Gurdjieff's mission and his person seems to beggar description in words. The cosmological ideas are only one indication that what is at issue is a level of consciousness and energy within man and the universe that is unknown to modern psychology. There exists a particular Gurdjieffian "atmosphere" in his own writings and in most accounts of his work with pupils, which evokes in some readers the same overall feeling and intellectual intuition that accompanies those unique experiences in life in which the whole sense of oneself, including one's familiar religious sense and sense of mystery, breaks down and when for a moment an unnameable emptiness and silence are experienced. The Gurdjieff teaching may perhaps be understood as a journey into and beyond that silence along with and by means of the demand to attend to the ordinary life of ourselves as we are. In any case, this central aspect of his teaching explains in part why at a certain level no comparisons of his teaching with traditional spiritualities are possible, while at deeper levels his ideas are being claimed by some activist followers of all the traditions and denied by others as spiritually invalid. The point is that this special "atmosphere" represents and manifests *being* and calls to that in a person which yearns for "something" that does not seem possible for one to find under most "known" forms of religion, science, psychology, and occultism.

After a brief period in Constantinople, Gurdjieff and his group of pupils made their way through Europe and finally settled in France where, in 1922, he established his Institute for the Harmonious Development of Man at the Chateau du Prieuré at Fontainebleau near Avon, just outside Paris. The brief, intense period of activity at the Prieuré has been described in numerous books, but even for those familiar with these accounts, the establishment and day-to-day activities of the Prieuré still evoke astonishment. It was during this period that Gurdjieff developed many of the methods and practices of group work that have retained a central place in the work of Gurdjieff pupils throughout the world today, including many of the movements or sacred dances that he reconstituted on the basis of his initiatic experience in monasteries and schools of awakening in Asia and the Levant. All serious accounts of the conditions Gurdjieff created at the Prieuré give the impression of a community life pulsating with the uncompromising search for truth engaging all sides of human nature—demanding physical work, intensive emotional interactions, and the study of a vast range of ideas about humanity and the universal world. These accounts invariably speak of the encounter with oneself that these conditions made possible and the experience of the self which accompanied this encounter.

The Prieuré attracted numerous artists and literary figures from America and England, many of whom were sent by P. D. Ouspensky who by that time had broken with Gurdjieff and was leading his own groups in London. Concerning his break with Gurdjieff, which is described with forceful compactness in *In Search of the Miraculous,* and pending a survey discussion below of Gurdjieff's leading pupils, there are many indications that at the deepest personal level Ouspensky maintained a spiritual connection with Gurdjieff. But, as one close observer has remarked,

> As early as 1918 . . . Ouspensky began to feel that a break with Gurdjieff was inevitable, that "he had to go"—to seek another teacher or to work independently. The break between the two men, teacher and pupil, each of whom received much from the other, has never been satisfactorily explained. They met for the last time in Paris in 1930.[2]

The rationale that lay behind the conditions Gurdjieff created for his pupils, that is to say, the idea of the Fourth Way, can perhaps be characterized by citing the descriptive brochure published at the Prieuré in 1922:

> The civilization of our time, with its unlimited means for extending its influence, has wrenched man from the normal conditions in which he should be living. It is true that civilization has opened up for man new paths in the

domain of knowledge, science and economic life, and thereby enlarged his world perception. But, instead of raising him to a higher all-round level of development, civilization has developed only certain sides of his nature to the detriment of other faculties, some of which it has destroyed altogether . . .

Modern man's world perception and his mode of living are not the conscious expression of his being taken as a complete whole. Quite the contrary, they are only the unconscious manifestation of one or another part of him.

From this point of view our psychic life, both as regards our world perception and our expression of it, fail to present a unique and indivisible whole, that is to say a whole acting both as a common repository of all our perceptions and as the source of all our expressions.

On the contrary, it is divided into three separate entities, which have nothing to do with one another, but are distinct both as regards their functions and their constituent substances.

These three entirely separate sources of the intellectual, emotional or moving life of man, each taken in the sense of the whole set of functions proper to them, are called by the system under notice the thinking, the emotional and the moving centers.[3]

It is difficult conceptually, and in a few words, to communicate the meaning of this idea of the three centers, which is so central to the Gurdjieffian path. The modern person simply has no conception of how self-deceptive a life can be that is lived in only one part of oneself. The head, the emotions, and the body each have their own perceptions and actions, and each, in itself, can live a simulacrum of human life. In the modern era this has gone to an extreme point and most of the technical and material progress of our culture serves to push the individual further into only one of the centers—one third, as it were, of one's real self-nature. The growth of vast areas of scientific knowledge is, according to Gurdjieff, outweighed by the diminution of the conscious space and time within which one lives and experiences oneself. With an ever-diminishing "I," man gathers an ever-expanding corpus of information about the universe. But to be human—to be a whole self possessed of moral power, will, and intelligence—requires all the centers, and *more*. This *more* is communicated above all in Gurdjieff's own writings in which the levels of spiritual development possible for man are connected with a breathtaking vision of the levels of possible service that the developing individual is called on to render to mankind and to the universal source of creation itself.

Thus, the proper relationship of the three centers of cognition in the human being is a necessary precondition for the reception and realization of what in the religions of the world has been variously termed the Holy Spirit, Atman, and the Buddha nature.

The conditions Gurdjieff created for his pupils cannot be understood apart from this fact. "I wished to create around myself," Gurdjieff wrote, "conditions in which a man would be continuously reminded of the sense and aim of his existence by an unavoidable friction between his conscience and the automatic manifestations of his nature."[4] Deeply buried though it is, the awakened conscience is the *something more* which, according to Gurdjieff, is the only force in modern man's nearly completely degenerate psyche that can actually bring parts of his nature together and open him to that energy and unnameable awareness of which all the religions have always spoken as the gift that descends from above, but which in the conditions of modern life is almost impossible to receive.

The most active period of the Prieuré lasted less than two years, ending with Gurdjieff's nearly fatal motor accident on July 6, 1924. In order to situate this period properly, it is necessary to look back once again to the year 1909 when Gurdjieff had finished his twenty-one years of traveling throughout Asia, the Middle East, Africa, and Europe meeting individuals and visiting communities who possessed knowledge unsuspected by most people. By 1909 Gurdjieff had learned secrets of the human psyche and of the universe that he knew to be necessary for the future welfare of humanity, and he set himself the task of transmitting them to those who could use them rightly. After trying to cooperate with existing societies, he decided to create an organization of his own. He started in 1911 in Tashkent, where he had established a reputation as a wonder-worker and an authority on "questions of the Beyond." He moved to Moscow in 1913 and after the revolution of February 1917 there began his astonishing journeys through the war-torn Caucasus region, principally Essentuki and Tiflis, leading a band of his pupils to Constantinople and finally to France, where he reopened his institute at the Chateau de Prieuré at Avon. His avowed aim during this period was to set up a worldwide organization for the dissemination of his ideas and the training of helpers. The motor accident of July 1924 occurred at this critical juncture.

When he began to recover from his injuries, Gurdjieff was faced with the sheer impossibility of realizing his plans for the institute. His health was shattered; he had no money; and many of his friends and pupils had abandoned him. He was a stranger in Europe, neither speaking its languages nor understanding its ways. He made the decision to find a new way of transmitting to posterity what he had learned about humanity, human nature, and human destiny. This was to be done by writing. His period as an author began in December of 1924 and continued until, in May 1935, he stopped writing and changed all his plans.

Gurdjieff's Writings

While he was still recuperating from his injuries, Gurdjieff began his work as a writer, dictating to his secretary Olga de Hartmann the opening lines of his most important book, *Beelzebub's Tales to His Grandson.* His two later books, *Meetings with Remarkable Men* and the unfinished *Life Is Real Only Then When 'I Am,'* have major aspects about them that are accessible only to pupils of the teaching—this is overwhelmingly true of the latter. But *Beelzebub* was written for the world.

It is an immense and unique work in every sense of the term. Cast as an allegory, it is the narrative of the once fiery rebel Beelzebub, who for his youthful indiscretion spent long years in our solar system, where, among his other activities, he had occasion to study that very minor planet Earth and its inhabitants. In these tales to his young grandson, Beelzebub comes back constantly to the causes of man's alienation from the sources of his own life and, at the same time, points in the direction toward which man could consciously evolve. Touching on one after another of the myriad aspects of human history from its earliest beginnings to modern times, Beelzebub continually brings his perceptions back to the same cosmic laws that govern both the working of nature and the psychic life of humans and, in so doing, bodies forth the picture of a living and conscious universe. In this universe, humanity, falling further away from an understanding of its source and the place it can occupy, has forgotten its function and lost all sense of its direction.

Beelzebub traces this failure with compassion and often with superb humor. His tenderness toward the undeveloped possibility represented by his grandson strikes the underlying note of the book, which is one of deep concern for the fulfillment of the individual human life.

This bare summary can give no impression of the extraordinary nature of this book. Intentionally written in complex, intricate style and making frequent use of strange-sounding neologisms, the book gradually yields its meanings only after repeated readings. Each reading of it opens new facets of Gurdjieff's teaching, not only in intellectual terms but at deep, subconscious levels.

Gurdjieff's Influence

During the writing of *Beelzebub's Tales,* Gurdjieff continued to live and receive pupils at the Prieuré and remained based there until 1933. During this period—between 1924 and 1933—A. R. Orage had gone to America, where he attracted a number of serious pupils, and where he made known the Gurdjieff teaching to some of America's leading artists and writers. At the same time, Ouspensky was in London lecturing and working to form his own school (it was through Ouspensky that Orage had first come into contact with the Gurdjieff teaching). Among the other well-known figures who studied under Ouspensky were Maurice Nicoll, Kenneth Walker, and P. L. Travers. Nicoll later went on to lead his own groups and write several influential books that reflected his work with the Gurdjieff ideas: *The New Man*, a pioneering study of the parables of Christ, and *Living Time*, which developed Ouspensky's theories about the dimensions of space and time.

In France, during the 1920s, Gurdjieff's institute had already suffered some notoriety when he accepted the dying Katherine Mansfield into the community of the Prieuré. Although Gurdjieff shunned publicity, a number of press accounts of life at the Prieuré, some foolish and slanderous, appeared in France and England in the early 1920s. After the automobile accident, however, and the consequent closing down of the intensive activities of the institute, Gurdjieff's work as a teacher attracted less public attention. In the late 1920s and early 1930s several other well-known writers became pupils, notably René Daumal, Margaret Anderson, and Kathryn Hulme. Daumal's writings, especially his unfinished masterpiece, *Mount Analogue*, are among the most vital and reliable literary expressions of certain key aspects of the Gurdjieff teaching.

In 1932 Gurdjieff left the Prieuré and settled in Paris, which was to remain his base until his death in 1949. By 1933, Orage had separated from Gurdjieff after some years of working with groups in America. He died in England in 1934. The work of Ouspensky, however, went on in London and then later also in New York. Ouspensky's book *Tertium Organum* had been published with considerable success in England in the early 1920s and had established his reputation as a writer about metaphysical subjects. This book, much of it written before he had met Gurdjieff, maintained its popularity throughout the 1930s and 1940s and deserves special consideration both as an important philosophical work in its own right and as a clue to the nature of Gurdjieff's influence upon those who became his close pupils.

Writing in the early part of the twentieth century, long before experiments with altered states of consciousness became a widespread aspect of the "new religions" movement, Ouspensky was seriously experimenting with altered states of consciousness and their effect on perception and cognition. His own experiences brought him to the conclusion that new forms and categories of thought were needed, quite apart from the two modes of thought (classical and positivistic) that had dominated Western civilization for over two thousand years. *Tertium Organum* is the fruit of these experiments. The book is dominated by the idea of higher dimensions, "eternal recurrence," and the insight that higher forms of knowledge must inevitably be associated with the development of the capacity for feeling—that is to say, the perception of truth is inseparable from the development of inner moral power. These basic ideas are developed in full in the book and, in one form or another, have entered as an influence into the writings of many modern philosophers and writers both in the West and in Russia. What distinguishes this book is not only the force of Ouspensky's vision but the fact that it was rooted in his own experience, rather than solely from reflecting on traditional ideas. Thus Ouspensky may be considered a modern pioneer in what can be called "inner empiricism," a mode of philosophizing about the kind of metaphysical issues which scientific thought has largely dismissed, but which retains the scientific attitude that seeks to base all theory on actual experience and carefully conducted experiments. Ouspensky's inner world was his own metaphysical laboratory.

Of particular significance here, however, is the fact that the book, written before Ouspensky became a pupil of Gurdjieff, contains numerous ideas and formulations which later appear intact in Ouspensky's account in *In Search of the Miraculous* as elements of the Gurdjieff teaching. This raises the question of the kind of help that Gurdjieff offered to those who followed him and shows the exceptional degree to which Ouspensky was prepared for such a teaching. In Ouspensky's case, there is no doubt that he opened himself to the vast body of new ideas which Gurdjieff brought forth. But it is also clear that, at the same time, he retained a great deal of his own previously acquired understanding of the human situation and the universal order. Somehow, under Gurdjieff, the questions that Ouspensky had wrestled with and the new ideas he had come to were now situated in a broader and more balanced perspective, taking on subtle new shadings that made them, in his mind, far more precise and integrated within an immensely more comprehensive worldview. When compared with *Tertium Organum*, *In Search of the Miraculous* does not, therefore, represent a rupture in Ouspensky's thinking so much as an extraordinary flowering of it, whereby it became, so to say, an instrument serving a new aim and the vehicle for another quality of energy. He began as an imposing thinker, and after Gurdjieff he remained a powerful thinker who has also become a different kind of man. Comparable observations are germane as well in the case of the composer Thomas de Hartmann, the quality of whose musical talent underwent an astonishing transformation under Gurdjieff.

These observations may be of help to anyone trying to assess the extent and nature of Gurdjieff's influence, both on those who worked with him and on those who have come after him, as well as his place in spiritual currents of modern civilization. Much grief is in store for investigators who try to trace Gurdjieff's influence on the culture under more conventional rubrics. It is true that a growing number of people now espouse what might be called a Gurdjieffian philosophy or psychology, but to focus on this aspect of his influence is to miss the essential aspect of his work and the only true standard by which his impact on our culture can really be measured. Like the founders of every great spiritual path, he sought to awaken rather than to indoctrinate. The course of his life as teacher does not follow the logic of an individual seeking merely to spread a doctrine.

When, therefore, it is admitted that Gurdjieff's influence has affected a great many fields and disciplines—such as religion, literature, psychology, philosophy, the visual arts, music, dance, etc.—it must be added that this influence does not represent a fanatical adherence to "Gurdjieffian" standards or ideals which are alien to the field at hand. The influence of Gurdjieff would show itself, rather, in certain underlying values and concerns—that is to say, in a deeper understanding of the work at hand rather than an eccentric understanding.

How, then, to regard the most externally visible ways in which his ideas and formulations have entered into modern culture? It can be argued, for example, that the world "consciousness" acquired the spiritual connotations which it now has because of Gurdjieff's use of the term to designate an aspect of the mind higher than ordinary thought. Or, as mentioned above, it is clear that his notion of the Fourth Way, that is, a rigorous spiritual discipline conducted in the midst of an individual's ordinary life activities, has been adopted by numerous religious and psychoreligious groups throughout the West. His emphasis on the role of self-observation has also had widespread influence, to the extent that there is a vague, but common, understanding among spiritual seekers today that the alternatives of introspection or positivistic behaviorism by no means exhaust the possibilities of one's ability to study and know oneself. In addition, modern concepts of group dynamics were strongly influenced by what he brought; indeed, the whole idea of the need for group work in order to affect psychological or behavioral change of any kind may be traced, in part, to Gurdjieff's emphasis on the group, rather than the Oriental guru–disciple relationship, as indispensable to Western spiritual development. But just as Gurdjieff's influence cannot be measured by the number of individuals who espouse his ideas, neither can his influence on the culture be measured by verbal formulations or concepts which he originated and which enjoy a certain fashion. Either Gurdjieff helped to create authentic men and women or he did not. The extent to which he did so is the extent to which his influence is to be valued.

Gurdjieff's School

Having opened the question of how to regard the influence of Gurdjieff, it is now possible to speak briefly about the chief means by which his influence may become a factor in our civilization. Obviously the term "school," when applied to the Gurdjieff teaching, does not and cannot refer only to a loosely connected group of followers sharing intellectual beliefs or attitudes. The term has a very precise meaning in the Gurdjieff teaching, somewhat akin to the meaning of "monastery," "ashram," or "brotherhood" as they are used in the history of religions tradition, or as they are applied, say, to the school of Pythagoras or the schools of the medieval and Renaissance painters. It is through a group of individuals studying and working together at varying levels that the transmission of his teaching was intended to take place. As has already been noted, it is clear that he did not believe Western man could be spiritually helped past a certain point by the traditional Eastern forms of relationship between a guru and an individual pupil. At the same time, he strongly emphasized that guidance was indispensable and that no one individual could hope to attain liberation working alone. A "school," considered to be a dynamic ordering of precise moral, psychological, and physical conditions within which a relatively small number of individuals can interact for the sake of self-development, became the principal form of transmission. Only such conditions, Gurdjieff taught, could allow older, more experienced pupils to pass on their understanding as part of their own inner work, while enabling all parties to take into account the ever-present tendencies to inattention, suggestibility, and fantasy. The Gurdjieff "school" thus represents an attempt to establish a school of awakening specifically adapted to modern life--with all the tension and paradox that phrase suggests when taken within the overwhelmingly materialistic context of modern civilization, that is, its overwhelming and omnipresent tendency to draw men and women out of themselves toward externals, instead of calling them back to the sources of the spirit.

Although a number of well-known individuals have been and are associated with the Gurdjieff *Work*, as the school is called following the meaning of the word in the alchemical tradition, many of Gurdjieff's leading pupils have chosen to remain unknown to the public, as have many of the leaders who represent the second and third generation of the teaching. Attempts to portray the nature of the membership by citing only those figures known to the public can therefore be misleading. As a general rule, those engaged in the Work pursue their ordinary lives without calling attention to their affiliation.

The Gurdjieff Foundation

After Gurdjieff's death in Paris in 1949, his work was carried on by his closest pupil and collaborator, Jeanne de Salzmann, under whose guidance centers of study were gradually established in Paris, New York, London, and Caracas. Over the past thirty years other centers of work have radiated from them in major cities of the Western world. The pupils living in America established the Gurdjieff Foundation of New York in 1953. Shortly thereafter, groups were started on the West Coast and in Canada. Similar branches of varying size have been formed throughout the world and at present there may be between five and ten thousand persons in the Americas, Europe, Asia, Africa, Australia, and the Middle East studying this teaching under the guidance of pupils who worked personally with Gurdjieff when he was alive. The main centers of study remain Paris, New York, and London because of the relatively large concentration of first-generation Gurdjieff pupils in these cities. Other groups maintain close correspondence with the principal centers, usually in relationship to one or two of the pupils who often travel to specific cities in order to guide the work of these groups. The general articulation of these various groups, both within America and throughout the world, is a cooperative one, rather than one based on strictly sanctioned jurisdictional control.

The Foundation offers its students a variety of activities whose form and emphasis change to some extent in response to cultural conditions and individual needs. Usually, inquiries and experiments are conducted in small groups under conditions that have the potential for developing in each individual the faculty of attention. As has already been indicated, the Gurdjieff teaching offers a remarkably comprehensive psychology of levels of attention and a many-sided practical method for developing access to this power in relationship to the three basic sources of perception in the human psyche—the three centers.

From the outset, pupils are encouraged and assisted in the study of the liberation of attention, which remains unexplored in the conditions of modern life. Such work is understood to be indispensable for what Gurdjieff called "self-observation." In fact, as has also been indicated, Gurdjieff taught that this is a universal and essential discipline, which was conveyed by Socrates and ancient teachings in the words of the Delphic oracle—"Know thyself"— as well as in the Gospels under the cryptic one-word command *gregoreite* (awake) and in Buddhism under the designation *nana dhasana* (vision). But although clear enough to initiates in these ancient traditions, it is practically inaccessible to a modern Western-educated individual. The many and various forms of work offered by the Gurdjieff Foundation are understood as a way for modern people to grasp and put into practical use this discipline which is said to be literally indispensable to real progress in the regenerate life.

The Gurdjieff Foundation approaches the question of obedience and authority, which is of such concern in the modern world, in this context. By voluntarily subjecting oneself to such a work of self-study, the student may come to realize that not only is one responsible for one's own work and that on one level the student can and must rely only on himself or herself but also that on a larger scale the student is entirely dependent on the help of others similarly engaged. Thus, in essence and in actual practice, nothing is given to a student unless the student asks for it, and then only after the student has studied the theory of the teaching sufficiently to understand intellectually the nature of the help being asked for.

Related to this orientation is the basic Gurdjieff idea of a "Way in Life," which, as has been mentioned, has exerted considerable influence, under varying interpretations, on many new religious and psychological movements in the Western world. As practiced by the Foundation, it means that the student seeks to understand life as it is, without attempting to alter anything in the name of inner development. Relationships to family, vocation, personal ties, and obligations are, at least to start with, left intact both for the material they provide for self-understanding and for the ultimate value and force that all human relationships contain when they are engaged in with a more central and harmonious attention.

The activities of the Foundation include the study of the Gurdjieff ideas, group meetings, study of the movements and sacred dances left by Gurdjieff, music, crafts and household work, the study of traditions, public demonstrations of work, and work with children and young people.

In group meetings students verify the authenticity of their observations through expressing them in the presence of others. The place of group leader is taken by one or several experienced pupils, and great care is taken that these meetings do not revolve around the person of the leader or turn into speculative, psychological discussions or encounters. These meetings have little in common with either group therapy sessions or with religious/ spiritual meetings in their known forms.

Crafts and household work are engaged in principally as a means of throwing light on the details of everyday life and to expose the cumulative force of self-illusion and passivity that holds sway even in the most "favorable" stations of life.

Gurdjieff reconstituted the "movements" exercises he had met with in Central Asia for his own pupils under intensive conditions of inner discipline. Through the guidance of Jeanne de Salzmann and Jessmin Howarth, the Foundation has taken precautions to transmit these exercises under comparable conditions as part of the central aim of developing the moral and spiritual power of individuals through the study and growth of the attention factor in the human organism. It is assumed that without the help of prepared teachers and without a solid connection to the ideas and the inner work, the practice of the movements cannot give the results intended. Therefore, at present, the movements are studied mainly at the principal established centers. Under Jeanne de Salzmann, a series of films documenting the movements has been made in order to preserve a record of the quality of inner work that the movements demand.

Group meeting and, where they are taught, the movements are comparatively invariant forms of practice of the Gurdjieff Foundation. The numerous other forms show more variety from center to center, depending on the makeup of the group and the specific line of inquiry that is held to be most useful at a given time or place.

The membership of the Gurdjieff Foundation worldwide exhibits considerable diversity with respect to social class, age, occupation, and educational background, although exact statistics are unavailable. Like Gurdjieff himself during his life, the Foundation attracts the interest of a surprisingly wide variety of people.

Notes

1. Review of the film *Meetings With Remarkable Men,* in *Material for Thought* 8 (Spring 1980) 86 (San Francisco: Far West Editions).
2. John Pentland, entry on P. D. Ouspensky in *The Encyclopedia of Religion* (New York: Macmillan, 1987) 11:143.
3. *G. Gurdjieff's Institute for the Harmonious Development of Man: Prospectus No. 1,* p. 3 (privately printed, ca. 1922).
4. G. I. Gurdjieff, *Meetings with Remarkable Men,* 270.

Bibliography

There now exists a vast and growing body of literature relating to Gurdjieff. Readers wishing to pursue the secondary literature are referred to the excellent and comprehensive *Gurdjieff: An Annotated Bibliography,* by J. Walter Driscoll and The Gurdjieff Foundation of California (New York: Garland, 1985).

Sources

Gurdjieff, G. I. *Beelzebub's Tales to His Grandson: An Objectively Impartial Criticism of the Life of Man.* New York: Dutton, 1978.
———. *Life is Real Only Then, When "I Am."* New York: Dutton, 1982.
———. *Meetings with Remarkable Men.* New York: Dutton, 1969.

——. *Views from the Real World: Early Talks in Moscow, Essentuki, Tiflis, Berlin, London, Paris, New York and Chicago.* As recollected by his pupils. New York: Dutton, 1975.

Studies

Bennett, William. *Gurdjieff: Making a New World.* New York: Harper & Row, 1976.

Daumal, René. *Mount Analogue: An Authentic Narrative.* Boston: Shambhala, 1986.

Hartmann, Thomas de. *Our Life with Mr. Gurdjieff.* San Francisco: Harper & Row, 1983.

Moore, James. *Gurdjieff: The Anatomy of a Myth.* Dorset, England: Element Books, 1991. [I am grateful to Mr. Moore for his help in establishing the chronology of Gurdjieff's life.]

Nicoll, Maurice. *Living Time.* Boulder and London: Shambhala, 1984.

——. *The New Man.* Boston and London: Shambhala, 1986.

Ouspensky, P. D. *In Search of the Miraculous: Fragments of an Unknown Teaching.* New York: Harcourt, Brace, 1949.

——. *A New Model of the Universe.* New York: Random House, 1971.

——. *Tertium Organum.* New York: Alfred A. Knopf, 1981.

——. *The Psychology of Man's Possible Evolution.* New York: Random House, 1981.

Vaysse, Jean. *Toward Awakening: An Approach to the Teaching Left by Gurdjieff.* New York: Arkana, 1990.

Webb, James. *The Harmonious Circle.* New York: Putnam's, 1980.

14

C. G. Jung in the Context
of Christian Esotericism
and Cultural History

GERHARD WEHR

SSOCIATING CARL GUSTAV JUNG (1875–1961), the founder of
analytical or archetypal psychology, with Christian esotericism
is not entirely without its problems. Jung never saw himself as
an "esoteric"; at any rate he did not want to be confused with
those pseudo-esoterics who veil the mysteries of human beings and the
world, nature, spirit, and psyche in a secretive way and declare themselves
the ones who are "knowing" and "initiated."[1]

Jung saw himself primarily as a doctor who was concerned with the
sickness of human beings and his time. He saw himself as a psychotherapist
concerned for cures that corresponded to the reality of particular suffering.
Psychopathological investigations led him to raise historical symbols and
figures from the dust of their graves. Above all he was concerned to incor-
porate into his researches, indeed to make the focus of his studies, those
dimensions of the unconscious which point far beyond the individual with
his or her personal problems. This special attention to the transpersonal or
collective unconscious directed his attention to basic themes and contents
of the esotericism of all times, in both religious and cultural history. Jung
was not the first to be struck by the fact that, for example, there are
products of the unconscious, like dreams, which have parallels with myths
or with religious traditions and images of revelation. Beyond question it
was Jung's achievement to demonstrate the inner correspondence between
individual spiritual and psychological experiences and the spiritual traditions of the peoples and make fruitful use of them in connection with
human healing or self-realization (individuation). This is already to enter
the sphere of esotericism. Accordingly depth psychologists and psycho-
therapists cannot function without a careful knowledge of spiritual and

cultural associations. They are themselves drawn into the event, the content of which is the texts and traditions, the images and symbols.

Thus one may speak of Jung's connection with esotericism—specifically with Christian esotericism—and cultural history in two ways: (1) In his extensive life's work Jung made a thorough survey of religious and cultural history. He took motives and contents from the spiritual tradition both to compare and to interpret the products of the unconscious, not only the unconscious of his patients but his own and that of all those who were concerned for a deeper knowledge of themselves. (2) The experience of depth psychology, the process of individuation that must be undergone, is itself an esoteric event which changes people to the depth of their being, extends their consciousness, and brings their personality to the maturity of the whole person. The comparison with the processes of transformation and initiation in the mysteries of antiquity but also in the processes of transmutation in mysticism and alchemy are obvious. C. G. Jung exploited this possibility to an abundant degree. To become clear about this, one has to see how this happens only in one or other of his main works, for example, *Psychology and Alchemy* (1944), *Aion* (1951), *Symbols of Transformation* (1952), *Answer to Job* (1952) or the great work of his old age, *Mysterium Coniunctionis* (1955).

Even if we keep in mind that Jung's concerns to evaluate esoteric material are motivated by his work in psychology and psychotherapy, it nevertheless cannot be denied that Jung's works to a large extent also open up valuable perspectives to anyone who approaches these books with problems relating to theology and the history of religion and culture, or with an interest in their esoteric aspects. So it is not surprising that there are dialogical and synoptic contributions from these specialist fields in particular; I am referring to works in which the attempt is made at a conversation between the disciplines (e.g. the study of religion, theology, mythology, anthroposophy, etc.) or at a survey of the insights which are gained in both areas.[2]

Encounter and Discussion with Christian Esotericism

C. G. Jung came into contact with relevant literature at a fairly early stage. In his autobiographical comments *Memories, Dreams, Reflections* he recalls his student days, in which he was already preoccupied with the question of the reality of the soul. Whereas philosophy had nothing to say about the objective nature of the soul, he arrived at his first conclusions from quite another side:

The observations of the spiritualists, weird and questionable as they seemed to me, were the first accounts I had seen of objective psychic phenomena. Names like Zoellner and Crookes impressed themselves on me, and I read virtually the whole of the literature available to me at the time. . . . The world gained depth and background. Could, for example, dreams have anything to do with ghosts? Kant's *Dreams of a Spirit Seer* came just at the right moment.[3]

Nor was that to be all, since soon there were added the writings of the Munich philosopher and psychologist Carl du Prel (1839–1899). With his book *Rätsel des Menschen* (*The Human Riddle*, 1892), he provided a brief introduction to occultism. As a collaborator on the journal *Sphinx*, edited in Germany from 1886 by Wilhelm Hübbe-Schleiden, C. du Prel had made contact with the theosophical movement in Germany, an offshoot of H. P. Blavatsky's Theosophical Society. However, Jung himself did not find this Anglo-Indian Theosophy congenial. During his university studies he was much more interested in the writings of Carl Eschenmayer, the Frankfurt doctor Johann Carl Passavant, the Swabian doctor Justinus Kerner, who made a name for himself through his account of "Prevost's Seer," and the books of Joseph Görres, who was interested in the history of myths and mysteries. These references point to a group of people who with Schelling, Franz von Baader, Gotthilf Heinrich Schubert and others devoted themselves to romantic natural philosophy and psychology. Moreover, Jung did not omit to point out in his biographical account that at that time he had also read "seven volumes of Swedenborg." And it is no surprise that Goethe's *Faust* began to fascinate the rising doctor and psychologist.

All this opened up the way to his later activity, at least on the speculative side. The young C. G. Jung regarded the principle of experience as even more important than speculation. He experimented with a medium.[4] These early studies found expression in his medical doctoral dissertation "On the Psychology and Pathology of Supposed Occult Phenomena." Of course, for Jung these were only preliminary and provisional stages of his real career as a doctor and researcher into depth psychology. But he had a sense of the esoteric from his early childhood days. On reading the first chapter of *Memories, Dreams, Reflections* one gets the impression of a searcher attempting to understand his inner experience with the help of spiritual texts from the past, especially since there is no one around him who could help him as a kind of spiritual director. He must, so to speak, give birth to this guru, this spiritual director, from himself, a necessity and a process that were to continue into the crisis period of Jung's mid-life. The world of dreams and imagination kept breaking into the external events of his life and calling. In his autobiography he says of himself: "These form the *prima materia* of my scientific work. They were the fiery magma out of which the stone that had to be worked was crystallized."[5] For Jung the "stone" is a symbol of a particular kind, namely, the *"lapis philosophorum,* the Philosophers' Stone," for which the esoteric alchemists had striven.

Jung's mid-life crisis was characterized by an event that was to be a turning point for him and the beginning of his self-discovery: his separation from Sigmund Freud (1912/1913). For Jung it was not just a matter of rejecting the exaggerated sexual theory of his teacher or making it presentable. From then on, two factors and elements of Christian esotericism above all became important for him: the central theme of the new birth or rebirth as a birth "from above" (in terms of John 3) instead of the Freudian incest theory, and the Damascus event. In both cases human beings experience a far-reaching change.☐For whereas the Christian with an exoteric orientation is concerned to receive the sacrament and blessing from a consecrated priest who is in the apostolic succession, a Christian esoteric like the apostle Paul lives by the immediacy of the divine spirit; he lives by the fact that Christ is *in him* (Galatians 2:20). Like Paul (Galatians 1), he or she is relatively independent of church tradition.

However, in order to interpret and integrate his own experiences breaking in on him from the unconscious in dreams and imagination, after his break with Freud, Jung looked around for historical prefigurations in which inner experience is in some way "prefigured." He is concerned to decipher the "primal" or archetypal images and symbols that rise up in him as landmarks on the inner way toward the maturing of the soul (individuation). For years Jung was deeply concerned with the documents of early Christian Gnosticism. These were primarily the texts (for the most part preserved only in fragments) of those esoteric Christians who in some cases from about the middle of the first century and in others from the middle of the second century saw Gnosis (spiritual knowledge) as a way which helped the sparks of the soul imprisoned in the earthly body to become conscious of themselves and thus paved the way for redemption and a return to the realm of light.

In the 1920s Jung had to recognize that the gulf in consciousness which separates a second-century Gnostic from a twentieth-century man or woman in search of self-knowledge is too great. In these texts, what is dominant above all is speculation about original spiritual experience. It is significant for the history of spirituality that quite unexpectedly, a way out opened up for Jung from the side of East Asian spirituality. Through the Sinologist Richard Wilhelm, in 1928 Jung made the acquaintance of a Taoist text which should be regarded as an alchemistic tractate, *The Secret of the Golden Flower.*[7] This text made it possible for the psychologist to pick up the lost thread again. But instead of following the Sinologist and from then on borrowing from the world of Asiatic spirituality, Jung turned to medieval alchemy, that is, to a specifically Western form of Christian esotericism. In *Memories, Dreams, Reflections* he has this to say:

> My encounter with alchemy was decisive for me, as it provided me with the historical basis which I had hitherto lacked. . . . As far as I could see, the tradition that might have connected Gnosis with the present seemed to have been severed, and for a long time it proved impossible to find any bridge that led from Gnosticism—or neo-Platonism—to the contemporary world. But when I began to understand alchemy, I realized that it represented the historical link with Gnosticism, and that a continuity therefore existed between past and present. Grounded in the natural philosophy of the Middle Ages, alchemy formed the bridge on the one hand into the past, to Gnosticism, and on the other into the future, to the modern psychology of the unconscious. . . .
>
> When I pored over these old texts everything fell into place: the fantasy-images, the empirical material I had gathered in my practice, and the conclusions I had drawn from it. I now began to understand what these psychic contents meant when seen in historical perspective. My understanding of their typical character, which had already begun with my investigation of myths, was deepened. The primordial images and the nature of the archetype took a central place in my researches, and it became clear to me that without history there can be no psychology, and certainly no psychology of the unconscious.[8]

Yet again, it must be stressed that Jung looked at these trends of an esoteric Christianity not as, say, a historian of culture or of the spirit but as someone who for years had been confronted with the products of his unconscious, which were endangering his psychic balance. So threatening was this imagination in detail that Jung called it the *prima materia* for a life's work. There is no question that over and above his specific aims in psychotherapy, he has made available to the cultural historian material that is as strange as it is valuable—for example, in his studies of the alchemical circle of forms and canon of symbols.

Thus Jung proves to be not just someone who is familiar with Christian esotericism because such content appears abundantly in his books and is interpreted by him as a physician of souls in his work of psychotherapy. For what is important here is not what is consciously presented to individuals, but only what so extends the consciousness that human existence with all its light and dark sides can be affirmed and shaped, and the meaningfulness of life can be experienced. Experience of self and experience of God correspond on this level. The focus of the doctor, like that of the spiritual director, is on experience, and this is a central category of the esoteric.

Now it should be accepted that Jung's analytical psychology does not raise any kind of religious claims, not even claims that might be interpreted as the rivalry of one esoteric movement or another. Indeed, simply to preserve its scientific character, it must be concerned to keep clear of any influence stemming from a religion or worldview. Above all, the sphere of freedom for human individuality must be respected in the psychotherapeutical process. So there can be no question of suggestion or indoctrination.

Alongside this, another fact of experience needs to be taken into account in the narrower definition of what is religious. On the one hand, it is the case that sometimes the earliest legacy of the human soul can emerge in archetypal images: this is not to be confused with the remnants of personal recollection of the personal unconscious (for example, in dreams). One might think, for example, of a pagan pre-Christian symbolism, or of theriomorphic motives (motives in animal form). On the other hand, the Christ phenomenon of the psyche of Western individuals has sometimes made a far deeper mark than is assumed. Thus pagan motives and Christian mentality are set side by side in the unconscious of Western men and women. A contemporary who in his or her everyday religious awareness seems to be particularly religious may have dreams that can have a truly pagan and barbaric stamp. On the other hand, declared atheists can be very much more "Christian" in their unconscious than they themselves suspect.

There is another aspect that should be taken into account in this connection. The fashionable trend as a result of which Eastern and Near Eastern spirituality has been revered in the West as a kind of substitute religion or as a substitute for a church proclamation that has become ineffective can easily mislead us about the deeper situation. For preoccupation with Asiatic philosophies and methods of training in spirituality (Zen, Yoga, etc.) and religions, however intensive, cannot alter the fact that the Christian image of God has left clear traces in the unconscious of Western men and women. Conversely, the Asian who is turning toward Western life-style and civilization should not succumb to the illusion that in this way basic attitudes of religion and worldview are done away with and that it is possible to become assimilated to Western men and women. As a rule this adaptation comes about only on the level of rational everyday awareness and not in the depths of the soul. An external religious "conversion" all too often proves to be a delusion.

Jung himself gives an example of what I have just said in his autobiographical reflections. It proves how deeply he felt that he was rooted in specifically esoteric Christian spirituality. During his journey to India in the 1930s Jung had abundant opportunity to study the makeup of the soul and spirit of Indian men and women and to experience the impressive testimony of Asian spirituality at first hand. In *Memories, Dreams, Reflections* he reports on the "overwhelming variety of impressions of India" but also on how he was visited by a surprising dream in which he had to swim alone and unaided across a channel to get the "Grail." Thus his own unconscious had again called him back into the sphere of Christian esotericism. He himself comments on the experience in his dream:

> This fact had impressed me all the more when I realized the concordance between this poetic myth and what alchemy had to say about the *unum vas* (the one vessel), the *una medicina* (the one medicine), and the *unus lapis* (the one philosopher's stone). Myths which day has forgotten continue to be told by night. . . . The dream wiped away all the intense impressions of India and swept me back to the too-long-neglected concerns of the Occident, which had formerly been expressed in the quest for the Holy Grail as well as in the search for the philosopher's stone.

And now there follows in Jung's account the sentence that contains the definition of his spiritual position in respect of his relationship to Christian spirituality. He continues:

> I was taken out of the world of India, and reminded that India was not my task, but only a part of the way—admittedly a significant one—which should carry me closer to my goal. It was as though the dream were asking me, "What are you doing in India? Rather seek for yourself and your fellows the healing vessel, the *salvator mundi* (saviour of the world), which you urgently need. For your state is perilous; you are all in imminent danger of destroying all that centuries have built up."[9]

Without doubt the dream and its interpretation express in an unmistakable way how Jung's work itself belongs in the living tradition of Christian esotericism. Here it is not a matter of the work of an early Christian Gnostic or one who retells or fashions stories of the Grail, but a contemporary physician. Aniela Jaffe, Jung's longtime colleague and biographer, commented on the special significance of alchemy:

> Alchemy could hardly have formed such a broad basis for Jung's researches into the unconscious and its forms and played so decisive a role as the historical test of his knowledge had there not been a genuine affinity between him and the adepts of the old Hermetic world. . . . However, in contrast to the alchemists, for Jung the fascination was not the material but the soul. For the scientist it was the object of strict empirical research; as a doctor he allowed it to offer help from deep understanding; as a human being he was a master and servant of its changes.[10]

This judgment by Aniela Jaffe is adequately backed up by Jung's own testimony. Thus he once commented in amazement that the experiences of the old masters of alchemy had been basically his own. If they experimented in the alchemists' kitchen, by going through the stages on the way to the Philosopher's Stone and the great Arcanum (the great mystery of the adepts), in Jung a similar psychic process took place, rich in inner trials and upheavals: "The process through which I had passed at that time corresponded to the process of alchemical transformation."[11]

What he means is particular phases of individuation which include the confrontation with one's own darkness (shadow) and the confrontation with the image of the soul of the opposite sex: the *animus* in the case of the woman and the *anima* in the case of the man.

So Jung takes his place in the circle of those who experience the process of a change of personality as an esoteric development in oneself, in order to be able to offer leadership and guidance on this inner way to others. Anyone who compares similar remarks about the process in Jacob Boehme will be surprised at the parallelism between what is depicted in the two instances.[12] What distinguishes Jung and Boehme from one another is their different position in the history of consciousness—quite apart from their personal destiny and role in life. Boehme's *Weg zu Christo*, which in a work of the same name he denotes by the Latin title *Christosophia* and elucidated in more detail in his *Theosophical Letters*,[13] may have been timely in the first quarter of the seventeenth century. It is still impressive today. That is also true of the Rosicrucian manifestos of the Swabian Johann Valentin Andreae (*Fama Fraternitatis; Confessio Fraternitatis; Chymische Hochzeit Christiani Rosenkreutz*),[14] which formed the basis of Rosicrucianism and which Jung mentioned a number of times. The Jungian way to individuation, which leads to the formation and knowledge of the human self, is contemporary to the degree that in the postconfessional age it guides both Christians and non-Christians, religious and nonreligious, to the reality of the soul and the spirit, without ruling out external—for example, church—forms of piety. And it is precisely here that one of the great significances of modern Christian esotericism lies, as it was practiced by Jung as a doctor of the soul and as a depth analyst.

Now and again Jung made very skeptical remarks about "Christianity" — it would be wrong to overlook the quotation marks which he himself uses! However, these remarks relate primarily to the Christianity of the church, which he came to know thoroughly in all its dark side as the son of a Protestant Reformed pastor. Jung did not simply outgrow at an early stage this exoteric form, which all too often calls for faith and fails to note the value of personal religious experience. He continually looked hopefully toward a possibility of the growth of the Christian myth. Here Jung went so far as to compare the psychology of the unconscious with an "incarnation or realization of the Logos" (that is, the pneumatic Christ). In a letter of August 24, 1953, to the former Greek Orthodox priest Gerhard P. Zacharias, in which this is hinted at, Jung actually wrote:

As Origen understands Holy Scripture as the body of the Logos, so the psychology of the unconscious is also to be interpreted as a manifestation of reception. Here, however, the Christ image which was formerly known has not made an appearance through human mediation, but the transcendental ("total") Christ has made itself a new, more specific body. The kingdom of Christ or the realm of the Logos is "not of this world," but a meaning which transcends the world.[15]

And even at the age of fifty-eight Jung wrote to a reader in London:

I am aware of my unconventional way of thinking and understand that it gives the impression that I am not a Christian. But I regard myself as a Christian, since my thinking is wholly rooted in Christian conceptions. In precise terms, I regard myself as a Christian, but I am at the same time convinced that present-day Christianity does not represent the ultimate truth; that is demonstrated by the chaotic situation of our time. The present situation seems to me to be intolerable; therefore I think that a fundamental further development of Christianity is absolutely necessary.[16]

Confrontation with Eastern Spirituality

When I said that even during his stay in India Jung felt himself to be intrinsically bound up with Christianity, I did not mean that he had closed himself to Eastern spirituality. Rather, his name is a symbol of great openness to any form of psychical or spiritual experience. For example, one significant indication of his attitude to the spirituality of the East is the address which he gave on May 10, 1930, in Munich on the occasion of the memorial service for Richard Wilhelm. In it he said that for any understanding of Asian spirituality and culture it was necessary to overcome existing prejudices and at the same time be open to alien spiritualities; that is, there was a need for an "understanding dedication, beyond all Christian resentment, beyond all European arrogance." He knows from experience that "all average figures lose themselves either by blindly uprooting of themselves or in an equally uncomprehending search for blame." Moreover:

The spirit of Europe is not helped merely by new sensations or a titillation of the nerves. What it has taken China thousands of years to build cannot be acquired by theft. If we want to possess it we must earn the right to it by working on ourselves. Of what use to us is the wisdom of the Upanishads, or the insight of Chinese Yoga, if we desert our own foundations as though they were errors outlived and settle with thievish intent on foreign shores like homeless pirates?[17]

Jung is no less clear in his remarks when in this connection he points to the need to expand the European concept of *Wissenschaft*, academic science or discipline, and then continues:

> We need a truly three-dimensional life if we are to experience the wisdom of China as living. Therefore we probably first need European wisdom about ourselves. Our way begins with European reality and not with Yoga exercises which are meant to deceive us about our reality.

Jung suspected as early as 1930 that the spirit of the East was already at the gates, and he saw two possibilities which lay in the imminent encounter between East and West. It could have a hidden healing power within it, but also "a dangerous infection." Accordingly the diagnostician and doctor left it to the capacity of his "patients" (that is, Western men and women) for decision and their human maturity to make what they could of this possibility.

Five years later, in February 1936, Jung published the article "Yoga and the West," in the English-language paper *Prabuddha Bharata,* which appeared in Calcutta. If at an earlier stage studies with Richard Wilhelm and the Indologist Heinrich Zimmer had stimulated him to investigate the nature of the East Asian tradition, this short article shows his estimation as a Western psychologist of the spiritual and physical system of training in India. Here he sees first of all the development which has led Western men and women into the conflict between faith and knowledge, between religious revelation and knowledge obtained by thought. Jung speaks of a "lack of direction bordering on psychic anarchy. . . . Through his historical development, the European has become so far removed from his roots that in the end his mind was split into faith and knowledge, in the same way that psychological exaggeration breaks up into its inherent opposites."[18] In saying this Jung is not denying that in this way it is possible to arrive at aspects of the historical consciousness, which are examined more closely by Jung's famous pupil Erich Neumann.[19]

Jung's result, which significantly he published in an Indian journal, at the relevant point reads thus:

> The split in the Western spirit therefore makes it impossible at the outset for the intentions of Yoga to be realized in any adequate way. . . . The Indian not only knows his nature, but he knows also how much he himself is nature. The European, on the other hand, has a science of nature and knows astonishingly little of his own nature, the nature within him.

There is thus a clear demand for a picture of human nature which spans the whole of reality. Moreover, the psychologist looks for the various "dispositions of the soul" which are quite different in Eastern men and

20. Carl G. Jung.

women from those in Western men and women. Therefore his advice is to study Yoga carefully, but also to examine the question of practicing it. His thoughts come to a climax in the dictum, "In the course of the centuries the West will produce its own Yoga, and it will be on the basis laid down by Christianity."[20] Whether this will prove to be a practical method or exercises comparable to Indian Yoga is another matter. However, it is important that Jung explicitly points to a discipline founded in Christian esotericism which is appropriate to the psychological presuppositions of Western men and women. He himself did not develop such practices of initiation, apart from the so-called active imagination.[21] However, this serves explicit psychological ends and should therefore be carried out under the direction of a doctor. Jung did not feel that he was called to renew culture or to found a modern discipline of initiation.

An investigation of the spiritual methods of training practiced in the West would have been desirable from a psychologist with a broad vision of his own. Evidently Jung was never asked for such an investigation and interpretation. We do, however, have psychological commentaries written by him on texts from Eastern religions. He wrote on the psychology of Eastern meditation and also produced a series of lengthy prefaces, for example, to books by D. T. Suzuki and Heinrich Zimmer or to the *I Ching*. By contrast—leaving aside later medieval alchemy—he mentioned the religious doctrines of the West all in the same breath, in a sweeping way which was sometimes even confusing for those who were not professionals. Thus, for example, Jung speaks of the "mass imports of exotic systems of religion"; he mentions the religion of Abdul Bahai, the representatives of the Sufi sects, the Ramakrishna mission, Western Buddhism, the American Christian Science and the Anglo-Indian Theosophy of H. P. Blavatsky and Annie Besant alongside the anthroposophy of Rudolf Steiner, which takes up the central European spiritual heritage. This sweeping summary must cause perplexity, especially as Jung dismisses or ignores both directions as being pseudo-esoteric. It is obvious that the great analyst and physician must have raised critical questions here. At all events, in this respect he left the high level of his analyses and interpretations of the reality of soul and spirit. Or should we regard this refusal as an indication that his task, the task of a physician of the soul, is a different one?

Further Aspects in the History of Ideas

Although Jung's work raises critical questions, it cannot be denied that analytical psychology as a whole is, above all, a contribution to a universal picture of reality that embraces human beings and the world, psyche and matter. This is where its topicality and its future lie. Both the encounter with Eastern and Far Eastern spirituality and access to the context of alchemy directed Jung the psychologist to the one complex reality. Jung applied to it the alchemistic term *unus mundus* (the one world). What he means is the reality that can at one time be described as material being and at another as a dynamic of the psyche. This *unus mundus* was to play a role above all in Jung's later works, when he had a fruitful exchange with the physicist and Nobel prize winner Wolfgang Pauli.[22] The studies produced in this connection show that the depth psychologist discloses possibilities of knowledge that point far beyond the original task of the physician and therapist.

Jung's collaboration proved to be fruitful because a parallelism of thought models arose in psychology and physics. Jung became convinced that the same unconscious that harbors the archetypical primal images of great religious relevance must also be connected with inorganic matter. He thought that in the last resort psyche and matter are to be seen as the two poles of one and the same reality, the alchemistic *unus mundus*. Jung demonstrated that the archetypes of the collective unconscious display a "psychoid" aspect (that is, not just a spiritual but also partially a material aspect), which produces the phenomenon of so-called synchronicity. This is a meaningful ordering of spiritual and material facts. In this connection Wolfgang Pauli pointed out that the theory of the evolution of life also called for consideration of the concept of synchronicity as Jung developed it. Accordingly there would be purposeful and thus "meaningful chance mutations" in the course of evolution. Even if such matters must initially be restricted to the discussion of specialists, they do open up perspectives on a new understanding of what is presented in the late-Pauline letters (e.g., Ephesians and Colossians) as an image of the cosmic Christ.[23]

Another central theme of Jung's analytical psychology which at the same time belongs at the center of Christian esotericism is the great theme of transformation. It is certainly no coincidence that it was in connection with this theme that Jung parted company with Sigmund Freud and from then on went his own way as a psychotherapist and researcher. One of the places where he stated his program was in the early work "Transformations and Symbols of the Libido." The later revised version is called "Symbols of Transformation."[24] It is basically the same theme that in the ancient mysteries, in the spiritual schools in East and West, denotes the method and aim of human maturing. In the language of the New Testament it is *metanoia*, the transformation of human beings at the depth of their beings.

All this subject matter is, of course, well known to academic theology. But the real problem is that it is not enough merely to deal with the testimonies of the religious or spiritual tradition by means of the known methods of philology and historical and textual criticism. That would be to seek to grasp the mystery of Christianity purely in external terms, that is, exoterically. However, esoteric spirituality that is worthy of the name is primarily concerned with the development of personal inwardness, with one's own experience and with transformation. A theology without experience is hardly in a position to mediate that spiritual knowledge and spiritual direction which nowadays is sought more than ever. For Jung, the son of a Reformed pastor, this insight had grown out of his own experience and sufferings. There are also some illuminating remarks about this in his autobiography *Memories, Dreams, Reflections:*

> I was equally sure that none of the theologians I knew had ever seen "the light that shineth in the darkness" with his own eyes, for if they had they would not have been able to teach a "theological religion," which seemed quite inadequate to me, since there was nothing to do with it but believe it without hope. This was what my Father had tried valiantly to do and had run aground. . . . I recognized that this celebrated faith of his had played this deadly trick on him, and not only on him but on most of the cultivated and serious people I knew. The arch sin of faith, it seemed to me, was that it forestalled experience.[25]

Let us leave aside the question of how Jung understood the Christian concept of faith; his particular merit as a depth psychologist lies in the fact that he showed the theology of his time a way to understand Christianity not only as a theological doctrine or as an ethical norm but as a unique possibility of personally undergoing a process of change and taking an inner way. Therefore the number of those who entered into conversations and correspondence with Carl Gustav Jung from both Protestant and Catholic theology was great. To one such Protestant theologian, Walter Uhsadel, he wrote:

> It seems to me that the most important task of anyone who trains souls in the present is to show people a way of getting to the primal experience which for example Paul encountered most clearly on the Damascus Road. In my experience this way opens up only in the process of the development of the individual soul.[26]

Thus, the esoteric Christian—which is what C. G. Jung undoubtedly was—becomes the inaugurator of a "depth theology," that is, a theology that takes part in that extension of consciousness which is not just limited to the rational basis of theological-exegetical work and proclamation and is not exhausted in charitable or social and political activities but is open to the dimension of spiritual depth, to esoteric Christianity. Only with a changed consciousness is it also possible to change external relations, interpersonal relations. Change begins within. It begins with the people who are to be changed.

At this point it can be asked what reception Jung's approach found. Instead of referring to the Jungian school in the narrower sense of the term, which includes Marie Louise von Franz, Aniela Jaffe, James Hillman, Ulrich Mann, Esther Harding, Erich Neumann, Jolande Jacobi, and others, I would like to take as a representative figure the person and work of Karlfried Graf Dürckheim. On the one hand, Dürckheim recognized the therapeutic relevance of Jungian analytical psychology and made it an ingredient of his own praxis; on the other hand, the theme of initiation comes so much to the fore that the basis of Christian esotericism comes into play, though he does not always put particular emphasis on this.

Karlfried Graf Dürckheim, who was born in Munich in 1896, was originally a philosopher and psychologist. In 1932 he became professor of psychology in Kiel, and from 1937 to 1945 he worked in Japan, where he encountered Zen Buddhism. After 1951 he developed and practiced the "initiation therapy," which he inaugurated with Maria Hippius in Todtmoos-Rütte in the Black Forest. This was based on a metaphysical anthropology in which basic experiences from a spiritual encounter with the mysticism of Meister Eckhardt, of Zen, and of the analytical psychology of C. G. Jung come together. Along with a system of practical work which involves the body, initiation therapy represents a way to self-realization. The practitioner focuses on the experience of being, that is, an experience which initiation therapy has in common with mysticism. The aim is transformation. At the same time, the experiential knowledge of the East applies, for the way is the goal. Graf Dürckheim observes:

> It is also necessary for those ultimately responsible for spiritual life, its knowledge and its realization, to learn to distinguish in theory and in practice (i.e. also in themselves) between the two levels on which human life inevitably is played out: the natural, limited by space and time, given to human beings to know, master and shape, and that beyond time and space, which transcends all human ability, but which is given to human beings for experience, obedience and self-realization in a life which testifies to transcendent life in our existence in space and time.[27]

Along with Jung, Dürckheim is guided by a concern to avoid psychologizing religion. It cannot be the task of either to seek to grasp religious experience only by means of psychological contemplation and analysis. Being open to the spiritual and transcendent calls for an extension of vision and consciousness which is not normally present but is achieved or prepared for only by practicing. However, the mystery of transformation in both cases transcends human capabilities. In religious terms, esoteric presence comes about in the sphere of grace. This grace is not striven for, nor is it fought for or earned, but rather is given. The human being can only clean the mirror; he or she can only open hands in preparation to receive. Anything else would be makeshift.

But this points to the transpersonal horizon before which authentic esotericism becomes event. At the same time it marks the limits inherent in a therapeutic praxis, a spiritual method or a system of knowledge. Such a discipline can never grasp the total extent of that which can be experienced—not even Jungian psychology. Rather, it represents one possibility among many. It may therefore be counted among those possibilities which are to be regarded as an extension of psychoanalysis or even humanistic psychology. The term "transpersonal psychology," though less than satisfactory, is an attempt to identify this perspective.[28]

Now while Graf Dürckheim was able to integrate the Jungian legacy into his work of initiation therapy and make fruitful use of it in the framework of his activities, the capacity of analytical psychology for further synopses (ways of seeing things together) and syntheses (putting things together) was in no way exhausted. Its capacity for dialogue nowhere emerges more clearly than in connection with the so-called Eranos Conferences, which, thanks to the initiative of Olga Fröbe-Kapteyn (who died in 1962), have taken place every year since 1933 in Ascona-Moscia on Lake Maggiore in Switzerland.[29] The biologist Adolf Portmann described this spiritual activity, which took place every year at the Casa Eranos until 1988, as "accepting the mystery of the spirit with reverence, saying what can be said and knowing that the unutterable is present: this is the spirit of the work of Eranos." Here is a place for exchanging ideas, in which natural scientists and figures from the humanities, students of religion, researchers into myths and psychologists carry on dialogue. Jung was part of the organizing body from 1933 on, when he spoke about the foundations of the procress of individuation, that is, about something at the heart of his psychology.

So far no synoptic approach has been developed which brings together the different ways to knowledge, namely, that of a synopsis of analytical psychology and the anthroposophy of Rudolf Steiner. I have explained elsewhere why this is burdened with many problems on both sides.[30] But the great inner affinity between analytical psychology and anthroposophy could also be demonstrated and reasons given for it. One of those reasons for this affinity is that Carl Gustav Jung and Rudolf Steiner not only developed a total picture of human beings and reality but also showed that human beings can follow the way to becoming completely themselves. At first sight the two methods of the psychologist and the spiritual teacher seem to be mutually exclusive, and the differences should not be taken too lightly. However, these differences represent only one aspect, especially as the two men went separate ways in their lives and each could not or did not want to know too much about the other. Often (though not always) when Steiner uses the metaphor of "height" to communicate "the knowledge of higher worlds,"[31] Jung prefers the metaphor of "depth," as this is already expressed in the term "depth psychology." But in the realm of the soul and spirit there is no spatial above or below. The deciding factor is what the particular metaphor used seeks to convey.

Therefore the differing use of the words "high" or "deep" need not express any contradiction. In both cases the sphere of the soul and spirit is entered, the sphere that extends far beyond the rational consciousness of the everyday self. The decision whether and to what degree it is possible and practicable to take Jung's and Steiner's epistemologies together cannot, however, be taken solely on the grounds of theoretical discussion but must also be taken in the sphere of concrete experience. That can best be confirmed by those who on the one hand adopt the approach of anthroposophy and are therefore trained in anthroposophical modes of knowledge and meditation, and those on the other hand who also come to be intensively preoccupied with their unconscious as Jung understands it. Both ways are viable; one and the same person can use both perspectives. Of course I am not talking here about an undisciplined moving to and fro between them. However, it is a fact of experience that those who have arrived at insights in one field of knowledge and bring with them the necessary degree of lack of prejudice are also in a position to be open to another method of knowledge. It is only a narrow-minded, hair-splitting approach to concepts, devoid of any personal experience, which cannot see the possibility of spiritual bridge building. There is an ecumene of the spirit! It allows a bridge to be built from one side to the other. It makes a synopsis possible.

Such an overall view is highly significant not least in connection with Christian esotericism, since both Jung and Steiner did not arrive, say, at a new understanding of Christ on the basis of speculation or mental games. Rather, both had an experience of Christ, each in an individual way, which marked a turning point in their lives and which can be of symbolic significance to men and women today who are alienated from the traditional church, for whom "God is dead" (Nietzsche).

This esoteric relationship to Christ independent of external tradition is undeniable in Jung;[32] in Steiner the "Christ impulse" may be termed the spiritual center and main feature of all anthroposophical activities. Neither Jung nor Steiner can be measured by the principles and norms of academic theology. In many respects that is a hopeful sign, not least in connection with the synopsis between analytical psychology and anthroposophy which has still to be worked out. The spirit blows where it wills.

Translated by John Bowden

Notes

1. For an introduction to Jung's life and work, see, e.g., Gerhard Wehr, *Jung: A Biography* (Munich, 1985; Boston, 1987); idem, *An Illustrated Biography of C. G. Jung* (Zurich and Boston, 1989).

2. Hans Schär, *Erlösungsvorstellungen und ihre psychologischen Aspekte* (Zurich, 1950); Ulrich Mann, *Theogonische Tage: Entwicklungslinien des Gottesbewusstseins in der altorientalischen und biblischen Religion* (Stuttgart, 1976); Gerhard Wehr, *C. G. Jung und Rudolf Steiner* (Stuttgart, 1972; reissued Zurich, 1990, and Hudson, NY, 1991).

3. C. G. Jung, *Memories, Dreams, Reflections* (New York and London, 1963) 119–20.

4. Stefanie Zumstein-Preiswerk, *C.G. Jungs Medium* (Munich, 1975).

5. Jung, *Memories, Dreams, Reflections*, 18.

6. Gerhard Wehr, *Tiefenpsychologie und Christentum – C. G. Jung* (Augsburg, 1990).

7. First English edition, London, 1931.

8. Jung, *Memories, Dreams, Reflections*, 226–27, 231–32.

9. Ibid., 313. See also Emma Jung and Marie-Louise von Franz, *Die Gralslegende in psychologischer Sicht* (Zurich, 1960). In this connection it should be noted that the Grail stories already represent a synthesis of Western Celtic and Eastern/Near-Eastern traditions.

10. Aniela Jaffe, *Aus Leben und Werkstatt von C.G.Jung* (Zurich, 1968) 82–83.

11. Jung, *Memories, Dreams, Reflections*, 236.

12. See Gerhard Wehr, *Jakob Böhme in Selbstzeugnissen und Bilddokumenten* (Reinbek, 1971, 1985) (with extensive bibliography).

13. Jacob Boehme, *Christosophia: Ein christlicher Einweihungsweg*, edited with a commentary by G. Wehr (Frankfurt, 1992); idem, *Theosophische Sendbriefe I/II* (Freiburg, 1980) (complete edition of all the Boehme letters).

14. *Die Bruderschaft der Rosenkreuzer: Esoterische Texte*, edited with an introduction by Gerhard Wehr (Cologne and Munich, 1984) (the edition contains the complete texts of *Fama Fraternitatis* [1614], *Confessio Fraternitatis* [1615], *Chymische Hochzeit Christiani Rosenkreutz* [1616]). An excellent edition in English is *The Chemical Wedding of Christian Rosenkrentz*, translated by Joscelyn Godwin (Grand Rapids: Phanes Press, 1992). See also the accounts by Frances A. Yates, *The Rosicrucian Enlightenment* (London and Boston, 1972); Gerhard Wehr, *Esoterisches Christentum: Aspekte, Impulse, Konsequenzen* (Stuttgart, 1975). The account ranges from the gospels and testimonies of earliest Christianity through medieval esotericism, Jacob Boehme and the Rosicrucians to the present; see Gerhard Wehr, *Die deutsche Mystik* (Munich, 1988).

15. Jung, *Letters*, vol. 2, ed. Aniela Jaffe and Gerhard Adler (London, 1976) 338–39.

16. Jung, *Letters*, vol. 3, ed. Aniela Jaffe and Gerhard Adler (London, 1977) 323.

17. Jung, in the preface to *The Secret of the Golden Flower*, viii. See Richard Wilhelm, "In Memoriam," in *Collected Works* 15 (London, 1966) 58.

18. Jung, *Collected Works* 11 (London, 1958) 532–34.

19. E. Neumann, *Ursprungsgeschichte des Bewusstseins* (Zurich, 1949). Reference should also be made here to the works of J. Gebser, *Ursprung und Gegenwart I/II* (Stuttgart, 1949, 1953) (there have been recent new editions in the context of the Gebser edition).

20. Jung, *Collected Works* 11:537.

21. The active imagination is an important therapeutic method of analytical psychology. Jung began to develop it from 1916 on. It is described in his study "The Transcendent Function," contained in *Collected Works* 8 and in his late work *Mysterium Coniunctionis*. With the help of the active imagination contents of the unconscious can be brought to consciousness. Here the ego engages in active interplay with the images and symbols that arise, as if these were living beings in the objective world. Here the archetypical depths of the psyche can be animated. See A. N. Ammann, *Aktive Imagination: Darstellung einer Methode* (Olten-Freiburg, 1978).

22. See C. G. Jung and Wolfgang Pauli, *Naturerklärung und Psyche* (Zurich, 1952); Marie-Louise von Franz, *Zahl und Zeit: Psychologische Überlegungen zu einer Annäherung von Tiefenpsychologie und Physik* (Stuttgart, 1970); Ernst Anrich, *Die Einheit der Wirklichkeit: Moderne Physik und Tiefenpsychologie* (Fellbach-Stuttgart, 1980).

23. See Gerhard Wehr, *Esoterisches Christentum* (Stuttgart, 1975) 33–34.

24. C. G. Jung, *Symbols of Transformation,* now in *Collected Works* 5.

25. Jung, *Memories, Dreams, Reflections,* 114.

26. Jung, *Letters,* vol. 1, ed. Aniela Jaffe and Gerhard Adler (London, 1973) 278–79.

27. Karlfried Graf Dürckheim, "Religiöse Erfahrung," in *Synopse: Beiträge zum Gespräch der Theologie mit ihren Nachbarwissenschaften: Festschrift für Ulrich Mann* (Darmstadt, 1975) 62. For an introduction, see especially Rüdiger Müller, *Wandlung zur Ganzheit: Die Initiatische Therapie nach Karlfried Graf Dürckheim und Maria Hippius* (Freiburg, 1982) (with an extensive bibliography); Manfred Bergler, *Die Anthropologie des Grafen Karlfried von Dürckheim im Rahmen der Rezeptionsgeschichte des Zen-Buddhismus in Deutschland,* philosophical dissertation for the University of Erlangen-Nuremberg, 1981 (with an extended bibliography); Gerhard Wehr, *Karlfried Graf Dürckheim: Leben im Zeichen der Wandlung* (Munich, 1988).

28. Transpersonal psychology, which originated in the United States in the middle of the 1960s, sets out to combine the insights of various psychological disciplines and to relate the insights of psychology, the humanities, and religion, and not least esotericism in its manifold forms. See Charles T. Tart, *Transpersonal Psychologies* (New York, 1975).

29. The lectures given at the Eranos Conferences, which take place every year, are documented in the *Eranos Jahrbuch,* which has been published since 1933 in the original languages (German, English, French). For Jung's connections with Eranos, see Aniela Jaffe, *C. G. Jung, Bild und Wort* (Olten-Freiburg, 1977).

30. Gerhard Wehr, *Jung und Steiner.* This study was a commission from the International Society for Depth Psychology in Stuttgart. It is this society of physicians, psychologists, theologians, and social scientists that is indebted to the work of Jung and which encourages open conversations between disciplines and academic viewpoints.

31. Rudolf Steiner, *Knowledge of Higher Worlds* (1904); there have been numerous editions and translations. For the anthroposophical method of meditation and knowledge, see Gerhard Wehr, *Die innere Weg: Anthroposophische Erkenntnis* (Reinbek, 1987); idem, *Rudolf Steiner: Eine Biographie* (Munich, 1987).

32. For Jung's work on Christ and on his pointer to Christ, see Wehr, *Tiefenpsychologie und Christentum;* idem, *Wege zur religiöser Erfahrung: Analytische Psychologie im Dienste der Bibelauslegung* (Darmstadt and Olten-Freiburg, 1974). The attempt is made here to extend the theological exegesis of the New Testament with the equipment of the depth psychology of C. G. Jung, in order to arrive at the spiritual dimension which the Bible expresses in the form of symbols and parables. Texts from the Gospel of John are used as an illustration.

Contributors

Antoine Faivre, coeditor of this volume, is Professor of Germanic Studies at the University of Haute-Normandie and Director of Studies at the Ecole Pratique des Hautes Etudes (Sorbonne), where he holds the chair of the History of Esoteric and Mystical Trends in Modern and Contemporary Europe. He is vice-president of the Association for Research and Information on Esotericism (ARIES) and associate editor of its journal, *ARIES*, as well as director of Cahiers de l'Hermétisme, published by Albin Michel. Among his many books are *Eckartshausen et la théosophie chrétienne* (1969), *L'Esotérisme au 18è siècle* (1973), *Accès de l'ésotérisme occidental* (1986) and *Toison d'Or et Alchimie* (1991)–the latter two forthcoming in English–and *The Eternal Hermes* (also forthcoming).

Jacob Needleman, coeditor of this volume, is Professor of Philosophy at San Francisco State University and former Director of the Center for the Study of New Religions at Graduate Theological Union, Berkeley, California. He is the author of many books, including *The New Religions* (1970), *A Sense of the Cosmos* (1979), *Lost Christianity* (1980), *The Heart of Philosophy* (1982), *The Way of the Physician* (1985), and *Money and the Meaning of Life* (1991).

Karen Voss, associate editor of this volume, is Adjunct Professor of Religious Studies at San Jose State University. Her publications include "Is There a 'Feminine' Gnosis?: Reflections on Feminism and Esotericism" (*ARIES*, June 1992) and "The *Hierosgamos* Theme in the Images of the *Rosarium philosophorum*," in *Alchemy Revisited* (1990).

Françoise Bonardel is Professor of Philosophy and Religion at the University of Paris I, Sorbonne. She is the author of *L'Hermétisme* (1985), *Antonin Artaud ou la fidélité à l'infini* (1987), *La Philosophie de l'Alchimie* (in press), and various articles on modern art and culture in the light of traditional alchemy.

Jean Borella teaches metaphysics at the University of Nancy II. He is the author of *La charité profanée* (1979) and *Le sens du surnaturel* (1986), and has pursued the elaboration of a symbolic ontology in *Le mystère du signe* (1989) and *La crise du symbolisme religieux* (1990). He has also written numerous articles on Christian gnosis and on the history of religious ideas.

Pierre Deghaye is Professor at the University of Caen, where he directs the Department of German Studies. He is the author of *La doctrine ésotérique de Zinzendorf* (1969), *La naissance de Dieu ou la doctrine de Jacob Boehme* (1985), as well as numerous studies on German spirituality, notably on Friedrich Christoph Oetinger. He has also written the introduction to the new French edition of Joseph Görres's *Christliche Mystik*.

Roland Edighoffer is Professor at the Sorbonne and Chair of the Department of German Studies at the University of Paris III. He is president of the Association for Research and Information on Esotericism (ARIES) and associate editor of its journal, *ARIES*. An expert on Rosicrucian movements since the seventeenth century, he is the author of *Rose-Croix et*

Société idéale selon Johann Valentin Andreae (2 vols., 1982 and 1987) and *Les Rose-Croix* (3d edition 1991).

DIETRICH VON ENGELHARDT is University Professor and Director of the Institute for the History of Medicine and Science at the Medical University of Lubeck. His works include *Hegel und die Chemie* (1976), *Historisches Bewusstsein in der Naturwissenschaft von der Aufklärung bis zum Positivismus* (1979), and, with Heinrich Schipperges, *Die inneren Verbindungen zwischen Philosophie und Medizin im 20. Jahrhundert* (1980).

JEAN-PIERRE LAURANT is a scholar in religious studies at the Ecole Pratique des Hautes Etudes (Sorbonne). He is the author of, among other works, *Le sens caché dans l'oeuvre de René Guénon* (1992) and *L'Esotérisme chrétien en France au 19è siècle* (1992).

ROBERT A. MCDERMOTT is president of the California Institute of Integral Studies, professor emeritus and former chair of the Department of Philosophy, Baruch College, CUNY, executive editor of *ReVision* magazine, and president of the Rudolf Steiner Institute. His publications include *The Essential Steiner* (1984) and *The Essential Aurobindo* (1987).

G. MALLARY MASTERS is Professor of Romance Languages and Comparative Literatures at the University of North Carolina at Chapel Hill. He is the author of *Rabelaisian Dialectic and the Platonic-Hermetic Tradition* (1969) and *La Lignée de Saturne ... de Jehan Thenaud* (1973), and editor of several works, including *Le Parcours des Essais: Montaigne, 1588-1988,* International Colloquy, Duke University–University of North Carolina at Chapel Hill, 7-9 April 1988 (1989).

EDMOND MAZET is Professor of Mathematics and the History of Science at the University of Lille III. Since 1978 he has been a frequent contributor to two journals devoted to the history of Freemasonry, *Cahiers Villard de Honnecourt* and *Renaissance Traditionnelle*.

HEINRICH SCHIPPERGES is Emeritus Director of the Institute of Medicine at the University of Heidelberg. He has written extensively on medicine in the Arabic and Latin Middle Ages, the history of psychiatry, and the development of modern medicine.

EMILY B. SELLON has been an editor, writer, lecturer, and long-time student of theosophy and Eastern philosophy. For many years she edited the journal *Main Currents in Modern Thought* and also served on the Board of Directors of the Theosophical Society of America.

RENÉE WEBER is Professor of Philosophy at Rutgers University. She is the author of *Dialogues with Socrates and Sages: The Search for Unity* (1986, 1990) and of many articles in the fields of Eastern philosophy and philosophy of religion.

GERHARD WEHR is the author of many works on Christian spirituality, depth psychology, and anthroposophy. He is the editor of the works of Jacob Boehme and has written biographies of C. G. Jung, Martin Buber, Rudolf Steiner, and K. Graf Duerckheim. Among his works are *Jakob Böhme* (1971), *Esoterisches Christentum* (1975), *C. J. Jung: Leben, Werke, und Wirkung* (1985), *Rudolf Steiner: Leben, Erkenntnis, Kulturimpuls* (1987), and *An Illustrated Biography of C. G. Jung* (1989).

Photographic Credits

The editors and publisher wish to thank the custodians of the works of art for supplying photographs and granting permission to use them. In particular, the art editor wishes to acknowledge the research assistance of Alice Buse, Librarian, The Philosophical Research Society, Los Angeles.

1. Courtesy of Swiss Museum of History of Pharmacy, Basel, Switzerland.
2. Courtesy of the Bibliotheca Philosophica Hermetica, Amsterdam.
3. Courtesy of the Bibliotheca Philosophica Hermetica, Amsterdam.
4. Collection of Antoine Faivre, Meudon.
5. Collection of Antoine Faivre, Meudon.
6. Courtesy of the Manly P. Hall Collection of the Philosophical Research Society, Los Angeles.
7. Courtesy of the Manly P. Hall Collection of the Philosophical Research Society, Los Angeles.
8. Courtesy of the Manly P. Hall Collection of the Philosophical Research Society, Los Angeles.
9. Collection of Antoine Faivre, Meudon.
10. Collection of Antoine Faivre, Meudon.
11. Collection of Antoine Faivre, Meudon.
12. Courtesy of Deutsches Freimaurer-Museum, Bayreuth.
13. Courtesy of Philosophisch-Anthroposophischer Verlag am Goetheanum.
14. Courtesy of the Manly P. Hall Collection of the Philosophical Research Society, Los Angeles.
15. Collection of Antoine Faivre, Meudon.
16. From *René Guénon,* ed. Jean-Pierre Laurant, *Cahier de L'Herne* n. 61 (Paris: Editions de L'Herne, 1985). Courtesy of L'Herne, Paris.
17. From James Moore, *Gurdjieff: The Anatomy of a Myth* (Rockport: Element, 1991), p. 179.
18. From P. D. Ouspensky, *Fragments of an Unknown Teaching* (New York: Harcourt, Brace and Co., 1949), p. 137.
19. From P. D. Ouspensky, *In Search of the Miraculous* (New York: Harcourt, Brace and Co., 1949), p. 190.
20. From Gerhard Wehr, *An Illustrated Biography of C. G. Jung.* © 1989 by René Coeckelberghs Verlag AG, Lucerne, Switzerland.

Indexes

Subjects

Alchemical esotericism, 71–99
Alchemical texts, 75–79
  ancient, Berthelot's rediscovery of,
    85
  nineteenth century, 85–87
  twentieth century, 86
Alchemy, 71–99
  Aquinas on, 42–43
  Christianity and, 74
  and creation, 93–95
  during Enlightenment, 59–62
  in fifteenth century, 77
  in fourteenth century, 77
  Hermes and, 189
  Hermetism and, 31–33
  Jung's interest in, 382, 393
  as mediator between matter and
    Spirit, 74
  medicine and, 171
  "modern," 72–73, 89–90, 92
  in nineteenth-century Germany, 82
  origin of word, 74–75
  Paracelsus on, 159, 161–62
  in Renaissance, 64, 65–68
  symbolic Masonry and, 268–69
  theosophy and, 311
  in thirteenth century, 47–48, 77
  traditionalist approaches to, 89–90,
    92
  in twelfth century, 32–33
  usage of word, 73–74
  Western, beginning of, 6–7
Alexander (mythical figure), 33–34

Alexandria, 3, 6
Amaurism, 39
Ambigua (Maximus the Confessor),
  20, 21
AMORC, 208
Analytical psychology. *See also* Jung,
  Carl Gustav
  anthroposophy and, 396–98
  on archetypal primal images, 393
  picture of reality of, 392–93
  on transformation, 393
Ancient sources of esoteric
  movements, 1–24
Anthroposophic Movement, 295
Anthroposophic Press, 309
Anthroposophical Society, 289, 295,
  308–9
Anthroposophy
  analytical psychology and, 396–98
  meaning of, 289
  principles of, 303–7
  Steiner and, 288–309
Arabs
  and Hermetism, 22–24
  science of, 28
Art and theosophy, 326–27
Arthurian legends, 34, 36. *See also*
  Grail, theme of
Assembly of Brothers, 234–35
Astrology
  in fourteenth century, 59
  Hermetic, 5, 6
  modern, 5

Names